Time Out
Paris

Penguin Books

PENGUIN BOOKS

Published by the Penguin Group
Penguin Books Ltd, 27 Wrights Lane, London W8 5TZ, England
Penguin Books USA Inc., 375 Hudson Street, New York, New York 10014, USA
Penguin Books Australia Ltd, Ringwood, Victoria, Australia
Penguin Books Canada Ltd, 10 Alcorn Avenue, Toronto, Ontario, Canada M4V 3B2
Penguin Books (NZ) Ltd, 182-190 Wairau Road, Auckland 10, New Zealand

Penguin Books Ltd, Registered Offices: Harmondsworth, Middlesex, England

First published 1989
First Penguin edition 1990
Second edition 1992
Third edition 1994
Fourth edition 1995
Fifth edition 1997
Sixth edition 1998
Seventh edition 1999
10 9 8 7 6 5 4 3 2 1

Printed and bound by William Clowes Ltd, Beccles, Suffolk NR34 9QE

Get packing

Get there

Eurostar operates up to 18 daily services from London St Pancras International to **Paris Gare de Nord** with return fares from £69 (*www.eurostar.com/08432 186186*).

Stay

Hotel Saint Paul is a friendly, affordable three-star hotel on a historic street in the Latin Quarter with 31 cosy ensuite rooms, plus air-conditioning and free wi-fi. It's a few minutes from plenty of bustling bars, cafés and brasseries, the Jardin du Luxembourg, the Panthéon and the Sorbonne. Sputnik, the resident cat, seems as much part of the furniture as the seventeenth-century walls. Check the website for special offers and discounts.

Hotel Saint Paul, 43 rue Monsieur le Prince, 75006 (+33 1 43 26 98 64/ www.hotelsaintpaulparis.com). Metro Odéon. Doubles from €154.

Eat

Le Restaurant. Exquisitely presented French fare in a Michelin-starred restaurant in the stately L'Hotel, which counts Oscar Wilde and Argentinian writer Jorge Luis Borges among its former guests. Book for the good-value lunch if you're on a budget; starters might include foie gras or scallops, seasonal mains feature skate wing or chicken and your meal will come with a perfectly prepared *amuse bouche* and freshly baked bread rolls.

Le Restaurant, L'Hotel, 13 rue des Beaux Arts, 75006 (+33 1 44 41 9900/www.l-hotel.com). Metro St Germain-des-Prés. Two-course lunch €42 per person.

Definite article *Michelin-starred food is served at Le Restaurant in L'Hotel*

Travel

www.parisaddress.com

Short term apartment rentals in Paris
Live in Paris like a true Parisian!
You wish to live Paris from "within", like a true Parisian?
Saint-Germain-des-Prés, the Latin Quarter, the Marais...

Paris Address invites you to discover picturesque
and lively central apartments.

Prices all included, instant availability and easy-booking
on the website.

Travel

Edited and designed by
Time Out Paris
100 rue du Fbg-St-Antoine
75012 Paris
Tel: +33(0)1.44.87.00.45
Fax: +33(0)1.44.73.90.60
e-mail: paris@timeout.com

Editor Natasha Edwards
Production Editor Dan Fielder
Sub Editor/Research Sue Nottingham
Additional Research Frances Dougherty, Lucia Scazzocchio, Rowan Tomlinson

Art Director Richard Joy
Ad Design Matthias Lechner

Advertising Manager Philippe Thareaut
Advertising Executives Susanne Twerenbold, Katherine Spenley

Managing Director Karen Albrecht

For
Time Out Guides Ltd
Universal House
251 Tottenham Court Road
London W1P 0AB
Tel: +44(0)171 813 3000
Tel: +44(0)171 813 6001
http://www.timeout.com
e-mail: guides@timeout.com

Editorial Director Peter Fiennes
Art Director John Oakey

Group Advertisement Director Lesley Gill
Sales Director Mark Phillips

Publisher Tony Elliott
Managing Director Mike Hardwick
Financial Director Kevin Ellis
Marketing Director Gillian Auld
General Manager Nichola Coulthard
Accountants Catherine Bowen, Bridget Carter

Features for the seventh edition were written or updated by:
History Dan Fielder, Natasha Edwards (Millennium party?), Carol Mann (Traces of the Belle Epoque).
Architecture Natasha Edwards. **War of the Words** Patrick Amine (translated by Simon Cropper). **The Seine**
Stephen Mudge. **Forever Paris** Alex Taylor. **Islands, Right Bank, Left Bank, Beyond the Périphérique,**
Parks Natasha Edwards, Susan Bell (Clignancourt: flea market mania), Jean O'Sullivan (Itineraries).
Museums Natasha Edwards, Stephen Mudge, Carol Pratl, Carol Mann (Not to be missed). **Art Galleries**
Natasha Edwards. **Accommodation** Sue Nottingham. **Restaurants** adapted by Rosa Jackson from *Time Out*
Eating & Drinking in Paris Guide, Alexander Lobrano (A Century of Brasseries). **Cafés & Bars** Adapted by
Rosa Jackson from *Time Out Eating & Drinking in Paris Guide*, Hannah Godfrey (I drink... therefore I am).
Fashion Julie Street, Rowan Tomlinson. **Specialist Shopping** Julie Street (Tati by name....). **Food & Drink**
Rosa Jackson. **Cabaret, Circus & Comedy** Tom Baker, Simon Cropper. **Children** Jean O'Sullivan. **Clubs**
Hugh Miles, Rebecca Carmen (Reality check). **Dance** Carol Pratl. **Film** Toby Rose, Simon Cropper (Ten for
the century). **Gay & Lesbian** Toby Rose. **Music: Classical & Opera** Stephen Mudge. **Music: Rock, Roots &**
Jazz Patricia Brien. **Sport & Fitness** Sue Nottingham. **Theatre** Annie Sparks. **Trips Out of Town** Natasha
Edwards, Stephen Mudge (Princes, paupers, folies des grandeurs). **Directory** Sue Nottingham.

The editors would like to thank the following for help and information:
Anna of Ladies Room, Lemisse Al-Hafidh, Sarah Charsley.

Photography by Tom Craig, Jon Perugia. **Additional photography** François Bourru, Laurence Guillot,
Francesca Yorke, Chris Kutschera, Nathalie Jacquault, Caroline Irby, Dawn Moon, Pacome Lajotte,
Colm Pierce. **Additional photos courtesy** Pierre Ferbos/Editions Flammarion, Hervé Lewandowski/
Photothèque des Musées de la Ville de Paris, Musée Carnavalet, Mahoudeau/Opéra National de Paris.
Maps p332-343 by Mapworld, p344-6 courtesy RATP.

Contents

About the Guide

The *Time Out Paris Guide* is one of an expanding series of guides that includes *London, Amsterdam, Barcelona, Berlin, Madrid, Prague, Rome, New York, Los Angeles* and *Sydney*. This seventh edition has been thoroughly revised and updated by staff and freelance writers resident in Paris. More than just a book for tourists, it is also for frequent visitors or long-term residents. It covers all the major sights and attractions, but also takes you to the city's more obscure and eccentric venues, as well as shops, restaurants, cafés, bars and clubs.

For up-to-the-minute weekly listings and reviews, look out for the *Time Out Paris* section (in English) inside the French listings magazine, *Pariscope*. For more on the city's best bars, bistros brasseries and bakeries, the *Time Out Eating & Drinking in Paris Guide* is a foodlover's bible.

PRACTICAL GUIDE

Above all, we've tried to make this book as useful as possible. Addresses, telephone numbers, transport details, opening times, admission prices and credit card details are all included in our listings. And, as far as possible, we've given details of facilities, services and events.

All the information in the guide was checked and correct when we went to press; but please bear in mind that owners and managers can change their arrangements at any time. If you want to be really sure, it's a good idea to phone before you set out to check opening times, dates of exhibitions, admission prices and the like. The same applies to information on disabled access; it's wise to phone first to check your needs can be met.

BOLD TYPE

Where we mention important places or events also listed elsewhere in the guide, or in detail later in the chapter, they are usually highlighted in **bold**.

ADDRESSES

Paris is divided into 20 *arrondissements* or districts, which form a tight snail-shell spiral beginning at Notre Dame and finishing at the Porte de Montreuil on the eastern edge of the city limits. Paris addresses include the *arrondissement* in the postcode, which begins with the prefix 750. So for example an address in the 1st *arrondissement* would have the postcode 75001, and one in the 20th would be 75020. Always use this form when writing letters. In this Guide we have referred to the *arrondissements* as 1st, 2nd, 3rd, 4th and so on. Addresses within the area covered in the large-scale map have also been given map references, but it is often equally simple to locate a street by seeing which *arrondissement* it is in, or looking for the nearest Métro.

PRICES

The prices listed throughout the guide should be used as guidelines. If prices vary greatly from those we've quoted, ask whether there's a good reason why. If not, go elsewhere. Then, please let us know. We try to give the best and most-up-to date advice, so we always want to hear if you've been badly overcharged. You'll also increasingly come across prices indicated in Euros (1 Euro = 6.55957F). Euro cheques are accepted in some places, but full transition to the European currency and the arrival in circulation of Euro coins and notes will take place only on 1 January 2002.

TELEPHONES

All French phone numbers have ten digits. From outside France, dial the country code (33) and leave off the zero at the start of the number.

CREDIT CARDS

Throughout this guide, the following abbreviations have been used for credit cards: **AmEx** American Express; **DC** Diners' Club; **MC** Mastercard; **V** Visa/Barclaycard. Note that shops, restaurants, cafés and museums will often not accept credit cards for sums of less than 100F.

LET US KNOW

It shold be stressed that the information we give is impartial. *Time Out* maintains a strict policy of editorial independence, and advertisers are never guaranteed special treatment of any kind. No organisation or enterprise has been included in this guide because the owner or manager has advertised in our publications. Their impartiality is one of the reasons why our guides are so successful and well respected.

We hope you enjoy the *Time Out Paris Guide* and that it makes your stay more enjoyable. However, if you disagree with any of our reviews, or have found somewhere you love and think should be included, let us know; your views on places you visited are always welcome. There's a reader's reply card in the book for your comments.

There is an online version of this guide, as well as weekly events listings for several international cities, at http://www.timeout.com.

Introduction

From my flat, on one side, beyond the courtyard and the mansard roofs, I can pick out the domes of the Panthéon, Observatoire and Val de Grâce; from the other, past the broad, tree-lined boulevard, muffled by the haze of pollution, glimmer the 30-storey tower blocks of Chinatown. One side historic, the other modern; that's the paradox of Paris, a centuries-old city known the world over for its monuments, museums and golden-stone buildings, yet a vibrant modern city that has never ceased to change. The Eiffel Tower marks the cityscape, but it is surrounded by a sea of apartment buildings that are home to millions of lives.

Of course, Paris *is* about the Eiffel Tower, the Louvre, the unfathomable *Mona Lisa*, the mythic Champs-Elysées and St-Germain, but it is also the myriad people of what remains an unusually lived-in city. It's worth going beyond the 'love France, loath the French' attitude of many tourists to see how the city really works, lives and plays.

Just as the city is not uniform but a series of different *quartiers*, so is its population diverse. While many talk about Paris' *embourgeoisement*, the city is still inhabited by a broad mix of classes and characters. You'll come across *parigot* workers'

cafés, Breton bars or Basque rendez-vous, just as you'll find gourmet temples filled with business magnates and the cocktail haunts of the glitterati. Africans, North Africans and Asians are only the most visible immigrants; they were preceded by Italians in the nineteenth century and Spanish, Portuguese and Russians in the early twentieth century. All this makes Paris an exciting, culturally rich – if sometimes uneasy – melting pot.

Stay a while in the city and you cannot help but get a sense of this variety, whether by visiting the street markets that remain an important focus of local life or by attending the most highbrow of theatre. You'll also come across Paris as the capital of France, both different from its regions and a sum of their parts. Political and cultural heart of the nation, Paris is the forum where social and political issues are argued out in public, in the passionately held right of anyone – and seemingly everyone – to demonstrate and strike, about, seemingly, everything. A contradictory blend of conservatives and revolutionaries, Parisians love to argue and to complain, but deep down, they are convinced there is nowhere else in the world to live.
Natasha Edwards.

A DAZZLING SHOW!

LIDO® *de Paris*

Dinner dance + Champagne + Show : *from 815 FF* (Dinner : 8 p.m. - Show : 10 p.m.
Show + Champagne : *560 FF* (Show : 10 p.m. & 12 p.m.)
Show from the Bar with 2 drinks : *385 FF*

Reservations: **01 40 76 56 10** - Champs-Élysées - Paris - http://www.lido.j

In Context

Paris by Season

The Parisian calendar of events is a rich miscellany of marathons and masses, fairs and festivals, high kitsch and high art.

Paris may still revel in its traditions of political radicalism and intellectual rigour, but for all that it is still a place that's capable of being really quite silly. The lighthearted **Course des Garçons et Serveuses de Café**, the freak shows of the **Foire du Trône**, the colourful antics of **Gay Pride**... all these events show a side of the French character that won't take itself too seriously. Not that culture vultures need ever go hungry, however. Alongside such highbrow set pieces as the **Festival d'Automne** and the **Festival du Film**, the Grand Palais is presenting exhibitions of Daumier, Chardin and Egyptian art. Look out, too, for a season of Moroccan art and culture, spanning several venues and media. And there'll be opportunities galore to celebrate two big anniversaries – Balzac's 200th and Poulenc's 100th.

While summer is the best time to do Paris on foot, the serious arts season closes down from mid-July to the end of August, resuming in the autumn with new shows and productions. But over Christmas or New Year the city keeps buzzing; theatres, museums and concert halls open as usual. Look out for two-for-one promotions such as **La Mairie de Paris vous invite au concert** (Jan or Sept) and **La Mairie de Paris vous invite au théâtre** (May). The Office de Tourisme de Paris (127 av des Champs-Elysées, 8th/01.49.52.53.54) will have extra info on events, as does the *Time Out Paris* section inside *Pariscope*. *See also chapters* **Dance, Film, Music: Classical & Opera, Music: Rock, Museums & Galleries, Roots & Jazz** *and* **Sport & Fitness.**

Public Holidays

On *jours fériés* banks, many museums, most shops and some restaurants close, and public transport runs as on Sunday. New Year, May Day, Bastille Day and Christmas are the most fully observed holidays, the others tend to depend on the day of the week. **New Year's Day** (Jour de l'An) 1 Jan; **Easter Monday** (Lundi de Pâques); **May Day** (Fête du Travail) 1 May; **VE Day** (Victoire 1945) 8 May; **Ascension Day** (Jour de l'Ascension); **Whit Monday** (Lundi de Pentecôte); **Bastille Day** (Quatorze Juillet) 14 July; **Feast of the Assumption** (Jour de l'Assomption) 15 Aug; **All Saints' Day** (Toussaint) 1 Nov; **Remembrance Day** (L'Armistice 1918) 11 Nov; **Christmas Day** (Noël) 25 Dec.

Spring

late Feb-early Mar: Salon de l'Agriculture

Paris-Expo, porte de Versailles, 15th (01.49.09.60.00). M° Porte de Versailles. **Admission** 55F.
Rural France comes to town to create the largest farm in the

world. Farmers inspect gigantic bulls, perfectly groomed sheep and manicured pigs, then repair to the food and drink hall to sample regional produce. If there's an election in the offing, politicians will be out in force too.

mid Mar: La Nuit des Publivores

Grand Rex, 1 bd Poissonnière, 2nd (01.44.88.98.00). M° Bonne-Nouvelle. **Admission** 200F.
New and old ads from around the world are screened in this massive venue all night, with breaks for ice cream. In the fun atmosphere, fave ads get applause and the cheesey ones get hisses. Themes in 1999 include Paris itself, the circus, and banned ads.

Mar: Foire Internationale à la Brocante et aux Jambons

Ile de Chatou (01.47.70.88.78). RER Chatou-Coissy. **Admission** 20F.
The spring jumble sale on the Ile de Chatou, north-west of La Défense, is a favourite source of bric a brac, unusual collectables and dusty furniture, together with a ham fair from the Middle Ages. There's another *foire* in autumn too.

Mar-early Apr: Banlieues Bleues

Seine St-Denis and area. **Information** (01.49.22.10.10). **Admission** free-150F.
Held in the Paris suburbs, this festival draws some of the greatest and most interesting names in classic jazz, blues, r 'n' b, soul, funk, flamenco, world music and gospel. Among many attractions in 1999: Marilyn Crispell, Dianne Reeves, Ahmad Jamal, Ali Farka Touré and Archie Shepp.

end Mar-early Apr: Festival EXIT

Maison des Arts et de la Culture de Créteil, pl Salvador Allende, 94000 Créteil (01.45.13.19.19). M° Créteil-Préfecture. **Tickets** 40F-200F.
This avant-garde dance, theatre and performance festival has made a big impact with its radical multinational programme.

1 Apr: Poisson d'Avril

On April Fool's Day in France the big joke is to try to stick a paper fish to some unsuspecting sucker's back. French journos pride themselves on their seasonal hoaxes.

early Apr: Festival du Film de Paris

Cinéma Gaumont Marignan, 27 av des Champs-Elysées, 8th (01.42.65.12.37). M° Franklin D Roosevelt **Admission** 35F/day. Week pass 150F.
A chance for the public to see unreleased international films, as well as meet directors, actors and key technicians. Stars and speakers to be confirmed.

mid Apr-end May: Foire du Trône

pelouse de Reuilly, 12th (01.46.27.52.29). M° Porte Dorée. **Admission** free; rides 10F-20F.
The largest funfair in France has it all: a huge Ferris wheel, haunted houses, *barbe à papa* (candy floss), plus old-fashioned attractions from fortune tellers to bearded ladies.

Good Friday: Le Chemin de la Croix

square Willette, 18th. M° Anvers or Abbesses. **Information** *(Sacré-Coeur 01.53.41.89.00).*
A crowd follows the Archbishop of Paris from the bottom of

The international tennis circus descends on Paris for the French Grand Slam tournament. A very glitzy event.

end May: Les Cinq Jours de l'Objet Extraordinaire

rues du Bac, de Lille, de Beaune, des Sts-Pères, de l'Université, de Verneuil, quai Voltaire, 7th. M° Rue du Bac or St-Germain-des-Prés. **Information** *(01.42.61.18.77).*
For five days, the upmarket antique dealers of the elegant Carré Rive Gauche each showcase one item according to theme. Special evening and Sunday openings.

early June-early July: Foire St-Germain

pl St-Sulpice and other venues in St-Germain-des-Prés, 6th. M° St-Sulpice. **Information** *(01.40.46.75.12).*
An echo of the medieval fair, with an antiques fair by the fountain, the Marché de la Poésie poetry salon, concerts and open-air theatre. For children there's a circus and miniature train.

early June: Festival Parade(s)

Various venues in Nanterre. RER Nanterre Ville. **Information** *(01.41.37.94.53).* **Admission** free.
A weekend of suburban street theatre and circus acts.

early June: Portes Ouvertes à la Garde Républicaine

12 bd Henri IV, 4th (01.49.96.13.13). M° Sully-Morland.
Polished horses, gleaming weaponry, booming brass as the historic regiment and presidential guard opens its doors.

June-July: Festival de St Denis

Various venues in St-Denis. M° St-Denis Basilique. **Information** *(01.48.13.12.10).* **Admission** 50F-250F.
Hear top classical choirs and orchestras amid the Gothic splendour of St-Denis Basilique and other historic buildings nearby.

20 June-14 July: Festival Chopin à Paris

Orangerie de Bagatelle, parc de Bagatelle, Bois de Boulogne, 16th. M° Porte Maillot, then bus 244. **Information** *(01.45.00.22.19).* **Admission** 80F-150F.
An annual treat for piano lovers, staged in the Orangerie of the Bagatelle gardens. This year's theme: the works of Chopin as a whole. Look out for candlelit evening concerts.

21 June: Fête de la Musique

All over Paris. **Information** *(01.40.03.94.70).*
Steel bands, Celtic rock, Yiddish singers, wandering accordionists and classical string quartets all join in on the longest day of the year, when thousands of musicians give free concerts all over the city (and country). Rising local rock, ragga and fusion talent plays at place Denfert-Rochereau, Arab and *raï* musicians at the Institut du Monde Arabe, but more anarchic gigs put on by local cafés or by street musicians often offer the best entertainment. Classical venues include Sainte-Chapelle, the Musée d'Orsay and the Palais de Justice.

mid-June: Feux de la St-Jean

quai St-Bernard, 5th (01.43.29.21.75). M° Gare d'Austerlitz. **Admission** free.
The feast of St John the Baptist is traditionally celebrated in France with fireworks, in Paris along the Seine.

end June: Gay Pride March

Information *Centre Gai et Lesbien (01.43.57.21.47).*
The parade grows more colourful by the year and draws big crowds, despite squabbling among the organisers. The route usually takes in République and the Bastille, but is subject to last-minute change, followed by an official fête and club events.

end June: Course des Garçons et Serveuses de Café

starts and finishes Hôtel de Ville, pl de l'Hôtel de Ville, 4th. M° Hôtel-de-Ville. **Information** *(01.42.96.60.75).*
A highlight of the alternative sporting year as over 500 bona

---

All play for the workers on **May Day.**

Montmartre up the steps to the Sacré Coeur, as he performs the fourteen traditional stations of the cross.

Apr: Marathon de Paris

starts around 9am, av des Champs-Elysées, first runners finish 11am, av Foch. **Information** *(01.41.33.15.68).*
20,000 runners huff round one of the world's biggest marathons, taking in the Bois de Boulogne and the quais.

end April-early May: Foire de Paris

Paris Expo, pl de la porte de Versailles. M° Porte de Versailles. **Information** *(01.49.09.61.21).* **Admission** 50F.
This is the biggest *salon*, a kind of amalgam of the Ideal Home Exhibition and Food & Wine fairs. A public showcase for every sector of commerce and industry – gastronomy, tourism, multimedia – there'll be plenty to taste and try out.

1 May: Fête du Travail

Labour Day is far more ardently maintained than Christmas or New Year. All museums (except the Eiffel Tower) close while unions and leftist groups stage a colourful march through working-class eastern Paris via the Bastille. Lilies of the valley are sold on street corners and given to mum.

30 May: La Course au Ralenti

departs 10am, rue Lepic, arrives pl du Tertre, 18th. M° Abbesses or Anvers. **Information** *(01.46.06.79.56).*
Beautiful vintage cars crawl up the steep streets of Montmartre. Last car to sputter over the 300m course wins.

Summer

end May-early June: French Tennis Open

Stade Roland Garros, 2 av Gordon-Bennett, 16th (01.47.43.48.00). M° Porte d'Auteuil. **Admission** 45F-280F.

fide café waiters and waitresses in uniform – bow ties, aprons, the lot – and tray in hand race over an 8km circuit via the *Grands Boulevards* and St-Germain-des-Prés.

July, Aug & Sept: Grandes Fêtes de Nuit de Versailles

Bassin de Neptune, Parc du Château de Versailles. RER C Versailles Rive Gauche. **Information** *(01.30.83.78.88).* **Admission** 70F-250F.

The sound and light spectacular in the gardens of Versailles (*see chapter* **Trips Out of Town**) attempts to recreate the spirit of the lavish court pageants given by Louis XIV. Costume scenes, dance and music are acted out against a background of fireworks and Le Nôtre's Baroque fountains.

end June-early July: La Goutte d'Or en Fête

square Léon, 18th. M° Barbès-Rochechouart. **Information** *(01.53.09.99.22).* **Admission** free.

Young locals and established names play *raï*, rap and reggae in the largely Arab and African Goutte d'Or district.

early July: Jazz à La Villette

211 av Jean-Jaurès, 19th (08.03.07.50.75/01.44.84.44.84). M° Porte de Pantin. **Admission** free-160F.

After twelve years, the Halle That Jazz festival has now colonised the entire La Villette complex. Big jazz, blues and Latin names perform in the Grande Halle, more experimental crossover types at the Cité de la Musique, and freebie events in smaller bar spaces or in the park itself.

13, 14 July: Le Quatorze Juillet (Bastille Day)

The French national holiday commemorates the storming of the Bastille prison on 14 July 1789, start of the French Revolution and a foretaste of bloodier events to come (*see chapter* **History**). On the evening of 13 July, Parisians dance at place de la Bastille. More partying takes place at firemen's balls: the stations of rue de Sévigné, rue du Vieux-Colombier, rue Blanche and bd du Port-Royal are particularly renowned (usually 13 and 14 July). There's a big Gay Ball on quai de la

Tournelle (5th). At 10am on the 14th, crowds line the Champs-Elysées as the President reviews a military parade from the Arc de Triomphe to Concorde. (Note: the Métro stops on the Champs are closed.) In the evening, thousands gather on the Champ-de-Mars for the firework display at Trocadéro.

14 July: Miss Guinguette Contest

Guinguette de l'Ile du Martin-Pêcheur, 41 Quai Victor-Hugo, 94500 Champigny-sur-Marne (01.49.83.03.02) RER Champigny-sur-Marne. 4pm on. **Admission** 40F.

Contestants at this hip dancehall on the Marne are judged on dancing ability, dress and knowledge of guinguette culture.

14 July-15 Aug: Paris, Quartier d'Eté

Various venues. **Information** *(01.44.94.98.00).* **Admission** free-100F.

Classical and world music concerts, dance, circus and other entertainment take place, often outdoors in the Jardins du Luxembourg, Palais-Royal and Tuileries and other parks, involving a wildly eclectic international array of participants.

mid-July-end Aug: Le Cinéma en Plein Air

Parc de la Villette, 19th (01.40.03.76.92). M° Porte de Pantin. **Admission** free.

Lie on the grass or recline in a deckchair for La Villette's tenth outdoor film festival, where movies are projected on to a huge screen. Focus this year is on European directors.

end July/early Aug: Le Tour de France

finishes av des Champs-Elysées, 8th. **Information** *(01.41.33.15.00).*

After 1998's drug-scandal riddled race, the great bike ride has a slightly toned down route for 1999 – but still finishes, as ever, with a last burst up the Champs-Elysées.

15 Aug: Fête de l'Assomption

Cathédrale Notre Dame de Paris, pl Notre Dame, 4th (01.42.34.56.10). M° Cité. **Admission** free.

On Assumption Day, Notre Dame becomes once again a place of religious rather than touristic pilgrimage. A procession parades around the Ile de la Cité behind a statue of the Virgin.

La Fête des Vendanges... *it's all to do with a vineyard and fancy dress. Anyway, cheers!*

Autumn

mid-Sept: Fête de L'Humanité
Information *(01.49.22.72.72)*.
With two ministers in the Jospin government, the French Communist Party remains a rare force in Europe and the jamboree put on by its newspaper *L'Humanité* is a celebration of all things left. Expect political debate, street artistes, lots of food stalls and concerts by big names and lots of homegrown pop, jazz and world music talent. Venue to be confirmed.

mid-Sept: Journées du Patrimoine
All over France.
This is the weekend when thousands queue for hours to reach the parts the public usually cannot. Not only are government ministries usually inaccessible but many are also in beautiful historic buildings. The longest waits are for the Palais de l'Elysée (home of the President), Matignon (home of the PM), Palais-Royal (Ministry of Culture and Conseil d'Etat) and Palais du Luxembourg (Senate). If you don't like waiting, seek out the more obscure embassies, ministries, private mansions or opulent corporate headquarters. This year's theme is citizenship. The Marais and Fbg-St-Germain are particularly ripe for mansion hopping. *Le Monde* and *Le Parisien* give detailed info, as does the Hôtel de Sully, 62 rue St-Antoine, 4th.

mid-Sept: Techno Parade
Information *(08.36.68.91.99)*.
The brainchild of ex-culture minister Jack Lang, and inspired by Berlin's Love Parade, last year's first Techno Parade gave the *genre* its official consecration. An estimated 200,000 revellers and floats by some twenty Parisian and provincial clubs and international guests joined in.

mid September: FIAC
Paris Expo, Pavillon du Parc, Porte de Versailles. 15th. Mº Porte de Versailles. Information *OIP (01.41.90.47.80)*. Admission 70F.
Around 160 French and international galleries participate at the Paris contemporary art fair. FIAC has moved to the Pavillon du Parc while repairs are carried out on the Grand Palais. After some staid years, a slimmed-down fair has put the emphasis back on the contemporary with a special section for young galleries. *See also chapter* **Galleries**.

15 Sept-31 Dec: Festival d'Automne
Various venues. Information *156 rue de Rivoli, 1st (01.53.451.7.00)*. Admission 100F-250F.
A highbrow challenge to the senses as world-class performers present experimental theatre, music and contemporary dance at such prestige venues as the Théâtre de la Ville, Odéon and the suburban public theatres.

early Oct: Fête des Vendanges à Montmartre
rue des Saules, 18th. Mº Lamarck-Caulaincourt. Mairie du XVIIIème, 1 pl Jules-Joffrin, 18th. Mº Jules-Joffrin. Information *(01.46.06.00.32)*.
The grape harvest at the last remaining vineyard in Montmartre is celebrated with great pomp in a parade from townhall to vineyard and back. Local residents dress up in pseudo-historic garb, bands parade and speeches are made.

early Oct: Prix de l'Arc de Triomphe
Hippodrome de Longchamp, Bois de Boulogne, 16th (01.49.10.20.30). Mº Porte d'Auteuil + free shuttle bus. Admission *lawns* free, *enclosure* 50F.
France's premiere horse race, where *le tout Paris* take their best frocks and champagne coolers out for a canter.

end Oct Salon du Chocolat
Espace Eiffel Branly, 23 quai Branly, 7th (01.45.03.21.26). Mº Alma-Marceau. Admission 50F.
A feast of chocolate to satisfy all gluttons.

Oct: Open Studios
Bastille area (11th, 12th); Ménilmontant (11th, 20th); 13th. Information *Artistes à la Bastille (01.53.36.06.73); Génie de la Bastille (01.40.09.84.03); Ménilmontant (01.40.03.01.61); 13ème Art (01.45.86.17.67)*. Admission free.
Open studio weekends are an interesting way to discover hundreds of painters, sculptors, engravers, photographers and designers – of wildly differing styles and standards – and the places where they work. The longest established scheme is around the Bastille, but there are others in the heavily artist-populated areas of Ménilmontant and the 13th.

early Oct: Mondial de l'Automobile
Paris-Expo, porte de Versailles, 15th. Mº Porte de Versailles. Information *(01.56.88.22.40)*. Admission 50F.
Next in 2000, the vast biennial, international motor show is a must for all who like fast things on wheels.

mid-Oct: Salon du Champignon
Jardin des Plantes, 36 rue Geoffroy-St-Hilaire, 5th (01.40.79.36.00). Mº Gare d'Austerlitz. Admission free.
Autumn means wild mushroom season and even in the Paris area, the keen head off to the Forest of Fontainebleau to seek them out. At the salon, hundreds of specimens are on show and mycologists on hand to help identify those safe to eat.

1 Nov: All Saints' Day
Although a full-blown US-style Hallowe'en has suddenly caught on, the more traditional remember the dead on 1 Nov, a public holiday when cemetery visiting, traditionally accompanied by chrysanthemums, is big business.

Nov: Mois de la Photo
Information *Maison Européenne de la Photographie (01.44.78.75.01)*. Admission varies.
Every two years (next 2000), themed photography exhibitions are put on in museums and commercial galleries all over town, with an emphasis on contemporary art photography.

early Nov: Festival Fnac-Inrockuptibles
La Cigale and other venues. Admission varies.
Indie rock and retro pop are the name of the game at the rock festival which has introduced such acts as Beck, Fiona Apple and Morcheeba to Paris. *Les Inrocks* has also proved itself open to new influences like easy listening and trip hop.

early Nov: Marjolaine
Parc Floral de Paris, Bois de Vincennes, 12th. Mº Château de Vincennes. Information *(01.45.56.09.09)*. Admission 40F.
Alternative/green living *à la parisienne*. In an atmosphere like a giant crafts fair, 450 stands dispense organic foods and wines, handmade gifts, household, health and beauty products and inform on environmental organisations from Greenpeace to cycling campaigns. Lectures range from earnest to plain odd.

11 Nov: Armistice Day
Arc de Triomphe, 8th. Mº Charles de Gaulle-Etoile.
At the remembrance ceremony for the dead of both World Wars, wreaths are laid by the President at the Tomb of the Unknown Soldier under the Arc de Triomphe. The remembrance flower is not the poppy but the *bleuet* (cornflower) after the colour of the pantalons worn by World War I infantry. *See also Compiègne in chapter* **Trips Out of Town**.

Nov: Lalique Skating Trophy
Palais-Omnisports de Paris-Bercy, 8 bd de Bercy, 12th (01.44.68.44.68). Mº Bercy. Admission 75F-245F.
Fancy things on ice by international champs and contenders.

Nov: Fête du Beaujolais Nouveau
The arrival of Beaujolais Nouveau on the third Thursday in November is no longer the much-hyped event of a few years

Savour authentic Vietnamese cuisine from Saigon, Hanoi and Hué

Le Santal

La Grande Tradition de
la Gastronomie Vietnamienne

Le Santal - Opéra
8 rue Halévy, 9th.
Mº Opéra
Tel: 01.47.42.24.69
Fax: 01.42.71.51.82

Le Santal - Côté Mer
6 rue de Poissy, 5th.
Mº Maubert-Mutualité
Tel: 01.43.26.30.56
Fax: 01.42.71.51.82

ago, but wine bars and cafés are still thronged (some from midnight on Wednesday, but especially Thursday evening) as customers gather to 'assess' the new vintage.

Winter

early Dec: Salon Nautique de Paris
Paris-Expo, porte de Versailles, 15th (01.41.90.47.10). M° Porte de Versailles. **Admission** 30F-60F.
Take to the seven seas as the international boat show shows off luxury yachts, leisure cruisers and record-breaking cats, among displays of windsurfing and other watery sports.

early Dec: Salon du Cheval, du Poney et de l'Ane
Paris-Expo, porte de Versailles, 15th (01.49.09.64.27). M° Porte de Versailles. **Admission** 50F-65F.
Everything you'll ever need to satisfy the equestrian-minded members of the family.

mid-Dec-early March: Patinoire de l'Hôtel de Ville
pl de l'Hôtel de Ville, 4th (01.42.76.40.40). M° Hôtel-de-Ville. **Admission** free (skate hire 30F).
First in the Tuileries, and since outside the city hall, the outdoor ice rink is just the thing for a chilly winter evening, surrounded by a forest of fir trees to give the illusion that you are far from the city. There are also a couple of merry-go-rounds for the little ones.

late Dec: Africolor
Théâtre Gérard Philipe, 59 bd Jules-Guesde, 93200 St-Denis (01.48.13.70.00). M° St-Denis Basilique. **Admission** 50F.
This annual African music fest promises a melting pot of traditional and Western-influenced sounds from across the African continent, culminating in a big all-night party on Christmas Eve.

late Dec: Festival Mondial du Cirque du Demain
Chapiteau Arlette Gross/Pelouse de Reuilly, 12th. (M° Porte Dorée. **Information** *(01.44.61.06.00).* **Admission** 70F-150F.
Young circus *artistes* teeter on high wires, clown, juggle or contort to catch the eye of any ringmaster in the audience. This is the springboard for many innovative talents who go on to join top modern troupes like Plume or Archaos.

24, 25 Dec: Christmas
Christmas is a family affair in France, with a dinner (on Christmas Eve) that traditionally involves *foie gras* or oysters, goose or turkey and a rich chocolate yule log (*bûche de Noël*). On Christmas Eve, Notre Dame Cathedral is packed for the 11pm service.

31 Dec: New Year's Eve
On *Réveillon* or the *Fête de la St-Sylvestre*, thousands of tourists and teenagers crowd the Champs Elysées and let off bangers, while nightclubs and restaurants put on expensive *soirées*. More oysters, *foie gras* and bubbly. As 1999 turns into 2000, look out for special events around Paris, such as at the Eiffel Tower.

1 Jan: La Grande Parade de Paris
leaves 2pm from Porte St-Martin, 2nd. M° Strasbourg-St Denis (01.43.65.10.10).
This colourful parade had its debut in Montmartre on 1 Jan 99, inspired by and twinned with London's Lord Mayor's Show. It offers over-the-top floats, vintage cars, jugglers, clowns, pompom girls plus festive music. The year 2000 parade, winding down the Grands Boulevards to Opéra and Madeleine will be even bigger and better, with 400-piece marching bands, giant balloon characters and more.

Chase the dragon at **Chinese New Year.**

6 Jan: Fête des Rois (Epiphany)
Pâtisseries sell thousands of *galettes des rois*, a flaky pastry cake with frangipane filling in which a *fève* or tiny charm is hidden. Whoever finds the charm dons a cardboard crown, becomes king or queen for a day, and chooses a consort.

Jan: Commemorative Mass for Louis XVI
Chapelle Expiatoire, 29 rue Pasquier, 8th (01.42.65.35.80). M° St-Augustin.
On the Sunday closest to 21 January, anniversary of the beheading of Louis XVI, members of France's aristocracy gather with die-hard royalists and assorted other far-right crackpots to mourn the end of the monarchy. Firm republicans are supposed to mark the day by eating *tête de veau*.

Jan or Sept: La Mairie de Paris vous invite au concert
Information *(01.42.76.67.00).*
Annual concert promotion offers two tickets for the price of one at hundreds of classical and jazz concerts all over Paris.

Jan/Feb: Nouvel An Chinois
Around av d'Ivry and av de Choisy, 13th. M° Porte de Choisy or Porte d'Ivry.
Chinatown comes alive to the clash of cymbals, as dragon dancers snake between the tower blocks to usher in Chinese New Year. Festivities are put on by the local businesses and take place on the nearest weekend(s) to the actual date.

early Feb: Festival Présences
Maison de Radio France, 116 av du Président-Kennedy, 16th (01.42.20.42.20). RER Kennedy-Radio France. **Admission** Free.
Risk the contemporary at this two-week long annual free festival of musical creation, performed by Radio France's resident orchestras, guest ensembles and soloists.

Key Events

c250 BC Lutétia founded on the Ile de la Cité by a Celtic tribe, the Parisii
52 BC Paris conquered by the Romans
260 St Denis executed on Mount Mercury (Montmartre)
361 Julian, Governor of Lutétia, becomes Roman Emperor
451 Attila the Hun nearly attacks Paris
496 Frankish king Clovis baptised at Reims
508 Clovis makes Paris his capital
543 Monastery of St-Germain-des-Prés founded
635 King Dagobert establishes Fair of St-Denis
800 Charlemagne becomes first Holy Roman Emperor. Moves capital from Paris to Aix-la-Chapelle (Aachen)
845-880 Paris sacked by the Vikings
987 Hugues Capet, Count of Paris, first King of France
c1100 Abélard meets Héloïse
1136 Abbot Suger begins Basilica of St-Denis
1163 Building of Notre Dame begins
1181 Philippe-Auguste establishes market at Les Halles
1190-1202 Philippe-Auguste constructs new city wall
1215 University of Paris recognised with Papal Charter
1246-48 Louis IX (St-Louis) builds the Sainte-Chapelle
1253 Sorbonne founded during the reign of Louis IX
c1300 Philippe IV Le Bel rebuilds the Conciergerie
1340 Beginning of Hundred Years' War with England
1357 Revolt by Etienne Marcel
1364 Charles V moves royal court to the Louvre and builds Bastille and Vincennes fortresses
1420-36 Paris under English rule
1463 First printing press in Paris
1528 François 1er begins rebuilding of Louvre
1572 St Bartholemew's Day massacre of Protestants
1593 Henri IV becomes a Catholic, ending Wars of Religion
1605 Building of place des Vosges
1610 Henri IV assassinated
1634 Académie Française founded by Cardinal Richelieu
1643 Cardinal Mazarin becomes Regent
1648-53 Paris occupied by the *Fronde* rebellion
1661 Louis XIV begins personal rule; fall of Fouquet
1667 Paris given its first street lighting
1672 Creation of Grands Boulevards on line of Charles V's city wall. Portes St-Denis and St-Martin built
1680 Comédie Française founded
1682 Louis XIV transfers Court to Versailles
1685 Colbert commissions place des Victoires
1700 Beginning of War of the Spanish Succession
1715 Death of Louis XIV; Philippe d'Orléans regent
1720 John Law's bank scheme collapses
1751 First volume of Diderot's *Encyclopédie* published
1753 Place Louis XV begun, later place de la Concorde
1785 Fermiers Généraux Tax Wall built around Paris
1789 First meeting of Etats-Généraux called since 1614
1789 14 July: Paris mob takes the Bastille. Oct: Louis XVI forced to leave Versailles for Paris. Population of Paris is about 600,000
1791 20 June: Louis XVI attempts to escape from Paris
1792 September Massacres. 22 Sept: Republic declared
1793 Execution of Louis XVI and Marie-Antoinette. Louvre museum opens to the public
1794 The Terror – 1300 heads fall in six weeks
1794 July: Jacobins overthrown; Directoire takes over
1799 Napoléon stages coup, and becomes First Consul
1804 Napoléon declares himself Emperor
1806 Napoléon orders building of the Arc de Triomphe
1814 Napoléon defeated; Russian army occupies Paris; Louis XVIII grants Charter of Liberties

1815 Napoléon regains power (the 'Hundred Days'), before defeat at Waterloo. Bourbons restored, with Louis XVIII
1828 Paris given first horse buses
1830 July: Charles X overthrown: Louis-Philippe of Orléans becomes king
1836 Completion of Arc de Triomphe
1837 First railway line in Paris, to St-Germain-en-Laye
1838 Daguerre creates first daguerreotypes
1848 Louis-Philippe overthrown: Second Republic, most men get the vote. Louis-Napoléon Bonaparte elected President
1852 Following coup, Louis-Napoléon declares himself Emperor Napoléon III: Second Empire.
1853 Haussmann appointed Prefect of Paris
1862 Construction of Palais Garnier begins
1863 Manet's *Déjeuner sur l'Herbe* first exhibited
1866 *Le Figaro* daily newspaper founded
1870 Prussian victory at Sedan. Napoléon III abdicates
1871 Commune takes over Paris after the Prussian siege
1874 First Impressionist exhibition on bd des Capucines
1889 Paris Exhibition on centenary of Revolution: Eiffel Tower built. Moulin Rouge opens
1894-1900 Dreyfus case polarises public opinion
1895 Dec: world's first public cinema screening in Paris by the Lumière brothers
1900 Paris World Exhibition: population of Paris then two million. First Métro line opens
1904 Pablo Picasso moves to Paris
1914 As World War I begins, Germans beaten back from Paris at Battle of the Marne
1918 11 Nov: Armistice signed in forest of Compiègne
1919 Peace conference held at Versailles
1934 Fascist demonstrations
1936-37 France elects Popular Front government under Leon Blum; first paid holidays
1940 Germans occupy Paris
1941-42 Mass deportations of Paris Jews
1944 25 Aug: Paris liberated
1946 Fourth Republic established. Women given the vote
1947 Dior's New Look
1949 Simone de Beauvoir publishes *The Second Sex*
1955-56 Revolt begins in Algeria; demonstrations on the streets in Paris
1957 Opening of CNIT in new La Défense business district
1958 De Gaulle President: Fifth Republic
1959 France founder member of the EEC (European Economic Community)
1968 May: student riots and workers' strikes in Paris and across France
1969 De Gaulle resigns, Pompidou becomes President; Les Halles market closes
1973 Boulevard Périphérique around Paris inaugurated
1977 Centre Pompidou opens. Jacques Chirac elected Mayor of Paris
1981 François Mitterrand elected President; abolition of the death penalty
1986 Musée d'Orsay opens
1989 Bicentenary of the Revolution celebrated: Louvre pyramid and the Opéra Bastille both completed
1992 Disney theme park opens outside Paris
1995 May: Jacques Chirac elected President
1996 Dec: Opening of new Bibliothèque Nationale François Mitterrand
1997 Socialist government elected under Lionel Jospin
1998 France wins football World Cup at Stade de France

History

The story of Paris is a bloody and vibrant tapestry of radicalism and revolt – social, political, religious, artistic.

PRE-HISTORY

Traces of habitation in the Paris basin have been found from the fourth and second millenia BC in Montmorency and Villejuif. Within Paris, Neolithic canoes, evidence of early river traffic, were discovered at Bercy in the early 1990s. Bronze age tombs and artefacts have also been discovered.

C 250BC: CELTIC PARISII

In about 250BC a Celtic tribe called the **Parisii,** probably driven from lands further east by the more powerful Belgae, established a fishing settlement named **Lutétia** on the Ile de la Cité. Sited on a route between Germany and Spain at the confluence of the Seine and the Marne, it was a natural crossroads. The Celts were canny traders, and grew prosperous – witness the hoard of gold coins from the first century BC in the **Musée des Antiquités Nationales**, St-Germain-en-Laye.

ROMAN CONQUEST

Its strategic position also made the city a prime target. By the first century BC the Romans had arrived in northern Gaul. Julius Caesar mentions the city of the Parisii, situated on an isle in the Seine, known as Lutétia, in his *Gallic Wars*. In 53BC when the Celtic tribes, the Senones and the Carnutes, refused to send delegates to the Assembly of Gaul at Amiens, he ordered the assembly to keep watch over the rebellious tribes. In 52BC, the Celt Vercingétorix spearheaded a revolt, joined by Camulogenus, who took control of Lutétia, while his army camped on Mons Lutetius, now site of the Panthéon. Caesar's lieutenant Labienus crushed the rebels at Melun, and marched downstream, camping in an area now occcupied by the Louvre's Cour Carrée. In a brief battle by the Champ de Mars, Camulogenus and his army were massacred, and Vercingétorix captured; thereafter the Parisii tribe and Gaul were under Roman rule.

Lutétia thrived. The Roman town centred on what is now the Montagne Ste-Geneviève on the Left Bank, fanning out either side of the *cardus maximus* (main thoroughfare), the present **rue St-Jacques**. Many of its villas were of masonry, brick and mortar, some embellished with frescoes and mosaics. A model of the ancient city, along with architectural vestiges, is on view at **Musée Carnavalet**. Around AD50-200 Lutétia acquired its grandest public buildings. The remains have been uncovered in a forum

on rue Soufflot, a trio of bathing establishments (rue des Ecoles, rue Gay-Lussac, boulevard St-Michel) and parts of the city wall and a hypocaust (heating system) at the Archaeological Crypt of Notre Dame. There was also a temple to Jupiter, where the cathedral now stands. Only the 10,000-seat **Arènes de Lutèce**, where Romans saw Christians slaughtered by lions, and the **Thermes de Cluny** reflect any of this former glory today.

CHRISTIANITY & ST DENIS

Christianity appeared in the third century AD, when Athenian St Denis, first bishop of Lutétia, was sent to evangelise its people. Legend has it that in 260, he and two companions began to knock pagan statues off their pedestals. They were arrested and decapitated on Mount Mercury, thereafter known as Mons Martis (Mount of Martyrs), later Montmartre. Plucky Denis picked up his head and walked away, chanting psalms. He finally fell at a seemingly predestined site north of Paris, where a pious Christian woman buried him. A sanctuary was later erected on the spot, since replaced by the **Basilique St-Denis**.

Roman power weakening, Lutétia (renamed Paris in 212) was under increasing attack from barbarians from the east. Many inhabitants retreated to their ancestral island, and a wall was built around the Cité. In 313 Emperor Constantine effectively made Christianity the new religion of the Empire.

357-363: EMPEROR JULIAN

In 357, a new governor, Constantine's nephew Julian, arrived in Lutétia (as he still called it). He improved the city's defences, and sought to return to Platonic ideals in opposition to what he saw as the brutality of Constantine and subsequent Christian emperors. In 361, after victories over the barbarians, his army declared him Roman Emperor in Paris. Condemned by Christian historians as 'Julian the Apostate', he could do little to turn back the new faith or the decline of Rome; he was killed in battle in 363.

STE-GENEVIEVE & ATTILA THE HUN

By the early fifth century, Roman rule had effectively collapsed in northern Gaul, its cities left to fend for themselves. In the ensuing chaos, the exemplary life of Ste Geneviève – and the threat of war – helped confirm many converts in the new faith. As the legend goes, in 451 Attila the Hun and his army were approaching Paris. Its people prepared to flee, but Geneviève told them to stay, saying the

Hun would spare their city so long as they repented of their sins and prayed with her. Miraculously, Attila did not attack but moved off to the south. Geneviève was acclaimed saviour of Paris.

CLOVIS & THE MEROVINGIANS

It was only a temporary reprieve. In 464 Childeric the Frank attacked Paris, and in 508 his son Clovis made it his capital, seated at the old Roman governor's palace on the Ile de la Cité. The now-aged Geneviève converted the new king to Christianity; he was baptised by St Rémi in **Reims**, 496. Clovis (ruled 481-511) began the Merovingian dynasty, of 'Long-haired kings' (they never cut their hair, apparently). On the Left Bank he founded the abbey of St-Pierre et St-Paul (later Ste-Geneviève), where he, queen Clotilde and Geneviève could be buried side by side. The **Tour de Clovis**, within the Lycée Henri IV, is a last relic of the basilica. Ste Geneviève, who died about 512, remains the patron saint of Paris; a shrine to her and relics are in the church of **St-Etienne-du-Mont** (originally adjoining the abbey). Clovis' son and successor Childéric II founded the equally renowned abbey of St-Germain-des-Prés. Not that the Merovingians were especially pious: under their law an inheritance had to be divided equally among heirs. This led to regular bloodletting and infanticide between royal princes, dowager queens and uncles, and the eventual snuffing-out of the line in 751. Most productive of the dynasty for Paris was Dagobert (628-638), who established the important annual Fair of St-Denis.

CAROLINGIANS V VIKINGS

Next came the Carolingians, named after Charles Martel ('the Hammer'), credited with halting the spread of Islam with his victory over the Moors at Tours, 732. In 751 his son Pepin 'the Short' was proclaimed King of all the Franks. His heir Charlemagne extended the Frankish kingdom and was made Holy Roman Emperor by the pope in 800. As his capital, however, he chose Aix-La-Chapelle (Aachen), entrusting sidelined Paris to a hereditary Count.

After Charlemagne, the Carolingian empire gradually fell apart, helped by famine, flood and marauding Vikings (the Norsemen or Normans), who sacked the city repeatedly between 845 and 885 and looted wealthy abbeys like **St-Germain-des-Prés**. When Emperor Charles II the Bald showed little interest in defending the city, Parisians sought help from Robert the Strong, Count of Anjou. His son Eudes (Odo), succeeded him as Count of Paris, and led the defence of the city in a ten-month long Viking seige in 885, sharing the throne 893-898 with Charles III the Simple. The feudal lords thus came to outpower their masters. In 987, the Count of Paris, Hugues Capet, great-grandson of Robert the Strong, was elected King of France by his peers at **Senlis**, and made Paris his capital. A new era was beginning.

THE CAPETIANS

The ascension of Hugues Capet, founder of the Capetian dynasty, is the point from which 'France' can be said to exist. For a long time, however, the kingdom consisted of little more than the Ile-de-France. Powerful local lords – in Normandy, Burgundy, the south, and later the possessions of the Kings of England – would defy royal authority for centuries. 'France' would largely be created through the gradual extension of Parisian power.

Paris continued to grow in importance, thanks to its powerful abbeys and the fairs of St-Germain and St-Denis. By the twelfth century, three distinct areas were in place: religion and government on Ile de la Cité, intellectual life around the various Left Bank schools, and commerce and finance on the Right Bank, close to Paris' main port at La Grève (by the present Hôtel de Ville) and its main market. The booming city was seeing a spectacular renaissance.

ABBOT SUGER

A major figure in this expansion was Suger, Abbot of St-Denis and minister to a series of weak monarchs, Louis VI (the Fat) and Louis VII (the Younger). The latter unwisely divorced the first of his three wives, Eleanor of Aquitaine, who then married Henry II of England, bringing a vast portion of southwest France under English control. Suger did much to hold the state together and give it an administration; as priest, he commissioned the new **Basilique St-Denis** in 1136, to house pilgrims flocking to the shrine. Considered the first true Gothic building, St-Denis set the style across France and northern Europe for four centuries. In 1163, Bishop Sully of Paris began building **Notre Dame**, embodiment of the High Gothic aesthetic.

ABELARD & HELOISE

Paris was also developing a reputation as a centre of learning. The abbeys had kept scholastic traditions alive, and by the eleventh century the Canon school of Notre Dame was already widely admired. By about 1100, scholars began to move out from the cathedral school and teach independently in the Latin Quarter. One such was Pierre Abélard, a brilliant logician and dialetician who had rooms in the **rue Chanoinesse** behind Notre Dame (still preserved to this day). He would be forever remembered for his part in one of the world's great love stories, a star-crossed saga of forbidden sex, castration and classical philosophy.

In 1118, at 39, Abélard (a nickname meaning 'honey-mouthed', referring to his debating skills) was taken on by Canon Fulbert of Notre Dame as tutor to his 17-year-old niece Héloïse. The pair began a passionate affair, but were found out by the Canon. Twice he enjoined them to celibacy, twice they disobeyed him. Following an illegitimate pregnancy and a secret marriage, the enraged father had Abélard castrated and his daughter consigned to a

Together at last: **Abélard & Héloïse***'s remains in Père-Lachaise cemetery.*

monastery. Abélard went on to write refined works of medieval philosophy, while Héloïse continued to send tormented, poetic missives to her lost lover. The two were reunited in death at the Paraclete, the oratory-cum-convent which Abélard had himself established and given to Héloïse, who became a famous abbess, and her nuns. In 1817, at the end of a circuitous route, their remains came to rest in a fanciful neo-Gothic tomb in **Père Lachaise cemetery**.

In 1215 the Paris schools combined in a more formally organised 'university' under papal protection. The greatest medieval thinkers attended this 'New Athens': German theologian Albert the Great, Italians Thomas Aquinas and Bonaventure, Scot Duns Scotus, Englishman William of Ockham. Most famous of the schools was the **Sorbonne**, founded in 1253 by Robert de Sorbon, Louis IX's chaplain.

PHILIPPE AUGUSTE

The first great Capetian monarch Philippe II (Philippe Auguste 1165-1223) became king in 1180. He won Normandy from King John of England and added Auvergne and Champagne.The first great royal builder to leave a mark on Paris, he built a new, larger fortified city wall, chunks of which can still be seen in **rue des Jardins-St-Paul** in the Marais and **rue Clovis** in the Latin Quarter. He began a new fortress on the Right Bank, the **Louvre**, but his main residence was still on Ile de la Cité (*see* **Conciergerie**). In 1181, he established the first covered markets, Les Halles, on the site they occupied until 1969; food merchants, drapers and other trade corporations followed. He also sought to do some-

thing about the city's mud and foul odours, ordering the first paving of streets in post-Roman Paris, and closing the most pestilential cemeteries.

LOUIS IX (ST LOUIS)

Philippe's grandson Louis IX (1226-70) was famed for his extreme piety. When not on crusade, or scouring Europe for holy relics, he put his stamp on Paris, commissioning the **Sainte-Chapelle**, convents, hospices and student hostels. But it was his grandson, Philippe IV (Le Bel, 1285-1314) who transformed the fortress on the Cité into a palace fit for a king, with the monumental Salle des Gens d'Armes in the **Conciergerie**. The end of his reign, however, was marred by insurrection in Paris and riotous debauchery at Court. In suspiciously quick succession, his three sons ascended the throne. The last, Charles IV, died in 1328 leaving no male heir.

THE VALOIS KINGS

All this proved irresistible to the English, who claimed the French crown for young Edward III, son of Philippe IV's daughter. The French refused to recognise his claim, as Salic law barred inheritance via the female line. Philippe de Valois, the late king's cousin, claimed the crown for himself (Philippe VI, 1328-50), and thus began the Hundred Years' War.

The Black Death arrived in Europe in the 1340s and, in Paris, outbreaks of the plague alternated with battles, bourgeois revolts, popular insurrections, and bloody vendettas between aristocratic factions. In 1355, Etienne Marcel, a rich draper, *prévôt* of the Paris merchants (a kind of mayoral precursor) and member of the *Etats-généraux* (it had met for the first time in Paris in 1347) seized Paris. His aim was to limit the power of the throne and gain a constitution for the city from Dauphin Charles (then regent, as his father Jean II had been captured by the English). In January 1357 Marcel declared a general strike and armed his merchants, speaking out against corrupt royal counsellors and demanding the release of Charles 'The Bad', King of Navarre, direct descendant of the Capetians, ally of the English – and prisoner of the French king. The Dauphin grudgingly accepted the *Etats'* extended powers but, after Charles of Navarre escaped prison and received a glorious welcome in Paris, offered to defend the city only if the *Etats* footed the bill. The city was divided, with Marcel's partisans donning a blue-and-red hood in solidarity. Suspicion, treachery and murder ensued, until in 1358 the Dauphin's supporters retook the city, and Marcel and his followers were savagely executed. So France's first popular revolution died with its leader.

CHARLES V (1364-80)

The former Dauphin distanced himself from the Paris mob by transferring his residence to the Louvre, where he installed his library and precious works of art. He further extended the city walls and had a new stronghold built on the eastern edge of Paris, the **Bastille**. Despite political turmoil, the arts flourished. Parisian artisans produced peerless miniatures, tapestries, manuscripts, together with gold, silver and carved ivory *objets*.

1420-36: ENGLISH RULE

After the battle of Agincourt in 1415 the English, in alliance with the Dukes of Burgundy, seemed to prevail. From 1420 to 1436 Paris was under English rule (as was most of France), with the Duke of Bedford as governor. In 1431, Henry VI of England was crowned King of France in Notre Dame. But the city was almost constantly besieged by the French, at one time helped by Joan of Arc. Eventually, Charles VII (1422-61) retook his capital.

RENAISSANCE & HERESY

Booksellers Fust and Schöffer brought printed books to the city in 1463, supported by wily Louis XI (1461-81) against the powerful scribes' and booksellers' guilds. In 1470, Swiss printers set up a press at the Sorbonne; others soon followed. By the end of the sixteenth century Parisian printers had published 25,000 titles.

In the last decades of the fifteenth century the restored Valois monarchs sought to reassert their position. Masons erected Flamboyant Gothic churches (*see chapter* **Architecture**), as well as impressive mansions commissioned by nobles, prelates and wealthy bourgeois, such as **Hôtel de Cluny** and **Hôtel de Sens**. The city's population tripled over the sixteenth century and the *faubourgs* outside the city walls also grew.

Henri IV: *converted for the capital.*

FRANCOIS 1ER

Most spectacular Valois was François 1er (1515-47), epitome of a Renaissance monarch. He engaged in endless wars with great rival Emperor Charles V, but also built sumptuous châteaux at **Fontainebleau**, Blois and **Chambord**, and gathered a glittering court of knights, poets and Italian artists, such as Leonardo da Vinci and Benvenuto Cellini. He also set about transforming the Louvre into the palace we see today, where he hung his Titians, Raphaels and the *Mona Lisa*. A native school of portraiture also developed, led by François Clouet.

François 1er's grandeur, however, was unable to prevent the advance of Protestantism, even if ever more heretics were sent to the stake in place de Grève. Huguenot (French Protestant) strongholds were mostly in the west; Paris, by contrast, was a citadel of virulent, often bloodthirsty Catholic orthodoxy, complicated by interwoven aristocratic squabbles between the factions of the Huguenot Prince de Condé and the Catholic Duc de Guise, supported by François 1er's successor Henri II (1547-60).

THE WARS OF RELIGION

By the 1560s, the situation had degenerated into open warfare. Henri II's scheming widow Catherine de Médicis, regent for the young Charles IX (1560-74), was the power behind the throne. Savagery was seen on both sides, and paranoia was rife. In 1572, a rumour ran round that Protestant Huguenots were plotting to murder the royal family and sack the city; in anticipation, on 23 August, St-Bartholomew's Day, Catholic mobs turned on anyone suspected of Protestant sympathies, slaughtering over 3000 people. When Henri III (1574-89) sought a compromise between the two sides, Paris turned on its sovereign and forced him to flee the Louvre. In August 1589 he was assassinated by a fanatical monk, so ending the Valois line.

HENRI IV & THE BOURBON DYNASTY

Henri III had recognised his ally Henri of Navarre, a Huguenot, as heir. He in turn proclaimed himself King Henri IV, founding the Bourbon dynasty. Fervently Catholic Paris continued to resist in a siege that dragged on nearly four years. Its inhabitants ate cats, rats, donkeys and even grass. Henri IV agreed to become a Catholic in 1593, and was received into the church at St-Denis, declaring that 'Paris vaut bien une messe' (Paris is well worth a mass). On 22 March 1594, he entered the city.

Aided by minister Sully, Henri IV undertook to unify the country and re-establish the monarchy's power. In Paris, he set about changing the face of his ravaged capital. He commissioned **place Dauphine** and Paris' first enclosed, geometrical square – the place Royale, now **place des Vosges**, cue for the building-up of the elegant Marais around it. But he never got round to improving the city's congested streets, habitually clogged with pedestrians, horses, donkeys and coaches. In 1610, after at least 23 other assassination attempts had failed, the King was stabbed to death by a Catholic fanatic while caught in a bottleneck on the **rue de la Ferronnerie**. The *ancien régime* began as it would end: with regicide.

LOUIS XIII & CARDINAL RICHELIEU

On Henri's death son Louis XIII (1610-43) was only eight years old, and Henri's widow, Marie de Médicis, became regent. She commissioned the self-aggrandising **Palais du Luxembourg**, and a series of 24 panels glorifying her role painted by Rubens, now in the Louvre. In 1617 Louis XIII, still only 16, was encouraged to take over. But the real power lay with Cardinal Richelieu, who in 1624 became the king's chief minister.

Richelieu won the confidence of tormented Louis XIII, who stuck by his minister through numerous plots hatched by his mother, wife Anne of Austria, assorted princes and disgruntled grandees. A brilliant administrator, he created a strong, centralised monarchy, paving the way for the absolutism of Louis XIV and steadily grinding down what he perceived as the two major enemies of the monarchy: abroad, Spain, and the independence of the aristocracy (especially u the Huguenots) at home. A great architectural patron, he commissioned Jacques Lemercier to build him a palace, which became the **Palais-Royal**, and rebuilt the **Sorbonne**. This was the height of the Catholic Counter-Reformation, and architects were commissioned to create such lavish Baroque churches as the **Val-de-Grâce**.

The literary lights of the *Grand Siècle* often found their patrons in the elegant Marais *hôtels particuliers*, where salons hosted by lettered ladies like Mlle de Scudéry, Mme de la Fayette, Mme de Sévigné and the erudite courtesan Ninon de l'Enclos, rang with witty asides and political intrigue. By comparison, Richelieu's Académie Française (founded 1634) was a fusty, pedantic reflection of the establishment.

CARDINAL MAZARIN & LA FRONDE

Richelieu died in 1642. Next year Louis XIII died, leaving five-year-old Louis XIV as heir. Anne of Austria became regent, with Cardinal Mazarin (a Richelieu protegé whose palace is part of the **Bibliothèque Nationale Richelieu**) as chief minister.

In 1648 the royal family was made to flee Paris by the **Fronde**, a rebellion of peasants and aristocrats led by the prince de Condé against taxes and growing royal power. Parisians supported the revolt at first – traditionally thought the root of Louis XIV's dislike of his capital – but soon tired of anarchy. When Mazarin's army entered Paris in 1653 with the boy-king, they were warmly received. Mazarin died in 1661, shortly after long-standing enemy Spain had been decisively defeated, leaving France stronger than ever and with military capacity to spare.

LOUIS XIV THE SUN KING

This was the springboard for Louis XIV's absolute rule, with the classically megalomaniac statement 'L'Etat, c'est moi' ('The State is me'). Military expansion was essential to Louis XIV's concept of greatness, and France was engaged in continual wars against the Dutch, Austria and England.

An essential figure in Louis' years of triumph was minister of finance Jean-Baptiste Colbert. He amassed most of the other important ministries over the 1660s and determined to transform Paris into a 'new Rome', with grand, symmetrical vistas – a sort of expression of absolute monarchy in stone. In the 1680s, he commissioned the finely proportioned **place des Victoires** and **place Vendôme** to glorify the king, and opened up the first boulevards along the line of Charles V's wall, with triumphal arches at **Porte St-Denis** and **Porte St-Martin**.

Louis XIV took little interest in Colbert's schemes. Such was his aversion to Paris that from the 1670s he focused on **Versailles**, whither he transferred the court, and into which he poured vast wealth. A place at court was essential for a successful career; the ambitious had no choice but follow the monarch.

The arts flourished. In 1659 Molière's troupe of actors settled in Paris under the protection of the King, presenting plays for both court and public. After the playwright's death in 1673, they became the **Comédie Française**. Favoured composer at Versailles was the Italian Lully, granted sole right to compose operas (in which the King himself often appeared). Other composers included Rameau and Charpentier, while Mme de Maintenon encouraged the tragedies of Racine.

Despite Colbert's efforts, endless wars left the royal finances in permanent disorder, reflected in growing poverty, vagrancy and a great many crippled war veterans. The **Invalides** was built to house them on one side of town, and the **Salpêtrière** on the other to shelter fallen women. Colbert died in 1683, and the military triumphs of earlier years gave way to the grim struggles of the War of the

Spanish Succession. Life at Versailles soured under dour Mme de Maintenon, Louis' last mistress, whom he secretly married in 1684. Nobles began sneaking away to modish **Faubourg-St-Germain**.

PHILIPPE D'ORLEANS

Louis XIV had several children, but not long before his own death, both his son and grandson died, leaving five-year-old great-grandson Louis XV (1715-74) as heir. The Regent, Philippe d'Orléans, an able general and diplomat, speedily returned the Court to Paris. Installed in the Palais-Royal, his lavish dinners regularly degenerated into orgies. The pleasure-loving courtiers and the Parisians who aped them spawned a large service population of dressmakers, jewellers, hairdressers, decorators and domestic servants. Tales of country youths corrupted by the city where they came to seek their fortune inspired writers from Marivaux to Rousseau, Restif de la Bretonne to the Marquis de Sade: Paris was the *nouvelle Babylone*, the modern Sodom.

1720 THE SOUTH SEA BUBBLE

The state remained chronically in debt, though the Regent sought to avoid further military entanglement. Taxation came mainly in duties on such commodities as salt. Collection was farmed out to a kind of private corporation, the *Fermiers généraux*, who passed an amount to the state and kept a proportion for themselves. This system bore down on the poor, was riddled with corruption and never produced the required resources; nevertheless none of the *ancien régime*'s ministers was ever able to abolish it. The Regent thought he had a remedy with Scottish banker John Law's investment scheme in the French colonies, which inspired a frenzy of wheeler-dealing. But in 1720, a run on the bank revealed that very little gold and silver was on hand to back up the paper bills. Panic ensued. Law was expelled from France, and the Regent, and to some extent royal government, were deeply discredited. The South Sea Bubble had burst.

LOUIS XV & THE ENLIGHTENMENT

As soon as he was his own man, Louis XV left Paris for Versailles, which once again saw sumptuous festivities in its new opera. But in the Age of Enlightenment, Paris was the real capital of Europe. 'One lives in Paris; elsewhere, one simply vegetates,' wrote Casanova. Paris' salons became the forum for intellectual debate under renowned hostesses like the Marquise du Deffand on rue de Beaune and Mme Geoffrin on rue St-Honoré. The King's mistress, the beautiful Marquise de Pompadour (1721-64), was a friend and protectress of Diderot and the *encyclopédistes*, of Marivaux and Montesquieu, and corresponded with Voltaire. She encouraged Louis XV to embellish his capital with monuments, such as Jacques Ange Gabriel's **Ecole Militaire** and place Louis XV (**place de la Concorde**). Intellectual activity was matched by a flour-ishing of fine and decorative arts with painters like Boucher, Van Loo and Fragonard setting the style.

LOUIS XVI

The great failure of Louis XV's reign was the defeat in the Seven Years' War (1756-63), in which France lost most of its colonies in India and Canada to Britain. As his grandson Louis XVI (ruled 1774-91), began his reign, France was expanding economically and culturally. Across Europe, people craved Parisian luxuries. In the capital, roads were widened, lamps erected, gardens and promenades created. Nobs indulged in horse racing (a taste acquired from the English) at **Vincennes** and the **Bois de Boulogne**. On boulevard du Temple, all classes watched dancers, singers, acrobats and trained monkeys. The city was obsessed with the new, from ballooning (begun by the Montgolfier brothers in 1783) to the works of Rousseau. Even royal princes flirted with the new sensibilities, as Louis-Philippe d'Orléans developed the **Palais-Royal** as a kind of open house for different classes, entertainments and ideas.

But France's intervention in the American War of Independence drove finances further towards bankruptcy. In 1785, at the behest of the *Fermiers généraux*, a tax wall was built around Paris, which only increased popular discontent (*see chapter* **Architecture**). Louis XVI's only option was to appeal to the nation; first through the *parlements* or regional assemblies of lawyers, and if all else failed the *Etats-généraux*, the representation of the Nobility, Clergy and Commoners, which had not met since 1614, and which would inevitably alter the relationship between society and a monarchy that believed it had an absolute right to command. Louis XVI continued to prevaricate, as 1789 began.

EARLY 1789

The spring of 1789 found Louis XVI increasingly isolated as unrest swept through France. In Paris, the people were suffering the results of a disastrous harvest, and there were riots in the Faubourg St-Antoine. The king finally agreed to convene the *Etats-généraux* at Versailles in May. The members of the Third Estate, the commoners, aware that they represented a far larger proportion of the population than nobility and clergy, demanded a system of one vote per member. Discussions broke down, and a rumour went round that the King was sending troops to arrest them. On 20 June 1789, at the Jeu de Paume at Versailles, the Third Estate took an oath not to separate until 'the constitution of the kingdom was established'. Louis backed down, and the *Etats-généraux*, newly renamed the **Assemblée Nationale**, set about discussing a Constitution.

Debate also raged in the streets among the poor *sans-culottes* (literally, without breeches: only the poor wore long trousers). It was assumed that any concession by the King was intended to deceive.

Louis had posted foreign troops around Paris, and on 11 July dismissed his minister, Jacques Necker, considered the commoners' sole ally. On 13 July an obscure lawyer named Camille Desmoulins leapt on a café table in the Palais-Royal. Likening Necker's dismissal to another St-Bartholomew's Day, he called the excited crowd: 'Aux armes!' 'To arms!'

STORMING THE BASTILLE

On 14 July, the crowd marched on **Les Invalides**, carrying off thousands of guns, then moved on to the hitherto invincible **Bastille**, symbol of royal repression. Its governor, the Marquis de Launay, refused to surrender, but the huge crowd outside grew more aggressive. It seems that one nervous Bastille sentry fired a shot, and within minutes there was general firing on the crowd. The mob brought up cannon to storm the fortress. After a brief battle, and the deaths of 87 revolutionaries, Launay offered his surrender. He was immediately killed, and his head paraded through Paris on a pike. Inside only seven prisoners were found. Nevertheless, the Revolution now had the symbolic act of violence that marked a break with the past.

Political debate proliferated on every side, above all in the rapidly multiplying political clubs, such as the Cordeliers, who met in a Franciscan monastery in St-Germain, or the radical Jacobins, who had taken over a Dominican convent on rue St-Honoré. Thousands of pamphlets were produced, read avidly by a remarkably literate public.

But there was also real hardship among the poor. As disruption spread through the country, wheat deliveries were interrupted, raising bread prices still further. In October, an angry crowd of women marched to Versailles to protest – the incident when Marie-Antoinette supposedly said, 'let them eat cake'. The women ransacked part of the palace, killing guards, and were only placated when Louis XVI appeared with a revolutionary red-white-and-blue cockade and agreed to be taken to Paris. The royal family were now virtual prisoners in the Tuileries.

In the Assembly, the Girondins, who favoured an agreement with the monarchy, originally prevailed, but came under intense attack from the openly Republican Jacobins. On 20 June 1791, Louis and his family tried to leave Paris by night, hoping to organise resistance from safety abroad. They got as far as the town of Varennes, where they were recognised and returned to Paris as captives.

In 1792, the monarchies of Europe formed a coalition to save Louis and his family. A Prussian army marched into France; the Duke of Brunswick threatened to raze Paris if the King came to harm. Paranoia reigned and anyone who showed sympathy for Louis could be accused of conspiring with foreign powers against the people. On 10 August, an army of *sans-culottes* demanded the Assembly officially depose Louis. This was refused, and the crowd attacked the Tuileries. The royal family were imprisoned in the **Temple** by the radical Commune de Paris, led by Danton, Marat and Robespierre, who thus became the dominant force in the Revolution.

1792-94: THE TERROR

The next month, as the Prussians approached Paris, saw the 'September Massacres'. Revolutionary mobs invaded the city's prisons to eliminate anyone who could possibly be a 'traitor' in a bloodletting that accounted for close to 2000 people. The monarchy was formally abolished on 22 September 1792, proclaimed Day I of 'Year I of the French Republic' in the all-new calendar. Soon after the French citizen army defeated the Prussians at Valmy.

This was the beginning of the most radical phase of the Revolution. The Jacobins proclaimed the need to be implacable with 'the enemies within', and so Dr Guillotin's invention took its place in the *place de la Révolution* (formerly Louis XV, now Concorde). Louis XVI was executed on 21 January 1793, followed in October by Marie-Antoinette.

In September 1793 the Revolutionary Convention, replacing the Assemblée Nationale, put 'terror on the agenda', in response to demands for more decisive action against foreign spies. The Revolution, as the Jacobin St-Just said, 'devoured its own children': most of the leading Girondins, Philippe-Egalité of Orléans, and even Jacobins such as Danton and

Me, myself and I: **Louis XIV**

Camille Desmoulins would meet the scaffold. In the Grande Terreur of 1794, 1300 heads fell in six weeks.

THE AGE OF REASON

Cultural transformation now proceeded apace; churches were confiscated in November 1789, made like Notre Dame into 'Temples of Reason' or put to practical uses. Many were vandalised; the carved bookcases from the Celestins convent were transferred to the Bibliothèque Nationale, while the Sainte-Chapelle became a storehouse for flour. The place du Trône (now **place de la Nation**) became place du Trône Renversé (Overturned Throne) and an 'Altar of the Fatherland' was installed on the Champ de Mars. All titles were abolished – *monsieur* and *madame* became *citoyen* and *citoyenne*. Artists participated in the revolutionary cause: as well as painting portraits of revolutionary figures and the *Death of Marat*, David organised the Fête de la Régénération in August 1793 at the Bastille.

THE DIRECTOIRE

The collective psychosis of the Terror could not endure. In July 1794 a group of moderate Republicans led by Paul Barras succeeded in arresting Robespierre, St-Just and the last Jacobins, who were immediately guillotined amid expressions of generalised hatred for these erstwhile popular heroes.

The wealthy, among them some Revolutionary *nouveaux riches*, emerged blinking into the city's fashionable corners. Barras and his colleagues set themselves up as a five-man Directoire to rule the Republic. In 1795, they were saved from a royalist revolt by an ambitious young Corsican general Napoléon Bonaparte, in a shootout at the **Eglise St-Roch**. France, if no longer the fire-breathing Republic of the Jacobins, was still at war with most of the monarchies of Europe. Bonaparte was sent to command the army in Italy, where he covered himself with glory. In 1798, he took his army to Egypt, which he almost succeeded in conquering.

EMPEROR NAPOLEON

When he returned to France, he found a Republic in which few had any great faith, while many were prepared to accept a dictator who had emerged from the Revolution. There had always been two potentially contradictory impulses behind the Revolution: a desire for a state that would be a democratic expression of the people, but also for one that would be an effective, powerful defender of the nation. Under Napoléon, the former impulse was put on hold, while France was given the most powerful centralised, militaristic state it had ever seen.

In November 1799 Bonaparte staged a coup, and in 1800 he was declared First Consul. Between continuing military campaigns, he set about transforming France – the education system (with the *Grandes Ecoles*), civil law (the *Code Napoléon*) and administration all bear the Napoleonic stamp to this day. In 1804, he crowned himself Emperor in an ostentatious ceremony in Notre Dame. Napoléon's first additions to the city were characteristically practical: the **Canal St-Martin**, *quais* and fine bridges, notably the **Pont des Arts**. He desired to be master of the 'most beautiful city in the world', complete with palaces, broad boulevards, colossal monuments and temples evoking the splendour of Augustan Rome – as seen in the **Madeleine** and the **Bourse**. The Emperor's official architects, Percier and Fontaine, also designed the **rue de Rivoli** and put up fountains all over the city.

Parisian society regained its *brio*. Egyptomania swept town after Bonaparte's Egyptian campaign, seen in Empire-Style furniture and in architectural details in the new area around rue and **passage du Caire**, while fashionable ladies mixed transparent Greek draperies and couture *à l'égyptienne*.

The Napoleonic epic was inseparable from military expansion. In 1805, he crushed Austria and Russia at Austerlitz, the victory he wished to commemorate with the **Arc de Triomphe** (although completed only in 1836 by royalist Louis-Philippe). But he overreached himself in the disastrous invasion of Russia in 1812, and in 1814 Paris was occupied, for the first time since the Hundred Years' War, by the Tzar's armies. Napoléon had one last throw, with his escape from confinement in Elba, return to Paris, and the 'hundred days' that ended in 1815 with defeat by Wellington at Waterloo.

MONARCHY RESTORED

In 1814, and then again in 1815, after Waterloo, the Bourbons were restored to the throne of France, in the shape of an elderly brother of Louis XVI, who had spent the Revolution in exile as Louis XVIII. Although his 1814 Charter of Liberties recognised that the pretensions of the *ancien régime* were lost forever, he and his ministers still sought to establish a repressive, Catholic regime that would in some way turn back the clock, hoping to find support in more conservative rural France.

Paris, however, still nurtured a strong feeling of rebellion. Over 60 years, a pattern would be repeated, already seen to some extent in 1789: Paris, especially the working-class east, was far more radical than anywhere else in the country. Its disproportionate weight in French affairs meant it was often seen as imposing its radicalism on the nation at large. At the same time, this radicalism was fed by a progressive press, liberal intellectuals – among them artists and authors Hugo, Daumier, Delacroix and Lamartine – radical students and a growing, poor, anarchic underclass. When provoked, this volatile coalition could explode into revolutionary violence.

THE 1830 REVOLUTION

Another brother of Louis XVI, Charles X became king in 1824. He proved reactionary, aided – to his downfall – by absolutist minister Prince Polignac who on 25 July 1830 abolished freedom of the

*Not a good time to be royal: the storming of the **Tuileries**, 1792.*

press, dissolved the Chamber of Deputies and altered the election laws, all in violation of the Charter of Liberties. Next day, 5000 printers and press workers were in the street. Three newspapers defiantly published. When police tried to seize copies, artisans and shopkeepers joined the riot. On 28 July, the disbanded National Guard came out rearmed, Republicans organised insurrection committees, and whole regiments of the Paris garrison defected. Charles hid out in St-Cloud as a provisional government raised the *tricolore* at the Hôtel de Ville, Notre Dame and on bridges. There then followed three days of fighting, known as 'Les Trois Glorieuses', till Charles was forced to abdicate in favour of his heir.

1830-48: LOUIS-PHILIPPE

Another eccentric leftover of the *ancien régime* was winched onto the throne: Louis-Philippe, Duc d'Orléans, son of Philippe-Egalité. A father of eight, who never went out without his umbrella, he was eminently acceptable to the Paris bourgeoisie. But the workers, who had spilled their blood in 1830 only to see quality of life worsen, simmered with rancour and frustration throughout the 'July Monarchy'.

In the first half of the century, the population of Paris doubled to over a million, as a building boom – in part on land seized from the nobility and clergy – brought floods of provincial workers. After 1837, when France's first railway line was laid between Paris and St-Germain-en-Laye, there were stations to build too. The overflow emptied into the poorest quarters. Novelists such as Balzac,

Hugo and Eugène Sue were endlessly fascinated by the city's underside, penning hair-raising accounts of dank, tomb-like hovels where the sun never shone, and of dismal, dangerous streets.

The well-fed, complacent bourgeoisie (mordantly caricatured in Daumier's lithographs) regarded this populace with fear. For while the Bourse, property speculation and industry flourished after 1830, workers were still forbidden from forming unions or striking. Gaslight cheered up the city streets but enabled the working day to be extended to fifteen hours-plus. Factory owners pruned salaries to the limit and exploited children, unfettered by legislation. Unemployed or disabled workers and their families were obliged to beg, steal or starve. An 1831 cholera epidemic claimed 19,000 victims, and aggravated already bitter class divisions. The rich blamed workers, beggars and immigrants for breeding disease; the poor hated the bourgeoisie who could afford to escape the city's fetid air, or move to the spacious new neighbourhoods in the 8th and 9th *arrondissements*. The stage was set for a battle.

Louis-Philippe's *Préfet* Rambuteau made a pitch to win Bonapartist support, finishing the **Arc de Triomphe** and the **Madeleine**, and also initiated some projects of his own, notably the **Pont Louis-Philippe** and **Pont du Carrousel**.

1848: REVOLUTION AGAIN

On 23 February 1848 nervous troops fired on a crowd on boulevard des Capucines. Again, demonstrators demanded blood for blood and barricades covered the city. The Garde Nationale defected to

The 1871 Commune: *rebels and republican guards clash in Père Lachaise cemetery.*

the rebels' side. In the Tuileries, Louis-Philippe abdicated, abandoning palace, capital and country – just as Charles X had done 18 years earlier.

The workers' revolution of 1848 briefly made France a republic again. The Second Republic was given a progressive provisional government, which included Romantic poet Lamartine and a mechanic – the first French proletarian to hold such a position. They abolished slavery in the colonies and the death penalty for political crimes, gave most French men (but only men) the vote, and set up National Workshops to guarantee jobs for all workers. But the capital had not counted on the reaction of the provinces. In May 1848, general elections put a conservative commission at the head of the Republic. An early official acts was to disband the 'make work' scheme as too costly and allied with socialism.

Desperate workers took to the streets in the 'June Days'. And this time the insurgents got the worst of it: thousands fell under the fire of the troops of General Cavaignac, and others were massacred in reprisals after the combat had ended.

LOUIS-NAPOLEON (NAPOLEON III)

At the end of 1848, to widespread surprise, new elections gave an overwhelming mandate to a new President of the Republic, Louis-Napoléon Bonaparte, nephew of the great Emperor. After consolidating his position, he decided he didn't merely want to preside but to reign, seizing power in a *coup d'état* on 2 December 1851. In 1852, the Prince-Président moved into the Tuileries Palace as Emperor of France: *Vive Napoléon III.*

At home, Napoléon III combined authoritarianism with crowd-pleasing social welfare in true Bonapartist style. Abroad, his policies included absurd adventures such as the attempt to make Austrian Archduke Maximilian Emperor of Mexico. Napoléon III had grandiose plans for Paris too. His ideas included completing the **Louvre**, landscaping the **Bois de Boulogne**, constructing new iron market halls at **Les Halles**, and opening up a series of new boulevards and train stations. To carry out these daunting tasks he appointed an Alsatian Protestant named Baron Haussmann, Préfet de la Seine from 1853. Haussmann set about his programme with unprecented energy, giving the aged, malodorous city its greatest-ever transformation (*see chapter* **Architecture**).

The new Paris was a showcase city, with the first department stores and the International Exhibition of 1867. With so much building work, there was plenty of opportunity for speculation. The world capital of sensual pleasure was again decried as a 'New Babylon'. Even Haussmann was not above reproach, forced to resign in 1869 after some of his projects were shown to be based on highly questionable accounts. The combination of sensuality and indulgent opulence of the Second Empire can well be seen in the regime's most distinctive single building, Charles Garnier's **Palais Garnier**, though Napoléon III did not see it completed.

THE FRANCO-PRUSSIAN WAR

In 1870, Napoléon III was maneouvred into war with the German states, led by Bismarck's Prussia. At Sedan, on 4 September 1870, the French army was crushed, and the Emperor abdicated.

Days later, a Parisian crowd demanded and won a new Republic, proclaimed to much cheering at the Hôtel de Ville. A provisional government was formed, yet within weeks Paris was under Prussian siege. Beleaguered Parisians shivered and starved through winter. In January 1871, Prussian artillery bombarded the southern *arrondissements.* The French government negotiated a temporary armistice with Bismarck, then hastily arranged elections for a National Assembly mandated to make peace. Paris voted republican, but the majority went to conservative monarchists. The peace terms signed at Versailles on 28 January 1871 – a five billion-franc indemnity, occupation by 30,000 German troops and ceding of Alsace-Lorraine to the newly united Germany– were seen as betrayal by disgusted Parisian patriots. Worse, the new Assembly under Adolphe Thiers spurned the mutinous capital and chose to set up in Versailles instead.

THE PARIS COMMUNE

Paris was marked by revolution in the nineteenth century and none proved bloodier nor more consequential than the last, which lasted nine weeks from March to May 1871 and which remains engraved in the collective memory of the Left and the French working class, a revolt rivetingly portrayed in posters, prints and newspapers at the **Musée de l'Art et d'Histoire de St-Denis**.

The turning point came on 18 March 1871, when Thiers sent a detachment of soldiers to Montmartre to collect two hundred cannons from the Garde Nationale, which had been paid for through public subscription to defend the city during the German siege. The abortive mission ended disastrously as insurrectionists led by heroine schoolteacher Louise Michels fended off the troops, killing two generals (a feat recorded in a plaque on rue du Chevalier-de-la-Barre, behind Sacré-Coeur).

Thiers immediately ordered all government officials and the regular army to leave Paris for Versailles, leaving the city in the hands of the poor and a wide-ranging spectrum of radicals. On 26 March, the Commune of Paris was proclaimed at the Hôtel de Ville. As Louis Blanc said: 'The Hôtel de Ville was the place chosen for the consecration of all revolutionary powers, the way Reims was formerly chosen for the coronation of kings.' The Commune's Assembly comprised workers, clerks, accountants, journalists, lawyers, teachers, artists, doctors and a handful of small business owners, who decreed the separation of Church and State, the secularisation of schools, abolition of night work in bakeries, creation of workers' cooperatives, and a moratorium on debts and rents. Yet,

there was never any question of abolishing private property, since the worker's fundamental aim was to become proprietor of an atelier.

Even artists got swept up in Commune fever. A federation of artists established in April 1871 attracted such talents as Corot, Daumier, Manet, Millet and the caricaturist André Gill (later of the **Lapin Agile** in Montmartre). Its mission: to urge the suppression of the Academy and the Ecole des Beaux-Arts, in favour of art freed of governmental sanctions. Courbet reopened the Louvre and the **Muséum d'Histoire Naturelle**. On 12 April, the column on place Vendôme celebrating Napoléon's victories was knocked down with great fanfare.

While support for the Commune was palpable among thousands of disenfranchised workers and inflamed intellectuals, their lack of organisation and political experience proved fatal, and they were also significantly outnumbered. It was only a matter of days when Thiers and his Versaillais troops began their assault on the city. On 4 April, the Commune's two principal military strategists, Flourens and Duval, were taken prisoner by the Versaillais and executed. By 11 April, Thiers' troops had retaken the suburbs and successfully dismantled forts at Issy and Vanves, which had withstood the Prussian siege.

LA SEMAINE SANGLANTE

Soon, barrages of artillery encircled the city, while inside Paris barricades of sandbags and barbed wire sprung up everywhere, from the heights of Montmartre to place de la Concorde. Men, women, and even children were caught up in house-to-house street fighting. On 21 May, in the week that would go down as the 'Semaine sanglante' (Bloody Week), Thiers' Versaillais entered the city through the Porte de St-Cloud, and occupied the prosperous west of the city, capturing Auteuil, Passy and the 15th *arrondissement.* Within three days of street fighting, more than half the city was retaken. The last line of resistance was along Fbg-St-Antoine, the Canal St-Martin and boulevard Richard-Lenoir. Marquis Gallifet, 'the butcher of the Commune' did a brutal 'mop-up' job in the parc des Buttes-Chaumont. On 28 May, among the tombs of the **Cimetière Père Lachaise**, 147 Communards were cornered and executed, against the 'Mur des Fédérés', today a moving memorial to the insurrection. The final battle played itself out in a narrow square formed by the rues de Belleville, Fbg-du-Temple and Oberkampf. The last serious resistance ended in the afternoon on the Fontaine-au-Roi, by place de la République.

An estimated 3000-4000 Communards or *fédérés* were killed in combat, compared with 877 Versaillais. The Commune retaliated by kidnapping and killing the Archbishhop of Paris and other members of the clergy, setting fire to a third of the city. 'Paris will be ours or Paris will no longer exist!'

vowed 'the red virgin' Louise Michel. The Hôtel de Ville was set ablaze, as well as the Tuileries, the Cour des Comptes and the Palais de la Légion d'Honneur. Although the Hôtel de Ville was rebuilt, the Tuileries was not and was ultimately torn down in 1880.

During the Semaine sanglante, thousands of insurrectionists were singled out and shot. At the Châtelet, Mazas and Roquette prisons, the Jardins du Luxembourg, Parc Monceau, Ecole Militaire and Panthéon, at least 10,000 Communards were shot en masse, many buried under public squares and pavements. There were over 40,000 arrests and over 5000 deportations, including Louis-Michel to New Caledonia for seven years.

THE THIRD REPUBLIC

The Third Republic, established in 1871, was an unloved compromise, although it survived for 70 years. The right yearned for the restoration of some kind of monarchy; to the left, the Republic was tainted by its suppression of the Commune.

Rapidly changing Paris – its busy boulevards, new railway stations and café life – also provided the perfect subject matter for the Impressionist painters, led by Monet, Renoir, Manet, Degas and Pissarro, then art's avant-garde. Rejected by the official Salon, their first group exhibition took place in 1874 in the atelier of the photographer Félix Nadar, on boulevard des Capucines.

Paris celebrated its faith in science and progress with two World Exhibitions, a follow-up to two held during the Second Empire. The 1889 exhibition was designed to mark the centenary of the Revolution and confirm the respectability of the Third Republic. Centrepiece was a giant iron structure, the **Eiffel Tower**, erected in the face of protests, such as that of writer Maupassant, who denounced it as a 'barbaric mass'.

On 1 April 1900, another World Exhibition greeted the new century. A futuristic city sprang up on the banks of the Seine, of which the **Grand** and **Petit Palais**, ornate **Pont Alexandre III** and grandiose Gare d'Orsay (now **Musée d'Orsay**) remain. In July 1900 the first line of the Paris Métro ferried passengers from Porte Maillot to Vincennes, in the unheard-of time of 25 minutes. The 1900 Exhibition drew well over 50 million visitors, who marvelled at the wonders of electricity, rode on the exciting new Ferris wheel, and drank in the heady atmosphere of Paris. Cafés and restaurants like **Julien**, **Le Train Bleu** at Gare de Lyon and Pharamond were spruced up for the occasion.

THE DREYFUS CASE

After the defeat of 1870, many circles were obsessed with the need for 'revenge' and the recovery of Alsace-Lorraine; a frustration also expressed in xenophobia and anti-semitism. These strands came together in the Dreyfus case, which polarised French society for years. In 1894, a Jewish army officer, Captain Alfred Dreyfus, was accused of spying for Germany, quickly condemned and sent off to Devil's Island. As the facts emerged, suspicion pointed clearly at another officer. Leftists and liberals took up Dreyfus' case, such as Emile Zola, who published his defence of Dreyfus, *J'Accuse* in *L'Aurore* in January 1898; rightists were bitterly opposed, sometimes taking the view that even if he were innocent it was imperative that the honour of the army should not be questioned, although divisions were not always clear cut: radical future prime minister Clemenceau supported Zola, but so did the prince of Monaco. Such were the passions this case mobilised that fights broke out in the street; nevertheless, Dreyfus was eventually vindicated, and released in 1900.

THE NAUGHTY 90S

Paris of the naughty nineties was synonymous with illicit pleasures inaccessible elsewhere. In 1889, impresario Maurice Zidler opened the **Moulin Rouge**, which successfully repackaged a half-forgotten dance called the *chahut* as the can-can. In 1894 what is believed to have been the world's first strip joint opened nearby on rue des Martyrs, the Divan Fayouac, with a routine titled *Le Coucher d'Yvette* (*Yvette Goes to Bed*). At the trial of Oscar Wilde in 1895, the mere fact he owned 'French books' was held as evidence against him.

The *belle époque* ('beautiful era', a phrase coined in the 1920s in a wave of nostalgia after World War I) – and most of all the decade before 1914 – was a time of prestigious artistic activity (*see p27*). When Countess Greffulhe (model for Proust's Princesse de Guermantes in *Remembrance of Things Past*) bestowed her patronage on Debussy, Mussorgsky, Diaghilev and his Ballets Russes, it was seen to be chic to favour avant-garde artists and musicians.

THE GREAT WAR

On 2 August 1914, France learned that war with Germany was imminent. Many Parisians rejoiced, for it seemed simply that the long-awaited opportunity for 'revenge' had finally come. However, the Allied armies were steadily pushed back. Paris filled with refugees, and by 2 September the Germans were on the Marne, just 15 miles from the city. The government took refuge in Bordeaux, entrusting the defence of the capital to General Galliéni. What then occurred was later glorified as the 'Miracle on the Marne'. Troops were ferried to the front in Paris taxis, one of which is now in the Musée de l'Armée. By 13 September, the Germans were pushed back to the Oise, and Paris was safe. In the trenches battles raged on, and Paris industrialised to produce weapons and chemicals.

After the catastrophic battle of Verdun in 1916 had inflicted appalling damage on the French army, a strong current of defeatism emerged.

Vassilieff's **Le Bal des Quat'zarts***: arty time was party time in interwar Montparnasse.*

Parisian spirits were further sapped by a flu epidemic and the shells of 'Big Bertha' – a gigantic German cannon levelled at the city from 75 miles away. The veteran Clemenceau was made prime minister in 1917 to restore morale. On 11 November, the Armistice was finally signed in the forest of **Compiègne**. Celebrations lasted for days, but the war had cut a swathe through France's male population, killing over 1 million men.

THE INTERWAR YEARS

Paris emerged from the War with a restless energy expressed in an artistic scene that was more dynamic and more cosmopolitan than ever. The city's continuing fascination with the new was seen in its enthusiastic embrace of Art Deco. Artistic life centred on Montparnasse (*see chapter* **Left Bank**), a bohemian whirl of colourful emigrés and daring nightclubs and cabarets. Cars became more frequent in the capital and the cinema a popular pastime, with the construction of grand picture palaces like **Le Grand Rex**.

The Depression did not hit France until after 1930, but when it arrived, it unleashed a wave of political violence. On 6 February 1934, Fascist and extreme right-wing groups demonstrated against the Republic and tried to invade the Assemblée Nationale. Fire hoses and bullets beat them back. Fifteen were killed, 1500 wounded. Socialists and Communists united in the face of Fascism and the economic situation to create the Popular Front. In 1936, socialist Léon Blum was elected to head a Popular Front government. In the euphoric 'workers' spring' of 1936; workers were given the right to form unions, higher salaries, a 40-hour week and, for the first time, paid holidays.

By the autumn, debates about the Spanish Civil War had split the coalition, and the economic situation was deteriorating. Blum's government fell in June 1937. France seemed within an inch of revolution. The working class was disenchanted, and right-wing parties grew on the back of fear of Communism, which to many seemed a far more immediate threat than Hitler. Tragically, each camp of a France that was divided into right and left feared the enemy within far more than the real enemy that was waiting on its doostep.

THE SECOND WORLD WAR

Britain and France declared war on Germany in September 1939, but for months this meant only the *drôle de guerre* (phoney war), characterised by rumour and inactivity. On 10 May 1940, the Germans invaded France, Belgium and Holland. By 6 June, the French army had been crushed and the Germans were near Paris. A shell-shocked government left for Bordeaux, archives and works of art were hurriedly hidden or bundled off to safety. Thousands of Parisians threw belongings into cars, carts, prams and bikes and began their own exodus south. Overnight the city emptied out. Whereas the population of Greater Paris in 1936 was 4.96 million, by the end of May 1940 it was 3.5 million, and by 27 June, stood at about 1.9 million.

Paris fell on 14 June 1940 with virtually no resistance. The German Army marched along the **Champs-Elysées**. At the Hôtel de Ville, the tricolore was lowered and the swastika raised. The French cabinet voted to request an armistice, and Maréchal Pétain, an elderly hero of the First War, dissolved the Third Republic and took over the government. The Germans occupied two-thirds of

France, while the French government moved south to Vichy. Some cabinet members left for North Africa to try and set up a government-in-exile, while a young, autocratic general, Charles De Gaulle, went to London to organise a Free French movement in open opposition to the occupation.

The Nazi insignia soon hung from every public building and monument, including the Eiffel Tower. Hitler visited Paris only once, on 23 June 1940, taking in the Palais Garnier, the Madeleine, Eiffel Tower and Napoléon's tomb at the Invalides. Leaving the city, he observed: 'Wasn't Paris beautiful?... In the past, I often considered whether we would not have to destroy Paris. But when we are finished in Berlin, Paris will only be a shadow. So why should we destroy it?'

THE OCCUPATION

For most Parisians, the occupation meant going without creature comforts. For the Germans, Paris was their western headquarters, and a very attractive assignment compared to, for example, Russia. They lapped up luxury goods, and swamped Paris' best nightspots, restaurants and hotels. There was no shortage of Parisians who accepted them, and warmed to an enemy who offered a champagne lifestyle and sustained Paris' traditional glitter. In the entertainment world, Maurice Chevalier and the actress Arletty were later condemned for having performed for, or having still closer contacts with, the Germans, as was couturier Coco Chanel.

Private cars were banned, to be replaced with horse-drawn carriages and *vélo-taxis*, in which a cart was towed behind a bicycle. Bread, sugar, butter, cheese, meat, coffee and eggs were rationed. City parks and rooftops were made into vegetable gardens and a substitute for coffee, dubbed 'café national' made with ground acorns and chickpeas.

Occupied Paris also had its share of pro-Vichy bureaucrats who preferred to work with the Germans than embrace what many saw as a futile opposition. There were also *attentistes* (wait and see-ers) and black marketeers, who became rich on the back of Nazi rationing. Even so, many were prepared to risk being hauled off to the Gestapo torture chambers at rue des Saussaies, avenue Foch or rue Lauriston. By the summer of 1941, the first executions of French underground fighters by the Germans had begun, in response to the activities of the patriots, organised from Britain.

DEPORTATION OF JEWS

There was also the rounding-up and deportation of Jews, in which the role of the Vichy authorities remains a sensitive issue to this day. On 29 June 1940, Jews were ordered to register with the police; on 11 November, all Jewish businesses were required to post a yellow sign. The wearing of the yellow star was introduced in May 1942, soon followed by regulations prohibiting Jews from restaurants,

bars, concerts, cinemas, theatres, beaches and other forms of entertainment, as well as most jobs.

The first deportations of Jews (most foreign-born) took place on 14 May 1941. In August, 6000 Jews were rounded up in the 11th *arrondissement* and interned in the suburb of Drancy, before being sent on to Auschwitz. In July 1942, 12,000 Jews were summoned to the Vélodrome d'Hiver (the winter cycling stadium) in Paris. The Vichy Chief of Police ensured that not only Jews aged over 18, but also thousands of young children not on the original orders, were deported in what is known as the Vél d'Hiv. A monument commemorating the event was commissioned by the French government and installed on the quai de Grenelle in July 1994, near where the Vélodrome once stood.

Still, not all Parisians stood for the persecution of the Jews. Many Jews were hidden during the war, and a number of government officials tacitly assisted them with ration cards and false papers. While one-third of French Jews were deported and killed in concentration camps during the war, the remaining two-thirds were saved, largely through the efforts of French citizens and the Résistance.

THE LIBERATION

In June 1944, the Allies invaded Normandy. German troops began to retreat east, and Parisians saw a real opportunity to retake their city. On 10 to 18 August there were strikes on the Métro and of public services. There was no radio broadcasting and no news, but people began to sense that liberation was finally at hand.

On 19 August, a tricolore was hoisted at the Hôtel de Ville, and the Free French forces launched an insurrection, occupying several buildings. On 23 August, Hitler ordered Von Choltitz, the German commander, to destroy the French capital. Von Choltitz stalled, for which inaction he would later be honoured by a grateful French government. On 25 August, General Leclerc's French 2nd Armoured Division, who had been carefully put at the head of the US forces approaching Paris in order that it would be French troops who would first enter the city, made their way into Paris by the Porte d'Orléans. The city went wild. There were still snipers hidden on rooftops, but in the euphoria of the moment no-one seemed to care. Late in the afternoon, De Gaulle arrived to make his way down the Champs-Elysées to the Hôtel de Ville. 'We are living minutes that go far beyond our paltry lives,' he cried out to an ecstatic crowd.

DE GAULLE & THE POST-WAR YEARS

In the immediate post-war years, those who had led the fight against Vichy and the Germans felt that now was the time to build a new society and a new republic. The National Resistance Council's postwar reform programme was approved by most parties from left to right, and De Gaulle was

Traces of the Belle Epoque

Music halls, impressionists, cabarets, the can-can, Folies-Bergère… for many, these images of the glorious decades preceding the first world war still seem to conjure up the quintessential Paris. The city was all French kisses and saucy *danseuses*, an immovable feast of oysters and champagne – at least until August 1914. But what remains now of the dizzying legend?

For one thing the restaurants, where luxurious conviviality still typifies a very Parisian notion of cuisine. Seek out the **Train Bleu** in the Gare de Lyon, all chandeliers, dripping stuccoes, triumphant frescoes, deep leather settees. The only comparable place still extant was also part of a rail complex, the Gare d'Orsay, today the Musée of the same name, which boasts a fabulous ballroom and one of the prettiest restaurants in town.

For a rare glimpse of Impressionist Paris, the irrepressible *bouillon* **Chartier** in rue Montmartre (and the smarter **Bouillon Racine** at Odéon) seems to have popped straight out of a Toulose-Lautrec painting. Here *bouillon* refers to a kind of cheap eating-house, where then as now food

is practically thrown at you by bow-tied waiters in ankle-length white aprons. Note the miles of tiny stacked drawers, once designed to store the Bordeaux-stained napkins of regular guests. The restaurants **Bofinger, Julien,** les Ministères and Grand Colbert (to name but a few) have been tastefully restored in keeping with the style of the period. (*See chapter* **Restaurants**.)

Otherwise, the Belle-Epoque has to be sought out with care: much was knocked down in the 1920s-30s in the name of rectilinear good taste. Often a relevant detail creates a distinct period feel: in many areas, a street corner might be crowned by a peaked rotunda and extravagant floral detailing. Look out for the Cheret-inspired *grisette* on the one-time Elysée Montmartre theatre, today a discount clothes shop on the Bd Clichy. Walk up the Butte and spend an evening in the **Lapin Agile,** haunt of the avant-garde of the period. The songs have been cleaned up and the absinthe banned, but the rest is intact, including the perilously slippery cobblestones.

The Belle-Epoque celebrated the conspicuous display of wealth. Department stores looked like a cross between a basilica and an opera house. The **Samaritaine,** le **Printemps,** les **Galeries Lafayette** boast cupolas, *verrières*, mosaics and spectacular vistas atop historic staircases. Grocer Felix Potin contributed some grand decors to the Paris scene: today they have been taken over by **Tati** (rue de Rennes branch) and the Monoprix at the Réamur-Sébastopol crossing, where several other period buildings may still be found.

Art Nouveau never really conquered Paris. The buildings erected for the Paris exhibition are more in the styles of the Grand Palais, where major art shows are put on today. Nevertheless, a welter of typical stone tendrils envelop the architecture. Hector Guimard's lush green metal foliage graces the entrance of traditional Métro stations. See, too, the (then) low-price housing estate he built in 1897, the Castel Beranger (14 rue la Fontaine/16th). The rapturous facade on 29 avenue Rapp (7th, luxury flats designed by Jules Lavirotte, a stylistic exception by French Art Nouveau standards) is worth a detour, as is the decor of the Fouquet jewellery shop on display at the **Musée Carnavalet** (mornings only). Perhaps the place that typifies the era best is little-known Passage d'Enfer (behind the incredible art-studios in car-free rue Campagne-Première). Here nothing has changed for over a century – not even the disgruntled concierges.

Chartier, *then as now.*

proclaimed provisional President. At first vigilante justice prevailed and accusations of collaboration began to fly, mock trials were set up, and severe punishments doled out to *collabos*, but many former Vichy officials escaped trial and rose within the administration.

As the economy began to revive, post-war Paris became a magnet for thousands of French men and women for whom the capital represented a new opportunity. The population rose dramatically: in 1946, there were 6.6 million inhabitants in greater Paris, but by 1950 that number had increased by 700,000. In response, the state built Villes Nouvelles (new towns) and low-income housing.

THE ALGERIAN WAR

De Gaulle relinquished office in 1946, and the Fourth Republic was established. Thereafter, French troops were constantly engaged in a losing battle to save France's disintegrating Empire. Vietnam was lost in 1954, but after revolt broke out in Algeria in 1956 socialist prime minister Guy Mollet sent in almost half a million troops. Algeria also became a major issue for intellectuals, and it was only a matter of time before the battles were reflected in Paris. Mutinous army officers, opposed to any 'sell-out' of the French settlers or *colons* in Algeria, took over government headquarters in Algiers. It was time, decided the Fourth Republic, to admit defeat and wheel the old demagogue out of retirement. In May 1958 De Gaulle came back, with the understanding that he was to be allowed to rewrite the constitution and give France the republic he thought she deserved.

DE GAULLE & THE FIFTH REPUBLIC

De Gaulle used time-honoured tactics, appearing to promise one thing to settlers in Algeria, while negotiating with rebel leaders for their country's independence, not without hiccups. On 17 October 1961, the pro-independence FLN demonstrated in Paris, police shot on the crowd. Officially only three were killed, but recently released archives show that over 300 bodies were fished out of the Seine alone. In 1962 Algeria was proclaimed independent, some 700,000 embittered colonists came straggling back to France. Yet De Gaulle emerged crowing victory and was re-elected in 1965 on the new system of presidential election by universal suffrage.

De Gaulle beamed down from his presidential throne like the monarch he wasn't. He commanded foreign policy, intervened in domestic policy when he felt like it, and reported to the nation by means of carefully orchestrated press conferences or appearances on television, which had by now muscled its way into many French homes.

The state was again under pressure to provide housing. Radical urbanisation plans were hastily drawn up for Paris. Although historic areas were considered sacrosanct, large areas succumbed to the ball and chain: the 'Manhattanisation' of Paris was under way. André Malraux, Minister of Culture, however undertook a major series of measures to ensure the preservation of the historic Marais.

The post-war mood of crisis was over, and into the breach thundered a sharp, fresh 'new wave' of cinema directors, novelists and critics – Truffaut, Melville, Godard, Resnais were among the filmmakers who quickly gained international status.

MAY 1968

By 1968, youth chafed against their yokes, as their numbers swelled the over-stretched French educational system. Dissatisfaction was widespread, not just with education, but also with the authoritarian nature of the state and of French society, in contrast to the 60s mood of counter-culture. In early May the students erupted first at Nanterre, then at the **Sorbonne**, and took to the streets. On 3 May, paving stones were torn up, perhaps inspired by the Situationist group's slogan '*sous les pavés, la plage*' ('beneath the paving stones, the beach'). Confrontations continued all week along boulevard St-Michel and rue Gay-Lussac in the Latin Quarter. By mid-May, workers and trade unions at **Renault** and Sud-Aviation had joined the protest and by 20 May, six million people were on strike across France. After negotiations failed, De Gaulle's proposal for a referendum was rejected with the worst night of violence. However, by 30 May, the tide began to turn with an anti-strike demonstration on the Champs-Elysées. By 5 June, workers began to go back to their factories. Even today, barely a week goes by without you hearing a French person evoke *soixante-huit*. If not a political revolution, May 68 was a cultural and social uprising that surprisingly allied France's students, intellectuals and working-class trade unionists. It profoundly shook the country's institutions and ruling classes, forcing a previously unheard-of attitude of open debate and forming a new generation, many of whom constitute the French establishment, especially the media, today. After losing a referendum in early 1969, De Gaulle retired to his provincial retreat, where he died in 1970.

1970: GEORGES POMPIDOU

Georges Pompidou or Pom-Pom – as De Gaulle's successor was often called – didn't preside over any earth-shattering political developments. What Pompidou (a conservative) did do was begin the process that radically changed the architectural face of Paris, implanting an uncompromisingly avant-garde building, the **Centre Pompidou**, in the heart of one of Paris' oldest neighbourhoods. It was the age of the motorway: Pompidou built the expressways along the Seine and gave the go-ahead to the redevelopment of Les Halles.

Read all about it: *the end of World War II is officially announced.*

VALERY GISCARD D'ESTAING

Valéry Giscard d'Estaing became president in 1974, on the sudden death of Pompidou. He made clear his desire to transform France into an 'advanced liberal society'. Notable among his decisions were those to transform **Gare d'Orsay** into a museum, and the creation of a high-tech science museum in the vast abattoirs at **La Villette**.

FRANÇOIS MITTERRAND

In an abrupt political turn-around, the Socialists, led by François Mitterrand, swept into power in 1981. The mood in Paris was initially electric, although after nationalising some banks and industries, Socialist France of the prosperous 1980s turned out to be not wildly different from Gaullist France. In Paris, the period was defined politically by the on-going feud between Mitterrand and Jacques Chirac, Paris' right-wing mayor since 1977.

From the very beginning of his presidency, Mitterrand cherished ambitions for transforming Paris: the *Grands Projets*. His first operation was the most daring: open-heart surgery on the Louvre. The **Louvre Pyramid** in turn carried with it a corollary, the transfer of the Ministry of Finance to a new complex at **Bercy**. If the **Grande Arche** gave a monument to La Défense in the west, Bercy was part of a vast programme for the renewal of eastern Paris along with **Opéra Bastille**. Last and most controversial *Grand Projet* was the new national library (**Bibliothèque Nationale François Mitterand**), completed after Mitterrand's death in January 1996.

Despite policies of decentralisation, especially in the arts, Paris remained very much the intellectual and artistic hub of France, helped in part by the long rivalry between left-wing central government and the right-wing Mairie de Paris, that saw Paris-funded exhibitions at the Petit Palais and Musée d'Art Moderne de la Ville de Paris rival the national Grand Palais and Centre Pompidou, and Châtelet develop as a rival to the Opéra Bastille.

THE CHIRAC ERA

The last years of the Mitterrand era were marked by the President's ill health, and a seeping away of his prestige. The new President Jacques Chirac elected in May 1995 is famous for being all things to all men and women, but came into power in an atmosphere very different from the expansive early 1980s. The start of his presidency was marked by social strife, with strikes in the autumn of 1995, terrorist attacks, corruption scandals and a prime minister Alain Juppé whose unpopularity exceeded even that of previous record holder – France's only woman prime minister Edith Cresson.

In May 1997, Chirac in a massive strategic miscalculation called a general election a year early. A Socialist coalition under new man Lionel Jospin won by a landslide, leaving Chirac sidelined into a largely ceremonial role in the 'cohabitation' and the Gaullist party in total disarray. The Socialist coalition (which includes Greens and Communists) started its reign with a record number of leading female ministers and unprecedented popularity. The relation with Europe continues to evolve, the transition from the franc to the Euro having begun on 1 January 1999. With the right still split over Europe and the far right Front National involved in fratricide between Jean-Marie Le Pen and his former cohort Bruno Mégret, the Socialists' chief challenges come from within – disagreements over implementation of the disputed 35-hour week (an unproven job creation project), social security, immigration and the rise of juvenile crime – Paris is not France, however, and the capital *intra muros* remains immune to the worst of social strife.

Millennium party?

The top restaurants may have been booked for years, but Parisian authorities have been surprisingly slow to get Millennium celebrations together. Plans for glittery fish in the Seine, a tree in the Bois de Boulogne for every Parisian, and a new wooden tower in the east to rival Eiffel's in the west have all been shelved.

As often in Paris, though, state rivals city in its schemes and the Ministry of Culture stole a march with the proposal (greeted with little enthusiasm) of twelve *portes* or gateways down the Champs-Elysées to be designed by artists and designers, including Deschamps and Makeieff (of Les Deschiens fame) and choreographer Philippe Decouflé. On a national level, several culture cities are planned; and a green meridian of trees is being planted from north to south. Other (unconfirmed) ideas go from the picturesque to the hare-brained: an egg suspended from the Eiffel Tower, or a proposal from two architects to complete planned but never constructed spires on Notre Dame with temporary structures in carbon fibre.

The lack of foresight is puzzling, given France's love of *grands projets*, but perhaps it comes as a relief: no mind-bogglingly tedious opening ceremony *à la* World Cup, no enormously expensive temporary dome *à la* London... Perhaps everyone will just congregate on the Champs as usual, skirting the bangers and guzzling the bubbly.

Rather, Jean Tiberi, mayor of Paris, has announced 2000 as a long-term reflection on what the city should become. Celebrations, muted on New Year's Eve, will continue throughout the year: big 14 July party and a free concert from (who else?) Johnny Hallyday.

Architecture

What is so visibly a historic city is also a very modern one, as centuries of planners and different rulers have left their mark.

Whether with walls, squares and boulevards, or *Grands Projets* to develop neglected corners of the city, periods of planning have formed Paris; its apparent homogeneity stems from use of the same materials over the centuries: local yellow limestone and slate – later zinc – roofs. It was only early this century that brick became widely used and, with a few exceptions like the Eiffel Tower, only since the war that large-scale use of glass, concrete and steel have created more obtrusive landmarks.

The Romanesque

The medieval city was centred on the Ile de la Cité and the Latin Quarter. The main thoroughfares of the medieval, and even the modern, street plan of the area, in the rue St-Jacques and rue Mouffetard, followed those of Roman Paris. Paris had several powerful Romanesque abbeys outside the city walls, but existing remains of this simple style are sparse. The tower of **St-Germain-des-Prés**, although topped by a later spire, still has its rounded arches, while some decorated capitals survive in the typically solid-feeling nave.

Gothic Paris

It was in the **Basilique St-Denis**, begun in 1136, under the patronage of the powerful Abbot Suger, that the Gothic trademarks of pointed arches, ogival vaulting and flying buttresses were combined for the first time. In technical terms, Gothic vaulting allowed buildings to span large spaces and let light in, bringing with it an aesthetic of brightness and verticality and new styles of ornament. A spate of building followed with cathedrals at **Chartres**, Sens and Laon, as well as **Notre Dame**, which incorporated all the features of the style: twin-towered west facade, soaring nave, intricate rose windows and buttressed east end.

Shortly after work on Notre Dame had commenced, in the 1190s, King Philippe-Auguste began the building of the first **Louvre**, with a solid defensive keep, part of which can be seen in the Louvre today. In the following century, ribbed vaulting became ever more refined and columns more slender, in the Rayonnant or High Gothic style. One of the few master mason/architects whose name is known is Pierre de Montreuil, who continued work on St-Denis with the magnificent rose windows.

His masterpiece, the 1246-48 **Sainte-Chapelle**, takes the Gothic ideal to its height. The fifteen stained glass windows of the upper chapel virtually create a wall of glass and reduce the stone tracery to a minimum. An impressive example of secular building of the time is the Salle des Gens d'Armes in the **Conciergerie**, completed in 1314.

The later Flamboyant Gothic style of the late fourteenth century saw little structural innovation, but a wealth of decoration. **Eglise St-Séverin**, with its twisting spiral column, is particularly original. The pinnacles and gargoyles of the early sixteenth-century **Tour St-Jacques** and the porch of **St-Germain-l'Auxerrois** are also typical.

Paris' two finest medieval mansions date from the end of the fifteenth century. Hôtel de Cluny (now **Musée National du Moyen-Age**) and **Hôtel de Sens** were both urban palaces for powerful abbots. With living quarters at the back of an enclosed forecourt, Cluny is a precursor of the domestic style of the sixteenth century. On a more humble note, the 1407 house of alchemist Nicolas Flamel, at **51 rue de Montmorency**, is one of the earliest surviving private houses in Paris.

Hôtel de Sully, *courtliest of courtyards.*

The Renaissance

The influence of the Italian Renaissance came late to Paris, and was largely due to the personal impetus of François 1er. He installed Leonardo da Vinci at **Amboise** and brought over Primaticcio and Rosso to work on his palace at **Fontainebleau**. It was not until 1528 that he established the court in Paris and set about updating the **Louvre**, with the Cour Carrée, by Pierre Lescot. The pretty, hybrid church of **St-Etienne-du-Mont** shows that Renaissance style remained a largely superficial effect: the structure is Flamboyant Gothic, the balustrade of the nave and the elaborate roodscreen (possibly by Delorme), with its spiral staircases and lacy fretwork, are Renaissance. A heavier hybrid is the massive **St-Eustache**. The **Hôtel Carnavalet**, altered by Mansart next century, and the **Hôtel Lamoignon**, both in the Marais, are Paris' best remaining examples of Renaissance mansions.

The *Ancien Régime*

France's first Bourbon king Henri IV had great plans for modernising his capital. He built the **Pont-Neuf** and laid out two major squares, the **place Dauphine** on the Ile de la Cité and the **place des Vosges** in the Marais. Both followed

St-Etienne-du-Mont: *check out the rood bits.*

a symmetrical plan, with vaulted galleries and steeply pitched roofs, and represented a departure from the untidy squares of medieval Paris. Their use of red brick was short-lived, in contrast with the classical Baroque stone that later filled the area.

The seventeenth century was a high point in French power; the monarchy desired buildings that reflected its grandeur, a need satisfied by the Baroque style. Great architects emerged under court patronage: Salomon de Brosse, François Mansart, Jules Hardouin-Mansart (his nephew), Libéral Bruand and Louis Le Vau, the decorator Charles Lebrun and landscape architect André Le Nôtre.

Even at **Versailles**, French Baroque never reached the level of excess seen in Italy or Austria. French architects followed the Cartesian principles of harmony, order and balance, with a preference for symmetry seen both in royal palaces and in the grand private houses put up in the Marais.

The **Palais du Luxembourg**, built by de Brosse in Italianate style for Marie de Médicis, combines classic French château design with elements of the Pitti Palace in Marie's native Florence. Counter-Reformation churches like the **Eglise St-Paul-St-Louis** or the **Chapelle de la Sorbonne** followed the Gésu in Rome. The **Eglise de Val-de-Grâce**, designed by Mansart, and later Jacques Lemercier, is one of the grandest examples of Baroque architecture in Paris. In the adjoining monastery, you can see the characteristic double-pitched 'Mansard roofs', a feature of French architecture ever since.

Nouveaux-riches flocked to build mansions in the Marais and, later, the Ile-St-Louis. Those in the Marais follow a symmetrical U-shaped plan, with a secluded courtyard: look through the archways to the *cour d'honneur* of the **Hôtel de Sully** or **Hôtel Salé**, where facades are richly decorated, in contrast with their street faces. Those on the Ile-St-Louis often broke with this plan to benefit from quai-side views.

Along **rue du Faubourg-St-Antoine** a different style developed. The buildings that furniture-makers lived and worked in here were tall, with cobbled courtyards lined with workshops.

Under Colbert, Louis XIV's chief minister, the creation of stage sets to magnify the Sun King's power proceeded apace. The Louvre grew as Claude Perrault created the sweeping west facade, while Hardouin-Mansart's **place des Victoires** and **place Vendôme,** an elegant octagon of arches and Corinthian columns, were both designed to show off equestrian statues of the king

Rococo & Neo-Classicism

In the early eighteenth century, the Faubourg-St-Germain overtook the Marais in fashion: mansions were built in rues de Grenelle, St-Dominique and de Varenne. Most are now ministries or embassies; today you can visit the Hôtel Bouchardon (**Musée Maillol**), which has some original carved panelling.

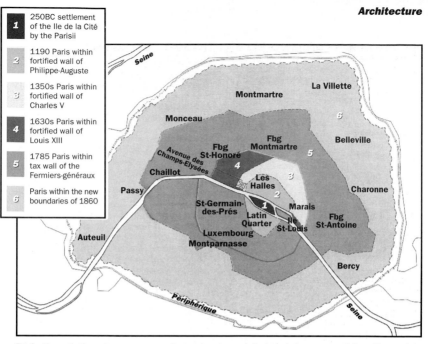

1	250BC settlement of the Ile de la Cité by the Parisii
2	1190 Paris within fortified wall of Philippe-Auguste
3	1350s Paris within fortified wall of Charles V
4	1630s Paris within fortified wall of Louis XIII
5	1785 Paris within tax wall of the Fermiers-généraux
6	Paris within the new boundaries of 1860

Paris *through the ages, as successive ramparts and ring-roads have spread from the centre.*

Under Louis XV, the severe lines of the previous century wcrc softened by rounded corners and decorative detailing, such as satyr masks over doorways, at the Hôtel Chenizot (51 rue St-Louis-en-l'Ile) and Hôtel d'Albret (31 rue des Francs-Bourgeois). The main developments came in interior decoration, with the frivolous French version of Rococo style. The best example is the **Hôtel de Soubise**, with panelling, plasterwork and paintings by artists including Boucher, Restout and Van Loo.

From the 1750s geometry was back as Ancient Rome inspired another monument to royal majesty, Jacques Ange Gabriel's Neo-Classical **place de la Concorde**, and Antoine's Hôtel des Monnaies (1767-75). Soufflot's huge, domed **Panthéon** (1755-92) was inspired by the one in Rome.

One late addition by the *ancien régime* was the tax wall, the *Mur des Fermiers Généraux*, built around the city in 1785. Utopian Claude-Nicolas Ledoux's **toll gates** played games with pure geometrical forms; circular at Parc Monceau and La Rotonde de la Villette, and rectangular pairs at place Denfert-Rochereau and place de la Nation.

The Nineteenth Century

The Revolution largely confined itself to pulling buildings down or appropriating them for new purposes. Royal statues bit the dust along with the Bastille prison, and churches became 'Temples of Reason' or grain stores. Napoléon, however, soon brought Paris back to a proper sense of its grand self. Land confiscated from aristocracy and church, especially in the 8th and 9th *arrondissements*, was built up. As the Emperor compared himself to the Caesars, a stern Classicism was preferred for the **Arc de Triomphe**, the Greek-temple inspired **Madeleine** and Brongniart's **Bourse**.

By the 1840s Classical style was under challenge from a Gothic revival closely associated with the restoration of medieval buildings and led by Eugène Viollet-le-Duc. Despite his detailed research, critics accused him of creating a romanticised notion of the medieval; his use of colour was felt to pollute these monuments – though actually in part a return to painted interiors of the period. Judge for yourself in the choir of Notre Dame and the Sainte-Chapelle, or his designs in the Musée d'Orsay, or visit the castle he (re)built largely from scratch at **Pierrefonds**.

Historical eclecticism ruled, though, with the neo-Renaissance **Hôtel de la Païva**, the **Hôtel de Ville** or the **Eglise de la Trinité**. Hittorff chose Antique polychromy in the **Cirque d'Hiver**; Byzantium and the Romanesque made a comeback in church architecture from the 1870s.

Engineering innovations made the use of iron frames in buildings increasingly common. An avant-garde precursor was the 1809 dome of the **Bourse du Commerce**, but Henri Labrouste's innovative reading room at the **Bibliothèque**

Ste-Geneviève (1844-50), in place du Panthéon, was one of the first to use iron for the entire structure, prefiguring his **Bibliothèque Nationale**. Baltard's new market pavilions (*see p35*) proudly proclaimed their iron and glass structure, but most often ironwork was hidden behind stone exteriors, allowing spacious interiors full of light. Stations like Hittorrf's **Gare du Nord** (1861-65) and such apparently massive stone structures as the Galerie d'Evolution (**Muséum d'Histoire Naturelle**) and **Musée d'Orsay** are but shells around an iron frame. The most daring, emphatic iron structure of them all was the **Eiffel Tower**, built in 1889, then the tallest structure in the world.

The Twentieth Century

Paris has always been about show and the twentieth century began with an outburst of extravagance for the 1900 Exposition Universelle. Laloux's Gare d'Orsay (now **Musée d'Orsay**) and the **Train Bleu** brasserie were ornate examples of the heavy Beaux-Arts floral style of the turn of the century. The **Grand Palais** (1900) itself has elements of the new Art Nouveau trend in its sinuous metal stairway, but the heavily sculptured exterior is firmly within official monumental style; the **Petit Palais** was closer to Baroque revival.

Genuine Art Nouveau architecture in Paris is quite rare, although some fine interiors exist, such as the **Bouillon Racine** or eateries like **Julien**, spruced up for the Exposition Universelle. Art Nouveau at its most fluid and flamboyant can be seen in Guimard's Métro stations and his 1901 **Castel Béranger**, the entrance to the luxury apartment block by Jules Lavirotte at **29 avenue Rapp**, or in shop 2 of **La Samaritaine**, built 1905-10 by Frantz Jourdain, with its whiplash-style staircase, recently restored *verrière* and peacock-adorned fresco. Weirdest of all is **14 rue d'Abbeville**, with green-glazed ivy climbing up the facade.

It was all a long way from the roughly contemporary work of Henri Sauvage, unmistakably innovative but too eclectic to be identified with any one movement. After the 1904 **Cité Commerciale Argentine** flats, with a geometrical decoration that recalls Macintosh and prefigures Modernism, his unusual tiled apartment block at **6 rue Vavin** (1911-12) was the first to use stepped-back terraces as a way of getting light into the different storeys. From this he went to a bigger social housing project in rue des Amiraux, which even included a swimming pool, and tiled artists' studios and flats in rue La Fontaine, as well as the more overtly Art Deco 1920s extensions of La Samaritaine.

Social housing began to be put up in many areas of Paris, funded by philanthropists, such as the Rothschilds in rue du Prague, or by the city where the Thiers fortifications (today just within the *Périphérique*) were demolished.

The Modern Movement

After World War I, two names stand out for their innovation, and influence – Auguste Perret and Le Corbusier. A third, Robert Mallet-Stevens, stands unrivalled for his elegance. Paris is one of the best cities in the world for Modern Movement houses and studios (often in the 16th and western suburbs like Boulogne and Garches), but also in a more diluted form for public buildings, such as town halls, low-cost public housing and in numerous schools built in the socially minded 1930s.

Perret stayed largely within a classical aesthetic, but his frank use of reinforced concrete (which he had previously used less visibly for the **Théâtre des Champs-Elysées**) gave scope for more varied facades than traditional walls. Most interesting is his **Conseil Economique et Social** at place d'Iéna, a circular pavilion with an open horseshoe staircase. Paris was spared his 1922 Maisons-Tours scheme, which would have transformed the city into an avenue of skyscrapers.

Le Corbusier tried out his ideas in early private houses such as the **Villa La Roche** and Villa Savoy at Poissy, with their interesting volumes and built-in furniture. His Pavillon Suisse at the **Cité Universitaire** can be seen as an intermediary point between these villas and the mass housing schemes of his *Villes Radieuses*, which became so influential and so debased in projects across Europe after 1945 (his plans included replacing swathes east of the Bastille by diagonal slabs).

Other notable Modern Movement houses and apartments include Adophe Loos' house for the Dadaist poet Tristan Tzara in avenue Junot, supposedly the epitome of his maxim 'ornament is crime', Chareau's influential Maison de Verre (31 rue St-Guillaume, 7th, not visible from the street), houses by Lurçat and Perret near the Parc Montsouris, Pierre Patout's steamboat style apartments (3 bd Victor, 15th) – the machine was part of the modern aesthetic – and Studio Raspail at 215 bd Raspail by Elkouken; the latter look like artists' studios but were built for the enlightened bourgeoisie in the studio style then fashionable.

The geometrical influence and love of chrome, steel and glass found its way into Art Deco cafés and brasseries, like **La Coupole**, or the Eldorado theatre and **Grand Rex** cinema. The 1930s also saw a return to vaguely totalitarian-looking Neo-Classical monumentalism, such as the **Palais de Tokyo** and **Palais de Chaillot** built for the 1937 exhibition.

Post-War Paris

As France revived from the trauma of World War II, the aerodynamic aesthetic of the 1950s saw the 1958 **UNESCO** building, by Bernard Zehrfuss, Pier Luigi Nervi and Marcel Breuer, and the beginnings of La Défense, with the construction of the **CNIT**. The *bidonvilles* or shanty-towns that had

The tales of Haussmann

Few figures in Paris history have had a worse press than Georges-Eugène Haussmann (1809-1891). First, he's charged with the glitzy *Grands Boulevards* – which have existed since Louis XIV – and then he's blamed for destroying Paris. Yet much of Paris as we know it is due to his transformations under the Second Empire. What would café society have been without the boulevard St-Germain or May 68 (so much for preventing revolution) without boulevard St-Michel? Not to mention arriving at Gare du Nord or benefitting from his sewers.

Appointed Napoléon III's *Préfet de la Seine* in 1853, Haussmann was not an architect but an administrator. Aided by architects and engineers including Baltard, Hittorff, Alphand and Belgrand, he set about making Paris the most modern city of its day. Broad boulevards were cut through the old city, often taking the eye to a focal point such as the new Palais Garnier, the Gare de l'Est or the Arc de Triomphe, continuing the principle established by Colbert and Hardouin-Mansart. Ile de la Cité was decimated, but some old districts were left largely unaltered. An estimated 27,000 houses were demolished and some 100,000 built during this period.

The **Cirque d'Hiver** *elected to go eclectic.*

The motives for this unprecedented exercise in urban and social engineering were a mixture of authoritarianism and paternalism. The wide boulevards and removal of the shabbiest city centre streets were in part anti-revolutionary measures against the politically volatile working classes, forcing them to move to the outer *faubourgs* and making construction of barricades more difficult. The new streets also answered real communication and health problems in a city that had grown from 500,000 in 1789 to 1 million in 1850, was disease-ridden and needed transport links. From an aesthetic angle, they added the varied viewpoints, and quality of light characteristic of Paris today.

There were more prosaic measures too; Haussmann constructed asylums (Hôpital Ste-Anne, 14th), prisons (Prison de la Santé, 14th), new schools, churches (**Eglise St-Vincent de Paul**), hospitals, the water and sewage systems, and gave Paris its new market pavilions at **Les Halles**, so much missed since their demolition in 1969. Paternalism extended to fresh air, as with the aid of Alphand, he landscaped the Bois and gave Paris an entirely new series of parks. Haussmann financed his vision by some dubious credit operations, which ultimately led to his downfall as he was forced to resign in 1869 after exposure of highly questionable accounts.

Architecturally, although historical eclecticism remained the style of the day, Haussmann also proved he could be an innovator. He persuaded Baltard to build the Les Halles not in stone as the architect wanted, but using a visible iron structure (a material Baltard thought undignified). It was such a success that Verlaine described the ten pavilions put up between 1854 and 1874 as 'the lace of Vulcan', and the style was soon copied in local markets, like the **Marché St-Quentin**, across the city.

Amidst the upheaval, one building epitomised Second-Empire style, though finished only after both Napoléon III and Haussmann had fallen from power. Charles Garnier's sumptuous **Opéra** of 1862-75 perfectly expresses the ambition of mid-century Paris – especially when viewed from the broad avenue leading up to it.

The city also acquired the Haussmanian apartment block, which has lasted until well into this century. Regulations of 1859 controlled the pitch of the roof, and ratio of building height to street width. It's a form that has been highly adaptable to different styles, budgets and sites.

Notre Dame de l'Espérance: *it takes divine inspiration to come up with something new.*

sprouted around the city, many occupied by immigrant workers, cried out for a solution. In the 60s and 70s, tower blocks and housing bars sprouted in the suburbs and the ring of new towns: Sarcelles, Mantes la Jolie, Cergy-Pontoise, Evry, Melun-Sénart and Créteil. Redevelopment inside the city was more limited, although new regulations allowed taller buildings, noticeably in Montparnasse and in the 13th and 19th (since altered to prevent another **Tour Montparnasse**).

In a decade that produced such monstrosities as the glass-faced towers of the Fronts de Seine, Piano and Rogers' high-tech **Centre Pompidou**, opened in 1977, was the first of the radical prestige projects that have become a trademark of modern Paris, introducing international architects, and establishing public competitions for big commissions.

The 1980s & Beyond

Mitterrand's *Grands Projets* dominated the 1980s and early 90s as he sought to leave his stamp on the city with Nouvel's **Institut du Monde Arabe**, Sprecklesen's **Grande Arche de la Défense**, as well as Ott's more dubious **Opéra Bastille** (a mastodon), Perrault's **Bibliothèque Nationale** (a curious throwback to the 60s) and Chemetov's Bercy finance ministry. Urban renewal has transformed previously industrial areas in an attempt to return the balance of Paris eastwards.

Stylistically, the buzz word has been 'transparency' – from I M Pei's **Louvre Pyramid**, and Nouvel's **Fondation Cartier** with its clever slices

of glass, to Armstrong Associates' new **Maison de la Culture du Japon** – while also allowing styles as diverse as Portzamparc's **Cité de la Musique**, with geometrical blocks round a colourful internal street, Ricardo Bofill's postmodern neo-classicism or Richard Meier's neo-Modernist **Canal+** headquarters. The city has also privileged public housing by both French and internally renowned foreign architects (often with far more interesting results than private developments). Of note are the human-scale housing round Parc de la Villette and Parc André-Citroën, Piano's red-tile and glass ensemble around a courtyard in rue de Meaux (19th), La Poste's apartments for young postal workers designed by young architects such as Frédérick Borel (rue Oberkampf) and Patrick Chavannes (av Daumesnil), Architecture Studio's lodgings for students, or recent housing in the suburb of Clichy by Fuksas and by Odile Decq.

Curiously, some of the most impressive buildings of the late 1990s have been either sacred or sporting. It's not easy to develop a new religious vernacular; Architecture Studio at Notre Dame de l'Espérance in the 15th and Botta at the new **Evry Cathedral** (the first built in France since World War II) have responded with more or less successful geometrical solutions. Sports facilities have been boosted by Henri and Bruno Gaudin's streamlined Stade Charléty and Zublena and Macary's **Stade de France**. The Métro has also made a return to style not seen since Guimard's station entrances, with Antoine Grumbach's and Bernard Khon's stations for the new Météor line.

War of the Words

It's hard to imagine it happening anywhere else, but in France the current literary scene is the focus of heated debate.

Inflamed by *Les particules élémentaires*, **Michel Houellebecq**'s second novel, the literary temperature in France has been unusually feverish. The literary *rentrée* of autumn 1998 was marked by a media fizz and endless discussions about Houellebecq's book and the state of modern French fiction. Suddenly the once stagnant world of letters was in turmoil, generating television and newspaper polemics the like of which had not been seen since the *Nouveau roman* movement in the 50s.

The flash-point came in August, when *Les particules* was published. It won the Prix Novembre (a literary prize guided by more 'modern' criteria than the prestigious Prix Goncourt), but opinions were far from unanimous. Shortly after the novel's publication, its self-styled *déprimiste* author was booted out of the literary review *Perpendiculaire,* to which he had been a regular contributor: the editors refused to condone his prevailing 'nihilism' and theses about reproduction, cloning, love and sexuality. The book follows two half-brothers, Bruno and Michel, one a depressive professor of literature, the other an eminent biologist interested in the latest research into cloning and quantum mechanics. The tale is set in the near future, a standpoint which lets the narrator look back over the last two decades of the twentieth century, weighing up society and the behaviour of feminists, naturists and other *fin de siècle* species, and providing a surprising twist in the final pages.

Houellebecq's book has a sociological quality, examining a whole range of modern social ills – eccentric behaviour, frustration, the death of desire, a new version of the will to power, suicide, degradation of the body, pornography and the exacerbated tensions between men and women. The book's excessive realism and lack of cosmetic touches did not go down well with many readers. On the other hand the book is the vehicle for a flood of ideas that, if nothing else, has proved unusually rich food for discussion – a French pastime *par excellence*. Perhaps it is this, more than anything else, that has appealed to so many diverse readers, who perhaps recognise themselves in its dilemmas.

In any case, the words 'writer for a new generation' are on many people's lips. In 1994, this generation (meaning 25- to 40-year olds) had found in Houellebecq a novelist who touched a new readership, with his first novel *Extension du domaine de la lutte* (recently translated into English as *Whatever*), championed by *Les Inrockuptibles* mag-

Houellebecq: *heaven knows he's miserable.*

azine, as was *Les particules*. He and other writers were slowly identified as an embryonic movement, distinguishable by their weariness of ideological engagements, a discernible mood of disillusion and despair, and a realistic, almost blunt written style which stands out starkly from the norm.

Another example is **Virginie Despentes**. Despite claiming to be misunderstood by her publisher Grasset, she won the Prix du Café de Flore with her novel *Les Jolies Choses*, the tale of twin sisters, Pauline a rebel, porn actress, Claudine who takes life in a go and commits suicide. Pauline in her way absorbs the identity of her dead sister in a descent into hell, written in everyday spoken argot. The prevailing impression was of a generation searching for an ideal, starting from a base of ordinary and far from sulphurous 'realism'.

The *affaire Houellebecq* also drew attention to a growing literary trend – notably among women writers – that often draws on individual experience to explore identity crises and questions of sexual uncertainty – an autobiographical approach and interest in the banal and mundane that find parallels in the work of photographer Sophie Calle and numerous young contemporary artists. **Marie Darrieussecq** was the literary sensation of 1996 with *Truismes* (*Pig Tales*), the story of a woman who metamorphoses into a pig which takes an often disturbingly ambivalent approach to feminism. Other examples are Despentes' earlier *Les chiennes savantes* and **Lorette Nobécourt**'s *La Conversation*, while **Linda Lê**'s *Voix*, subtitled 'une crise', is a psychological trauma seen from the inside, less a tale than a beautifully written, nightmarish series of impressions awash with morbid images and mad ravings.

Mixing reality and fiction, **Christine Angot** drives the nail home, taking herself as her main theme, in *Sujet Ango*. It's an approach which she had already applied in the powerful *Vu du ciel*, a tale of incest that feels autobiographical, and in *Interview*, where she puts the accent intensely on the body of the writer, the most deeply buried *moi*, a vision of the self which overturns its apparent journalistic objectivity.

Yet despite all the heavy issues, French writers are not without a sense of humour. 28-year-old **Laurent Gautier**'s *Notices, manuels techniques et modes d'emploi* has a jaunty style closer to the spoken than the written word. It's the story of a Paul, a young man apprenticed to write instruction manuals in the editorial department of an electrical appliance factory. Paul (who incidentally has the same surname as the author) starts turning out

garbled, nonsensical texts, which mislead customers, cause accidents, and lead to his arrest and a strangely poignant incarceration. The short story is told with tongue firmly in cheek, but the frivolous tone is misleading, as the narrative is intercut with short reflections on language and technology.

In an equally theoretical vein, **Christophe Donner** attacks frivolity in his literary manifesto *Contre l'imagination*, which berates authors who hide behind imagination to do nothing more daring than entertain.

Donner presumably does not read books like **Guillaume Clémentine**'s first novel *Le Petit Malheureux*, the antithesis of the serious fare provided by Houellebecq and others that nevertheless shares their self-centred approach. Clémentine's hero is a cynical, rough-and-ready party animal on the dole, with no principles beyond selfishness and a gift (born of inertia) for riotous flights of fancy (he becomes a protegé of Saddam Hussein). None of all this clouds his lucidity: 'My life is spent in the conditional tense: I would love, I would like, I would be. I do nothing. I expect nothing. I hope for nothing.' Clémentine paints a self-deprecating picture of his own weakness and parodies the France of *fonctionnaires* and state benefits.

A more wistful approach comes from **Arnaud Oseredczuk**, whose seductively freeform *59 Préludes à l'évidence* consists of short texts which recount fleeting pleasures, a succession of failed chat-up attempts and amorous disappointments, voyages and flashes of understanding. It's a sort of little portable geography, a log book of spiritual escape, an ensemble driven by a search for truth.

In a different vein, **Denis Robert** is both investigative journalist and novelist. *Pendant les affaires, les affaires continuent* was an enquiry into corruption scandals, while his novels *Je ferai un malheur* and *Notre héros au travail* recount his trials as a young journalist tracking down lies. The overlap continues in his recent *Tout va bien puisqu'on est encore en vie*, a novel which blends fiction and reality.

If not all these remarkable new authors have earned the favour of the public, others are raking in the royalties. One that has is **Philippe Delerm**'s *La Première Gorgée de bière ou des plaisirs minuscules* (a charmingly written, poetic series of everyday experiences), which has sold a massive 650,000 copies in French (as well as being translated into around twenty languages), while *Les Particules* has sold over 250,000 copies.

Even if the current vogue is for extreme confrontations – under the guise of polemics – this itself perhaps hides a certain conformism in literature, ideology and politics, which is quietly spreading out. The prevailing impression remains one of a generation that is searching for an ideal, starting from self-analysis and a base of everyday 'realism'. Anti-literature, if you will.

Despentes: *pretty young things?*

Sightseeing

In Perspective

Parisians traditionally divide their city – as we have done in this guide – into Right Bank (*Rive Droite*) and Left Bank (*Rive Gauche*), with the Seine and its islands running through the middle. Each has its own image and many Parisians – although they may live one side and work the other – are passionately attached to their Left or Right Bank identity. The Right Bank has long symbolised commerce and entertainment, clubs and cabaret. The Left Bank is more literary and intellectual, with its universities, famous cafés and arthouse cinemas.

The divisions are of course more complex, with the grand and the intimate, the old and the new, the sacred and the profane mingling on both sides of the river. On the Right Bank, the popular Faubourg-St-Antoine, with its craftsmen's alleyways and tradition of revolt, is a long way from the bourgeois, residential 16th, itself light years from gaudy Pigalle, while even the business-dominated area near the Bourse shifts imperceptibly into the rag trade of Sentier, or south with the quiet passages surrounding the Palais-Royal. Indeed, one can argue for an East-West division: the bourgeois, businessy west versus the working-class east with its immigrant mix. Here again, there's a grain of truth and plenty of exceptions. What you will find everywhere is a lived-in city made up of distinctive *quartiers*: it's not just a question of monuments, but the people who throng there, that make the different districts fascinating to explore.

The city continues to evolve, in both planned developments and a more organic process. Bookshops and cinemas still line the Latin Quarter, but smart fashion groups associated with Faubourg-St-Honoré have colonised St-Germain-des-Prés. Artists and students have moved on to the cheaper, anarchic bars of Ménilmontant and philosophers now argue it out at the Bastille, while the Marais, known for its museums and historic mansions, also hosts Paris' ever-more visible gay pulse.

Paris has always gone through waves of urban planning, be it Charles V putting up a defensive wall in the fourteenth century or Haussmann cutting through new roads in the nineteenth. Planning continues today, as different areas are in their turn developed. Despite its historical aura, Paris is a modern city, with some of the bravest recent architectural interventions in Europe, a whole wave of new parks, new museums and housing projects breathing life into previously neglected corners.

Luckily for the visitor, Paris is easy to get around and its geography easy to comprehend. The city is divided into 20 *arrondissements* which form a snail-shell spiral beginning at Notre Dame and finishing at Porte de Montreuil, on the eastern edge of the city limits. Public transport is plentiful and it's easy to walk between many of the major sights. The Seine, whose banks are easily bridged, is at the heart of the city's past, and at the forefront of its plans for the future.

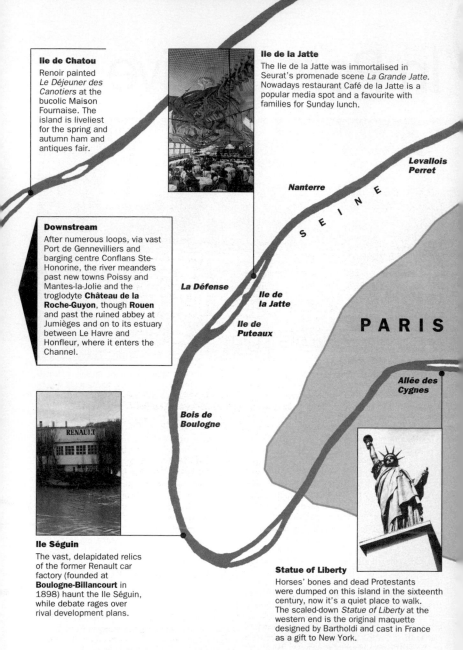

Ile de Chatou

Renoir painted *Le Déjeuner des Canotiers* at the bucolic Maison Fournaise. The island is liveliest for the spring and autumn ham and antiques fair.

Ile de la Jatte

The Ile de la Jatte was immortalised in Seurat's promenade scene *La Grande Jatte*. Nowadays restaurant Café de la Jatte is a popular media spot and a favourite with families for Sunday lunch.

Levallois Perret

Nanterre

S E I N E

Downstream

After numerous loops, via vast Port de Gennevilliers and barging centre Conflans Ste-Honorine, the river meanders past new towns Poissy and Mantes-la-Jolie and the troglodyte **Château de la Roche-Guyon**, though **Rouen** and past the ruined abbey at Jumièges and on to its estuary between Le Havre and Honfleur, where it enters the Channel.

La Défense

Ile de la Jatte

Ile de Puteaux

PARIS

Allée des Cygnes

Bois de Boulogne

RENAULT

Ile Séguin

The vast, delapidated relics of the former Renault car factory (founded at **Boulogne-Billancourt** in 1898) haunt the Ile Séguin, while debate rages over rival development plans.

Statue of Liberty

Horses' bones and dead Protestants were dumped on this island in the sixteenth century, now it's a quiet place to walk. The scaled-down *Statue of Liberty* at the western end is the original maquette designed by Bartholdi and cast in France as a gift to New York.

'The water of the Seine sometimes purges foreigners slightly. What they see as a bad thing is however a benefit; it is a gentle natural purgation, which calms the nerves and the digestive system affected by partaking in too large quantity of new food'. **(Dr Audin Rovière, seventeenth century)**

The Seine

The Seine is the lifeblood of Paris: not simpy of its historic heart, but also of the new Paris fast being built up around Bercy and the new Bibliothèque Nationale. Most of the city's great sights line its banks – one reason why you'll now see more tourist boats than freight barges. Beside the river, the cobbled *berges* make a pleasant breather from the streets above. They were the brainchild of the Comte de Laborde, who envisaged 'the splendours of antiquity combined with the delights of Benares on the banks of the Ganges.'

Péniches

The artistic or bohemian enjoy abondoning terra firma for the watery life. Boats, moored at various points along the Seine, range from shabby to sophisticated but are often capable of casting off on trips. If anyone should fall overboard, there is a separate river police to fish them out.

Ile de la Cité

Ile St-Louis

Passerelle de Solférino

Paris' newest footbridge is due to open autumn 1999 linking the **Tuileries** on the *Rive Droite* to **Musée d'Orsay** on the *Rive Gauche*.

Bridges

36 bridges cross the Seine within Paris (due to be joined by the Solférino and Bercy footbridges). The oldest surviving bridge is the paradoxically named **Pont Neuf**, opened by Henri IV in 1605, and the first not to have houses atop it. Most romantic is the metal **Pont des Arts** footbridge between the Institut de France and the Louvre. Most ornate is the **Pont Alexandre III**, built for the 1900 Exposition Universelle. Most practical is rebuilt **Pont de l'Alma** – the Zouave statue measures the height of the water when the river floods.

Musée de Sculpture en Plein Air

Despite works by Zadkine, Schoffer and César, the outdoor sculpture show on quai St-Bernard often seems more popular with courting couples than art lovers.

Charenton-le-Pont

MARNE

Upstream

Just outside Fontainebleau, the Yonne meets the Seine. The Yonne is longer than the Seine and therefore should have given its name to the capital's great artery, but tradition has proved stronger than logic; besides, the Seine emerges romantically from the vineyards of Burgundy, whereas the Yonne draws its source from undistinguised hills in the Nièvre.

The Marne

This tributary is famous for popular riverside *guinguette* dance halls, where families go at weekends to be inebriated by the sound of the accordion and the clink of full glasses.

Forever Paris

TV presenter, media pundit and fervent Europhile, France's favourite Englishman Alex Taylor on the city he loves to hate.

Forget the clichés! Forget the Louvre, Montmartre and the *caille aux truffes* halfway up the Eiffel Tower – if you've decided to move to Paris, you'd better get a life – down and out with the rest of us piled up on this side of the Périphérique.

Paris is about all that. Paris is sitting in an *embouteillage* (traffic jam) with some oink trying to muscle in from the taxi lane, stuck on the voie 'Express' Georges Pompidou, which for you has long since replaced the notion of *Rive Droite* you thought you'd be driving to work along. Paris is about listening to FIP in the car, occasionally interrupting its peculiar mix of Schubert and jazz for those women with impossibly sexy delivery to tell you that the 'big axis points of the capital are totally saturated', as is the air pollution index.

Paris is wondering why on earth French TV is still churning out two-and-a-half hour-long variety shows most evenings, presented – just like they were when you first arrived here twenty years ago – by Michel Drucker, and still featuring Dave warbling away at the high notes on 'Vanina' – the whole filled in with more posthumous tributes to Dalida. It's wondering what inane conception of TV scheduling could have led the two major channels to put out the same news, at the same time, and asking yourself why no-one has ever told presenter Patrick Poivre d'Arvor's make-up person to do his ears the same *après-ski* colour as the rest of his face.

Paris is about being rude about all the car number plates (92s especially) 'in' on Saturday evenings from the *banlieue*, or even worse from *la province*. It's about buying a greasy merguez and chip sandwich at 4am on rue de Lappe, blearily bumping into someone you only see at your office 'cafette' at lunch.

Paris is about listening to your taxi driver chat about the PSG football team's performance, while he speeds you at dawn across the place de la Concorde, and wondering who's staying at the Crillon.

Paris is getting freaked out when the cute CRS officers only ever ask Arabs to 'prove their identity' in the Forum des Halles. It's cursing the mayor for seemingly employing people to walk in zigzags down the pavements on Saturday afternoons when you've just emerged, full of bags, from the Samaritaine, and finding out that the 72 bus doesn't run down that part of the street on Saturdays.

Paris is moments of nostalgia you thought you'd never have – picking up microwaveable roly-poly puddings from M&S, or trying to explain Grant's accent on *Eastenders* to patient French friends.

Paris is about Métro strikes on rainy Thursday mornings, it's about never having filled in the right form at your local Crédit Lyonnais when all you want to do is put money into your account. It's about staying calm when employees from EDF or GDF tell you 'c'est pas possible.'

It's about worrying you're going to forget a redundant 'ne' in a subjunctive clause every time all you want is a demi at your local café *zinc*.

It's about spending sunny Sunday afternoons on the terrace of the Café Beaubourg, looking at badly dressed people passing by, and sending the cappuccino back because it hasn't got enough froth.

Paris is about never being seen dead going to the Louvre or the Comédie Française, it's about going to cinemas in the 15th *arrondissement* on Mondays when it's 30 per cent cheaper.

It's about living in the world's most beautiful big city and pretending not to notice it any more. That's what being a true Parisian is all about, so come here and have a ball.

The Islands

The Ile de la Cité and the Ile St-Louis nestle side by side in the heart of the city, yet lead quite different lifestyles.

Ile de la Cité

In the 1st and 4th arrondissements.

The Ile de la Cité was the site of the settlement that grew into Paris, first founded in around 250 BC by the Parisii, and centre of political and religious power under the Romans and in the Middle Ages.

When Victor Hugo wrote *Notre Dame de Paris* in 1831, the Ile de la Cité was a bustling medieval quarter of narrow streets and tall wooden houses: 'the head, heart and very marrow of Paris'. Baron Haussmann put paid to that; he supervised the expulsion of 25,000 people from the island, razing homes, flattening some twenty churches and obliterating most streets. The lines of the old streets in front of Notre Dame are traced into the parvis.

The people were forced to resettle in the east of the city, leaving behind a few large buildings – the **Conciergerie**, the law courts, the Hôtel Dieu hospital, the police headquarters and, of course, **Notre Dame**. The island now plays host to hordes of tour coaches during the day, but otherwise it can often seem rather sad and soulless.

The most charming spot is the western tip, where the **Pont Neuf** spans the Seine above a leafy triangular garden known as the **square du Vert-Galant**. With a wonderful view of the river, it's a great spot for summer picnics. In the centre of the bridge is a statue of Henri IV on his horse, first erected in 1635, destroyed in the Revolution, and then replaced in 1818. On the island-side of the Pont Neuf is the strangely secluded **place Dauphine**. André Malraux had a Freudian analysis of its appeal – 'the sight of its triangular formation with slightly curved lines, and of the slit which bisects its two wooded spaces. It is, without doubt, the sex of Paris.' Built in red brick and stone, it was, like the place des Vosges, commissioned by Henri IV, who named it in honour of his son, the Dauphin and future King Louis XIII.

Moving along the *quais* towards the centre of the island, the view is dominated by the severe classical **Palais de Justice**, and lining the Seine on the island's north bank, the medieval towers of the **Conciergerie**, both originally parts of the palace complex of the Capetian kings, on what had been the Roman governor's house. In 1358, after Etienne Marcel's uprising caused Charles V to move the royal retinue into the Louvre, it became a prison where people were incarcerated before being executed. Much of the facade is a nineteenth-century

Taking a break on the banks of the Seine.

pseudo-medieval reconstruction, but the original fourteenth-century clock tower remains, and the interior is worth visiting for the vaulted Salle des Gens d'Armes, vast kitchens and recreated prison cells.

Nearby, surrounded by the law courts of the Palais de Justice, is the **Sainte-Chapelle**, Pierre de Montreuil's masterpiece of stained glass and slender Gothic columns. It was built as a royal chapel to house relics brought back from the Crusades by France's sainted king Louis IX. The two-tiered structure is awash with colour and light. Still the centre of the French legal system, the **Palais de Justice** evolved alongside the Conciergerie, enclosing the chapel and entirely blocking off the chapel's north side. After going through security, you can wander through the marble corridors, and sit in on cases in the civil and criminal courts.

Across the boulevard du Palais, **place Louis Lépine** is now filled by a flower market (9.30am-6.30pm Mon-Sat), and a twittering bird market on

Sundays. To the south is the Préfecture de Police, known by its address, quai des Orfèvres, and immortalised in Simenon's *Maigret* detective novels. East of the market sprawls the **Hôtel Dieu**, founded in the seventh century. During the Middle Ages, once inside, your chances of survival were slim. Today it's one of the main hospitals for central Paris, but a much quieter and safer place.

The eastern end of the island is dominated by **Notre Dame**. Walk round the back for the best views of its structure. Don't miss the ascent to the roof to admire the ghoulish gargoyles and fine view. Look for the bronze marker in front of the cathedral, known as Kilomètre Zéro, the point from which all distances are measured. The **Crypte Archéologique** under the parvis gives a sense of the multi-layered past, when the it was a tangle of alleys, houses, churches and cabarets.

To the north-east of the cathedral are a few medieval streets untouched by Haussmann, such as **rue Chanoinesse** – built to house canons of Notre Dame, **rue des Ursins** and the narrow **rue des Chantres**. Steps away from the cathedral at rue du Cloître-Notre-Dame is **Le Vieux Bistro**, one of the best traditional bistros in Paris. At **9 quai aux Fleurs** Héloïse lived with her uncle Canon Fulbert, who had her lover Abélard castrated.

On the eastern tip of the island is the **Mémorial de la Déportation** (10am-noon, 2-5pm daily), a tribute to the thousands deported to death camps during World War II. Visitors descend a blind staircase to river level, where there are simple chambers inscribed with the names of the deportees.

Cathédrale Notre Dame de Paris

pl du Parvis-Notre-Dame, 4th (01.42.34.56.10).
M° Cité/RER St-Michel-Notre-Dame. **Open** 8am-6.45pm daily. **Admission** free. *Towers* (01.44.32.16.70) entrance at foot of north tower. **Open** 10am-4.30pm daily. **Admission** 35F; 25F 12-25s; free under-12s. **No credit cards. Map J7**
Catholics and tourists from all over the world come to pay homage to the Gothic masterpiece. Begun in 1163 by Bishop Maurice de Sully, keen to outdo the impressive new abbey at **St-Denis**, it was not completed until 1345. The cathedral straddles two architectural eras, echoing the great galleried churches of the twelfth century and the buttressed cathedrals which followed. Among its famous features are the three glorious rose

Leering streetlife on **rue St-Louis-en-l'Ile**.

windows. During the Revolution, the cathedral was turned into a temple of reason and a wine warehouse, and the statues of the kings were destroyed – those seen today are nineteenth-century replicas. Several of the originals were discovered in 1979 and are now on show at the **Musée National du Moyen Age**. The cathedral was returned to its ceremonial role for Napoléon's coronation as Emperor in 1804, but by the nineteenth century, the structure had fallen into such dilapidation that artists, among them Victor Hugo, petitioned King Louis-Philippe to restore the cathedral, which was masterfully done by Viollet-le-Duc. During the Nazi occupation, the stained-glass windows were removed, numbered and replaced with sandbags to save them from destruction. Renovation continues, as sculptures are cleaned or replaced after centuries of pollution and pigeons (the last scaffolding should be removed by the end of 1999). The north bell tower, leading to a gallery adorned with gargoyles, should reopen in May or June 1999.

La Conciergerie

1 quai de l'Horloge, 1st (01.53.73.78.50).
M° Cité/RER Châtelet-Les Halles. **Open** Apr-Oct 9.30am-6.30pm daily; Nov-Mar 10am-5pm daily. **Admission** 35F; 23F 12-25s, students; free under-12s; 50F combined ticket with Sainte Chapelle. **No credit cards. Map J6**
The Conciergerie looks like the forbidding medieval fortress and prison it once was. Yet, much of the gloomy facade was added last century; the thirteenth-century Bonbec tower was part of the palace of the Capetian kings and Tour de l'Horloge, built in 1370, was the first public clock in Paris. A visit takes you through the huge medieval kitchens, the Salle des Gardes and the Salle des Gens d'Armes, an impressive vaulted Gothic hall built in 1301-15 for Philippe le Bel. It gradually became a prison under the watch of the Concierge. Inside you can see the cell where Marie-Antoinette was held during the Revolution. Her enemies Danton and Robespierre later ended up here too, following thousands of others who were guillotined under the Terror. The wealthy could pay for a private cell with their own furniture. A list of Revolutionary prisoners, including a florist and a hairdresser, shows that far from all were nobles. The Chapelle des Girondins contains Marie-Antoinette's crucifix and a guillotine blade.

La Crypte Archéologique

pl du Parvis-Notre-Dame, 4th (01.43.29.83.51).
M° Cité/RER St-Michel-Notre-Dame. **Open** Apr-Oct 10am-5.30pm; Nov-Mar 10am-4.30pm. **Admission** 32F; 21F 12-25s; free under-12s. **No credit cards. Map J7**
The excavations under the parvis span sixteen centuries, from the remains of Gallo-Roman ramparts and a hypocaust, complete with furnace and brick piles, to a nineteenth-century drain. They give a good idea of the city's evolution, with fifteenth-century cellars built into old Roman walls and remains of medieval streets alongside foundations of an eighteenth-century foundling hospital.

Sainte-Chapelle & Palais de Justice

4 bd du Palais, 1st (01.53.73.78.50). M° Cité or Châtelet. **Open** Apr-Sept 9.30am-6.30pm daily; Oct-Mar 10am-5pm daily. **Admission** 35F; 23F 12-25s, students; free under-12s; 50F combined ticket with Conciergerie. **Credit** (shop) MC, V. **Map J6**
Inside a courtyard of the Palais de Justice is the exquisite Sainte-Chapelle. France's devout King Louis IX (1226-70), later as St Louis, was a collector of holy relics, some of doubtful authenticity. In the 1240s he ordered Pierre de Montreuil to design a suitable church in which to house the Crown of Thorns, which he had just bought. The chapel was built on two levels, the upper one for the monarch, his family and the canons, the lower chapel for the palace servants. The chapel is a monument to High Gothic style, and the upper level seems to be built almost entirely of stained glass. Bring binoculars, and come on a sunny day to best view the windows, which depict Biblical scenes. The chapel is used for concerts by early music ensembles.

*The river route to **Notre Dame**.*

Ile St-Louis

In the 4th arrondissement. Best M° stations Pont-Marie, Sully-Morland.

The Ile St-Louis is one of the most exclusive residential addresses in the city – discreet and self-contained rather than show-off. Delightfully unspoiled, it has a mix of fine architecture, narrow streets and magnificent views from the tree-lined *quais*.

For hundreds of years the island was a swampy pasture belonging to Notre Dame and a retreat for fishermen, boaters, swimmers and lovers, known as the Ile Notre Dame. In the fourteenth century Charles V built a fortified canal through the middle, thus creating the Ile aux Vaches ('Island of Cows'). Its real-estate potential wasn't realised until 1614, when speculator Christophe Marie persuaded Louis XIII to fill in the canal and plan streets, bridges and houses. The island was renamed in honour of the King's pious predecessor and, although Marie went bankrupt, the venture proved a huge success. It became highly fashionable as a site for elegant new residences from the 1630s on, thanks to the interest shown by society architect Louis Le Vau, who lived on the island and designed many of the hotels on quai d'Anjou, quai de Bourbon and quai de Béthune, as well as the church St-Louis-en-l'Ile; by the 1660s the island was filled.

Nowadays the Ile St-Louis is like a set from a *grand siècle* period drama, without a Métro or many modern shops. Instead there are *quais* lined with plane trees and poplars, fine houses with carved stone doorways, quirky gift shops, quaint tea shops and some lively bars and restaurants.

Running lengthways through the island is the **rue St-Louis-en-l'Ile**. No 54 was once a real ten-nis court, now the **Hôtel du Jeu de Paume**. At No 31 is Berthillon, purveyor of the best ice cream in town, while at the western end are the Flore en l'Ile tea room, and the popular **Brasserie de l'Ile St-Louis**, which draws Parisians and tourists alike, including many rugby fans.

Among the finest buildings on the island are the Hôtel Chenizot, at 51 rue St-Louis-en-l'Ile, with fabulous *rocaille* doorway adorned by a bearded faun and balcony decorated with grim-faced monsters; the Hôtel Lambert at No 2, built by Le Vau in 1641 for Louis XIII's secretary, with stone lions and palm trees; and **Hôtel de Lauzun**, a rare building in Paris to have retained its seventeenth-century interior. In the 1840s, it was owned by literary aficionado Jérôme Pichon, who rented out rooms to artists and writers, among them Baudelaire.

Eglise St-Louis-en-l'ile

19bis rue St-Louis-en-l'Ile, 4th (01.46.34.11.60). M° Pont-Marie. **Open** 3-7pm Mon; 9am-noon, 3-7pm Tue-Sun. **Map L7**

Built 1664-1765, following plans by Louis Le Vau and completed by Gabriel Le Duc. The interior follows the classic Baroque model with Corinthian columns and a sunburst over the altar, and is a popular classical concert venue.

Hôtel de Lauzun

17 quai d'Anjou, 4th. M° Pont-Marie. **Map L7**

This 1657 *hôtel particulier* has gilded, scaled sea-serpent drainpipes on the exterior and lavish *trompe l'oeils* inside, including the *Allégorie du printemps* in the Small Cabinet and four tiers of nymph-like children on the bedroom walls. Here lived La Grande Mademoiselle, cousin of Louis XIV and mistress of the dashing Duc de Lauzun, whose salon was frequented by Racine, Molière and La Fontaine. Later, Baudelaire wrote part of *Les Fleurs du Mal* here. The *hôtel* is open during occasional exhibitions (none in 1999) and offers special group visits (reserve months or even years ahead with Mme Lesieur at the Hôtel de Ville on 01.42.76.57.99).

The Right Bank

With palaces, mansions, revolutionary hotspots and the latest

The Louvre to Concorde

In the 1st arrondissement.

When the monarchs moved from the Ile de la Cité to spacious new quarters on the Right Bank, the Louvre and secondary palaces of the Tuileries and Palais Royal became the centre of royal power, in an area still full of royal and imperial survivors.

Now a Mecca for art-lovers, the **Louvre** remains *the* Parisian palace, with huge state rooms, fine courtyards and galleries stretching to the **Jardin des Tuileries**. Part of Philippe-Auguste's original twelfth-century fortress can be seen within the palace walls, though the Louvre only became the main royal residence in the fourteenth century, and later monarchs divided loyalties between it, the place des Vosges and Versailles. François 1er and his successors replaced the old fortress with a more luxurious residence, the Cour Carrée, perhaps Paris' best example of Renaissance architecture, and the gallery along the Seine leading to the Tuileries Palace to the west. The Louvre was first opened to the public as a museum by the Revolutionary Convention in 1793, though the palace continued to be used by governments, royal, imperial or republican. Two hundred years later, the *Grand Louvre* scheme added IM Pei's pyramid in the Cour Napoléon, doubled the exhibition space and constructed the subterranean **Carrousel du Louvre** shopping mall, auditorium and food halls. Despite initial opposition, the pyramid has become part of the cityscape surprisingly quickly. The steel and glass structure is fascinating for its technical brilliance and the tricks it plays with the fountains. Floodlit by night, it has a mesmerising glow.

Most people now approach the Louvre by the Cour Napoléon from Palais Royal (*see below*), but it's also worth walking through the peaceful Cour Carrée out to rue du Louvre. The Lescot (western) facade is François 1er's original wing adorned with writhing Mannerist figures, while through the southern archway you can see over the Pont des Arts to the Institut de France. On place du Louvre, opposite the palace, is **St-Germain-l'Auxerrois**, once the French kings' parish church, and home to the only original Flamboyant-Gothic porch in Paris, built in 1435. Mirroring it to the left is the nineteenth-century Neo-Gothic 1st *arrondissement* town hall, alongside chic new bar **Le Fumoir**.

The *Grand Louvre* has also rejuvenated the **Musée des Arts Décoratifs**, **Musée de la Mode et du Costume** and shortly-to-open **Musée de la Publicité**, and restored the **Arc du Carrousel**, a mini-Arc de Triomphe built 1806-09 by Napoléon and surmounted by the famous Roman bronze horses taken from St Mark's in Venice. France was obliged to return them in 1815; they were replaced with replicas in 1828. Through the arch you can now appreciate the extraordinary perspective through the **Jardin des Tuileries** all along the **Champs-Elysées** up to the **Arc de Triomphe** and beyond to the **Grande Arche de la Défense**. Originally stretching to the Tuileries palace (burnt down in the Commune), the Tuileries gardens were laid out in the seventeenth century and remain a living space with cafés, ice cream

quartiers *on the rise, this is ever the right place to be.*

stalls and summer fun fair. On the flanks of the Tuileries overlooking place de la Concorde stand the **Orangerie**, noted for its series of Monet water lilies (closing for renovation late 1999), and the **Jeu de Paume**, originally built to play real tennis, now used for chic exhibitions of contemporary art.

Along the north side of the Louvre, the **rue de Rivoli**, created by Napoléon for military parades, is remarkable for its uniform, arcaded facades, designed by Imperial architects Percier and Fontaine. It runs in a perfect line to **place de la Concorde** in one direction, to the Marais in the other, where it merges into rue St-Antoine. Though most shops here now sell souvenirs, elegant, old-fashioned hotels still remain, as do gentlemen's tailors, bookshops **WH Smith** and **Galignani**, and the famous tea room **Angelina**. The area formed a little England in the 1830s-40s as aristocracy, writers and artists flooded across the Channel after the Napoleonic Wars. They stayed at the Hôtel Meurice or in smart new rue de la Paix and rue Castiglione, reading the daily paper published by bookseller Galignani and dining in the restaurants of the Palais-Royal; at the time the area was described as 'a true quarter of London transposed to the banks of the Seine.'

At the western end of the Louvre, at the junction of rue de Rivoli and rue des Pyramides, have a look at place des Pyramides. The shiny gilt equestrian statue of Joan of Arc is one of four statues of her in the city – designed, along with Rodin's *Burghers of Calais*, to make Brits feel guilty. Running parallel to rue de Rivoli, ancient **rue St-Honoré** is one of those streets that changes style in different districts – all smart shops towards place Vendôme, local cafés and inexpensive bistros towards Les Halles. At No 296, the Baroque church of **St-Roch**, is pitted with bullet holes left by Napoléon's troops when they put down a royalist revolt in 1795. With its old houses, rue St-Roch still feels like *vieux Paris*; a couple of shops are even built into the side of the church. Crossing the road, at 263bis, the 1670-76 Chapelle de l'Assomption has an outsize dome, so disproportionate that contemporaries dubbed it 'dumb dome' (*sot dôme*), a pun on Sodom. Just west of here, much talked-about, pristine-white boutique **Colette** at No 213 has given a shot of adrenaline to the area's rather staid clothes shops. Opposite is rue du Marché St-Honoré, where **Le Rubis** wine bar hosts the scrum to taste Beaujolais Nouveau every November. It formerly led to the covered Marché St-Honoré (on the site of the Couvent des Jacobins, a famous revolutionary meeting-place), but the market has recently been replaced by the shiny glass and steel offices of the Paribas bank by Spanish architect Ricardo Bofill. There are several bistros in the square; behind, quiet streets such as rue Danielle-Casanova contain some fine, rather forgotten eighteenth-century *hôtels particuliers*.

Further west along rue St-Honoré lies wonderful, eight-sided **place Vendôme**, one of Louis XIV's main contributions, with a perspective that now goes from rue de Rivoli up to Opéra. A place Vendôme address has, perhaps, the highest snob value in the city, home to bankers, jewellers, the Ministry of Justice and the Ritz hotel.

At the west end of the Tuileries, the **Place de**

la Concorde, laid out by Jacques Ange Gabriel for Louis XV, is a brilliant exercise in the use of open space. André Malraux called it 'the most beautiful architectural complex on this planet', and it's impossible not to recognise its grandeur, especially at night. At the entrance to the Champs-Elysées are the winged Marly horses, copies of the originals by Guillaume Coustou, now in the Louvre. There are plans to redo the place and remove some of the traffic, although full pedestrianisation is unlikely.

Fashion boutiques, china and silverware shops and luxury hotels fill the area. Leading to the Madeleine is smart rue Royale, with stuffy tea room **Ladurée** and the legendary but now disappointing **Maxim's** restaurant (featured in Lehár's opera *The Merry Widow)*. There are more smart shops and fashion-haunt **Buddha Bar** in rue Boissy d'Anglas, while the ultimate sporting luxuries can be found at **Hermès** (note the horseman on its parapet) on rue du Fbg-St-Honoré (westward extension of rue St-Honoré), plus fashion names Guy Laroche, Karl Lagerfeld, Lanvin and Lolita Lempicka, and fine porcelain and tea rooms on the recently revamped Galerie Royale and Passage Royale.

Eglise St-Germain-l'Auxerrois

2 pl du Louvre, 1st (01.42.60.13.96). M° Pont-Neuf or Louvre. **Open** 8am-8pm daily. **Map H6**
Standing back from the street, this pretty church facing the Louvre was for centuries the royal church. Its architecture spans several centuries of construction. Most striking is the elaborate Flamboyant Gothic porch. Inside see the thirteenth-century Lady Chapel and splendid canopied, carved bench designed by Le Brun in 1682 for the royal family. The church achieved notoriety on 24 Aug 1572, when the signal for the St-Bartholomew's Day massacre was rung from here.

Eglise St-Roch

296 rue St-Honoré, 1st (01.42.44.13.20). M° Pyramides or Tuileries. **Open** 8.30am-7.30pm daily. **Map G5**
Curious rather than beautiful, this surprisingly long church begun in the 1650s was designed mainly by Jacques Lemercier, although the Lady Chapel was designed c1700 by Hardouin-Mansart and the north facade added by Robert de Cotte a few years later. The area was then the heart of Paris, and illustrious parishioners and patrons left notable funerary monuments: Le Nôtre, Mignard, Corneille and Diderot are all here. Look for busts by Coysevaux and Coustou and Falconet's statue *Christ on the Mount of Olives.* Paintings include works by Chassériau, Vignon and Le Sueur. There are a kitsch Baroque pulpit and cherub-adorned retable behind the rear altar. In 1795, a bloody shoot-out occurred in front of the church between royalists and conventionists, led by Napoléon, leaving bullet holes that still pit the facade.

Palais du Louvre

entrance through Pyramid, Cour Napoléon, 1st (01.40.20.50.50/recorded information 01.40.20.51.51). M° Palais-Royal. **Open** 9am-6pm Mon, Thur-Sun; 9am-9.45pm Wed. *Temporary exhibitions, Medieval Louvre* 10am-9.45pm Mon, Wed-Sun. **Admission** 45F (until 3pm); 26F Mon, Wed-Sat after 3pm, Sun; free under-18s first Sun of month. **Credit** MC, V. **Map H5**
Arguably the world's greatest art collection. The miles of galleries take in Antiquities and such icons as the *Mona Lisa* and Delacroix's *Liberty Leading the People (see chapter* **Museums**). The palace, built over centuries, was home to generations of French monarchs from the fourteenth century. A section of the massive keep, built in the 1190s by

Philippe-Auguste and turned into a royal residence in the mid-fourteenth century by Charles V, part of his new fortifications, is now open to view in the new underground complex. In the 1540s, François 1er asked Pierre Lescot to begin a Renaissance palace (now the western wing of enclosed Cour Carrée). Continued by his successors, the different facades are etched with royal monograms – H interlaced with C and D for Henri II, his queen Catherine de Médicis and favourite Diane de Poitiers. Henri IV and Louis XIII completed the Cour Carrée and built the wing along the Seine, although contemporary engravings show that some of the medieval fortified towers remained. The pedimented facade along rue du Louvre was added by Perrault under Louis XIV, who also brought in Le Vau and Le Brun to refurbish the interior. After the court left for **Versailles** under Louis XIV, the royals abandoned the palace and the apartments were often occupied by artists and state servants. After the Revolution, Napoléon added the grand stairway by his architects Percier and Fontaine (only the ceilings of the former landing, now Salles Percier et Fontaine, remain) and built the galleries along rue de Rivoli, complete with imperial figures (this wing houses the independently run **Musée des Arts Décoratifs, Musée de la Mode et du Textile** and **Musée de la Publicité**). His nephew Napoléon III added the Cour Napoléon.

The collection was first opened to the public in 1793, but the Ministry of Finance remained in the palace until the 1980s, when the Louvre's latest great transformation, the *Grand Louvre* project, began. One major feature was the opening of the Richelieu Wing in 1993, which doubled the exhibition area; another is the glass pyramid in the Cour Napoléon, opened in 1989 (bicentenary of the Revolution) and now the main entrance.

Place de la Concorde

1st/8th. M° Concorde. **Map F5**
Planned by Jacques Ange Gabriel for Louis XV in 1753, the place de la Concorde is the largest square in Paris, with grand perspectives stretching east-west from the Louvre to the Arc de Triomphe, and north-south from the Madeleine to the Assemblée Nationale across the Seine. Its construction required several years, and disaster marred the fireworks planned to celebrate the 1770 marriage of the Dauphin to Marie-Antoinette, when over a hundred people were crushed falling into a ditch in the unpaved *place.* Gabriel also designed the two grandiose colonnaded mansions on either side of rue Royale: the one on the west houses the exclusive **Crillon** hotel and an automobile club, the other is the Navy Ministry. The *place* was embellished last century with the tiered wedding-cake fountains, depicting river and maritime navigation, and sturdy classical lamp-posts. The obelisk in the centre, from Luxor, was a present from the Viceroy of Egypt in the 1830s. Best view is by night, from the terrace by the Jeu de Paume at the end of the Tuileries gardens.

Place Vendôme

1st. M° Tuileries or Opéra. **Map G4**
Elegant place Vendôme got its name from the *hôtel particulier* built by the Duc de Vendôme previously on this site. Inaugurated in 1699, the eight-sided *place* was conceived by Hardouin-Mansart to show off an equestrian statue of the Sun King. This statue was torn down in 1792, and in 1806 the Colonne de la Grande Armée was erected, modelled on Trajan's column in Rome, and illustrated with a spiral comic-strip illustrating Napoléon's military exploits, made out of 1250 Russian and Austrian cannons captured at the battle of Austerlitz. During the 1871 Commune this symbol of 'brute force and false glory' was pulled down by the revolutionaries. The present column is a replica from three years later, retaining most of the original frieze. Hardouin-Mansart only designed the facades; the buildings behind were put up by various nobles and speculators. Today the square is home

---

IM Pei's **Pyramide du Louvre:** *a pointed excuse to discover the museum inside-out.*

to Cartier, Boucheron, Van Cleef & Arpels, Trussardi and other prestigious jewellers and fashion names, international banks, the Justice Ministry and the Ritz. Chopin died at No 12, in 1849. The *place* was recently given a facelift, and an underground *parking* has removed cars from its surface.

Palais-Royal & Financial Paris

In the 1st and 2nd Arrondissements.

Across the rue de Rivoli from the Louvre, past the Louvre des Antiquaires antiques superstore stands the Palais-Royal, once Cardinal Richelieu's private mansion and now the Conseil d'Etat and Ministry of Culture; on the southwest corner is the Comédie Française theatre. The company created by Louis XIV in 1680 moved here in 1790, a spiritual homecoming, as Molière died nearby at 40 rue de Richelieu, commemorated in the Molière fountain. The brass-fronted Café Nemours on place Colette is popular with thespians. George Sand used to buy her tobacco across the square at cigar shop A la Civette.

Now cherished for their tranquility, in the 1780s the Palais-Royal was a rumbustious centre of Parisian life, where aristocrats and the grubby inhabitants of the *faubourgs* rubbed shoulders in subversive abandon. The coffee houses in its arcades attracted radical debate. Here Camille Desmoulins called the city to arms on the eve of Bastille Day. After the Napoleonic Wars, Wellington and Field Marshal von Blücher supposedly lost so much money at the gambling dens that Parisians claimed they had won back their entire dues for war reparations. Only **Grand Véfour**, the sumptuously panelled haute cuisine restaurant, survives from this era, although there are simpler places to eat *al fresco*, like the Muscade tea room and **Restaurant du Palais-Royal**. Wander under the arcades to browse in this eccentric world of antique dealers, philatelists and specialists in tin soldiers and musical boxes, luxury perfumerie **Shiseido**, the period housewares and kitsch contemporanea of Galerie Jean de Rohan-Chabot or vintage clothes specialist **Didier Ludot**. Go through the arcades to rue de Montpensier to the west, and the neo-rococo Théâtre du Palais-Royal. Opposite, next to busy bar **L'Entracte**, is one of several narrow, stepped passages that run between this road and rue de Richelieu, which with parallel rue Ste-Anne is a focus of Paris' Japanese community, all sushi restaurants and noodle bars. On the east side off Galerie Valois, the Passage Verité archway leads from sober place de Valois towards Les Halles via the **Galerie Véro Dodat** or the rue St-Honoré.

Squeezed between the elegant calm of the Palais-Royal and the frenzied Grands Boulevards lies Paris' traditional business district, beating at a considerably less frantic pace than Wall Street. The **Banque de France**, France's central bank, has occupied the seventeenth-century Hôtel de Toulouse since 1811. Very little of the original remains, but its long gallery

is still hung with old masters. Nearby the pretty **place des Victoires** was designed, like place Vendôme, by Hardouin-Mansart, forming an intimate circle of buildings today dedicated to fashion. The two worlds now meet in bistro **Chez Georges**, where bankers and fashion moguls rub shoulders. West of the place, explore the shop-lined covered **Galerie Vivienne** and **Galerie Colbert** (*see page 57, Rites of Passage*) and the **Bibliothèque Nationale Richelieu**, with its exhibition spaces in what was Cardinal Mazarin's mansion, now largely deserted since the bulk of the national library was transferred to the Left Bank. On the corner of Galerie Vivienne and rue de la Banque is luxury *épicerie* and wine merchant **Legrand**. Take a detour along the passage des Petits Pères to see the Notre-Dame-des-Victoires church, all that remains of an Augustine convent demolished in 1859. This church has a remarkable cycle of paintings by Van Loo.

Rue de la Banque now leads to **La Bourse** (stock exchange), behind a commanding Neo-Classical colonnade. Otherwise the area has a relaxed feel, at weekends positively sleepy. For business lunches and after-work drinks, stockbrokers and journalists converge on the **Vaudeville** brasserie. On rue des Colonnes, you'll find a quiet street lined with graceful porticos and acanthus motifs dating from the 1790s. Across the busy rue du Quatre-Septembre, stands the huge 70s concrete and glass HQ of **Agence France-Presse**, France's biggest news agency. This street and its continuation rue Réaumur were built up by the press barons with some striking Art Nouveau buildings. Most newspapers have since left; *Le Figaro* remains in rue du Louvre.

Bibliothèque Nationale Richelieu

58 rue de Richelieu, 2nd (01.47.03.81.26). M° Bourse.
Open *Galerie Mansart/Mazarine* 10am-7pm Tue-Sun. *Cabinet des Médailles* 1-5pm Mon-Sat; noon-6pm Sun.
Admission *Galerie Mansart/Mazarine* 35F; 24F under-26s, over-60s. *Cabinet des Médailles* 22F; 15F students, over-60s, under-26s. **No credit cards. Map H4**
The genesis of the French National Library dates from the 1660s, when Louis XIV's finance minister Colbert brought together the manuscripts of the royal library in the lavish town house which was once Cardinal Mazarin's. First opened to scholars in 1720, by 1724 the institution had received so many new acquisitions that the neighbouring Hôtel de Nevers was added. Some of the original painted decoration can still be seen in Galeries Mansart and Mazarine, now used for exhibitions of manuscripts and prints. Coins, medals and curious royal memorabilia can be seen in the **Cabinet des Médailles**. The complex was transformed in the 1860s by the innovative circular, iron-framed, vaulted reading room designed by Henri Labrouste, but the library is now curiously empty as the books have moved to the gigantic new **Bibliothèque Nationale François Mitterrand** on the Left Bank. Only the precious manuscripts and collections of engravings, drawings, music scores and photographs remain.

La Bourse

Palais Brongniart, pl de la Bourse, 2nd (01.40.41.62.21). M° Bourse. **Guided tours** 1.15-4pm Mon-Fri. **Admission** 30F; 15F students. **No credit cards. Map H4**
After a century at the Louvre, the Palais-Royal and rue Vivienne, the stock exchange found its home in 1826 in this

Take time for some serious reflection at the **Jardin des Tuileries.**

building designed by Alexandre Brongniart under Napoléon, a dignified testament to First Empire taste for Ancient Greece with Corinthian columns and female allegorical statues representing Business, Justice, Agriculture, Industry. It was enlarged in 1906 to create a cruciform interior, where brokers buzzed around a central enclosure, the *corbeille*. Computers have made it obsolete, but the atmosphere remains frenetic.

Louvre des Antiquaires

2 pl du Palais-Royal, 1st (01.42.97.27.00). M° Palais-Royal. **Open** *11am-7pm Tue-Sun.* **Map H5**
This upmarket antiques centre behind the facade of an old *grand magasin* houses 250 dealers. Louis XV furniture, tapestries, Sèvres and Chinese porcelain, silver and jewellery, model ships and tin soldiers can all be found here for a price.

Palais-Royal

main entrance pl du Palais-Royal, other entrances in rue de Montpensier, rue de Beaujolais, rue de Valois, 1st. M° Palais-Royal. **Open** *Gardens only dawn-dusk daily.* **Admission** free. **Map H5**
The Palais-Royal has a rich history. Built for Richelieu by Jacques Lemercier, it was known as the Palais Cardinal. Richelieu left it to Louis XIII, whose widow preferred it to the chilly Louvre and gave it its name. The Orléans rebuilt the facades in the 1750s. In the 1780s, the Duc d'Orléans enclosed the gardens in a three-storey peristyle. Housing cafés, theatres, sideshows, shops and apartments, its arcades came into their own as a society trysting place. Its cafés saw pre-revolutionary plotting, and the Palais-Royal became known as a hot-bed of gambling and prostitution. Today the gardens offer a surprisingly tranquil spot in the heart of Paris, while many surrounding shops specialise in prints and antiques. The former palace houses the Conseil d'Etat and the Ministry of Culture. Daniel Buren's sculpture of 280 black and white striped columns of different heights graces the main courtyard.

Place des Victoires

1st, 2nd. M° Bourse. **Map H5**
Louis XIV introduced the grand Baroque square with circu-lar place des Victoires, commemorating victories against Holland, designed in 1685 by Hardouin-Mansart to set off an equestrian statue of the king. The original disappeared in the Revolution; today's statue dates from 1822. Today, the sweeping facades shelter such names as Kenzo and Thierry Mugler.

Opéra & Les Grands Boulevards

Mainly in the 2nd, 8th and 9th arrondissements.
One of Napoléon III's architectural extravaganzas, the wedding cake of Charles Garnier's **Palais Garnier** opera house, and its feast of sculpture inside and out, perfectly illustrate the excesses of its reactionary patron. It evokes the mood of opera at its grandest, and it's not hard to see why the Phantom of the Opera legend started here. Garnier also designed the **Café de la Paix**, overlooking place de l'Opéra, the interior of which still gives a sense of stepping back into the 1860s. Behind, in the Jockey Club (now Hôtel Scribe, 14 rue Scribe), the Lumière brothers held the world's first public cinema screening in 1895. Opposite on the corner of boulevard des Capucines extends the wooden frontage of the delightfully old-fashioned emporium Old England. Inside it has antiquated wooden counters, Jacobean-style plaster ceilings and equally dated goods and service. **Olympia** concert hall, at 28 boulevard des Capucines, is the legendary venue of Piaf and other greats. The auditorium was recently knocked down and rebuilt a few metres from the original. Across the road at No 35, pioneering portrait photographer Nadar opened a studio in the 1860s, soon frequented by writers, actors and artists – Dumas père, Doré, Offenbach – and

in 1874 the setting for the ground-breaking first Impressionist exhibition.

Like a classical temple at the end of the boulevard stands the **Madeleine**, a vaguely religious monument to Napoléon. Its huge Corinthian columns mirror the **Assemblée Nationale** over the Seine, while the interior is a riot of marble, cluttered with side altars to saints who look like Roman generals. Most come to ogle **Fauchon**, Paris' most extravagant delicatessen, **Hédiard**, **La Maison de la Truffe**, and the other luxury foodstores, or for haute cuisine restaurant **Lucas Carton**, with Art Nouveau interior by Majorelle. Near here too is the **Chapelle Expiatoire** built by Louis XVIII in memory of Louis XVI and Marie-Antoinette.

Just behind the Opéra, the *grands magasins* (department stores) **Printemps** and **Galeries Lafayette** opened in the late nineteenth century. Awash with tourists all year and with Parisians at Christmas and in the sales, both are much altered. Printemps still has an imposing domed entrance and Lafayette an impressive stained glass dome. Behind the latter, on rue Caumartin, stands the austere, newly cleaned facade of Lycée Caumartin, designed as a convent in the 1780s by Bourse architect Brongniart to become one of Paris' most prestigious lycées under Napoléon. West along Haussmann's boulevard, the Second Empire church of **St-Augustin** is a clever exercise in cast iron by Baltard, architect of the Les Halles market pavilions.

Palais Garnier: *aria all on your own?*

Chapelle Expiatoire

29 rue Pasquier, 8th (01.42.65.35.80). M° Madeleine. **Open** 1-5pm Thur-Sat. **Map F3**
Commissioned from Fontaine in 1815 by Louis XVIII in memory of his executed predecessors Louis XVI and Marie-Antoinette. Their remains, along with almost 3000 revolutionary victims, including Philippe-Egalité, Charlotte Corday, Mme du Barry, Camille Desmoulins, Danton, Malesherbes and Lavoisier, were found in 1814 on the exact spot where the altar stands. Two marble statues represent Louis XVI supported by an angel and Marie-Antoinette, kneeling at the feet of Religion, represented by the King's sister, Mme Elisabeth. The chapel draws royalists for a memorial service every January.

Eglise St-Augustin

46 bd Malesherbes, 8th (01.45.22.23.12). M° St-Augustin. **Open** 8.30am-6.45pm Mon-Fri; 8.30am-1pm, 2.30-6.45pm Sat, Sun. **Map F3**
Designed by Victor Baltard in 1860-71, St-Augustin is not what it first seems. The domed, neo-Renaissance stone exterior, curiously getting wider towards the rear to adapt to the triangular site, is merely a shell. Within, Baltard used an iron vault structure, as at Les Halles; even the decorative angels are cast in metal. Note the William Bougereau paintings in the transept.

Eglise de la Madeleine

pl de la Madeleine, 8th (01.44.51.69.00). M° Madeleine. **Open** 7.30am-7pm Mon-Sat; 9am-1pm, 3.30-7pm Sun. **Map G4**
The building of a giant church on this site began in 1764. In 1806 Napoléon continued the project as a 'Temple of Glory' dedicated to his Grand Army, and commissioned Barthélemy Vignon to design a semi-Athenian temple. After the Emperor's fall construction slowed, but the church was finally consecrated in 1845. The gigantic colonnades of the facade are mirrored by those of the Assemblée Nationale across the river.

Inside are three and a half giant domes and pedimented, pseudo-Grecian side altars amid a sea of multicoloured marble. The painting by Ziegler in the chancel depicts the history of Christianity, Napoléon prominent in the foreground. The church is a favourite for celebrity weddings and funerals.

Palais Garnier

pl de l'Opéra, 9th (01.44.73.13.04). M° Opéra. **Open** 10am-5pm daily. **Guided tours** in French (01.40.01.22.63) 1pm Tue-Sun, 60F. **Admission** 30F; 20F 10-25s, over-60s; free under-10s. **No credit cards. Map G4**
Awash with gilt, satin, red velvet and marble, the opulent Palais Garnier, with its sumptuous grand staircase, sculptures and glittering chandeliers, is a monument to the ostentation of the Second Empire French *haute bourgeoisie*. Designed by Charles Garnier in 1862, it has an immense stage and an auditorium for over 2000 people. The exterior is equally opulent, with sculptures of music and dance on the facade, a gaudy Apollo topping the copper dome, nymphs holding torches, and a ramp up the side of the building on rue Scribe for the Emperor to drive his carriage to the royal box. Carpeaux's sculpture *La Danse* shocked Parisians with its frank sensuality, and in 1869 someone threw a bottle of ink over its marble thighs; the original is safe in the **Musée d'Orsay**. Since renovation in 1996, opera fans rejoice that Garnier again hosts lyric productions as well as ballet. Visitors can see the library, museum, Grand Foyer, Grand Staircase and the auditorium with its controversial false ceiling, painted with scenes from opera and ballet by Chagall in 1964 – there's occasional talk of returning to the original, still underneath.

Quartier de l'Europe

This area north of Opéra around Gare St-Lazare has streets named after various European capitals.

Described in Zola's *La Bête Humaine*, it is *the* Impressionist *quartier*, if hardly a tourist draw now. The exciting new steam age was depicted by Monet in the 1870s in *La Gare St-Lazare* and *Pont de l'Europe*; Caillebotte and Pissarro painted views of the new boulevards, and Manet had a studio on rue de St-Petersbourg, where he entertained sitters and exhibited works. This is an area built up in the late nineteenth century, then known for its prostitutes or *lorettes* (*see below*, **La Nouvelle Athènes**); rue de Budapest remains a sleazy red light district, while rue de Rome has long been home to Paris' stringed-instrument makers. Just east of Gare St-Lazare, look out for the imposing **Eglise de la Trinité** and Art Nouveau brasserie Mollard.

Eglise de la Trinité

pl Estienne d'Orves, 9th (01.48.74.12.77). M° Trinité. **Open** 7.15am-7.30pm Mon-Sat; 8.30am-1pm, 5-8pm Sun. **Map G3** Dominated by the tiered wedding-cake belltower, the church was built 1861-67 by Théodore Ballu in a neo-Renaissance style, typical of the era's historical eclecticism, and is famous as the church where composer Olivier Messiaen (1908-92) was organist for over 30 years. Guided tours on Sundays.

The Grands Boulevards

Contrary to popular belief, the string of *Grands Boulevards* between Madeleine and République (des Italiens, Montmartre, Poissonnière, Bonne-Nouvelle, St-Denis, St-Martin) were not built by Haussmann but by Louis XIV in 1670, replacing the fortifications of Charles II's city wall. This explains the strange changes of level of the eastern segment, as steps lead up to side streets or down to the road on former traces of the ramparts. The boulevards burgeoned in the early nineteenth century, witness some fine Neo-Classical facades and the network of covered galleries (*see page 57*, **Rites of Passage**), often built on lands repossessed from aristocrats or the church after the Revolution. The boulevards feel rather anonymous today, although they still have a gaudy character, with theatres, burger joints, chain restaurants and sleazy discount stores. The area is up for renovation on the city's agenda. Towards Opéra, the grandiose domed banking halls of disaster-prone Crédit Lyonnais, being rebuilt after a serious fire in 1996, and the Sociéte Générale reflect the business boom of the late nineteenth century.

Tucked between busy boulevard des Italiens and rue de Richelieu is pretty place Boïeldieu and the **Opéra Comique**. Originally built 1781-83 as the Comédie Italienne, the theatre was rebuilt in 1894-98 as a Neo-Classical confection with caryatids and ornate lamp-posts. Alexandre Dumas *fils* was born across the square at No 1 in 1824.

On the other side of boulevard Montmartre, past the eighteenth-century Mairie du 9ème (6 rue Drouot), stands the spiky modern construction of the **Drouot** auction house. Around it are the offices of numerous specialist *commissaires-priseurs*, antique shops and **Les Caves Drouot**, where auction

goers and valuers congregate. There are several grand if a little delapidated *hôtels particuliers* on rue de la Grange-Batelière, which leads on one side down curious **Passage Verdeau** and on the other back to the boulevards via picturesque **Passage Jouffroy**: second-hand book and print dealers, toy shops, quaint **Hôtel Chopin** and the colourful carved entrance of the **Musée Grévin** waxworks museum. Over the other side is the **Passage des Panoramas**. At 7 rue du Fbg-Montmartre is the budget eaterie **Chartier** and at No 35, vintage sweetshop **A la Mère de Famille**, founded in 1761 and still with its *fin de siècle* facade. Wander down cobbled Cité Bergère, built in 1825 as desirable residences; though most are now budget hotels, the pretty iron and glass *portes-cochères* remain. The area is home to kosher restaurants, and livens up with the Folies-Bergère (currently offering musicals rather than cabaret) and **Pulp** and **Rex Club** nightclubs. The palatial Art Deco cinema **Le Grand Rex** offers an interesting backstage tour. East of here are Louis XIV's triumphal arches, the **Porte St-Martin** and **Porte St-Denis**, recently unveiled after renovation, and a cacophony of levels, as narrow rue de Cléry and rue d'Aboukir lead towards Les Halles.

Le Grand Rex

1 bd Poissonnière, 2nd (08.36.68.70.23). M° Bonne Nouvelle. **Tour** *Les Etoiles du Rex* every 10 mins 10am-7pm Wed-Sun, public holidays, daily in school holidays. **Admission** 40F; 35F under-12s; 65F tour and film; 60F under-12s. **Map J4**
Opened in 1932, the huge Art Deco cinema was designed by Auguste Bluysen with fantasy Hispanic interiors by US designer John Eberson. See behind the scenes in the 40-minute Les Etoiles du Rex tour, a wacky high-tech experience. After a presentation about the construction of the auditorium, visitors ascend behind the big screen, taking in newsreel footage of Rex history and an insight into film production tricks with sensurround effects to jolt the strongest nerves.

Hôtel Drouot

9 rue Drouot, 9th (01.48.00.20.20/ recorded information 01.48.00.20.17). M° Richelieu-Drouot. **Open** 11am-6pm Mon-Sat. **Map H4**
A spiky aluminium and marble-clad concoction is the unlikely setting for the hub of France's secondary art market. The architects Biro and Fernier, who designed it in the early 80s to replace the crumbling former premises, wanted to achieve a 'surrealist interpretation of Haussmann'. Inside, shiny escalators whizz you up small salerooms, where medieval manuscripts, eighteenth-century furniture, Oriental arts, modern paintings and fine wines might be up for sale. Drouot makes a great free exhibition, with pieces of varying quality crammed in together. Details of forthcoming sales are published in weekly *Gazette de L'Hôtel Drouot*, sold at news stands. The French auction system is currently undergoing radical change. The European Union insisted French auction barriers be opened, and Sotheby's and Christie's should in theory have been allowed to enter the French market since 1998 but have as yet been prevented from holding auctions by legal technicalities.
Branches: Drouot-Montaigne 15 av Montaigne, 8th (01.48.00.20.80); Drouot Nord 64 rue Doudeauville, 18th (01.28.00.20.90).

Porte St Denis + Porte St Martin

corner rue St-Denis/bd St-Denis, 2nd/10th; 33 bd St-Martin, 3rd/10th.

Rites of Passage

The picturesque glass-roofed *galeries* that thread their way between Paris' boulevards recall the atmosphere of the Romantic era. Most were built by speculators in the early nineteenth century, when properties confiscated from the church or nobility under the Revolution brought vast tracts of land onto the market. The *galeries* or *passages* allowed strollers to inspect novelties safe from rain, mud and horses. Astute pedestrians can still make their way entirely undercover from the Grands Boulevards to the Palais-Royal. Over 100 *galeries* existed in 1840; less than 20 remain today, mostly in the 1st, 2nd and 9th, but renovation has brought them back into fashion. A later example is the 1904 Galerie Commerciale Argentine at 111 rue Victor-Hugo, 16th, while in the 8th there's the upmarket Galerie Royale. Visit in daytime: most are locked at night and on Sundays.

Galerie Véro-Dodat
2 rue du Bouloi/19 rue Jean-Jacques-Rousseau, 1st. Mº Louvre or Palais-Royal. **Map G5**
Véro and Dodat, prosperous *charcutiers*, built this arcade in the Restoration, equipping it with gaslights and charging astronomical rents. The tiled floor and wooden shopfronts, decorated with Corinthian colums and arcaded arched windows, are beautifully preserved along with the *loge du*

Galerie Vivienne: *the grandest of 'em all.*

gardien and little stairways leading up to apartments. Attractions include vintage **Café de l'Époque**, antique dolls and teddies at Capia, shops selling architectural salvage, sleek modern make-up **By Terry** and a printer.

Galerie Vivienne & Galerie Colbert
rue 6 Vivienne/4 rue des Petits-Champs and 5 rue de la Banque, 2nd. Mº Bourse. **Map G4**
Opened in 1826, and still upmarket. Vivienne, with its stucco bas-reliefs and mosaic pavement, houses Gaultier's couture, the fabrics of Wolff et Descourtis, **Pylones** gift shop and pretty tea-room A Priori Thé. Running in a parallel L-shape is Galerie Colbert, with its huge glass dome.

Passage du Caire & Passage du Ponceau
2 pl du Caire/33 rue d'Alexandrie and 119 bd de Sébastopol/212 rue St-Denis, 2nd. Mº Réaumur-Sébastopol. **Map J/K4**
Now taken up by Sentier clothing workshops, Passage du Caire is interesting for the Egyptian motifs at the entrance and Ponceau for its narrow walkway and high ceiling.

Passage de Choiseul
40 rue des Petits-Champs/23 rue St-Augustin, 2nd. Mº Pyramides or Quatre-Septembre. **Map G4**
Famed for its colourful depiction in Céline's *Mort à Crédit* (named Passage des Bérésinas), this is the *passage* where the writer grew up. Its charm lies in the very ordinariness of its clothing stores and discount shops.

Passage du Grand-Cerf
10 rue Dussoubs/145 rue St-Denis, 2nd. Mº Etienne-Marcel. **Map H5**
A less ornate *passage* near the rue Montorgueil street market, built in 1835 and notable for its height (originally giving access to a hostel above the shops), wrought iron work and hanging lanterns. It has recently been restored with some unusual shops selling fabrics and design objects.

Passage des Panoramas
10 rue St-Marc/11 bd Montmartre, 2nd. Mº Richelieu-Drouot. **Map H4**
The earliest surviving example is named for the giant circular illuminated paintings of capitals, created by Robert Fulton and Pierre Prévost and exhibited here when the passage opened in 1800. Take in the superb premises of Stern, engraver since 1830, and L'Arbre à Cannelle tea room.

Passage des Princes
5 bd des Italiens/97-99 rue de Richeliue, 2nd. Mº Richelieu-Drouot. **Map H4**
Opened in 1860, but since over-restored and often deserted.

Passage Jouffroy & Passage Verdeau
10-12 bd Montmartre/9 rue de la Grange-Batelière, 9th. Mº Richelieu-Drouot. **Map H4**
Built 1845-46, with a grand barrel-vaulted glass and iron roof. Past **Musée Grévin** and Café Zephyr, there's old-fashioned printsellers, antiquarian bookshops, traditional toy shops and the curiosities of Thomas Boog.

Passage Brady & Passage du Prado
46 rue du Fbg-St-Denis/43 rue du Fbg-St-Martin, 16 rue du Fbg St-Denis/16 bd St-Denis, 10th. Mº Château d'Eau or Strasbourg-St-Denis. **Map J4**
Brady is packed with Indian grocers, barbers and inexpensive curry houses; Prado boasts Art Deco motifs.

These twin triumphal gates were erected in 1672 and 1674 at important entry points as part of Colbert's strategy for the aggrandisement of Paris to the glory of Louis XIV's victories on the Rhine. Modelled on the triumphal arches of Ancient Rome, the Porte St-Denis designed by François Blondel is particularly harmonious, based on a perfect square, with a single arch, bearing Latin inscriptions and decorated with military trophies and battle scenes. Porte St-Bernard on the Left Bank has since been demolished and a gateway planned for the Fbg-St-Antoine never came to pass.

Les Halles & Sentier

In the 1st and 2nd arrondissements.

Few places epitomise the transformation of central Paris more than Les Halles, wholesale fruit and veg market for the city since 1181, when the covered markets were established by king Philippe Auguste. Zola called it the 'belly of Paris', the nerve centre of life in the capital, a giant covered market graced with Baltard's green iron pavilions. In 1969 the trading market moved to a new wholesale market in the southern suburb of Rungis, leaving a giant hole – long nicknamed *le trou des Halles* (slang for arsehole) – that was only filled in the early 80s, by the miserably designed **Forum des Halles** mall, after long political dispute. One pavilion was saved and reconstructed in the suburbs at Nogent-sur-Marne (*see chapter* **Beyond the Périphérique**).

After an initial burst of cool, the giant complex has become seedier by the year. As 'social exclusion' has risen as one of France's major problems, the Forum has become a mecca for the homeless, punks and junkies, the epitome of the Paris seen in Luc Besson's 1985 movie *Subway*, making surviving market restaurants L'Escargot Montorgueil (recognisable by the gilded snail above the door) and Pharamond look increasingly incongruous. In fact, the colourful market crowd and prostitutes of rue St-Denis always made this a seedy area. East of the Forum is the place des Innocents, centred on the Renaissance **Fontaine des Innocents**. The four-sided roofed structure was designed by Pierre Lescot who also worked on the Louvre for François 1er (Jean Goujon's original reliefs are in the Louvre). It was moved here from the city's main burial ground, nearby Cimetière des Innocents, demolished in 1786 after flesh-eating rats started gnawing into people's living rooms, and the bones transferred to the **Catacombes**. Pedestrianised rue des Lombards is a centre for nightlife, with bars, restaurants and the **Baiser Salé**, **Sunset** and **Duc des Lombards** jazz clubs. In ancient rue de la Ferronnerie, king Henri IV was assassinated in 1610 by Catholic fanatic François Ravaillac (who had followed the royal carriage held up in the traffic). The street has now become an extension of the Marais gay circuit with the thriving **Banana Café** and other gay bars.

Les Halles gardens seem inhabited largely by the homeless. Looming over them is the **Eglise St-Eustache**, with Renaissance motifs inside and chunky flying buttresses without. At the western end of the gardens is the circular **Bourse du Commerce**, once the main corn exchange, now a busy commodity market for coffee and sugar, world trade centre and Paris Chamber of Commerce office. It was built on the site of a palace belonging to Marie de Médicis, recalled in the astronomical column outside.

West of Les Halles is packed with clothes shops – **Agnès b**'s empire extends along most of rue du Jour, more streetwise outlets like **Kiliwatch** on rue Tiquetonne, **Junk** on rue Etienne-Marcel and further designer names west at place des Victoires (*see above* **Palais-Royal**). Hints of the market past linger in the 24-hour brasserie Au Pied de Cochon, now more geared to tourists, and restaurant supply shops, like *foie gras* specialist **Comptoir de la Gastronomie** or kitchen equipment emporia **A Simon** and **E Dehillerin**. East of here, pedestrianised **rue Montorgueil**, all food shops and cafés, is an irresistible place to while away a few hours.

At 20 rue Etienne-Marcel is the **Tour de Jean Sans Peur**, a strange relic of the fortified townhouse (1409-11) of Jean, Duc de Bourgogne, though over-restoration now rather hides its age.

The ancient easternmost stretch of the **rue St-Honoré** runs into the southern edge of Les Halles. The Fontaine du Trahoir designed by Soufflot in 1767 with neo-Renaissance icicles stands at the corner with rue de l'Arbre-Sec. Opposite, the fine Hôtel de Truden (52 rue de l'Arbre-Sec) was built in 1717 for a wealthy wine merchant, with wrought iron balcony and carved armorials. In the courtyard, a shop sells historic issues of old papers and mags. Such ancient little streets south of the gardens, like rue des Lavandiers-Ste-Opportune running towards the Seine and narrow rue Jean-Lantier, show a human side of Les Halles that has yet to be destroyed in cleaning up programmes. By the Pont-Neuf is **La Samaritaine** department store. It's chaotically organised inside but has a fantastic Art Nouveau staircase and glass *verrière*. The tea room at the top offers a panoramic view. From here quai de la Mégisserie leads towards Châtelet, lined with horticultural suppliers and pet shops.

Eglise St-Eustache

rue du Jour, 1st (01.40.26.47.99). Mº/RER-Les Halles. **Open** *May-Oct* 9am-8pm Mon-Sun. *Nov-Apr* 9am-7pm Mon-Sun. **Guided Tour** 3pm free (phone ahead). **Map J5**
This barn-like church (built 1532-1640) dominates Les Halles. Its elaborately buttressed and monolithic vaulted structure is essentially Gothic, but the decoration with Corinthian capitals is distinctively Renaissance. Paintings in the side chapels include a *Descent from the Cross* by Luca Giordano; works by Thomas Couture adorn the early nineteenth-century Lady Chapel. During the Revolution the church became the Temple of Agriculture. A favourite with music-lovers, it boasts a magnificent 8000-pipe organ (free recitals 5.30pm Sun).

Forum des Halles

1st. Mº/RER Châtelet-Les Halles. **Map J5**
This labyrinthine concrete mall extends three levels underground and includes the **Ciné Cité** multiplex, the **Forum des Images** and a swimming pool, as well as mass-market

The **Eglise St Eustache**, *on the face of it.*

clothing chains, branches of **Fnac**, Habitat and – a result of empty outlets – the **Forum des Créateurs**, a section given over to young designers. The first part of the centre was completed in 1979, the second phase by the Bourse du Commerce added in 1986. Both are now severely shabby, but you're bound to end up here sometime, if only to use the vast Métro and RER interchange which disgorges thousands of commuters and shoppers every day through the Forum's depths.

Rue St-Denis & Sentier

Away from the crowded malls of Les Halles, the Sentier is a virtual Parisian backwater. For years the district was all crumbling houses, run-down shops and downmarket strip-joints. In recent years, the prostitutes and peep-shows have been partly pushed back by energetic pedestrianisation.

The tackiness is pretty unremitting along the traditional red-light district of rue St-Denis (and northern continuation rue du Faubourg-St-Denis), which snakes north from the Forum. Kerb-crawlers gawp at the neon adverts for *l'amour sur scène*, and size up sorry-looking prostitutes in doorways.

Between rue des Petits Carreaux and rue St-Denis is the site of what was once the Cour des Miracles, where paupers would return after a day's begging to 'miraculously' regain use of their eyes or limbs. An abandoned aristocratic estate, it was a refuge for the underworld for decades until cleared out in 1667 by Louis XIV's chief of police, La Reynie. The surrounding Sentier district is centre of the rag trade, a surprising island of manufacturing where sweatshops copy the cat walks and the streets fill with porters carrying linen bundles over their shoulders. Streets like rue du Caire, rue d'Aboukir and

rue du Nil, testifying to a fit of Egyptomania after Napoléon's Egyptian campaign, are connected by a maze of passages lined with wholesalers. The area attracts hundreds of illegal and semi-legal foreign workers, who line up for work in place du Caire.

Fbg-St-Denis to Gare du Nord

North of **Porte St-Denis**, which celebrates Louis XIV's victories on the Rhine (*see above* **Grands Boulevards**), there's an almost souk-like feel to frenetic rue du Fbg-St-Denis with its food shops, narrow passages and sinister courtyards. The brasserie **Julien** boasts one of the finest Art Nouveau interiors in Paris, with wood carved by Majorelle, stunning painted panels, and eternally fashionable status, while up dingy cobbled Cour des Petites-Ecuries, theatre-goers flock to **Brasserie Flo**. Garishly lit **Passage Brady** is a surprising piece of India, full of restaurants and hairdressers. Rue des Petites-Ecuries ('stables street') was once known for saddlers but now has Turkish shops and cafés as well as top jazz venue the **New Morning**. This is one version of an authentic Paris *quartier*.

Just north, rue de Paradis has long had showrooms for crystal and porcelain makers and still glistens with discount glass and china outlets. At No 18 is the extravagant glazed facade of the former Magasin des Faïenceries de Choisy-le-Roi Boulenger. A little further, the **Musée Baccarat** is full of the excesses – and technical brilliance – of nineteenth-century crystal manufacture. The area is decidedly rundown, but unusual Empire-style

Hôtel de Bourrienne hidden at 58 rue d'Hauteville (open 1-6pm 1-15 July, Sept or by appointment/01.47.70.51.14) points to a grander past.

The top of rue d'Hauteville affords one of the most unexpected views in Paris. **Eglise St-Vincent de Paul**, with its twin towers and cascading terraced gardens, is about as close as Paris gets to Rome's Spanish Steps. Just behind on rue de Belzunce are the excellent modern bistro **Chez Michel** and offshoot Chez Casimir. On boulevard Magenta, the **Marché St-Quentin** is one of the busiest surviving covered iron markets, built in the 1860s, as the area was transformed under the Second Empire.

Boulevard de Strasbourg was one of Haussmann's new roads designed to give a grand perspective up to the new Gare de l'Est and soon built up with popular theatres – the mosaiqued neo-Renaissance Théâtre Antoine-Simone Berriau and the Art Deco Eldorado. At No 2, another neo-Renaissance creation houses Paris' last fan makers and the **Musée de l'Eventail**. Sandwiched between Gare de l'Est and Canal St-Martin stand the near derelict remains of the **Couvent des Récollets** and its former gardens – now the Square Villemin, a small park.

Couvent des Récollets

bd de Strasbourg, 10th. **Map L3**
This seventeenth-century Franciscan convent served as woman's shelter, barracks and hospital after the Revolution, but the last tenant, an architectural school, moved out in 1990. In July 1997, an artists' association held Sunday open events in the gardens. The convent's future is under evaluation, with the artists supporting plans for a Cité Européenne de la Culture.

Eglise St-Vincent de Paul

pl Franz-Liszt, 10th (01.48.78.47.47). M° Gare du Nord.
Open 8am-noon, 2-7pm daily. **Map K2**
Imposingly set at the top of terraced gardens, the church was begun in 1824 by Lepère and completed 1831-44 by Hittorff, replacing an earlier chapel to cater to the newly populous district. Twin towers, pedimented Greek temple portico and evangelist figures on the parapet are in classical mode. Original enamel paintings by Jules Jollivet were deemed too risqué, and removed. The interior has a double storey arcade of columns, murals by Flandrin, and church furniture by Rude.

Gare du Nord

rue de Dunkerque, 10th (01.53.90.20.20). M° Gare du Nord. **Map K2**
The grandest of the great nineteenth-century train stations (and Eurostar terminal since 1994) was designed by Haussmann's pet architect Hittorff in 1861-64. A vast, bravura iron and glass vault hides behind a much more conventional stone facade, with Ionic capitals and statues representing towns of northern France and Europe served by the station.

Beaubourg & the Marais

In the 3rd and 4th arrondissements.
Between boulevard Sébastopol and the Bastille lies Beaubourg – the historic area in which the Centre Pompidou landed in 1977 – and the Marais, built up between the sixteenth and eighteenth centuries and now a magnet for unusual boutiques, interesting museums and trendy bars.

Beaubourg & Hôtel de Ville

Contemporary Parisian architecture began with the **Centre Pompidou**, opened in 1977 in a formerly rundown area still known by its medieval name Beaubourg ('beautiful village'). This international benchmark of high-tech was always intended to be as much of an attraction as its contents. Sadly most of the centre is closed until 2000; much of the surrounding streetlife has dried up too. Out on the piazza is the **Atelier Brancusi**, the reconstructed studio which the sculptor left to the state on his death in 1956, recently joined by *Le Pot Doré*, a giant gilded flowerpot artwork by Jean-Pierre Raynaud.

The other side of the piazza, peer down rue Quincampoix for its art galleries, bars and curious passage Molière. It was here that Scottish financier John Law ran his speculative venture that crashed when the South Sea Bubble burst in 1720; hounded by the mob he took refuge in the Palais-Royal. Beside the Centre Pompidou is place Igor Stravinsky, with the red brick **IRCAM** contemporary music institute and the playful **Fontaine Stravinsky**, designed by Nikki de Saint Phalle and Jean Tinguely. It's full of whirring machines and multi-coloured gadgets including a *Nana* and a snake that move and squirt water. On the south side of the square is the church of **St-Merri**, with a Flamboyant Gothic facade complete with an androgynous demon leering over the doorway. Inside are some fine vaulting,

Passage Brady: *ever a slice of India.*

a carved wooden organ loft, the oldest bell in Paris (1331), and sixteenth-century stained glass. There are free chamber music concerts most weekends.

Between Beaubourg and **rue de Rivoli** is a maze of narrow pedestrianised streets. On the river side of rue de Rivoli stands **Tour St-Jacques**, alive with Gothic gargoyles, and **place du Châtelet**, an Egyptian-style fountain in the centre. Site of a notorious prison in the Middle Ages (demolished in the early nineteenth century), it houses twin theatres designed by Davioud in the 1860s: **Châtelet Théâtre Musical de Paris**, a classical and opera venue, and leading dance space, **Théâtre de la Ville**.

Beyond Châtelet looms the **Hôtel de Ville**, of which the Mayor's apartment occupies an entire floor. Centre of municipal rather than royal (or republican) power since 1260, it overlooks a square of the same name, once known as place de Grève, by the original Paris port. Here disgruntled workers once gathered – hence the French for 'strike' (*grève*). Protestant heretics were burnt in the *place* during the Wars of Religion, and the guillotine first stood here during the Terror, when Danton, Marat and Robespierre made the Hôtel their seat of government. Revolutionaries made it their base in the 1871 Commune, but the building was wrecked in savage fighting. It was rebuilt on a grander scale in fanciful neo-Renaissance style with statues representing French cities along the facade.

Despite the heavy traffic, quai de l'Hôtel de Ville has some popular inexpensive bistros, Trumilou and Louis-Philippe Café, with excellent views to the Ile de la Cité. From here, there's a door on rue des Barres into the **Eglise St-Gervais-St-Protais**.

Centre Pompidou

rue Beaubourg, 4th (01.44.78.12.33). Mº Hôtel-de-Ville or Rambuteau/RER Châtelet-Les Halles. **Open** noon-10pm Mon, Wed-Fri; 10am-10pm Sat, Sun, holidays. Closed 1 May. **Admission** *Temporary exhibitions* fee varies. **Credit** (shop) AmEx, MC, V. **Map K5**
The primary colours and exposed pipes and air ducts make the Centre Pompidou one of the most instantly recognisable buildings of Paris. Commissioned in 1968 by President Pompidou, it opened in 1977. The Italo-British duo of Renzo Piano and Richard Rogers won the competition for its design with their notorious 'inside-out', boilerhouse approach, which put air-conditioning, lifts and escalators outside, leaving a freely adaptable space for galleries, cinema, performance and library within. Most of the centre is closed until 1 Jan 2000, although an exhibition space remains open. The BPI library is temporarily housed nearby. The 'teepee' on the piazza explains the changes going on inside and is used for occasional lectures and dance events. *See also chapter* **Museums**.

Eglise St-Gervais-St-Protais

pl St-Gervais/rue des Barres, 4th (01.48.87.32.02). Mº Hôtel de Ville. **Open** 5am-10pm daily. **Map K6**
This church takes on different characters from different sides: late Gothic from rue des Barres, classical on place St-Gervais, where the facade added in 1621 was the first in Paris to use the three orders (Doric, Ionic, Corinthian). Inside is an impressive triple nave and series of side chapels, together with a central choir with carved choir stalls. The Couperin dynasty of composers were organists here. Adjoining the church on rue des Barres are the remains of the charnel house.

Tour St-Jacques

pl du Châtelet, 4th. Mº Châtelet. **Map J6**
Much-loved by the Surrealists, this solitary gargoyle-covered Flamboyant Gothic bell-tower is the remains of the St-Jacques-La-Boucherie church, built for the powerful Butchers' Guild in 1523. Pascal carried out experiments on the weight of air here in the seventeenth century. A weather station now crowns the 52-metre high tower, which can only be admired from outside.

The Marais

East of Roman rue St-Martin and rue du Renard lies the Marais, a truly magical area whose narrow streets are dotted with aristocratic *hôtels particuliers (see page 64)*, art galleries, fashion boutiques and stylish cafés. The big city slows down here, giving you time to notice the beautifully carved doorways and the early street signs carved into the stone.

The Marais, or 'marsh', started life as an uninhabited piece of swampy ground used for market gardening, inhabited only by a few religious foundations. In the sixteenth century the elegant **Hôtel Carnavalet** and **Hôtel de Lamoignan** prefigured its phenomenal rise as an aristocratic residential area after Henri IV began constructing the **place des Vosges** in 1605. Soon nobles began building smart townhouses where famous literary ladies like Mme de Sévigné and Mlle de Scudéry and influential courtesan Ninon de l'Enclos held court. The area fell from fashion a century later; happily, many of the narrow streets were essentially unchanged as mansions became industrial workshops, schools, tenements, even a fire station. The current renaissance dates from 1962 and a preservation order from then-Culture Minister André Malraux, which safeguarded many endangered buildings for use as museums. Now one of the liveliest, most international *quartiers*, property prices have soared into the luxury bracket.

An ideal starting point is the **place des Vosges**, a perfectly proportioned arcaded square of red-brick townhouses once popular for duels. At one corner is **Maison de Victor Hugo**, once occupied by the author. Luxurious **Ambroisie** restaurant is for special treats; much simpler but charming and touristy is **Ma Bourgogne**. An archway leads from the southwest corner to the elegant **Hôtel de Sully**. The main courtyard, adorned with stone carvings of the elements and seasons, leads off rue St-Antoine.

West of place des Vosges, the **rue des Francs-Bourgeois** runs right through the Marais. The street soon forgets its Les Halles legacy in the food shops of rue Rambuteau to become a street packed with elegant mansions and original shops: fashion boutiques **Et Vous**, **Blanc Bleu**, **Plein Sud** and **Abou Dhabi**, flower arrangements and garden gadgets at Millefeuilles, the delectable bathroom accessories of **Bains Plus**, the funky knick-knacks of **La Chaise Longue**... The tea room **Les Enfants Gâtés** ('spoiled children') sums up the mood. For a little culture, seek out two of Paris' most elegant early eighteenth-century residences, full of Rococo lightness: **Hôtel d'Albret** (No 31) and **Hôtel de Soubise** (No 60), the national archives, where interiors by Boucher and Lemoine can be seen as part of the **Musée de l'Histoire de France**.

Just behind Hôtel de Soubise, the **Hôtel Guénégaud** (60 rue des Archives) was built in 1654 for Louis XIV's Secretary of State by Mansart, and now houses the **Musée de la Chasse et de la Nature**. Look out for one of the city's few remaining Gothic cloisters adjoining classical Eglise des Billettes, sandwiched at No 22 between the cafés and gay bars, and the curious Gothic turret on the corner of rue des Francs-Bourgeois and rue Vieille-du-Temple – the remains of the Hôtel Hérouët built c1500 for Jean Hérouët, Louis XII's treasurer. Huge Medusa-adorned oak doors at No 47 lead to the **Hôtel des Ambassadeurs de Hollande**, where Beaumarchais wrote *The Marriage of Figaro*.

Even workaday rue du Temple, once the road leading to the Templars' church, is full of surprises. Near rue de Rivoli, the **Latina** specialises in Latin American films. At No 41 an archway leads into the courtyard of the former Aigle d'Or coaching inn, now the **Café de la Gare** café-théâtre, **Le Studio** Tex-Mex and dance studios. Across the street, chilled-out recent arrival **L'Epicerie** showcases young fashion designers and artists. Further north among bag and accessory wholesalers, the imposing **Hôtel de St-Aignan** at No 71 contains the new Jewish museum. Just beyond it is the Hôtel du Montmor at No 79. Round the corner, **Hôtel de Hallwyl** is a rare domestic building by Ledoux. Also worth a look is austere **Hôtel de Lamoignon**, on the corner of rue Pavée and rue des Francs-Bourgeois. Built in 1585 for Diane de France, Henri II's illegitimate daughter, it now houses the **Bibliothèque Historique de la Ville de Paris**.

The district's two most important museums are also in ex-*hôtels*. The **Musée Carnavalet** on rue de Sévigné, dedicated to Paris history, runs across the **Hôtel Carnavalet**, once home to famous letter-writer Mme de Sévigné, and the later **Hôtel le Peletier de St-Fargeau**. Curiosities include faithful reconstructions of Proust's bedroom and the Fouquet jewellery shop. The **Hôtel Salé** on rue de Thorigny, built and named in 1656 for a salt tax collector, has been finely restored and extended to house the **Musée National Picasso**. The original ornate staircase remains, as do two fine sphinxes in the entrance courtyard. Nearby is pretty **Hôtel Libéral Bruand**, while there are several early seventeenth-century houses on rue du Parc Royal.

The Marais is also home to Paris' oldest Jewish community, centred on rue des Rosiers, rue des Ecouffes and rue Pavée (where there's a synagogue designed by Guimard). Originally mainly Eastern European Ashkenazi Jews who arrived last century after the pogroms (many later deported during World War II), the community expanded in the 1950s and 60s with a wave of Sephardic Jewish

immigration following French withdrawal from North Africa. Thus there are now many *falafel* shops alongside the Jewish bakers and delis, as well as several fast-encroaching, designer clothes shops.

The lower ends of rue des Archives and rue Vieille-du-Temple are the centre of café life and happening bars, like cutesy **Petit Fer à Cheval** and cosmopolitan **La Chaise au Plafond** and **Café du Trésor** in the neighbouring impasse du Trésor. This area, especially rue Ste-Croix-de-la-Bretonnerie and rue du Temple, is the hub of the Paris gay scene, particularly thriving at night. Also good for a drink is rue du Bourg-Tibourg, with US-style **Lizard Lounge** and wine bistro **Le Coude Fou**. Charming place du Marché Ste-Catherine is worth seeking out for the characterful Bar de Jarente and Jewish/East European restaurant Pitchi-Poï.

Place des Vosges

4th. M° St-Paul. **Map L6**

The first planned square in Paris was built 1605-12 by Henri IV. With its beautifully harmonious red-brick and stone arcaded facades and steeply pitched roofs, the intimate square is quite distinct from the pomp of later Bourbon Paris. Perfectly symmetrical – the Pavillon du Roi over the rue de Birague mirrored by the Pavillon de la Reine on the other side – the actual plots behind the facades were let out to speculators. Originally the place Royale, the square's name dates from the Napoleonic Wars, when the Vosges was the first region of France to pay its war taxes. Mme de Sévigné, salon hostess and letter writer, was born here in 1626. Then the garden saw duels and romantic trysts; now it attracts *boules* players and children. In the centre is Henri IV's successor Louis XIII.

The Temple & Arts et Métiers

The northern, less gentrified half of the Marais stretching up towards place de la République is home to tiny local bars, costume-jewellery and ragtrade wholesalers and industrial workshops, alongside recently arrived fashion designers. The Quartier du Temple was once a fortified, semi-independent entity under the Knights Templar. The round church and keep have long been replaced by Square du Temple and the Carreau du Temple clothes market. The keep became a prison in the Revolution, where the royal family were held in 1792. On rue de Bretagne are food shops and fashionable couscous restaurant **Chez Omar**; the nearby Marché des Enfants Rouges is due to reopen in 1999. The **Web Bar** on rue de Picardie runs exhibitions and concerts, while tucked behind secretive courtyard entrances in the fine hôtels along rue Vieille-du-Temple and rue Debelleyme are the lofty spaces of many of Paris' most avant-garde art galleries.

Back towards Beaubourg is the Arts et Métiers area, originally the powerful Abbey of St-Martin-des-Champs, transformed after 1789 into the **Musée des Arts et Métiers** (closed for renovation and archaeological digs). The adjacent fifteenth-century church of St-Nicolas-des-Champs has a superb Baroque altarpiece. This area is not as forgotten as it may look, with the classic bistro Ami Louis, and

Pompidou *piping is under wraps (for once).*

trendy Latin restaurant **Anahi**. No 3 rue Volta was thought the city's oldest house; recent analysis puts its half-timbered structure in the sixteenth century. The earliest domestic dwelling is nearby **Auberge Nicolas Flamel** (51 rue de Montmorency), now a bistro, built in 1407 for alchemist Nicolas Flamel.

The St-Paul District

In 1559, Henri II was mortally wounded in a jousting tournament on what is now broad, busy rue St-Antoine. He is commemorated in a grieving marble Virgin by Pilon commissioned by his widow Catherine de Médicis, now in the Jesuit church of **St-Paul-St-Louis**. The former convent buildings are now part of Lycée Charlemagne. Towards the Bastille, the heavily domed church of the Visitation Ste-Marie was designed in the 1630s by Mansart. South of rue St-Antoine is a more sedate residential area known as St-Paul. There are still plenty of fine houses, but the overall mood is more discreet. The **Village St-Paul**, a colony of antique sellers spread across small interlinked courtyards between rues St-Paul, Charlemagne and quai des Celestins, is a promising source of 1930s and 50s furniture, kitchenwares and wine gadgets (open Mon, Thur-Sun). On rue des Jardins-St-Paul is the largest surviving section of the **wall of Philippe-Auguste**. The infamous poisoner Marquise de Brinvilliers lived at Hôtel de Brinvilliers (12 rue

Charles V) in the 1630s. She killed father and brothers to get her hands on the family fortune, and was only caught after her lover died... of natural causes.

Two of the Marais' finest mansions are on rue François-Miron, an ancient fork of rue St-Antoine. **Hôtel de Beauvais**, No 68, is still being restored, while **Hôtel Hénault de Cantorbe** has been renovated with a striking modern extension as the **Maison Européenne de la Photographie**. Down rue de Fourcy towards the river, see the formal gardens of the **Hôtel de Sens**, a fanciful ensemble of Gothic turrets decorated with stone wolves and monsters, which now houses the Bibliothèque Forney. Across from the tip of the Ile St-Louis is the **Pavillon de l'Arsenal**, built by a rich timber merchant to put on private art shows to rival the offical *salons* and now used for shows on Paris architecture.

Eglise St-Paul-St-Louis

99 rue St-Antoine, 4th (01.42.72.30.32). M° Bastille or St-Paul. **Open** *7.30am-8pm Mon-Wed, Sat; 7.30am-10pm Thur; 9am-8pm Sun.* **Map L7**
The domed Baroque Counter-Reformation church, completed in 1641, is modelled like all Jesuit churches on the Gesù in Rome, with its three-storey hierarchical facade bearing (replacement) statues of saints Louis, Anne and Catherine, single nave and side chapels. Its dome was the first important Baroque dome in Paris. The hearts of Louis XIII and XIV were stolen from here in the Revolution. Most of the original paintings and furnishings were removed then too, when the church became a temple of reason. In 1802 it became a church again and now houses Delacroix's *Christ in the Garden of Olives*. The shell stoups were a gift from Victor Hugo.

Fortified Wall of Philippe-Auguste

rue des Jardins-St-Paul, 4th. M° Pont Marie or St-Paul. **Map L7**
King Philippe-Auguste (1165-1223) was the first great Parisian builder since Roman times, enclosing the growing city on Left and Right banks within a great defensive wall. The largest surviving section, complete with towers, extends along rue des Jardins-St-Paul. Another chunk can be seen at 3 rue Clovis in the Latin Quarter, and odd remnants of towers are dotted around the Marais and St-Germain-des-Prés.

Mémorial du Martyr Juif Inconnu

17 rue Geoffroy l'Asnier, 4th (01.42.77.44.72). M° St-Paul or Pont-Marie. **Open** *10am-1pm, 2-5pm Mon-Fri, Sun; 10am-1pm, 2.5pm Fri. Closed Sat, Jewish holidays.* **Admission** *15F.* **No credit cards.** **Map K6**
A reminder that many of the Jews rounded up in World War II (originally for foreign Jews, later extended to French Jews) were residents of the Marais, this monument also serves as an archive and exhibition centre on the deportations.

The Bastille & Eastern Paris

Mainly in the 11th and 12th arrondissements.
Traditionally a boundary point between central Paris and the more proletarian east, **place de la Bastille** has remained a potent symbol of popular revolt ever since the prison-storming that inaugurated the Revolution, and is still a favoured spot for demos and gatherings. Since the 1980s, it has also been a magnet for new cafés, restaurants, galleries and bars, so transforming the area from one of craft workshops into a youthful hotspot.

Merry Marais mansions

Many of the finest Marais *hôtels particuliers* can be visited as museums, while the courtyards of others are often visible from the street. For some of the more private buildings, try a walking tour, or join the queues on the Journées du Patrimoine in September (*see chapter* **Paris by Season**).

Hôtel d'Albret
31 rue des Francs-Bourgeois, 4th. M⁰ St Paul.
Map L6
The courtyard facade was built 1635-50, while the streetside facade was reconstructed in pure Rococo style in the 1740s with an elegant ironwork balcony supported on a rocaille cartouche and lions' heads. In the 1650s, Mme de Montespan, mistress of Louis XIV, was introduced here to Françoise d'Aubigné, widow of writer Scarron, who became governess to her eight illegitimate children. Françoise worked her way up via court governess to become the king's new official mistress, Mme de Maintenon. Now used by the cultural affairs department of the Ville de Paris, you can wander into the courtyard in the week. Occasional jazz concerts in summer.

Hôtel des Ambassadeurs de Hollande
47 rue Vieille-du-Temple, 4th. M⁰ St Paul. **Map K6**
Aka Hôtel Amelot de Bisseuil, this house (not open to the public) was built 1650-1660 by Pierre Cottard. Here in 1778 Beaumarchais wrote *The Marriage of Figaro;* seen as a narrowly disguised criticism of the court, it was initially censored. In the Revolution the *hôtel* became a dance hall. Behind the two massive oak doors decorated with Medusas are two courtyards, the first with sundials and stone figures of Romulus and Remus. The interior includes a grand bedchamber and sumptuously decorated Galerie de Psyché.

Hôtel Beauvais
68 rue François-Miron, 4th. M⁰ St-Paul. **Map K6**
Now being restored, this sumptuous mansion was built in the 1650s for Catherine-Henriette Bellier, a chambermaid of Anne of Austria who had married ribbon merchant Pierre de Beauvais. From here, Anne watched her newly married son Louis XIV arrive with bride Marie-Thérèse in 1660. Later the young Mozart performed here. From the street you can admire the central balcony adorned with goats' heads; the most innovative element is the courtyard, marked by a rotunda over the doorway and semi-circular bay at the other end.

Hôtel Carnavalet
23 rue de Sévigné, 3rd. M⁰ St-Paul. **Map L6**
Begun c1550 for Jacques de Ligneries by Pierre Lescot (Louvre architect), Carnavalet's U-shaped layout set the model for the Paris *hôtel particulier*: main building at the rear of a courtyard, lateral wings with stables and kitchens, entrance doorway closing the court from the street. The sculptures of the four seasons on the main facade are attributed to Jean Goujon. In the 1660s, Mansart rebuilt the streetside building and added the grand staircase. Famous letter writer Marquise de Sévigné (1626-96) spent her last twenty years here. Since 1866, Carnavalet has been the museum of Paris history. *See also* **Musée Carnavalet.**

Hôtel Donon
8 rue Elsévir, 3rd. M⁰ St-Paul. **Map L6**
Built for the royal buildings inspector, this pretty, sober *hôtel* built in 1598 gives an overall impression of verticality with its long windows, steeply pitched roof and two narrow wings. Now housing the **Musée Cognacq-Jay**, it is one of the best places to see eighteenth-century panelled interiors. Famous courtesan Ninon de l'Enclos lived at No 14.

Hôtel Guénégaud
60 rue des Archives, 3rd. M⁰ Rambuteau. **Map K5**
A spare, almost sombre building from the outside, the Hôtel Guénégaud has been attributed to François Mansart for its harmonious proportions. The building fell into a state of dereliction but has been beautifully restored. Inside, stuffed animal trophies belonging to the **Musée de la Chasse** looming over the grand stairway add to the effect.

Hôtel de Hallwyll
28 rue Michel-le-Comte, 3rd. M⁰ Rambuteau. **Map L6**
A rare example of domestic architecture by Nicolas Ledoux, known for toll gates around the city, who modified the earlier Hôtel de Bouligneux, previously home to the influential Enlightenment salon of Mme Necker and her daughter Mme de Staël. In the 1760s Ledoux brought the three-storey building into line with severe, geometrical Neo-Classical style, creating an Antique inspired colonnade at the rear.

Hôtel Hénault de Cantorbe
5-7 rue de Fourcy, 4th. M⁰ St-Paul. **Map L6**
Built in the early 1700s for the *fermier général* (tax collector) Hénault de Cantorbe, this *hôtel* suffered a typical Marais decline, housing a cheese shop, ic-cream maker and rundown flats, but has since been rescued to house the **Maison Européenne de la Photographie** with a well-adapted modern extension by Yves Lion. The grand stairway and

Mozart once busked at **Hôtel Beauvais.**

facades are listed – simple on rue de Fourcy, more elaborate on the rue François-Miron, where there's a superb balcony supported by a helmeted head.

Hôtel Lamoignan

24 rue Pavée, 4th. M° St-Paul. **Map L6**
One of the earliest noble Marais mansions, it was built in 1585 for Diane de France, illegitimate daughter of Henri II. Jutting out into the street is a curious square turret. The courtyard is magisterial, with giant Corinthian pilasters (for the first time in Paris) and a Greek key frieze. Writer Alphonse Daudet had rooms here in the nineteenth century. The monumental building is now home to the **Bibliothèque Historique de la Ville de Paris**, and the reading room still has its original painted beamed ceiling.

Hôtel Libéral Bruand

1 rue de la Perle, 3rd. M° St-Paul. **Map L6**
Built in 1685 by the architect of Les Invalides and the Salpêtrière for himself. At the rear of a pretty arcaded courtyard, the lovely main facade has a pediment decorated with cherubs round an *oeil de boeuf* window, arched windows and niches containing antique-style busts. There's a collection of locks and keys inside (*see* **Musée de la Serrure**).

Hôtel de Soubise/Hôtel de Rohan

60 rue des Francs-Bourgeois, 3rd. M° Hôtel de Ville. **Map L6**
Actually an assemblage of three different mansions. By the time the **Hôtel de Soubise** was begun in 1704, the nobs were already switching loyalty to Versailles and Fbg-St-Germain, but it is still one of the grandest of *hôtels*. Built for the Prince and Princesse de Soubise, architect Delamair incorporated the turreted medieval gateway of the **Hôtel de Clisson** into one side of the colonnaded *cour d'honneur*, while the Rococo apartments (visible within the **Musée de l'Histoire de France**) were decorated by Boucher, Natoire, Restout and Van Loo. The adjoining **Hôtel de Rohan** (87 rue Vieille-du-Temple) also by Delamair, for Soubise's son, Bishop of Strasbourg, later Cardinal de Rohan, has a wonderful relief by Robert Le Lorrain, *The Horses of Apollo*, over the stables in the courtyard. The *Cabinet des Singes* by Christophe Huet can occasionally be seen during exhibitions. It was here that one of the Cardinal's successors was implicated in the scandal of the queen's necklace in 1785.

Hôtel de St-Aignan

71 rue du Temple, 3rd. M° Rambuteau. **Map K6**
Apart from the winged and bearded heads on the doors, the austere street facade gives few hints at the grandeur within, but once in the newly restored courtyard you get the impression this *hôtel* was built for giants. Though most of the original interiors have been destroyed, the elegant cuboid entrance hall remains and frescoes in the vaulted dining room (an early example of such a room) were rediscovered during renovation. The grand staircase has been reconstructed, including a never-executed *trompe l'oeil* ceiling on architect Pierre Le Muet's original plans of 1647. In 1998 the *hôtel* opened as the **Musée d'Art et d'Histoire du Judaïsme**, which includes a tribute to the numerous Jewish families deported from their flats here during World War II.

Hôtel Salé

5 rue de Thorigny, 3rd. M° Chemin-Vert or St-Paul. **Map M6**
Although officially the Hôtel Aubert de Fontenay, this *hôtel* built 1656-59 by architect Jean Boullier soon acquired the

Tax cash, salted away, built **Hôtel Salé**.

name *salé* from the salt tax which made tax collector Fontenay his fortune. A spectacular semi-circular courtyard is overlooked by sphinxes; the stunning grand stairway is carved with garlands and cupids. *See also* **Musée Picasso**.

Hôtel de Sens

1 rue du Figuier, 4th (01.42.7814.60). M° St-Paul or Pont-Marie. **No credit cards. Map L7**
This rare example of Parisian medieval architecture was built 1475-1519 as a *pied à terre* for the wealthy Archbishops of Sens. Its fanciful turrets owe something to nineteenth-century restorers' imagination, but it has superb windows, elaborately carved dormers and vaulted Gothic entrance. In the Wars of Religion, the Guise brothers hatched many an anti-royalist plot within its walls. Queen Margot lived here after she was repudiated by Henri IV, having failed to provide him an heir. Today, the *hôtel* is home to the **Bibliothèque Forney**, devoted to applied and graphic arts. *See also* **Museums**.

Hôtel de Sully

62 rue St-Antoine, 4th (01.44.61.20.00). M° St-Paul or Bastille. **Open** *courtyards* 8am-6.30pm daily. **Map L7**
Designed by Jean Androuet du Cerceau in 1624, this perfectly restored *hôtel particulier* was bought by Henri IV's former minister the Duc de Sully. Today it houses the Caisse Nationale des Monuments Historiques and the Mission du Patrimoine Photographique. The fine interior is closed to the public, but walk through the two beautifully proportioned courtyards, with allegorical reliefs of the seasons and the elements. At the rear of the second courtyard is a rare orangery.

The site of the prison itself is now a Banque de France office and the gap left by the castle ramparts forms the present-day square, dominated by the massive **Opéra Bastille**. Opened in 1989 on the bicentennial of Bastille Day, it remains a highly controversial *Grand Projet* – although many productions sell out, and along with the creation of the Port de l'Arsenal marina to the south it has undoubtedly contributed to the area's rejuvenation.

Rue de Lappe typifies the Bastille's tranformation, as the last remaining furniture workshops, the 1930s **Balajo** (Bal à Jo) dance hall, old Auvergnat bistro La Galoche d'Aurillac and grocer Chez Teil hold out against a dizzy array of theme bars, gift shops and pseudo-Cuban and American cafés.

You can still catch a flavour of the old working-class district at the Sunday morning market on **boulevard Richard Lenoir** or up rue de la Roquette. Rue du Fbg-St-Antoine still has numerous furniture-makers' ateliers and gaudy furniture stores, but is being colonised by clothes shops and bars: one can't but help feel a twinge of regret for when the last neo-Louis XV chair or nubian slave candelabra disappears. Rue de Charonne has trendy bars and bistros like **La Fontaine, Chez Paul, Pause Café**, and turn-of-the-century **Bistro du Peintre**, as well as art galleries and shops full of weird 60s furniture and designer bits. Along with rue Keller, the patch is a focus for record shops, streetwear and, increasingly, young fashion designers. There's still something of a village spirit as the in-crowd hang out at the Pause Café and the Planète Keller committee hold street parties.

But the main thoroughfares tell only half the story, for the area developed its own distinctive style of architecture. Behind narrow street frontages are quaintly named cobbled alleys, dating back to the eighteenth century, lined with craftsmen's workshops or quirky bars and bistros. Investigate the Cours de l'Ours, du Cheval Blanc, du Bel Air (with hidden garden), de la Maison Brûlée or the Passage du Chantier on Fbg-St-Antoine, where a gaggle of salesmen try to lure unsuspecting customers into its workshops, the rustic-looking Passage de l'Etoile d'Or and the Passage de l'Homme with old wooden shop fronts on rue de Charonne. This land originally lay outside the city walls on the lands of the Convent of St-Antoine (parts of which survive as the Hôpital St-Antoine), where in the Middle Ages skilled furniture makers were free from the city's restrictive guilds, beginning a tradition of independence and free-thinking that made this area a powder keg during the Revolution. Now, however, many of the workshops are the studios of artists, architects, designers or ad agencies.

East of Ledru-Rollin Métro is the bustling North African-flavoured market of **place d'Aligre** and covered Marché Beauvais, whose cast-iron structure dates from 1843. Nearby are lively wine bar **Le Baron Rouge** and modish bistro **Le Square**

Trousseau, whose *belle époque* interior has featured in many an ad. The Faubourg runs east to **place de la Nation**, a traffic junction and red-light district interesting for its two square pavilions and Doric columns, remnants of the tax-collectors' wall built by Ledoux pre-Revolution. It was originally called place du Trône to commemorate the arrival here of Louis XIV with his wife Marie-Thérèse in 1660. During the Terror the guillotine was for a time here in what became Place du Trône Renversé ('overturned throne'). Centre is Dalou's grandiose allegorical *Triomphe de la République*, commissioned for the Revolution's centenary, 1889.

Boulevard Beaumarchais separates rowdy Bastille from the elegant Marais. Look out for the wonderful polygonal **Cirque d'Hiver** designed in imitation of antique polychromy by Hittorrf to house the circus in winter, and still used today. Further east, beyond place Voltaire, on rue de la Roquette, a small park and playground surrounded by modern housing marks the site of the former prison de la Roquette. The gateway has been preserved and a plaque remembers the 4000 resistance members imprisoned here in World War II.

Opéra Bastille

pl de la Bastille, 12th (box office 08.36.69.78.68/guided visits 01.40.01.19.70). Mº Bastille. **Guided Tour** phone for details. **Admission** 50F; 30F students, under-16s, over-60s. **No credit cards. Map M7**

The megalithic Opéra Bastille has been a controversial *Grand Projet* for several reasons: the cost of upkeep, its scale, the quality of the architecture, the opera productions. Opened in 1989, some thought it a stroke of socialist genius to implant a high-culture edifice in a traditionally working-class district; others thought it a typical piece of Mitterrand skulduggery. Recent attention has centred on the building itself: netting was put up to stop granite slabs falling on people below, suggesting major repairs are already needed. Although intended as an 'opera for the people', that has never really happened; opera and ballet are now shared with the Palais Garnier.

Place de la Bastille

4th/11th/12th. Mº Bastille. **Map M7**

Nothing remains of the infamous prison which, on 14 July 1789, was stormed by the forces of the plebeian revolt. Though only a handful of prisoners remained, the event provided the rebels with gunpowder, and gave the insurrection momentum. It remains the eternal symbol of the Revolution, celebrated here with a lively street *bal* every 13 July. The prison was quickly torn down, its stones used to build Pont de la Concorde, though supposedly pieces could be bought from local entrepreneurs afterwards. Vestiges of the foundations can be seen in the Métro; there's part of a reconstructed tower at square Henri-Galli, near pont de Sully (4th). The Colonne de Juillet, topped by a gilded *génie* of Liberty, in the square's centre, remembers the Parisians killed in the revolutions of July 1830 (when Charles X was overturned after three days' fighting) and 1848.

South of the Bastille

A newish attraction here is the **Viaduc des Arts**, a former railway viaduct now containing craft and design boutiques. Further along, avenue Daumesnil

Place des Vosges: *an arcade to amuse all architecture aficionados.*

is fast becoming a silicon valley of computer outlets. Atop the viaduct, the **Promenade Plantée** continues through the Jardin de Reuilly and east to the **Bois de Vincennes**. At No 186, Eglise St-Esprit is a curious 1920s concrete copy of the Hagia Sophia in Istambul. At No 293 the underappreciated **Musée des Arts d'Afrique et d'Océanie** contains fantastic tribal art and an aquarium beloved of kids.

It's hard to believe now that as late as the 1980s, wine was still unloaded off barges at Bercy; sadly, only a couple of the old brick warehouses are preserved. This stretch of the Seine is firmly part of redeveloped Paris with the massive Ministère de l'Economie et du Budget and **Palais Omnisports de Paris-Bercy**, a pyramid-shaped sports stadium and concert venue. The dramatic American Center, designed by Frank Gehry to overlook the **Parc de Bercy**, is to be the new Maison du Cinéma, film museum and library.

Le Viaduc des Arts

15-121 av Daumesnil, 12th. Mº Bastille, Ledru-Rollin or Gare de Lyon. **Map M8**

Under the arches of a disused railway viaduct, chic glass-fronted workshops opened in 1995 now provide a showroom for designers and craftspeople, continuing the long tradition of furniture trades in the Faubourg St-Antoine. Some outlets are rather twee, but the variety is fascinating: from contemporary furniture designers to picture frame gilders, tapestry restorers, porcelain decorators, architectural salvage and a French hunting horn maker, as well as design gallery **VIA** and the **Viaduc Café**. The last arches by the Bastille will be incorporated in 1999. Along the top of the viaduct, the planted promenade offers a traffic-free view into Parisian lives and continues east to Bois de Vincennes (*see chapter* **Parks**).

The Champs-Elysées

In the 8th, 16th and 17th arrondissements.

Parisians (who don't often go there) can barely mention the avenue des Champs-Elysées without adding: 'the most beautiful avenue in the world'. If, on

Itinerary: Cheapskate champions

Who said Paris was pricey? Tighten your belt and have a low-budget day out, the better to indulge the next extravagance…

•Start the day at the **Marché d'Aligre**, one of the cheapest and liveliest street markets in Paris, open every morning except Monday. Breakfast (orange juice, coffee and a croissant) at the **Aouba Café** (21 rue d'Aligre) will set you back 15F. Check out **Chaussures HP** for cut-price Timberland shoes and go down rue d'Aligre to the flea market section. Lots of junk, but keep your eyes peeled for a first edition or hand-painted china. Pick-up a baguette and whatever fruit is in season, and explore the century-old covered Marché Beauvais for cheese, *charcuterie* and other picnic goodies.

•Head down Fbg-St-Antoine to the Bastille. Catch a film at MK2, 4 bd Beaumarchais, 29F instead of 45F before noon.

•Tuck into your picnic with a glass of beer (9F), wine (8F) or soda (7F) at **Ah! Ca Ira!** on place de la Bastille or splash out on their 27F *formule* (sandwich, drink and coffee).

•Catch a **No 20** bus – one of the few with an open platform at the back – from Bastille to République, to explore **Tati**'s vast emporium of trash and treasure, from household goods to the truly terrifying wedding department.

•Continue your bus ride along the **Grands Boulevards** for the free, constantly changing exhibiton of antiques and *objets d'art* at the **Hôtel Drouot**, and the secondhand booksellers of **passage Jouffroy**.

•By now your appetite is whetted for the quintessential low-budget dining experience of Chartier. Other humble *bouillons* of the *belle époque* shot upmarket year's ago, but Chartier's working-class feel, bustling atmosphere and low prices are still intact. Just don't expect haute cuisine. *Bon appétit.*

Marché Beauvais: *picnic fixings.*

first, tourist-filled sight, the 'Elysian Fields' can be a disappointment, the avenue remains the symbolic gathering place of a nation – for France's victory in the 1998 football World Cup (the biggest crowd since the Liberation), New Year, 14 July or the final stage of the Tour de France. Despite the many burger bars, over-priced cafés, car showrooms and malls, vestiges of erstwhile grandeur remain in the impressive, nighttime vista stretching from floodlit place de la Concorde to the Arc de Triomphe, with the crowds lining up for the glitzy **Lido** cabaret, **Queen** nightclub and various cinemas. One of Jacques Chirac's worthier mayoral efforts was a major facelift here, with new underground car parks and smart granite paving. Upmarket shops and hotels have moved back in the past couple of years, including branches of **Louis Vuitton, Sephora, Fnac**, the Ladurée tea room and Marriott hotel.

The great spine of western Paris started life as an extension to the Tuileries gardens, laid out by Le Nôtre as far as the Rond-Point in the seventeenth century. By the Revolution, the avenue had been laid along its full stretch, but was more a place for a Sunday walk than a street. Shortly before the Revolution the local guard worried that its dark corners offered 'to libertines and people of bad intentions a refuge that they can abuse'. During the Second Empire, the Champs-Elysées became a focus of fashionable society, with smart residences and hotels along its upper half, together with street lights, pavements, sideshows, concert halls, theatres and exhibition centres, plus military parades and royal processions, and the avenue of world repute was born. Bismarck was so impressed when he arrived with the conquering Prussian army in 1871 that he had a replica, the Kurfürstendamm, built in Berlin. The Prussian army in 1871 and Hitler's troops in 1940 both made a point of marching down it, to a silently hostile reception, but loud celebrations accompanied the victory march along the avenue in 1944. The windows of Guerlain's perfume house have fine cast-iron decoration; though marred by a foreign exchange bureau at the front, the grand house at No 25 was built for the Marquise de Païva, celebrated nineteenth-century courtesan, and is now the smart Travellers' Club; while the grand CCF bank was once a hotel.

South of the avenue, the glass-domed **Grand Palais** and **Petit Palais**, both built for the 1900 Exposition Universelle and still used for major shows, create an impressive vista across elaborate Pont Alexandre III to Les Invalides. The rear wing of the Grand Palais opening onto avenue Franklin D Roosevelt contains the **Palais de la Découverte**, a fun science museum that's a real hit with children.

To the north is a Paris of smart shops and officialdom. On circular place Beauvais a gateway leads to the Ministry of the Interior. At 55-57 rue du Fbg-St-Honoré lurks the eighteenth-century **Palais de l'Elysée**, the official presidential res-

Barrels of fun with the **Bastille**'s *Red Baron.*

idence with gardens extending to the edge of the Champs-Elysées. Nearby are the equally palatial British Embassy and adjoining ambassadorial residence, once the Hôtel Borghèse, as well as pricey fashon outlets, antique shops and hotels.

The lower, landscaped reach of the avenue hides two theatres and haute cuisine restaurants **Laurent** and **Ledoyen** in fancy Napoléon III pavilions. At the **Rond-Point des Champs-Elysées**, Nos 7 and 9 give some idea of the splendid mansions that once lined the avenue. From here, the dress code leaps a few notches as **avenue Montaigne** reels off its array of haute-couture houses: Ungaro, Mugler, Dior and Chanel and recent ready-to-wear arrivals 51 Montaigne, Prada and Calvin Klein in smart *hôtels particuliers*. Look for the lavish Plaza Athénée hotel and Auguste Perret's innovative 1911-13 **Théâtre des Champs-Elysées** concert hall topped by the fashionable Maison Blanche restaurant.

At the western end, the **Arc de Triomphe** towers above place Charles de Gaulle, better known as l'Etoile. Begun to glorify Napoléon, the giant triumphal arch was modified after his disgrace to celebrate the armies of the Revolution. The *place* was commissioned later by Haussmann and most of its harmonious facades, designed by Hittorff, are well preserved. From the top, look down on great swathes of prize Paris real estate: the swanky mansions along the grassy verges of the avenue Foch – the city's widest street – or the prestige office buildings of avenues Hoche and Wagram.

Arc de Triomphe
pl Charles de Gaulle (access via underground passage), 8th (01.43.80.31.31). M° Charles de Gaulle-Etoile. **Open** *Apr-Oct* 9.30am-11pm daily. *Nov-Mar* 10am-10.30pm daily. Closed public holidays. **Admission** 40F; 32F 12-25s; free under-12s. **Credit** MC, V. **Map C3**
The Arc de Triomphe forms the centrepiece of Paris' grand east-west axis from the Louvre, through the Arc du Carrousel and the place de la Concorde up to the Grande Arche de la Défense. The Arc is 50m tall, 45m wide and decorated with a giant frieze of battle scenes and sculptures on its flanks, including Rude's *Le Départ des Volontaires*, also known as *La Marseillaise*. Commissioned by Napoléon in 1806 as a tribute to his own military victories, it was completed only in 1836. In 1920 the Tomb of the Unknown Soldier was laid at the arch's base, and an eternal flame burns to commemorate the dead of World Wars I and II. The manic drivers zooming around the arch turn the *place* into a race track, but fortunately there's a subway. From the top, there's a wonderful view of the twelve avenues radiating out from its focal point.

Grand Palais
av Winston-Churchill, av du Général-Eisenhower, 8th (01.44.13.17.17/01.44.13.17.30). M° Champs-Elysées-Clemenceau. **Map E5**
You can't miss the immense glass dome and galloping bronze horses pulling chariots atop the Grand Palais, built for the 1900 Exposition Universelle. Its three different facades were designed by three different architects, which explains the highly eclectic wealth of decoration. The wing on avenue du Général-Eisenhower is used for blockbuster art shows; the avenue Franklin D Roosevelt wing holds the **Palais de la Découverte**; the avenue Winston-Churchill wing is still undergoing renovation. *See chapter* **Museums**.

Petit Palais
av Winston-Churchill, 8th (01.42.65.12.73). M° Champs-Elysées-Clemenceau. **Open** 10am-5.40pm. Tue-Sun. **Admission** 45F; 35F 7-16s, students; free under-7s. **Map E5**
Also built for the 1900 Exposition Universelle, only here the style is rather more charmingly Rococo. Look for the grandiose barrel-vaulted entrance hall with painted ceilings and an attractive semi-circular courtyard garden surrounded by a marble-columned arcade. *See chapter* **Museums**.

Monceau & Batignolles

At the far end of avenue Hoche is intimate **Parc Monceau** (main entrance bd de Courcelles), with its Antique follies and large lily pond. The park is usually full of neatly dressed children and nannies, and surrounded by some of the dearest apartments in Paris, part of the planned late nineteenth-century expansion of the city over the plaine Monceau. Newly renovated **Musée Jacquemart-André** on boulevard Haussmann gives an idea of the extravagance of the area when newly fashionable. There are two other worthwhile museums nearby: **Musée Nissim de Camondo** (eighteenth-century decorative arts) and **Musée Cernushi** (Chinese art). There are some nice exotic touches, such as the unlikely red lacquer **Galerie Ching Tsai Too** (48 rue des Courcelles, 8th), built in 1926 for a Chinese art dealer near the fancy wrought-iron gates of Parc Monceau, or the onion domes of the Russian Orthodox **Alexander Nevsky Cathe-**

dral on rue Daru. Built in the mid-nineteenth century when a sojourn in Paris was an essential part of the education of every young Russian aristocrat, it is still at the heart of an emigré little Russia. The Fbg-St-Honoré contains the Salle Pleyel concert hall. At 11 rue Berryer stands the 1870s mansion built for Salomon de Rothschild, now the **Centre National de la Photographie**. The pedimented Neo-Classical church of St Philippe de Roule takes one back down rue La Boétie to the Champs-Elysées.

The Quartier de Batignolles to the northeast of Parc Monceau, far from the clichéd image of the 17th arrondissement, is much more working-class, with rue de Lévis street market, tenements overlooking the deep railway canyon and the attractive square de Batignolles with its church overlooking a small semi-circular *place*.

Alexander Nevsky Cathedral
12 rue Daru, 8th (01.42.27.37.34). M° Courcelles. **Open** 3-5pm Tue, Fri, Sun. **Map D3**
With enough onion domes and gilding, icons and frescoes to make you think you were in Moscow, this Russian Orthodox church was built 1859-61 in the Neo-Byzantine Novgorod-style of the 1600s, on a Greek-cross plan by the Tsar's architect Kouzmine, architect of the St-Petersburg Beaux-Arts Academy, and Strohm.

The 16th Arrondissement

South of Arc de Triomphe, avenue Kléber leads to the monumental buildings and terraced gardens of the Trocadéro, with spectacular views over the river to the Eiffel Tower. This is another museum-filled area: the main building, the vast symmetrical 1930s **Palais de Chaillot** dominates the hill, housing four museums and the **Théâtre National de Chaillot**. Across place du Trocadéro is the small **Cimetière de Passy**, whose illustrious inhabitants include Manet and Berthe Morisot.

The slightly dead area behind Trocadéro holds a few surprises. Hidden among the shops on avenue Victor-Hugo, behind a conventional looking apartment block, is the jungle-like garden and African art collection of the **Musée Dapper**, and at No 111 the Galerie Commerciale Argentine, a brick and cast-iron apartment block and shopping arcade, now mostly empty, designed by ever-experimental Henri Sauvage and Charles Sarazin in 1904.

At place d'Iéna stands the circular Conseil Economique, an example of the concrete architecture of Auguste Perret, opposite the rotunda of the **Musée Guimet**, with its collection of Asian art (closed for renovation). Avenue du Président-Wilson is home to the **Musée d'Art Moderne de la Ville de Paris** in the Palais de Tokyo. The collection includes Dufy's *La Fée Electricité* and two versions of Matisse's *La Danse*, and there are excellent exhibitions of modern and contemporary art. Opposite (though the entrance is on the other side), the fancy round pavilion of the Palais Galliera,

Opéra Bastille: *never knowingly over-praised...*

Musée de la Mode et du Costume, houses temporary fashion-related exhibitions. On avenue Marceau, the 1930s church of St-Pierre de Chaillot is a massive neo-Byzantine structure with reliefs by Henri Bouchard. Paris acquired a new monument at place de l'Alma after the fatal accident of Princess Diana and Dodi Al-Fayed in the Alma tunnel on 31 August 1997. Proposals have been put forward for an official memorial, but the golden flame (a replica of that on the Statue of Liberty given as a return hommage by the city of New York) at the junction with avenue de New-York has been covered in flowers and messages ever since.

Cimetière de Passy

2 rue du Commandant-Schloesing, 16th (01.47.27.51.42). M° Trocadéro. **Open** 8am-5.15pm daily. **Map B5**
Behind a 30s Modernist portal, tombs include those of composers Debussy and Fauré, painters Manet and his sister-in-law Berthe Morisot, designer Ruhlmann and writer Giraudoux, among numerous generals and politicians.

Palais de Chaillot

pl du Trocadéro, 16th. M° Trocadéro. **Map C5**
Looming across the river from the Eiffel Tower, the immense pseudo-classical Palais de Chaillot was built by Azéma, Boileau and Carlu for the 1937 international exhibition. It is typical of the monumental, neo-totalitarian architecture of the time, though it actually stands on the foundations of an earlier complex put up for the 1878 World Fair. It is home to the **Musée de la Marine** (marine and naval history) and **Musée de l'Homme** (ethnology, anthropology, human biology) in the western wing, and in the eastern **Musée des Monuments Historiques** (closed for renovation) and **Théâtre National de Chaillot**. The **Cinémathèque** repertory cinema has reopened after a fire, but the Musée du Cinéma, currently closed, is likely to move to Bercy. The Trocadéro gardens

below are a little dilapidated, but the impressive pool with bronze and stone statues showered by powerful fountains form a spectacular ensemble with the Eiffel Tower and Champ de Mars across the river. Watch out for roller-bladers!

Passy & Auteuil

West of here, most of the 16th *arrondissement* is pearls-and-poodle country, plus some important curios, avant-garde architecture and classy shops.

When Balzac lived at 47 rue Raynouard (now **Maison de Balzac**), Passy was a country village where people came to take cures for anaemia at its mineral springs – a name reflected in the rue des Eaux. Many Parisians, however, perversely preferred the dubious delights of drinking the Seine. Nearby the **Musée du Vin** is of interest for its location in the cellars of a wine-producing monastery destroyed in the Revolution. Passy was absorbed into the city in 1860 and today is full of smart Haussmannian apartment blocks. Centre of life is rue de Passy, the former village high street, with **Franck et Fils** department store, upmarket fashion and food shops and the covered **Marché de Passy**. The apartment of French statesman and journalist Georges Clemenceau can be visited at 8 rue Benjamin-Franklin (01.45.20.53.41/Tue, Thur, Sat, Sun 2-7pm). Many of the best things, however, take a bit of searching out: exclusive residential cul-de-sacs or 'villas' of small houses and gardens affordable only by old money or those with film star incomes. Explore the Villa Beauséjour, where three Russian wooden *dachas* by craftsmen from St-Petersburg were rebuilt after the 1867 Exposition

Architectural innovators in the 16th: Le Corbusier designed this house in **rue Mallet-Stevens.**

Universelle, then join local families-plus-dogs for lunch at trendy **La Gare** restaurant in the former Passy-La Muette station on the *Petite Ceinture*.

West of the Jardins du Ranelagh (originally high-society pleasure gardens, modelled on the bawdy eighteenth-century London version) is the **Musée Marmottan** (rue Louis-Boilly), which features a fabulous collection of Monet's late water lily canvases, other Impressionists and Empire furniture.

Next to the Pont de Grenelle is **Maison de Radio-France**, the giant Orwellian home to the state broadcasting bureaucracy opened in 1963. You can attend concerts or take guided tours (*see* **Musée de Radio France**) round its endless corridors; employees nickname the place 'Alphaville' after the Godard film. From here, in upmarket Auteuil, go up rue Fontaine, the best place for specimens of Art Nouveau architecture by Hector Guimard. Despite extravagant iron balconies, Castel Beranger at No 14 was originally low-rent lodgings; Guimard designed outside and in, right down to the wallpaper and stoves. He also designed the less-ambitious Nos 19, 21 and tiny Café Antoine at No 17.

The area around Métro Jasmin is the place to pay homage to the area's other prominent architect Le Corbusier. The **Fondation Le Corbusier** is in two of his avant-garde houses in the square du Dr-Blanche, while a little further up rue du Dr-Blanche, rue Mallet-Stevens is almost entirely refined houses by Robert Mallet-Stevens. Most have been rather altered, but one has a fantastic stained glass stairwell. There are plenty of exclusive villas in Auteuil, too, like Villa Montmorency with its little gardens

off boulevard de Montmorency and winding Avenue de la Réunion off rue Chardon-Lagache. At the western edge of Auteuil by the *Périphérique* ring road are Parc des Princes sports stadium, home to Paris St-Germain football club; Roland Garros tennis courts, home of the French tennis open; and **Les Serres d'Auteuil** greenhouses and gardens, once part of Louis XV's nurseries and still the municipal florist.

West of the 16th, across the *Périphérique*, sprawls the **Bois de Boulogne**, once a royal hunting reserve and made into a park by Napoléon III, though much is still woodland cut by paths and roads. It's usually packed at weekends with Parisians walking dogs. It contains Longchamp and Auteuil racecourses, several restaurants and the rose gardens of the Jardins du Bagatelle.

Fondation Le Corbusier

Villa La Roche, 10 square du Dr-Blanche, 16th (01.42.88.41.53). M° Jasmin. **Open** 10am-12.30pm, 1.30-6pm Mon-Fri (library 1.30-6pm). Closed Aug. **Admission** 15F; 10F students. **No credit cards.**
This house, designed by Le Corbusier in 1923 for a Swiss art collector, shows the architect's ideas in practice, in drawings, paintings, sculpture and furniture. Here are all the typical *pilotis*, roof terraces, split volumes, internal balconies and built-in furniture, though no stereotype Modernist white – the interior is muted pinks, greys, greens. Adjoining Villa Jeanneret – also by Le Corbusier – houses the Foundation's library.

Montmartre & Pigalle

Mainly in the 9th and 18th arrondissements.
Montmartre, away to the north of the city centre on the tallest hill in the city, is the most unabashedly

romantic district of Paris. Despite the onslaught of tourists who throng **Sacré-Coeur** and place du Tertre, it's surprisingly easy to get away from the main tourist drag. Climb and descend quiet stairways, peer into little alleys, steep stairways and deserted squares or find the ivy-clad houses with gardens to catch some of its old village atmosphere, or explore streets like rue des Abbesses, with its young, arty community.

For centuries, Montmartre was a quiet, windmill-packed village. Then, as Haussmann sliced through the city centre, working-class families began to move out from the old city in search of accommodation and peasant migrants poured into industrialising Paris from across France. The hill was absorbed into Paris in 1860, but remained fiercely independent. In 1871, after the Prussians capitulated, the new right-wing French government sought to disarm the local National Guard by taking away its cannons installed in Montmartre. An angry crowd led by teacher and radical heroine Louise Michel drove off the government troops, killing two generals and taking over the guns, thus starting the **Paris Commune**, commemorated by a plaque on rue Chevalier-de-la-Barre. From the 1880s artists moved in. Toulouse-Lautrec patronised Montmartre's bars and immortalised its cabarets in his posters; later it was frequented by artists of the Ecole de Paris, Utrillo and Modigliani. The *vie de bohème* of Montmartre is no longer a byword for TB and bitter winters, but Montmartre hasn't entirely surrendered to modern chic either.

The best starting point is the **Abbesses** Métro, one of only two in the city (along with Porte Dauphine) to retain its original Art Nouveau glass awning designed by Hector Guimard. Across place des Abbesses as you emerge from the station is the Art Nouveau church of **St-Jean de Montmartre**, with its turquoise mosaics around the door and brick facade disguising a reinforced-concrete structure.

Along rue des Abbesses and adjoining rue Lepic, which winds its way up the *butte* (hill), are many excellent food shops, wine merchants, busy cafés, including the heaving **Sancerre**, and quirky boutiques devoted to offbeat designers, such as **Bonnie Cox** or crazy hat shop **Têtes en l'Air**. Along impasse Marie-Blanche there's a strange neo-Gothic house. In rue Tholozé is the famous **Studio 28** cinema, opened in 1928. Buñuel's *L'Age d'Or* had a riotous première here in 1930; you can still see footprints made by him and Cocteau in the foyer.

In the other direction from Abbesses, at 11 rue Yvonne-Le-Tac, is the **Chapelle du Martyr**, where, according to legend, St Denis picked up his head after his execution by the Romans in the third century. Montmartre probably means 'hill of the martyr' in his memory, or it may derive from temples to Mars and Mercury in Roman times. The present convent dates from 1887, but on the same site in 1534, the Spanish soldiers Ignatius Loyola and François Xavier founded the Jesuit Order.

Around the corner, the cafés of rue des Trois Frères are popular for an evening drink. The street leads into place Emile-Goudeau, whose staircases, wrought-iron street-lights and old houses are particularly evocative, as is the unspoiled bar Chez Camille. At No 13 stood the Bateau Lavoir, named after the medieval washing stands along the Seine. Once a piano factory, it was divided in the 1890s into a warren of studios where artists lived in total penury, among them Braque, Picasso and Juan Gris. Among the ground-breaking works of art created here was Picasso's *Desmoiselles d'Avignon*. The building burned down in 1970, but its replacement still rents out space to artists. Further up the hill on rue Lepic are the village's two surviving windmills, or *moulins*. The **Moulin de Radet** moved here in the seventeenth century from its hillock in rue des Moulins near the Palais-Royal. The **Moulin de la Galette**, made famous by Renoir's painting of an evening's revelry, is now a restaurant.

On top of the hill, the area round **place du Tertre** is all that's worst about Montmartre today. Dozens of so-called artists compete to sketch your portrait or try to flog lurid sunset views of Paris, and the streets are packed with souvenir shops and tacky restaurants. Here you'll also find the café A la Bonne Franquette, a billiard hall in the last century.

Just off the square is the oldest church in the district, **St-Pierre-de-Montmartre**, whose columns have grown bent with age. Founded by Louis VI in 1133, it is a fine example of early Gothic, and a striking contrast to its extravagant neighbour and Montmartre's most prominent landmark, **Sacré-Coeur**, standing on the highest point in the city. If you're climbing up from square Willette, avoid the main steps and try the less-crowded steps of rue Foyalter or rue Maurice-Utrillo on either side.

On the north side of place du Tertre in rue Cortot is the quiet manor housing the **Musée de Montmartre**, devoted to the area and its former inhabitants, with original Toulouse-Lautrec posters. Dufy, Renoir and Utrillo all had studios here. Nearby in rue des Saules is the Montmartre vineyard, planted in 1933 in memory of the vineyards that covered the hillside ever since the Gallo-Roman period. The grape-picking each autumn is an annual ritual (*see chapter* **Paris by Season**). As for the wine itself, a local ditty proclaims that for every glass you drink, you pee twice as much out.

Further down the hill amid rustic, shuttered houses is the **Lapin Agile** cabaret at 22 rue des Saules, another legendary meeting point for Montmartre artists, which is still going strong today. A series of pretty squares leads to rue Caulaincourt, towards **Montmartre Cemetery**, a curiously romantic place. Winding down the back of the hill, the wide avenue Junot is lined with exclusive houses, among them the one built by Adolf Loos for Dadaist poet Tristan Tzara at No 15, a monument of modernist architecture.

Cimetière de Montmartre

20 av Rachel, access by stairs from rue Caulaincourt, 18th (01.43.87.64.24). M° Blanche. **Open** *summer* 9am-5.45pm daily; *winter* 9am-5.15pm daily. **Map G1**

This small, romantic ravine was once quarries, then a communal burial pit. Here you will find Sacha Guitry, Truffaut, Nijinsky, Berlioz, Degas, Greuze, Offenbach, Feydeau, Dumas *fils*, German poet Heine and many other writers and artists, reflecting the area's theatrical and artistic past. There's also *La Goulue*, real name Louise Weber, first great star of the cancan and model for Toulouse-Lautrec, celebrated beauty Mme Récamier, and the consumptive heroine Alphonsine Plessis, inspiration for Dumas' *La Dame aux Camélias* and Verdi's *La Traviata*. Flowers and poems are still left daily for Egyptian diva Dalida, who lived nearby.

Sacré-Coeur

35 rue du Chevalier-de-la-Barre, 18th (01.53.41.89.00). M° Abbesses or Anvers. **Open** *Crypt/dome* Oct-Mar 9am-6pm; *Apr-Sept* 9am-7pm daily. **Admission** *Crypt* 15F; 8F 6-16s, students; free under-6s. *Dome* 15F; 8F 6-25s, students; free under-6s. *Crypt/dome* 25F; 13F 6-25s; free under-6s. **No credit cards. Map J1**

The icing sugar-white dome is one of the most visible landmarks in Paris, and dominates the *butte Montmartre*. Begun as an act of penance after the nation's defeat by the Prussians in 1870 (and the takeover by the Commune next year), Sacré-Coeur wasn't finished until 1914; consecration was finally in 1919. A jumble of architects worked on the mock Romano-Byzantine edifice. The interior, lavishly adorned with gaudy Neo-Byzantine mosaics, the crypt and the gallery in the dome, where the view is even better, are all open to visitors.

Pigalle

Straddling the 9th and 18th *arrondissements* from busy place de Clichy with its multiplex cinema and glitzy Brasserie Wepler, along boulevards de Clichy and de Rochechouart, Pigalle has long been the most important sleaze centre of Paris. By the end of last century, of the 58 houses on rue des Martyrs, 25 were cabarets (a few such as **Michou** and **Madame Arthur** remain today); others were dubious hotels used for illicit liaisons. Flashing neon signs still offer live shows, and coachloads of tourists file along to inspect the sex shops. The **Moulin Rouge**, once the image of naughty *fin de siècle* Paris, has become a tourist draw. Its befeathered dancers still cancan across the stage but are no substitute for La Goulue and Joseph Pujol – the *pétomane* who could fart melodies – of earlier times.

This brash area has recently become a trendy night spot inhabited by the mediarati. The Moulin Rouge's old restaurant has become the **MCM Café**, the **Folies Pigalle** cabaret is a hip club. What was once the Divan Japonais, depicted by Toulouse-Lautrec, has been transformed into **Le Divan du Monde**, a streetwise nightclub and music venue. Laidback youth pile into **La Fourmi** bar, while the old **Elysée Montmartre** music hall puts on an eclectic array of bands and one-nighters.

La Nouvelle Athènes

Just south of Montmartre and bordered by the slightly seedy area around Gare St-Lazare (*see above*, **Quartier de l'Europe**) lies this mysterious, often overlooked *quartier* that was once beloved of artists and artistes of the Romantic era. Long-forgotten actresses and *demi-mondaines* had *bijoux* mansions built there on their own money or gold *Louis* put up by wealthy admirers. Some of the prettiest can be found in tiny rue de la Tour-des-Dames, which refers to one of the many wind-

---

Itinerary: Kids' Montmartre

•Start at **place des Abbesses** and stroll along rue Yvonne le Tac. Browse in Gaspard de la Butte at No 10 bis, with its irresistible handmade clothes for under-sixes, and la Boutique des Anges at No 2, which sells only angel-themed objects. Continue along rue Tardieu to place Suzanne Valadon, which boasts a funicular.

•Ride the sumptuous baroque merry-go-round in **Square Willette** with its splendid uphill view.

•View the naive paintings at **Halle St-Pierre,** the ultimate child-friendly museum. Have lunch in the café (savoury tarts and gratins 35F-45F).

•At the Marché St-Pierre, stock up on sequins and tulle for dressing-up – or pick that longed-for Bambi/Barbie/Batman curtain fabric.

•Board the funicular (price: a Métro ticket) or take the steps to the top of the Butte, and one of the best views of Paris. Pick out landmarks before visiting the mosaic-studded interior of the Sacré Coeur; climb the dome for an even better view.

•Turn right on rue St Eleuthère, taking in the Roman **Arènes de Montmartre** en route for rue Norvins and the quaint *petit train* for a guided tour of Montmartre (adults 30 F, kids 18F).

•Back at place du Tertre the children will enjoy watching the street artists; if you commission a sketch of your child, set a limit of 100F-150F.

•As an antidote to wide-eyed urchins, head to rue Poulbot and the **Espace Dalí**, whose zany, Surrealist exhibits are light years away.

•Hungry parents and children can double back to **Place du Tertre** for reasonably-priced *crêpes* or *jambon frites* at No 17, Chez Eugène. Then meander down narrow winding streets back to place des Abbesses with Paris twinkling at your feet.

Give a long (or medium) wave to... **Radio France.** *See p72.*

mills owned by the once-prosperous Couvent des Abbesses. The windmill stood until 1822, by when superstars such as the legendary Mlle Mars had moved in. She had a splendid place built at No 1, replete with skylight and deliciously lurid fake marble, which can be glimpsed through the glass door. Well-known academic painters Horace Vernet and Paul Delaroche also had houses built here. Wander through the adjoining streets and passageways to catch further angles of these miniature palaces and late eighteenth-century *hôtels particuliers*, especially on rue La Rochefoucauld.

The area round the Neo-Classical Eglise Notre-Dame-de-Lorette, which includes rue Taitbout, haunt of Balzac's fallen heroine in *Splendeurs et Misères des Courtisanes*, built up in Louis-Philippe's reign and was famous for its courtesans, known as *lorettes*. From 1844 to 1857, Delacroix had his studio at 58 rue Notre-Dame-de-Lorette (next to the house, at No 56, where Gauguin was born in 1848). The painter later moved to place de Furstenberg in the 6th *arrondissement* (now **Musée Delacroix**).

Just off rue Taitbout stands square d'Orléans, a remarkable housing estate built in 1829 by English architect Edward Cresy. This ensemble of flats and artists' studios attracted the glitterati of the day, including the divine Taglioni, Pauline Viardot, George Sand and her lover Chopin. The couple each had first-floor flats and could wave at each other from their respective drawing rooms. The **Musée de la Vie Romantique** in nearby rue Chaptal displays the writer's mementoes in a perfect setting. Take in place Gustave-Toudouze, with pleasant tea room Thé Folies, and glorious circular place St-Georges, home to the true Empress of Napoléon III's Paris, the notorious Païva, who lived in the richly sculpted Neo-Renaissance No 28, already thought outrageous at the time of its construction in 1840 (before she moved to an equally extravagant house on the Champs-Elysées).

The **Musée Gustave Moreau**, meanwhile, is grounds alone for a visit. Originally the artist's studio, it was actually planned by him to become a museuem to house several thousand works which he bequeathed to the nation. Fragments of *la bohème* can still be gleaned in the neighbourhood, though the Café La Roche, where Moreau met Degas for drinks and rows, has been downsized to the utterly forgettable La Jaconde on the corner of rues La Rochefoucault and La Bruyère. Degas painted most of his memorable ballet scenes round the corner in rue Frochot and Renoir hired his first decent studio at 35 rue St-Georges. A couple of streets away in Cité Pigalle, a charming collection of studios, stands Van Gogh's last Paris house (No 5), from where he moved to Auvers-sur-Oise. There is a plaque here, but nothing on the building in rue Pigalle where Toulouse-Lautrec drank himself to death in 1903.

La Goutte d'Or

For a very different experience, head for Barbès-Rochechouart Métro station and the area north of it, known as the Goutte d'Or. In Zola's day this was (and it still is) one of the poorest working-class districts in the city. Zola used it as a backdrop for *L'Assommoir*, his novel set among the district's laundries and *absinthe* bars, and his *Nana* grew up on the rue de la Goutte d'Or itself.

Now it's primarily an African and Arab neighbourhood, with plenty of colour to make up for the modest housing. Depending when you come it can seem like a colourful slice of Africa or a state under constant police siege, with frequent sweeps on *sans-papiers* or suspected Islamic terrorists. Rue de la Goutte-d'Or itself has been done up, but other parts are still slums. Down rue Doudeauville, you'll find African musical shops, rue Polonceau has African grocers and Senegalese restaurant **Chez Aïda**, while Square Léon is the focus for **la Goutte d'Or en Fête** every June which tries to harness some of the cosmopolitan local talent. Some bands, such as Africando and the Orchestre National de Barbès, have become well known across Paris.

There's a lively street market under the Métro tracks (Mon, Wed, Sat mornings) and boxes of bargain clothes store **Tati** to rummage through. From here rue Orsel leads back to Montmartre via **Marché St-Pierre**. The covered market hall is now used for exhibitions of naïve art, but in the street, outlets like Dreyfus and Moline vie with discount fabrics.

On the northern edge of the city at Porte de Clignancourt is Paris' largest flea market, the **Marché aux Puces de St-Ouën** (*see page 79*).

North-East Paris

In the 10th, 11th, 19th and 20th arrondissements.
The old working-class area north and east of République is in transformation, mixing pockets of charm with grotty or even dangerous areas. Main attraction is **Père Lachaise cemetery**. Ménilmontant, the area around it, and neighbour Belleville, once villages where Parisians escaped at weekends, were absorbed into the city in 1860.

Canal St-Martin to La Villette

Canal St-Martin, built 1805-25, begins at the Seine at Pont Solval, disappears underground at the Bastille, then re-emerges at rue du Fbg-du-Temple east of place de la République. This stretch has the most charm, lined with shady trees and crossed by iron footbridges and locks. Most of the old warehouses have closed, but the area is still semi-industrial and a bit shabby, with the odd barge puttering into view. Designers have begun snapping up old industrial premises and unusual bars like **Atmosphère** and La Marine have multiplied.

You can take a boat up the canal between the Port de l'Arsenal and the Bassin de la Villette. Between the fifth and sixth locks at 101 quai de Jemmapes is the **Hôtel du Nord**, which inspired Marcel Carné's 1938 film, though most locations were recreated in a studio. The hotel has reopened as a lively bar, used for **Laughing Matters** comedy evenings. East here is the **Hôpital St-Louis** (main entrance rue Bichat), founded in 1607 to house plague victims, and built as a series of isolated pavilions to stop disease spreading. A mishmash of buildings has been added to the original brick and stone pavilions, but an effort at restoration is now being made. Behind the hospital, the rue de la Grange-aux-Belles housed the infamous Montfaucon gibbet, built in 1233, where victims were hanged and left to the elements. Much of the area has been redeveloped, but today the street contains music cafés **Chez Adel** (No 10) and Apostrophe (No 23), plus the **Squart** art squat (No 31), which contains artists' studios and performance space. Only the inconspicuous Le Pont Tournant, on the corner with quai de Jemmapes overlooking the swing bridge, still seems to hark back to canal days of old.

East lies the **Parti Communiste Français**, place du Colonel-Fabien, a curved glass curtain raised off the ground on a concrete wing, designed in 1968-71 by Brasilia architect Oscar Niemeyer with Paul Chemetov and Jean Deroche. It is the HQ of perhaps the only influential CP left in Europe.

To the north, place de Stalingrad was landscaped in 1989 to expose the **Rotonde de la Villette**, one of Ledoux's grandiose toll houses which now houses exhibitions and archaeological finds. Here the canal widens into Bassin de la Villette, built for Napoléon in 1808, bordered by new housing developments, as well as some of the worst of 60s and 70s housing. At the eastern end of the basin is an unusual 1885 hydraulic lifting bridge, the Pont de Crimée. Thursday and Sunday mornings inject some vitality with a canalside market, place de Joinville. East of here, the Canal de l'Ourcq (created in 1813 to provide drinking water as well as for freight haulage) divides: Canal St-Denis runs north through St-Denis towards the Seine, Canal de l'Ourcq runs through **La Villette** and suburbs east. A couple of meat-heavy, old-style bistros and the Grande Halle de la Villette, now used for festivals and exhibitions, are all that remains of the old meat-market. The area has been revitalised in the last decade by the **Cité des Sciences et de l'Industrie** science museum, an activity-filled postmodern park and **Cité de la Musique** concert hall and music museum.

La Villette
Cité des Sciences et de l'Industrie *30 av Corentin-Cariou, 19th (01.40.05.70.00/ 01.36.68.29.30). Mᵒ Porte de la Villette.* **Cité de la Musique** *(01.44.84.45.00).* *Grande Halle de la Villette (01.40.03.75.03), 211-219 av Jean-Jaurès, 19th. Mᵒ Porte de Pantin.* **Guided tours of park** *(01.40.03.75.05)* 3pm Wed from junction of Canal de l'Ourcq and Canal St-Martin. **Open** 10am-6pm/7pm Mon, Wed-Sat, Sun. Closed Tue. **Price** 50F; 35F under-26s, students, over-60s. **Map insert**
A giant arts and science complex, La Villette's programmes range from avant-garde music to avant-garde circus. The site of Paris' main cattle market and abattoir, it was to be replaced by a high-tech slaughterhouse but was then turned into the **Cité des Sciences et de l'Industrie**, a futuristic, interactive science museum. Outside are the shiny spherical Géode cinema and Argonaute submarine and the park, dotted with red *folies*, draws entertainments from outdoor *bals* to outdoor film (*see chapter* **Paris by Season**). Across large lawns south of the canal are the aircraft-hangar-like **Zénith**, used for pop concerts, and the Grande Halle de la Villette, used for trade fairs, exhibitions and the Villette Jazz Festival, which is the last remaining part of the old meat market. It is winged by the Conservatoire de la Musique music school on one side and on the other the **Cité de la Musique**, designed by Christian de Portzamparc, with its concert halls, rehearsal rooms, **Musée de la Musique** and Café de la Musique.

Ménilmontant & Charonne

Once some houses on a hill where vines and fruit trees were cultivated, Mesnil-Montant (uphill farm) expanded with bistros, workers' housing, balls and bordellos. It was incorporated in Paris in 1860 with Belleville and has a similar history: workers' agita-

It's all up and downs in **Montmartre**.

tion, resistance in the Commune, large immigrant population. Today it's a thriving centre of alternative Paris, popular with artists and young Parisians.

The area mixes 1960s and 70s monster housing projects and older dwellings, some gentrified, some derelict. Below rue des Pyrénées, the Cité Leroy or Villa l'Ermitage are calm houses with gardens and an old carpenter's workshop. At its junction with rue de Ménilmontant there is a bird's-eye view into the centre of town. Follow rue Julien-Lacroix to place Maurice-Chevalier and nineteenth-century Notre-Dame-de-la-Croix church.

For a restful glass, try laidback **Lou Pascalou** (14 rue des Panoyaux), **La Buvette** (same street) or **Le Soleil** on the boulevard (No 136). While side streets still display male-only North African cafés, old *parigot* locals and half-bricked up houses, the rue Oberkampf has had a meteoric rise, drawing queues to some of the city's hippest bars. Young international trendies have followed the artists and **Le Mecano**, **Mercerie** and **Scherkhan** bars have followed the success of **Café Charbon** and **La Cithéa** club, while a more cultural concentration is growing on rue Boyer with the Maroquinerie literary café and bistro Chez Jean.

East of Père-Lachaise is Charonne, which joined Paris in 1859. The medieval **Eglise St-Germain de Charonne**, place St-Blaise, is the city's only church, apart from St-Pierre de Montmartre, still to have its own graveyard. The rest of Charonne, centred on rue St-Blaise, is a prettified backwater of quiet bars and bistros. Towards Porte de Bagnolet, the **Flèche d'Or** bar in a former railway station has injected a dose of arty *branchitude*, as has grungy **Le Gambetta** next door. Cross the Périphérique at Porte de Montreuil for the suburban **Puces de Montreuil**, most junky of Paris' fleamarkets.

Cimetière du Père Lachaise

main entrance bd de Ménilmontant, 20th (01.43.70.70.33). M° Père-Lachaise. **Open** 9am-5.30pm daily. **Map P5**
With thousands of tightly packed tombs arranged along cobbled lanes and tree-lined avenues, this is said to be the world's most visited cemetery. Named after the Jesuit Père de la Chaise, Louis XIV's confessor, it was laid out by the architect Brongniart in 1804 with trees and curving alleys. The *Colombarium* (crematorium) was added in 1889. The presumed remains of medieval lovers Abélard and Héloïse were moved here in 1817, along with those of Molière and La Fontaine, in a bid to gain popularity for the site. Famous inhabitants soon multiplied: Sarah Bernhardt, Champollion, Delacroix, Ingres, Géricault (in a tomb with bronze reliefs of his best-known works), Bizet, Balzac, Proust, Chopin (his empty tomb), Colette and Piaf. Jim Morrison, buried here in 1971, still attracts a flow of spaced-out pilgrims; follow the graffiti. Oscar Wilde's headstone, carved by Epstein, is a winged, naked, male angel which was considered so offensive that it was neutered by the head keeper, who used the offending member as a paper-weight. The Mur des Fédérés got its name after 147 members of the Paris Commune of 1871 were shot against it. Nearby is a memorial to resistance members deported in World War II.

Eglise St-Germain-de-Charonne

4 pl St-Blaise, 20th. M° Porte de Bagnolet. **Open** 9am-7pm daily.

A village church was built in the ninth century on this charmingly bucolic site. What's there today is mainly early fifteenth century, when the nave was rebuilt in simple Gothic style, but the buttressed square tower is thirteenth century.

Puces de Montreuil

M° Porte de Montreuil. **Open** 7.30am-7pm Mon, Sat, Sun.
Very second-hand clothing, contraband videos, broken chairs and miscellaneous rubbish dominate this grungy flea market sprawling alongside the Périphérique. It's much more anarchic than Clignancourt and little here is pre-1900, but you may find fun collectables like pastis jugs.

Belleville

Until the eighteenth century, Belleville was largely agricultural. Enormous growth in the early nineteenth century increased its population to 60,000. Incorporated into the rapidly expanding city in 1860, Belleville became a work and leisure place for the lower classes, while many bourgeois still had country houses in the area. Despite attempts to dissipate workers' agitation by splitting the former village between 11th, 19th and 20th *arrondissements*, it was the centre of opposition to the Second Empire – and the last *quartier* to surrender during the Commune. Cabarets, artisans, cinemas and workers' housing typified *fin de siècle* Belleville. Legend has it Piaf was literally born on the pavement outside 72 rue de Belleville in 1915, commemorated in a stone tablet above the door. In the 30s and 40s, Belleville was the place to dance to the music of Piaf or Chevalier. The **Java**, now a salsa club, once a Piaf haunt, still has its original *bal-musette* décor.

A promenade in the *hauts de Belleville* could begin at the top of the Parc de Belleville, with the panoramic view from rue Piat. The park runs down the hill in wavy terraces. Below, on animated boulevard de Belleville, Chinese and Vietnamese restaurants and supermarkets rub shoulders with Muslim and Kosher groceries, butchers and bakers, *couscous* and *falafel* eateries. On market day (Tue, Fri mornings), Belleville can seem like a slice of Africa.

On the small streets off the rue de Belleville, old buildings hide many courtyards and gardens. Rue Ramponeau mixes new housing and relics of old worker's Belleville. At No 23, down a crumbling alley, an old iron smithy has become **La Forge**, a squat for artists, many of whom are ardent members of La Bellevilloise association, which is trying to maintain the community and preserve the area from redevelopment. But as many of the buildings are falling apart, they may still suffer the same fate as countless other corners of Belleville.

Up the avenue Simon Bolivar is the eccentric **Parc des Buttes-Chaumont** (main entrance rue Botzaris), one of the most attractive and least-known landscaping feats of Baron Haussmann's designers. East of the park, between place des Fêtes and place de Rhin et Danube, are a number of tiny, hilly streets lined with small houses and gardens that still look positively provincial.

Clignancourt: flea market mania

Mº Porte de Clignancourt. Open 7am-6pm Mon, Sat, Sun

Sifting through other people's junk is, after the cinema, France's most popular pastime. It is such an integral part of French life that there is a special word for it: *chiner*, 'to hunt for antiques.' And although the days when priceless artefacts could be picked up for a song from naive dealers are long gone, the beautiful and the bizarre can still be found.

Even if you do not plan to buy, the *Marché aux puces* at the Porte de Clignancourt, actually located in suburban St-Ouen, provides an aesthetic feast for anyone who is interested in history or fashion or is just plain curious about other people's lives. The largest antiques market in the world, it boasts over 2000 stands and is in fact thirteen markets, each with its own distinctive character and atmosphere. Do not be discouraged by the ramshackle stalls which line the route from the Métro, but continue past the gypsy fortune teller and the hot dog stands, pass under the thundering Périphérique and turn left into the rue des Rosiers, the main drag off which most of the markets open.

'Never mind the quality...'

Marché Vernaison

If you have time for only one market, choose this, the oldest and most charming. Small shops spill an intriguing mishmash of eye-catching objects out into the labyrinth of narrow alleyways. Vernaison is particularly good for china dolls, Steiff teddy bears, elegant Art Deco light fixtures, old train sets, vintage advertising posters and exquisite fabrics. Pascal Evenu (150bis, Allée 7) has an extensive array of French kitsch, including 50s ashtrays advertising Dubonnet or Gauloises. Antik'art (157, Allée 2) stocks bakelite radios. Francine (stand 121-123, Allée 7), has an excellent collection of fine bedlinen, old lace and embroidered silks.

Marché Malik

The vintage clothes market has sadly been largely taken over by stands selling cheap modern fashions. However, it is worth visiting for the couple of gold mines which remain. Top Paris designers, including Gaultier and Galliano, regularly scour Malik for inspiration. Go to Violette et Sarah (42 rue Paul Bert) for beautiful nineteenth-century silk gowns, 1940s rayon dresses and embroidered velvet evening bags. Brigitte (3 rue Jules-Vallès) often has pretty things at more affordable prices, as does her neighbour, Monique.

Marché Serpette

The carpeted and heated Serpette is the most luxurious and expensive of the markets and for sheer comfort is the place to head on a cold, rainy day. There is a lot of highly polished Art Deco, Vuitton luggage, paintings and jewellery. Go to number 13, allée 3, where the extravagantly moustachioed Alain Broussaille repairs and sells old lighters and fountain pens. One of his own paintings forms a stunning background to his Gothic stand.

Marché Paul Bert

Prices are lower at the open-air market next to Serpette. Here you might find anything: a stuffed leopard in a glass case, a 50s jukebox or an oversized clock from a Paris street corner, while one stall is a treasure trove of high-quality if pricey old French kitchenwares from earthenware terrines and copper moulds to curious wine implements.

Best of the Rest

The alleyways of the **Marché Biron** are not as grand as they once were, but it is still the place to find over-the-top Louis XV gilt chairs, an ormolu candelabra, crystal glasses, expensive jewellry. Built in 1989 and 1991, **Malassis** and **Dauphine** lack the old-world charm of Vernaison or Paul Bert, but are still worth a visit. For lunch, don't miss **Chez Louisette**, a wonderfully kitsch old café tucked away at the end of the Marché Vernaison where you can listen to ageing crooners perform renditions of Piaf or Aznavour while savouring an excellent rabbit in mustard sauce.

Making the most of your visit:

•Do not underestimate how much there is to see: set aside at least an entire morning or afternoon.
• Always bargain. As a rough guide, most dealers will knock 10 to 15 per cent off the marked price.
•Take cash. Dealers will almost always give a better price if you pay *en liquide*.
•Be wary of pickpockets, especially in the crowded Marché Malik.

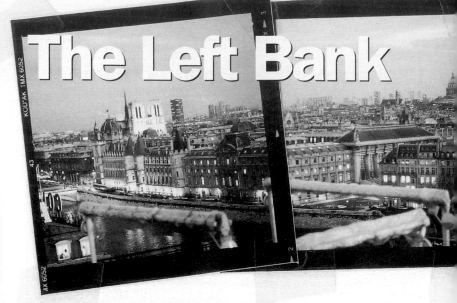

The Left Bank

The romantic Rive Gauche offers up myth and modernity, lives

The Latin Quarter

In the 5th arrondissement.

This section of the Left Bank east of boulevard St-Michel is probably so named because students here spoke Latin until the Revolution. Or the name may allude to the vestiges of Roman Lutétia, of which this area was the heart. The first two Roman streets were on the site of present-day rue St-Jacques (later the pilgrims' route to Compostella) and rue Cujas. The area still boasts many medieval streets and the city's best Roman remains: the Cluny baths, now part of **Musée National du Moyen Age** – Thermes de Cluny, and **Arènes de Lutèce** amphitheatre.

Quartier de la Huchette

The area is full of tourists, who pour down boulevard St-Michel and adjoining streets in summer. The boulevard has largely been taken over by fast-food giants and downmarket shoe and clothes chains, though giant book emporium **Gibert Joseph** is over a century old, and the fountain with its statue of St Michael slaying the dragon in place St-Michel is an ever-popular meeting point. Down pedestrianised rue de la Huchette and rue de la Harpe you'll find more Greek restaurants and café tables than evidence of medieval learning. Above the kebabs and taverna signs of rue de la Harpe, look for elegant eighteenth-century wrought-iron balconies and carved masks. Find, too, rue du Chat-Qui-Pêche, supposedly Paris' nar-

rowest street; rue de la Parcheminerie, named for the parchment sellers and copyists who once lived here; rue Galande with its over-hanging medieval buildings and **Studio Galande** cinema, famed for weekly screenings of *The Rocky Horror Picture Show*; and tiny **Théâtre de la Huchette** (on rue de la Huchette), which has been playing the original production of Ionesco's *The Bald Prima Donna* ever since 1957.

There are also two outstanding churches. **St-Séverin** was built over 450 years, ending up with an exuberant Flamboyant Gothic vaulted interior. In its garden are the remains of a Gothic charnel house, where bodies dug up in communal pits were stored before burial in the adjacent cemetery. **St-Julien-le-Pauvre**, off rue Galande, is one of Paris' oldest churches, built as a resting place for pilgrims in the twelfth century. There's a fine view of Notre Dame from the square Viviani garden next door.

Across boulevard St-Germain stands the **Musée National du Moyen Age – Thermes de Cluny**, a magnificent collection of medieval art housed in the Gothic mansion of the Abbots of Cluny, itself built over ruined Roman baths. The imposing remains are visible from boulevard St-Michel.

Down by the river, back from the *bouquinistes* or book sellers who line the *quais*, and with a fine view of Notre Dame, is second-hand English book-shop **Shakespeare & Co** (37 rue de la Bûcherie), a port of call for expatriate literati, though no relation to the rue de l'Odéon original. At 13 rue de la Bûcherie is the circular Old Faculty of Medicine,

of the literary, artists' dens and Latin lovers.

where students used to examine corpses that had been stolen from graveyards.

East of here place Maubert, now a morning marketplace (Tue, Thur, Sat), was used in the sixteenth century to burn books and hang heretics, particularly Protestants. The little streets between here and the traffic-heavy *quais* are among the city's oldest. The picturesque galleried houses of rue de Bièvre chart the course of the river Bièvre, which flowed into the Seine at this point in the Middle Ages, and was only fully covered over in 1912. Religious foundations once abounded; remnants of the Collège des Bernardins can be seen in rue de Poissy. On the quai de la Tournelle, look for the elegant seventeenth-century Hôtel Miramion at No 53, now the **Musée de l'Assistance Publique**, telling the history of Paris hospitals. There's food for all pockets, from the illustrious **Tour d'Argent** (No 15, a restaurant since 1582, though the present building dates from the 1900s) to the Tintin shrine café-tabac **Le Rallye** (No 11). Below, moored in this former dock for hay and wood, are numerous houseboats and barges.

Eglise St-Julien-le-Pauvre

rue St-Julien-le-Pauvre, 5th (01.43.54.52.16). M° Cluny-La Sorbonne. **Open** 10am-7.30pm daily. **Map J7**
One of Paris' oldest churches, St-Julien was formerly a sanctuary offering hospitality to pilgrims en route for Compostella. The present church dates from the late twelfth century, on the cusp of Romanesque and Gothic. Originally part of a Cluniac priory, it became the university church when colleges migrated to the Left Bank from Notre Dame. In the later Middle Ages, it was used for student assemblies that became so raucous the church was closed in 1524. Since 1889, it has been used by the Greek Melchite church, its icons giving an exotic air. The

sober outside looks rather bashed up, but inside is relatively well-preserved. The capitals are richly decorated with vine and acanthus leaves; one even has winged female harpies.

Eglise St-Séverin

1 rue des Prêtres-St-Séverin, 5th (01.42.34.93.50). M° Cluny-La Sorbonne or St-Michel. **Open** 11am-7.45pm Mon-Fri; 8am-9.30pm Sat; 9am-9.30pm Sun. **Map J7**
The Primitive and Flamboyant Gothic styles merge in this complex, composite little church, mostly built between thirteenth and fifteenth centuries, though further alterations in the 1680s were paid for by Louis XIV's cousin the 'Grande Mademoiselle'. The double ambulatory is famed for its remarkable 'palm tree' vaulting and unique double spiral column. The windows include some modern stained glass by Jean Bazaine.

Musée National du Moyen Age – Thermes de Cluny

6 pl Paul-Painlevé, 5th (01.53.73.78.00). M° Cluny-La Sorbonne. **Open** 9.15am-5.45pm Mon, Wed-Sun. **Admission** 28F; 20F 18-25s, all Sun; free under-18s, CM. **Guided tours** *Museum* 3.30pm Wed, Sat, Sun. *Baths* 2pm Wed, Sat, Sun. 36F; 21F under-18s, plus entry charge. **Credit** (shop only) V. **Map J7**
Along with the Hôtel de Sens in the Marais, this crenellated building is Paris' only other remaining example of important fifteenth-century secular architecture. It was built – atop an earlier Gallo-Roman baths complex dating from the second and third centuries – by Jacques d'Amboise in 1485-1498 at the request of the Abbé de Cluny, for lodging priests passing through the capital. It set new standards for domestic comfort and, with its main building behind a courtyard, was a precursor of the Marais *hôtels particuliers*. Admire the polygonal staircase, Gothic mullioned windows and balustrade lined with gargoyles in the main courtyard. The baths are the most important Roman remains in Paris, and three large rooms and parts of the hypocaust system are visible – the impressive vaulted frigidarium (cold bath); tepidarium (warm bath) and caldarium (hot bath). After the Revolution, a printer, a laundry and cooper set up shop here in 1807, before it

became a museum in 1844. The structure remains largely intact, including the Flamboyant Gothic chapel on the first floor. Still commonly known as Cluny, it now houses an exceptional collection of medieval art, with the *Lady and the Unicorn* tapestries and superb goldwork, architectural fragments and artefacts. *See also chapter* **Museums**.

The Sorbonne & the Montagne Ste-Geneviève

Ever-studenty Montagne-Ste-Geneviève still contains a remarkable concentration of academic institutions today, from the Sorbonne to research centres to *Grandes Ecoles* such as the Ecole Normale Supérieure. But in the thirty years since May 68, its warren of narrow streets has attracted the well-heeled, pushing accommodation beyond most students' pockets. The intellectual tradition persists, though, in the countless specialist book stores and the art cinemas of rue Champollion and rue des Ecoles, such as **Action Ecoles**, **Le Champo** with its eternal Hitchcock retrospectives, the **Reflet Médicis Logos** and film-themed café **Le Reflet**.

The district began its long association with learning in about 1100, when a number of scholars, including Peter Abélard, began to live and teach on the Montagne, independent of the established Canon school of Nôtre Dame. This loose association of scholars began to be referred to as a University. The Paris schools soon attracted scholars from all over Europe, and the 'colleges' – really just student residences – multiplied, until the University of Paris was given official recognition with a charter from Pope Innocent III in 1215.

By the sixteenth century, the university – now known as the **Sorbonne**, after the most famous of its colleges – had been co-opted by the Catholic establishment. A century later, Cardinal Richelieu rebuilt the Sorbonne, but the place slowly dwindled and slid into decay. After the Revolution, when the whole university was forced to close, Napoléon resuscitated the Sorbonne as the cornerstone of his new, centralised, exclusively French-language education system. The university participated enthusiastically in the uprisings of the nineteenth century, and was also a seedbed of the May 1968 revolt; students battling with police ripped up the cobbles of the boulevard St-Michel (since paved over). Nowadays the university is much quieter, not least because the Sorbonne is now only one of 18 faculties of the University of Paris dotted around city and suburbs. The present buildings (entrance: rue de la Sorbonne) are mostly late nineteenth century; only the Baroque Chapelle de la Sorbonne, where Richelieu is buried, survives from his rebuilding. The courtyard is open to the public; you can sometimes sneak into lectures in the main amphitheatre.

Also on rue des Ecoles stand the late eighteenth-century buildings of eminent, independent **Collège de France**, founded in 1530 with the patronage of François 1er by a group of humanists led by Guillaume Budé to revive the study of classical authors. Recent notables have included Claude Lévi-Strauss, Emmanuel Le Roy Ladurie and Georges Duby. Lectures are open to the pubic (11 pl Marcelin-Berthelot/01.44.27.12.11). For intellectual fodder, neighbouring **Brasserie Balzar** remains fashionable; regulars here even set up Les Amis du Balzar in protest at its 1998 acquisition by the Groupe Flo.

Climb up rue St-Jacques to the south or by winding rue de la Montagne-Ste-Geneviève to the huge domed **Panthéon**, originally commissioned by Louis XV as a church for the city's patron Ste Geneviève, but converted in the Revolution into a secular temple for France's *grands hommes*. There's a superb view from the top. In place du Panthéon, conceived by the Panthéon's architect Soufflot, is the elegant classical *mairie* (town hall) of the 5th *arrondissement*, mirrored by the law faculty. On the north side, on the site of a college where Erasmus, Calvin and Ignatius Loyola all studied, is the **Bibliothèque Ste-Geneviève**, with a fine collection of medieval manuscripts and magnificent nineteenth-century iron-framed reading room. On the other side is the **Hôtel des Grands-Hommes**, where Surrealist André Breton invented 'automatic writing' in the 1920s.

To the east of the square stands the more intimate church of **St-Etienne-du-Mont**, with a remarkable Renaissance rood screen. Pascal and Racine are both

Panthéon: *easier to get into if you're a man.*

buried here, as are the remains of Ste Geneviève. Parisians still come to ask her for favours. Jutting behind, in the grounds of Lycée Henri IV, is the Gothic-Romanesque **Tour de Clovis**, the only remaining part of the once giant abbey of Ste-Geneviève, though parts of a cloister have recently been excavated in the grounds. The Lycée, one of the most prestigious schools in the city, is closed to the public, though you can admire its gardens from the swimming pool, Piscine Jean Taris. Further along rue Clovis is a chunk of Philippe-Auguste's twelfth-century city wall (the other main surviving section is in the Marais). Of the other medieval streets, rues du Cardinal-Lemoine and Descartes were both inhabited by Ernest Hemingway. At 65 rue du Cardinal-Lemoine, the severe former Collège des Ecossais, founded to house Scottish students, is the resting place for the brain of James II, who died at St-Germain-en-Laye. At No 75 hides the charming **Hôtel des Grandes-Ecoles**. Cheap eats abound here; **L'Ecurie**, opposite the Ecole-Polytechnique at 2 rue Laplace, is housed in an underground network of medieval stables.

Beyond rue Soufflot is one of the most picturesque stretches of the rue St-Jacques containing several ancient buildings. Note the elegant *hôtel* at No 151 with elaborate balcony, but also good food shops, vintage bistro **Perraudin** and Aussie bar **Café Oz**. Turn off up hilly rue des Fossés-St-Jacques for pleasant place de l'Estrapade tucked behind the Panthéon.

Eglise St-Etienne-du-Mont

pl Ste-Geneviève, 5th (01.43.54.11.79). M° Cardinal-Lemoine/RER Luxembourg. **Open** 8am-noon, 2-7.15pm Tue-Sat; 9am-noon 2.30-6.30pm Sun. No visits during services. **Map J8**

An important pilgrimage site since the Dark Ages for the shrine of Ste Geneviève. The present church was built – in an amalgam of Gothic and Renaissance styles – between 1492 and 1626, and originally adjoined the abbey church of Ste-Geneviève. The curiously charming facade mixes Gothic rose window, classical columns and pediment. The stunning Renaissance roodscreen is the only one left in Paris, and possibly the work of François 1er's architect Philibert Delorme. Look for the double spiral staircase, ornate stone fretwork, and Germain Pilon's wooden Baroque pulpit (1651), with massive female figures of the virtues. The elaborate brass-covered shrine to the right of the choir, surrounded by plaques giving thanks for miracles Geneviève has performed. In the ambulatory are tablets to Racine and Pascal. A passageway, lined with nineteenth-century glass scenes depicting Ste Geneviève's life, leads to a Catechism Chapel designed by Baltard.

Le Panthéon

pl du Panthéon, 5th (01.44.32.18.00). *RER Luxembourg.* **Open** *Apr-Sept* 9.30am-6.30pm daily; *Oct-Mar* 10am-5.30pm daily. **Admission** 35F; 23F 12-25s; free under-12s. **Credit** MC, V. **Map J8**

Soufflot's Neo-Classical megastructure was the architectural *Grand Projet* of its day. A grateful Louis XV had it built to thank Ste Geneviève for helping him recover from illness. But events caught up with its completion in 1790, and post-Revolution it was re-dedicated as a 'temple of reason' and the resting-place of the nation's great men. It was definitively secularised in 1885, in a neat reversal of the history of Rome's famed Pantheon, upon which it was modelled, which started as a pagan temple only to be turned into a Catholic church.

St-Etienne-du-Mort: *home of Paris' patron.*

In the recently restored interior admire the elegant Greek columns and domes which give the building an airy grandeur, as well as the nineteenth-century murals by Puvis de Chavannes depicting the life of Ste Geneviève. The crypt of greats includes statesmen, politicians and thinkers; Voltaire, Rousseau, Victor Hugo and Zola. New heroes are added rarely: Pierre and Marie Curie's remains were transferred here in 1995, she being the first women to be interred here in her own right; André Malraux, De Gaulle's culture minister, arrived in 1996. The steep spiral stairs up to the colonnade around the dome lead to wonderful views over Paris.

La Sorbonne

47 rue des Ecoles, 5th (01.40.46.20.15). M° Cluny-La Sorbonne. **Open** *courtyards* 9am-4.30pm Mon-Fri. **Map J7**

Founded in 1253 by the cleric Robert de Sorbon as one of several separate theological 'colleges' in the area, the University of the Sorbonne was at the centre of the Latin Quarter's intellectual activity from the Middle Ages until May 1968, when its premises were occupied by students and stormed by the CRS (riot police). The authorities subsequently splintered the University of Paris into less-threatening suburban outposts, but the Sorbonne remains home to the Faculté des Lettres. Rebuilt by Richelieu and reorganised by Napoléon, the present buildings mostly date from 1885 to 1900 and include a labyrinth of classrooms and quaint lecture theatres, as well as an observatory tower, visible from the rue St-Jacques. The elegant dome of the seventeenth-century chapel dominates place de la Sorbonne. The chapel is closed to the public except for occasional concerts and exhibitions; Cardinal Richelieu is buried in an ornate tomb inside. Members of the public who wish to visit the Sorbonne should reserve a month in advance and confirm in writing to Mme Bolot.

Mouffetard

At the top of rue du Cardinal-Lemoine is picturesque **place de la Contrescarpe** (named after the embankments of Philippe-Auguste's fortifications), a famous rendez-vous since the 1530s, when writers Rabelais, Ronsard and Du Bellay frequented the cabaret de la Pomme de Pin at No 1, and still known for its lively cafés. Off to the south winds the **rue Mouffetard**, one of the oldest and most characterful streets in the city. This area was once a mixture of plain poverty and penniless bohemia. Cheap student- and tourist-filled bistros, fondue and Greek restaurants and ethnic knick-knack shops still give it a bohemian air, but it's rather more touristy than when Hemingway described it as 'that wonderful narrow crowded market street'. The lower half, towards the late Gothic church of **St-Médard**, has a busy street market that seethes at weekends. One of the narrow streets off rue Mouffetard is rue du Pot-de-Fer, where (at No 6) George Orwell stayed in a cheap boarding house in 1928-29 during his time as a *plongeur*, and vividly depicted it in *Down and Out in Paris and London* as 'a ravine of tall, leprous houses'. Take a detour along rue Tournefort with its elegant houses.

To the west of this knot of narrow streets, broad rue Gay-Lussac, a hot spot in the May 1968 riots, leads to the **Jardins du Luxembourg**. The rue d'Ulm houses the elitist intellectual Ecole Normale Supérieure, which was taken hostage in demos by the unemployed in January 1998, when several students joined the occupiers in an echo of 1968. Further down rue St-Jacques is another eminent landmark, the **Val-de-Grâce**, least-altered and most ornate of all Paris' Baroque churches.

Eglise St Médard

141 rue Mouffetard, 5th (01.44.08.87.00). M° Censier-Daubenton. **Open** 9am-noon, 2-.30-7pm Tue-Sat; 9am-noon Sun. **Map K9**
The original chapel here was a dependency of the Abbaye de Ste-Geneviève, but rebuilding at the end of the fifteenth century created a much larger late Gothic structure, with light-filled clerestory and elaborately vaulted ambulatory. Some of the capitals were fluted to suit 1780s Neo-Classical fashion.

Eglise du Val-de-Grâce

pl Alphonse-Laveran, 5th (01.40.51.47.28). RER Port-Royal. **Open** *mass* 9am, 11am Sun; *museum and church* noon-7pm Tue, Wed; 1.30-7pm Sat, Sun. **Map J9**
This church and its surrounding Benedictine monastery – now a hospital and interesting medical museum – were built by François Mansart and Jacques Lemercier, to fulfil Anne of Austria's vow to erect 'a magnificent temple' if God blessed her with a son. He promptly presented her with two. Extraordinarily expensive and built over several decades, the recently restored church is the most luxuriously Baroque of the city's seventeenth-century domed churches, closely influenced by the Redentore in Venice, with a few Bernini-esque touches like the baldaquin with six barleysugar spiral columns borrowed from St Peter's in Rome. Bernini greatly admired Pierre Mignard's dome fresco, calling it 'the masterpiece of French art'. Its swirling colours and forms are meant to prefigure heaven. The monastic buildings are best viewed, flood-lit by night, from the boulevard du Port-Royal.

The Jardin des Plantes District

At the eastern end of rue des Ecoles, east of rue Monge and rue des Fossés St-Bernard, you move into a quieter area that nonetheless contains Roman relics, several major academic institutions, and is a focus for Paris' Muslim community. Nestling between the Seine and the 1960s-70s slab architecture of Paris university's campuses VI and VII (known as Jussieu), large parts of which are closed for asbestos removal, is the striking modern **Institut du Monde Arabe**, with a busy programme of concerts and exhibitions related to the Arab world.

The Paris mosque is not far away, although you may want to stop off on the way at the **Arènes de Lutèce**, the Roman amphitheatre, entered from rue

Monge or rue des Arènes. Rediscovered in 1869 during the building of rue Monge, the central arena and many tiers of stone seating remain. The green-roofed **Mosquée de Paris** was built in 1922, partly after Granada's Alhambra, though the popular Moorish tea room within is a very Parisian experience.

The mosque looks out onto the **Jardin des Plantes**, Paris' botanical garden. Established in 1626 as a garden for medicinal plants, it features an eighteenth-century maze, a winter garden brimming with rare plant species and the brilliant renovated Galerie de l'Evolution of the **Museum National d'Histoire Naturelle**. There's also the **Ménagerie** zoo founded in the Revolution, home to evil-looking vultures, as well as big cats, bears and reptiles. Botanical and zoological hints abound in the area, from street names like Buffon and Linné (botanists) to the charming Fontaine Cuvier on rue Cuvier (paleontologist) with a figure of Natural History supported on smiling lion and grinning crocodile.

Arènes de Lutèce

entrances rue Monge, rue de Navarre, rue des Arènes, 5th. M° Cardinal-Lemoine or Jussieu. **Open** 10am-dusk daily. **Map K8**
Once the Roman arena, where roaring beasts and wounded gladiators met their deaths. The site was discovered in 1869, and if you enter via the passageway at 49 rue Monge you'll feel you've stumbled on a secret – just you and the gangs of kids playing ball, skateboarders, *boules*-players and drunks.

Institut du Monde Arabe

1 rue des Fossés-St-Bernard, 5th (01.40.51.39.53). M° Jussieu. **Open** 10am-6pm Tue-Sun. *Library* 1-8pm Tue-Sat. *Café* 2.30-6.30pm Tue-Sat; noon-3pm Sun. **Admission** *Building, rooftop terrace, library* free. *Museum* 25F; 20F 12-25s, students; free under-12s, CM. *Exhibitions* 45F; 35F students, over-60s. **Map K7**
This wedge-shaped *Grand Projet* was purpose-designed by French architect Jean Nouvel in 1980-87. It's a clever blend of high-tech steel and glass architecture and Arab influences. Nouvel took his inspiration from the screens of Moorish palaces and devised an intriguing high-tech version based on the principle of a camera aperture, using programmed photoelectic cells so that they would adjust automatically to admit constant amounts of daylight. Inside is a permanent collection of Middle Eastern art, archaeological finds, temporary exhibition spaces, a specialist library and café. There's an active performing arts programme of dance and classical Arab music, and great views from the rooftop terrace.

La Mosquée de Paris

1 pl du Puits-de-l'Ermite, 5th (01.45.35.97.33/Tea room 01.43.31.38.20/Turkish baths 01.43.31.18.14). M° Censier-Daubenton. **Open** *tours* 9am-noon, 2-6pm Mon-Thur, Sat, Sun (closed Muslim holidays). *Tea room* 10am-midnight daily. *Turkish baths women* 10am-9pm Mon, Wed-Sat; *men* 2-9pm Tue; 10am-9pm Sun. **Admission** 15F; 10F 7-25s, over-60s; free under-7s. *Tea room* free. *Turkish baths* 85F. **No credit cards. Map K8**
Built 1922-26, the mosque's green-and-white minaret oversees the centre of the Algerian-dominated Muslim community in France. Built in Hispano-Moresque style, with elements inspired by the Alhambra and Fez' Mosque Bou-Inania, the mosque is a series of buildings and courtyards in three sections: religious (grand patio, prayer room and minaret); scholarly (Islamic school and library); and, entred from rue Geoffroy-St-Hilaire, commercial (domed *hammam* or Turkish baths, shop and relaxing Moorish tea room).

*Feeling moorish? Go for tea at the **Mosquée**.*

St-Germain & Odéon

Ever chic St-Germain-des-Prés is where the great myths of Paris café society and intellectual life grew up. In cafés here Verlaine and Rimbaud went drinking and, a few generations later, Sartre, Camus and de Beauvoir scribbled their first masterpieces. (St-Germain also epitomised Paris' postwar jazz boom in the musicians grouped around writer, critic and trumpeter Boris Vian.) Even the Métro station has literary pretensions, with illustrations of printing pionneers and local literary lions. For the visitor the area is ideal for a stroll around the art galleries and decorators of the rue des Beaux-Arts, rue de Seine and rue Bonaparte; the fine clothes shops around St-Sulpice; the jazz clubs along rue St-Benoît; the classy street market on rue de Buci; or the elegant lawns and fountains of the Luxembourg gardens.

But St-Germain is changing. Earnest types still stride along clutching weighty tomes, but so prestigious and expensive has the area become that any writers who inhabit it are either well-established or rich Americans pretending to be Hemingway. Recently, luxury fashion groups long associated with the Right Bank and 'commerce' have moved in, often replacing venerable bookshops. **Emporio Armani** has taken over the old Drugstore, Dior a bookshop, Cartier a classical record shop and Louis Vuitton has unpacked its bags at 6 place St-

Germain. In 1997 a band of intellectuals, led by 60s singer Juliette Gréco, founded SOS St-Germain to try and save the area's soul. But the literary-fashion split is not always clear: Sonia Rykiel is among the campaigners, Paco Rabanne hopes to revive Le **Montana** jazz club and Karl Lagerfeld has just opened his own photo gallery in rue de Seine. Let's hope that rather than just preserving the area in aspic, they can make it swing again.

From the Boulevard to the Seine

Nerve centre of the district is boulevard St-Germain, cut through by Haussmann in 1855, with politicians' favourite **Brasserie Lipp** (No 151), **Café de Flore** (No 172), which likes to think of itself as the birthplace of existentialism, and **Les Deux Magots** (6 pl St-Germain-des-Prés) either side of late-night bookshop **La Hune** (No 170). During World War II, hit by shortages of coal, Sartre descended from the ivory tower of his apartment on rue Bonaparte to save a bundle in heating bills. 'The principal interest of the Café de Flore,' he noted, 'was that it had a stove, a nearby Métro and no Germans', De Beauvoir was notorious for hogging the table nearest the heater. Although you can now spend more on a few coffees there than you would on a week's central heating, it remains a favourite with the literati, especially the quiet room upstairs, where philosophical debate has recently been revived by English-speaking enthusiasts. Earlier this century it was also frequented by Picasso, Apollinaire and the Surrealists. The Deux Magots, named after the two statues of Chinese mandarins inside, now provides an interesting sociological cross-section of tourists, but can no longer really claim to be a hotbed of intellectual life.

Across from the terrace of the Deux Magots is the oldest church in the city, **St-Germain-des-Prés**, dating back to the sixth century. By the eighth century it was one of the most important Benedictine monasteries in France and host to an important medieval fair. What you see today (mainly eleventh and twelfth century) is a shadow of its former glory, as the church was severely damaged by a Revolutionary mob in 1792.

Part of the Abbot's palace, built in 1586, and traces of the cloister remain behind the church on rue de l'Abbaye. The charming place Furstenburg (once the stableyard of the Abbot's palace), now shades the house where the painter Delacroix lived at the end of his life (*see* **Musée Delacroix**). Rue de l'Echaudé shows a typical St-Germain mix: cutting-edge fashion at **L'Eclaireur** (No 24) and bistro cooking at ancient L'Echaudé-St-Germain (No 21). The elegant seventeenth-century *hôtels* of rue Jacob contain specialist book and design shops, pleasant hotels and bohemian throwbacks like *chansonnier* bistro **Les Assassins**. Illustrious former residents include Ingres, Wagner and Colette.

Further east along the boulevard at Odéon, the rue de Buci contains a top-class food market, running into rue de Seine with a lively scene centred around the **Bar du Marché** and Chai de l'Abbaye cafés. Rue Bonaparte (where Manet was born at No 5 in 1832), rue de Seine and the rue des Beaux-Arts are still packed with small art galleries, specialising in twentieth-century abstraction, tribal art and Art Deco furniture. Oscar Wilde died 'beyond his means' at what was then the inexpensive Hôtel d'Alsace, now the fashionably over-the-top **L'Hôtel** in rue des Beaux-Arts. **La Palette** and **Bistro Mazarin** are good stopping-off points with enviable terraces on rue Jacques-Callot. Rue Mazarine, with interesting shops of lighting, vintage toys and jewellery, is home to Conran's much talked about new brasserie **L'Alcazar** (No 62). At the northern end of rue Bonaparte is the entrance to the seventeenth-century building, once a monastery, of the **Ecole Nationale Supérieure des Beaux-Arts**,

Paris' main fine arts school. Complementing it on the quai de Conti is the **Institut de France**, recently cleaned to reveal its crisp classical decoration. Built with money bequeathed by Louis XIV's minister Cardinal Mazarin, it now houses eminent institutions including the Académie Française, jealous guardian of the French language. Next door is the Neo-Classical Hôtel des Monnaies, originally the country's mint (1777-1973), where medals and special editions are struck. Now it's the **Musée de la Monnaie**, an engrossing coin museum. Opposite, the iron Pont des Arts leads across to the Louvre.

On rue de l'Ancienne-Comédie is the famous Café Procope, where coffee was first brought to the Parisian public in 1686 following its introduction to the royal court by the Turkish ambassador. Frequented by Voltaire, Rousseau, Benjamin Franklin, revolutionary Danton and later Verlaine, it is now a disappointing restaurant aimed at tourists, although it does contain some remarkable

---

Itineraries: Literary luminaries

•Start the day rummaging among the books, old magazines, postcards and prints of the **bouquinistes** on quai de Montebello.
•Cross to **Shakespeare & Co** on rue de la Bûcherie, a ramshackle bookshop that's good fun.
•Head down boulevard St-Michel and stop for a coffee at **Café de la Sorbonne** in the square in front of the university's chapel.
•Walk up rue Soufflot and pay your respects to Voltaire, Rousseau and Zola at the **Panthéon**.
•Back across boulevard St-Michel, then down rue de Médicis to **Odéon, Théâtre de l'Europe**.
•A moment's silence at 12 rue de l'Odéon, site of Shakespeare & Co (the original) where Sylvia Beach published Joyce's *Ulysses* in 1922.
•Cross boulevard St Germain to 13 rue de l'Ancienne Comédie for lunch at **Le Procope**, patronised by Voltaire and Diderot.
•Sip a digestif in the shadow of Sartre, Camus and de Beauvoir on boulevard St Germain at **Café de Flore** or **Les Deux Magots**.
•Walk it off in the Jardins du Luxembourg. Continue on to rue de Fleurus, where expat high priestess Gertrude Stein held court at no 27.
•A coffee in café-bookshop La Bibliothèque (weekday afternoons, 52 rue d'Assas), amidst a mix of philosophy, crime novels and Judaïca.
•With a nod to Strindberg's former home at No 62, head for Port Royal, on the fringes of Montparnasse, the other 'Republic of Letters'. Have an apéritif in the recently renovated **Le Bullier**, where Joyce had many a drink.

•You have earned dinner at Hemingway's table, across the road at the **Closerie des Lilas**, still a classy canteen for authors and their publishers. You may be sitting near the next Prix Goncourt.
•Head for **Le Select**, unofficial headquarters of the Lost Generation and one of Beckett's haunts. Have a cocktail in their memory. Cheers.
•Incurable browsers can hop a taxi back to St-Germain and leaf through glossy art books and French literature till midnight at **La Hune**.

*Late-night literary leanings at **La Hune**.*

---

memorabilia, including Voltaire's desk and a post-card from Marie-Antoinette. The back opens onto the cobbled passage du Commerce St-André and the adjoining courtyards of the Cour de Rohan, home to toy shops, jewellers and tea rooms. Delightful today, it has a more sinister past. In the eighteenth century, Dr Joseph-Ignace Guillotin first tested out his notorious execution device (on sheep), supposedly in the cellars of what's now the Pub St-Germain.

To the east, a charming web of narrow streets centres on winding rue St-André-des-Arts, historically and in spirit part of the Latin Quarter rather than St-Germain, with ancient houses, gift shops and an arts cinema. Look up to see some grand doorways and iron balconies, especially at Nos 47 and 49. The rue Gît-le-Coeur ('here lies the heart') is so called because one of Henri IV's mistresses lived here. At No 9 is the Hôtel du Vieux Paris, unofficially known as the 'Beat Hotel', where William Burroughs and pals revised *The Naked Lunch*.

Ecole Nationale Supérieure des Beaux-Arts (Ensb-a)

13 quai Malaquais, 6th (01.47.03.52.15). M° Odéon or St-Michel. **Open** *Courtyard* 8.30am-8pm Mon-Fri. *Exhibitions* 1-7pm Tue-Sun. *School visits* Mon, by appointment. **Admission** *Exhibitions* 20F; free under-12s, students. *School visits* 25F. **Credit** V. **Map H6**
Paris' most prestigious fine arts school is installed in what remains of a seventeenth-century convent, the eighteenth-century Hôtel de Chimay and some later additions. After the Revolution, the buildings were transformed into a museum of French monuments and in 1816 into the Ecole. Today it's often used for exhibitions (*see chapter* **Museums**), but at other times only the courtyard is open to visitors.

Institut de France

23 quai de Conti, 6th (01.44.41.44.41). M° St-Germain-des-Prés. **Guided** tours 9am, 2pm Sat, Sun (call ahead). **Admission** 20F. **No credit cards. Map H6**
Designed by Le Vau, the classical Baroque building housing the Institut de France dates from 1663-84. Overlooking the Seine, the semi-circular structure dominated by its dome was founded by Mazarin as a school for provincial children. In 1805 the five academies of the Institut were transferred here; most prestigious is the Académie Française, renowned for outbursts against Franglais, and whose 40 eminences work steadily on the dictionary of the French language. Inside is Mazarin's ornate tomb by Hardouin-Mansart, and the Bibliothèque Mazarine, which holds 500,000 volumes. Surprisingly, access to the library is open to anyone over 18 who turns up with ID, two photos and 100F for a one-year library card.

Eglise St-Germain-des-Prés

pl St-Germain-des-Prés, 6th (01.43.25.41.71). M° St-Germain-des-Prés. **Open** 8am-7pm daily. **Guided tour** 3pm third Sun of the month. **Map H7**
On the advice of Germain (later bishop of Paris), Childebert, son of Clovis, had a basilica and a monastery built towards 543. The oldest church in Paris, for many years it was known as St-Germain-le-Doré because of its copper roof. The original church was pillaged by Normans, to be rebuilt around the year 1000 in Romanesque style. Most of the present structure is twelfth century, albeit heavily altered after the Revolution, when the abbey was burnt and a saltpetre refinery installed in the church. Today, only some ornate carved capitals and the tower remain of the eleventh-century church. The top was altered during clumsy nineteenth-century restoration, when a spire was added, as were the frescoes in

Stalking fashion in **St-Sulpice**.

the nave by Hippolyte Flandrin. The Gothic choir was inspired by the one at St-Denis. Some interesting tombs include that of Jean-Casimir, deposed king of Poland who became abbot of St-Germain in 1669, and Scottish nobleman William Douglas. Under the window in the second chapel is the funeral stone of the philosopher Descartes, whose ashes (bar his skull) have been in the church since 1819.

St-Sulpice & the Luxembourg

South of boulevard St-Germain between Odéon and Luxembourg is a quarter that epitomises civilised Paris, full of historic buildings and interesting shops. Just off the boulevard lies the old covered market of St-Germain, once the site of the important St-Germain Fair. Following redevelopment it now houses an underground swimming pool, a few surviving food stalls hidden in the centre and a rather soulless shopping arcade, although the Irish pub **Coolín** is a pleasant stopping-off point. Rue Guisarde is nicknamed *rue de la soif* (street of thirst) thanks to the merry carrousers who swarm its bars and bistros by night. Rue Princesse and rue des Cannettes are a beguiling mix of lively bistros, like **Mâchon d'Henri** and **Chez Fernand**, plus budget eateries where *plats du jour* are cooked up for students, and some well-hidden late-night haunts including the Birdland bar, lively Argentine La Milonga and the notoriously elitist **Castel's** nightclub.

Dawdle past the fashion boutiques, antiquarian book and print shops and high-class pâtisseries and you come to **St-Sulpice**, a surprising eighteenth-century exercise in classical form with two uneven turrets and a colonnaded facade. Delacroix painted the frescoes, in the first chapel on the right. The square contains Visconti's imposing, lion-flanked Fontaine des Quatre-Points Cardinaux – its name a pun on the compass points and four clerics who didn't (*ne point*) become cardinal – and is used for an antiques fair and a poetry fair every summer as part of the Foire St-Germain. The innocuous looking **Café de la Mairie** remains a favourite with local intellectuals and students, a classic example of essential anti-chic, while between shops of religous artefacts, the chic boutiques along place and rue St-Sulpice include Yves Saint-Laurent, Christian Lacroix, **Agnès b**, perfumier Annick Goutal, the furnishings of **Catherine Memmi** and milliner **Marie Mercié**. Most of the houses date from the eighteenth century. Look out for the doorway of No 27, the Hôtel de Forgères, adorned with carved garlands of fruit.

To the west, prime shopping territory continues: the clothes shops of rue du Four, leather and accessory shops of rue du Dragon, rue du Cherche-Midi and rue de Grenelle, including fashion-victim essentials like **Prada**, Patrick Cox and **Stéphane Kélian**, although if you see a queue into the street it's most likely for the bread of **Poîlane**.

To the south, the wide rue de Tournon, lined by some very grand eighteenth-century residences, such as the elegant Hôtel de Brancas (now the **Institut Français de l'Architecture**) with allegorical figures of Justice and Prudence over the door, opens up to the **Palais du Luxembourg** and its adjoining park. Built for Marie de Médicis, the palace now serves as the French Senate. Ever popular with joggers and *dragueurs*, the **Jardins du Luxembourg** are much beloved of a population starved of greenery, with formal paths, legions of sculptures and a pond for sailing toy boats on. On the southern side the long, thin extension, the Jardins de l'Observatoire, contain the elaborate Fontaine de l'Observatoire, with figures of the continents sculpted by Carpeaux, surrounded by thrashing sea beasts and water-spouting turtles.

Heading north towards boulevard St-Germain, you pass the Neo-Classical **Odéon, Théâtre de l'Europe** built in 1779, now one of Paris' leading subsidised theatres. Beaumarchais' *Marriage of Figaro* was first performed here in 1784. The semicircular place in front was home to revolutionary hero Camille Desmoulins, at No 2, now La Mediterranée restaurant, decorated by Jean Cocteau.

A more seedy, studenty hangout is Le Bar Dix among the antiquarian bookshops on rue de l'Odéon. James Joyce's *Ulysses* was first published in 1922 at No 12 by Sylvia Beach at the legendary, original Shakespeare & Co.

Back on the boulevard St-Germain is a statue of Danton, who lived on the site before the construction of the boulevard. Now it's a popular meeting point, thanks to numerous cinemas and cafés. Up the street at 12 rue de l'Ecole-de-Médecine is the colonnaded Neo-Classical Université René Descartes (Paris V) medical school, designed in the late eighteenth century by Jacques Gondoin and home to the **Musée d'Histoire de la Médicine**. Across the street, the refectory remains from the **Couvent des Cordeliers** (No 15), an important Franciscan priory in the Middle Ages and later hotbed of Revolutionary plotting by the Club des Cordeliers. It is now part of the medical faculty, but open to the public for art exhibitions. Marat, one of the club's leading lights, met his waterloo in the tub at his home in the same street (then called rue des Cordeliers), when he was stabbed in 1793 by Charlotte Corday, but gained eternity through David's celebrated painting of his wet demise. Look out for the magnificent doorway of the neighbouring *hôtel* and the domed building at No 5, once the barbers' and surgeons' guild. Climb up rue André-Dubois to rue Monsieur-le-Prince, which follows the ancient ramparts of Philippe-Auguste's fortifications, for the popular budget **Polidor** at 41, which has been feeding students and tourists since 1845. On rue Racine, the **Bouillon Racine**, once a working-class dining hall with sinuous Art Nouveau woodwork, has been restored as a Belgian eatery .

Eglise St-Sulpice

pl St-Sulpice, 6th (01.46.33.21.78). M° St-Sulpice.
Open 8am-7.30pm daily. **Map H7**
Work on this giant church began in 1646, but it was only completed 120 years later, after six architects had toiled on it. The grandiose Italianate facade with its double colonnade is the creation of Jean-Baptiste Servandoni, from 1733-45, although the two towers remained unfinished at his death. The one on the right has never been completed, and is still five metres short of its neighbour. Servandoni had originally planned to construct a semi-circular *place* in front of the church, but this was never carried out and the present one was designed in the last century by Visconti, who also designed the fountain. The interior is famed for the three murals by Delacroix in the first chapel on the right of the entrance, depicting Jacob's fight with the Angel, Heliodorus chased out of the temple and St Michael killing the Dragon. Don't miss the two giant shell water stoops – a gift from the Doge of Venice to François 1er in the sixteenth century.

Palais du Luxembourg

rue de Vaugirard, 6th. M° Odéon/RER Luxembourg.
Map H8
The Palais du Luxembourg was built for Henri IV's widow Marie de Médicis in the 1620s by Salomon de Brosse, on the site of the former mansion of the Duke of Luxembourg. Its Italianate style, with ringed columns and rustication, was intended to resemble the Pitti Palace in her native Florence, although she did not live here for long, as Richelieu had her exiled to Cologne. The palace and its grounds, the **Jardins du Luxembourg**, remained in royal hands until the 1789 Revolution, when they passed to the state. The palace now houses the French Senate.

St-Sulpice: *crossroads for churchmice, café society and would-be World Cup champs.*

The Monumental 7th & West

Smart townhouses spread west from St-Germain into the 7th *arrondissement*, as the vibrant street and café life subsides in favour of residential blocks and government offices. The 7th easily divides into two halves. The more intimate Faubourg St-Germain to the east became part of the city with the creation of the 'boulevards du Midi' in 1704, and was soon colonised by the nobility. It still contains many beautiful mansions and fine upmarket shops. To the west, built up in the nineteenth century, the windswept expanses of wide avenues number the most famous sight of all, the Eiffel Tower.

The Faubourg St-Germain

Often written off by Proust as a symbol of staid, haute-bourgeois and aristocratic society, this area (despite the Revolution) remains home to some of Paris' oldest and grandest families, although most of its eighteenth-century *hôtels particuliers* have now been taken over by embassies and government ministries. You can admire their stone gateways and elegant courtyards, especially on rues de Grenelle, St-Dominique, de l'Université and de Varenne. Among the most beautiful is the 1721 Hôtel Matignon (57 rue de Varenne), residence of the Prime Minister; the elegant facade with central bay at the rear of the *cour d'honneur* is sometimes visible through the entrance portal. The nearby Cité Varenne at No 51 is a lane of exclusive houses with private gardens. To see the decorative interiors and private gardens of others like the Hôtel de Villeroy (Ministry of Agriculture, 78 rue de Varenne), Hôtel Boisgelin (Italian Embassy, 47 rue de Varenne), Hôtel d'Estrée (residence of the Russian ambassador, 79 rue de Grenelle), built for the Duchesse d'Estrées by Robert de Cotte, 1720 Hôtel de Avaray (residence of the Dutch ambassador, 85 rue de Grenelle), or 1777 Hôtel de Monaco (Polish Embassy, 57 rue St-Dominique), you'll have to wait for the **Journées du Patrimoine**.

Two *hôtels* that can be visited are the Hôtel Biron, (*see below*) and Hôtel Bouchardon, now **Musée Maillol** (59-61 rue de Grenelle), which retains wooden panelling and a curved entrance around Bouchardon's Fountain of the Four Seasons.

This area boasts the famous **Bon Marché** department store, Paris' first, and the chic food and design shops of rue du Bac, including a branch of Hédiard, the **Conran Shop**, the colourful tablewares of **Dîners en Ville** and, towards the river, stuffed animal emporium **Deyrolle**. Along rue du Cherche-Midi are agreeable shops and tea rooms, and the **Musée National Hébert** of interest for its setting in a mid-eighteenth-century house as much as for the paintings. There are further smart shops on boulevard Raspail, along with Paris' most successful *Marché biologique* on Sunday mornings. You may see coaches lined up beside the Bon Marché; these come not to shop but to pay pilgrimage at the **Chapelle de la Médaille Miraculeuse**.

Towards the Seine, high-quality antiques dealers abound in the Carré Rive Gauche, the quadrangle enclosed by the quai Voltaire (often known as *quai des antiquaires*) and rues des Sts-Pères, du Bac and de l'Université (*see chapter* **Paris by Season**). Shops full of Baroque finery, tapestries, chandeliers and statuary make fine window shopping. This area also contains one of Paris' most important cultural sights, the **Musée d'Orsay**, a *fin-de-siècle* railway station now home to the national collection of Impressonist and nineteenth-century art. A new footbridge being built across to the Tuileries is due to open in autumn 1999.

Across rue de Bellechasse is the **Musée de la Légion d'Honneur**, devoted to France's honours system, with a quirky, semi-circular pavilion.

Continuing westwards along the Seine, facing the Pont de la Concorde and the place de la Concorde across the river, is the **Assemblée Nationale**, the lower house of the French parliament. Originally the Palais Bourbon, its pedimented Neo-Classical facade was added in 1806 to mirror that of the Madeleine across the river, but the entrance on place du Palais-Bourbon, through which you can see its *cour d'honneur*, shows its more domestic origins. Nearby, the church of Ste-Clotilde on rue des Las-Cases was an early example of nineteenth-century Gothic Revival, much decried at the time.

Beside the Assemblée is the Foreign Ministry, often referred to by its address, the quai d'Orsay. Beyond it stretches the long, grassy esplanade leading up to the golden-domed **Invalides**, the vast military hospital complex which now houses the **Musée de l'Armée**. Cannons line the grand pavilions of the 196-metre-long facade, decorated with allegorical tributes to Louis XIV. The two churches inside – St-Louis-des-Invalides and the Eglise du Dôme – glorify the various French monarchs and their armies. Inside the Eglise du Dôme is Napoléon's tomb. The esplanade gives a perspective across ornate, cherubim-laden **Pont Alexandre III** to the Grand and Petit Palais, all constructed for the 1900 Exposition Universelle.

Just beside Les Invalides, a far cosier place to visit is the **Musée Rodin**, housed in the charming eighteenth-century Hôtel Biron and its huge gardens. Rodin was invited to move here in 1908 on the understanding that he would bequeath his work to the state. As a result, you can now see many of his great sculptures, including *The Thinker* and *The Burghers of Calais*, in a beautiful setting. Not far from here on rue de Babylone, an interesting architectural oddity is La Pagode cinema, a genuine Japanese pagoda constructed in 1895. It is currently closed for renovation, but the exotic structure can be admired from the outside. Film buffs will enjoy the shop across the street, specialising in vintage film posters.

Assemblée Nationale

33 quai d'Orsay, 7th (01.40.63.60.00). M° Assemblée Nationale. **Guided tours** 10am, 2pm, 3pm Sat when Chamber not in session; ID required; arrive early. **Map F5**
The Palais Bourbon has been home to the lower house of the French parliament since 1827, and was the seat of the German military administration during the Occupation. Built in 1722 for Louis XIV's daughter, the Duchesse de Bourbon, the palace was extended by the Prince de Condé, who added the Hôtel de Lassay, now official residence of the Assembly's president. The Greek-style facade facing the Seine was stuck onto the building in 1806 to echo that of the Madeleine across the river; the real entrance is via the place du Palais Bourbon. Inside, the library is decorated with Delacroix's *History of Civilisation*. Visitors can attend debates.

Chapelle de la Médaille Miraculeuse

Couvent des Soeurs de St-Vincent-de-Paul, 140 rue du Bac, 7th (01.49.54.78.88). M° Sèvres-Babylone. **Open** 7.45am-1pm, 2.30-7pm daily. **Map F7**
A series of reliefs to the left of the entrance recounts the life of saintly nun Catherine Labouré. In 1830 she had a visit from the Virgin, who gave her a medal which performed many miracles. The Chapelle is one of the most visited pilgrimage sites in France, with two million faithful every year. It's an extraordinary concoction of statues, mosaics and murals, where the bodies of Catherine and her mother superior lie embalmed. You can buy your own miraculous medal for a few francs.

Les Invalides

esplanade des Invalides, 7th (01.44.42.54.52/Musée de l'Armée 01.44.42.37.67). M° Invalides. **Open** *Apr-Sept* 10am-6pm daily; *Oct-Mar* 10am-5pm daily. **Admission** 37F; 27F 11-18s, students under-26; free under-11s, CM. **Credit** MC, V. **Map E6**
Visible miles away because of the gleaming Eglise du Dôme (regilded for the 1989 bicentenary of the Revolution), the classical-style Hôtel des Invalides, designed by Libéral Bruand (1671-76) for Louis XIV as a military hospital and retirement home for the wounded, at one time housed up to 6000 invalids (hence the name). Part of it is still a hospital but much of it contains the **Musée de l'Armée**, with its staggering display of weapons and war-time paraphernalia, and Musée de l'Ordre de la Libération. The Eglise du Dôme is a highly decorated example of French architecture under Louis XIV. Designed by Hardouin-Mansart, with a square ground plan, it is one of the grandest Baroque churches in the city. Since 1840 it has been dedicated to the worship of Napoléon, whose body was brought here from St Helena 19 years after he died. It now lies beneath the coffered dome, in a red porphyry sarcophagus in a hushed circular crypt. The church of St-Louis is also known as the Church of the Soldiers, decorated with captured flags, its crypt filled with the remains of military men.

Musée d'Orsay

62 rue de Lille, 7th (01.40.49.48.14/recorded information 01.45.49.11.11). M° Solférino/RER Musée d'Orsay. **Open** 10am-6pm Tue, Wed, Fri, Sat; 10am-9.30pm Thur; 9am-6pm Sun. **Admission** 40F; 30F 18-25s, over-60s, Sun; free under-18s. **Credit** (shop) AmEx, MC, V. **Map G6**
The Musée d'Orsay was originally a train station, designed by Victor Laloux as part of the enormous works for the 1900 Exposition Universelle. You can still see the names of cities it once served on the Seine-side facade. Trains ceased to run there in the 50s as its platforms proved too short, and for a long time it was threatened with demolition, until in the late 70s President Giscard d'Estaing bowed to public pressure and scrapped plans to demolish the fine Beaux-Arts edifice, with its distinctive twin clock towers. It was decided instead to turn it into a museum spaning the fertile period 1830-1914, in a boldly redesigned interior by Italian architect Gae Aulenti. Opened in 1986, the main attraction is the skylit Impressionist gallery on the upper floor, filled with masterpieces by Monet, Degas, Renoir, Pissarro and Van Gogh. *See also chapter* **Museums**.

West of Les Invalides

To the west of the Invalides is the massive **Ecole Militaire**, the military academy built by Louis XV where Napoléon graduated, and which is still in army use today. Designed in 1751 by Jacques Ange Gabriel, this stern, imposing exercise in classicism isn't open to the public. Opposite its south entrance are the Y-shaped **UNESCO** building, built in 1958, and, another monumental structure, the 30s Modernist Ministry of Labour. Off the wide avenues de Suffren, Rapp and de la Bourdonnais, there's some sense of residential life in this quarter of officialdom, on rue St-Dominique, with old-fashioned bistro **Thoumieux** at No 79, a favourite with local families, or among the smart food shops and *traiteurs* of rue Cler; on Thursday and Saturday mornings the avenue de Saxe offers up one of the most scenic street markets in Paris.

In rue Surcouf the **Musée de la Seita**, a tobacco museum and art gallery, occupies the site where France's first cigarettes were manufactured in 1845.

From the north-western side of the Ecole Militaire begins the vast Champ de Mars, a former market garden converted into a military drilling ground in the eighteenth century and used after the 1789 Revolution for Bastille Day celebrations. Now it forms a spectacular backdrop to the most famous Parisian monument of them all, the **Eiffel Tower**, tallest building in the world from 1889 until New York's skyscrapers began sprouting in the 30s. It was intended only as a temporary structure, a bravura show of the new-found mastery of iron construction. Maupassant claimed he left Paris because of it; William Morris visited daily to avoid having to see it from afar, yet it is the satisfyingly phallic Eiffel Tower that has become the most potent international symbol of Paris.

Les Egouts de Paris

entrance opposite 93 quai d'Orsay, by Pont de l'Alma, 7th (01.53.68.27.81). M° Alma-Marceau/RER Pont de l'Alma. **Open** 11am-4pm Mon-Wed, Sat, Sun. Closed three weeks in Jan. **Admission** 25F; 20F students, 5-16s, over 60s; free under 5s. **Map D5**
For centuries water sellers were a part of Paris street life; the main source of drinking water (more popular than the springs of Passy) was the Seine, which was also the main sewer. Construction of the Paris sewers began in 1825, to be taken efficiently in hand by Haussmann and his engineers from 1853. Today, the Egouts de Paris have been made into one of the smelliest museums in the world. Each sewer is marked with a replica of the street sign above it, making the 2100km system a real city beneath a city.

Eiffel Tower

Champ de Mars, 7th (01.44.11.23.45/recorded information 01.44.11.23.23). M° Bir-Hakeim/RER Champ-de-Mars. **Open** *Jan-12 June* 9am-11pm; *13 June-Aug* 9am-midnight; *Sept-Dec* 9am-11pm daily. **Admission** *By lift* 1st storey 20F; 11F 4-12s; 2nd storey 42F; 21F 4-12s; 3rd storey 59F; 30F 4-12s; free under-4s. *By stairs* 1st & 2nd storeys only 14F. **Credit** AmEx, MC, V. **Map C6**
What for many is the symbol of Paris was the tallest building in the world at 300m when built in 1889 for the Exposition Universelle on the centenary of the Revolution. Now,

Les Invalides: *Napoléon's last resting-place.*

Fronts de Seine

Downstream from the Eiffel Tower, the 15th *arrondissement* has few tourist sites. Near the Pont Bir-Hakeim on quai Branly stands the high-tech **Maison de la Culture du Japon**. The riverfront has been taken over by 70s tower block developments, some of the most jarring clashes with modernity in Paris. Signs of improvement further west are the sophisticated headquarters of the Canal+ TV channel, 2 rue des Cévennes, designed by American Richard Meier, and, surrounded by well-thought out modern housing, the **Parc André Citroën**, opened in 1992. Created on the site of a former Citroën car factory, the park has been laid out as a contemporary formal garden with a geometric design, water gardens and two large glasshouses. You'll be able to go up in a balloon here for the Millenium celebrations.

with its aerial, it reaches to 321m. The view of it from Trocadéro across the river is monumental, but the distorted aspect from its base most dramatically shows off the graceful ironwork of Gustave Eiffel. Be prepared for a long wait for a ride in the lifts – in 1998 the tower beat its previous record to receive six million visitors, its present popularity contrasting with the indignation which greeted its construction. The lifts travel 100,000km a year. To save time and money you can stop at the first or second platform, but those who go on to the top can view Eiffel's cosy salon and enjoy amazing panoramas: over 65km on a good day and a vision of the Paris of millions of lives. The queue is not so long at night, when the city lights against the Seine live up to their romantic image. There's the Altitude 95 bistro on the first level, and the smart Jules Verne restaurant on the second, as well as a post office and souvenir shops.

UNESCO

pl de Fontenoy, 7th (01.45.68.10.00). M° Ecole-Militaire or Ségur. **Open** 9am-6pm Mon-Fri. **Map D7**
The Y-shaped UNESCO headquarters was built in 1958 by a multi-national team – an American (Breuer), an Italian (Nervi) and a Frenchman (Zehrfuss). A giant construction in concrete and glass, it's worth visiting for the sculptures by Picasso, Arp, Giacometti, Calder and others in the lobbies. Inside it buzzes with palpable postwar idealism. Behind there's a Japanese garden, with contemplation space (a concrete cylinder) by Japanese minimalist Tadao Ando.

Village Suisse

38-78 av de Suffren, 15th. M° La Motte-Picquet-Grenelle. **Open** 10.30am-7pm Mon, Thur-Sun. **Map D7**
The site of the Swiss Village erected for the 1900 Exposition Universelle, this conglomeration of roughly 150 boutiques offers antiques and collectables from Asian and African art to engravings, furniture and jewellery. Sundays tend to be busy as the village with its gardens makes a pleasant walk.

Montparnasse & Beyond

In the early 1900s artists like Picasso, Léger and Soutine, as well as the poet Apollinaire came to 'Mount Parnassus' to escape the rising rents of Montmartre, bringing cutting-edge intellectual life to the area. Between the wars they were joined by Chagall, Zadkine and other escapees from the Russian Revolution, who set up the lively restaurant **Dominique**, and by Americans Man Ray, Henry Miller, Ezra Pound and Gertrude Stein. The neighbourhood symbolised modernity: jazz, *bal nègre*, Surrealism, and *fureur de vivre*. Mondrian claimed he moved here in 1926 to indulge in the charleston.

To some extent their legacy has lived on, but Montparnasse is a sadder, more disparate place now. The high-rise **Tour Montparnasse**, Paris' failed tribute to Manhattan, is the most visible of several infelicitous projects of the 70s; at least there are good views of the city from the top. The old Montparnasse railway station, where the Germans surrendered Paris on 25 August 1944, has been transformed into a maze of steel and glass corridors, with the new **Jardin de l'Atlantique** suspended over the TGV tracks. This is the main point of arrival from Brittany, as reflected in the numerous *crêperies* scattered around. Fronting the boulevard is a shopping complex and sports centre. To the west is Ricardo Bofill's circular place de Catalogne, typical of his postmodern version of Classicism.

Nearby rue de la Gaîté, once renowned for its cabarets, has fallen prey to strip joints and sex shops, although boulevard Edgar-Quinet has pleasant cafés and a street market (Wed, Sat mornings). The boulevard du Montparnasse still buzzes at night, thanks to its many cinemas and its legendary brasseries: the famed **Dôme** at No 108, now a luxurious fish restaurant and bar; giant Art Deco brasserie **La Coupole** at No 102, which opened in 1927 with columns decorated by different artists and daring basement dancehall is ever busy despite the construction of a block of flats on top; and classic late-night café **Le Select** No 99. Further east legendary literary café **La Closerie des Lilas**, opened as a dance hall in the 1840s, was a favourite with everyone from Lenin and Trotsky to Picasso and Hemingway and still draws politicians and publishers today. Le Nègre de Toulouse and the Dingo are long gone but there's still a sense of the *louche* at the **Rosebud** in rue Delambre. Near boulevard du Montparnasse, boulevard Raspail boasts Rodin's 1898 *Balzac;* his rugged, elemental rendition of the novelist caused such a furore that it wasn't displayed in public for 40 years.

If artists met at the cafés along the boulevard, their studios were actually dispersed over much of the 14th *arrondissement*, as well as parts of the 6th, 13th and 15th. Large windows testify to studios now frequently converted into apartments, such as the strange tiled studio building at 31 rue Campagne-Première (once home to Man Ray and featured in Godard's *A bout de Souffle*), around the courtyard at 126 boulevard du Montparnasse, on boulevard Raspail and rue Notre-Dame-des-Champs, or the old academies of rue de la Grande-Chaumière, where young artists too broke to hire a model went to draw from the nude. One of these academies survives, untouched and poignantly atmospheric at 14 rue la Grande-Chaumière, where you can still go and sketch by the hour, just next to where Modigliani died at No 8 in less than picturesque misery. Russian artist Marie Vassilieff ran her avant-garde Academie Vassilieff in the row of ivy-hung studios at 21 avenue du Maine (recently saved from redevelopment as the **Musée du Montparnasse**), the scene of lively fêtes with Picasso, Braque and Modigliani. The former studios of sculptors Zadkine (100bis rue d'Assas) and Bourdelle (16 rue Bourdelle) are now interesting museums, while Brancusi's studio, originally in the 15th, has been rebuilt outside the Centre Pompidou (*for all see chapter* **Museums**). A more recent addition is the glass and steel **Fondation Cartier** on boulevard Raspail, headquarters to Cartier and an exhibition centre for contemporary art. Laurens, Picasso and Maillol had studios at the rustic-looking cité Fleurie (65 boulevard Arago), which is still occupied by artists today. It's closed to the public, but you can peer through the gate into the gardens.

Inexpensive clothes and a **Fnac** can be found on rue de Rennes. There are numerous shoe, food and children's shops on rues Vavin and Bréa which lead to the Jardins du Luxembourg. Stop for a coffee at Café Vavin and look at Henri Sauvage's white tiled apartment building at 6 rue Vavin, built in 1911-12.

While the rest of the neighbourhood has gone a bit downhill, Montparnasse cemetery has grown in status as a resting place for the famous. It's calmer and less crowded than Père-Lachaise, but still counts numerous literary and artistic greats.

Cimetière de Montparnasse

3 bd Edgar-Quinet, 14th (01.44.10.86.50). M° Edgar-Quinet or Raspail. **Open** *16 Mar-6 Nov* 9am-6pm daily; *6 Nov-15 Mar* 9am-5.30pm daily. **Map G9**
Pay homage to writers Jean-Paul Sartre and Simone de Beauvoir, Baudelaire, Maupassant and Tristan Tzara, composers César Frank and Saint-Saëns, sculptors Dalou, Rude, Batholdi, Laurens and Zadkine, the unfortunate Captain Alfred Dreyfus, André Citroën of car fame, and Mr and Mme Pigeon reposing in their double bed. More recent occupants include Jean Seberg, waiflike star of *A bout de souffle*, beloved comic Coluche and *provocateur* Serge Gainsbourg. In the northeast corner, one of Brancusi's best known sculptures, *Le Baiser* (The Kiss), adorns one of the tombs. The ruins of a windmill are a relic of a more rural past.

Tour Maine-Montparnasse

33 av du Maine, 15th (01.45.38.52.56). M° Montparnasse-Bienvenüe. **Open** 9.30am-10.30pm daily. **Admission** *exhibition only* 36F; 30F over-60s; 27F 14-20s, students; 22F 5-14s; free under-5s. *exhibition/terrace* 46F; 38F over-60s; 34F 14-20s, students; 30F 5-14s; free under-5s. **No credit cards. Map F9**
Built in 1974 on the site of the former Gare Montparnasse, this steel-and-glass monster, at 209m high, is lower than the Eiffel Tower, but more central, and offers excellent views over Right and Left Banks. A lift whisks you up to the 56th floor, where you'll find a display of aerial views of Paris, allowing you to see how the city has changed since 1858, and there's a terrace on the 59th floor. There's rarely a queue.

Denfert-Rochereau & Montsouris

A spookier kind of burial ground can be found at place Denfert-Rochereau (instantly recognisable by the large bronze lion, sculpted by Bartholdi of Statue of Liberty fame, which dominates the traffic junction), entrance to the **Catacombs**. The bones of six million people were transferred here from overcrowded Paris cemeteries before the Revolution. During World War II the Résistance hid out here; in the 1980s, the catacombs became popular for illicit concerts and parties. The entrance is next to one of the toll gates of the **Mur des Fermiers-généraux** built by Ledoux in the 1780s, marking what was then the boundary of the city.

Returning towards Montparnasse along the avenue Denfert-Rochereau you'll come to the **Observatoire de Paris** (62 av de l'Observatoire), built by Perrault for Louis XIV's minister Colbert in 1668 (open to the public by appointment only, first Sat of the month). This is where the moon was first mapped, where Neptune was discovered and the speed of light first calculated. The French meridian mapped by politician and astronomer François Arago in 1806 (in use before the Greenwich meridian was adopted as an international standard) runs north-south through the building. Both Arago and the meridian have an unusual minimalist memorial by Dutch artist Jan Dibbets in the form of 135 bronze medallions, embedded along the Paris meridian line, on its route through the 18th, 9th, 2nd, 1st, 6th and 14th

*The **Eiffel Tower** towers serenely over all manner of other Parisian attractions.*

arrondissements, passing through some of the city's most celebrated sites, including Sacré Coeur, Palais Royal, the Louvre and Jardins du Luxembourg. One is in the square de l'Ile de Sein (where the meridian crosses boulevard Arago) on the empty base of the original statue to Arago, melted down during World War II. Next door the Maison du Fontainier (42 rue de l'Observatoire), was part of Marie de Médicis' underwater reservoir, designed to feed her fountains just as much as the people. The reservoir is now dry(ish) and can be visited on the **Journées du Patrimoine**.

The 14th *arrondissement* to the south of place Denfert-Rochereau is a mainly residential but pleasantly spacious area. The small but lively food market and several cafés on **rue Daguerre** are a favourite local rendez-vous, especially on Sunday. The area around rue Hallé, formerly part of the village of Montrouge incorporated into the city in 1860, was laid out in little crescents in an early attempt at a garden city. In the 30s, writers and lovers Henry Miller and Anaïs Nin and sculptor Chana Orloff lived in villa Seurat, off rue de la Tombe-Issoire, where architect André Lurçat built several of the houses, and where Seurat once lived. Off rue d'Alésia, now better known for its discount clothes stores, there are some un-Parisian-looking townhouses, while foodies make the trek to rue Jean-Moulin for bistro **La Régalade**. At 4 rue Marie Rose is the **Maison de Lénine** (01.42.79.99.58/by appointment), where Lenin lived 1909-12 with Nadejda Krpskaïa and her mother. Once a compulsory stop for East European dignitaries, today it's a forlorn place financed by the French Communist party, exhibiting his crockery and modest furniture, some of which looks as if it would be more suitable for the flea market at the **Puces de Vanves** on the southwest edge of the *arrondissement*.

The 14th *arrondissement* also boasts a lovely large park, the **Parc Montsouris**. On the park's opening day in 1878 the man-made lake suddenly and inexplicably emptied and the engineer responsible promptly committed suicide. Many of the artists who gave Montparnasse its reputation actually lived around here. Around the western edge of the park are several small streets such as rue du Parc Montsouris and rue Georges-Braque that were built up in the early 1900s with charming small villas and artists' studios, many by distinguished avant-garde architects, including the Villa Ozenfant (53 av Reille), designed in 1922 by Le Corbusier for painter Amédée Ozenfant, and the elegant Villa Guggenbuhl (14 rue Nansouty) designed in 1926-27 by Lurçat. Once mainly occupied by artists, they're now more likely to be the homes of lawyers and doctors. On the southern edge of Montsouris the **Cité Universitaire**, home to 6000 foreign students, is worth visiting for its themed pavilions, designed by eminent architects, and for its landscaped grounds.

Les Catacombes

1 pl Denfert-Rochereau, 14th (01.43.22.47.63).
M° Denfert-Rochereau. **Open** 2-4pm Tue-Fri; 9-11am, 2-4pm Sat, Sun. Closed public holidays. **Admission** 27F; 19F 8-25s, over-60s; free under-7s, CM. **No credit cards.** **Map G10**
The miles of dank, subterranean passages have existed, originally as stone quarries, since Roman times. In the 1780s, the contents of the over-crowded Paris cemeteries were transferred here. Stacks of bones alternate with tidy rows of skulls, while macabre quotations (Lamartine, Virgil, etc) on stone tablets add philosophical reflections. There's barely word of God, other than a couple of underground altars. There are supposedly bits of six million people down here, including victims of the Terror. Another section was used by the Résistance during World War II. Avid 'cataphiles' are renowned for finding obscure entrances for underground parties, but would you really want to spend a night down here?

Cité Universitaire

bd Jourdan, 14th. RER Cité Universitaire.
The Cité Universitaire was founded on an interwar ideal of internationalism and a desire to attract foreign students. Among landscaped gardens, the 40 pavilions were designed in supposedly national style, some by architects of the country like the De Stijl Collège Néerlandais by Willem Dudok, others in exotic pastiche, like the Pavillon Asie du Sud-Est with its Khmer sculptures and bird-beaked roof. The Pavillon Suisse (1935) and Brazilian Pavilion (1959) by Le Corbusier reflect his early and late styles. You can visit the Swiss pavilion (01.44.16.10.16; 8am-noon, 2-8pm Mon-Fri; 10am-noon, 2pm-8pm Sat, Sun) which has a tiled Le Corbusier mural on the ground floor.

Marché aux Puces de Vanves

av Georges Lafenestre (on bridge after Périphérique) and av Marc-Sangrier, 14th. M° Porte de Vanves. **Open** 7.30am-7pm Sat, Sun.
Smaller than St-Ouen or Montreuil and perhaps the friendliest of Paris' flea markets, Vanves is a good source of small decorative and household items.

15th Arrondissement

The 15th is Paris' largest *arrondissement* and the one that probably has the least for the tourist. It's worth making a detour to passage de Dantzig to visit **La Ruche** ('beehive'), designed by Eiffel as a wine pavilion for the 1900 exhibition. Afterwards it was acquired by philanthropic sculptor Alfred Boucher, who had it rebuilt on this site and let it out as studios for 140 artists. Chagall, Soutine, Brancusi and Modigliani all spent periods here, and the studios are still much sought after by artists today. Near here on rue des Morillons the **Parc Georges Brassens** was opened in 1983 on the site of the former Abattoirs de Vaugirard. The old market pavilions are used for a busy antiquarian and second-hand bookmarket at weekends. In one corner a vineyard produces around 200 bottles of Clos des Morillons every year. The reason many people come here, though, is for the huge trade fair centre **Paris Expo** at the Porte de Versailles .

Paris Expo

Porte de Versailles, 15th (01.43.95.37.00). M° Porte de Versailles. **Map B10**
The vast exhibition centre hosts everything from fashion to medical equipment fairs. Many are open to the public, such as the Foire de Paris and the Salon de l'Agriculture.

Lazy days at **Parc Montsouris**.

The 13th Arrondissement

A working-class area that became one of the most industrialised parts of Paris in the nineteenth century, the 13th has been one of the most marauded areas of Paris since World War II, from the tower blocks of Chinatown to the new national library and the burgeoning development zone around it.

Gobelins & La Salpêtrière

Although its image may be of tower blocks, the 13th also contains some historic parts of Paris, expecially where it borders on the 5th (*see above*, **Latin Quarter**). The **Manufacture Nationale des Gobelins** is home to the French state weaving companies. The tapestries and rugs produced here (usually on government commission) continue a tradition dating back to the fifteenth century, when Jean Gobelin set up his dyeing works by the river Bièvre. Followed by tanneries and other industries, the river became notorious for its pollution until covered over in 1912, while the slums were depicted in Hugo's *Les Miserables*. The area was tidied up in the 30s, when the **Square Réné Le Gall**, a small park, was laid out on former tapestry-workers' allotments. On rue des Gobelins, where Gobelin lived, the so-called **Château de la Reine Blanche** is a curious medieval relic.

On the western edge of the *arrondissement*, next to the Gare d'Austerlitz, sprawls the huge Hôpital de la Pitié-Salpêtrière, one of the oldest hospitals in Paris, founded in 1656, and where Princess Diana was brought after her fatal crash. Its most striking feature is the **Chapelle St-Louis-de-la-Salpêtrière**, designed by Libéral Bruand.

The busy road intersection of place d'Italie has seen more developments with the Centre Commercial Italie, opposite the town hall, a bizarre high-tech confection designed by Japanese architect Kenzo Tange, which contains the Gaumont Grand Ecran Italie cinema, and the Arapaho music venue, as well as shops. There's a good food market on boulevard Auguste-Blanqui (Tue, Fri, Sun mornings) and the sharply contrasting attractions of Chinatown and the Butte aux Cailles.

Chapelle St-Louis-de-la-Salpêtrière

47 bd de l'Hôpital, 13th (01.42.16.04.24). Mº Gare d'Austerlitz. **Open** 8.30am-6.30pm daily. **Map L9**
The austerely beautiful chapel was designed by Libéral Bruand in 1657-77 with an octagonal dome in the centre and eight separate naves in order to separate the sick from the insane, the destitute from the debauched. Around the chapel are some of the seventeenth- and eighteenth-century buildings of the Hôpital de la Pitié-Salpêtrière, founded on the site of a gunpowder factory (hence its name from saltpetre) by Louis XIV to round up poor, vagrant and unwanted women, becoming a research centre of the insane in the 1790s. Charcot pioneered neuro-psychology here, receiving a famous visit from Freud. It is now one of Paris' main teaching hospitals, but the chapel is regularly used for contemporary art exhibitions.

Château de la Reine Blanche

17 rue des Gobelins, 13th. Mº Gobelins. **Map K10**
Through a gateway you can spot the turret and overhanging first floor of an ancient house. The curious relic is named after Queen Blanche of Provence who had a château here, but was probably rebuilt in the 1520s for the Gobelin family.

Manufacture des Gobelins

42 av des Gobelins, 13th (01.44.08.52.00). Mº Gobelins.
Tours 2-2.45pm Tue-Thur. **Admission** 45F; 35F 7-25s, over-60s; free under-7s. **No credit cards. Map K10**
Tapestries have been woven on this site almost continuously since 1662 when Colbert, Louis XIV's jack of all trades, set up the Manufacture Royale des Meubles de la Couronne. Also known as the Gobelins after Jean Gobelin, a dyer who previ-

ously owned the site, the factory was at its wealthiest during the *ancien régime* when tapestries were produced for royal residences under the direction of artists such as Le Brun and Oudry. Today tapestries are still woven (mostly for the state) and visitors can watch weavers at work on pieces destined for French ministries and embassies. The guided tour (in French) through the 1912 factory gives you a chance to understand the complex weaving process and includes a visit to the Savonnerie carpet workshops next door. The tour also takes in the eighteenth-century chapel and the Beauvais tapestry workshops. Arrive 30 minutes before your tour.

Chinatown

South of the rue de Tolbiac is Paris' main Chinatown, centred between the 60s tower blocks along avenues d'Ivry and de Choisy, and home to a multi-Asian community. The bleak modern architecture could make it one of the most depressing areas of Paris, yet it's a fascinating piece of South-East Asia, lined with kitsch restaurants, Vietnamese *phô* noodle bars and Chinese patisseries, as well as the large **Tang Frères** supermarket on avenue d'Ivry. Less easy to find is the Buddhist temple with its large golden Buddha, hidden in an underground car park beneath the tallest tower block (Autel de la culte de Bouddha, av d'Ivry, opposite rue Frères d'Astier-de-la-Vigerie, open 9am-6pm daily). To see the area at its busiest, come here for the traditional lion and dragon dances at Chinese New Year (*see* **Paris by Season**).

La Butte aux Cailles

In striking contrast to nearby Chinatown, the villagey Butte aux Cailles is a neighbourhood of old houses, winding cobblestone streets and funky bars and restaurants, just southwest of the Place d'Italie. This workers' neighbourhood, home in the 1800s to many small factories, including a tannery, was one of the first to fight during the 1848 Revolution and the Paris Commune. The Butte has preserved its insurgent character and, in recent years, has resisted the aggressive forces of city planning and construction companies. The steep, cobbled rue de la Butte-aux-Cailles and the rue des Cinq-Diamants are the headquarters of the arty, *soixante-huitard* bohemian forces. For a complete village tour, saunter down the rustic rues Alphand, Buot, and Michal as well. Villa Daviel contains neat little villas, while the cottages built in 1912 in a mock-Alsatian vernacular style, clustered around a garden square at 10 rue Daviel, were one of the earliest public housing schemes in Paris. Behind the small garden at the place Paul-Verlaine lies an attractive brick Arts-and-Crafts style swimming pool fed by an artesian well. Explore passage Vandrezanne, the square des Peupliers, and the rue Dieulafoy, whose houses and gardens offer calm to those persistent enough to find them.

To discuss art, music or the most recent workers' strikes, the Butte offers a selection of relaxed, inexpensive bistros: Le Temps des Cérises, run as a cooperative, busy **Chez Gladines** and more upmarket Chez Paul. Two feisty bars **La Folie en Tête** and **Le Merle Moqueur** offer music, cheap beer on tap and youthful crowds spilling outside.

The Developing East

Dominique Perrault's massive **Bibliothèque Nationale de France François Mitterrand**, the last of the *Grands Projets*, opened, roughly on time, in December 1996. It was the first in a series of developments intended to liven up this desolate part of the Left Bank formerly taken up by railway yards. Other features of the plan, called ZAC Rive Gauche, include new housing and office developments, the covering-over of some of the remaining railway lines, the swallowing-up of existing industrial buildings in the area, such as Les Frigos former refrigerated warehouses (now containing artists' studios) and the majestic Moulins de Paris, mysteriously partly burnt down in 1996. The area's isolation should be reduced by the new high-speed Météor link and the construction of a footbridge between the library and Bercy across the river. Much of the area resembles a building site and is in a state of constant flux as new blocks appear overnight, shops open and roads change names. Happily, a growing flotilla of music bars moored on the Seine, the **Guinguette Pirate**, **Péniche Blues Café** and **Péniche Makara**, provide signs of new life in the air. Across the railway tracks, a pioneering art nucleus **ScèneEst** is burgeoning among the offices, with the arrival of six adventurous young galleries on rue Louise-Weiss. An unlikely monument (despite rumours of its destruction) is the rue Watt. Once used for offbeat happenings, it is famed as the lowest road in Paris.

Bibliothèque Nationale de France François Mitterrand
11 quai François-Mauriac, 13th (01.53.79.53.79).
M° Bibliothèque François Mitterrand or Quai de la Gare.
Open 10am-7pm Tue-Sat; noon-6pm Sun. **Admission** *day* 20F; *annual* 200F. **Map M10**
Opened in December 1996 by President Chirac, the gigantic new French national library (dubbed 'TGB'or *Très Grande Bibliothèque*) was the last of Mitterrand's *Grands Projets* and also the most expensive and most controversial. Architect Dominique Perrault was criticised for his curiously dated-looking design, which hides readers underground and stores the books in four L-shaped glass towers (intended to resemble open books), necessitating the installation of wooden shutters to protect them from sunlight. In the central void is a garden (open only to researchers) filled with 140 trees, uprooted from Fontainebleau at a cost of 40 million francs. The research section, below the public reading rooms, opened in autumn 1998, whereupon the massive computer system failed to get the right books to the right person and staff promptly went on strike. The library houses over ten million volumes, 420km of shelves and room for 3000 readers. Books, newspapers and periodicals are on public access to anyone over 18. An audio-visual room allows the public to browse through photo archives, film documentaries or sound recordings, and there are regular concerts and exhibitions. *See chapters* **Museums** *and* **Directory**. *Wheelchair access.*

Beyond the Périphérique

The suburban sprawl of the banlieue is a world apart from Paris, but it hides some surprises – from avant-garde villas to medieval castles.

Boulogne & the West

Paris' most desirable suburbs lie to the west of the city, supposedly the result of prevailing winds which carried industrial grime eastwards. Between the wars, the middle classes began to build expensive properties here, and further out there are large expanses of forest. Decentralisation also means that La Défense, Neuilly, Boulogne, Levallois and Issy-les-Moulineaux have become work places for residents of Paris, especially in the service, advertising and media industries.

Neuilly-sur-Seine is the most sought-after residential suburb, where smart apartment blocks have gradually replaced the extravagant mansions built around the Bois de Boulogne. Expect to see lots of velvet hairbands and Hermès scarves.

Boulogne-Billancourt is the most important town in the region outside Paris. In 1320 the Gothic Eglise Notre Dame was begun in tribute to a statue of the Virgin washed up at Boulogne-sur-Mer. By the eighteenth-century, the village of Boulogne was known for its wines and its laundries and early this century for its artist residents (Landowski, Lipchitz, Chagall, Gris), while Billancourt was known for its industries (cars, aviation and cinema). The famous film studios where Abel Gance shot *Napoléon* were recently demolished. Between Boulogne and Sèvres across the Seine on the Ile Séguin, the now-disused Renault factory sits in the river like a long ocean liner or, since closure in 1992 (future redevelopment is still undecided), rather more of a beached whale. Near the Bois de Boulogne are elegant villas, and some fine examples of 1920s and 30s architecture by Le Corbusier, Mallet-Stevens, Perret, Lurçat and others, well pinpointed by plaques around the town. In the town centre, the white Modernist town hall was designed by Tony Garnier in 1934. Next door, the **Musée des Années 30** focuses on artists and architects who lived in the town at that time.

Just across the Seine is **St-Cloud**, site of a château that burnt down in the Franco-Prussian war. There remains a marvellous park overlooking the river (*see chapter* **Parks**) and in prosper-

Corporate high-rises cluster in **La Défense.**

ous St-Cloud and neighbouring Garches, streets of often romantic villas. South of St-Cloud is Sèvres, site of the famous porcelain factory, now the **Musée National de Céramique**. Although an avenue of lime trees points to the demolished château of the Ducs de Guise, **Meudon** is often associated with sculptors, including Rodin, whose Villa des Brillants is now a museum, and abstract sculptor Jean Arp, whose house and studio was designed by his wife Sophie Taeuber-Arp.

The **Château de Malmaison** at Rueil-Malmaison was a favourite residence of Napoléon and Josephine, who transformed its interior in Empire style. The eccentric **Château de Monte**

Cristo (01.30.61.61.35) at Port Marly was built for Alexandre Dumas with a tiled Moorish room. In the grounds, the strange Château d'If is inscribed with the titles of his numerous works.

The town of **St-Germain-en-Laye** is a smart commuter suburb, with a historic centre dominated by the forbidding château, upmarket shops and the **Musée Départemental Maurice Denis**, home of the Nabi painter. Henri II lived in the château, with his wife Catherine de Médicis and his mistress Diane de Poitiers, and Louis XIV was born here. Mary Queen of Scots grew up here, and the dethroned James II lived here from 1689 until his death in 1701. It was restored by Napoléon III, who turned it into the **Musée des Antiquités Nationales**. The château overlooks the Grande Terrasse, laid out by Le Nôtre, on the edge of a huge forest.

La Défense

Paris' mini-Manhattan is only a hop, skip and a jump from central Paris, but as you emerge from the depths of the RER, its giant skyscrapers and walkways feel like a different world. Even if somewhat cold and anonymous, it is surprisingly lively: overwhelmingly businessy during the week, filled with visitors and shoppers on the weekends.

La Défense (named after a stand against the Prussians in the 1870 Franco-Prusian war) has been a showcase for French business since the mid-50s, when the triangular **CNIT** exhibition hall (01.46.92.11.11/open 9am-6pm daily) was built for trade shows. It was a landmark in its day, and still has the largest concrete vault in the world (a 230-metre span). Successive governments developed the idea of giving Paris a new, separate district for modern business, and it soon proved popular with big corporations such as Elf, Gan and Fiat.

Today, over 100,000 people work on this reservation, and another 35,000 dwell in the futuristic blocks of flats on the southern edge. None of the skyscrapers display any great architectural distinction, although together they make an impressive sight. Jean Nouvel's plans for La Tour Sans Fin, a never-ending skyscraper destined to merge into the clouds, remain on the drawing board.

The **Grande Arche de la Défense**, completed for the bicentenary of the Revolution in 1989, is now a major tourist attraction with a superb view from the top. Outside on the giant forecourt are fountains and sculptures by artists including Miró, Serra, Calder and César's *Thumb*. Even more fun are the kitsch computer-controlled fountains and Takis' flashing light poles. The **Info-Défense** kiosk (01.47.74.84.24/open 9.30am-1pm, 2-5.30pm Mon-Fri) in front of CNIT has maps and guides of the area.

La Grande Arche de la Défense

92400 Paris la Défense (01.49.07.27.57). M° La Défense. **Open** 10am-7pm daily (last ride to the rooftop at 6pm). **Admission** 40F; 32F under-18s, students. CM. **Credit** AmEx, MC, V.

Planned to complete the axis of the Champs-Elysées and the Arc de Triomphe – and then skewed at a slight angle – the Grande Arche is simultaneously one of the most pointless and most successful of the *Grands Projets* and catapulted obscure Danish architect Johan Otto von Spreckelsen to fame. Only from close up do you realise how vast the structure is. A stomach-churning ride in high-speed glass lifts soars up through the 'clouds' to the roof where there is a bird's eye view into Paris and out to the city's western reaches.

St-Denis & the North

The suburbs north and east of Paris were the first to be industrialised, from the 1860s onwards, and they remain the grimmest parts of the greater Paris region. In the 1950s, huge estates of tower blocks were built swiftly on cheap industrial land to meet the post-war housing crisis and accommodate newly arrived immigrant labour. Most famous is Sarcelles, long a symbol of urban misery.

In amongst this suburban sprawl, at the heart of the old town of **St-Denis**, stands one of the treasures of Gothic architecture: the **Basilique St-Denis**, where most of France's monarchs were buried. St Denis also boasts the innovative **Musée de l'Art et d'Histoire de St-Denis** in the scrupulously preserved buildings of a Carmelite convent founded in 1625, a busy covered market, some fine contemporary buildings, such as Niemeyer's 1989 headquarters for Communist newspaper *L'Humanité* and Gaudin's extension to the town hall, and a gleaming new tramway. Across the canal is the elegant new **Stade de France** football stadium, with flying-saucer-like roof, designed for the 1998 World Cup. The *département* of Seine St Denis also has a lively cultural scene, notably the Théâtre Gérard Philipe at St-Denis and MC93 at Bobigny, and hosts prestigious jazz and classical music festivals, while the Parc de la Corneuve hosts the annual Fête de l'Humanité in September. **Le Bourget**, home to Paris' first airport (still used for VIP and private aircraft) contains the brilliant **Musée de l'Air et de l'Espace**.

North of Sarcelles, **Ecouen**, noted for its Renaissance château, now the **Musée National de la Renaissance**, gives glimpses of a rural past. **Enghien-les-Bains**, set around a large lake where you can hire rowing boats and pedalos, provided a pleasure haven last century with the development of its spa as a cure for ulcers, a casino (still the only one in the Paris region) and a racecourse.

Basilique St-Denis

2 rue de Strasbourg, 93200 St-Denis (01.48.09.83.54). M° St-Denis-Basilique. **Open** *Apr-Sept* 10am-7pm Mon-Sat; noon-7pm Sun. *Oct-Mar* 10am-5pm Mon-Sat; noon-5pm Sun. **Admission** *nave* free. *Royal tombs* 32F; 21F 12-25s, students; free under-12s. **Guided tours** 11.15am, 3pm daily (25F audio guide in English). **No credit cards.** Legend has it that when St-Denis was beheaded, he picked up his head and, accompanied by a choir of angels, walked to Vicus Catulliacus (now St-Denis), where he wished to be buried. The first church on this site was built over his tomb in around 475. The present edifice is regarded as the first

La Grande Arche de La Défense; *not much use but difficult to miss.*

example of true Gothic architecture. The basilica was begun by Abbot Suger in the twelfth century; in the middle of the following century master mason Pierre de Montreuil erected the spire and rebuilt the choir, nave and transept, with elaborate rose windows. This was the burial place for all French monarchs between 996 and the end of the *ancien régime* (apart from three), so the ambulatory amounts to a veritable museum of French funerary sculpture. The basilica was badly damaged during the Revolution in 1792 when the tombs were desecrated and the royal remains thrown into a communal pit nearby. Part of the fifth-century Merovingian church can be seen in the crypt.

Cimetière des Chiens

4 pont de Clichy, 92600 Asnières (01.40.86.21.11). *M° Mairie de Clichy.* **Open** *Apr-Oct* 10am-6pm Mon, Wed-Sun; *Nov-Mar* 10am-5pm, Mon, Wed-Sun. **Admission** 16F; 8F 6-12s. **No credit cards.**
Paris has 200,000 dogs and some of them, along with many cats, a horse and a monkey, end up here on a slightly forlorn island in the Seine. A decaying neo-Byzantine entrance points to a grander past: just within lies a grand monument, a small girl draped over a large dog: Barry the St Bernard 'who saved the lives of 40 people. He was killed by the 41st.' Here we are in a poignant otherworld of Trixies, Oscars and much-missed Fidos, redolent of beloved animals and lonely lives. There is even room for 'the errant dog', who one summer day in 1958 died at the gates of the cemetery and was the 40,000th beast to be buried here.

Eglise Notre Dame du Raincy

av de la Résistance, 93340 Le Raincy (01.43.81.14.98). *SNCF Raincy-Villemomble.* **Open** 8.30am-6pm daily.
This little-known Modernist masterpiece by Auguste Perret was built 1922-23 as a low-budget war memorial. Its structure is of brick and concrete, with impressively simple interior traversed by simple ribbed concrete columns; even the altar is of reinforced concrete. In place of conventional stained glass, the windows designed by Maurice Denis are coloured glass blocks that create fantastic reflections on the interior.

Stade de France

rue Francis de Pressensé, 93200 St-Denis (01.55.93.00.45). M° St Denis Porte de Paris/RER B La Plaine Stade de France/RER D Stade de France St Denis. **Open** 10am-5.30pm daily (except during events). **Admission** 35F; 28F 6-17s, students; free under 6s. *Coulisses du Stade* (10am, 2pm, 4pm) 90F; 65F 6-17s, students; free under 6s (reserve for visits in English). **Credit** MC, V.
The flying-saucer Stade de France landed on the edge of Paris just in time for the 1998 football World Cup. Architects Zubléna, Macary, Regembal and Constantini pipped Jean Nouvel to the post in a controversial competition and the stadium was put up in record time (31 months). It has quickly become a landmark with its spectacular steel and aluminium oval roof suspended from masts, with a great view from the A1 when floodlit by night. The modulable design means the Stade can be adapted for various sports and festivities, seating 76,000 for athletics, 80,000 for soccer and rugby matches and over 100,000 for rock concerts. The 90-minute guided visit takes in the stands and VIP box, changing rooms and entry tunnel – be prepared to climb 200 steps.

Vincennes & the East

The more upmarket residential districts in the east surround the Bois de Vincennes, such as **Vincennes**, dominated by its imposing medieval castle and home to Paris' main zoo. Riverside **Joinville-le-Pont**, once famed for its rowing clubs and for movie studios where Marcel Carné shot *Les Enfants du Paradis*, and neighbour **Champigny-sur-Marne** draw Parisians at weekends for the footpaths along the banks of the Marne and *guinguette* dance halls like **Chez Gégène** or hipper **La Guinguette de l'Ile du Martin-Pêcheur** on its own little island.

In Champigny-sur-Marne, the Musée de la Résistance Nationale (88 av Marx-Dormoy/01.48.81.00.80) tells the history of the French Résistance. Look out for two architectural curiosities: the surving Baltard pavilion from Les Halles at **Nogent-sur-Marne** and Chinagora, a mock pagoda which has recently gone bust but whose green glazed tiles still stand out in Alfortville. Further out, Créteil, a planned new town, was built in the 1960s around a man-made lake.

Château de Vincennes
av de Paris, 94300 Vincennes (visits 01.48.08.31.20). M° Château de Vincennes. **Open** Nov-Mar 10am-5pm daily; Apr-Oct 10am-6pm daily. **Admission** 32F; 25F (Ste-Chapelle only). **No credit cards.**
An imposing curtain wall punctuated by towers encloses this medieval fortress, still home to a French garrison. Few traces remain of Louis VII's first hunting lodge, or the fortified manor built by Philippe-Auguste. The square keep was begun by Philippe VI and completed by defence-obsessed Charles V, who also added the curtain wall and began rebuilding the pretty Flamboyant Gothic Ste-Chapelle (open on guided visits). The keep (closed for restoration) originally housed elaborate royal apartments and is where Henry V of England died in 1422. Louis XIII used the château for a hunting lodge and had the Pavillon du Roi and Pavillon de la Reine built by Louis Le Vau (completed 1658). Both were sumptuously decorated, but along with the rest of the castle were transformed into barracks in the nineteenth century.

Pavillon Baltard
12 av Victor Hugo, 94130 Nogent-sur-Marne (01.48.73.45.81). RER Nogent-sur-Marne. **Open** during salons/exhibitions only.
In the 1970s when Les Halles were demolished someone had the foresight to save one of Baltard's iron and glass market pavilions (No 8: the egg and poultry shed), and resurrect it in 1977 in the Paris suburbs. Since augmented by the grandiose organ built in 1930 for the Gaumont Palace cinema, the pavilion is used for salons, concerts and exhibitions.

Sceaux & the South

Interwar and post-war urbanisation transformed this area as former villages – like Sceaux, Antony and Vanves – and a ring of defensive fortresses – Forts d'Issy, Vanves, Montrouge, Bicêtre and d'Ivry – metamorphosed from a past of vineyards, agriculture and aristocratic residences to areas of workers' housing. Bordering Paris, the 'red' (left wing) suburb of Malakoff is home to numerous artists. Leafy **Sceaux** was formerly the setting for a sumptuous château built in the seventeenth century for Louis XIV's finance minister Colbert. The present building housing the Musée de l'Ile de France (01.46.61.06.71) dates from 1856 but the park with its Grand Canal and waterfalls more or less follows Le Nôtre's original design. Nearby at **Châtenay-Malabry**, the 1930s Cité de la Butte-Rouge garden-city estate was a model of its time for social housing. Writer Chateaubriand, forced to leave Paris for his criticism of Napoléon, lived in a pretty villa in the romantically named Vallée-aux-Loups (*see chapter* **Museums**), where the spectacularly landscaped park is evidence of his passion for gardening.

The south-eastern suburbs boomed during nineteenth century industrialisation, witness **Ivry-sur-Seine** with its warehouses and the Manufacture des Oeillets, a former rivet factory that is now a theatre and art gallery. The picturesque windmill (place du 8 mai 1845) testifies to an agricultural past – but Ivry is today known for its enlightened social policies, in housing projects like L'Atelier built in the 70s with a multiplicity of levels and roof gardens.

The bleak new town of **Evry**, 30km south of Paris, was created in 1969. It is of note for then-radical housing projects like Les Pyramides and the modern **Cathédrale de la Résurrection**.

Aqueducs d'Arcueil
Spanning the Bièvre valley through Arcueil and Clamart is the impressive double-decker structure that brings water from Wissous to Paris, along the same route as in Roman times. The first aqueduct, built in the second or third century AD, existed a few metres from this one. In 1609 Henri IV decided to reconstruct the Roman aqueduct, a project continued by his widow Marie de Médicis. By 1628 the aqueduct provided water through fourteen fountains on the Left Bank and two on the Right Bank.

Cathédrale de la Résurrection
1 clos de la Cathédrale, 91000 Evry (01.64.97.93.53). SNCF Evry-Courcouronnes. **Open** 10am-1pm, 2-6pm Mon-Fri; 10am-noon, 2-6pm Sat; 2.30-6.15pm Sun.
Completed in 1995, this was the first new cathedral built in France since the war, and aims to give a new aesthetic to religious architecture, in Swiss architect Mario Botta's rather heavy, truncated, red-brick cylindrical form.

The tramway is desirable in **St-Denis**.

Parks

From historic terraces and sculpture shows to postmodern prairies and herb gardens, Paris parks provide a sensory feast.

Paris is not often thought of as a green city, yet its parks have gone through several waves of conscious planning. Le Nôtre set the way with the **Tuileries** in the seventeenth century. During the Second Empire, Haussmann with typical energy set out to 'ventilate' the city and spruced up the royal hunting forests of **Bois de Boulogne** and **Bois de Vincennes**, redesigned **Parc Monceau** and created the **Parcs Montsouris** and **Buttes-Chaumont**. The socially aware 1930s saw a wave of small squares and gardens for the people, such as Square Willette (18th), Square René Le Gall (13th) and Butte du Chapeau Rouge (19th), while over the past two decades, an unprecedented spate of garden building has seen derelict industrial sites and even aerial spaces turned into new public parks. Over the centuries, the informal *jardin à l'anglaise* has vied for popularity with the paths and terraces of Le Nôtre's *jardin à la française* in the **Tuileries**. Today's adventurous new gardens, like the **Parc André Citroën**, use both traditions in a contemporary reinterpretation. Other gardens lurk behind palatial *hôtels particuliers* or within courtyards; among them, the **Musée Rodin** and the **Hôtel de Sens** can be visited today.

Most parks are open daily from early morning until dusk (often until 8 or 9pm in summer, 4 or 5pm in Dec).The Mairie de Paris publishes a brochure of guided visits to Paris gardens (in French), available from the Service des Visites, 3 av de la Porte d'Auteuil, 16th/01.40.71.75.23. The famous keep-off-the-grass rules have been abolished in most of the city parks, except in the Tuileries, Luxembourg, Palais-Royal and Parc Monceau.

Classic Parks

Jardin des Tuileries
rue de Rivoli, 1st. M° Tuileries or Concorde. **Map G5**
Stretching between the Louvre and place de la Concorde, the gravelled alleyways here have been a fashionable promenade since they opened to the public in the sixteenth century. The gardens were laid out in roughly their present form by André Le Nôtre, who began his illustrious career as royal gardener here in 1664, before going on to such exalted commissions as **Versailles** and **Vaux-le-Vicomte**, creating the prototypical *jardin à la française* with its terraces and central vista running through round and octagonal ponds, and continuing along what would become the Champs-Elysées; when the Tuileries palace was burnt down by the Paris Commune in 1871, the park was expanded. As part of the *Grand Louvre* project, the most fragile sculptures, including Coysevox's winged horses, have been transferred to the Louvre and

*An a-maze-ing view in the **Jardin des Plantes**.*

replaced by copies, the Maillol sculptures have returned to the Jardin du Carrousel (nearest to the Louvre), while replanting has restored parts of Le Nôtre's design and renewed trees damaged by pollution. Today, the Tuileries still have a pleasure-garden feel, with pony rides, *boules* players, cafés, ice cream kiosks and a big funfair in summer. Several modern sculptures have just been added to develop a 'living museum', including bronzes by Laurens, Moore, Ernst, Martin and Giacommetti and Dubuffet's *Le Bel Costumé*. Works by Picasso and Calder are to follow, along with pieces commissioned from contemporary sculptors. Gardeners should note the specialist bookshop by place de la Concorde.

Jardin des Plantes
pl Valhubert, rue Buffon or rue Cuvier, 5th (01.40.79.30.00). M° Gare d'Austerlitz or Jussieu. **Map L8**
Although small and slightly run-down, the Jardin des Plantes contains over 10,000 species of plants, including winter and Alpine gardens and tropical greenhouses (open selected days and hours). Originally planted by Louis XIII's doctor as the royal medicinal plant garden in 1626, the Jardin opened to the public in 1640. It contains a small zoo and the **Muséum National d'Histoire Naturelle**, of which the magnificent Grande Galerie de l'Evolution sits like a palace at the end of formal beds. Behind, an eighteenth-century yew maze,

designed by botanist Buffon, spirals up a little hill to an iron gazebo. Several ancient trees include a cedar planted in 1734.

Jardins du Luxembourg

pl Auguste-Comte, pl Edmond-Rostand or rue de Vaugirard, 6th. M° Odéon/RER Luxembourg. **Map H8**
Part formal garden with terraces and gravel paths, part 'English garden' of lawns and part amusement centre for gardenless Parisians, the Jardins du Luxembourg are the quintessential Paris park. The gardens were created for Marie de Médicis at the same time as the **Palais du Luxembourg**, but were much reworked by Chalgrin last century. Dotted around the park is a veritable gallery of French sculpture from the looming Cyclops on the 1624 Fontaine de Médicis, to wild animals, queens of France, a mini *Statue of Liberty* and a monument to Delacroix. There are orchards, with over 300 varieties of apples, and an apiary where you can take courses in beekeeping. Even if you're not into greenery, the Luxembourg is a must for those with an interest in social anthropology. You can watch chessplayers, joggers and martial arts practictioners. Children enjoy pony rides, sandpits and roundabouts, and sail toy boats; there are tennis courts, *boules* pitches, a café and bandstand, while the green park chairs are beloved of booklovers and *dragueurs*.

Parc Montsouris

bd Jourdan, 14th. RER Cité-Universitaire.
One of Haussmann's parks on the southern edge of the city, with obligatory lake and artificial cascades. Its gently sloping lawns descend towards a lake, with turtles and ducks, and the variety of bushes, trees and flowerbeds make it the most colourful of the capital's parks. Spot the bed planted with different roses for French newspapers and magazines.

Les Serres d'Auteuil

3 av de la Porte d'Auteuil, 16th (01.40.71.75.23). M° Porte d'Auteuil. **Open** 10am-5pm daily. **Admission** 5F; 2.50F 6-18 years; free over-60s, under-6s. **No credit cards.**
These wonderfully romantic glasshouses were opened in 1895 to cultivate plants for parks and public spaces across Paris. Today there are seasonal displays of orchids and begonias. Best of all is the steamy tropical central pavilion with palm trees, birds and a pool of Japanese ornamental carp.

Parc Monceau

bd de Courcelles, 17th. M° Monceau. **Map E2**
Surrounded by grand *hôtels particuliers*, Monceau is a favourite with well-dressed *BCBG* children and their nannies. It was laid out in the late eighteenth century for the Duc de Chartres (Philippe-Egalité) in the English style that was then fashionable, with an oval lake, spacious lawns and a variety of follies: an Egyptian pyramid, a Corinthian colonnade, Venetian bridge and ancient tombs. At the main entrance is one of the tax pavilions constructed by Ledoux.

Parc des Buttes-Chaumont

rue Botzaris, rue Manin, rue de Crimée, 19th. M° Buttes-Chaumont. **Map N3**
This fantasy wonderland is the perfect, picturesque meeting of nature and the artificial, with meandering paths and vertiginous cliffs. It was designed for Haussmann in the 1860s on the site of a gypsum quarry, rubbish tip and sinister public gibbet. Waterfalls cascade out of a man-made cave, complete with fake stalactites, while out of the artificial lake rises a 50m-high rock reached by an impressive suspension bridge. Climb up to the little classical gazebo, modelled on the Temple of the Sibyl at Tivoli, from where there are superb views of Sacré-Coeur and the surrounding area.

Beyond the Périphérique

Les Jardins Albert Kahn

14 rue du Port, 92100 Boulogne (01.46.04.52.80). M° Boulogne-Pont St Cloud. **Open** *May-Sept* 11am-7pm

Tue-Sun; *Oct-Apr* 11am-6pm Tue-Sun. **Admission** 22F; 15F students, over-60s; free under-8s. **No credit cards.**
Painted red bridges, coloured maples, bamboos, Japanese shrines, cascading streams and geometric landscaping – yet somehow never twee. Instead there's an enormous variety of habitats, species and moods crammed in a small space. The famed Japanese garden precedes a quadrangle of roses and fruit trees, then leads via the Blue Forest – where misty spruces and tall cedars cast an undeniably blue haze – via marshy Marais to the boulders, ferns and pines of the Vosgeian forest, like a lump of Alsace transplanted. Water and evergreens dominate the gardens, making them interesting even in winter.

Parc de St-Cloud

St-Cloud (01.41.12.02.90). M° Pont de Sèvres and cross river. **Open** *Mar-Oct* 7.30am-9pm (until 10pm *May-Aug*); *Nov-Feb* 7.30am-8pm. **Admission** free; 20F for cars. **No credit cards.**
This is a rare park where you can play football or frisbee, walk or picnic on the grass, cycle or hire a peddle car. Yet this is another classic French park laid out by Le Nôtre, and all that remains of a royal château that belonged to 'Monsieur', brother of Louis XIV. It was destroyed by fire in 1870, three months after the Franco-Prussian war was declared in the château. There are complex avenues that meet in stairs, long perspectives, stepped terraces, a great view over Paris from the Rond-Point du Balustrade and a series of pools and fountains: most spectacular is the Grande Cascade, a multi-tiered feast of dolphins and sea beasts, switched on at 4pm on the second and fourth Sundays of the month from May to September.

Into the Twenty-First Century

These adventurous futuristic parks may occasionally allow you to walk on the grass, but don't ever forget their intellectual flavour.

Parc de Bercy

rue de Bercy, 12th. M° Bercy. **Map N9**
On the site of the Bercy warehouses across the river from the new national library, Bercy combines French love of geometry with that of food. There's a large lawn crossed by paths with trees and pergolas, and a grid with square rose, herb and vegetable plots, an orchard, and gardens representing the four seasons. Brick paths with iron wagon tracks have been preserved, to guard the memory of barrels wheeled in from boats on the Seine, as have some century-old trees. The adjacent American Center (currently closed), designed by Frank Gehry, is due to become the Maison du Cinéma.

La Promenade Plantée

av Daumesnil, 12th. M° Bastille, Ledru-Rollin, Gare de Lyon or Daumesnil. **Map M/N8**
There's life above art as the railway tracks atop the **Viaduc des Arts** have been replaced by a promenade planted with roses, shrubs and clumps of rosemary. The walk offers great high-level views into neighbouring apartments. It continues through the Jardin de Reuilly and the Jardin Charles Péguy on to the **Bois de Vincennes** at the Porte Dorée in the east. Rollerbladers are banned but no one seems to have noticed.

Jardin de l'Atlantique

entry from Gare Montparnasse or pl des Cinq-Martyrs-du-Lycée-Buffon, 15th. M° Montparnasse-Bienvenüe. **Map G9**
Perhaps the hardest of all to find, the Jardin de l'Atlantique, opened in 1995, takes the Parisian quest for space airbound with an engineering feat suspended 18 metres over the railway tracks of Montparnasse station. It provides a small oasis of granite paths, trees and bamboo in an urban desert enclosed by modern apartment and office blocks. There's an interesting sculptural thermometer and small openings allowing you to peer down on the TGVs below.

Anticipating the computerised water jets has become a local sport at **Parc André Citroën**.

Parc André Citroën

*rue Balard, rue St-Charles, quai Citroën, 15th. M° Javel
or Balard.* **Map A9**
Laid out in 1993 on the site of the Citroën car factory, this is
the twenty-first-century equivalent of a French formal garden,
comprising two large glasshouses, computerised fountains,
waterfalls, black and white gardens, a wilderness and a series
of small glasshouses and gardens planted with different-
coloured plants and even sounds. What at first seems cold
merits exploration for modern-day Le Nôtres (Gilles Clément
and Alain Prévost) have been at play: stepping stones and
water jets prove that this is a garden for pleasure as well as
philosophy. The park will eventually extend to the Seine.

Parc Georges Brassens

rue des Morillons, 15th. M° Porte de Vanves. **Map D10**
Built on the site of the former Abbatoirs de Vaugirard, Parc
Georges Brassens prefigured the industrial recuperation of
André Citroën and La Villette. The old gateways crowned by
bronze bulls have been kept, as have a series of iron meat market pavilions, which house a busy second-hand book market
at weekends. The interesting Jardin des Senteurs is planted
with aromatic species, while on one side, the vineyard produces around 200 bottles of Clos des Morillons every year.

Parc de la Villette

*av Corentin-Cariou, 19th. M° Porte de la Villette. or av
Jean-Jaurès, 19th. M° Porte de Pantin.* **Map inset**
Dotted with the quirky, bright-red pavilions or *folies*
designed by Swiss architect Bernard Tschumi, the Parc de
la Villette is a postmodern feast between the Cité des Sciences
et de l'Industrie in the north and the Cité de la Musique in
the south, all on the site of former abattoirs. The design may
have originated from a complicated deconstructionist theory of points, lines and surfaces, but the result is fun. The
folies serve as glorious climbing frames in addition to such
uses as first-aid post, burger bar and children's art centre.
Kiddies shoot down a Chinese dragon slide and a meandering suspended path follows the Canal de l'Ourcq that bisects
the park. As well as big lawns or *prairies*, there are ten

themed gardens with evocative names such as the Garden
of Mirrors, of Mists, of Acrobatics and of Childhood Fears.

The Woods

Bois de Vincennes

12th. M° Porte-Dorée or Château de Vincennes.
East of the city is Paris' biggest park. Formerly the royal
forest of the Valois, it was made into a park in 1860 by
Napoléon III, and owes much to Haussmann's landscape
architect Alphand, who added the lake and cascades that are
a major part of its charm. Boats can be hired on the lake, and
there are various cycle paths, a Buddhist temple, a racetrack,
baseball pitch and flower gardens. It also contains Paris'
main **Zoo** and the **Cartoucherie** theatre. Next to the park
is the imposing **Château de Vincennes**, where England's
Henry V died in 1422. The **Parc Floral de Paris** (esplanade
du Château, 12th/01.43.43.92.95) boasts horticultural displays, summer concerts, a picnic area, exhibition space, children's amusements and crazy golf.

Bois de Boulogne

16th. M° Porte-Dauphine or Les Sablons.
Covering over 865 hectares, the Bois, a series of gardens
within sometimes scrubby woodland, had its origins as the
ancient hunting Forêt de Rouvray and was landscaped in the
1860s when grottoes and cascades were created around the
Lac Inférieur, where you can hire rowing boats in summer.
Within the Bois, the Jardins de Bagatelle (route de Sèvres à
Neuilly, 16th/01.40.67.97.00. open 9am-5.30pm), surrounding
a château that formerly belonged to Richard Wallace, the
Marquis of Hertford, are famous for their roses, spring daf-
fodils and water lilies. The **Jardin d'Acclimatation** is an
amusement park for kids. The Bois also has two racecourses (Longchamp and Auteuil), restaurants, 140,000 trees and
tracks and paths for horse riders and cyclists. Packed at
weekends with dog walkers, picnickers and sports enthusiasts, at night it's more seedy, and despite clean-up attempts
is still associated with kerb-crawling.

FONDATION CLAUDE MONET
GIVERNY

Visit Claude Monet's House, Gardens and Studio

The foundation is open daily from 10am - 6pm
from April 1st to Oct 31st.
closed Mon. except April 5th (Easter) & May 24th 1999 (Whit).

**Train 1 hr to Vernon from Paris Gare St. Lazare
Giverny , 27620. Tel: 02.32.51.28.21 Fax: 02.32.51.54.18**

Museums & Galleries

Museums

Swot up on art history, local history, medical gore and the latest contemporary creations in Paris' rich array of exhibits.

As well as world-famous mega collections of the fine and decorative arts, and a whole clutch of museums dealing with the city's artistic and literary greats and less greats (often in the houses where they lived), there are museums here for the most demanding specialist. Paris boasts at least four museums of medicine and medical history, not to mention collections of fans, glasses, radios, locks and criminal evidence, and science and transport displays which remind us that France is the birthplace of Ariane as much as of Poussin.

Action continues on the museum front. The mammoth **Louvre** rehang has virtually finished, but the *Grand Louvre* project continues to unfold at the **Musée de la Publicité** and **Musée des Arts Décoratifs**. The **Orangerie** is also due for a revamp, the long-awaited **Musée d'Art et d'Histoire du Judaïsme** has finally opened in its grand Marais home, while in the much longer term Chirac's grand scheme for a Musée des Arts et des Civilisations (the politically correct expression for 'tribal art') has resurfaced, and an architectural contest has been launched for a new museum on the quai Branly. Exhibitions for 1999 include Daumier and Chardin at the **Grand Palais**, Burne-Jones at the

Musée d'Orsay, Robert Delaunay at the **Centre Pompidou**, part of a Moroccan season at the **Petit Palais**, and a celebration of the bicentenary of Balzac's birth at the **Maison de Balzac**.

Note that most museums are closed on Monday or Tuesday. To avoid queues, try to visit major museums and exhibitions during the week, especially at lunch time or evening; reduced rates on Sundays often generate big crowds. Guided tours in English tend to be available only in the larger museums (*see chapter* **Directory** for guided tours

in English that sometimes include museums). There are reduced admission charges for certain categories of people (pensioners, students), but make sure you have an identity card or a passport proving your status. Most ticket counters close 30-45 minutes before closing time. Note that pre-booking is now often possible – and sometimes essential – for major shows at the Grand Palais. It's also possible to prebook tickets for the Louvre.

Paris Carte Musées et Monuments (CM)

Price one day 80F, three days 160F, five days 240F.
This card gives free entry into 70 museums and monuments all around Paris (indicated below by CM), and allows you to jump queues. It's very good value if you're in Paris for a few days and plan on intensive museum visiting, although you have to pay extra for special exhibitions. It can be bought at museums, monuments, tourist offices, branches of Fnac and principal Métro and RER stations.

Fine Art

Centre Pompidou – Musée National d'Art Moderne

rue Beaubourg, 4th (01.44.78.12.33). Mº Hôtel-de-Ville or Rambuteau/RER Châtelet-Les Halles. **Open** *temporary exhibitions only; museum reopens 1 Jan 2000.* noon-10pm Mon, Wed-Fri; 10am-10pm Sat, Sun, public holidays. Closed Tue, 1 May. **Admission** *varies.* **Credit** MC, V. **Map K6**

After celebrating its twentieth anniversary in 1997, the high-tech monument closed for a major rearrangement of the interior spaces. In the meantime, some of the 30,000 works of modern and contemporary art in the Musée National d'Art Moderne (including major holdings of Matisse, Picasso, Surrealists, *Nouveaux Réalistes*, Pop Art, Minimalism and Arte Povera, design and architecture) are on loan to other Paris collections and external exhibitions. The museum reopens in 2000 with a slightly enlarged display area. The Galeries Sud remain open for temporary exhibitions including David Hockney (Jan-Apr 1999) and Robert Delaunay (June-Aug 1999) and an exhibition on the theme of time (spring 2000). *See also chapters* **Right Bank** *and* **Architecture**. *Shop. Children's workshops. Wheelchair access.*

Musée d'Art Moderne de la Ville de Paris/ARC

11 av du Président Wilson, 16th (01.53.67.40.00/ recorded information 01.40.70.11.10). M° Iéna or Alma-Marceau. **Open** 10am-5.30pm Tue-Fri; 10am-6.45pm Sat, Sun. *Temporary exhibitions* 10am-6.45pm Tue-Sun. Closed Mon, some public holidays. **Admission** 27F; 14.50F 18-25s; free under-18s, CM. *Temporary exhibitions* varies. *Combined ticket* 45F; 35F students; free under-7s. **Credit** (shop) AmEx, DC, MC, V. **Map D5**
This monumental museum was built as the Electricity Pavilion for the 1937 Exposition Universelle, and Dufy's vast mural *La Fée Electricité* can still be seen in a curved room. Today the building holds the municipal collection of modern art, which is strong on the Cubists, Fauves, the Delaunays, Rouault, Soutine, Modigliani and the Ecole de Paris, with some recently discovered panels from an early version of Matisse's *La Danse*, alongside his later reworking (1932-33). Contemporary artists such as Boltanski, Lavier, Sarkis, Hantaï and Buren are also represented. The museum is particularly reputed for its dynamic exhibition programme, with major names of modern art (from *Die Brücke* to Rothko), while ARC (Animation, Recherche, Confrontation) puts on adventurous contemporary shows, ranging from established names to first museum shows of young artists. Until mid-Sept 1999, 200 works from the Musée National d'Art Moderne (Centre Pompidou) have replaced most of the permanent collection, although *La Fée Electricité* and *La Danse* are still on view. *Bookshop. Café. Concerts. Wheelchair access.*

Musée Cognacq-Jay

Hôtel Donon, 8 rue Elzévir, 3rd (01.40.27.07.21). M° St-Paul. **Open** 10am-5.40pm Tue-Sun. Closed Mon, public holidays. **Admission** 17.50F; 9F 18-25s; free under-18s, over-60s, CM. **No credit cards. Map L6**
This intimate museum in the carefully restored Hôtel Donon houses the collection put together early this century by Ernest Cognacq, founder of La Samaritaine, and his wife Louise Jay. Their tastes stuck mainly to the eighteenth century; although some English (Reynolds, Lawrence, Romney), Dutch and Flemish (Rembrandt, Ruysdael, Rubens) have slipped in, the focus falls on French Rococo artists such as Watteau, Fragonard, Boucher, Greuze and Quentin de la Tour, with a sprinkling of Canalettos and Guardis for good measure. The pictures are displayed in period panelled rooms (some original to the *hôtel*, some rescued from other locations) alongside furniture, ceramics, tapestries and sculpture to give a good impression of how these items would have looked in their original private house context. *Bookshop. Children's workshops.*

Musée Départemental Maurice Denis, 'Le Prieuré'

2bis rue Maurice Denis, 78100 St-Germain-en-Laye (01.39.73.77.87). RER A St-Germain-en-Laye. **Open** 10am-5.30pm Wed-Fri; 10am-6.30pm Sat, Sun. Closed 1 Jan, 1 May, 25 Dec. **Admission** 25F; 15F 12-25s, students, over-60s; free under-12s, CM (35F and 25F during exhibitions). **No credit cards.**
Out in the genteel commuterland of St-Germain-en-Laye, this former royal hospital became home and studio to Nabi painter Maurice Denis in 1915. The remarkable collection, housed in ancient wards and attics, comprises paintings, prints and decorative objects by the Nabis (a group that also included Sérusier, Bonnard, Vuillard, Roussel and Vallotton). There are also paintings by their forerunners Gauguin and the Pont-Aven school, and by Toulouse-Lautrec. The collection is rich in works by Denis, who also painted the frescoes and designed the stained glass in the small chapel. *Bookshop. Wheelchair access.*

Fra Angelico awaiting art worshippers at the Louvre.

Musée Jacquemart-André

158 bd Haussmann, 8th (01.42.89.04.91). M° Miromesnil or St-Philippe-du-Roule. **Open** 10am-6pm daily. **Admission** 47F; 35F 7-17s, students; free under-7s. **Credit** AmEx, MC, V. **Map E3**
The magnificent collection gathered by Edouard André and his wife Nélie Jacquemart is as worth visiting for its illustration of the life of the nineteenth-century *haute bourgeoisie*, as for the paintings and other treasures they unearthed in salerooms or on tours through Europe. André had the magnificent Hôtel André constructed in the 1870s in the newly desirable neighbourhood outlined by Baron Haussmann. On the ground floor are the circular Grand Salon, rooms of tapestries and French furniture, Boucher mythological fantasies, and the library with Dutch paintings including Rembrandt's *The Pilgrims of Emmaus*, smoking room with Moorish stools and English portraits and the magnificent polychrome marble winter garden with double spiral staircase. Up on the

Not to be missed

A wealth of unlikely treasures are tucked away in seemingly minor museums or in the back rooms of the more renowned ones: here's a dozen masterpieces to get you exploring...

● **Camille Claudel's** marble bust of a young girl – sensitivity from Rodin's mistress and pupil (Musée Rodin).

● *The Communal Kitchen* by Ilya Kabakov – an installation that tells you all about communal life in dank Moscow apartments (Musée Maillol).

● *Lady with the Unicorn* – tapestry alive with flowers, rabbits as well as mythical beasts (Musée National du Moyen Age).

● **Louis XIV's Dogs** – portraits of Bonne, Nonne, Pomme, Nonette, Lise, Folie and Mite by Desportes (Musée de la Chasse et de la Nature).

● **Medieval Miniatures** – jewel-like detail in clear contrast to Monet's breadth (Musée Marmottan).

● *Miss O'Murphy's Foot* by Boucher – a sensual study of Louis XV's fifteen-year-old mistress (Musée Carnavalet).

● **Napoléon's Imperial Barge** – dreams of empire (Musée de la Marine).

● **Pasteur's Tomb** – a neo-Byzantine extravagance at the former home of the scientist (Musée Pasteur).

● **Rembrandt's** *Balaam's Ass* – unexpected in a museum mainly devoted to the French eighteenth century (Musée Cognacq-Jay).

● *Salomé* by Gustave Moreau – multiple versions of the Bible's most spoilt brat (Musée Gustave Moreau).

● **World War I field station** – blood and guts medicine vividly presented (Musée du Service de Santé des Armées).

● **Zadkine's** *Woman with a Fan* – 3D Cubism at its best (Musée Zadkine).

Learning to love the Louvre

Although the Louvre first opened to the public in 1793, before the Richelieu wing was even built, President Mitterrand's *Grand Louvre* project doubled the exhibition space and transformed this venerable institution into one of the world's most modern museums. The collections are based around the original royal collections, augmented by revolutionary seizures and later acquisitions. It's important to be selective, as the museum is truly huge, and you could easily spend days or even weeks just gazing at French or Italian painting or Antiquities.

The museum is organised into wings – Richelieu (along rue de Rivoli), Sully (round the Cour Carrée), Denon (along the Seine) – which lead off on three sides from beneath the glass pyramid. Each department is colour coded and labelled, and illustrated signs point to key works, such as the *Mona Lisa* or *Winged Victory of Samothrace*, for those planning on a lightning tour. It's almost impossible not to get lost at some point, so be sure to pick up the useful free orientation leaflet at the entrance.

French Painting
Richelieu, Sully: second floor; Denon: first floor.
A quick survey of French painting begins in the Richelieu and Sully wings, starting with late medieval and Renaissance work, including the striking *Diana the Huntress* by an unknown artist, thought to be an idealised portrait of Diane de Poitiers, and portraits by Clouet. There are landscapes by Claude Lorrain, as well as *The Four Seasons* and other Biblical and mythological canvases by Poussin. Le Nain's peasant scenes and Georges de la Tour's strikingly lit *Les Tricheurs* (card cheats) and *Angel Appearing to St-Joseph* from the 1640s give way to the Rococo frivolity of Watteau, Fragonard and Boucher.

Smaller nineteenth-century works including Ingres' erotic *The Turkish Bath* are also in the Sully wing, while large format paintings are in the Denon wing. Neo-Classicists – David's *Sabine Women* and monumental representation of the coronation of Napoléon in Notre Dame, along with his portraits *Mme Récamier* and *Juliette de Villeneuve*, Ingres' the *Grande Odalisque* and Gros' rendition of Napoléon on campaign – are pitted against Romantics – including Géricault's *Raft of the Medusa* (inspired by a real shipwreck where the survivors resorted to cannibalism) and Delacroix's *Liberty Leading the People*, celebrating the Revolution of 1830 – in the battle of the styles.

French Sculpture
Richelieu: ground floor.
The most dramatic feature of the Richelieu wing are its two magnificent sculpture courts covered by a high-tech glazing system. The Cour Marly gives pride of place to Guillaume Coustou's *Chevaux de Marly* of 1745, two giant naturalistic horses being restrained by grooms in a freeze-frame of rearing struggle, which contrasts with the courtly correctness of the two winged horses opposite, *Fame* and *Mercury*, created by Coysevox, Coustou's uncle, for Louis XIV in 1706. In the Cour Puget, admire the four bronze captives that originally adorned a statue in place des Victoires and Clodion's Rococo frieze. Spacious side rooms are devoted to medieval tomb sculpture, including the remarkable fifteenth-century tomb of Burgundian aristocrat Philippe Pot supported by ominous black-cowled figures, and the original Renaissance reliefs by Jean Goujon for the Fontaine des Innocents in Les Halles, pompous eighteenth-century official portraiture, Neo-Classical mythological subjects and wild animal studies by Barye.

The Mona Lisa is still puzzling the hordes with that enigmatic smile.

Objets d'Art & the Nineteenth Century

Richelieu: first floor, second floor; Sully: first floor.
Highlight is the medieval Treasure of St-Denis. There are also Renaissance enamels, furniture and early clocks, and later decorative art. Napoléon III's opulent apartments have been preserved with chandeliers and upholstery intact.

Italian Painting

Denon: first floor.
Two new rooms of Renaissance frescoes by Botticelli, Fra Angelico and Luini open the fantastic Italian collections, leading the way to Florentine Early Renaissance paintings by, among many, Cimabue, Fra Angelico and Filippo Lippi, and Uccello's *Battle of San Romano* with its caparisoned horses and grid of lances. The Grande Galerie includes Leonardo's *Virgin on the Rocks* and *The Virgin, The Child and St-Anne*, two delectable tiny Raphaels, Mantegna, Ghirlandaio and Perugino, and in a side room of Siennese art, Piero della Francesca. In the Salle des Etats, the *Mona Lisa* in a bulletproof case tends to monopolise attention but in 2001-02 will be given its own small room, leaving space to appreciate Venetian masterpieces, such as Titian's early *Fête Champêtre* and portraits, Tintoretto and Veronese's magisterial *The Marriage at Cana*.

Northern Painting

Richelieu: second floor.
The Dutch, Flemish and German schools have been given new breathing space, although many major works are still tucked away in small rooms or *cabinets*: Bosch's *Ship of Fools*, a Dürer self-portrait, Holbein's *Anne of Cleves*, Rembrandt self-portraits and Vermeer's *Lacemaker* and *The Astronomer*. Rubens' 24 typically bravura canvases commissioned by Marie de Médicis for the Palais du Luxembourg to celebrate her own virtues are displayed in the Galerie Médicis. From the year 2000, three new rooms will hold the eighteenth- and nineteenth-century collections.

Spanish & English Painting

Denon: first floor.
The small collection of English painting (Fusseli, Turner, Lawrence) currently hangs with part of the Spanish collection (Velasquez, Ribera, Goya) but new Spanish galleries, including a Goya room, are due to open in 1999.

Non-French European Sculpture

Denon: lower-ground floor, ground floor.
Michelangelo's *Dying Slave* and *Rebel Slave*, created for the tomb of Pope Julius II in 1513-15, are the best-known works of post-Classical sculpture, but there are also pieces by Donatello, Cellini, Giambologna, Della Robbia, Neo-Classical, Spanish and northern European works.

Greek, Etruscan & Roman Antiquities

Denon: lower-ground and ground floors; Sully: ground and first floors.
Greek treasures include the *Venus de Milo*, the magnificent *Winged Victory of Samothrace* on her ship's prow at the top of the grand staircase and over 2000 painted vases. Massive halls of Roman sculpture and sarcophagi are drawn largely from the Borghèse (*Borghèse Vase* and *Borghèse Gladiator*) and Richelieu collections. The charming Etruscan terracotta sarcophagus of a *Married Couple* depicts a couple reclining at a banquet. There are mosaics from Carthage, Pompeii and Antioch.

Lovelorn Psyche and Cupid *by Canova.*

Egyptian & Oriental Antiquities

Sully: ground and first floors; Denon: lower-ground floor; Richelieu: ground floor.
The huge Egyptian department had its beginnings in Champollion's voyages in Egypt. Arranged thematically on the ground floor, chronologically on the first floor, exhibits include the bust of Amenophis IV (all that remains of a colossal statue), the Giant Sphinx, sarcophagi and a whole room of mummified cats, birds and even fish. The Coptic section, including the church from Baouit, and Roman Egypt section, are in Denon, due to be joined in early 2000 by works from Syria, Palestine, Nubia and Sudan. Anatolian, Iranian and Mesopotamian art is in Richelieu around a magnificent reconstruction of the courtyard of Khorsabad, with breathtaking Assyrian winged bulls.

Islamic Art

Richelieu: lower-ground floor.
The Islamic collections include early glass, Iznik ceramics, Iranian blue and white ware, intricately inlaid metalwork, carpets and funerary stele and pierced screens.

Musée du Louvre

entrance through Pyramid, Cour Napoléon, 1st (01.40.20.50.50/recorded information 01.40.20.51.51/ advance booking 01.49.87.54.54). M° Palais-Royal. **Open** 9am-6pm Mon, Thur-Sun; 9am-9.45pm Wed; . *Temporary exhibitions, Medieval Louvre, bookshop* 10am-9.45pm Mon, Wed-Sun. Closed Tue, some public holidays. **Admission** 45F (until 3pm); 26F (after 3pm & Sun); free under-18s, CM, first Sun of the month. *Temporary exhibitions* varies. **Credit** MC, V. **Map G5**

stairway three newly restored Tiepolo frescoes depict the arrival of Henri III in Venice. Upstairs, what was to have been Nélie's studio (she gave up her brushes on marriage) became their 'Italian museum': a small, exceptional Early Renaissance collection that includes Uccello's exquisite *St George and the Dragon*, virgins by Perugino, Botticelli and Bellini, Mantegna's *Ecce Homo*, a superb Schiavone portrait, a Carpaccio panel and Della Robbia terracottas. The audio-guide (available in English) is extremely informative.
Audio guide. Bookshop. Café (11.30am-5.30pm).
Wheelchair access (by appointment).

Musée Marmottan – Claude Monet

2 rue Louis-Boilly, 16th (01.42.24.07.02). M° La Muette. **Open** 10am-5.30pm Tue-Sun. Closed Mon, 1 May, 25 Dec. **Admission** 40F; 25F 8-25s, over-60s; free under-8s. **Credit** (shop) MC, V.
This museum achieved fame with Michel Monet's bequest of 165 works by his father, including a breathtaking series of late water-lily canvases, displayed in a special basement room. Sit and absorb the intensity of viridian green and electric blue: these exercises in pure colour show Monet at his most daring and closest to abstraction. The collection also contains Monet's *Impression Soleil Levant*, which gave the Impressionist movement its name, and Impressionist canvases by Sisley, Renoir, Pissarro, Caillebotte and Berthe Morisot as well as some by the nineteenth-century Realists. The rest of the collection should not be ignored. There's a room containing the Wildenstein collection of medieval illuminated manuscripts, the recently restored ground- and first-floor salons house smaller Monets, early nineteenth-century gouaches, a curious clock and other fine First Empire furnishings in keeping with the house, much of it adorned with pharaohs' busts, eagles and sphinxes, under the influence of Napoléon's Egyptian campaigns.
Shop. Partial wheelchair access.

Musée de Montparnasse

21 av du Maine, 15th (01.42.22.91.96). M° Montparnasse-Bienvenüe or Falguière. **Open** *during exhibitions* 1-7pm Wed-Sun. **Admission** 20F; 15F 6-16s, students, over-60s; free under-6s. **No credit cards. Map F8.**
This row of ivy-hung studios is a relic of the artists' alleyways that once threaded Montparnasse. The museum opened in May 1998 with paintings by former resident Marie Vassilieff, whose avant-garde Académie Vassilieff dispensed with formal teaching for classes given by the pupils themselves. During World War I she ran a canteen for impoverished artists (a meal for 50c), scene of lively fêtes with Picasso, Braque and Modigliani, and in the 20s was famed for artistic *bals* (Bal Banal, Bal Transmental, etc). There's only a limited permanent collection (consisting largely of archive films and photos), but temporary exhibitions are linked to past and present artists working in the area.

Musée de l'Orangerie

Jardin des Tuileries, 1st (01.42.97.48.16). M° Concorde. **Open** *3 May-4 Aug 1999* 9.45am-5.15pm Mon, Wed-Sun. Closed Tue, public holidays. **Admission** 30F; 20F 18-25s, over-60s, all visitors Sun; free under-18s; CM. **Credit** (shop) MC, V. **Map F5**
Monet's eight huge, late *Nymphéas* (water lilies) *(see also above* **Musée Marmottan***)*, conceived especially for the Orangerie's oval rooms were left by the artist to the nation as a 'spiritual testimony'. Presented to the public in 1927, they still have an extraordinary freshness today and will be the centrepiece of a special exhibition from 3 May to 4 August 1999, after which the museum will close until the end of 2001 for a major overhaul. On reopening the Jean Walter and Paul Guillaume collection of Impressionism and the Ecole de Paris (Soutine, Renoir, Cézanne, Sisley, Picasso, Derain, Matisse, Rousseau, Modigliani) will also go on show again, complemented by furniture and decorative objects.
Guided tours in English. Shop. Wheelchair access.

Musée d'Orsay

1 rue de Bellechasse, 7th (01.40.49.48.14/recorded information 01.45.49.11.11). M° Solférino/RER Musée d'Orsay. **Open** 10am-6pm Tue, Wed, Fri, Sat; 10am-9.45pm Thur; 9am-6pm Sun. Closed Mon, some public holidays. **Admission** 40F; 30F 18-25s, all on Sun; free under-18s; CM. **Credit** (shop) AmEx, MC, V. **Map G6**
Opened in 1986, the Musée d'Orsay fills a Beaux-Arts train station built for the 1900 Grand Exposition, saved from demolition to become Paris' museum devoted to the pivotal years 1848-1914. Milanese architect Gae Aulenti remodelled the interior, inserting postmodern partitions and lift shafts, keeping the iron-framed coffered roof and creating galleries off either side of a light-filled central canyon. Twelve years on, the drawbacks of her conversion have become apparent and some of the materials are looking a little shoddy, but the museum still draws long queues. Much of the problem is that most visitors come to see the famous Impressionists and Post-Impressionists cramped, knee-deep in tourists upstairs, while too much space and prestige are given downstairs to *art pompier* – the languid nudes of Cabanel and Couture or the grandiose history paintings of Meissonier and Chassériau. The museum is planned along a more-or-less chronological route, starting on the ground floor, running up to the upper level and finishing on the middle floor, thus showing both the continuities between the Impressionists and their forerunners, the Realists and the Barbizon School, and making apparent their revolutionary use of light and colour.
The right (Lille side) of the central aisle is dedicated to the Romantics and history painters. Cool portraits by Ingres contrast with the Romantic passion of Delacroix's North African period, and his pupil Chassériau. Further on are examples of early Degas, and melancholy mystical works by the Symbolists Gustave Moreau and Puvis de Chavannes.
The first rooms to the left (Seine side) of the central aisle are given over to the Barbizon landscape painters Corot and Daubigny, and Millet's idealised depictions of rural virtue, including *L'Angélus*. Don't miss the set of clay busts by Daumier caricaturing notables of his time. One room is dedicated to Gustave Courbet, with *The Artist and his Studio* and his monumental *Burial at Ornans*, which seem to form a bridge with the Impressionists. A recent acquisition, his sexually explicit *L'Origine du Monde* still has tremendous power to shock today. This floor also covers pre-1870 works by the Impressionists (Monet, Pissarro, Van Gogh, Manet) and precursor Boudin, several of whom are shown in Fantin-Latour's *Un atelier aux Batignolles*.
Standing out in the central aisle is the work of sculptor Jean-Baptiste Carpeaux, whose faces have an almost rococo sensibility, including his controversial *La Danse*, which shocked nineteenth-century moralists with its naked dancers. A model of the Palais Garnier reveals just how much of the building is taken up by reception rooms and the lavish stairway and how little by the auditorium.
Escalators whisk you upstairs, where you can see masterpieces by Pissarro, Renoir and Caillebotte, Manet's controversial *Déjeuner sur l'Herbe* and wonderful portrait *Berthe Morisot* (a recent aquisition), several of Monet's paintings of Rouen cathedral, in which he explored the changing qualities of light at different times, and depictions of his garden at **Giverny**, and paintings, pastels and sculptures by Degas, whose Japanese-influenced backstage ballet scenes broke all previous rules of composition. The riches continue with the Post-Impressionists. Among the boiling colours and frantic brushstrokes of Van Gogh are his *Church at Auvers* and his last painting *Crows*. There are Cézanne still lifes, Gauguin's Breton and Tahitian periods, recently augmented by the *Self-Portrait with Yellow Christ*, Toulouse-Lautrec's depictions of Montmartre lowlife and the Moulin Rouge, the Pointillists Seurat and Signac, the mystical works of Redon and the primitivist jungle of the Douanier Rousseau.
On the mezzanine are the Nabis painters, Vallotton, Denis, Roussel, Bonnard and Vuillard, treating religious and

No one bothers to get dressed up for the **Musée d'Orsay**'s *sculpture feast.*

domestic scenes in a wonderfully flat, decorative style. Several rooms are given over to the decorative arts with a mouth-watering collection of Art Nouveau and Jugendstil furniture and fine paintings by Munch and Klimt, as well as rooms devoted to architectural drawings and photography. The sculpture terraces include powerful busts by Rodin with his *Gates of Hell* and *Balzac* (also in the Musée Rodin), heads by Rosso and bronzes by Bourdelle and Maillol.

Temporary exhibitions widen the perspective: after Whistler, with Burne-Jones (Mar-June 1999). Finally, visit the ornate reception room of the former station hotel and the museum's Café des Hauteurs. *See also chapter* **Left Bank**. *Audioguide. Bookshop. Café-restaurant. Concerts. Guided tours. Library (by appointment). Wheelchair access.*

Musée du Petit Palais

av Winston-Churchill, 8th (01.42.65.12.73). M° Champs-Elysées-Clemenceau. **Open** 10am-5.40pm Tue-Sun. Closed Mon, some public holidays. **Admission** 27F; 14.50F 18-25s, students; free under-18s, over-60s, CM. *Temporary exhibitions* 45F; 35F 7-25s, students, over-60s; free under-7s. **Credit** (shop) MC, V. **Map E5**

Standing across the road from the Grand Palais *(see below* **Exhibition Centres**), and likewise constructed for the 1900 Grand Exposition, the Petit Palais contains a hotchpotch of collections belonging to the city, including Greek painted vases and Antique sculpture, Chinese porcelain, Beauvais tapestries, French furniture, paintings by Delacroix, Millet, Géricault, Daumier, Courbet, Redon, works by Vuillard and Bonnard, a selection of Impressionists, plus maquettes for public sculpture around Paris. Most visitors come for stylishly presented temporary exhibitions, from Ancient Egypt and Tiepolo in 1998 to Morocco in 1999.

Bookshop. Guided tours. Library. Wheelchair access.

One-Man Shows

Atelier Brancusi

piazza Beaubourg, 4th (01.44.78.12.33). M° Hôtel-de-Ville or Rambuteau/RER Châtelet-Les Halles. **Open** noon-10pm Mon, Wed-Fri; 10am-10pm Sat, Sun. Closed Tue. **Admission** 30F; 20F under-26s; free under-16s. **No credit cards. Map K6**

When Constantin Brancusi died in 1956 he left his studio in the 15th *arrondissement* and all its contents, including sculptures, maquettes, tools, photos, his bed and his wardrobe, to the state. Rebuilt first within the Palais de Tokyo and then in 1977 outside the Centre Pompidou, the studio has since been completely reconstructed as a faithful reproduction of the artist's living and working spaces. His fragile works in wood and plaster, including his celebrated endless columns and streamlined bird forms, show how Brancusi revolutionised sculpture early this century.

Atelier-Musée Henri Bouchard

25 rue de l'Yvette, 16th (01.46.47.63.46). M° Jasmin. **Open** 2-7pm Wed, Sat. Closed last two weeks of Mar, June, Sept and Dec. **Admission** 25F; 15F students, under-26s; free under-7s. **No credit cards.**

This small, dusty museum is housed in the studio where sculptor Henri Bouchard worked from 1924 to his death in 1960. The studio is crammed with works in bronze, plaster, stone and marble in every shape and size, while the entrance hall is used for changing thematic displays. Bouchard is best known for his monumental Apollo at the **Palais de Chaillot** (1937), but the atelier also contains more intimate, realistic works and some expressive clay figures.

Espace Dali Montmartre

11 rue Poulbot, 18th (01.42.64.40.10). M° Anvers or Abbesses. **Open** 10am-6pm daily. **Admission** 35F; 25F 8-25s, students; free under-8s. **Credit** (shop only) AmEx, DC, MC, V. **Map H1**

The black-walled interior, artistically programmed lighting and specially composed soundtrack make it clear that this is a high-marketing presentation of the artist's work. Don't come expecting to see Dali's celebrated Surrealist paintings: the museum concentrates on sculptures (mainly bronzes) from the 70s, at the tacky end of his career. There are also reproductions of his book illustrations – La Fontaine's fables, Freud, de Sade, Dante and *Alice in Wonderland* – where he fully exploited his taste for the fantastic and the sexual. *Shop.*

Fondation Jean Dubuffet

137 rue de Sèvres, 6th (01.47.34.12.63). M° Duroc. **Open** 2-6pm Mon-Fri. Closed Aug, public holidays. **Admission** 25F. **No credit cards. Map E8**

Changing display of drawings and sculptures by the French artist (1901-85), plus maquettes of the monumental architectural sculptures from his *L'Hourloupe* cycle. *Archives (by appointment). Bookshop.*

Musée Bourdelle

16-18 rue Antoine-Bourdelle, 15th (01.49.54.73.73). M° Montparnasse-Bienvenüe or Falguère. **Open** 10am-5.40pm Tue-Sun. Closed Mon, public holidays. **Admission** 17F; 9F students, over-60s (30F and 20F during exhibitions); free under-7s, CM. **No credit cards. Map F8**

An interesting museum devoted to Rodin's pupil, sculptor Antoine Bourdelle, who produced monumental works, like the Modernist relief friezes at the **Théâtre des Champs-Elysées**. Housed around a small garden in a mix of buildings, the museum includes the artist's studio and apartments, a 1950s extension revealing the evolution of Bourdelle's monument to General Alvear in Buenos Aires, and bronzes and maquettes in a new wing by Christian de Portzamparc. Other artists also had studios here, including briefly Chagall. *Bookshop. Children's workshops. Reference library (by appointment). Wheelchair access.*

Musée Delacroix

6 pl Furstenberg, 6th (01.44.41.86.50). M° St-Germain-des-Prés. **Open** 9am-5pm Mon, Wed-Sun. Closed Tue, public holidays. **Admission** 23F; 18F 18-25s, over-60s; free under-18s, CM. **No credit cards. Map H6**

Eugène Delacroix moved to the pretty place Furstenberg in 1857 to be nearer to the **Eglise St-Sulpice** where he was painting murals, and lived here until his death in 1863. The Louvre and the Musée d'Orsay house his major paintings, but the collection displayed in his apartment and the studio he had built in the garden includes small oil paintings (among

them a self-portrait as Hamlet and a portrait of his housekeeper), some free pastel studies of skies and sketches for larger works, and still conserves some of the atmosphere of the studio as it must have been. Other displays relate to his friendships with Baudelaire and George Sand. Recent extension has added a documentation room.

Musée Maillol

59-61 rue de Grenelle, 7th (01.42.22.59.58). M° Rue du Bac. **Open** 11am-6pm Mon, Wed-Sun. Closed Tue. **Admission** 40F; 26F students, over-60s; free under-18s. **Credit** (shop) AmEx, MC, V. **Map G7**

Dina Vierny met sculptor Aristide Maillol (1861-1944) at the age of 15, and for the next ten years was his principal model, idealised in such sculptures as *Spring, Air* and *Harmony*. In 1995 she opened this museum in a carefully restored eighteenth-century *hôtel*, displaying his drawings, pastels, a decorative faïence fountain and wooden cradle, engravings, tapestry panels and his early Nabis-related paintings (a delectable *Jeune Fille au chapeau* noir), as well as numerous sculptures and studies. There are also works by his contemporaries (Vierny also sat for Matisse, Dufy and Bonnard) including Picasso, Rodin, Gauguin, Bonnard, Degas, Cézanne, Matisse and Dufy; some rare Surrealist documents and multiples by Marcel Duchamp and Villon; naïve painters like Camille Bombois and André Bouchart; and works by the Russian artists Vierny has championed from Kandinsky and Poliakoff to Ilya Kabakov, whose installation *The Communal Kitchen* recreates the atmosphere and sounds of a shared Soviet kitchen. Interesting temporary exhibitions have included Basquiat, Valloton and the School of London. *Bookshop. Café. Wheelchair access.*

Musée Gustave Moreau

14 rue de la Rochefoucauld, 9th (01.48.74.38.50). M° Trinité. **Open** 11am-5.15pm Mon, Wed; 10am-12.45pm, 2-5.15pm Thur-Sun. Closed Tue, public holidays. **Admission** 22F; 15F students, over-60s; free under-18s, CM. **Credit** MC, V. **Map G3**

Most eccentric of all the one-man museums, this is not only where Symbolist painter Gustave Moreau (1825-98) lived, worked and taught, but was also designated by the artist to become a museum after his death – the first curator was his former pupil Rouault. The enormous double-height studio, with a further storey above reached by an impressive spiral staircase, is crammed wall to wall with Moreau's paintings and there are thousands more of his drawings and watercolours to pull out from shutters on the walls. The museum will transport visitors back into the mystical movement that peaked in the late nineteenth century. Moreau developed a personal mythology, filling his detailed canvases with images of *St John the Baptist, St George*, and lascivious *Salomé*, griffins and unicorns, using jewel-like colours that, like those of the Pre-Raphaelites, owed much to the rediscovery of the early Italian masters. Don't miss the small private apartment where he lived with his parents. *Bookshop. Library (by appointment).*

Musée National Hébert

85 rue du Cherche-Midi, 6th (01.42.22.23.82). M° St-Placide or Vaneau. **Open** 12.30-5.30pm Mon, Wed-Fri; 2-5.30pm Sat, Sun and public holidays. Closed Tue, 1 Jan, 1 May, 25 Dec. **Admission** 16F; 12F 18-25s; free under-18s, CM. **No credit cards. Map F7**

Now largely forgotten, Ernest Hébert (1817-1908) was a painter of Italian landscapes and figurative subjects, who bent to the fashion of the time with pious portraits and depictions of sentimental shepherdesses during the mid-century, and brightly coloured, Symbolist-influenced muses, Ophelias and Impressionist-tinged ladies towards the end of his career. The endless watercolours and oils are mostly unremarkable, if an interesting testament to nineteenth-century taste – though the run-down house, built in 1743, is strangely appealing.

Musée National Jean-Jacques Henner

43 av de Villiers, 17th (01.47.63.42.73). Mº Malesherbes or Monceau. **Open** 10am-noon, 2-5pm, Tue-Sun. Closed Mon, some public holidays. **Admission** 21F; 15F students under 25; free under-18s, CM. **No credit cards. Map E2**

Henner's nephew bought artist Dubufe's studio in 1920 to house his uncle's work. Very popular in his own day (critic Véron called him 'a nineteenth-century Leonardo'), Henner (1829-1905) today seems less interesting than his Post-Impressionist contemporaries. His sketches, drawings and letters give an insight into his creative process and appeal more than his society portraits, nymphs and naïads.

Musée National Picasso

Hôtel Salé, 5 rue de Thorigny, 3rd (01.42.71.25.21). Mº Chemin-Vert or St-Paul. **Open** 9.30am-5.30pm Mon, Wed-Sun. Closed Tue. **Admission** 30F; 20F 18-25s, all on Sun (38F and 28F during exhibitions); free under-18s, CM. **Credit** (shop) MC, V. **Map L6**

The unparalleled collection of paintings and sculpture by Pablo Picasso (1881-1973) and one of the grandest mansions in the Marais are an unbeatable combination. The collection represents all phases of the master's long and varied career, the nucleus acquired by the French state in lieu of inheritance taxes, including a superb gaunt blue period self-portrait, son *Paolo as Harlequin,* his Cubist and classical phases, surreal *Nude in an Armchair,* plus the boldly drawn and unabashedly ribald pictures he produced in his later years, wonderful beach pictures of the 1920s and 30s and portraits of his favourite models Marie-Thérèse and Dora Maar. The unusual pasted wallpaper collage *Women at their Toilette,* originally intended as a cartoon for a tapestry, gets its own small room. The drawings for the pivotal *Demoiselles d'Avignon* are here, as well as prints and ceramics that demonstrate his versatility. But it is perhaps the sculpture

Convoluted company at **Musée Picasso**.

which stands out above all, from the vast plaster head on the staircase to a girl skipping and a small cat. Look closely at the sculpture of an ape – you'll see that its face is made out of a toy car. Picasso is exceptional for his continual inventiveness and, rare in great art, his sense of humour. Also here is Picasso's collection of tribal art – juxtaposed with the 'primitive' wood figures he carved himself – and paintings, with works by Matisse and Douanier Rousseau.
Audio-visual room. Bookshop. Outdoor café June-Oct. Wheelchair access.

Musée Rodin

Hôtel Biron, 77 rue de Varenne, 7th (01.44.18.61.10). Mº Varenne. **Open** *Apr-Sept* 9.30am-5.45pm Tue-Sun; *Oct-Mar* 9.30am-4.45pm Tue-Sun. Closed Mon, public holidays. **Admission** 28F; 18F 18-25s, all on Sun; free under-18s, art students, CM. *Gardens only* 5F. **Credit** (shop) AmEx, MC, V. **Map F6**

One of Paris's most pleasant museums, the Rodin occupies the stately *hôtel particulier* where Rodin actually lived and sculpted at the end of his life. The famous *Kiss,* the moving *Cathedral,* Rodin's studies of *Balzac* and other pieces of note occupy the rooms indoors, accompanied by several works by Rodin's mistress and pupil Camille Claudel, and paintings by Van Gogh, Monet, Renoir and Rodin himself. In the recently replanted gardens are the moving *Burghers of Calais,* the elaborate *Gates of Hell,* the final proud portrait of *Balzac,* and the eternally absorbed – and absorbing – *Thinker, Orpheus* under a shady stretch of trees, as well as several unfinished nymphs seemingly emerging from the marble. Rodin fans can also visit the Villa des Brillants at Meudon (01.41.14.35.00 Apr-Sept, 1-6pm Fri-Sun), where he worked from 1895, with sculptures, plaster casts and sketches.
Bookshop. Garden café (summer). Partial wheelchair access. Visits for visually handicapped (by appointment).

Musée Zadkine

100bis rue d'Assas, 6th (01.43.26.91.90). Mº Notre Dame des Champs/RER Port Royal. **Open** 10am-5.30pm Tue-Sun. Closed Mon, public holidays. **Admission** 17.50F; 9F students (27F and 19F during exhibitions); free under-18s, CM. **No credit cards. Map G8**

Arresting works by the Russian-born Cubist sculptor Ossip Zadkine are displayed around the garden (his largest sculptures) and over the tiny house he inhabited from 1928 until his death in 1967. Zadkine's compositions include musical, mythological and religious subjects and his style varies with his materials: bronzes tend to be geometrical, wood more sensuous, flowing with the grain. Sculptures and preparatory studies are cleverly displayed on ledges around the rooms at eye-level, along with drawings by Zadkine and some paintings by his wife Valentine Prax. The studio has been converted for temporary exhibitions of contemporary art.
Library (by appointment). Certain works accessible and captioned for the visually handicapped.

Photography

Caisse des Dépôts et Consignations

13 quai Voltaire, 7th (01.40.49.41.66). Mº Rue du Bac. **Open** noon-6.30pm Tue-Sun. Closed public holidays. **Admission** free. **No credit cards. Map G6**

This hugely wealthy quango has substantial collections of contemporary photography. Month-long displays are supplemented by three-day solo shows by contemporary artists, photographers and video-makers that have so far included Bill Viola, Claude Closky and Marie-Ange Guilleminot. *Wheelchair access.*

Centre National de la Photographie

Hôtel Salomon de Rothschild, 11 rue Berryer, 8th (01.53.76.12.32). Mº Charles de Gaulle-Etoile. **Open**

noon-7pm Mon, Wed-Sun. Closed Tue, 1 May, 25 Dec. **Admission** 30F; 15F 10-25s, over-60s; free under-10s. **Credit** MC, V. **Map D3**
Housed on what appears to be a long-term temporary basis in a former Rothschild mansion, the national photography centre under new director Régis Durand has taken a more contemporary line since 1996 and also organises the international Biennial de l'Image (next in 2000). Following major monographic exhibitions by Hannah Collins, Sophie Calle and Thomas Struth, Jean-Marc Bustamente and Tracey Moffat are programed for late 1999, while the Atelier gives space to young artists exploring the new frontiers of photography in installation, video and digital images.

Maison Européenne de la Photographie
5-7 rue de Fourcy, 4th (01.44.78.75.00). M° St-Paul or Pont-Marie. **Open** 11am-8pm Wed-Sun. Closed Mon, Tue, public holidays. **Admission** 30F; 15F students, over-60s; free under-8s, all 5-8pm Wed. **Credit** MC, V. **Map L6**
This new institution in a restored Marais mansion with strikingly minimalist extension by architect Yves Lion has proved hugely successful since opening in 1996. There are usually several shows at once including historic and contemporary photographers, both on loan and from the institution's extensive reserves. Solo shows have included William Klein, Cartier-Bresson, Weegee and Pierre et Gilles. The cellars are used for experimental and multimedia works. Organises the biennial Mois de la Photo.
Auditorium. Café. Library. Wheelchair access.

La Mission du Patrimoine Photographique
Hôtel de Sully, 62 rue St-Antoine, 4th (01.42.74.47.75). M° Bastille or St-Paul. **Open** 10am-6.30pm Tue-Sun. Closed Mon. **Admission** 25F; 15F students, under-25s, over-60s. **Credit** MC, V. **Map L7**
Historic photographic shows are put on – often in association with bodies like the Royal Photographic Society – of individuals like Cecil Beaton, Jacques-Henri Lartigue, W Eugene Smith or on themes such as the Egyptian pyramids.

Decorative Arts

Musée des Antiquités Nationales
Château, pl du Château, 78100 St-Germain-en-Laye (01.39.10.13.00). RER A St-Germain-en-Laye. **Open** 9am-5.15pm Mon, Wed-Sun. **Admission** 25F; 17F 18-25s, all on Sun; free under-18s. **Credit** (shop) MC, V.
If you feel a touch of Millennium fever coming on, a visit to this museum is a humbling cure. Here thousands of years spin by from one cabinet to the next, putting our own era in awe-inspiring context. The museum is housed in the rambling château which dominates the attractive town of St-Germain-en-Laye. Don't be put off by the thought of vast arrays of broken pots and worked flints – there's much more besides. Some of the early Paleolithic animal sculptures and stone carvings existed long before the Ancient Egyptians. The museum goes on to include the Romans in Gaul, where the artefacts are more familiar but of fine quality, including an immaculate mosaic floor and jewellery, which since seems only to have been imitated and 'reinvented'. The collection is well presented and not short of amusing curiosities: massive antlers from a prehistoric Irish deer and a collection of eighteenth-century cork models of ancient sites, including the Orange amphitheatre prior to restoration.
Shop.

Musée des Arts Décoratifs
Palais du Louvre, 107 rue de Rivoli, 1st (01.44.55.57.50). M° Palais-Royal. **Open** 11am-6pm Tue, Thur, Fri; 11am-9pm Wed; 10am-6pm Sat, Sun. Closed Mon, some public holidays. **Admission** 35F; 25F 18-25s; free under-18s, CM. **Credit** AmEx, MC, V. **Map H5**

This rich collection of decorative arts is currently undergoing a major facelift as part of the Grand Louvre project. So far only the Renaissance and Middle Ages gallery is open, with jewellery due to follow in autumn 99 and the remaining departments scheduled for 2001. The current display whets the appetite. Aside from religious works, the specificity of the collection is that, unlike the Louvre where many works have a royal origin, here the collection is essentially a representation of bourgeois life. In addition to fine sixteenth-century Venetian glass and Flemish tapestries, there are two reconstructions of period rooms, one a panelled Gothic Charles VIII bedchamber complete with tapestries and furniture, the other a Renaissance room in fake marble as existed in Italian and French homes of the fifteenth century. The religious art is dominated by the Gothic collection of architect and decorator Emile Peyre, a gift from the begining of the century, notable for a wonderful altarpiece of the life of John the Baptist by Luis Borassa.
Library. Shop. Wheelchair access (105 rue de Rivoli).

Musée National de la Céramique
pl de la Manufacture, 92310 Sèvres (01.41.14.04.20). M° Pont de Sèvres. **Open** 10am-5pm Mon, Wed-Sun. Closed Tue, some public holidays. **Admission** 22F; 15F 18-25s; free under-18s, CM. **Credit** (showroom) MC, V.
Founded in 1738 as a private concern, the porcelain factory moved to Sèvres from Vincennes in 1756 and was soon taken over by the state. Finely painted, delicately modelled pieces that epitomise French Rococo style, together with later Sèvres, adorned with copies of Raphaels and Titians, demonstrate extraordinary technical virtuosity. The collection also includes Delftware, Italian majolica, Meissen, Della Robbia reliefs, Oriental and Hispano-Moorish pieces. Don't miss the outstanding Ottoman plates and tiles from Iznik and the elegantly decorated, eighteenth-century faïence commode.
Shop and showroom. Wheelchair access.

Musée de la Chasse et de la Nature
Hôtel Guénégaud, 60 rue des Archives, 3rd (01.53.01.92.40). M° Rambuteau. **Open** 11am-6pm Tue-Sun. Closed Mon, public holidays. **Admission** 30F; 15F 16-25s, students under 26, over-60s; 5F 5-16s; free under 5s. **No credit cards. Map K5**
Housed on three floors of a beautifully proportioned mansion built by François Mansart in 1654, this museum brings together a group of objects ranging from Stone Age arrow heads to Persian helmets via Louis XV console tables under the common theme of hunting – nature, unless in the form of an alarming array of stuffed animals, doesn't get much of a look-in. The highlight is the collection of wonderfully ornate weapons: crossbows inlaid with ivory and mother-of-pearl, guns decorated with hunting scenes, swords engraved with arabesques or masks, all reminders that hunting was a luxury sport and its accoutrements were important status symbols. There are also French hunting pictures by artists, like Chardin, Oudry and Desportes, and a Rembrandt sketch.
Bookshop.

Musée du Cristal Baccarat
30bis rue de Paradis, 10th (01.47.70.64.30). M° Poissonnière. **Open** 10am-6pm Mon-Sat. Closed Sun, public holidays. **Admission** 15F; 10F 12-25s, students; free under-12s. **Credit** (shop) AmEx, DC, MC, V. **Map H5**
The showroom of celebrated glassmaker Baccarat, with a museum attached. The main interest here is in seeing which fallen head of state or deposed monarch used to drink out of Baccarat glasses. There are also some kitsch but technically magnificent pieces produced for the great exhibitions last century. Baccarat moved its glass workshops here in 1832, and this street remains full of glassware and china outlets.
Shop.

*Dinner is on the stairway at the **Musée de la Chasse et de la Nature**.*

Musée de l'Eventail

Atelier Hoguet, 2 bd de Strasbourg, 10th (01.42.08.90 20). M° Strasbourg-St-Denis. **Open** 2-6pm Mon, Tue, Wed. *Workshop* 9am-12.30pm, 2-6pm Mon-Fri. Closed Aug, public holidays. **Admission** 30F; 20F students under 18. **No credit cards. Map K4**

The fan-making Hoguet family's collection is housed in the *atelier*'s neo-Renaissance showroom complete with its original 1893 walnut fittings. Exhibits go from eighteenth-century painted fans with mother-of-pearl and ivory sticks to contemporary fans by designers such as Karl Lagerfeld. There's also an interesting display on the techniques and materials used to make these luxury items – which until the French Revolution only the nobility were permitted to use. *Shop.*

Musée des Lunettes et Lorgnettes

2 av Mozart, 16th (01.45.27.21.05). M° La Muette. **Open** *from Apr/May 1999* 10am-noon, 2-6pm Tue-Sat. Closed Aug, public holidays. **Admisssion** 20F. **No credit cards. Map A6**

Currently moving to a new address, this collection gathers every conceivable type of sight-enhancing gadget, including eighteenth-century glasses, nineteenth-century monocles and telescopes in tooled leather cases, through to Brigitte Bardot's black and white plastic sun specs. An eyeful.

Musée de la Mode et du Costume

Palais Galliéra, 10 av Pierre 1er de Serbie, 16th (01.47.20.85.23). M° Iéna or Alma-Marceau. **Open** during exhibitions 10am-6pm Tue-Sun. Closed Mon, public holidays. **Admission** 45F; 32F 8-25s, over-60s; free under-8s. **Credit** MC, V. **Map C5**

Opposite the Musée d'Art Moderne de la Ville de Paris (*see above* **Fine Art**), this fanciful 1890s mansion opens its doors to the public during exhibitions that go from historical periods to individual dress designers, or themes like marriage (Apr-Aug 1999). The permanent collection has an emphasis on nineteenth-century town clothes, but the exhibitions often include items loaned from other institutions.

Musée de la Mode et du Textile

Palais du Louvre, 107 rue de Rivoli, 1st (01.44.55.57.50). M° Palais-Royal. **Open** 11am-6pm Tue, Thur, Fri; 11am-10pm Wed; 10am-6pm Sat, Sun. Closed Mon. **Admission** 25F; 16F 18-25s, over-60s; free under-18s, CM. **Credit** (shop only) AmEx, MC, V. **Map G5**

The new-look fashion museum has moved into a much bigger space as part of the *Grand Louvre* project, so that for the first time part of a vast collection is on permanent show. The display is rotated annually: since 1998 it has concentrated on the exotic touches that have been a frequent feature of Western fashion since the Middle Ages, with patterns like paisley and cuts like the kimono or recent chinoiseries by John Galliano. New display Gardes Robes starts in May 1999. *Research centre (by appointment). Shop. Wheelchair access (105 rue de Rivoli).*

Musée National du Moyen Age – Thermes de Cluny

6 pl Paul-Painlevé, 5th (01.53.73.78.00). M° Cluny-La Sorbonne/RER St-Michel. **Open** 9.15am-5.45pm Mon, Wed-Sun. Closed Tue, some public holidays. **Admission** 28F; 18F 18-25s, over-60s, all on Sun; free under-18s, CM. **No credit cards. Map J7**

Occupying the Paris mansion of the medieval abbots of Cluny, which was built into the ruins of third-century Roman baths, the museum of medieval art and artefacts retains a domestic scale suitable for the intimacy of many of its treasures. Its most famous pieces are the *Lady and the Unicorn* tapestries, depicting convoluted allegories of the five senses, beautifully displayed in a special circular room. The mille-fiore-style tapestry, filled with rabbits and flowers, is wrought in exquisite colour and detail. Elsewhere there are displays of enamel bowls and caskets from Limoges, carved ivories and gold reliquaries and church plate, medieval books of hours to leaf through, wooden chests and locks, while a new room is devoted to chivalry and everyday life at the end of the Middle Ages. There are also early fabrics, including ancient Coptic weaving from Egypt and heavily embroidered bishop's copes, medieval sculpture with capitals from

The Lady & the Unicorn *allegory of the senses at the* **Musée National du Moyen-Age**.

churches all over France, and heads of the kings of Judea from Notre Dame, which had been mutilated in the Revolution under the mistaken belief that they represented the kings of France, and were rediscovered by chance (minus their noses) in 1979. *Bookshop. Concerts. Guided tours.*

Musées des Parfumeries-Fragonard
9 rue Scribe, 9th (01.47.42.93.40) and 39 bd des Capucines, 2nd (01.42.60.37.14). Mº Opéra. **Open** 9am-5.30pm Mon-Sat. Closed Sun. **Admission** free. **Credit** (shop only) AmEx, MC, V. **Map G4**
Get on the scent at the two museums showcasing the collection of perfume house Fragonard. The five rooms at rue Scribe range from Ancient Egyptian ointment flasks to eighteenth-century vinaigrettes and Meissen porcelain scent bottles, while the second museum contains bottles designed by Lalique and Schiaparelli, among others. Both also have displays on scent manufacture and an early twentieth-century 'perfume organ' with rows of the bottled ingredients used by 'noses' when creating their valuable concoctions. *Shop.*

Musée de la Publicité
Palais du Louvre, 107 rue de Rivoli, 1st (01.44.55.57.50). Mº Palais-Royal. **Open** from end 1999, ring for details. **Admission** ring for details. **Map H5**
This museum started life as a poster museum in 1978, becoming an advertising museum in 1982, and has since relocated to a wing of the Louvre, arranged by Jean Nouvel, as part of the *Grand Louvre* programme. Posters from 1700 to 1945 will be complemented by ads and other recent items donated by graphic artists and advertising agencies.

Musée Nissim de Camondo
63 rue de Monceau, 8th (01.53.89.06.40). Mº Monceau or Villiers. **Open** 10am-5pm Wed-Sun. **Admission** 30F; 20F 18-25s; free under-18s, CM. Closed Mon, Tue, some public holidays. **Credit** V. **Map E3**
The Camondos were a rich banking family who moved to Paris from Constantinople in 1867. The collection put together by Count Moïse de Camondo exploits to the full a love for fine French furniture and ceramics, as well as loudly patterned Italian marble, and is named after his son Nissim, who died in World War I (the rest of the family died at Auschwitz). Moïse replaced the family's two houses near Parc Monceau with this palatial residence in 1911-14, and lived here in a style quite out of his time. A succession of grand first-floor reception rooms are crammed with furniture by leading craftsmen of the Louis XV and Louis XVI eras, including Oeben, Riesener and Leleu, huge silver services and sets of Sèvres and Meissen porcelain. All are set off by carpets and tapestries (Gobelins, Aubusson, Beauvais, Savonnerie), mostly in extremely good condition and a surprising riot of colour. Most remarkable is the circular Salon de Huet, overlooking Parc Monceau, adorned by eighteenth-century pastoral scenes. On the second floor are the rooms used daily by the family, including a spectacularly plumbed bathroom. *Bookshop.*

Musée National de la Renaissance
Château d'Ecouen, 95440 Ecouen (01.34.38.38.50). SNCF from Gare du Nord to Ecouen-Ezanville, then bus 269. **Open** 9.45am-12.30pm, 2-5.15pm Mon, Wed-Sun. Closed Tue, 1 Jan, 1 May, 25 Dec. **Admission** 25F; 17F 18-25s Sun; free under-18s, CM. **No credit cards**.
Overlooking an agricultural plain, yet barely outside the Paris suburbs, the Renaissance château built 1538-55 for Royal Constable Anne de Montmorency and his wife Margaret de Savoie is the authentic setting for a wonderful collection of sixteenth-century decorative arts. The display is low-key but there are some real treasures, arranged over three floors of the château (some parts only open in the morning or afternoon). Best of all are the imposing original painted chimneypieces, not unlike those at Fontainebleau, only

here the caryatids and grotesques as well as the Biblical and mythological scenes are painted. Complementing them are furniture, Limoges enamels, tin-glazed earthenware decorated with Classical and religious scenes, armour, embroideries, rare painted leather wall hangings with scenes of Scipio, and a magnificent cycle of ten tapestries depicting the story of David and Bathsheba.
Bookshop. Wheelchair access (call ahead).

Musée de la Serrurerie – Musée Bricard
Hôtel Liberal Bruand, 1 rue de la Perle, 3rd (01.42.77.79.62). Mº St-Paul. **Open** 2-5pm Mon; 10am-noon, 2-5pm Tue-Fri. Closed Sat, Sun, two weeks in Aug, public holidays. **Admission** 30F; 15F students, over-60s; free under-18s. **No credit cards. Map L6**
This museum is housed in the cellars of the elegant mansion that architect Libéral Bruand built for himself in 1685. The collection focuses on locks and keys from Roman times to the end of last century, but also takes in window fastenings, hinges, tools and the elaborate, gilded door handles from Versailles complete with Louis XIV's personal sun-burst.

Architecture & Urbanism

Musée des Années 30
Espace Landowski, 28 av André-Morizet, 92100 Boulogne-Billancourt (01.55.18.46.45). Mº Marcel Sembat. **Open** noon-6pm Tue; 10am-6pm Wed, Sat; 2-8pm Thur; 2-6pm Fri; 1-6pm Sun. Cosed Mon, 15 Aug-1 Sept, public holidays. **Admission** 30F; 20F students, students, over-60s; free under-16s. **No credit cards.**
In a building that also contains a library and cinema and smacks just a little too much of the municipal, the new Musée des Années 30 is a reminder that an awful lot of second-rate painting and sculpture were produced in the 1930s, notably the muscular nudes of the classical revival, alongside some curiosities like the 'colonial' works depicting France's imperial subjects. There are decent Modernist sculptures by the Martel brothers, graphic design drawings and Juan Gris still lifes and drawings, but the main interest is the 30s furniture and the drawings and models of the luxury Modernist houses and monumental town hall built by avant-garde architects including Perret, Le Corbusier, Lurçat, Mallet-Stevens and Fischer when this suburb was expanding in the 30s.
Shop. Wheelchair access.

Institut Français d'Architecture
6 rue de Tournon, 6th (01.46.33.90.36). Mº Odéon. **Open** (during exhibitions only) 12.30-7pm Tue-Sat. **Admission** free. **No credit cards. Map H7**
Exhibitions examining twentieth-century architects or aspects of the built environment. The emphasis is on modernist pioneers, joined by lectures and conferences.
Lectures. Library. Wheelchair access.

Musée des Monuments Français
Palais de Chaillot, pl du Trocadéro, 16th (01.44.05.39.10). Mº Trocadéro. **Open** should reopen 2001. **Admission** ring for details. **Map B5**
Founded by the Gothic revivalist Viollet-le-Duc to record the architectural heritage of France, the museum is closed for renovation. It is to reopen with an enlarged collection as the Centre pour le Patrimoine Monumental et Urbain.

Pavillon de l'Arsenal
21 bd Morland, 4th (01.42.76.33.97). Mº Sully-Morland. **Open** 10.30am-6.30pm Tue-Sat; 11am-7pm Sun. Closed Mon, 1 Jan. **Admission** free. **Credit** (shop) MC, V. **Map L7**
This centre presents imaginative exhibitions on urban design and architecture, in the form of drawings, plans, photographs and models, often looking at Paris from unusual perspectives, be it that of theatres, hidden courtyards, the use of

glass or the banks of the Seine. There's a 50-square metre model of Paris, and a recently updated, permanent exhibition 'Paris, la ville et ses projets' on the historic growth of the city. *Bookshop. Guided tours. Lectures. Wheelchair access.*

Ethnology, Folk & Tribal Art

Musée des Arts d'Afrique et d'Océanie
293 av Daumesnil, 12th (01.44.74.84.80/recorded information 01.43.46.51.61). M° Porte Dorée. **Open** 10am-5.20pm Mon, Wed-Fri; 10am-5.50pm Sat, Sun. Closed Tue, 1 May. **Admission** 30F; 20F 18-25s, over-60s, all on Sun; free under-18s, CM. **Credit** (shop) MC, V.

One of Paris' best-kept secrets, this museum has a winning combination of tropical fish and live crocs in the basement, stunning tribal art up above. The building was designed for the 1931 Exposition Coloniale, and the astonishing bas-relief on the facade reeks of colonialism; there are also two remarkable Art Deco rooms by Ruhlmann. On either side of a vast reception room are newly displayed Aboriginal art and art from the Pacific islands, including carved totems from Vanuatu, anthropomorphic vases from Nouvelle Caledonia and hanging hook figures from Papua New Guinea. Upstairs, the variety of African masks and statues is stunning, including Dogon statues from Mali, and pieces from Côte d'Ivoire and Central Africa, recently joined by Benin bronzes and other Nigerian art from the Barbier-Muller collection. There

Write on: literary lives

Maison de Balzac
47 rue Raynouard, 16th (01.42.24.56.38). M° Passy. **Open** *from 20 May 1999* 10am-5.40pm Tue-Sun. Closed Mon, public holidays. **Admission** 17.50F; 9F 18s-25s; free under-18s, over-60s, CM. **No credit cards. Map B6**
Honoré de Balzac (1799-1850) moved to this address in 1840 to avoid his creditors and established a password to sift friends from bailiffs. The pavilion makes a delightful showcase for a wide range of memorabilia, including first editions, letters, corrected proofs, portraits of friends and Polish mistress Mme Hanska, plus a 'family tree' of Balzac's characters that covers several walls. The study houses his desk, chair and the monogrammed coffee pot that fuelled all-night work on much of *La Comédie humaine.* 'La Toise du Savant et le Vertige du Fou' (May-Sept 1999) marks the bicentenary of the author's birth. *Library (by appointment).*

Maison de Victor Hugo
Hôtel de Rohan-Guéménée, 6 pl des Vosges, 4th (01.42.72.10.16). M° Bastille or St-Paul. **Open** 10am-5.40pm Tue-Sun. Closed Mon, public holidays. **Admission** 17.50F; 9F 7-18s, students; free under-7s, over-65s, CM. **No credit cards. Map L6**
Victor Hugo (1802-85) lived in this historic townhouse from 1832 until he was forced to flee – first elsewhere in Paris and then to Guernsey – after the 1848 Revolution. Here he wrote part of *Les Misérables* and a number of poems and plays. When not writing, Hugo clearly kept himself busy – as well as typical period portraits of the writer and his large family, the collection includes his own drawings, the carved pseudo-Oriental furniture he designed himself, and his and his sons experiments with the then new middle-class hobby of photography.

Musée de la Vie Romantique
16 rue Chaptal, 9th (01.48.74.95.38). M° Blanche. **Open** 10am-5.40pm Tue-Sun. Closed Mon, public holidays. **Admission** 17.50F; 9F over-60s, students (27F and 19F during exhibitions); free under-18s, CM. **No credit cards. Map G2**
When artist Ary Scheffer lived in this villa, this area south of Pigalle was known as the New Athens because of the concentration of writers, composers and artists living here. Baronne Aurore Dupin alias George Sand (1804-76) was a frequent guest at Scheffer's soirées, and the house is now devoted to the writer, her family and her intellectual circle, which included Chopin, Delacroix (art tutor to her son) and composer Charpentier. Quietly charming, the

museum reveals little of her writing or proto-feminist ideas, nor her affairs with Jules Sandeau, Chopin (represented by a marble bust) and Alfred de Musset; rather it presents a typical bourgeois portrait in the watercolours, lockets and jewels she left behind. In the courtyard, Scheffer's studio containing several of his *pompier*-type portraits and history subjects, is used for exhibitions. *Bookshop. Concerts (summer).*

Maison de Chateaubriand
La Vallée aux Loups, 87 rue de Chateaubriand, 92290 Chatenay-Malabry (01.47.02.08.62). RER B Robinson + 20min walk. **Open** (guided tours only except Sun) *Apr-Sept* 10am-noon, 2-6pm Wed, Fri-Sat, Sun; *Oct-Mar* 2-5pm Tue-Sun. Closed Mon, Jan. **Admission** 30F; 20F students, over-60s; free under-8s. **No credit cards.**
In 1807, attracted by the quiet Vallée aux Loups, Chateaubriand (1768-1848), author of *Mémoires d'outre tombe,* set about transforming a simple eighteenth-century country house into his own Romantic idyll and planted the park with rare trees as a reminder of his travels. The interior has been lovingly reconstructed. Most interesting are the over-the-top double wooden staircase, based on a maritime design, a reminder of the writer's noble St Malo birth, and the portico with two white marble Grecian statues supporting a colonnaded porch. Anyone familiar with David's *Portrait of Mme Récamier* in the Louvre will find the original chaise longue awaiting the sitter, who was one of Chateaubriand's numerous lovers, no doubt to the discomfort of his stern wife, Céleste. After a politically inflammatory work Chateaubriand was ruined and in 1818 had to sell his beloved valley.
Concerts/readings (spring, autumn). Shop. Tea room.

Musée Mémorial Ivan Tourguéniev
16 rue Ivan-Tourguéniev, 78380 Bougival (01.45.77.87.12). M° La Défense, plus bus 258. **Open** *21 Mar-mid Dec* 10am-6pm Sun. **Admission** 25F; 20F 12-26s; free under-12s. **No credit cards.**
The proverbial Russian soul, a blend of European extravagance and Oriental mysticism, persists in unexpected places like tranquil, Seine-side Bougival. Inhabited for several years by Russian novelist Ivan Turgenev until his death in 1883, this sumptuous *dacha* perched in a birch forest was a gathering spot for Romantic composers Saint-Saëns and Fauré, opera divas Pauline Viardot and Maria Malibran, and writers Henry James, Flaubert, Zola and Maupassant. As well as letters and editions (mainly in Russian), there's the music room where Viardot held court. *Bookshop. Concerts.*

are also fabrics, jewellery and embroidery from the Maghreb. The second floor is used for temporary displays, both traditional and contemporary. The tribal art will eventually become part of the Musée des Arts et des Civilisations. As for the crocs... *Aquarium. Shop. Wheelchair access.*

Musée des Arts et Traditions Populaires
6 av du Mahatma-Gandhi, 16th (01.44.17.60.00). Mº Les Sablons. **Open** 9.30am-5.15pm Mon, Wed-Sun. Closed Tue, some public holidays. **Admission** 22F; 15F 18-25s, over-60s; free under-18s, CM. (*Temporary exhibitions* 23F, 16F 18s-25s, over-60s; 10F 5-18s; free under-5s.) **Credit** (shop) AmEx, MC, V.
This important centre of French folk art, in the Bois de Boulogne, spotlights the traditions and popular culture of pre-industrial France, depicting rural life through agricultural tools, household objects, furniture, costumes and models. The liveliest sections are those devoted to customs and beliefs, which include a crystal ball, tarot cards, thunder stones and early medicines, and popular entertainment, with displays on the circus, sports, puppet theatres and music. *Auditorium. Shop. Library/sound archive (by appointment).*

Musée Dapper
50 av Victor-Hugo, 16th (01.45.00.01.50). Mº Victor-Hugo. **Open** closed until Sept 2000. **Admission** ring for details. **Map B4**
The Fondation Dapper usually organises one or two beautifully displayed, themed exhibitions of African art every year, but is currently closed for refurbishment.

Musée des Arts Forains
53 av des Terroirs de France, 12th (01.43.40.16.22). Mº Bercy. **Open** *groups only* reserve ahead. **Admission** 75F; 25F under-15s. **No credit cards. Map P10**
The collection of fairground art from 1880-1950 rescued by Jean-Louis Favand has moved to one of the last wine warehouses at Bercy, fortunately listed after the rest of the site had been demolished. There are several roundabouts (painted cows and pigs as well as horses) – some of which are operational – a tincan alley, a shooting range, *montagne russe* (precursor of the rollercoaster) and fairground organs. *Guided tours.*

Musée de l'Homme
Palais de Chaillot, pl du Trocadéro, 16th (01.44.05.72.72). Mº Trocadéro. **Open** 9.45am-5.15pm Mon, Wed-Sun. Closed Tue, public holidays. **Admission** 30F; 20F 5s-16s, over-60s; free under-4s. **Credit** (shop) MC, V. **Map B5**
Starting off with an exhibition on world population growth, this compendious museum goes on to consider birth control, death, disease, genetics and racial distinction before turning to tribal costumes, tools, idols and ornaments from all over the world. Displays and tableaux are arranged by continent, with Africa and Europe on the first floor and Asia and the Americas on the second. A section devoted to music provides curious instruments and recordings of the noises they make. The displays tend to be dowdy and could do with some labelling in English, but the variety of the collections (eventually due to form the core of Chirac's Musée des Arts et des Civilisations), including a shrunken head, a stuffed polar bear and a reconstruction of a Mayan temple, makes this an ideal departure point for exotic escapism on a rainy day. *Café. Cinema. Concerts. Lecture room. Library. Photo Library. Wheelchair access.*

Oriental Arts

Musée National des Arts Asiatiques – Guimet
6 pl d'Iéna, 16th (01.45.05.00.98). closed until 2000. *Galeries du Panthéon Bouddhique, 19 av d'Iéna, 16th (01.40.73.88.11). Mº Iéna.* **Open** 9.45am-5.45pm Mon,

Musée des Arts Forains: *life's roundabout.*

Wed-Sun. **Admission** 16F; 12F students, all on Sun; free under-18s, CM. **Credit** (shop) MC, V. **Map E5**
The stunning national collection of Oriental and Asian art, notably the Cambodian Khmer sculptures from the civilisation of Angkor Wat, is closed for renovation. The Panthéon Bouddhique remains open in a Neo-Classical *hôtel*: Emile Guimet's original collection tracing the religious history of China and Japan from the fourth to nineteenth centuries. *Shop. Wheelchair access.*

Musée Cernuschi
7 av Velasquez, 8th (01.45.63.50.75). Mº Villiers or Monceau. **Open** 10am-5.40pm Tue-Sun. Closed Mon; public holidays. **Admission** 17.50F; 9F 18-25s; free under-18s, over-60s, CM. *Temporary exhibitions* 35F; 25F 7-25s, over-60s; free under-7s. **No credit cards. Map E2**
Erudite banker Henri Cernuschi amassed the nucleus of this collection of Chinese art on a long voyage to the Far East in 1871 and housed it in his mansion near the Parc Monceau. It ranges from Neolithic terracottas to Han and Wei dynasty funeral statues – in which Chinese potters displayed their inventiveness by creating entire legions of animated musicians, warriors, dancers, animals and other accessories to take to the next world. Other highlights include refined Tang celadon wares, Sung porcelain, fragile paintings on silk, bronze vessels and jade amulets. Among recent additions is some contemporary Chinese painting. Until 27 June 1999, the collections are complemented by the Meiyintang collection of ceramics from the Sui to Yuan periods. *Wheelchair access (call ahead).*

Musée d'Ennery
59 av Foch, 16th (01.45.53.57.96). Mº Porte Dauphine. **Open** *from Apr 1999 (ring to check)* 2-5.45pm Thur, Sun. **Admission** free. **No credit cards. Map A4**
This extraordinary collection of Oriental decorative arts, put together by author Adolphe d'Ennery and his wife, is as interesting for what it says about late nineteenth-century taste as for the objects themselves. The 5000 items are still in the d'Ennery's lavish Napoléon III *hôtel* and many have been kept in their original rosewood and mother of pearl showcases. The collection, dating from the seventeenth to nineteenth centuries, includes lacquer, ceramics, crystal, jade, ivories, bronzes, masks, wood carvings and *netsuke.*

Musée de l'Institut du Monde Arabe
1 rue des Fossés-St-Bernard, 5th (01.40.51.39.53). Mº Jussieu. **Open** 10am-6pm Tue-Sun. Closed Mon, 1 May. **Admission** 25F; 20F 18-25s, students, over-60s (30F and 25F during exhibitions); free under-18s, CM. **Credit** (shop) AmEx, MC, V. **Map K7**
Opened in 1987 as another *Grand Projet*, the institute of the Arab world brings together a library, cultural centre, exhibitions and the 'Museum of the Arab Museums', displaying

items on long-term loan from museums in alternating Arab countries (Syria and Tunisia started the ball rolling) alongside its own permanent collection. The objects, covering a huge geographical (India to Spain) and historical (prehistoric to contemporary) span, are set off well in the high-tech space and include examples from almost every branch of the applied arts, calligraphy, metalwork, ceramics, textiles and miniatures. Particularly strong are the collections of early scientific instruments, nineteenth-century Tunisian costume and jewellery and contemporary fine art.
Bookshop. Cinema. Lectures. Library. Tea Room. Wheelchair access (call ahead).

History

Mémorial du Maréchal Leclerc de Hauteclocque et de la Libération de Paris & Musée Jean Moulin
23 allée de la 2e DB, Jardin Atlantique (above Grandes Lignes of Gare Montparnasse), 15th (01.40.64.39.44). M° Montparnasse-Bienvenüe. **Open** 10am-5.40pm Tue-Sun. Closed Mon, public holidays. **Admission** 17.50F; 9F students, over-60s (27F and 19F during exhibitions); free under-18s, CM. **No credit cards.** **Map F9**
A double museum dedicated to two men who were instrumental in the Liberation of Paris, from opposing sides of the political spectrum. General Leclerc commanded the French Division that was the first Allied unit to enter Paris; Moulin was a Communist resistance martyr. Both halves are full of war memorabilia with extensive photographic, documentary and film archive material.
Bookshop. Vidéothèque. Wheelchair access (call ahead).

Musée de l'Armée
Hôtel des Invalides, esplanade des Invalides, 7th (01.44.42.37.72). M° Varenne or Latour-Maubourg. **Open** *Apr-Sept* 10am-6pm daily; *Oct-Mar* 10am-5pm daily. Closed 1 Jan, 1 Nov, 25 Dec. **Admission** 37F; 27F under-18s, students under 26, over-60s; free under-7s, CM. **No credit cards.** **Map E6**
After checking out Napoléon's tomb under the vast golden dome of Les Invalides, many tourists don't bother to pursue their visit with the army museum, included in the ticket price. If you are interested in military history, the museum is a must, but even if sumptuous uniforms and armour are not your thing, the building is in itself a splendour. Besides military memorabilia from Antiquity on, the rooms are filled with fine portraiture (don't miss Ingres' masterpiece of Emperor Napoléon on his throne), some well recreated interiors, as well as the newly reopened museum of maquettes of fortifications (10am-noon, 2-6pm daily). Probably, the most immediate and moving rooms are those dedicated to the First and Second World Wars, where documents and photos bring the conflicts vividly to life. *See also* **Les Invalides** *in chapter* **Left Bank**.
Café. Films. Concerts. Lectures. Shop.

Musée de l'Art et d'Histoire de St-Denis
22bis rue Gabriel-Péri, 93200 St-Denis (01.42.43.05.10). M° St-Denis Porte de Paris. **Open** 10am-5.30pm Mon, Wed-Sat; 2-6.30pm Sun. Closed Tue, public holidays. **Admission** 20F; 10F students, over-60s; free under-16s. **No credit cards.**
This prizewinning museum in the suburb of St-Denis is housed in the former Carmelite convent that in the eighteenth century numbered Louise de France, daughter of Louis XV, among its incumbents. Although there are displays of local archaeology, prints and drawings about the Paris Commune, Modern and post-Impressionist drawings and documents relating to the poet Paul Eluard who was born in the town, the most vivid part is the first floor where the nuns' austere cells have been preserved.

Musée du Cabinet des Médailles
Bibliothèque Nationale Richelieu, 58 rue de Richelieu, 2nd (01.47.03.83.30). M° Bourse. **Open** 1-5pm Mon-Sat; noon-6pm Sun. Closed public holidays. **Admission** 22F; 15F students; free under-13s. **Credit** (shop) MC, V. **Map H4**
With attention now focused on the new Bibliothèque François Mitterrand the original building cuts a rather melancholy figure. On the first floor is the anachronistic Cabinet des Médailles; the extensive collection of coins and medals is for specialists, but efficient sliding magnifying glasses help bring exhibits to life. The strange aspect of the museum lies in its parallel Greek, Roman and medieval collections, which would seem to lie outside its brief, but which are probably the most interesting aspect for the general public. Oddities to discover include the Merovingian King Dagobert's throne and Charlemagne's chess set, nestling among Greek vases and miniature sculptures from all periods. Attendants seem slightly put out by visitors.
Shop. Partial wheelchair access.

Musée Carnavalet
23 rue de Sévigné, 3rd (01.42.72.21.13). M° St-Paul. **Open** 10am-5.40pm Tue-Sun. Closed Mon, some public holidays. **Admission** 27F; 14.50F students, 18-25s, over-60s; free under-7s, CM (exhibitions 35F; 25F; free under-7s). **Credit** (shop) AmEx, MC, V. **Map L6**
The museum of Paris history owes its origins to Baron Haussmann who, in 1866, persuaded the City of Paris to buy the Hôtel Carnavalet to house some of the interiors from buildings destroyed to make way for his new boulevards. Since then the museum has added a second *hôtel* and built up a huge collection which tells the history of the city from pre-Roman Gaul to the twentieth century, through archeological finds, *objets d'art*, prints, paintings and furnishings.
The Hôtel Carnavalet contains the main collection and retains much of its old atmosphere, with an attractive *cour d'honneur* and a formal garden. Carnavalet's most famous resident was Mme de Sévigné, whose letters to her daughter bring alive aristocratic life under Louis XIV. A good collection of related memorabilia includes portraits of the author and her circle, her Chinese-export, lacquered desk and some of her letters, displayed in the panelled first-floor gallery and salon. All that remains of the adjoining seventeenth-century Hôtel Le Peletier de St-Fargeau, linked since 1989, is the elegant grand staircase and one restored, panelled *cabinet*.
The displays are arranged chronologically. The original sixteenth-century rooms house the Renaissance collections with portraits by Clouet, and furniture and pictures relating to the Wars of Religion that dominated French politics for most of the period. The first floor covers the period up to 1789 with furniture, applied arts and paintings displayed in restored, period interiors. The bold, new colours, particularly in the oval *boudoir* from the Hôtel de Breteuil (1782), may come as a shock to people with pre-conceived ideas about subdued eighteenth-century taste; however the use of royal blues and vivid greens is correct as the colours have been copied from original paint samples. Interesting interiors include the Rococo *cabinet* painted for engraver Demarteau by his friends, Fragonard, Boucher and Huet in 1765, chinoiserie rooms and the Louis XIII-style Cabinet Colbert.
The collections from 1789 on are housed in the *hôtel* next door. The Revolutionary items are the best way of getting an understanding of the convoluted politics and bloodshed of the period from the calling of the Estates General through to the Directory. Here are portraits of all the major players, prints, objects and memorabilia including a bone model of the guillotine made by French prisoners of war in England, Hubert Robert's gouaches, commemorative china and a small chunk of the Bastille prison. Those of a sentimental bent should look at the pathetic souvenirs from the Temple prison where the royal family were held: among them, the Dauphin's lead soldiers and Louis XVI's shaving kit.

*Plenty of knights in shining armour at the **Musée de l'Armée**.*

The nineteenth-century collections range from items belonging to Napoléon, through views of Paris depicting the effects of Haussmann's programme to the early twentieth-century ballroom of the Hôtel Wendel. Highlights include the ornate cradle given by the city to Napoléon III on the birth of his son and the Art Nouveau boutique Fouquet designed by Mucha in 1901, with a sea-horse fountain. Rooms devoted to French literature finish the tour with portraits and room settings, including Proust's cork-lined bedroom.
Bookshop. Guided tours. Reference section (by appointment). Visits. Wheelchair access.

Musée Grévin

10 bd Montmartre, 9th (01.47.70.85.05). M° Grands Boulevards. **Open** *Term-time* 1-6.30pm daily. *School holidays* 10am-7pm daily. **Admission** 55F; 44F students; 36F 6-14s; free under-6s. **Credit** MC, V. **Map J4**
The French version of Madame Tussaud's with an easy-to-miss entrance is over a hundred years old, but is smaller than its London counterpart. Realism is variable (Depardieu's nose is well done but Gainsbourg's stubble particularly unconvincing), though the costumes are very good. There are some odd touches: spot the recurring black cats and the collection of famous revolutionaries' death masks. Although there is a fair quota of international film stars and well-known statesmen (Clinton, Kohl), the emphasis is on episodes from French history (the trial of Joan of Arc, the death of Marat) and personalities – in a recent bid for popularity popsters 2 Be 3 and Lara Fabian have arrived in the Galerie des Personnalités. A full list of all the figures is not available until you get to the souvenir stand at the end: it costs 10F.
Bookshop. Wheelchair access ground floor only.

Musée de l'Histoire de France

Hôtel de Soubise, 60 rue des Francs-Bourgeois, 3rd (01.40.27.62.18). M° Hôtel-de-Ville or Rambuteau. **Open** noon-5.45pm Mon, Wed-Fri; 1.45-5.45pm Sat, Sun. Closed Tue, public holidays. **Admission** 20F; 15F 18-25s, over-60s; free under-18s. **Credit** MC, V. **Map K6**
Housed in one of the grandest mansions in the Marais, this museum of French history is part of the National Archives. A display of historical documents covers themes like the Middle Ages, the Revolution and Republican politics; other rooms are used for temporary exhibitions. All slightly dry, but the Hôtel de Soubise also contains the finest Rococo interiors in Paris: the apartments of the Prince and Princesse de Soubise, decorated with superb plasterwork, panelling and paintings by prominent artists of the period including Boucher, Natoire, Restout and Van Loo.
Shop.

Musée National de la Légion d'Honneur

2 rue de Bellechasse, 7th (01 40 62 84 25). M° Solférino/RER Musée d'Orsay. **Open** *Mar-Oct* 2-7pm Tue-Sun; *Nov-Feb* 2-5pm Tue-Sun. Closed Mon, 1 Jan, 1 May, 1 Nov, 25 Dec. **Admission** 25F; free under-18s, students, CM. **Credit** (shop) MC, V. **Map G6**
Opposite the Musée d'Orsay is the museum devoted to France's honours system, housed in the stables of the superb Hôtel de Salm, bought by Napoléon in 1804. Groups can also organise visits to the private apartments, and the museum itself is undergoing a facelift, in time for the bicentenery of the Ordre de la Légion d'Honneur in 2002. The rich collection of official gongs and lookalike mayoral chains is enlivened by some superb portraiture, including an effective display which combines the cloak of the Ordre du St-Esprit and a fine eighteenth-century portrait by Van Loo of the creation of the Order, featuring the same costume. Napoléon has a room dedicated to his memory including a dashing representation by Gros and the pistols he presented to Tsar Alexander I. On the mezzanine a new space evokes World War I through moving sketches, portraits and medals.
Shop.

Musée de la Marine

Palais de Chaillot, pl du Trocadéro, 16th (01.45.53.31.70). M° Trocadéro. **Open** 10am-6pm Mon, Wed-Sun. Closed Tue. **Admission** 38F; 25F under-26s, over-60s; free under-5s, CM. **Credit** (shop) MC, V. **Map B5**
The ideal place to find your sealegs, the maritime museum

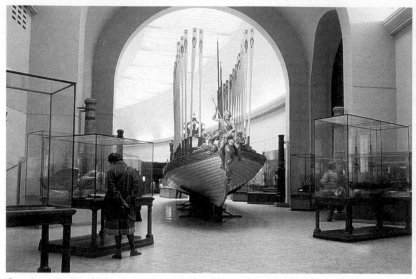

Sea the collection for boat people at the **Musée de la Marine**.

concentrates on French naval history via detailed carved models of battleships and Vernet's imposing series of paintings of the ports of France (1754-65) to a model of a nuclear submarine, as well as the impressive Imperial barge, built when Napoléon's delusions of grandeur were reaching their zenith in 1811. There are also carved prows, old maps, antique and modern navigational instruments, ships in bottles, underwater equipment and romantic maritime paintings plus a new area devoted to the modern navy.
Lectures. Shop.

Musée de la Monnaie de Paris

11 quai de Conti, 6th (01.40.46.55.35). Mº Pont-Neuf. **Open** 11am-5.30pm Tue-Fri; noon-5.30pm Sat, Sun. Ateliers, one-hour guided tour (in French) 2.15pm Wed, Fri (15F). Closed public holidays. **Admission** 20F; 15F students, over-60s; free under-16s, CM, all on Sun. **Credit** (shop) MC, V. **Map H6**
Housed in the handsome Neo-Classical mint built in the 1770s by Jacques-Denis Antoine, this high-tech museum tells the story of France's coinage from pre-Roman origins to the presesnt day through a series of sophisticated displays and audiovisual presentations. The history of the French state is directly linked to its coinage, and the museum is highly informative about both. If your French is sufficient for the tour, a visit to the still-functioning ateliers, taking in foundry, engraving and casting of coins and medals, is fascinating for all those interested in how things are made.
Shop. Visits (atelier). Partial wheelchair access.

Musée de Montmartre

12 rue Cortot, 18th (01.46.06.61.11). Mº Lamarck-Caulaincourt. **Open** 11am-6pm Tue-Sun. Closed Mon. **Admission** 25F; 20F students; free under-8s. **Credit** (shop) MC, V. **Map H1**
At the back of a peaceful garden, this seventeenth-century manor is a haven of calm after touristy Montmartre. The museum is administered by the Société d'Histoire et d'Archéologie du Vieux Montmartre, which since 1886 has aimed to preserve documents and artefacts relating to the

historic hilltop. The collection consists of a room devoted to Modigliani, who lived in rue Caulaincourt, the re-created study of composer Gustave Charpentier, some original Toulouse-Lautrec posters, porcelain from the short-lived manufacture at Clignancourt and a homage to the famous local bistro the Lapin Agile. The artist's studios above the entrance pavilion were occupied at various times by Renoir, Emile Bernard, Raoul Dufy and Suzanne Valadon with her son Maurice Utrillo and his friend, her husband André Utter. Recent temporary exhibitions have given a boost to this sweet if rather sleepy museum.
Archives (by appointment). Bookshop.

Musée de la Préfecture de Police

1bis rue des Carmes, 5th (01.44.41.52.54). Mº Maubert-Mutualité. **Open** 9am-5pm Mon-Fri; 10am-5pm Sat. Closed public holidays. **Admission** free. **No credit cards. Map J7**
The history of Paris is viewed via crime and its prevention since the founding of the Paris police force in the sixteenth century at this small museum on the upper floor of a police station. Among eclectic treasures here are prisoners' expenses from the Bastille, including those of dastardly jewel thief the Comtesse de la Motte, the exploding flowerpot planted by Louis-Armand Matha in 1894 in a restaurant on the rue de Tournon and the gory *Epée de Justice*, a seventeenth-century sword blunted by the quantity of noble heads chopped.

Music, Cinema & Media

Musée du Cinéma Henri Langlois

closed until further notice. **Admission** ring for details.
Cinema is a religion in Paris, and this museum is testimony to the devotion of its highest priest Henri Langlois, who assembled the **Cinémathèque**'s collection. The emphasis is on cinema's origins from precursors to the first animated cartoons, as well as posters, costumes and sets. After a fire in the Palais de Chaillot in 1997, the museum will probably reopen late 2000 in the former American Center near Bercy.

Musée Edith Piaf

5 rue Crespin-du-Gast, 11th (01.43.55.52.72).
Mº Ménilmontant. **Open** by appointment 1-6pm Mon-
Thur. Closed three weeks in Sept. **Admission** voluntary
donation. **No credit cards. Map N5**
Les Amis d'Edith Piaf run this tiny two-room museum in a
part of Paris familiar to the sometime street singer. Call a
couple of days ahead to visit. The collection of memorabilia
exudes love for the 'little sparrow', her diminutive stature
graphically shown by a lifesize cardboard cutout. Her little
black dress and tiny shoes are the most moving items, but
her letters, posters and photos all have a welcome personal
touch. There's a sculpture of the singer by Suzanne Blistene,
wife of Marcel who produced most of Piaf's films, and CDs
and books on sale for the devoted fan.
Shop.

Musée de la Musique

Cité de la Musique, 221 av Jean-Jaurès, 19th
(01.44.84.46.00). Mº Porte de Pantin. **Open** noon-6pm
Tue-Thur; noon-7.30pm Fri, Sat; 10am-6pm Sun. Closed
Mon, public holidays. **Admission** 35F; 25F 18s-25s; 10F
6-18s; free under-6s, over-60s, CM. **Credit** MC, V. **Map
insert**
Alongside the concert hall in the striking modern Cité de la
Musique is this innovative new music museum, its well-lit
galleries stacked under the dome. It houses the gleamingly
restored collection of instruments from the old Conservatoire,
interactive computers and scale models of opera houses and
concert halls. On arrival you are supplied with a set of headphones with commentary in a choice of languages. Don't
spurn this offer, for the musical commentary is an essential
part of the enjoyment, playing the appropriate music or
instrument as you approach the exhibit. The thrill of seeing
a superb three-manual Flemish harpsichord and hearing it
play is tremendous. Alongside the trumpeting brass, curly
woodwind instruments and precious strings are also more
unusual items, such as the Indonesian gamelan orchestra,
which so influenced Debussy and Ravel. The models of concert halls and opera houses appeal to all ages. The Baroque
opera at Versailles is particularly evocative. The route runs
with a model of IRCAM and some pioneering synthesisers,
now showing their age. Alongside the exhibits are simple-
to-use computers, providing basic information about composers and musical periods (albeit only in French). With a
shop well-stocked with music-themed gifts and a modern
research centre with more computers, this museum stands
proud among often dusty music museums elsewhere. One
of the concerts programmed in the museum's amphitheatre
use historic instruments from the collection. *See also chapters* **Right Bank** *and* **Music: Classical & Opera**.
Audioguide. Bookshop. Library. Wheelchair access.

Musée de l'Opéra

Palais Garnier, 1 pl de l'Opéra, 9th (01.40.01.24.93).
Mº Opéra. **Open** 10am-4.30pm daily. Closed some public
holidays. **Admission** 30F; 20F 10-25s, students, over-
60s; free under-10s. **No credit cards. Map G4**
The magnificently restored Palais Garnier houses small
temporary exhibitions relating to current opera or ballet productions, and a permanent collection of paintings, scores and
bijou opera sets in period cases. The picture gallery is of
unusually high quality, a sort of National Portrait Gallery
for musicians. The ticket also includes a visit to the auditorium (rehearsals permitting), although the splendour of the
building is greatly diminished without an audience.
Bookshop.

Religion

Musée d'Art et d'Histoire du Judaïsme

Hôtel de St-Aignan, 71 rue du Temple, 3rd
(01.53.01.86.53). Mº Rambuteau. **Open** 11am-6pm Mon-

Fri; 10am-6pm Sun. Closed Sat, Jewish holidays.
Admission 40F; 25F 18-26s; free under-18s. **Credit**
(shop) MC, V. **Map K5**
Opened in December 1998 in an imposing Marais mansion,
the new Jewish museum gives Jewish heritage a much more
visible showcase than before. Focusing on migrations and
communities, exhibits bring out the importance of ceremon-
ies, rites and learning, and show how styles were adapted
across the globe. A silver Hannukah lamp made in Frankfurt,
finely carved Italian synagogue furniture, embroidered Bar
Mitzvah robes, Torah scrolls and North African dresses put
the emphasis on fine craftsmanship but also on religious
practice, for which a certain familiarity with both Judaism
and the decorative arts is helpful. There are also documents
relating to the infamous Dreyfus case, from Zola's *J'Accuse*
to anti-Semitic cartoons, and an impressive array of paintings by the early twentieth-century avant-garde and the
Ecole de Paris (El Lissitsky, Mané-Katz, Modigliani, Soutine
and, above all, Chagall). The Shoah is side-stepped – with
the exception of a work by Christian Boltanski that commemorates the Jews who were living in the Hôtel St-Aignan
in 1939, thirteen of whom died in concentration camps, thus
bringing the collection back to the district in which it is set.
Auditorium. Café. Library. Shop. Wheelchair access.

Musée de la Franc-Maçonnerie

16 rue Cadet, 9th (01.45.23.20.92). Mº Cadet. **Open**
2-6pm Tue-Sat. Closed Mon, Sun, public holidays.
Admission 10F. **No credit cards. Map H3**
Situated at the back of the Grand Orient de France (French
Masonic Great Lodge) in a school hall-style room, this fair-
ly unsophisticated museum traces the history of freemason-
ry from early medieval stone masons' guild to the present.
Display cases include prints of famous masons (General
Lafayette and 1848 revolutionary leaders Blanc and Barbès),
insignia and ceremonial objects, but despite the potentially
interesting subject you still come out feeling none the wiser.
Bookshop.

Science, Medicine & Technology

La Cité des Sciences et de l'Industrie

Parc de la Villette, 30 av Corentin-Cariou, 19th
(01.40.05.80.00/01.40.05.12.12). Mº Porte de la Villette.
Open 10am-6pm Tue-Sun. Closed Mon, public holidays.
Admission 50F; 35F 7-16s, students under 25, over-60s;
free under-7s; *Cité/Géode Pass* 92F; 79F children; not
valid weekends or holidays. **Credit** MC, V. **Map insert**
Set within the Parc de la Villette, this ultra-modern science
museum has been riding high since its opening in 1986 and
pulls in over five million visitors a year. Originally intended as a modern abattoir, the expensive project was derailed
mid-construction and cleverly transformed the structure into
a gigantic, state-of-the-art science museum. **Explora**, the
permanent show, occupies the upper two floors, whisking
visitors through 30,000 square metres of 'space, life, matter
and communication', where scale models of satellites including the Ariane space shuttle, planes and robots make for an
exciting journey. There's an impressive array of interactive
exhibits on language and communication enabling you to
learn about sound waves and try out different smells. Put on
your Michael Fish act and pretend to be a weatherman in the
Espace Images, try out the delayed camera and other optical illusions in the Jeux de lumière, or draw 3D images on
computer. The Serre 'garden of the future' investigates futuristic developments in agriculture and bio-technology, such
as transgenic plants or the possibility of growing tomatoes
on glasswool. The **Espace** section, devoted to man's conquest of space, lets you experience the sensation of weight-
lessness. Other sections feature climate, ecology and the
environment, health, energy, agriculture, the ocean and vol-
canoes. The new Automobile gallery looks at the car both as
myth and as technological object, with driving simulator and

Dinosaurs go high-tech at the **Muséum National d'Histoire Naturelle** *(see p128).*

displays on safety, pollution and designs of the future. Remembering the industry of the name, the Cité also has links with various companies: in 1999, there's an exhibition about Michelin tyres. The lower floors house temporary exhibitions, a documentation centre and special children's sections. The Louis Lumière cinema shows films in 3-D, and there's a restored submarine moored next to the Géode. *See also chapters* **Right Bank**, **Film** *and* **Children**.
Bookshop. Café. Cinema. Conference centre. Library (multimedia). Wheelchair access & hire.

Musée de l'Air et de l'Espace

Aéroport de Paris-Le Bourget, 93352 Le Bourget Cedex (01.49.92.71.99/recorded information 01.49.92.71.71). Mº Gare du Nord then bus 350/Mº La Courneuve then bus 152/RER Le Bourget then bus 152. **Open** *May-Oct* 10am-6pm; *Nov-Apr* 10am-5pm Tue-Sun. Closed Mon, 1 Jan, 25 Dec. **Admission** 30F; 22F 8-16s, students; free under-8s. **Credit** MC, V.

The air and space museum is a potent reminder that France is a technical and military as well as cultural power. Housed in the former passenger terminal at Le Bourget airport, the collection begins with the pioneers, including fragile-looking biplanes, the contraption in which Romanian Vivia succeeded in flying twelve metres in 1906, and the strangely nautical command cabin of a Zeppelin airship. Outside on the runway are several Mirage fighter planes, a Boeing 707, an American Thunderchief with painted shark-tooth grimace and Ariane launchers 1 and 5. Within a vast hangar, walk through the prototype Concorde 001 and view wartime survivors including a Spitfire and German Heinkel bomber. Further hangars display military planes, helicopters, commercial jets and bizarre prototypes like the Leduc, designed to be launched off the back of another plane, sporting and acrobatic planes and finally space missiles and satellites. A section is devoted to hot air balloons, invented in 1783 by the Montgolfier brothers and quickly adopted for military reconnaissance. Dramatic displays make this museum great fun and most captions are summarised in English.
Shop. Wheelchair access.

Musée des Arts et Métiers

60 rue Réaumur, 3rd (01.40.27.22.20/01.53.01.82.20). Mº Arts et Métiers. **Open** closed until end 1999. **Admission** ring for details. **Map K5**

Occupying the medieval abbey of St-Martin-les-Champs, this historic science museum has a wealth of machines and models relating to great inventions from 1500 on, including automatons, Pascal's calculating machine, Blériot's plane and the first steam car. When the museum reopens, seven sections will cover different aspects of science and technology, with visits ending in the twelfth-century chapel.

Musée de l'Assistance Publique

Hôtel de Miramion, 47 quai de la Tournelle, 5th (01.46.33.01.43). Mº Maubert-Mutualité. **Open** 10am-5pm Wed-Sat. Closed Mon, Tue, Aug. **Admission** 20F; 10F students, over-60s; free under-13s, CM. **No credit cards. Map K7**

The history of Paris hospitals, from the days when they were receptacles for abandoned babies to the beginnings of modern medicine with anaesthesia, is explained in a surprisingly lively fashion through paintings, prints, various grisly medical devices and a reconstructed ward and pharmacy; texts are unfortunately in French only. Until 12 July 1999, an exhibition on aspects of hospital care marks the 150th anniversary of L'Assistance Publique.

Musée d'Histoire de la Médecine

Université René Descartes, 12 rue de l'Ecole-de-Médecine, 6th (01.40.46.16.93). Mº Odéon. **Open** 15 July-Sept 2-5.30pm Mon-Fri; *Oct-13 July* 2-5.30pm Mon-Wed, Fri, Sat. Closed Sun, public holidays. **Admission** 20F; free under-12s. **No credit cards. Map H7**

The medical faculty collection covers the history of medicine from ancient Egyptian embalming tools through to a 1960s electrocardiograph. There's a gruesome array of serrated-edged saws and curved knives used for amputations, stethoscopes and syringes, the surgical instruments of Dr Antommarchi, who performed the autopsy on Napoléon, and the scalpel of Dr Félix, who operated on Louis XIV.

Muséum National d'Histoire Naturelle

*57 rue Cuvier, 5th (01.40.79.30.00). M° Jusssieu or
Gare d'Austerlitz.* **Open** *Grande Galerie* 10am-6pm Mon,
Wed, Fri-Sun; 10am-10pm Thur. Closed Tue. **Admission**
Grande Galerie 40F; 30F 5-16s, students, over-60s; free
under-5s. *Other pavilions, each* 30F; 20F students, 4-16s,
over-60s. **No credit cards. Map K9**
Within the Jardin des Plantes botanical garden, the brilliantly renovated Grande Galerie de l'Evolution has taken Paris'
Natural History Museum out of the dinosaur age. Skeletons
and stuffed animals were restored and architect Paul
Chemetov successfully integrated modern lifts, stairways
and the latest lighting and audio-visual techniques into the
nineteenth-century iron-framed structure. As you enter, you
will be confronted with the 13.66 metre-long skeleton of a
whale: the rest of the ground floor is dedicated to other sea
creatures. Don't miss the unpleasant-looking swordfish, or
the narwhal with its two metre-long tusk. On the first floor
are the big mammals, organised by habitat (savannah, jungle, etc) mostly in the open – with the exception of Louis
XVI's rhinoceros, stuffed on a wooden chair frame shortly
after its demise (and that of monarchy) in 1793. Video screens
and interactive computer screens give information on life in
the wild. Glass-sided lifts take you up through suspended
birds to the second floor, which deals with man's impact on
nature and considers demographic problems and pollution.
The third floor traces the evolution of species, while a gallery
at the side, deliberately retaining old-fashioned glass cases,
displays endangered and extinct species. Striking a very neat
balance between fun and education, the museum is popular
with kids, with a 'discovery' room for the under-12s and
laboratories for teenagers. The long dusty departments of
geology, fossils, skeletons and insects housed in separate
pavilions over the park have just had a facelift. *See also chapters* **Left Bank**, **Parks** *and* **Children**.
*Auditorium. Bookshop. Café. Library. Wheelchair access
(Grande Galerie).*

Musée Pasteur

*Institut Pasteur, 25 rue du Dr-Roux, 15th
(01.45.68.82.82). M° Pasteur.* **Open** 2-5.30pm daily.
Closed public holidays, Aug. **Admission** 15F; 8F
students. **Credit** MC, V. **Map E9**
The apartment where the famous chemist and his wife lived
for the last seven years of his life (1888-95) has hardly been
touched since his death; you can still see their furniture and
possessions, family photographs, memorabilia and a room
of scientific instruments. The highlight is the extravagant,
Byzantine-style funerary chapel on the ground floor built to
house Pasteur's tomb; the brightly coloured mosaics illustrate some of his most important scientific achievements,
including pasteurisation and a vaccine against rabies.
Shop.

Musée de Radio-France

*116 av du Président-Kennedy, 16th (01.42.30.21.80). M°
Ranelagh/RER Kennedy-Radio France.* **Open** guided tours
10.30am, 11.30am, 2.30pm, 3.30pm, 4.30pm Mon-Sat. Closed
public holidays. **Admission** 20F; 15F 8s-25s, students,
over-60s. No under-8s. **No credit cards. Map A7**
When the cylindrical Radio France building was opened by
De Gaulle in 1963 it was a technological wonder and a visit
to the museum starts with an appreciation of its now rather
dated architecture. The history of audio and visual science
is clearly presented with an emphasis on French pioneers
such as Branly and Charles Cros, including documentary evidence of the first radio message between the Eiffel Tower
and the Panthéon. The exhibits, from primitive crystal sets
through suberb Art Deco radios and televisions to contemporary equipment, are illustrated by fascinating clips; particularly interesting is the London broadcast of the Free
French with its delightfully obscure coded messages. From
the museum you can look through double-glazed panels onto
the making of radio programmes, where 'noises off' are still

provided by *bruiteurs* with coconut shells and clattering
plates. The tour ends with a visit to the barnlike Salle Olivier
Messiaen concert hall. It is a shame that this museum is only
available as a guided tour, exhibits are clearly captioned and
a chance to linger or accelerate would be welcome.

Musée du Service de Santé des Armées

*Val de Grace, pl Alphonse-Laveran, 5th (01.40.51.40.00).
RER Port-Royal.* **Open** noon-5pm Tue, Wed, Sat, Sun.
Map J9
Admission 30F; 15F under-12s. **No credit cards.**
Don't be put off by the rather daunting title, for not only is this
an exemplary newly restored collection, but it is also housed
in one of the capital's finest Baroque buildings (for an extra
20F you can enjoy a guided tour of Anne of Austria's salon,
with monogrammed marble floor). The museum traces the history of military medicine, via recreations of field hospitals and
ambulance trains, and beautifully presented antique medical
instruments and pharmacy jars. World War I brings a chilling
insight into the horror of the conflict, when many buildings
were transformed into hospitals and, ironically, medical science progressed in leaps and bounds. The collection is also rich
in moving pictures of battlefield scenes. Exhibits are supported by audiovisual consoles (in French), which allow the visitor
to explore subjects from malaria to early surgical techniques.
If you've ever played doctors and nurses you'll be riveted.

Palais de la Découverte

*Grand Palais, av Franklin D Roosevelt, 8th
(01.40.74.80.00/01.40.74.81.73). M° Franklin D
Roosevelt.* **Open** 9.30am-6pm Tue-Sat; 10am-7pm Sun.
Closed Mon, 1 Jan, 1 May, 14 July, 15 Aug, 25 Dec.
Admission 27F; 17F 7-18s, students under 26; free
under-7s. *Planetarium* 13F. **Credit** MC, V. **Map E5**
Join hordes of schoolkids at Paris' original science museum,
housing designs from Leonardo da Vinci's extraordinary

Interact at the **Cité des Sciences**.

inventions onwards. Replicas, models, audiovisual material and real apparatus are used to bring the displays to life. Permanent displays cover man and his biology, light and the thrills of thermo-dynamism. The space Planète Terre space has been remodelled to take account of developments in meteorology and issues such as global warming, while one room is dedicated to all you could ever want to know about the sun. There is also a theatre, where on some days demonstrations of electrostatics are presented (11am, 1pm, 3pm, 5pm). Members of the audience are charged with electricity so that their hair stands on end or they give off long sparks. Housed at the back of the Grand Palais, it is far more conveniently located than the Cité des Sciences, if a bit old-fashioned by comparison, and teems with young children. In November 1997 the Planetarium reopened with a new projector and fibre optics to allow much more realistic representation of the starscape and planetary movement. *Café. Experiments. Shop.*

Eccentricities

Musée de la Contrefaçon

16 rue de la Faisanderie, 16th (01.56.26.14.00). Mº Porte-Dauphine. **Open** 2-5.30pm Tue-Sun. Closed Mon, and Sat, Sun in Aug. **Admission** 15F; free under-12s. **No credit cards. Map A4**
This small museum was set up by the Union des Fabricants, the French anti-counterfeiting association and puts a strong emphasis on the penalties involved (even for the buyer) in forgery. Although the oldest known forgery is displayed (vase covers from c.200 BC), the main focus is on contemporary copies of well-known brands – Reebok, Lacoste, Hermès, Vuitton, Ray Ban – with the real thing displayed next to the fake; even Babie doll, Barbie's illicit clone, gets a look in.

Musée de la Curiosité

11 rue St-Paul, 4th (01.42.72.13.26). Mº St-Paul or Sully Morland. **Open** 2pm-7pm Wed, Sat, Sun. Closed Mon, Tue, Thur, Fri. **Admission** 45F, 30F 3-12s; free under-3s. **No credit cards. Map L7**
A museum of magic at the heart of the Marais, with a show of card tricks, a talk (in French) on the history of magic going back to Egyptian times and a whole range of objects such as magic wands, a cabinet for cutting people in half, optical illusions and posters. The welcome is warm and enthusiastic, and you will be guided through the collection by specialists whose passion for their art is absolutely contagious. If you're lucky, they might even teach you a trick or two.

Musée de l'Erotisme

72 bd de Clichy, 18th (01.42.58.28.73). Mº Blanche. **Open** 10am-2am daily. **Admission** 40F; 30F students. **No credit cards. Map H2**
Opened in 1997 by Joseph Khalifa (a collector of erotic art) and his two associates, the erotic museum has been seen as an attempt to clean up the sleazy image of peep-show Pigalle. The diverse collection of erotic art, both sacred and profane, includes painting, sculpture, graphic art and *objets d'art* from Latin America, Asia, Europe to Nepal. Pieces run from Indian Hindu representations of lingam and yoni, African ceremonial masks, Japanese prints/paintings of courting couples, tiny Chinese ceramic *objets d'art* up to modern and contemporary works. Sadly, the pieces are organised haphazardly and labelling is at a minimum, making it difficult to decipher the origin, age and purpose (if any) of a piece. *Shop. Wheelchair access.*

Musée de la Poupée

Impasse Berthaud, 3rd (01.42.72.73.11). Mº Rambuteau. **Open** 10am-6pm Tue-Sun. Closed Mon. **Admission** 35F; 25F 18-25s; 20F 3-18s; free under-3s. **No credit cards. Map K5**
This private collection of French dolls puts the emphasis on

the late nineteenth century, with dolls by manufacturers Jumeau, Steiner and Gaultier. Ringlets, large eyes, rose-bud lips, arching eyebrows and peaches-and-cream complexions give a good idea of the period's concept of female beauty. The elaborate costumes and the selection of period dolls' houses, tea-sets and teddies, also give an insight into nineteenth-century middle-class life, although temporary shows, such as Barbie, have recently given doll society an update. *Bookshop. Wheelchair access.*

Musée de la SEITA

12 rue Surcouf, 7th (01.45.56.60.17). Mº Invalides or Latour-Maubourg. **Open** 11am-7pm Tue-Sun. Closed Mon. **Admission** free. *Temporary exhibitions* 25F; 15F students; free under-12s. **Credit** MC, V. **Map E5**
On the site of France's first cigarette factory, the museum of the French state tobacco company SEITA traces the development of the lowly weed that rose from relative obscurity to become a household name. In France, it's all thanks to Jean Nicot (of nicotine fame), who in 1561 first introduced tobacco to the country in his diplomatic bag. Smoking paraphernalia from around the world includes snuff boxes, tobacco graters, maiolica tobacco jars, hundreds of pipes (among them George Sand's favourite) and the changing designs of Gauloises and Gitanes packs. High-quality temporary art exhibitions – financed by but unrelated to smoking – have included Basquiat, Dix, Schiele and Kokoschka. *Bookshop. Wheelchair access.*

Musée du Vin

rue des Eaux, 5 square Charles-Dickens, 16th (01.45.25.63.26). Mº Passy. **Open** 10am-6pm Tue-Sun. Closed Mon, 25 Dec-1 Jan. **Admission** 35F; 29F over-60s; 28F 4-18s, students; free under-4s. **Credit** (shop/restaurant) AmEx, DC, MC, V. **Map B6**
The Ile-de-France was a wine producing area in the Middle Ages, as nearby rue Vineuse reminds. Now only a few bottles are produced at Suresnes, Parc Georges Brassens and Montmartre, which are of only anecdotal interest to modern tastes. The main appeal of the museum is the beauty of the building itself: the genuine, vaulted cellar of a wine-producing monastery that was destroyed during the Revolution. The ancient bottles, vats, corkscrews and cutouts of medieval peasants making wine are quickly seen, but at the end there is a *dégustation* (tasting) with some *foie gras*. There is some wine on sale, but thankfully no hard sell. *Restaurant (noon-3pm). Shop.*

Exhibition Centres

Most open only during exhibitions. Various cultural centres also mount shows related to the countries they represent. These include: Centre Culturel Calouste Gulbenkian (Portugal – 51 av d'Iéna, 16th/ 01.53.23.93.93); Centre Culturel Suisse (38 rue des Francs-Bourgeois, 3rd/01.42.71.38.38); Centre Wallonie-Bruxelles (127 rue St-Martin, 4th/ 01.53.01.96.96); Goëthe Institut (Germany – 17 av d'Iéna/ 16th/01.44.43.92.30/and Galerie Condé, 31 rue de Condé, 6th/01.40.46.69.60); Institut Finlandais (60 rue des Ecoles, 5th/01.40.51.89.08); Institut Néerlandais (121 rue de Lille, 7th/01.53.59.12.40); Maison de l'Amérique Latine (217 bd St-Germain, 7th/01.49.54.75.00).

Bibliothèque Forney

Hôtel de Sens, 1 rue du Figuier, 4th (01.42.78.14.60). Mº Pont-Marie. **Open** 1.30-8pm Tue-Sat. Closed Mon, public holidays, Aug. **Admission** 20F; 10F students under 28, over-60s; free under-12s.

*Dusty vintages at the **Musée du Vin**.*

No credit cards. Map L7
Set in the turrets and Gothic vaulting of this medieval mansion – the oldest in the Marais – the library specialises in the applied and graphic arts, and has a wing given over to temporary displays. *See also chapter* **Right Bank**. *Bookshop.*

Bibliothèque Nationale de France – Richelieu
58 rue de Richelieu, 2nd (01.47.03.81.26). **Open** 10am-7pm Tue-Sun. Closed Mon, two weeks in Sept, public holidays. **Admission** 35F; 24F 12-26s, students, over-60s. **Credit** MC, V. **Map H4**
Within the old Bibliothèque Nationale, the Galeries Mansart and Mazarine, once Cardinal Mazarin's art gallery and library, have regular exhibitions ranging from Indian miniatures or medieval manuscripts to contemporary etchings. *See also chapter* **Right Bank**.

Bibliothèque Nationale de France – François Mitterrand
quai François-Mauriac, 13th (01.53.79.59.59). *M° Bibliothèque Nationale or Quai de la Gare.* **Open** 10am-7pm Tue-Sat; noon-6pm Sun. Closed Mon, two weeks in Sept, public holidays. **Admission** 35F; 24F 12-26s over-60s; free under-12s. **Credit** MC, V. **Map M10**
The gigantic new library could not be more different from its historic parent, but shares a similarly erudite programme, which includes photography and an on-going cycle related to writing. *See also chapters* **Left Bank** *and* **Directory**. *Café. Wheelchair access.*

Chapelle St-Louis de la Salpêtrière
47 bd de l'Hôpital, 13th (01.42.16.04.24). *M° Gare d'Austerlitz.* **Open** 8.30am-5.30pm daily. **Admission** free. **No credit cards. Map L9**
Libéral Bruand's austere seventeenth-century chapel provides

a fantastic setting for contemporary art, notably installations by Bill Viola, Tadashi Kawamata and Anish Kapoor for various Festivals d'Automne. *See chapter* **Left Bank**. *Wheelchair access.*

Couvent des Cordeliers
15 rue de l'Ecole-de-Médicine, 6th (01.40.46.05.47). *M° Odéon.* **Open** hours vary, usually 11am-7pm Tue-Sun. Closed Mon. **Admission** 25F; 10F students, over-60s; free under-3s. **No credit cards. Map H7**
Administered by the Ville de Paris and the medical school, this barn-like refectory of a Franciscan convent is used for varied shows, in both style and quality, of contemporary art.

Ensb-a (Ecole Nationale Supérieure des Beaux-Arts)
13 quai Malaquais, 6th (01.47.03.50.00). *M° St-Germain-des-Prés.* **Open** 1-7pm Tue-Sun. Closed Mon. **Admission** 25F; 15F students, over-60s; free under-12s. **Credit** MC, V. **Map H6**
Exhibitions at France's central art college vary from the pick of recent graduates (May-June 1999) to theme shows of contemporary art (Corps social, autumn 1999) or from Ensb-a's rich holdings of prints and drawings (nude studies, Géricault, Dutch and Italian drawing). *See also chapter* **Left Bank**. *Bookshop.*

Espace Electra
6 rue Récamier, 7th (01.53.63.23.45). *M° Sèvres-Babylone.* **Open** noon-6.30pm Tue-Sun. Closed public holidays, Aug. **Admission** varies. **No credit cards. Map G7**
Originally built as an electricity substation and owned by the French electricity board, Espace Electra is used for varied art, graphic and design exhibitions, from garden designer Gilles Clément to photography or Latin American art.

Fondation Cartier pour l'art contemporain
261 bd Raspail, 14th (01.42.18.56.72/recorded information 01.42.18.56.51). *M° Raspail.* **Open** noon-8pm Tue, Wed, Fri-Sun; noon-10pm Thur. Closed Mon. **Admission** 30F; 20F under-25s, students, over-60s; free under-10s. **Credit** (shop) V. **Map G9**
Jean Nouvel's glass and steel building is as much a work of art as the exhibitions inside, which alternate between shows and installations by contemporary artists like Jean-Pierre Raynaud and Panamerenko or fashion designer Issey Miyake, to multi-cultural, century-crossing themes as wide-ranging as birds or love. The transparency of the ground floor means that many artists seem happier with the basement space. Concerts, dance and video are presented in the 'Soirées Nomades' at 8pm on Thursday between September and June. *Bookshop. Wheelchair access.*

Fondation Coprim
46 rue de Sévigné, 3rd (01.44.78.60.00). *M° St-Paul.* **Open** 10am-6pm Mon-Fri; noon-6pm Sat. Closed Sun, two weeks in Aug, public holidays. **Admission** free. **No credit cards. Map L6**
Coprim moved recently to a former print workshop in the Marais. The bent is towards contemporary figurative painting – opening show was Gérard Garouste's Rabelaisian cycle – and there's also an annual prize for young artists. *Bookshop.*

Fondation Mona Bismarck
34 av de New-York, 16th (01.47.23.38.88). *M° Alma-Marceau.* **Open** 10.30am-6.15pm Tue-Sat. Closed Mon, Sun, Jul, Aug, public holidays. **Admission** free. **No credit cards. Map C5**
Very chic setting for widely varied exhibitions of everything from Etruscan antiquities to Haitian painters, often lent by prestigious foreign collections.

Galéries Nationales du Grand Palais

Grand Palais, av du Général-Eisenhower, 8th (01.44.13.17.17). M° Champs-Elysées-Clemenceau. **Open** 10am-8pm Mon, Thur-Sun; 10am-10pm Wed. Pre-booking compulsory before 1pm. Closed Tue, 1 May, 25 Dec. **Admission** 50F; 35F students, all on Mon; *two exhibitions* 63F; 43F students, all on Mon. **Credit** (shop) V. **Map E5** Paris' premier venue for blockbuster exhibitions is a striking leftover from the 1900 Grand Exposition. The glass-domed central hall is closed for restoration, but two other exhibition spaces remain. 1999 sees exhibitions on Ancient Egypt, Daumier and Chardin. *See also chapter* **Right Bank**. *Audioguides. Bookshop. Café. Wheelchair access*

Halle St-Pierre – Musée d'Art Naïf Max Fourny

2 rue Ronsard, 18th (01.42.58.72.89). M° Anvers. **Open** 10am-6pm Mon-Sat. Closed Sun. **Admission** 40F; 25F students. CM. **Credit** (shop) AmEx, DC, MC, V. **Map J2** The former covered market specialises in Art Brut (a term coined by Dubuffet to describe self-taught *singuliers*, often from poor backgrounds with no formal training or those in prisons and asylums, who used poor or idiosyncratic materials) and *art-naïf* (self-taught artists who use more traditional techniques) from its own and other specialist collections (until July 1999: American Outsider Art). The link to children's art is reflected in workshops put on for youngsters. *Bookshop. Children's workshops.*

Jeu de Paume

1 pl de la Concorde, 1st (01.47.03.12.50). M° Concorde. **Open** noon-9.30pm Tue; noon-7pm Wed-Fri; 10am-7pm Sat, Sun. Closed Mon, some public holidays. **Admission** 38F; 28F students, over-60s; free under-13s. **No credit cards. Map F5** When the Impressionist museum moved from here to the Musée d'Orsay, the former real tennis court of the Tuileries Palace was redesigned by Antoine Stinco for contemporary and modern art exhibitions. The recent emphasis has been on the 1950s and 60s, with French establishment artists (Arman, César, Alechinsky) drawing an audience to match. A basement cinema mounts artists' film and video series. *Bookshop. Café. Cinema. Wheelchair access.*

Musée-atelier Adzak

3 rue Jonquoy, 14th (01.45.43.06.98). M° Plaisance. **Open** *depends on show.* The eccentric house and studio built by the late Roy Adzak resounds with traces of this conceptual artist's plaster body columns and dehydrations. Now a registered charity, it gives (mainly foreign) artists a first chance to exhibit in Paris.

Passage de Retz

9 rue Charlot, 3rd (01.48.04.37.99). M° Filles du Calvaire. **Open** 10am-7pm daily. **Admission** 35F; 20F students under 26, over-60s; free under-12s. **No credit cards. Map L5** A Marais mansion which became a toy factory and has now been resurrected as a gallery. Varied shows include contemporary design as well as fine art and fun theme offerings like techno-music-led Global Techno or a valentine show. *Café.*

Pavillon des Arts

101 rue Rambuteau, 1st (01.42.33.82.50). M° Châtelet-Les Halles. **Open** 11.30am-6.30pm Tue-Sun. Closed Mon, public holidays. **Admission** 30F; 20F 6s-25s, students, over-60s; free under-6s. **No credit cards. Map K5** Next to the Forum des Halles, this first-floor gallery hosts varied exhibitions from contemporary photography or Vietnamese art to Surrealism to the history of Paris. *Wheelchair access.*

Renn Espace d'Art Contemporain

7 rue de Lille, 7th (01.42.60.22.99). M° Rue du Bac. **Open** 3-7pm Tue-Sat. Closed Mon, Sun. **Admission** free. **No credit cards. Map G6** This well-designed space owned by film director Claude Berri hosts retrospective-style exhibitions, lasting six to nine months, devoted to modern abstract or conceptual masters such as Yves Klein, Sol LeWitt, Daniel Buren and Hantai.

Expect hair-raising discoveries at the **Palais de la Découverte** *(see p128).*

Art Galleries

Catch up on the latest multi-media trends, gallery powerhouses and new forms of exhibition as art goes streetwise.

Galleries are art laboratories. They are the places where you will see artists first, or can follow them over the long term. Paris galleries have long been aided by a strong state aquisition policy (now reduced), often to the detriment of a private buyers' market, and a system of grants for first shows. But there are increasing challenges to the traditional exhibition format, both by alternative projects or within galleries themselves (*see box*). The current art scene continues to involve a vast multiplicity of styles and media: painting, drawing, installation, readymades, photo and video, not to mention sound pieces and actions. The medium is simply means to an end, and appropriation – harking back to grand-daddy Marcel Duchamp – is open to all.

THE ART CIRCUIT

Like-minded galleries cluster together. For new, innovative work head for the northern part of the Marais. Galleries around the Bastille mainly present young artists; those around St-Germain-des-Prés, home of the avant-garde in the 1950s and 60s, now largely confine themselves to traditional sculpture and painting, while those around the Champs-Elysées, the centre before that, present big modern and contemporary names, but are unlikely to risk the untried. Those interested in the most conceptual side of young creation should keep an eye on rue Louise-Weiss, behind the new Bibliothèque Nationale, where six young galleries set up shop as **Scène Est** in 1997, tempting several thousand visitors with a shared calendar of show openings. Annual art fair FIAC in early October gives a quick fix on the gallery scene.

SQUATS & STUDIOS

Thousands of French and international artists continue to live and work in Paris, aided by subsidised studio projects, or heading for low-rent *quartiers*. Some start off in art 'squats', often becoming involved in saving the life of the district and gaining semi-official studio status, like Les Frigos (91 quai de la Gare, 13th/01.44.24.96.96), its future still uncertain in the ZAC Rive Gauche redevelopment; La Forge (rue Ramponneau, 20th); or the Squart/Collectif de la Grange (31 rue de la Grange-aux-Belles, 10th), currently fighting eviction but supported by the local Mairie. There are numerous chances to visit artists' studios. The Génie de la Bastille, Ménilmontant and the 13ème Art (*see* chapter **Paris by Season**) are the best known,

but there are also 'portes ouvertes' (often in May or October) in Belleville, St-Germain, the 14th and 18th *arrondissements* and the suburbs of Montrouge, Montreuil and Ivry-sur-Seine.

INFORMATION & MAGAZINES

Local publications include *Beaux Arts*, focusing on the historical and the art market, and the more contemporary bilingual *Art Press*. Trendy young mags *Blocnotes* and *Purple* take a more multi-disciplinary look, embracing design, philosophy, fashion, music and film in a break from white-cube gallery orthodoxy. Only a selection of the most active and consistent galleries can be listed here. For information on current shows, look for the leaflet *Galeries Mode d'Emploi* (Marais/Bastille/rue Louise-Weiss), the Association des Galleries fold-out (Left and Right Bank shows/suburban cultural centres) and the *Journal des Expositions*, which carries ads for some of the more alternative spaces. Virtually all galleries are closed in August. Ring to check in late July and early September.

Beaubourg & the Marais

Galerie Aréa
10 rue de Picardie, 3rd (01.42.72.68.66). M° Temple. **Open** 2-7pm Wed-Sat; 3-7pm Sun. **Map L5**
A small, two-level gallery bravely committed to French painters, usually with a figurative/expressionist bent. Also occasional literary events. More experimental works get short shows at the Réserve (50 rue d'Hauteville, 10th).

Brownstone Corréard & Cie
26 rue St-Gilles, 3rd (01.42.78.43.21). M° Chemin-Vert. **Open** 11am-1pm, 2-7pm Tue-Sat. **Map L6**
Minimalist aesthetics and fashion links are frequent trends in this glass-fronted gallery: John Armleder, photographer Seton Smith, Gottfried Honegger and Sylvie Fleury's interesting fashion statements.

Farideh Cadot
77 rue des Archives, 3rd (01.42.78.08.36). M° Arts et Métiers. **Open** 2-7pm Tue-Sat. **Map L5**
After 20 years, Farideh Cadot's shows still reflect personal taste and long-term loyalty to a particular set of artists, including Connie Beckley, Meret Oppenheim, Georges Rousse, Joël Fisher, Jorge Molder and Markus Raetz.

Galerie Cent 8
108 rue Vieille-du-Temple, 3rd (01.42.74.53.57). M° St-Sébastien-Froissart. **Open** 10.30am-1pm, 2.30-7pm Tue-Sat. **Map L5**
Consistently interesting since opening in spring 1998, with Christine Borland's anthropological explorations (back in 2000) and Laurent Parriente's white maze; Hans Hemmert and Xavier Zimmerman are coming up in 1999.

Chantal Crousel

40 rue Quincampoix, 4th (01.42.77.38.87). M° Châtelet-Les Halles. **Open** 11am-1pm, 2-7pm Tue-Sat. **Map J6**
This long-standing Beaubourg gallery hosts both internationally known Sigmar Polke, Tony Cragg, Sophie Calle, Annette Messager and Mona Hatoum, and some of the hottest of the new generation, Thomas Hirshhorn, Abigail Lane and Rikrit Tiravanija. Look out for Gabriel Orozco and a first show by Israeli Moshe Ninio in summer 1999. All media.

Galerie de France

54 rue de la Verrerie, 4th (01.42.74.38.00). M° Hôtel-de-Ville. **Open** 11am-7pm Tue-Sat. **Map K6**
One of the rare galleries to span the entire twentieth century, from Brancusi, the melting heads of Eduardo Rosso and erotic Surrealism of Mattà to contemporary artists like Cy Twombly, Rebecca Horn and sculptor Alain Kirili.

Galerie Marian Goodman

7 rue Debelleyme, 3rd (01.48.04.70.52). M° St-Sébastien-Froissart. **Open** 11am-7pm Tue-Sat. **Map L5**
Goodman introduced Europeans like Boltanski and Kiefer to New York. Now she brings some of them back for mini demonstrations. It's mainly established names (Baumgarten, Struth, etc) but she has also snapped up brilliant young Brit videomaker Steve McQueen. Changing address in May 1999.

Galerie Karsten Greve

5 rue Debelleyme, 3rd (01.42.77.19.37). M° St-Sébastien-Froissart. **Open** 11am-7pm Tue-Sat. **Map L5**
This historic Marais building is Cologne gallerist Karsten Greve's Parisian outpost and venue for retrospective-style displays of top-ranking artists such as Cy Twombly, Louise Bourgeois, John Chamberlain and Tony Cragg.

Galerie Ghislaine Hussenot

5bis rue des Haudriettes, 3rd (01.48.87.60.81). M° Rambuteau. **Open** 11am-1pm, 2-7pm Tue-Sat. **Map K5**
High-concept stuff is presented in a two-level warehouse space, from the date paintings of conceptual guru On Kawara and the sculptural forms of Franz West to the much-hyped fashion model performances of young Italian Vanessa Beecroft.

Galerie du Jour Agnès b

44 rue de Quincampoix, 4th (01.44.54.55.90). M° Châtelet-Les Halles. **Open** noon-7pm Tue-Sat. **Map J5**
Agnès b's gallery fills the modern space previously used by Galerie Jean Fournier (which returns for a show in July). Artists share the designer's interests in the Third World and social issues: British photographer Martin Parr, Africa's Felix Brouly Bouabré and Seydou Keïta, India's Vyakul, plus a few French such as the sound/light environments of Claude Lévêque.

Galerie Laage-Salomon

57 rue du Temple, 4th (01.42.78.11.71). M° Rambuteau. **Open** 2-7pm Tue-Sat. **Map K6**
Goes from land artists/sculptors Roger Ackling and Hamish Fulton to the feminist slogans of Claudia Hart, photographers Hannah Collins, Fariba Hajamadi and Candida Höfer.

Yvon Lambert

108 rue Vieille-du-Temple, 3rd (01.42.71.09.33). M° Filles du Calvaire. **Open** 10am-1pm, 2.30-7pm Tue-Fri; 10am-7pm Sat. **Map L5**
A succession of major names – Kiefer, Kosuth, Schnabel, Boltanski, Toroni, Goldin, Serrano – makes this warehouse-like gallery an essential stop. Photoworks and videos from Barbara Kruger and a new installation by Carl André started off 1999. Young artists in the Côté Rue gallery (2-7pm Tue-Sat).

Galerie Nikki Diana Marquardt

9 pl des Vosges/10 rue de Turenne, 4th (01.42.78.21.00). M° St-Paul or Bastille. **Open** 11am-6pm Mon-Fri; noon-6pm Sat. **Map L6**
Many shows in this former industrial space off place des Vosges have a political content. Sarajevo, Northern Ireland, Algeria and Palestine have figured as topics for group shows, with occasional film, poetry or music evenings.

Galerie Nelson

40 rue Quincampoix, 4th (01.42.71.74.56). M° Châtelet-Les Halles. **Open** 2-7pm Tue-Sat. **Map J6**
Mainly photoworks by Thomas Ruff, Thomas Schütte, Joseph Bartscherer, plus pieces by late Fluxus artist Filliou.

Galerie Nathalie Obadia

5 rue du Grenier-St-Lazare, 3rd (01.42.74.67.68). M° Rambuteau. **Open** 11am-7pm Mon-Sat. **Map K5**
Obadia supports young talents, often many women, like installation artist Nathalie Elemento and painter Valérie Favre, plus established names Jessica Stockholder and Bustamente.

Galerie Papillon-Fiat

16 rue des Coutures-St-Gervais, 3rd (01.40.29.98.80). M° St-Paul. **Open** 2-7pm Tue-Sat. **Map L6**
Claudine Papillon shows important contemporary European painters and sculptors, usually of Conceptual bent, such as Tony Carter, Erik Dietman, Michael Craig-Martin, Dieter Roth, Patrick Caulfield and Sigmar Polke.

Galerie Gilles Peyroulet

80 rue Quincampoix, 3rd (01.42.78.85.11). M° Rambuteau or Etienne-Marcel. **Open** 2-7pm Tue-Fri; 11am-7pm Sat. **Map K5**
Peyroulet shows works in all media but is often stronger with photo and sculpture-based pieces. Artists include Marin Kasimir, Alex Hartley, Markus Hansen and Robin Collyer.

Galerie Polaris

8 rue St-Claude, 3rd (01.42.72.21.27). M° St-Sébastien-Froissart. **Open** 1-7.30pm Tue-Fri; 11am-1pm, 2-7.30pm Sat. **Map L5**
Bernard Utudjian works over the long term with a few artists including photographers Stéphane Couturier and Anthony Hernandez and photo/performance artist Nigel Rolfe.

Galerie Jacqueline Rabouan-Moussion

110 rue Vieille-du-Temple, 3rd (01.48.87.75.91). M° Filles du Calvaire. **Open** 10am-7pm Mon-Sat. **Map L5**
Moussion alternates unusual Paris-based artists, such as Anne Ferrer, whose satin pigs touch on feminism and sexuality, gender stuff from Chrystel Egal, funny videomaker Pierrick Sorin, with some older French names, such as Jean Degottex, and Korean artists concerned with environmental art.

Galerie Rachlin Lemarié Beaubourg

23 rue du Renard, 4th (01.44.59.27.27). M° Hôtel-de-Ville. **Open** 10.30am-1pm, 2.30-7pm Tue-Sat. **Map K6**
When Galerie Beaubourg moved south, Rachlin and Lemarié took over its list including sculptors Arman and César and *nouvelle figuration* painter Combas, and added a few artists of their own, like François Boisrand and Nichola Hicks.

Galerie Thaddaeus Ropac

7 rue Debelleyme, 3rd (01.42.72.99.00). M° St-Sébastien-Froissart. **Open** 10am-7pm Tue-Sat. **Map L5**
Mainly features American Pop, neo-Pop and neo-Geo (Warhol, Baechler, Sachs), but has pulled off some coups with an installation by Kabakov and the museum-quality *New Testament Paintings* of Gilbert & George.

Daniel Templon

30 rue Beaubourg, 3rd (01.42.72.14.10). M° Rambuteau. **Open** 10am-7pm Mon-Sat. **Map K5**
A favourite with the French art establishment, Templon shows big-name painters. Salle, Alberola, Viallat and Le Gac are understandable, but it seemed a most unlikely spot for shockers Jake and Dinos Chapman's first Paris presentation.

Gilbert & George at **Thaddaeus Ropac** *– always better appreciated in France than the UK.*

Galerie Anne de Villepoix
11 rue de Tournelles, 4th (01.42.78.32.24). M° Bastille.
Open 11am-7pm Tue-Sat. **Map L7**
Anne de Villepoix alternates established older figures such as photographer John Coplans with younger artists in all media. Jean-Luc Moulène, Andrew Mansfield, Sam Samore, Gillian Wearing and Valérie Jouve are programmed for 1999.

Galerie Xippas
108 rue Vieille-du-Temple, 3rd (01.40.27.05.55). M° Filles du Calvaire. **Open** 10am-1pm, 2-7pm Tue-Fri; 10am-7pm Sat. **Map L6**
This unusual U-shaped gallery presents painters and photographers as varied as Thomas Demand, Nancy Dwyer, Joan Hernández Pijoan, Ian Davenport and Anne Deleporte.

Galerie Zurcher
56 rue Chapon, 3rd (01.42.72.82.20). M° Arts & Métiers.
Open 11am-7pm Tue-Sat. **Map K5**
Specialises in young artists including Camille Vivier and recent Ensb-a graduate Gwen Ravillous, young Swiss Michel Huellin, and young Brit painters Paula Kane and Dan Hayes.

Bastille

Chez Valentin
77 av Ledru-Rollin, 12th (01.43.44.15.38).
M° Ledru-Rollin. **Open** 2.30-7pm Tue-Sat. **Map N7**
Young artists. You might find Véronique Boudier's crushed neon tubes and mouldering jelly, other suprising media in the sound installations of Franck David, the naive portraits of Jean-Christophe Robert positively charm in comparison.

Durand-Dessert
28 rue de Lappe, 11th (01.48.06.92.23). M° Bastille.
Open 11am-7pm Tue-Sat. **Map M7**
A powerhouse of the French art scene, this gallery has long been committed to artists associated with arte povera (Pistoletto and Mario Merz), major French names François

Morellet, Gérard Garouste and Bertrand Lavier and photographers William Wegman, Patrick Tosani and Balthasar Burckhardt. There's an excellent art bookshop.

Galerie J & J Donguy
57 rue de la Roquette, 11th (01.47.00.10.94).
M° Bastille. **Open** 1-7pm Tue-Sat. **Map M6**
Idiosyncratic Donguy, one of the first to open in the area, concentrates on the photos and documents of *art corporel* (body art), including operation-crazy Orlan, and the Austrian action art scene such as now-imprisoned Otto Mühl.

Galerie Alain Gutharc
47 rue de Lappe, 11th (01.47.00.32.10). M° Bastille.
Open 2-7pm Tue-Fri; 11am-7pm Sat. **Map M7**
Gutharc shows a taste for the intimate, seen in the photos of Agnès Propeck, and has recently picked out the young photographers Delphine Kreuter and Greg Fielder.

Espace d'Art Yvonamor Palix
13 rue Keller, 11th (01.48.06.36.70). M° Bastille or Ledru-Rollin. **Open** 2-7pm Tue-Sat. **Map M6**
This Mexican gallerist's slickly presented artists, often American, mostly use computer-manipulated photography: Aziz+Cucher, Sandy Skogland, Joseph Nevchatel, Keith Cottingham and Richard Prince. Paris-based, British-born artist Lucy Orta's projects involve clothes and the homeless.

Galerie Jousse Seguin
34 rue de Charonne, 11th (01.47.00.32.35). M° Bastille or Ledru-Rollin. **Open** 11am-1.30pm, 2.30-7pm Mon-Sat.
Map N7
This dynamic gallery picks up on 90s issues like gender and identity (Chuck Nanney, Serge Conte's Post-it portraits, or Thomas Grunfeld's animal misfits), plus a few painters (Peter Hopkins, Richter pupil Karin Kneffel) and the multi-media sampling/actions of Mathieu Laurette. A hangar-like second space round the corner at 5 rue des Taillandiers is devoted to furniture and ceramics by architects and designers of the 1930s to 50s such as Charlotte Perriand and Jean Prouvé.

Le Sous-Sol

*9 rue de Charonne, 11th (01.47.00.02.75). M° Bastille or
Ledru-Rollin.* **Open** 2.30-7pm Tue-Sat. **Map M7**
After moving from its basement a year ago, the Sous-Sol continues to invite artists to create site-specific works that interact with the architecture, whether in its new location or in outside premises such as a recently converted Marais *hôtel.*

Champs-Elysées

Galerie Louis Carré et Cie

10 av de Messine, 8th (01.45.62.57.07). M° Miromesnil.
Open 10am-12.30pm, 2-6.30pm Mon-Sat. **Map E3**
This gallery was founded in 1938 and shows today largely focus on a small stable of contemporary French artists such as *nouvelle figuration* painter Hervé di Rosa and Haïtianborn sculptor Hervé Télémacque, although you'll also find Calder, Dufy, Delaunay and Léger among the artists in stock.

Galerie Lelong

13 rue de Téhéran, 8th (01.45.63.13.19). M° Miromesnil.
Open 10.30am-6pm Tue-Fri; 2-6.30pm Sat. **Map E3**
Lelong shows major, post-1945, international names. After recent shows by Kounellis, Alechinsky and Appel, Bernard Pagès, Sean Scully, James Brown and Eduardo Chillida are scheduled for 1999. Branches in New York and Zurich.

Galerie Jérôme de Noirmont

38 av Matignon, 8th (01.42.89.89.00). M° Miromesnil.
Open 10am-1pm, 2.30-7pm Mon-Sat. **Map E4**
Opening in moneyed avenue Matignon could arouse suspicions that Noirmont sells purely business art. But in three years, eye-catching shows by A R Penck, Clemente, Jeff Koons, Dermott & MacGough and the latest photo series of Pierre et Gilles, together with stylishly produced catalogues, have made this gallery worth the trip.

St-Germain-des-Prés

Galerie 1900-2000

*8 rue Bonaparte, 6th (01.43.25.84.20). M° Mabillon or
St-Germain-des-Prés.* **Open** 2-7pm Mon; 10am-12.30pm,
2-7pm Tue-Sat. **Map H7**
Marcel and David Fleiss present an eclectic range of twentieth-century art with a strong predilection for Surrealism, Dada, Pop art and the Fluxus movement. This is a place to find works on paper (drawings, collage) that might include anyone from Léger and De Chirico to Lichenstein or Rauschenberg.

Galerie Claude Bernard

*7 rue des Beaux-Arts, 6th (01.43.26.97.07). M° Mabillon
or St-Germain-des-Prés.* **Open** 9.30am-12.30pm, 2.30-6.30pm Tue-Sat. **Map H6**
This large gallery shows mostly realist, figurative paintings and drawings from the 1960s to the present, by the likes of Peter Blake, David Hockney, Xavier Valls and Balthus.

Galerie Jeanne Bucher

*53 rue de Seine, 6th (01.44.41.69.65). M° Mabillon or
Odéon.* **Open** 9am-6.30pm Tue-Fri; 10am-12.30pm,
2.30-6pm Sat. **Map H7**
One of the first galleries to set up on the Left Bank, in 1925. It now occupies a simple, airy space hidden in a courtyard, and specialises in post-war abstract and Cobra painters, with a few contemporary sculptors.

Galerie Jean-Jacques Dutko

*13 rue Bonaparte, 6th (01.43.26.96.13). M° Mabillon or
St-Germain-des-Prés.* **Open** 2.30-7pm Mon; 10.30am-1pm,
2.30-7pm Tue-Sat. **Map H7**

Exhibitions of abstract paintings or contemporary sculpture are conceived around an impressive display of Art Deco furniture and African or Oceanic tribal art. Atelier Bonaparte at No 11 is devoted to furniture by contemporary artists.

Galerie Jean Fournier

22 rue du Bac, 7th (01.42.97.44.00). M° Rue du Bac.
Open 10am-12.30pm, 2-7pm Tue-Sat. **Map G6**
Fournier has changed *quartier* but still specialises in the painters of the French 70s Support-Surface movement Claude Viallat and Pierre Buraglio, independents Hantaï, Piffaretti and the US West Coast abstractionists Sam Francis and Joan Mitchell, who spent part of their career in Paris.

Galerie Samy Kinge

54 rue de Verneuil, 7th (01.42.61.19.07).
M° Rue du Bac. **Open** 2.30-7pm Tue-Sat. **Map G6**
This small venue in the antiques district promotes European artists working in the Surrealist tradition, such as the late Victor Brauner and Eva Aëppli, plus some younger names.

Galerie Maeght

42 rue du Bac, 7th (01.45.48.45.15). M° Rue du Bac.
Open 9.30am-7pm Tue-Sat. **Map G6**
This world-famous gallery rests on past glories and today's shows unfortunately tend to pale compared to a past that once included Giacommetti and Miró. Recently, however they have have included some well-mounted historic shows, like Archipenko, alongside contemporary artists. The gallery continues the tradition of beautifully produced artists' books, printed in its own workshops.

Galerie Montenay-Giroux

31 rue Mazarine, 6th (01.43.54.85.30). M° Odéon.
Open 11am-1pm, 2.30-7pm Tue-Sat. **Map H7**
This expansive sky-lit gallery, which started out in life as a garage, now exhibits contemporary painters including Eric Dalbis and Jean-Pierre Pincemin, Ange Leccia and Markus Lüpertz.

Hains plays word games at **Daniel Templon.**

Galerie Denise René

196 bd St-Germain, 7th (01.42.22.77.57).
M° St-Germain-des-Prés. **Open** 10am-1pm, 2-7pm
Tue-Fri; 11am-1pm, 2-7pm Sat. **Map H7**
Something of an institution, Denise René has remained firmly committed to kinetic art and geometrical abstraction ever since Tinguely first presented his machines here in the 50s.
Branch: 22 rue Charlot, 3rd (01.48.87.73.94).

Galerie Darthea Speyer

6 rue Jacques-Callot, 6th (01.43.54.78.41). M° Mabillon
or Odéon. **Open** 11am-12.45pm, 2-7pm Tue-Fri;
11am-7pm Sat. **Map H6**
Often colourful, representational painting and sculpture and naive artists are the speciality here. It can be fairly kitsch, but at best features the politically committed expressionism of Leon Golub or the American dreams of Ed Paschke.

Georges-Philippe Vallois

36-38 rue de Seine, 6th (01.46.34.61.07). M° Mabillon
or St-Germain-des-Prés. **Open** 10.30am-1pm, 2-7pm Tue-Sat. **Map H7**
Son of Art Deco furniture and modern sculpture specialist Galerie Vallois (at No 41), Georges Philippe takes a more contemporary bent, mainly sculpture, some photography and video (Alain Bublex, Gilles Barbier, Paul McCarthy). No 38 takes a more historic line.

Galerie Lara Vincy

47 rue de Seine, 6th (01.43.26.72.51). M° Mabillon or
St-Germain-des-Prés. **Open** 2.30-7.30pm Mon; 11am-12.30pm, 2.30-7.30pm Tue-Sat. **Map H7**
Lara Vincy is one of the more eccentric characters of the area and one of the few to retain a sense of the 70s Fluxus-style 'happenings'. She puts on interesting theme shows, such as works involving music or literature, as well as solo shows by artists including master of the epigram, Ben.

ScèneEst: rue Louise-Weiss

Air de Paris

32 rue Louise-Weiss, 13th (01.44.23.02.77).
M° Chevaleret. **Open** 2-7pm Tue-Sat. **Map M10**
This gallery is named after Duchamp's famous bottle of air and, true to their namesake, shows here tend to be highly experimental, if not chaotic. A young stable includes Paul McCarthy, Philippe Parreno, Liam Gillick, Pierre Joseph and Carsten Höller, who play witty games with the concepts and language behind contemporary art.

Art: Concept

34 rue Louise-Weiss, 13th (01.53.60.90.30).
M° Chevaleret. **Open** 2-7pm Tue-Fri; 11am-7pm Sat.
Map M10
Originally from Nice, Art: Concept shows trendy young stuff, often in the art/club/fashion overlap like Michel Blazy or Jeffrey Deller, but still seems to be looking for a direction.

Galerie Almine Rech

24 rue Louise-Weiss, 13th (01.45.83.71.90).
M° Chevaleret. **Open** 11am-7pm Tue-Sat. **Map M10**
Almine Rech's gallery has proved one of the most consistent of the ScèneEst, with both solo and theme shows, often featuring photography/video or works on paper. International artists have included African-American Willie Cole, Swiss photographer Annelies Strba, Italian Ugo Rondinone and young French discovery Rebecca Bourgnigault.

Galerie Jennifer Flay

20 rue Louise-Weiss, 13th (01.44.06.73.60). M°
Chevaleret. **Open** 2-7pm Tue-Fri; 11am-7pm Sat. **Map M10**
New Zealander Jennifer Flay has a talent for picking up on interesting young artists, ensuring that this is a gallery people

Sweet nothings from Ben to **Lara Vincy.**

watch. Come here for a sampling of the French scene including Xavier Veilhan and Claude Closky, European photographers including Richard Billingham and Willie Doherty, plus John Currin, Cathy de Monchaux and Zoë Leonard.

Galerie Emmanuel Perrotin

30 rue Louise-Weiss, 13th (01.42.16.79.79). M°
Chevaleret. **Open** 2-7pm Tue-Fri; 11am-7pm Sat. **Map M10**
Perrotin shows young European artists, many of whom explore portraiture or autobiography, like Maurizio Cattelan and Alix Lambert, plus wacky Henrik Plenge Jakobsen and catman Alain Sechas. This is also the place to catch provocative young Japanese artists, such as Noritoshi Hirakawa, Takashi Murakami and glossy cyberpunkette Mariko Mori.

Galerie Praz-Delavallade

28 rue Louise-Weiss, 13th (01.45.86.20.00). M°
Chevaleret. **Open** 2-7pm Tue-Fri; 11am-7pm Sat. **Map M10**
Mainly young American artists, such as Meg Cranston, the cartoon-style antics of navel-gazing Chicago bad boy Jim Shaw, and feminist animal paintings by Erika Rothenberg.

Photo Galleries

Photoworks can also be found in many other galleries, while branches of Fnac mount surprisingly erudite photography shows. The biennial Mois de la Photo (next 2000) sees a vast range of photo exhibitions across the city.

Galerie 213

213 bd Raspail, 14th (01.43.22.83.23). M° Raspail. **Open**
11am-7pm Tue-Sat. **Map G9**
New photo gallery tries to make the art-fashion world link with photographers like Elaine Constantine.

Galerie Françoise Paviot

57 rue Ste-Anne, 2nd (01.42.60.10.01). M° Quatre-Septembre. **Open** 2.30-7pm Tue-Sat. **Map H4**
Françoise Paviot exhibits both historic classics like Brassaï and Man Ray and contemporary photographers like Dieter Appelt, Toshio Shibata and Anna and Bernhard Blume.

Michèle Chomette

24 rue Beaubourg, 3rd (01.42.78.05.62).
M° Rambuteau. **Open** 2-7pm Tue-Sat. **Map K5**
This second-floor gallery exhibits classical and experimental photographic work. Alain Fleischer, Eric Rondepierre, Lewis Baltz, Bernard Plossu, Holger Trulzch are regulars.

Espace Contrejour

96 rue Daguerre, 14th (01.43.21.41.88). M° Gaîté.
Open 10am-7.30pm Mon-Sat. **Map G10**

Off the main circuit, Contrejour specialises in living photographers, mainly French and Italian. The gallery also publishes catalogues and books, and has darkroom facilities.

Agathe Gaillard
3 rue du Pont-Louis-Philippe, 4th (01.42.77.38.24). Mº Pont-Marie or Hôtel-de-Ville. **Open** 1-7pm Tue-Sat. **Map K6**
This long-established gallery specialises in classic masters such as Gibson, Cartier-Bresson and Kertész. Recent shows include Edouard Boubat.

La Laverie
9 rue Keller, 11th (01.47.00.11.38). Mº Bastille or Ledru-Rollin. **Open** 2-7pm Tue-Sat. **Map M6**
This association run by four French and Chinese photographers promotes exchanges between France and Asia, with exhibitions and a photo archive. Darkroom.

Design Galleries

See also **Galerie Jean-Jacques Dutko**, above, and Colette in *chapter* **Specialist Shops**.

de/di/bY
22 rue Bonaparte, 6th (01.40.46.00.20). MºSt-Germain-des-Prés. **Open** 11am-7pm Tue-Sat. **Map H6**
This new gallery presents objects and furniture by contemporary design gurus: among others Kuramata, Sottsass, Pistoletto, Pesce, Arad and Charpin.

Galerie Néotu
25 rue du Renard, 4th (01.42.78.96.97). Mº Hôtel-de-Ville. **Open** 9am-7pm Mon-Fri; 11am-6pm Sat. **Map K6**
The contemporary furniture, ceramics and carpets shown here are as much art as function, with creations by designers including Kristian Gavoille, Martin Szekely as well as some younger arrivals.

VIA
29-37 av Daumesnil, 12th (01.46.28.11.11). Mº Gare de Lyon. **Open** 9am-7pm Mon-Sat; 11am-6pm Sun. **Map M8**
Now installed in three stylish arches within the Viaduc des Arts complex, VIA (Valorisation de l'Innovation dans l'Ameublement) promotes furniture design by providing information and showcasing talent, from recent graduates to big names like Wilmotte, Nouvel, Garouste et Bonetti and Hilton McConnico.

Galleries on the road

Ways of presenting contemporary art are increasingly being challenged. Indicative was the joint Dominique Gonzalez-Foerster, Pierre Huyghe and Philippe Parreno show at the Musée d'Art Moderne de la Ville de Paris, which replaced the exhibition as an assembly of individual artworks by the collectively conceived exhibition as totality, itself an artwork, yet composed of autonomous elements. At Rikrit Tirajanija's show at **Galerie Chantal Crousel** visitors were invited to bring along objects, add comments or play games. Mathieu Laurette's 'free sample' at **Galerie Jousse-Seguin** demonstrated his mode of living his art both through collecting freebies and by techno samples. Both involved interesting concepts about art exchanges and commerce, but also suffered from a lack of visual realisation.

A new questioning of the role of the gallery is leading to some exciting projects around town. **Projet 10**, whose show Propos Mobiles dispersed living modules and mobile artworks around the 10th *arrondissement*, is an ambitious effort to bring challenging yet accessible contemporary art to unexpected locations, from young artists Andrea Zittel and Franck Scurti to internationally renowned Vito Acconci. **Nøn_Facture**'s interventions in October 1998 in Centre Commercial Italie 2, aimed to show that art and commerce can meet, with inexpensive objects by young artists for sale on the escalators and around various departments of Printemps.

Acconci's lorry went public with **Projet 10**.

Artists' collective **Glassbox** (113bis rue Oberkampf, 11th/01.43.38.02.82) who opened in autumn 1997, specialises in politically oriented group shows that have included art poetry and designs for living. Meanwhile newly opened **Public** (4 impasse Beaubourg, 3rd) claims to be not an alternative space but a 'malleable space' encouraging engagement in the city. Galleries are also investigating new spaces. **Galerie Anton Weller** (57 rue de Bretagne, 3rd/ 01.42.72.05.62) has instigated a series of experimental exhibitions 'Chez l'un, L'Autre'. After presenting Bernard Lallemand in a shop in rue Debelleyme, it invited artists' groups (Glassbox, Attitudes), poetry and music reviews (*Java, Musica Falsa*), art agents (Ghislain Mollet-Viéville, Cyril Putman), curators (Alain Declerq), to show in a huge space in rue du Cherche-Midi.

Consumer

Accommodation

From former convents turned budget hotels to luxury palaces which pamper your every wish and whim, Paris has them all.

With almost 1500 hotels in central Paris, visitors have an unrivalled and sometimes bewildering choice. Some recreate the style and charm of a luxurious nineteenth-century private residence, others are resolutely modern. Even on a limited budget, it's possible to stay in an atmospheric historic building in the heart of the city or to follow in the footsteps of famous former residents.

Official star ratings are not listed here, because the French classification system (from no stars to four) is based on standard factors such as room size, the presence of a lift, services and so on, but not on cleanliness, warmth of welcome or tasteful décor. In addition, many hotels don't upgrade after renovation, so a two-star hotel may well be better (but not necessarily cheaper) than a three-star one. Justifiably named palace hotels drip with every service you can think of, let alone need, but luxury and often 100 rooms or more can lead to standardisation. If you prefer a more personal approach, the small family-run hotels which abound in Paris may be more your style.

Hotels are often booked solid in high season (May, June, Sept, Oct) and in particular for fashion weeks (Jan and early July for couture, Mar and Oct for *prêt-à-porter*) and trade fairs (mostly in spring and autumn). At these times it's best to book well ahead. During low season (late July, Aug, Nov-Feb), you may be able to find rooms at less than the prices listed here – it's always worth asking. Same-day reservations can be made in person at branches of the Office de Tourisme de Paris (*see chapter* **Directory**). A small fee is charged (8F-50F, depending on the hotel category). Prices quoted for a double room are for two people and, unless stated, all rooms have private shower or bath, and telephone. All hotels are also required to charge an additional room tax (*taxe de séjour*) of 1F-7F per person, per night, depending on the hotel type, although this is sometimes included in their prices.

Palace Hotels

Hôtel Ritz

15 pl Vendôme, 1st (01.43.16.30.30/fax 01.43.16.31.78). M° Concorde or Opéra. **Rates** *single 3000F-3300F; double 3600F-4000F; suite 4900F-32,900F; breakfast 190F-340F.* **Credit** AmEx, DC, MC, V. **Map G4**
Coco Chanel, the Duke of Windsor and Proust all stayed at the Ritz, as did Hemingway who reputedly said he hoped heaven would be as good. Now owned by Mohamed Al Fayed, it was here that Diana and Dodi spent the evening before their ill-fated ride. The Oriental-carpeted corridors go on for ever and the windows on place Vendôme are both sound and bullet-proof. There are 142 wonderfully luxurious bedrooms and 45 palatial suites, from the romantic 'Frédéric Chopin' to the glitzy Imperial.
Hotel services *Air con. Bars. Babysitting. Conference services. Change. Cookery school. Fitness centre/pool. Hairdresser. Laundry. Lift. Porter. Restaurant. Shops.* **Room services** *CD. Fax. Hairdryer. Jacuzzi. Minibar. Modem link. Radio. Room service (24-hr). Safe. TV/VCR.*

Le Bristol

112 rue du Fbg-St-Honoré, 8th (01.53.43.43.00/fax 01.53.43.43.01). M° Miromesnil. **Rates** *single 2600F-3000F; double 3250F-4000F; suite 4600F-36,000F; breakfast 175F-265F.* **Credit** AmEx, DC, MC, V. **Map E4**
Opened in 1924, the Bristol prides itself on discreet class rather than the flashy luxury of some of its palace rivals, attracting a business rather than pop-star clientele. The 180 rooms are exercises in quiet elegance *à la* Louis XV, with panelling and original prints and paintings. The best suites are larger than most Paris flats and some have private terraces. There's an indoor swimming pool on the glass-enclosed rooftop and a first-rate restaurant (*see chapter* **Restaurants**).
Hotel services *Air con. Babysitting. Bar. Conference services. Change. Fitness centre/pool. Hairdresser. Laundry. Lift. Parking. Porter. Restaurant. Sauna.* **Room services** *CD. Fax. Hairdryer. Minibar. Modem link. Radio. Room service (24-hr). Safe. TV/VCR.*

Hôtel de Crillon

10 pl de la Concorde, 8th (01.44.71.15.00/fax 01.44.71.15.02). M° Concorde. **Rates** *single 2950F-3400F; double 3500F-4300F; suite 4950F-31,000F; breakfast 170F-230F.* **Credit** AmEx, DC, MC, V. **Map F4**
The Crillon is located in a magnificent Neo-Classical palace commissioned by Louis XV in 1758 and built by Jacques Ange Gabriel. The clientele includes film stars and politicians, but the hotel continues with gilt-edged tradition. The chequered marble lobby dripping with chandeliers, the blue-draped Jardin d'Hiver tea room, the superb Ambassadeurs restaurant (*see chapter* **Restaurants)** and the grand presidential suites ooze prestige, echoed in all 123 rooms and 40 suites.
Hotel services *Air con. Babysitting. Bar. Business services. Change. Fitness centre. Laundry. Lift. Porter. Restaurants. Shop. Wheelchair access.* **Room services** *CD. Hairdryer. Minibar. Radio. Room service (24-hr). Safe. TV.*

Hôtel Plaza Athénée

25 av Montaigne, 8th (01.53.67.66.65/fax 01.53.67.66.66). M° Alma-Marceau. **Rates** *single 3000F; double 3700F-5800F; suite 7800F-16,000F; breakfast 160F-250F.* **Credit** AmEx, DC, MC, V. **Map H5**
Fashion favourite Plaza Athénée is in the midst of extensive refurbishments which should be completed by September 1999. Here, the dedicated shopper can fall straight out of bed and into the couture shops lining avenue Montaigne. The

Breakfast epiphanies? Dive straight into the lap of luxury at the inimitable Ritz.

205 rooms and suites are rich with comfort (with even more personal touches after the renovations). In summer, the Cour Jardin becomes a six-storey cascade of ivy – a romantic setting for lunch or tea – while Le Régence restaurant has creative haute cuisine among the grand-hotel pomposity. **Hotel services** *Air con. Babysitting. Bars. Conference services. Change. Fitness centre. Hairdresser. Laundry. Lift. Parking. Porter. Restaurants. Shops.* **Room services** *CD player. Hairdryer. Minibar. Modem link. Radio. Room service (24-hr). Safe. TV/VCR.*

Hôtel Royal Monceau

37 av Hoche, 8th (01.42.99.88.00/fax 01.42.99.89.90). M° Charles de Gaulle-Etoile. **Rates** *single* 2300F-3150F; *double* 2750F-4800F; *suite* 4900F-19,000F; *extra bed* 400F; *breakfast* 155F-215F. **Credit** AmEx, DC, MC, V. **Map D3**
With grey and white marble floor, Gobelins tapestries and huge flower arrangements in the entrance hall, the Royal Monceau is a temple to 20s-style opulence. The 219 rooms and suites are spacious and stylish, with hand-painted panels in some rooms. A large fitness centre overlooks a pretty sunken garden. A circular glass-walled garden restaurant and the Venetian-styled 'Carpaccio' cater for guests or visitors. **Hotel services** *Air con. Babysitting. Bar. Conference services. Hairdresser. Health club/pool. Parking. Restaurants.* **Room services** *Hairdryer. Minibar. Radio. Room service (24-hr). Safe. TV.*

Hôtel Raphaël

17 av Kléber, 16th (01.44.28.00.28/fax 01.45.01.21.50). M° Kléber. **Rates** *single or double* 2340F-5040F; *suite* up to 28,800F; *extra bed* 450F; *breakfast* 135F-175F. **Credit** AmEx, DC, MC, V. **Map C4**
The Raphaël is rich with antiques, sumptuous furnishings and handpainted panels and, with only 90 rooms, retains a sense of personal service and privacy. The imposing hallway is lined with mirrors, portraits and wood panelling, and there's even a Turner at the far end. Three unusual suites have recently been added, including a duplex and a triplex with private terraces. Numerous celebrities have stayed here since the hotel opened in 1925, including US presidents Ford and Bush, Serge Gainsbourg who wrote songs in his suite here, and singer Lenny Kravitz. Superb 360° views of Paris can be had from the 7th-floor terrace restaurant in summer. **Hotel services** *Air con. Babysitting. Bar. Conference services. Change. Laundry. Lift. Porter. Restaurant.* **Room services** *CD player. Fax. Hairdryer. Minibar. Modem link. Radio. Room service (24-hr). Safe. TV/VCR.*

Critics' choice

Hôtel de Banville Charming and family-run

Hôtel des Grandes Ecoles Serene garden

Hôtel Beaumarchais Stylish and bright

Hôtel d'Angleterre Low-key elegance in a former British embassy

Hôtel Delambre Modern touches and colours mixed with Montparnasse's arty heyday

Hôtel Caron de Beaumarchais Historic detail

Hôtel Pergolese Futuristic, designer shapes

Hôtel Chopin Cosy comfort in an old *passage*

Pavillon de la Reine Ivy-covered romance off the Place des Vosges

Hôtel de Nesle Wacky murals and hippy past

*The **Plaza Athénée** courtyard: ivy league.*

De Luxe/Expensive

Hôtel Costes

239 rue St-Honoré, 1st (01.42.44.50.00/fax 01.45.44.50.01). M° Tuileries. **Rates** *single* 1750F; *double* 2250F-4500F; *suite* 5250F-10,750F; *breakfast* 150F. **Credit** AmEx, DC, MC, V. **Map G5**
After the trend-setting Café Beaubourg and Café Marly, Jean-Louis Costes did it again with his instantly famous hotel, opened in 1995 and soon graced by top models and film stars. He teamed up with designer Jacques Garcia to create a mood of subtly contemporary historicism, from the Italianate central courtyard overlooked by Roman gods to the towering conservatory and a restaurant filled nightly with media and film folk. Bedrooms and bathrooms, resplendent with maroon and mahogany, are firmly in the opulent spirit of Napoléon III's Second Empire. Book well ahead.
Hotel Services *Air con. Bar. Change. Lifts. Laundry. Fitness centre/pool. Restaurant.* **Room services** *CD player. Fax. Hairdryer. Minibar. Modem link. Radio. Room service. Safe. TV.*

Hôtel Regina

2 pl des Pyramides, 1st (01.42.60.31.10/fax 01.40.15.95.16). M° Tuileries. **Rates** *single* 1080F-1680F; *double* 1380F-2300F; *suite* 2300F-4100F; *breakfast* 95F-145F. **Credit** AmEx, DC, MC, V. **Map G5**
Like the gilded statue of Joan of Arc in the square, the hotel, which has been completely refurbished over the last three years, is an extravagant relic of another age and retains its Art Nouveau allure. The old panel clock, which has a face for each of seven different cities, and the wooden change kiosk evoke the excitement of the first days of transatlantic steam travel. A pleasant bustle fills the entrance, while upper rooms offer great views over the Tuileries and Louvre. **Hotel services** *Air con. Babysitting. Bar. Conference services. Change. Garden. Laundry. Lift. Porter. Restaurant.* **Room services** *Hairdryer. Minibar. Radio. Room service (24-hr). Safe. TV.*

Pavillon de la Reine

28 pl des Vosges, 3rd (01.40.29.19.19/fax 01.40.29.19.20). M° Bastille. **Rates** *single* 1700F-1850F; *double* 1900F-2100F; *suite* 2050F-3900F; *breakfast* 110F-135F. **Credit** AmEx, DC, MC, V. **Map L6**

Walking through one of the elegant arches of the romantic Place des Vosges and into the leafy garden of this ivy-covered mansion is a magical experience, particularly at night when the facade is dramatically lit. Inside, lavish furnishings, rustic beams and tapestries contribute to the feeling of tasteful luxury. The 55 rooms and suites, some with romantic four-posters and all with magnificent antique chests sourced from *brocantes*, overlook flower-filled courtyards. **Hotel services** *Air con. Bar. Babysitting. Change. Laundry. Lift. Parking. Porter.* **Room services** *Hairdryer. Minibar. Room service (24-hr). Safe. TV/VCR. Wheelchair-adapted rooms.*

Hôtel du Jeu de Paume

54 rue St-Louis-en-l'Ile, 4th (01.43.26.14.18/fax 01.40.46.02.76). M° Pont Marie. **Rates** *single or double* 905F-1550F; *junior suite* 2500F; *breakfast* 80F. **Credit** AmEx, DC, MC, V. **Map K7**

This romantic hotel began life as a real tennis court, ordered by Louis XIII in 1634, when the Ile St-Louis was being developed with aristocratic homes. Subsequently a warehouse and then a craftsmen's workshop, in 1988 the timber-framed court was converted into a dramatic, airy breakfast room, centrepiece of this comfortable 32-room hotel. A serene garden adds to the sense of exclusivity. **Hotel services** *Babysitting. Bar. Conference services. Laundry. Lift. Porter. Sauna.* **Room services** *Hairdryer. Jacuzzi. Minibar. Radio. Room service (24-hr). TV.*

L'Hôtel

13 rue des Beaux-Arts, 6th (01.43.25.27.22/fax 01.43.25.64.81). M° Mabillon. **Rates** *single or double* 800F-2800F; *suite* 2000F-4000F; *breakfast* 110F. **Credit** AmEx, DC, MC, V. **Map H6**

Showbiz and fashion types flock to this just slightly over-the-top-hotel on a gallery-filled St-Germain street. In its shabbier days as the Hôtel d'Alsace, Oscar Wilde stayed here until his death in 1900, claiming he was dying 'beyond his means'. Guy-Louis Duboucheron acquired L'Hôtel in 1968, filled it with flamboyant flower arrangements and restored Wilde's room, as well as the Art Deco bedroom of music-hall star Mistinguett, with an opulence that borders on camp. **Hotel services** *Air con. Bar. Business services. Change. Laundry. Lift. Porter. Restaurant.* **Room services** *Hairdryer. Minibar. Radio. Room service. Safe. TV.*

Hôtel de l'Abbaye

10 rue Cassette, 6th (01.45.44.38.11/fax 01.45.48.07.86). M° St-Sulpice. **Rates** *single or double* 960F-1650F; *suite* 1900F-1950F; *breakfast included.* **Credit** AmEx, MC, V. **Map G7**

This tranquil hotel was originally part of a convent, and has been brought up to date without losing its charm. Wood panelling, well-stuffed sofas and an open fireplace add to the relaxed atmosphere but, best of all, there's a surprisingly large garden where breakfast is served in warmer months. Each of the 42 rooms and four duplex suites are tasteful and luxurious. The suites have pretty roof terraces. **Hotel services** *Air con. Babysitting. Bar. Change. Garden. Laundry. Lift. Porter. Safe.* **Room services** *Hairdryer. Radio. Room service. TV.*

Hôtel Buci Latin

34 rue de Buci, 6th (01.43.29.07.20/fax 01.43.29.67.44). M° St-Germain-des-Prés. **Rates** *single or double* 970F-1650F; *suite* 1750F; *breakfast included.* **Credit** AmEx, DC, MC, V. **Map H7**

In contrast to mock-ancient St-Germain hotels, the Buci Latin, above lively rue de Buci street market, is proudly post-

modern. From papier-mâché lamps to high-backed chairs and colourful sculpture, the emphasis is on humorous elegance. Designer graffiti decorates the stairwell and you recognise your room by the painting on the key ring. Room 140 is a duplex; suite 162 has giant jacuzzi and terrace. **Hotel services** *Air con. Babysitting. Bar. Change. Coffee shop. Laundry. Lift. Porter. Restaurant. Safe.* **Room services** *Hairdryer. Minibar. Modem link. Radio. Room service (24-hr). Safe. TV.*

Hôtel Lutétia

45 bd Raspail, 6th (01.49.54.46.46/fax 01.49.54.46.00). M° Sèvres-Babylone. **Rates** *single or double* 1800F-2300F; *suite* 2800F-15,000F; *extra bed* 450F; *breakfast* 75F-145F. **Credit** AmEx, DC, MC, V.

A masterpiece of Art Nouveau and early Art Deco architecture, the Lutétia opened in 1910 to serve shoppers coming to the Bon Marché, bringing Grand Hotel style to the Left Bank. In a less-glorious interlude, it was used by the Gestapo during the Occupation. Sybille de Margerie revamped its 250 rooms in purple, gold and pearl grey to maintain an elegant 30s feel. When artist Arman is not around, you can stay in the suite adorned with his sculptures and tribal art collection. **Hotel services** *Air con. Babysitting. Bar. Change. Conference services. Laundry. Lift. Parking. Porter. Restaurants.* **Room services** *Hairdryer. Minibar. Modem link. Radio. Room service (24-hr). Safe. TV.*

Relais St-Germain

9 carrefour de l'Odéon, 6th (01.43.29.12.05/fax 01.46.33.45.30). M° Odéon. **Rates** *single* 1290F; *double* 1600F-1850F; *suite* 2100F; *extra bed* 250F; *breakfast included.* **Credit** AmEx, DC, MC, V. **Map H7**

Near the Odéon theatre, this hotel has preserved the character of its seventeenth-century building. The 22 generous rooms are tastefully decorated, combining antique furnishings, beautiful fabrics and modern fittings; each is named after a French writer, such as the lovely 'Molière' suite, up its own rickety staircase. Discreet and accommodating service. **Hotel services** *Air con. Bar. Babysitting. Laundry. Lift. Porter. Safe.* **Room services** *Fax. Hairdryer. Minibar. Modem link. Radio. Room service. Safe. TV/VCR.*

Hôtel Duc de Saint-Simon

14 rue de St-Simon, 7th (01.44.39.20.20/fax 01.45.48.68.25). M° Rue du Bac. **Rates** *single or double* 1350F-1475F; *suite* 1900F-1950F; *breakfast* 70F. **Credit** AmEx, MC, V. **Map F6**

Stepping off the quiet side street into a pretty courtyard with iron furniture and bright cushions gives you a taste of the delights inside. A beautiful living room with the hotel's own-design yellow fabric is as relaxing as the 34 tasteful bedrooms, all individually decorated. Four rooms have terraces above a leafy garden, and the ancient cellars have been neatly converted into a small bar, salon and breakfast room. **Hotel services** *Babysitting. Bar. Fax. Laundry. Lift. Porter.* **Room services** *Hairdryer. Modem link. Room service. Safe. TV (on demand).*

Le Montalembert

3 rue de Montalembert, 7th (01.45.49.68.68/fax 01.45.49.69.49). M° Rue du Bac. **Rates** *single or double* 1750F-2300F; *suite* 2850F-4400F; *breakfast* 100F. **Credit** AmEx, DC, MC, V. **Map G6**

A successful fusion of traditional and modern lies behind the 1926 Beaux Arts facade of this luxurious hotel. A corner with comfy sofas and modern open fireplace, a sprinkling of tribal art and a young staff adds up to a pleasurable experience. Styles in the 56 rooms go from Louis-Philippe to contemporary, and bathrooms are all chrome and spotlights. **Hotel services** *Air con. Babysitting. Bar. Conference facilities. Change. Laundry. Lift. Porter. Restaurant.* **Room services** *Fax. Hairdryer. Minibar. Modem link. Radio. Room service (24-hr). Safe. TV/VCR.*

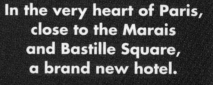

Hôtel Lancaster

7 rue de Berri, 8th (01.40.76.40.76/fax 01.40.76.40.00).
M° George V. **Rates** *single* 1650F-1950F; *double* 2350F-
2750F; *suite* 4500F-10,000F; *breakfast* 120F. **Credit**
AmEx, DC, MC, V. **Map D4**
Dating from 1889, this sumptuous, elegantly renovated townhouse has 60 individually designed rooms, offset by a private
collection of *objets d'art*, from Empire pieces to the paintings
of former resident Boris Pastoukhoff. Marlene Dietrich had a
suite here, still in her favourite lilac. The tone shies away from
glitz and provides the sense of an exclusive private club.
Hotel services *Air con. Conference services. Health*
club. Lift. Parking. Porter. **Room services** *Double*
glazing. Hairdryer. Minibar. Safe. TV/VCR.

Millennium Commodore

12 bd Haussmann, 9th (01.42.46.72.82/fax
01.47.70.23.81) M° Richelieu Drouot. **Rates** *single or*
double 1900F-3100F; *suite* 3900F-4900F; *extra bed* 550F;
breakfast 120F. **Credit** AmEx, DC, MC, V. **Map H4**
The Commodore reopened in 1998 after expensive refurbishment by Britain's Millennium group. The gold and white
cupola and superb Art Deco lift shaft and banisters from the
hotel's opening in 1927 have been kept, along with some carefully restored furniture in the 163 rooms. An aura of luxurious calm reigns, whether guests are reading in a fireside
basket chair or relaxing in the well-thought out bedrooms.
Hotel services *Air con. Babysitting. Bars. Change*
Conference services. Hairdresser. Laundry. Lift. Parking.
Porter. Restaurant. **Room services** *Hairdryer. Minibar.*
Modem link. Radio. Room service (24-hr). Safe. TV/VCR.

Hôtel Pergolèse

3 rue Pergolèse, 16th (01.53.64.04.04/fax 01.53.64.04.40).
M° Porte Maillot or Argentine. **Rates** *single* 1000F-
1300F; *double* 1100F-1500F; *junior suite* 1600F-1800F;
breakfast 70F-95F. **Credit** AmEx, DC, MC, V. **Map B3**
From the elegant stone exterior of this hotel near the Bois de
Boulogne, slip into a futuristic yet soothing interior. From the
lounge's leather sofas and dalek-like chairs you see a small
Japanese-style garden through a curved glass wall. The
breakfast room has dynamic Philippe Starck and Hilton Mc
Connico furniture. The 40 rooms combine grey, pinks and
peaches with warm ash and mahogany furniture. The bath-
rooms are a concentration of marble, glass and shiny steel.
Hotel services *Air con. Babysitting. Bar. Change.*
Laundry. Lift. Porter. **Room services** *Hairdryer. Minibar.*
Modem link. Radio. Room service (24-hr). Safe. TV.

Hôtel Square

3 rue de Boulainvilliers, 16th (01.44.14.91.90/ fax
01.44.14.91.99). M° Passy/RER Kennedy-Radio France.
Rates *single or double* 1400F-1800F; *suite* 2100F-2600F;
breakfast 50F-90F. **Credit** AmEx, DC, MC, V. **Map A7**
Though the polished granite curtain wall may look forbidding, the dramatic interior of this courageously modern hotel
is welcoming, combining luxurious touches with the individual service that comes with only 22 rooms. The exotic
woods, quality fabrics and paint finishes are striking and
original. The temporary exhibitions in the narrow atrium are
by leading contemporary artists, such as Ben and Viallat.
There's a direct entrance to the Zébra Square brasserie.
Hotel services *Air con. Bar. Babysitting. Conference*
services. Change. Laundry. Lift. Porter. Restaurant.
Room services *Fax. Hairdryer. Minibar. Modem link.*
Radio. Room service (24-hr). Safe. TV/VCR.

Terrass Hôtel

12-14 rue Joseph-de-Maistre, 18th (01.46.06.72.85/fax
01.42.52.29.11). M° Place de Clichy. **Rates** *single* 1110F-
1260F; *double* 1320F-1470F; *suite* 1760F; *breakfast*
included. **Credit** AmEx, DC, MC, V. **Map H1**
A stately building on a corner near the Montmartre cemetery, with superb views over Paris, the Terrass is owned by

Millennium Commodore: *glorious rebirth.*

the family who built it over 80 years ago. Of 101 rooms, 75
are air conditioned, and a whole floor is non-smoking.
Furnishings vary from old wooden furniture to lively stripes
and vivid colours. A piano bar entertains downstairs, but in
good weather go for the seventh-floor roof terrace restaurant.
Hotel services *Air con. Bar. Babysitting. Conference*
services. Change. Laundry. Lift. Porter. Restaurant. **Room**
services *Hairdryer. Minibar. Radio. Room service. TV.*

Moderate

Le Britannique

20 av Victoria, 1st (01.42.33.74.59/fax 01.42.33.82.65).
M° Châtelet. **Rates** *single* 725F; *double* 870F-995F; *extra bed*
130F; *breakfast* 60F. **Credit** AmEx, DC, MC, V. **Map J6**
A courteous welcome is offered by the young staff at this elegant hotel near place du Châtelet. From the stylish entrance
hall, a few steps lead down to the English-style sitting room
furnished with burgundy leather chesterfields, model ships
and old hat boxes. The 40 recently refurbished rooms have
plush vine-pattern curtains and bedcovers. The stand of burgundy umbrellas waiting to be borrowed on a rainy day provides a lovely, old-fashioned touch of class.
Hotel services *Laundry. Lift.* **Room services** *Double*
glazing. Hairdryer. Safe. Minibar. TV.

Hôtel Brighton

218 rue de Rivoli, 1st (01.47.03.61.61/fax
01.42.60.41.78). M° Tuileries or Concorde. **Rates** *single*
545F-915F; *double* 580F-950F; *triple* 1025F-1125F;
breakfast included. **Credit** AmEx, DC, MC, V. **Map G5**
The Brighton had been left behind by its luxurious neighbours, offering rue de Rivoli status and Tuileries views at low
prices; but a year-long renovation starts in March 1999 and
prices may rise afterwards. Half of the hotel will remain open,
so make the most of the huge rooms, mosaiqued hallway and
faux marble-columned *salon de thé* while work is going on.
Hotel services *Change. Laundry. Lift. Porter. Safe.*
Tearoom. **Room services** *Double glazing. Hairdryer.*
Minibar. TV.

Hôtel des Tuileries

10 rue St-Hyacinthe, 1st (01.42.61.04.17/fax
01.49.27.91.56). M° Pyramides. **Rates** *single* 790F-
1200F; *double* 890F-1200F; *triple* 1400F; *breakfast* 60F.
Credit AmEx, DC, MC, V. **Map G5**
This is a delightful small hotel on a quiet street between the
Tuileries and place du Marché St Honoré. Ethnic rugs, wall-
hangings, antique furniture and original pictures decorate the
lobby and the 26 rooms, and the centrepiece is a delicate, list-

ed spiral staircase. The cellar breakfast room gets natural light from an interior greenhouse. The sumptuous yet homely result is popular with the fashion world, so book ahead. **Hotel services** *Air con. Laundry. Lift. Porter. Small meeting room.* **Room services** *Double glazing. Hairdryer. Minibar. Safe. TV.*

Hôtel Baudelaire Opéra

61 rue Ste-Anne, 2nd (01.42.97.50.62/fax 01.42.86.85.85). M° Opéra or Pyramides. **Rates** *single* 500F-540F; *double* 640F-700F; *triple* 760F-830F; *breakfast* 42F. **Credit** AmEx, DC, MC, V. **Map H4**
To stay here is a history lesson: Baudelaire lodged here, writer Céline lived in the passage next door; during the Counter-Reformation, Protestants were forcibly converted to Catholicism in the basement. The 29 rooms are decorated with wood and bright colours, and five have mezzanines; No 22 has a salon below and wooden spiral stairway up to the bedroom. **Hotel services** *Lift. Safe.* **Room services** *Double glazing. Hairdryer. Minibar. TV.*

Hôtel Caron de Beaumarchais

12 rue Vieille-du-Temple, 4th (01.42.72.34.12/fax 01.42.72.34.63). M° St-Paul. **Rates** *single or double* 730F-810F; *breakfast* 54F, *brunch* 78F. **Credit** AmEx, DC, MC, V. **Map K6**
Named after the eighteenth-century playwright who lived just up the street, this charming Marais hotel recreates the refined tastes of Beaumarchais' era, from gilded mirrors to fabrics copied from period documents and Chinese-style bathroom tiling. The 19 simply styled rooms are comfortable if not always spacious. Dotted around are framed pages from first editions of the *Marriage of Figaro*, the opera based on Beaumarchais' play. Book early. **Hotel services** *Air con. Laundry. Lift. Safe.* **Room services** *Double glazing. Hairdryer. Minibar. TV.*

Hôtel des Deux-Iles

59 rue St-Louis-en-l'Ile, 4th (01.43.26.13.35/fax 01.43.29.60.25). M° Pont-Marie. **Rates** *single* 750F; *double* 860F; *breakfast* 52F. **Credit** AmEx, MC, V. **Map K7**
This refined, peaceful hotel in a seventeenth-century townhouse on Ile St-Louis has been done up in faintly colonial style with cane furniture, print curtains and a lovely fireplace in the lobby. The **Hôtel de Lutèce** at No 65 (01.43.26.23.52), under the same management, displays a similar sense of period style. **Hotel services** *Air con. Lift.* **Room services** *Hairdryer. Safe. TV.*

Hôtel St-Louis Marais

1 rue Charles V, 4th (01.48.87.87.04/fax 01.48.87.33.26). M° Sully-Morland or Bastille. **Rates** *single* 400F-550F; *double* 650F-750F; *triple* 950F; *breakfast* 45F. **Credit** MC, V. **Map L7**
At this restful corner hotel in the Marais, the reception is reminiscent of a stately home. The seventeenth-century beams, wooden furnishings and plush carpets give a homely feel to the 16 rooms, decorated in dark green or deep rose colour schemes. Look out for a section of arch originally part of an external doorway as you climb the old spiral staircase. **Hotel services** *Laundry. Safe.* **Room services** *Double glazing. Hairdryer. TV.*

Hôtel St-Merry

78 rue de la Verrerie, 4th (01.42.78.14.15/fax 01.40.29.06.82). M° Hôtel-de-Ville. **Rates** *single or double* 450F-1100F; *triple* 1300F; *suite* 1800F-2400F; *breakfast* 50F. **Credit** AmEx, MC, V. **Map K6**
Nestled against the Gothic church of the same name, the Saint-Merry basks in eccentricity. Built in the seventeenth century, it was first the church presbytery and later a brothel until bought in 1962 by Christian Crabbe, who has transformed the eleven rooms and one suite by scouring antique salesrooms for Neo-Gothic furniture and panels to incorpo-

rate in headboards or cupboard doors. A confessional box serves as a phone cubicle and iron candelabras, stone walls and beams add to the charm. The biggest surprise is the flying buttress straddling the bed in room 9. Book in advance. **Hotel services** *Safe.* **Room services** *Double glazing. Hairdryer.*

Hôtel du Vieux-Marais

8 rue du Plâtre, 4th (01.42.78.47.22/fax 01.42.78.34.32). M° Hôtel-de-Ville. **Rates** *single* 480F; *double* 560F-690F; *extra bed* 100F; *breakfast* 35F. **Credit** MC, V. **Map K6**
The renovations promised in 1998 were finally in full swing at this small hotel north of Hôtel de Ville when we visited in early 1999. The finished product (late spring 1999) should be delightful – the clean lines of oak furniture are being combined with grey carpets, cool cream walls and beige and red leather. A courtyard garden is promised, together with a pretty mosaic-tiled floor in the reception. Should be a winner. **Hotel services** *Air con. Lift.* **Room services** *Double glazing. Hairdryer. TV. Wheelchair access (1 room).*

Grand Hôtel Malher

5 rue Malher, 4th (01.42.72.60.92/fax 01.42.72.25.37). M° St-Paul. **Rates** *single* 490F-640F; *double* 590F-740F; *suite* 890F-990F; *breakfast* 47F. **Credit** AmEx, MC, V. **Map L6**
The glossy dark green frontage and grand doors are impressive as you step off the lively Marais street. In the airy reception there are large mirrors, a smart marble floor and elegant turquoise window drapes; steep stairs lead down to the seventeenth-century vaulted breakfast room. The 31 cosy rooms sport tasteful colour schemes and clean, simple bathrooms. **Hotel services** *Lift. Small conference room. No-smoking rooms. Safe.* **Room services** *Double glazing. Hairdryer. Minibar. TV.*

Hôtel des Grands Hommes

17 pl du Panthéon, 5th (01.46.34.19.60/fax 01.43.26.67.32). RER Luxembourg. **Rates** *single* 700F; *double* 800F; *triple* 900F; *suite* 1200F; *breakfast* 50F. **Credit** AmEx, DC, MC, V. **Map J8**
The Panthéon (resting place of the 'great men' of the name) looms over this elegant eighteenth-century hotel. André Breton invented automatic writing here in 1919. The 32 good-sized rooms are pretty with some exposed beams and iron bedheads, and awesome dome views from the sixth-floor balconies. **Hotel services** *Air con. Babysitting. Meeting room. Lift. Safe.* **Room services** *Hairdryer. Minibar. TV.*

Hôtel Jardins du Luxembourg

5 impasse Royer-Collard, 5th (01.40.46.08.88/fax 01.40.46.02.28). RER Luxembourg. **Rates** *single or double* 790F-840F; *breakfast* 50F **Credit** AmEx, DC, MC, V. **Map H8**
It would be hard to find a quieter location than this cul-de-sac near the Jardins du Luxembourg. The ground floor is welcoming, with kilim rugs, bright cushions, vivid paintwork and stripped floorboards. Jolly floor tiles show up in the inviting cellar breakfast room and also in the bathrooms, and the 26 bedrooms are colourful and attractive. Sigmund Freud stayed at this hotel (then called the Hôtel de la Paix) as a student in 1885. **Hotel services** *Air con. Laundry. Lift. Sauna.* **Room services** *Hairdryer. Minibar. Safe. TV.*

Hôtel d'Angleterre

44 rue Jacob, 6th (01.42.60.34.72/fax 01.42.60.16.93). M° St Germain des Prés. **Rates** *single or double* 700F-1200F; *suite* 1500F; *extra bed* 250F; *breakfast* 60F. **Credit** AmEx, DC, MC, V. **Map H6**
Low-key elegance prevails at this former British embassy where the US independence treaty was prepared in 1783 (and signed down the street, because it had to be signed on non-British ground). Climb the listed staircase or tinkle away at

the grand piano in the stately salon. Some of the 27 rooms look over the ivy strewn courtyard which is the heart of the hotel. Most rooms are a good size; the four cheapest are smaller. **Hotel services** *Lift (not to all rooms).* **Room services** *Double glazing. Hairdryer. Safe. TV.*

Hôtel Bonaparte
61 rue Bonaparte, 6th (01.43.26.97.37/fax 01.46.33.57.67). M° St-Sulpice. **Rates** *single* 490F-590F; *double* 620F-745F; *triple* 820F; *breakfast included.* **Credit** MC, V. **Map G7**
Fresh flowers grace this small hotel among the boutiques of St-Sulpice. Behind a Neo-Classical entrance are 29 spacious rooms, many furnished with *armoires*. The best are on the street side, with decorative fireplaces and gilt mirrors. **Hotel services** *Air con.* **Lift.** **Room services** *Double glazing. Hairdryer. Safe. TV.*

Hôtel du Danube
58 rue Jacob, 6th (01.42.60.34.70/fax 01.42.60.81.18). M° St Germain des Prés. **Rates** *single or double* 650F-880F; *suite* 1150F; *extra bed* 200F; *breakfast* 50F. **Credit** AmEx, MC, V. **Map H6**
This pretty, family-run hotel spreads over two eighteenth-century buildings around a small courtyard. Here the exiled head of the Polish government, General Sikorsky, lived 1939-1940. Styles vary from Chinese to Victorian, with lots of individually chosen furniture to give the 40 rooms a homely feel. Relax in the flowery chintz lounge or pretty breakfast room. **Hotel services** *Lift.* **Room services** *Hairdryer. TV.*

Hôtel Louis II
2 rue St-Sulpice, 6th (01.46.33.13.80/fax 01.46.33.17.29). M° Odéon. **Rates** *single or double* 555F-820F; *triple* 980F; *breakfast* 52F. **Credit** AmEx, DC, MC, V. **Map H7**
Beams and half-timbered partitions abound in this ancient corner building in St-Germain. Apart from the triple in the attic, rooms are small but light, and decorated with amusing, vaguely Gothic fittings and floral wallpaper. The salon has the endearing air of a provincial house, with big *armoire* and a clutter of small tables and upholstered chairs. **Hotel services** *Lift.* **Room services** *Hairdryer. Minibar. Safe. TV.*

Hôtel des Marronniers
21 rue Jacob, 6th (01.43.25.30.60/fax 01.40.46.83.56). M° St-Germain-des-Prés. **Rates** *single* 560F; *double* 755F-905F; *triple* 980F-1080F; *extra bed* 190F; *breakfast* 50F. **Credit** MC, V. **Map H6**
An oasis of calm in noisy, lively St-Germain, the Marronniers has a paved courtyard in front and a lovely conservatory and garden at the back, where you can find the chestnut trees of the name. The 37 rooms are mostly reasonably sized, some with pretty canopies and rich (almost garish) floral fabrics. **Hotel services** *Air con. Bar. Conference facilities. Garden. Lift. Safe.* **Room services** *Double glazing. Hairdryer. TV.*

Hôtel Récamier
3bis pl St-Sulpice, 6th (01.43.26.04.89/fax 01.46.33.27.73). M° St-Sulpice or Mabillon. **Rates** *single* 485F-665F; *double* 620F-700F; *extra bed* 155F; *breakfast included.* **Credit** MC, V. **Map H7**
Tucked into a corner of the square next to St-Sulpice, this flower-filled hotel (vases and wallpaper) has spacious, comfortable rooms. Lace curtains, grandfather clocks and mahogany furniture give a delightful olde-worlde feel. There are 30 rooms, the cheapest without en-suite shower or bath. **Hotel services** *Lift. Safe.*

Hôtel Lenox
9 rue de l'Université, 7th (01.42.96.10.95/fax 01.42.61.52.63). M° Rue du Bac. **Rates** *single or double* 680F-1100F; *duplex* 1500F; *breakfast* 45F. **Credit** AmEx,

DC, MC, V. **Map G6**
Arty types linger in the laidback lobby and bar of this stylish hotel, much as Hemingway is said to have done. Black and white photographs and a predominance of leather, wood and plants add to the air of earnest artistic endeavour. Some handpainted furniture brightens up the 34 tasteful rooms. Also owns the comfortable **Hôtel Lenox** in Montparnasse (15 rue Delambre, 14th/01.43.35.34.50/double 560F-690F). **Hotel services** *Babysitting. Bar. Change. Laundry. Lift. Safe.* **Room services** *Hairdryer. Radio. TV.*

Hôtel le Tourville
16 av rue de Tourville, 7th (01.47.05.62.62/fax 01.47.05.43.90) M° Ecole-Militaire. **Rates** *single* 690F-890F; *double* 790F-1390F; *suites* 1690F-1990F; *breakfast* 60F. **Credit** AmEx, DC, MC, V. **Map E7**
From a reception decked out with colourful sofas and well-placed lighting, the elegance continues, particularly in the larger suites, which enjoy a jacuzzi and private balcony. Prices vary widely, but cheaper rooms are still of a good standard. **Hotel services** *Air con. Bar. Laundry. Lift. Safe.* **Room services** *Hairdryer. TV.*

Hôtel de l'Université
22 rue de l'Université, 7th (01.42.61.09.39/fax 01.42.60.40.84). M° Rue du Bac. **Rates** *single* 500F-700F; *double* 850F-1300F; *triple* 1100F-1500F; *extra bed* 200F; *breakfast* 50F. **Credit** AmEx, MC, V. **Map G6**
A short walk from the Musée d'Orsay, this spacious 27-room hotel is full of snug corners. Chunky antique wardrobes, warm colours, velvety carpets and soft furnishings augment the splendour of this seventeenth-century building. The elegant vaulted cellar rooms can be hired for functions. **Hotel services** *Air con. Lift.* **Room services** *Hairdryer. Safe. TV.*

Hôtel Belle Epoque
66 rue de Charenton, 12th (01.43.44.06.66/fax 01.43.44.10.25). M° Bastille. **Rates** *single* 595F-800F; *double* 650F-820F; *triple* 970F; *breakfast* 55F-75F. **Credit** AmEx, DC, MC, V. **Map M7**
Behind an old facade near the Bastille, this modern hotel has 31 pleasant rooms decorated with Art Deco-style furniture based on Printz and Ruhlmann. The reception, with large club chairs, opens onto a small courtyard with vines and tables. **Hotel services** *Air con. Bar. Laundry. Lift. Meeting rooms.* **Room services** *Double glazing. Hairdryer. Minibar. Safe. TV.*

Hôtel Résidence Bouquet de Longchamp
6 rue du Bouquet de Longchamp, 16th (01.47.04.41.71/ fax 01.47.27.29.09). M° Boissière or Iéna. **Rates** *single* 456F-676F; *double* 512F-752F; *extra bed* 106F; *breakfast* 50F. **Credit** AmEx, DC, MC, V. **Map C5**
Hidden down a backstreet near the Palais de Chaillot is this hotel run by a friendly Austrian who speaks German, French and English. 17 cosy rooms are nicely decorated in pastel blues or yellows, with delicate fabrics on the walls. The breakfast room looks onto a tiny courtyard with climbing plants. **Room services** *Minibar. Room service (24-hr). TV.*

Hôtel de Banville
166 bd Berthier, 17th (01.42.67.70.16/fax 01.44.40.42.77). M° Porte de Champerret. **Rates** *single* 760F; *double* 890F-1050F; *suite* 1450F; *extra bed* 100F; *breakfast* 65F. **Credit** AmEx, DC, MC, V. **Map C1**
Marianne Moreau's mother and grandmother preceded her here and personal touches are painstakingly maintained. Each of the 38 rooms is individually designed, with iron or brass beds and warm Italianate colours. The breakfast room has a trompe l'oeil: you can (almost) imagine yourself amongst trees and climbing roses. A good escape from bustling central Paris. **Hotel services** *Air con. Laundry. Lift.* **Room services** *Safe. TV.*

Carefully wrought romance at the peaceful, family-run **Hôtel de Banville.**

Hôtel Regent's Garden
6 rue Pierre-Demours, 17th (01.45.74.07.30/fax 01.40.55.01.42). M° Charles de Gaulle-Etoile or Ternes. **Rates** *single* 710F-1030F; *double* 780F-1400F; *extra bed* 120F; *breakfast* 50F. **Credit** AmEx, DC, MC, V. **Map C3**
High ceilings and plush upholstery in the foyer hark back to the Second Empire, when this house was built for Napoléon III's physician. The refinement continues in 39 large bedrooms, some with gilt mirrors and fireplaces. With its walled garden, this is an oasis of calm ten minutes from the Arc de Triomphe. It is a Best Western, but doesn't feel at all like a chain. **Hotel services** *Air con. Change. Garden. Lift. Laundry. Parking. Safe.* **Room services** *Double glazing. Hairdryer. Minibar. Radio. TV.*

Inexpensive

Hôtel du Cygne
3 rue du Cygne, 1st (01.42.60.14.16/fax 01.42.21.37.02). M° Etienne Marcel or Châtelet. **Rates** *single* 280F-375F; *double* 420F-490F; *breakfast* 35F. **Credit** MC, V. **Map J5**
The Cygne occupies a pleasantly renovated seventeenth-century building in pedestrianised Les Halles. Exposed beams, abound, while furniture bought at *brocantes* by the two sisters who own the hotel adds interest. Rooms are on the small side, but all except the cheapest singles have bathrooms. The 490F 'La Grande' under the eaves is particularly delightful. **Room services** *Hairdryer. Safe. TV.*

Hôtel Vivienne
40 rue Vivienne, 2nd (01.42.33.13.26/fax 01.40.41.98.19). M° Bourse or Grands Boulevards. **Rates** *single* 450F; *double* 470F-515F; *triple* 650F; *breakfast* 40F. **Credit** MC, V. **Map H7**
Soft yellows and oranges in the reception, wood floors, chandeliers and wicker add to the charm of this hotel that seems to have stepped straight out of a Van Gogh. Barely a stone's throw from the Palais Garnier and the Grands Magasins. **Hotel services** *Lift. Safe.* **Room services** *Hairdryer. TV.*

Alhotel Vertus
5 rue des Vertus, 3rd (01.44.61.89.50/fax 01.48.04.33.72). M° Arts et Métiers. **Rates** *single* 450F-480F; *double* 550F-580F; *suite* 680F-710F; *breakfast* 38F. **Credit** AmEx, DC, MC, V. **Map K5**
In a renovated seventeenth-century building with beams and exposed stone walls, this small hotel is decked out with pale wood furniture and plush green carpets. Its nine rooms combine original features with modern conveniences. **Hotel services** *Laundry. Lift. Safe.* **Room services** *Double glazing. Hairdryer. TV.*

Grand Hôtel Jeanne d'Arc
3 rue de Jarente, 4th (01.48.87.62.11/fax 01.48.87.37.31) M° St-Paul. **Rates** *single* 300F-400F; *double* 305F-500F; *triple* 640F; *quad* 600F; *extra bed* 75F; *breakfast* 35F. **Credit** MC, V. **Map L6**
The attractive stone-built Jeanne d'Arc is on the corner of a pretty Marais street. Inside are interesting touches, from hand-crafted 3D door numbers and murals in the breakfast room to the heraldic mosaic mirror in the reception. The cheapest of the 36 rooms are small but still good value, and all are tastefully decorated. Friendly staff and a homely feel. **Hotel services** *Lift.* **Room services** *TV.*

Hôtel de la Place des Vosges
12 rue de Birague, 4th (01.42.72.60.46/fax 01.42.72.02.64). M° Bastille or St-Paul. **Rates** *single* 365F-485F; *double* 545F-580F; *breakfast* 35F. **Credit** AmEx, DC, MC, V. **Map L6**
A few steps from the place des Vosges is this former muleteer's house, dating from the same period. There is now an elegant reception, salon and breakfast area. The 16 bedrooms are plainer, but still comfortable. Bathrooms are being refitted in green and grey marble. There are views over the rooftops from the top floors, but the lift only goes to the 4th. **Hotel services** *Lift. Safe.* **Room services** *Hairdryer. TV.*

Hôtel Sansonnet
48 rue de la Verrerie, 4th (01.48.87.96.14/fax

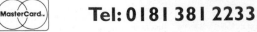

01.48.87.30.46). M° Hôtel-de-Ville. **Rates** *single* 270F-395F; *double* 400F-440F; *shower* 20F; *breakfast* 33F. **Credit** MC, V. **Map K6**
Behind the listed façade of this Marais building are 25 quiet rooms in a jumble of corridors and wrought iron staircases. The rooms are reasonably sized and simply furnished – most singles lack toilet or bathroom, but all doubles are en suite. The manager of 30 years gives guests a calm, patient welcome. **Hotel services** *Safe.* **Room services** *Double glazing. Hairdryer. Room service. TV.*

Hôtel du Septième Art
20 rue St-Paul, 4th (01.44.54.85.00/fax 01.42.77.69.10). M° St-Paul. **Rates** *single* 295F-670F; *double* 420F-670F; *suite* 620F-670F; *extra bed* 100F; *breakfast* 45F. **Credit** AmEx, DC, MC, V. **Map L7**
A movie buff's dream, the Septième Art is stuffed with film posters and Hollywood memorabilia. The theme continues with black-and-white checked floors in reception, while the 23 bedrooms are more sober in beige and paisley. The breakfast room doubles as a mini-shop where you can buy Chaplin statuettes or a miniature movie set. Popular with media types, this is a fun, upbeat hotel in the southern Marais. **Hotel services** *Bar. Washer/dryer (30F/35F).* **Room services** *Hairdryer. Safe. TV.*

Familia Hôtel
11 rue des Ecoles, 5th (01.43.54.55.27/fax 01.43.29.61.77). M° Maubert-Mutualité. **Rates** *single or double* 380F-550F; *triple* 620F-680F; *quad* 620F-750F; *breakfast* 30F, 35F in room.* **Credit** AmEx, DC, MC, V. **Map J7**
An enthusiastic welcome awaits you at this old-fashioned hotel where the balconies are hung with plants. Chatty owner Eric Gaucheron will help you with local lore, and is immensely proud of the sepia murals, well-polished mahogany furniture and tiny balconies in some of the hotel's 30 rooms. His latest project is to strip the stairwell to reveal natural stone. **Hotel services** *Lift. Safe.* **Room services** *Double glazing. Hairdryer. Minibar. TV.*

Hôtel Esmeralda
4 rue St-Julien-le-Pauvre, 5th (01.43.54.19.20/fax 01.40.51.00.68). M° St-Michel. **Rates** *single* 160F-420F; *double* 450F-490F; *triple* 550F; *quad* 600F; *breakfast* 40F. **No credit cards. Map J7**
This charming 1640 building looks onto a tree-lined square and over the Seine to Notre Dame. In the cosy, plant-filled entrance, the resident cat may be curled up in a velvet chair. Upstairs are 19 floral rooms with antique furnishings and uneven floors. Great location and good value, so book ahead. **Hotel services** *Safe.*

Hôtel des Grandes Ecoles
75 rue du Cardinal-Lemoine, 5th (01.43.26.79.23/fax 01.43.25.28.15). M° Cardinal-Lemoine. **Rates** *single or double* 530F-690F; *triple* 670F-790F; *quad* 890F; *extra bed* 100F; *parking* 100F; *breakfast* 45F. **Credit** MC, V. **Map K8**
Stroll through the arched entrance, along the cobbled lane and into an arena of calm. The Grandes Ecoles stands behind high walls and you can breakfast in the lovely garden in summer. Extended a few years ago, there are now 51 rustically furnished rooms in three buildings; the largest also houses the reception with its welcoming staff, and an old-fashioned breakfast room with gilt mirror and piano. **Hotel services** *Garden. Lift. Parking. Safe.* **Room services** *Double glazing. Hairdryer.*

Hôtel St-Jacques
35 rue des Ecoles, 5th (01.44.07.45.45/fax 01.43.25.65.50). M° Maubert-Mutualité. **Rates** *single* 250F-480F; *double* 420-580F; *triple* 580F-650F; *breakfast* 35F. **Credit** AmEx, DC, MC, V. **Map J7**
The enthusiastic new owner has kept the nineteenth-century atmosphere, while renovating to a high standard. The 35

rooms are spacious, with high ceilings, fresh fabrics and pastels. Original painted ceilings have been uncovered during renovation work and will be conserved. The handful of singles without bathrooms are a real bargain. Audrey Hepburn and Cary Grant were filmed here in the 50s comedy *Charade.* **Hotel services** *Lift. Safe.* **Room services** *Double glazing. Hairdryer (in most rooms). TV.*

Hôtel des Trois Collèges
16 rue Cujas, 5th (01.43.54.67.30/fax 01.46.34.02.99). RER Luxembourg or M° Cluny-La Sorbonne. **Rates** *single* 400F-610F; *double* 500F-700F; *triple* 800F; *breakfast* 42F. **Credit** AmEx, DC, MC, V. **Map J7**
On a quiet street in the Latin Quarter, this hotel has a modern lobby and contemporary furniture. The 44 rooms are modern and nicely decorated, if not large: corner and larger sixth-floor rooms are best. The breakfast room turns into a pleasant *salon de thé* in the afternoons. **Hotel services** *Lift. Safe. Tearoom.* **Room services** *Double glazing. Hairdryer. TV.*

Hôtel du Globe
15 rue des Quatre-Vents, 6th (01.43.26.35.50/fax 01.46.33.62.69). M° Odéon. **Rates** *single or double* 390F-565F; *breakfast* 45F. **Credit** AmEx, MC, V. **Map H7**
The Globe is an eccentric and appealing mix of styles. Gothic wrought-iron doors lead into florid corridors, and an unexplained suit of armour supervises guests from the tiny salon. The 15 rooms are individually styled, including a bamboo-clad 'Tahiti' room. A small, winding staircase may lead to suitcase trouble. Good value for a fun, eclectic hotel. **Room services** *Radio. TV.*

Hôtel du Lys
23 rue Serpente, 6th (01.43.26.97.57/fax 01.44.07.34.90). M° Odéon or St-Michel. **Rates** *single* 380F-490F; *double* 520F; *triple* 620F; *breakfast included.* **Credit** MC, V. **Map H7**
A seventeenth-century building near place St-Michel, with a flowered entrance, wooden beams and a winding staircase. The 22 rooms are tastefully decorated in pinks and blues, sprinkled with antique furniture. If you can brave the stairs, room 19 has a lovely balcony with plants. A faithful following makes reservations a must. **Room services** *Hairdryer. Safe. TV.*

Hôtel St-André-des-Arts
66 rue St-André-des-Arts, 6th (01.43.26.96.16/fax 01.43.29.73.34). M° Odéon. **Rates** *single* 370F; *double* 470F-510F; *triple* 580F; *quad* 640F; *breakfast included.* **Credit** MC, V. **Map H7**
In the thick of St-Germain and opposite a delightful passageway is this sixteenth-century building with an abundance of old beams and stone walls. Once occupied by the king's musketeers, the hotel now boasts 33 pleasant rooms and some smart new cream and green bathrooms (all rooms should have bathrooms by late 1999). **Hotel services** *Safe.*

Hôtel de Nevers
83 rue du Bac, 7th (01.45.44.61.30/fax 01.42.22.29.47). M° Rue du Bac. **Rates** *single* 430F; *double* 480F-540F; *extra bed* 100F; *breakfast* 35F. **No credit cards. Map G6**
This characterful eleven-room hotel was once an outbuilding of the Récollets convent. Everything is scaled down, with mini-wardrobes and neat bathrooms. Rooms are quite smart, but the paintwork on the winding staircase seems to suffer regular torment as guests carry luggage up. If you can make it to the 4th floor, two rooms have tiny terraces. **Hotel services** *Safe.* **Room services** *Minibar. TV.*

Hôtel des Arts
7 cité Bergère, 9th (01.42.46.73.30/fax 01.48.00.94.42). M° Grands Boulevards. **Rates** *single* 360F-380F; *double*

380F-400F; *triple* 530F; *breakfast* 33F. **Credit** AmEx, DC, MC, V. **Map J4**

In a tiny, tranquil alley of hotels, this is the best, if most unconventional, of the cheapies. Run by the friendly Bernard family, now in their fourth generation of hotel-keeping, the reception area is bohemian, with Babar the parrot, a bubbling fish tank, and a gaudy grandfather clock. The stairwells are pasted over with theatre and museum posters. The 26 rooms vary in size and species of flowery wallpaper, but all are fresh and clean, so you can forgive the cork headboards.
Hotel services *Laundry. Lift. Parking. Safe.* **Room services** *Double glazing. Hairdryer. Radio. TV.*

Hôtel Chopin

46 passage Jouffroy or 10 bd Montmartre, 9th (01.47.70.58.10/fax 01.42.47.00.70). M° Richelieu Drouot. **Rates** *single* 405F-455F; *double* 450F-490F; *triple* 565F; *breakfast* 38F. **Credit** AmEx, DC, MC, V. **Map J4**
Hidden beyond the Musée Grévin, old-fashioned toy shops, and printsellers, you find the delightful 36-room Chopin, built with the passage in 1846. The hall has kept its chesterfields, but rooms have been colourfully redone and (except one single) have shower or bath and toilet. Book ahead.
Hotel services *Hairdryer. Lift. Safe.* **Room services** *TV.*

Résidence du Pré

15 rue Pierre-Sémard, 9th (01.48.78.26.72/fax 01.42.80.64.83). M° Cadet. **Rates** *single* 425F; *double* 460F-495F; *triple* 600F; *breakfast* 50F. **Credit** AmEx, DC, MC, V. **Map J3**
On a street of nineteenth-century buildings festooned with ornate iron balconies, the efficient 40-room Résidence du Pré is the least expensive of three Hôtels du Pré. Rooms are spacious and sport strong reds and rusts with dark wood panelling. Convenient for the Gare du Nord.
Hotel services *Bar. Lift. Safe. Parking (60F).* **Room services** *Double glazing. TV.*

Hôtel Apollo

11 rue de Dunkerque, 10th (01.48.78.04.98/fax 01.42.85.08.78). M° Gare du Nord. **Rates** *single* 225F-325F; *double* 385F-445F; *triple* 445F-500F; *quad* 600F; *breakfast* 30F. **Credit** AmEx, DC, MC, V. **Map K2**
Opposite the Gare du Nord, the Apollo is a great find in an area full of doubtful budget joints. The 45-room hotel has true rustic charm; rooms are decorated with large wardrobes and florid wallpaper. English and German spoken.
Hotel services *Lift.* **Room services** *Double glazing. Minibar. Safe. TV.*

Hôtel Beaumarchais

3 rue Oberkampf, 11th (01.53.36.86.86/fax 01.43.38.32.86). M° Filles de Calvaire. **Rates** *single* 350F-400F; *double* 450F-500F; *suite* 700F; *breakfast* 35F. **Credit** AmEx, MC, V. **Map L5**
This stylish hotel was redesigned two years ago by its architect owner, with walls, fabrics, wavy headboards and Milan glass bedlamps all in bright reds, blues and yellows. 33 rooms range from small singles to a good-sized suite; some overlook a pretty courtyard. The reception, living and breakfast areas have clean lines and curves and an airy feel.
Hotel services *Air con. Lift.* **Room services** *Hairdryer. Safe. TV.*

Hôtel Delambre

35 rue Delambre, 14th (01.43.20.66.31/fax 01.45.38.91.76). M° Edgar-Quinet or Vavin. **Rates** *single* 395F; *double* 460F-550F; *mini suite* 750F; *extra bed* 80F; *breakfast* 42F. **Credit** AmEx, MC, V. **Map G9**
Elegant cast-iron touches in the 30 rooms and the breakfast area give this friendly hotel an individual style, much updated from the 1920s when Surrealist André Breton lived here. Room 7, with private terrace, and the family mini suite in the attic, are particularly appealing.
Hotel services *Lift. Safe.* **Room services.** *Hairdryer. Modem link. Safe. TV. Wheelchair access (one room).*

Hôtel Istria

29 rue Campagne-Première, 14th (01.43.20.91.82/fax 01.43.22.48.45). M° Raspail. **Rates** *single* 500F; *double*

Hôtel des Grandes Ecoles *is one of the Latin Quarter's best-kept secrets (see p.151).*

580F-600F; *breakfast* 45F. **Credit** AmEx, DC, MC, V.
Map G9
The Istria has been modernised but has kept the charm which attracted photographer Man Ray and poet Louis Aragon in Montparnasse's heyday. The 26 compact rooms are simply furnished. There's a cosy cellar breakfast room and a comfortable living area. The unusual tiled artists' studios next door featured in Godard's *A bout du souffle*.
Hotel services *Air con. Fax. Laundry. Lift.* **Room services** *Double glazing. Hairdryer. Safe. TV.*

Hôtel Keppler

12 rue Keppler, 16th (01.47.20.65.05/fax 01.47.23.02.29).
M° Kléber or George V. **Rates** *single or double* 430F-480F; *triple* 550F; *breakfast* 35F. **Credit** AmEx, MC, V. **Map C4**
The high ceilings and spacious rooms are typical of this prestigious neighbourhood, but don't often come at these prices. The 49 rooms are in pale blues and beiges, there's a spiral staircase and a vintage lift. The reception, salon and breakfast room are business-like but subtle lighting adds atmosphere.
Hotel services *Bar. Lift.* **Room services** *Hairdryer. Room service (24-hr). Safe. TV.*

Hôtel Ermitage

24 rue Lamarck, 18th (01.42.64.79.22/fax 01.42.64.10.33). M° Lamarck-Caulaincourt. **Rates** *single* 430F; *double* 500F; *triple* 630F; *quad* 730F; *breakfast included.* **No credit cards. Map H1**
This twelve-room hotel is only five minutes from Sacré-Coeur, but is on a peaceful street away from the tourist madness. Bedrooms are large, endearingly over-decorated and characterful. Ground-floor rooms give onto a garden, while back rooms on the upper floors have great views of the city.
Hotel services *Garden.* **Room services** *Double glazing. Hairdryer.*

Prima Lepic

29 rue Lepic, 18th (01.46.06.44.64/fax 01.46.06.66.11). M° Blanche or Abbesses. **Rates** *single* 350F-380F; *double* 380F-440F; *triple* 500F-600F; *quad/quin* 700F; *breakfast* 40F. **Credit** MC, V. **Map H1**
The Prima Lepic, on a lively street between the Moulin Rouge and Sacré Coeur, offers a nostalgic Montmartre experience. From the pretty tiled entrance to the breakfast room with white wrought-iron furniture and garden murals, the hotel is full of originality. Ribbons and flounces may not be everyone's taste, but the 38 rooms are clean and a reasonable size.
Hotel services *Lift. Safe.* **Room services** *Hairdryer. TV.*

Hôtel Regyn's Montmartre

18 pl des Abbesses, 18th (01.42.54.45.21/fax 01.42.23.76.69). M° Abbesses. **Rates** *single* 380F-400F; *double* 435F-475F; *triple* 575F-605F; *breakfast* 40F-45F. **Credit** AmEx, MC, V. **Map G1**
A great location opposite the Abbesses Métro in the heart of Montmartre. There is a pretty breakfast room decorated with murals of the Métro entrance and six of the 22 rooms have superb views. A few shabby edges, but full of character.
Hotel services *Lift.* **Room services** *Hairdryer. Safe. Radio. TV.*

Budget

Hôtel de Lille

8 rue du Pélican, 1st (01.42.33.33.42). M° Palais-Royal. **Rates** *single* 210F-290F; *double* 240F-290F; *extra bed* 80F; *shower* 30F; *no breakfast.* **No credit cards. Map H5**
None of the glamour of the Louvre or Palais-Royal, just a few steps away, has rubbed off on this 13-room hotel, but at these prices who's complaining? The fake flowers in the hall, worn rugs and Toulouse-Lautrec prints are nothing to write home about, but the doubles are a reasonable size. Some rooms have WC and shower, others just a washbasin. No phones.

Hôtel Tiquetonne

6 rue Tiquetonne, 2nd (01.42.36.94.58/fax 01.42.36.02.94). M° Etienne Marcel. **Rates** *single* 143F-213F; *double* 246F; *shower* 30F; *breakfast* 25F. **Credit** MC, V. **Map J5**
On a paved street near Les Halles, this superb-value hotel has 47 basic but clean rooms. Some are very large for the price, and high ceilings on the lower floors give even more sense of space. All doubles have bathrooms; some singles are without.
Hotel services *Lift.*

Hôtel du Séjour

36 rue du Grenier-St-Lazare, 3rd (01.48.87.40.36). M° Etienne Marcel or Rambuteau. **Rates** *single* 180F; *double* 240F-320F; *extra bed* 120F; *shower* 20F. *No breakfast.* **Map K5**
No frills, furbelows or phones here, but this 21-room hotel is a welcoming haven for travellers on a budget. Run by a friendly Portuguese couple for 25 years, most rooms and bathrooms have been nicely smartened up, and the tiny courtyard is freshly painted. Upper rooms get lots of sun.
Room services *Double glazing.*

Hôtel Castex

5 rue Castex, 4th (01.42.72.31.52/fax 01.42.72.57.91). M° Bastille. **Rates** *single* 240F-290F; *double* 320F-360F; *triple* 460F; *extra bed* 70F; *breakfast* 25F. **Credit** MC, V. **Map L7**
The Perdigãos have recently taken over this good-value Marais hotel and added a small salon with bamboo furniture. Neon-lit drinks and snacks machines are incongruous but no doubt handy. The spruced-up kitchen is also available to guests. The 27-rooms are plain but pleasant. A few still have no toilet but all have a shower or bath, the rest are en-suite.
Hotel services *Fax. Safe. TV.*

Hôtel de la Herse d'Or

20 rue St-Antoine, 4th (01.48.87.84.09/fax 01.48.87.94.01). M° Bastille. **Rates** *single* 160F; *double* 200F-295F; *triple* 320F; *shower* 10F; *breakfast* 25F. **Credit** V. **Map L7**
Enter this seventeenth-century building down a stone-walled corridor, and you'll find a cheap and cheerful hotel lacking much character but offering good-sized basic rooms in an excellent location. The 35-rooms (many without bathroom) look onto small dark courtyards or the noisy rue St-Antoine.
Hotel services *Safe.*

Hôtel Pratic

9 rue d'Ormesson, 4th (01.48.87.80.47/fax 01.48.87.40.04). M° St-Paul. **Rates** *single* 200F; *double* 245F-360F; *breakfast* 25F. **Credit** MC, V. **Map L6**
In a great location next to the place du Marché-Ste-Catherine in the Marais, this is a good budget option. Don't expect lavish décor or antiques at these prices, but the 24 rooms are simple and clean, and some have tiny bathrooms.
Room services *Double glazing. Safe.*

Hôtel de Nesle

7 rue de Nesle, 6th (01.43.54.62.41/fax 01.43.54.31.88). M° Odéon. **Rates** *single* 275F; *double* 350F-500F; *extra bed* 75F; *no breakfast.* **No credit cards. Map H6**
The eccentric Nesle draws an international backpacker clientele to be regaled with tales from Madame of its hippy past; Monsieur is responsible for the painted figures posturing on the walls of the 20 rooms (from colonial to Oriental, Molière to the Knights Templars). Toilets and showers on the same floor for rooms without. No phones in rooms and no reservations.
Hotel services *Garden.* **Room services** *Double glazing.*

Grand Hôtel Lévêque

29 rue Cler, 7th (01.47.05.49.15/fax 01.45.50.49.36). M° Ecole-Militaire. **Rates** *single* 270F; *double* 380F-450F; *triple* 550F; *breakfast* 35F. **Credit** AmEx, MC, V. **Map D6**
Located on a largely pedestrianised market street near the

Eiffel Tower, the Lévêque is good value for this chic area. The old-tiled entrance is charming, while the 50 newly refurbished rooms are well-equipped and comfortable with sparkling white bathrooms in all the doubles; singles just have a basin.
Hotel services *Lift.* **Room services** *Double glazing. Hairdryer. Safe. TV.*

Résidence Hôtel des Trois Poussins

15 rue Clauzel, 9th (01.53.32.81.81/fax 01.53.32.81.82). M° St-Georges. **Rates** *single* 380F-520F; *double* 520F-680F; *single studio* 480F-580F; *double studio* 580F-740F; *breakfast* 45F. **Credit** AmEx, MC, V. **Map H2**
The Résidence, between the banking centre of Opéra and picturesque Sacré-Coeur, offers a rare opportunity for self catering. Of the 40 beamed and floral rooms, 24 are studios, fully equipped with kitchens including microwaves.
Hotel services *Bar. Lift.* **Room services** *Double glazing. Hairdryer. Kitchen. Modem link. Safe. TV.*

Hôtel de Nevers

53 rue de Malte, 11th (01.47.00.56.18/fax 01.43.57.77.39). M° République. **Rates** *single* 160F-260F; *double* 180F-275F; *triple* 335F; *quad* 410F; *shower* 20F; *breakfast* 25F. **Credit** MC, V. **Map L4**
This is a friendly, good-value base ten minutes from the Marais. Three languid cats welcome you as one of the family. The 34 rooms are clean and comfortable; it's worth paying more for a bathroom. The vintage lift is an experience.
Hotel services *Lift. Porter.*

Hôtel des Batignolles

26-28 rue des Batignolles, 17th (01.43.87.70.40/fax 01.44.70.01.04). M° Rome. **Rates** *single* 200F-320F; *double* 320F-360F; *triple* 430F; *breakfast* 25F. **Credit** DC, MC, V. **Map F2**
This hotel still feels a little like the girls' boarding house it once was, with simple furnishings and plain bathrooms, but provides a good base within reach of Montmartre. The Batignolles is quiet and clean, with 33 spacious rooms and a tranquil courtyard with false-acacia trees for summer.
Hotel services *Safe.* **Room services** *Double glazing.*

Youth Accommodation

MIJE

Fourcy *6 rue de Fourcy, 4th (01.42.74.23.45/fax 01.40.27.81.64). M° St-Paul.* **Fauconnier** *11 rue du Fauconnier, 4th (01.42.74.23.45). M° St-Paul.* **Maubisson** *12 rue des Barres, 4th (01.42.74.23.45). M° Hôtel de Ville.* **Open** *hostels* 7am-1am daily. **Rates** *dormitory* 130F per person (18-30s sharing rooms); *single* 206F; *double* 316F; *triple* 142F per person; *membership* 15F; *breakfast* included. **No credit cards. Map L6, L7, K6**
Two seventeenth-century aristocratic Marais residences and a former convent are surely the most attractive budget sleeps in Paris. Plain but clean rooms sleep up to eight; all have a shower and basin. Fourcy has a beautiful vaulted dining hall.

BVJ Paris/Quartier Latin

44 rue des Bernardins, 5th (01.43.29.34.80/fax 01.53.00.90.91). M° Maubert-Mutualité. **Open** *24-hour, all year.* **Rates** *dormitory* 100F-120F per person; *single* 130F; *breakfast* included. **No credit cards. Map K7**
138 beds in bare modern dorms (for up to ten) and singles, a TV lounge and a work room. Discounts for over a month.
Branch: BVJ Paris/Louvre 20 rue Jean-Jacques Rousseau, 1st (01.53.00.90.90). 200 beds.

Young & Happy Hostel

80 rue Mouffetard, 5th (01.45.35.09.53/fax 01.47.07.22.24). M° Place Monge. **Rates** *dormitory* 107F per person; *double* 127F per person; *breakfast* included. **Open** 8am-11am, 5pm-

Hôtel Chopin: passage to the past.

2am daily. **Credit** MC, V (300F min). **Map J8**
This friendly hostel on an animated street offers 82 beds in slightly tatty surroundings. The dorms are a bit cramped but the young, international clientele ensures community atmosphere. There's a tiny kitchen in the basement.

Association des Etudiants Protestants de Paris

46 rue de Vaugirard, 6th (01.46.33.23.30/fax 01.46.34.27.09). M° Mabillon or St-Sulpice. **Open** *Office* 8.45am-noon, 3-7pm Mon-Fri; 8.45am-noon, 6-8pm Sat; 10am-noon Sun. *Hostel* 24 hours daily. **Rates** *dormitory* 80F per person; 2100F monthly; *breakfast* included. **No credit cards. Map G7**
In a good location by the Luxembourg gardens, the AEPP offers accommodation for students of 18-30 in dormitories of six to eight, plus basic cooking facilities, café and TV lounge. No reservations are accepted and membership is 10F, to be paid on arrival in addition to 200F deposit.

Auberge Internationale des Jeunes

10 rue Trousseau, 11th (01.47.00.62.00/fax 01.47.00.33.16). M° Ledru-Rollin. **Open** 24hrs daily; *rooms closed* 10am-3pm. **Rates** *Nov-Feb* 81F; *Mar-Oct* 91F; *breakfast* included. **Credit** AmEx, MC, V. **Map N7**
Cleanliness is a high priority at this hostel close to the Bastille, where there are rooms for two to six people. Larger ones have their own shower and toilet. No curfew.

Résidence Bastille

151 av Ledru-Rollin, 11th (01.43.79.53.86/fax 01.43.79.35.63). M° Voltaire. **Open** 7am-12.30pm, 2pm-1am daily. **Rates** *shared* 110F-125F per person; *single* 160F-175F; *breakfast* included. **Credit** MC, V. **Map N6**
Recently renovated, this modern hostel has 150 beds for under-35s. 10 per cent discount with a student card.

Auberge Jules Ferry
8 bd Jules-Ferry, 11th (01.43.57.55.60/fax 01.43.14.82.09). M° République or Goncourt. **Open** *Office* 8am-1am; *Hostel* 24 hrs daily, *rooms closed* 11am-2pm. **Rates** *shared* 115F per person; *double* 240F; *breakfast included.* **Credit** MC, V. **Map M4**
Friendly IYHF hostel has rooms for two to six and an Internet facility. No advance reservations, but they can usually find you a bed here or in another branch.

Bed and Breakfast

Alcove & Agapes
Le Bed & Breakfast à Paris, 8bis rue Coysevox, 18th (01.44.85.06.05/fax 01.44.85.06.14).
This new B & B service has more than 80 homes, mostly in central Paris (320F-500F for a double room). Carefully selected hosts range from artists renting out their spare room to grandmothers whose families have long since flown the nest.

Tourisme chez l'Habitant
15 rue des Pas-Perdus, BP 8338, 95804 Cergy Saint-(01.34.25.44.44/fax 01.34.25.44.45). **Open** 9.30am-6.30pm Mon-Fri; 10am-5pm Sat. **Credit** AmEx, MC, V.
Stay for a minimum of two nights in one of the 80 homes on the books, for 168F-206F per person, plus 60F booking fee.

Chain Hotels

Holiday Inn
Central reservations across Europe UK 0800-897121; France 0800-905999. **Rates** prices vary according to hotel: *single or double* 995F-1995F; *executive* 1695F-2500F; *breakfast* 45F-125F. **Credit** AmEx, DC, MC, V.
A dependable American-owned chain, with 20 hotels in Paris and suburbs. The grandest is at République (01.43.55.44.34).

Hôtel Ibis
Central reservations from the UK 0181.283.4550; from France 01.60.77.52.52/fax 01.69.91.05.63. **Rates** *single or double* 295F-495F; *breakfast* 39F. **Credit** AmEx, DC, MC, V.
This inexpensive French chain has 20 hotels within the Périphérique, and many more in the suburbs.

Libertel
Central reservations in the UK 0990 300200; from France 01.44.74.17.47. **Rates** *single or double* 470F-1700F depending on hotel; *breakfast* 45F-75F. **Credit** AmEx, DC, MC, V.
This Paris-based chain founded in 1991 has 30 hotels in the city ranging from the delightful 12-room **Prince de Condé** to the 243-room **Terminus Nord**.

Timhôtel
Central reservations 01.44.15.81.15/fax 01.44.15.95.26. **Rates** *single or double* 470F-680F; *triple* 595F-960F; *breakfast* 49F-60F. **Credit** AmEx, DC, MC, V.
A bit different from the hotel chain norm, Timhotels are individually decorated and well located. Picturesque Timhotel Montmartre has great views. Other handy branches are near the Jardin des Plantes, Louvre, Bourse and Gare du Nord.

Apart-Hotels & Short-Stay Rental

A deposit is usually payable on arrival.

Apparthotel Citadines
Central reservations (01.41.05.79.79/fax 01.47.59.04.70). **Rates** *one person studio* from 450F; *two* from 530F; *apartment for four* from 760F. **Credit** AmEx, DC, MC, V.

Ten modern complexes (Montparnasse, Montmartre, Opéra, etc) attract a mainly business clientele. Rooms are on the cramped side, but kitchenette and table also make them practical for those with children. Discounts for seven nights plus. **Hotel services** Double glazing. *Hairdryer. Kitchen. TV.*

Home Plazza Bastille
74 rue Amelot, 11th (01.40.21.20.00/fax 01.47.00.82.40). M° St-Sébastien-Froissart. **Rates** *single* 787F; *double* 894F; *suite* 1087F-1622F. **Credit** AmEx, DC, MC, V. **Map L5**
Aimed at both business people and tourists, this carefully constructed 'village' of 290 apartments built around a street is reminiscent of a stage set. Rooms are clean and modern with well-equipped kitchenette and spacious bathrooms. **Hotel services** *Air con. Bar. Business services. Garden. Parking. Restaurant.* **Room services** *Hairdryer. TV.*

Paris Appartements Services
69 rue d'Argout, 2nd (01.40.28.01.28/fax 01.40.28.92.01). **Open** 9am-6pm Mon-Fri; 10am-1pm Sat. **Rates** *studio* from 3850F per week; *apartment* from 5250F per week. **Credit** MC, V.
Furnished studios and one-bedroom flats in the 1st to 4th *arrondissements*, with weekly maid service, and a 24-hour helpline. Lower rates for over one month. Bilingual staff.

Camping

Camping du Bois de Boulogne
2 allée du Bord de l'Eau, Bois de Boulogne, 16th (01.45.24.30.81; fax 01.42.24.42.95). M° Porte-Maillot (then free shuttle-bus to campsite during summer) or bus 244. **Open** 24 hours daily. **Credit** AmEx, DC, MC, V.
It's unlikely that you'd really come to Paris to camp, but a campsite does exist on the western side of the Bois de Boulogne. A one- to two-person plot with electricity and water for a tent or caravan costs 127F-149F per night; 96F-133F without electricity. Add 24F-31F for each extra person.

Hôtel de Nesle: *still boho in St-Germain.*

Menu Lexicon

A gourmet glossary to French menu speak to help you order your meal like a true grenouille.

Abats offal. **Agneau** lamb. **Aiguillettes** (*de canard*) thin slices of duck breast. **Ail** garlic; **aioli** sauce made with ground garlic. **Aligot** mashed potatoes with melted cheese and garlic. **Aloyau** loin of beef. **Ananas** pineapple. **Anchoïade** spicy anchovy and olive paste. **Andouillette** chitterling sausage made from pig's offal. **Aneth** dill. **Anguille** eel. **Asperge** asparagus. **Assiette** plate. **Aubergine** aubergine (GB); eggplant (US).

Ballotine meat or fish boned, stuffed and rolled up. **Bar** sea bass. **Barbue** brill. **Bavarois** moulded cream dessert. **Bavette** beef flank steak. **Béarnaise** rich sauce of butter and egg yolk. **Beignet** fritter or doughnut. **Belon** smooth, flat oyster. **Betterave** beetroot. **Beurre** butter. **Biche** venison. **Bifteak** steak. **Bisque** shellfish soup. **Blanc** breast. **Blanquette** a 'white' stew made with eggs and cream. **Blette** Swiss chard. **Boudin noir/blanc** black (blood)/white pudding. **Boeuf** beef; – **bourguignon** beef cooked Burgundy style, with red wine, onions and mushrooms; – **gros sel** boiled beef with vegetables, similar to *pot-au-feu*. **Bouillabaisse** Mediterranean fish soup. **Bourride** a *bouillabaisse*-like soup, without shellfish. **Brebis** sheep's milk cheese. **Brochet** pike. **Brochette** kebab. **Bulot** whelk.

Cabillaud fresh cod. **Caille** quail. **Campagne/campagnard** country-style. **Canard** duck. **Cannelle** cinnamon. **Carbonnade** beef stew with onions and stout or beer. **Carré d'agneau** rack or loin of lamb. **Carrelet** plaice. **Cassis** blackcurrants, also blackcurrant liqueur used in *kir*. **Cassoulet** stew of haricot beans, sausage and preserved duck. **Céleri** celery. **Céleri rave** celeriac. **Cèpe** cep mushroom. **Cerise** cherry. **Cervelles** brains. **Champignon** mushroom; – **de Paris** button mushroom. **Charcuterie** cold cured meats, such as *saucisson* or pâté. **Charlotte** moulded cream dessert with a biscuit edge; also baked versions with fruit. **Chasseur** cooked with mushrooms, shallots and white wine. **Chateaubriand** thick fillet steak, usually served for two with a *béarnaise* sauce. **Chaud** hot. **Chaud-froid** a sauce thickened with gelatine or aspic, used to glaze cold dishes. **Cheval** horse. **à Cheval** with an egg on top. **Chèvre** goat's cheese. **Chevreuil** young roe deer. **Chou** cabbage. **Choucroute** sauerkraut, usually served *garnie* with cured ham and sausages. **Choufleur** cauliflower. **Ciboulette** chive. **Citron**

lemon. **Citron vert** lime. **Citronelle** lemongrass. **Civet** game stew. **Clafoutis** thick batter filled with fruit, usually cherries. **Cochon de lait** suckling pig. **Coco** large white bean. **Colin** hake. **Confit de canard** preserved duck. **Contre-filet** sirloin steak. **Coquelet** baby rooster. **Coquille** shell. **Coquilles St-Jacques** scallops. **Côte** chop; **côte de boeuf** beef rib. **Cornichon** pickled gherkin. **Crème anglaise** custard sauce. **Crème brûlée** creamy custard dessert with caramel glaze. **Crème Chantilly** sweetened whipped cream. **Crème fraîche** thick, slightly soured cream. **Crépinettes** small, flattish sausages, often grilled. **Cresson** watercress. **Crevettes** prawns (GB), shrimps (US). **Croque madame** sandwich of toasted cheese and ham topped with an egg; **croque monsieur** sandwich of toasted cheese and ham. **En croûte** in a pastry case. **Cru** raw. **Crudités** assorted raw vegetables.

Darne (de saumon) salmon steak. **Daube** meat braised slowly in red wine or stock. **Daurade** sea bream. **Dégustation** tasting or sampling. **Désossé** boned. **Dinde** turkey.

Echalote shallot. **Eglefin** haddock. **Endive** chicory (GB), Belgian endive (US). **Entrecôte** beef rib steak. **Entremets** cream or milk-based dessert. **Epices** spices. **Epinards** spinach. **Escabèche** sautéed and marinated fish, served cold. **Escargot** snail. **Espadon** swordfish. **Estouffade** meat that has been marinated, fried and braised.

Faisan pheasant. **Farci** stuffed. **Fauxfilet** sirloin steak. **Feuilleté** 'leaves' of (puff) pastry. **Fève** broad bean. **Filet mignon** beef tenderloin. **Fines de claire** crinkle-shelled oysters. **Fines herbes** mixture of herbs. **Flambé** food flamed in a pan in burning brandy or other alcohol. **Flétan** halibut. **Foie** liver; **foie gras** fattened liver of goose or duck. **Forestière** with mushrooms. **au Four** baked. **Fraise** strawberry. **Framboise** raspberry. **Friandises** sweets or petits-fours. **Fricadelle** meat-ball. **Fricassé** meat fried and simmered in stock, usually with creamy sauce. **Frisée** curly endive. **Frites** chips (GB); fries (US). **Froid** cold. **Fromage** cheese; – **blanc** smooth cream cheese. **Fruits de mer** shellfish. **Fumé** smoked.

Galantine boned meat or fish pressed together, usually with a stuffing. **Galette**

Menu Lexicon

round flat cake of flaky pastry, potato pancake or buckwheat savoury *crêpe*. **Garni** garnished. **Gâteau** cake. **Gelée** aspic. **Gésiers** gizzards. **Gibier** game. **Gigot d'agneau** leg of lamb. **Gingembre** ginger. **Girolle** prized species of chanterelle mushroom. **Glace** ice cream. **Glacé** frozen or iced. **Goujon** strips of fish, coated breadcrumbs and fried. **Granité** water-ice. **Gras** fat. **Gratin dauphinois** sliced potatoes baked with milk, cheese and garlic. **Gratiné** browned with breadcrumbs or cheese. **Grèque** (*à la*) vegetables served cold in the cooking liquid including oil and lemon juice. **Grenouille** (*cuisses de*) frogs' legs. **Griotte** morello cherry. **Groseille** redcurrant. **Groseille à maquereau** gooseberry.

Haché minced. **Hachis Parmentier** shepherd's pie. **Hareng** herring. **Haricot** bean; **– vert** green bean. **Homard** lobster. **Huître** oyster.

Ile flottante poached whipped egg white floating in vanilla custard.

Jambon ham; **– cru** cured raw ham. **Jarret de porc** ham shin or knuckle. **Julienne** vegetables cut into matchsticks.

Langoustine Dublin Bay prawns, scampi. **Lait** milk. **Lapin** rabbit. **Lamelle** very thin slice. **Langue** tongue. **Lard** bacon; **lardon** small cube of bacon. **Légume** vegetable. **Lentilles** lentils. **Lièvre** hare. **Lieu** pollack. **Limande** lemon sole. **Lotte** monkfish.

Mâche lamb's lettuce. **Magret** duck breast. **Maison** (*de la*) of the house. **Maquereau** mackerel. **Marcassin** young wild boar. **Mariné** marinated. **Marmite** small cooking pot. **Marquise** light mousse-like cake. **Marron** chestnut. **Merguez** spicy lamb/beef sausage. **Merlan** whiting. **Merlu** hake. **Meunière** fish seasoned, floured, sautéed in butter. **Miel** honey. **Mignon** small fillet of meat. **Moëlle** bone marrow; **os à la** – marrow bone. **Morille** morel mushroom. **Moules** mussels; **– à la marinière** cooked in white wine, shallots, parsley, butter and lemon juice. **Morue** dried, salted cod; **brandade de –** puréed with potato. **Mousseline** lightened with whipped cream or egg white. **Moutarde** mustard. **Mûre** blackberry. **Muscade** nutmeg. **Myrtille** bilberry/blueberry.

Nage aromatic poaching liquid. **Navarin** lamb and vegetable stew. **Navet** turnip. **Noisette** small round portion, usually meat; hazelnut. **Noix** walnut. **Noix de coco** coconut. **Nouilles** noodles.

Oeuf egg; **– en cocotte** baked egg; **– en meurette** egg poached in red wine; **– à la neige** see *Ile flottante*. **Oie** goose. **Oignon** onion. **Onglet** cut of beef, similar to *bavette*. **Oseille** sorrel **Oursin** sea urchin.

Pain bread. **Palourde** type of clam. **Pamplemousse** grapefruit. **Panaché**

mixture. **Pané** breaded. **en Papillote** cooked in paper packet. **Parfait** sweet or savoury mousse-like mixture. **Parmentier** with potato. **Pâtes** pasta or noodles. **Paupiette** slice of meat or fish, stuffed and rolled. **Pavé** thick steak. **Pêcheur** based on fish. **Perdrix** partridge. **Petit salé** salt pork. **Pied** foot (trotter). **Pignon** pine kernel. **Pintade/pintadeau** guinea fowl. **Pipérade** scrambled egg with Bayonne ham, onion and peppers. **Pistou** pesto-like basil and garlic paste. **Plat** dish; main course; **– du jour** daily special. **Pleurotte** oyster mushroom. **Poire** pear. **Poireau** leek. **Poisson** fish. **Poivre** pepper. **Poivron** red or green (bell) pepper. **Pomme** apple. **Pomme de terre** potato; **pommes lyonnaises** potatoes sliced and fried with onions. **Potage** soup. **Pot au feu** boiled beef with vegetables. **Poulet** chicken. **Poulpe** octopus. **Pressé** squeezed. **Prune** plum. **Pruneau** prune.

Quenelle light poached dumpling, usually made with fish, sometimes poultry. **Quetsch** damson. **Queue de boeuf** ox-tail.

Ragoût brown meat stew. **Raie** skate. **Raifort** horseradish. **Râpé** grated. **Rascasse** scorpion fish. **Réglisse** liquorice. **Reine-claude** greengage plum. **Rillettes** potted meat, usually pork and/or goose. **Ris de veau** veal sweetbreads. **Riz** rice. **Rognons** kidneys. **Rôti** roast. **Rouget** red mullet.

Sablé shortbread biscuit. **St Pierre** John Dory. **Salé** salted. **Sandre** pike-perch, a freshwater fish. **Sanglier** wild boar. **Saucisse** sausage. **Saucisson** small sausage. **Saucisson sec** dried sausage eaten cold. **Saumon** salmon. **Sec/sèche** dry. **Seiche** squid. **Sel** salt. **Suprême** (*de volaille*) fillets (of chicken) in a cream sauce. **Supion** small squid.

Tartare raw minced steak (also tuna or salmon). **Tarte aux pommes** apple tart. **Tarte Tatin** a warm, caramelised apple tart cooked upside-down. **Terrine** a rectangular earthenware dish or a pâté cooked in one. **Tête** head; **– de veau** calf's head, cooked in a white *court-bouillon*. **Thé** tea. **Thon** tuna. **Timbale** dome-shaped mould, or food cooked in one. **Tisane** herbal tea. **Tournedos** small slices of beef fillet, sautéed or grilled. **Tourte** covered pie or tart, usually savoury. **Travers de porc** pork spare ribs. **Tripes** tripe. **Tripoux** Auvergnat dish of sheep's tripe and feet. **Truffes** truffles. **Truite** trout.

Vacherin cake of layered meringue, cream, fruit and ice cream; a soft, cow's milk cheese. **Vapeur** steam. **Veau** veal. **Velouté** stock-based white sauce; creamy soup. **Viande** meat. **Vichyssoise** cold leek and potato soup. **Volaille** poultry.

Cooking time (La Cuisson)

Cru raw. **Bleu** practically raw. **Saignant** rare. **Rosé** pink (said of lamb, duck, liver, kidneys). **A point** medium rare. **Bien cuit** well done. **Très bien cuit** very well done.

Restaurants

From cosy bistro to bustling brasserie, from Auvergne to Argentina, we pick the Paris tables most likely to pleasure your palate.

Whatever you want in a restaurant – stimulating cooking, lively atmosphere, attentive service, a stunning setting – it's sure to exist in Paris, a city that worships food like no other. But with thousands of places to choose from, the perfect dining experience is not always easy to find. Some places, like **La Coupole**, seem eternal: even run by a big brasserie chain, it retains an authentic buzz. Others change personality with a new owner or chef, making the food scene particularly tricky to follow.

Even with a limited budget around 100F, you can easily eat a hearty three-course meal with wine at a café or small bistro. It's important to choose carefully, though, as the food at this price can vary from sloppy to sophisticated. The best places are easy to spot: usually down side streets, they are filled with locals who look as if they eat there every day.

A little more money (150F-250F) can buy you a memorable meal at a chef's bistro, a contemporary *genre* that offers affordable seasonal set *menus*. Some are annexes of luxury restaurants, such as Michel Rostang's **Bistrot d'à Côté** chain and Guy Savoy's bistros; others showcase talented young chefs, like **La Régalade**, **Chez Michel** and **Philippe Detourbe**. Feast on traditional food at old-world bistros such as **Chardenoux** or **Le Grizzli**, or dive into a seafood platter in an atmospheric brasserie. Paris dining has grown far more international in the past 25 years, so for a change try one the best Asian or North African restaurants.

If you really want to splash out there are plenty of classic restaurants, such as **La Tour d'Argent** and **Les Ambassadeurs,** serving refined traditional cuisine in romantic settings. For cutting-edge cooking that borrows subtly from other cultures, Alain Passard at **L'Arpège**, **Pierre Gagnaire** and **Alain Ducasse** are leaders on the scene.

Don't miss the opportunity to sample wines that would be impossible to find elsewhere at these prices, from celebrated Burgundy and Bordeaux vintages to wines from lesser-known regions such as Languedoc-Roussillon, the Jura and Alsace.

Restaurants are listed by *arrondissement* order within each category. For more detailed listings and a larger selection, see the annual *Time Out Eating & Drinking in Paris Guide.*

L'Impasse: *an out-of-the-way bistro worth looking out for. See page 160.*

Prices & Prix fixe

Prices are based on the cost of a starter (*entrée*), main course (*plat*) and dessert chosen *à la carte*, but do not include drinks. It is quite acceptable to order only an *entrée* and *plat*, or *plat* and dessert, rather than all three courses. *Prix fixe* refers to a *menu* or *formule*, which offers a more limited choice at a set price, again usually three courses, and may include wine. By law, all restaurant and cafés prices include a 12-15 per cent service charge, so any other tip you may leave (5F-10F in a bistro, more in grand restaurants) is optional. Tables at haute-cuisine and classic restaurants often need to be booked well in advance, but it's always worth trying your luck.

Bistros

La Tour de Montlhéry (Chez Denise)

5 rue des Prouvaires, 1st (01.42.36.21.82). RER Châtelet-Les Halles. **Open** 24 hours, 7am Mon-7am Sat. Closed 14 July-15 Aug. **Average** 220F. **Credit** MC, V. **Map J5**
This famous all-night mecca – a relic of Les Halles' market past – sees a cheerful rabble of regulars tucking into huge main courses like piles of lamb chops or hearty morsels of rabbit simmered in mustard sauce with *frites*. Reserve.

L'Epi d'Or

25 rue Jean-Jacques-Rousseau, 1st (01.42.36.38.12). Mº Louvre. **Open** noon-2.30pm, 7-11pm Mon-Fri; 7-11pm Sat. Closed Aug. **Average** 200F. **Credit** V. **Map H5**
The nicotine-brown walls and porcelain knick-knacks lend this Les Halles bistro a strong Parisian atmosphere, and the food is perfectly respectable. To sample forgotten French dishes, order the *salade parisienne* (boiled beef in a tasty vinaigrette), and the *chaudrée tourangelle*, a *bourguignon* with pork. Try the fat homemade *frites*, but skip dessert. Menu 105F till 9pm.

Chez Georges

1 rue du Mail, 2nd (01.42.60.07.11). Mº Bourse. **Open** noon-2pm, 7-9.30pm Mon-Sat. Closed three weeks in Aug. **Average** 220F. **Credit** AmEx, MC, V. **Map J5**
Finance and fashion powerbrokers love this excellent bistro with its *vieille France* atmosphere. The food never strays from tried-and-tested bistro faves. Starters come in pots, and veal sweetbreads with morel mushrooms or sea bass with *beurre blanc* are tasty and generous, if slightly uneventful. The wine is exciting, especially if you're not paying.

Aux Crus de Bourgogne

3 rue Bachaumont, 2nd (01.42.33.48.24). Mº Sentier or Les Halles. **Open** noon-2.30pm, 7.45-10.30pm Mon-Fri. **Average** 200F. **Credit** AmEx, MC, V. **Map J5**
Arriving at the iron-and-glass awning in the pedestrianised rue Montorgueil market zone feels like a homecoming and in summer tables spill onto the picturesque, car-free street. Regulars relish the fresh, reasonably priced lobster. Otherwise try the *pièce de boeuf* or a simmered daily special.

L'Auberge Nicolas Flamel

51 rue de Montmorency, 3rd (01.42.71.77.78). Mº Rambuteau. **Open** noon-2.30pm, 8-11.45pm Mon-Fri; 8-11.45pm Sat. **Average** 175F. **Prix fixe** 295F. **Lunch menu** 69F. **Credit** MC, V. **Map K5**
Thought to be the oldest house in Paris, this stylish restaurant was built in 1407 as an *auberge* for travellers and women in distress. Today, quietly *branché* Parisians come for the very good cuisine, like a copious, rustic *hochepot mediéval* and more modish *rôti de lotte*. Ask owner and host Natan for a hand with the wine list, as wine is his hobby. Excellent service.

Le Hangar

12 impasse Berthaud, 3rd (01.42.74.55.44). Mº Rambuteau. **Open** 7.30pm-midnight Mon, noon-3pm, 7.30pm-midnight Tue-Sat. Closed Aug. **Average** 200F. **No credit cards. Map K5**

You can afford to be seen at **Le Réconfort.**

Stunning food in a hidden and purposefully plain spot, tucked into a dark impasse next to the doll museum. It's impossible to resist the perfectly pan-fried *foie gras*, served with the creamiest potato and olive oil purée or with subtle lentil cream. *Filet de boeuf* is meltingly tender and fish just right. Save room for the *petit gâteau mi-cuit au chocolat* or the fruit crumble.

Le Réconfort

37 rue de Poitou, 3rd (01.42.76.06.36). Mº St-Sébastien-Froissart. **Open** noon-2pm, 8.15-11pm Mon-Fri; 8.15-11pm Sat. Closed two weeks in Aug. **Average** 200F. **Lunch menu** 69F, 89F. **Credit** MC, V. **Map L5**
This stylish bistro may fill with trendy, *très international* photographers and models, but the updated, cosmopolitan bistro classics are both very good and affordable. Follow the Moroccan-style *compote de légumes* with an excellent Argentine steak or fresh cod in a balsamic sauce.

Le Valet de Carreau

2 rue Dupetit-Thouars, 3rd (01.42.72.72.60). Mº Temple. **Open** noon-2.30pm, 8-10.30pm Mon-Fri; 8-10.30pm Sat. **Average** 150F. **Prix fixe** 130F, 180F (dinner, winter only). **Lunch menu** 75F. **Credit** MC, V. **Map L5**
On a square shaded by plane trees and graced by a green Wallace drinking fountain, the 'Jack of Diamonds' boasts a colourful interior and seats outside in summer. A sophisticated Marais set comes for dishes like *ravioles* with caramelised cauliflower cream and a haddock *millefeuille*.

Baracane – Bistro de l'Oulette

38 rue des Tournelles, 4th (01.42.71.43.33). Mº Bastille. **Open** noon-2.30pm, 7pm-midnight Mon-Fri; 7pm-midnight Sat. **Average** 200F. **Prix fixe (dinner)** 135F, 215F. **Lunch menu** 52F, 82F. **Credit** MC, V. **Map L6**
Marcel Baudis and Alain Fontaine of L'Oulette have kept these little premises going with aplomb, at a standard of

cooking way above bistro norm. Two superb-value, daily *menus du marché* might be typified by a wild mushroom velouté and lambs' kidneys in a madeira sauce, while a pricier *menu-carte* offers Southwestern classics, like *cassoulet*.

Le Colimaçon
44 rue Vieille du Temple, 4th (01.48.87.12.01)
M° St-Paul. **Open** 7.30pm-1am Mon, Wed-Sun **Prix fixe** 89F, 129F. Closed three weeks in Aug. **Average** 160F. **Credit** AmEx, DC, MC, V. **Map K6**
Walking up the spiral staircase here is like stepping back into the eighteenth century. Come here for reliable bistro fare in an area not renowned for it. Start with rich fish soup or *escargots*, and follow with veal *sauté*, grilled salmon or delicious *cassoulet*. Homely desserts include a good fruit tart.

Le Grizzli
7 rue St-Martin, 4th (01.48.87.77.56). M° Hôtel-de-Ville or *RER Chatelet-Les-Halles.* **Open** noon-2.30pm, 7.30-11pm Mon-Sat. **Average** 220F. **Prix fixe** 120F, 160F. **Map K6**
This bistro seems to have it all – a blissfully untouched old-world setting, quietly competent waiters and solidly good traditional food. The *fricot de veau* is a toothsome house speciality, as are all meat and fish dishes cooked *sur l'ardoise*, or on heated pieces of slate, as in the Auvergne.

L'Impasse (Chez Robert)
4 impasse Guéménée, 4th (01.42.72.08.45). M° Bastille.
Open 7.30-11pm Mon-Sat. Closed Aug. **Average** 200F. **Prix fixe** 145F. **Credit MC, V. Map L7**
You're unlikely to stumble upon this simple, beamed bistro by accident as it is tucked away in a cul-de-sac. Those in the know come here for traditional bourgeois fare with a refined touch. Try the *foie gras* to start, and follow with the house speciality, a duck leg in wine sauce with plums and apples.

Le Vieux Bistro
14 rue du Cloître-Notre-Dame, 4th (01.43.54.18.95).
M° Cité or RER St-Michel. **Open** noon-2pm, 7.30-11pm daily. **Average** 250F. **Credit MC, V. Map J7**
Though opposite Notre Dame, there are few tourists here to pay the high-seeming prices for conventional-sounding fare. But for your money you get welcoming service and true bistro glory, such as an excellent *frisée aux lardons* with a poached egg or some of the best *boeuf bourguignon* in Paris.

Le Bistrot d'à Côté
16 bd St-Germain, 5th (01.43.54.59.10). M° Maubert-Mutualité. **Open** 12.30-2pm, 7.30-11pm Mon-Fri; 7.30-11pm Sat. **Average** 200F. **Prix fixe** (dinner) 148F, 189F. **Lunch menu** 135F. **Credit** AmEx, MC, V. **Map J7**
Long-loved Chez Raffatin et Honorine now belongs to Michel Rostang's Bistrots d'à Côté group, but has kept its *bouchon* charm and densely packed marble-topped tables. Chic intelligentsia come for good food and talk. The menu is surprisingly wide-ranging and adventurous, including imposters like Asian-inspired squid sautéed with beansprouts and ginger.

Les Bouchons de François Clerc
12 rue de l'Hôtel-Colbert, 5th (01.43.54.15.34).
M° Maubert-Mutualité. **Open** noon-2pm, 7-10.30pm Mon-Fri; 7-10.30pm Sat. **Prix fixe** (dinner) 219F. **Lunch menu** 117F. **Credit** AmEx, MC, V. **Map J7**
Locals and tourists alike cram into this attractive beamed dining room for the fine Bordeaux and Burgundies sold at wholesale rates and the 219F four-course *menu*, typified by a *cou de canard farci* and a salmon *millefeuille*. The fine cheese selection is another highlight. Booking essential.

Le Reminet
3 rue des Grands-Degrès, 5th (01.44.07.04.24).
M° Maubert-Mutualité or St-Michel. **Open** 7.30-10.15pm Tue; noon-2pm, 7.30-10.15pm Wed-Sun. Closed one week in Aug, three weeks in Jan. **Average** 180F. **Prix fixe**

110F (dinner). **Lunch menu** 85F. **Credit** MC, V. **Map J7**
An excellent, moderately priced bistro, smartened up with chandeliers and mirrors. Proof of the kitchen's homely style is the guinea fowl with savoy cabbage and bacon, while the salt cod on a bed of chicory, cooked with lemon and honey, offers an enticing assortment of flavours.

Brasserie Fernand
13 rue Guisarde, 6th (01.43.54.61.47). M° Mabillon.
Open noon-2.30pm, 7-11.30pm Mon-Sat. Closed three weeks in Aug. **Average** 200F. **Credit** MC, V. **Map H7**
The latest incarnation of this warm, old-fashioned bistro is a roaring success. The daily offer runs to well-executed classics like green bean salad or asparagus followed by grilled swordfish with ratatouille or pork *filet mignon* with excellent Lyonnais potatoes. Very noisy but fun in a group. Book.

Le Christine
1 rue Christine, 6th (01.40.51.71.64) M° Odéon. **Open** noon-2.30pm, 7-11pm Mon-Fri, 7-11pm Sat. **Average** 175F. **Prix fixe** 155F, 185F. **Lunch menu** 99F. **Credit** MC, V. **Map H6**
A fine spot for a long, lingering meal: friendly, attentive service, generously spaced tables, and an inviting setting. Good main dishes include braised chicken and vegetables lightly scented with star anise, and Charolais steak with *haricot verts*. There's also a veggie menu. For dessert, try the unusual carrot-lemon mousse in tea sauce. Reliable wines by the carafe.

Le Mâchon d'Henri
8 rue Guisarde, 6th (01.43.29.08.70). M° Mabillon.
Open noon-2.30pm, 7-11.30pm daily. **Average** 130F.
No credit cards. Map H7
This bastion of tradition in the modish district behind place St-Sulpice draws yuppie couples and party-ready French Sloanes for its remarkable food. The *menu* changes daily, but might be marrow bones with coarse salt, plump anchovies on warm potato salad and juicy *rognons de veau*. Booking a must.

Au Bon Acceuil
14 rue de Monttessuy, 7th (01.47.05.46.11).
M° Alma-Marceau/RER Pont de l'Alma. **Open** noon-2.30pm, 7.30-10.30pm Mon-Fri. Closed Aug and one week in Jan. **Average** 225F. **Prix fixe** (dinner) 155F. **Lunch menu** 135F. **Credit** MC, V. **Map D6**
This pleasant bistro near the Eiffel Tower fills its tables each night with a mix of internationals and chic locals for its bargain 155F *cuisine du marché* menu. The offer changes twice daily but might be a superb red pepper mousse with aubergine caviar, *émincé de boeuf* and comforting *crème brûlée*. A la carte goes to grander roast turbot with asparagus and Jerusalem artichokes. Booking essential.

La Fontaine de Mars
129 rue St-Dominique, 7th (01.47.05.46.44). M° Ecole-Militaire. **Open** noon-3pm, 7.30-11pm daily. **Average** 200F. **Lunch menu** 90F. **Credit** AmEx, MC, V. **Map D6**
As well as the good food, warm welcome and efficient service from a sassy bunch of waiters, you might come here to watch the attractive crowd of French regulars. Try the sublime duck *foie gras* and tasty main courses like *onglet de veau* in garlic cream sauce. The wine list is outstanding, and there's a lovely terrace in summer. Booking essential.

Le Petit Troquet
28 rue de l'Exposition, 7th (01.47.05.80.39) M° Ecole-Militaire. **Open** 7-10.30pm Mon; noon-2pm, 7-10.30pm Tue-Sat. **Prix-fixe** 158F. **Credit** MC, V. **Map D6**
You'll find a gracious welcome in these two tiny rooms tastefully knitted out with *vieille France* bric-a-brac. Everything tastes bright and freshly cooked, and the market-inspired set *menu* is a bargain. We enjoyed a *feuilleté* of chicken livers and oyster mushrooms, sautéed duck breast, organic chicken and a nice crumble. Go with the 'wines of the month'.

Le Square Trousseau (see page 165): *yes, that bottle-blond crew cut really is Gaultier...*

Thoumieux
79 rue St-Dominique, 7th (01.47.05.49.75). M° La Tour-Maubourg. **Open** noon-3.30pm, 6.45pm-midnight Mon-Sat; noon-midnight Sun. **Average** 200F. **Prix fixe** 82F, 160F. **Credit** AmEx, V. **Map D6**
There's something poignantly beautiful about this large, old-fashioned bistro with its red velvet banquettes, white table-cloths, polite, black-jacketed waiters, and well-bred 7th *arrondissement* residents out *en famille. A la carte* is the best option, offering French classics like *blanquette de veau* or *cassoulet.* For dessert try the *flognarde,* an apple and raisin pie.

Chez Savy
23 rue Bayard, 8th (01.47.23.46.98). M° Franklin D Roosevelt. **Open** noon-3pm, 7.30-11pm Mon-Fri. Closed Aug. **Average** 200F. **Prix fixe** 110F, 135F, 168F. **Credit** AmEx, MC, V. **Map E4**
This may be the haunt of solicitors and of stars from the TV station opposite, but the welcome here is magnanimous and the rustic Auvergnat cuisine generally faultless. Start with *jambon d'Auvergne* and then be tempted by beef and lamb from the Cantal or the gigantic *jambonneau* with lentils.

Chez Jean
8 rue St-Lazare, 9th (01.48.78.62.73). M° Notre-Dame-de-Lorette. **Open** Mon-Fri noon-2.30pm, 7-11.30pm; 7pm-midnight Sat. Closed second week Aug. **Average** 250F. **Prix fixe** 185F. **Credit MC, V. Map G3**
This homely 1950s bistro is first-rate for a delicious meal and a relaxed night out. Starters are refreshing, like a *fondue* of leeks with *langoustines;* main courses feature unusual flavour combinations like lamb fillet with basil *persillade.* After, try the grapefruit *sablé* with whiskey sorbet. Excellent wine list too.

Au Gigot Fin
56 rue de Lancry, 10th (01.42.08.38.81). M° Jacques-Bonsergent. **Open** noon-2.30pm, 7.30-10.30pm Mon-Fri; 7.30-10.30pm Sat. Closed two weeks in Aug. **Average** 170F. **Prix fixe** 110F, 175F. **Lunch menu** 65F, 85F. **Credit** AmEx, MC, V. **Map L4**

With its lace curtains, zinc bar and vine-patterned staircase, little seems to have changed at this family-run bistro near the Canal St-Martin since it opened in the 1920s. The leg of lamb of the name, prepared in no less than seven ways, is still a speciality. Inexpensive wines add to the good mood.

Astier
44 rue Jean-Pierre-Timbaud, 11th (01.43.57.16.35). M° Parmentier. **Open** noon-2pm, 8-11pm Mon-Fri. Closed Aug, 23 Dec-5 Jan, ten days in Apr. **Prix fixe** 140F. **Lunch menu** 115F. **Credit** MC, V. **Map M4**
The wood-panelled walls badly need a makeover and the service can be frustrating, but the secret to Astier's devoted following is the food. The 140F four-course feast, with a stunning wine list, must be one of the best value meals in town. Try classics like *rognons de veau* or *lapin à la moutarde,* but leave room for the amazing cheese tray and desserts like a chocolate *feuillantine:* bitter chocolate layered with banana mousse.

Chardenoux
1 rue Jules-Vallès, 11th (01.43.71.49.52). M° Charonne. **Open** noon-2.30pm, 8-10.30pm Mon-Fri; 8-10.30pm Sat. Closed Aug. **Average** 250F. **Prix fixe** 165F (Sat dinner only). **Credit** AmEx, MC, V. **Map N7**
This pretty, turn-of-the-century bistro could succeed on its décor alone, but the cooking will turn gourmets misty-eyed. Chef Bernard Passavant's talent lies in lifting age-old French classics out of the ordinary, especially slow-cooked *daubes* and *salmis,* the meat totally impregnated by richly alcoholic sauces.

Chez Paul
13 rue de Charonne, 11th (01.47.00.34.57). M° Bastille. **Open** noon-2.30pm, 7pm-12.30am daily. **Average** 140F. **Credit** AmEx, MC, V. **Map N7**
This well-loved bistro's original red banquettes, amber walls and tiled floor are an echo of Bastille restaurants before the area went from working class to hip. An unposey, yet wildly fashionable, mix of ages and types feeds on decent, abundant food, like duck-laden Périgord salad, *steak au poivre* or rabbit stuffed with *chèvre.*

A Century of Brasseries

The metropolitan bustle of the brasserie is irrevocably associated with Parisian life. Names like **La Coupole**, **Bofinger** and **Brasserie Lipp** conjure up visions of huge trays of crushed ice covered with freshly shucked oysters, onion soup under a cap of melted cheese, and *choucroute garnie*, that signature dish of sauerkraut garnished with an assortment of *charcuterie*. Many brasseries are as well-known for their sumptuous interiors as they are for their food.

However, the past decade has seen a dizzying consolidation of brasseries into restaurant chains, with the relentless acquisition of many of Paris' surviving independents by Groupe Flo or the Frères Blanc. The purchase of **Brasserie Balzar** by Groupe Flo produced howls from its regulars, who even formed 'Les Amis du Balzar' to fight for its very special Parisian identity.

It's telling that 'Les Amis' are as interested in protecting the atmosphere of the place and the rights of its venerable waiters in long white aprons as they are its food. If the pre-Flo kitchen produced reliably straightforward *foie gras*, oysters and *raie au beurre*, no one ever came to the Balzar in search of gastronomy. In fact, most brasseries originally aspired to fast, filling meals, washed down with a mug of house beer. *Brasserie* means brewery; the earliest brasseries evolved in Alsace, the eastern region on the German border, with a long brewing tradition.

Paris' first true brasserie was founded in 1864 by Alsatian Frédéric Bofinger, soon becoming a fashionable after-theatre address. (The splendid listed interior with glass *verrière* in the main dining room dates from 1919.) The genus really took off after France lost the Franco-Prussian war in 1870 and Alsace was annexed by Germany, sending a stream of Alsatian refugees to the capital. **Chez Jenny** with its excellent draught beer, first-rate *choucroute*, costumed waitresses and 1930s marquetry by Strasbourgeois *ébéniste* Spindler, after-theatre favourite **Brasserie Flo** and unpretentious, independently owned **Brasserie de l'Ile St-Louis** all retain something of the Alsatian character. The genre thrived as trains brought more and more travellers to the capital: one reason so many Paris stations have a brasserie nearby. The grandiose **Train Bleu** in Gare du Lyon is the ultimate, built to welcome visitors to the 1900 Exposition Universelle and resplendent with painted ceiling and gilded cherubs.

Over the next 30 years, the brasserie's character took shape, with beer, shellfish and *choucroute* typically served until the late hours to a large dining capacity. In 1900, the city was spellbound by the dawning modernity of a new century, reflected in Art Nouveau, the decorative style that sought to break with the bourgeois past; the brasserie was to become one of its most enduring showcases. Endowed with beautiful new settings, the format emerged as a social idea: where dinner had previously often been taken in enclosed, almost private dining rooms, now everyone wanted to be able to see not only their immediate neighbours but the entire room. And their menus made them democratic – artists could dawdle over a plate of whelks and beers at one table, while a top-hatted industrialist spoiled his mistress with champagne and lobster across the room, the kind of juxtaposition to create an appealing frisson in the air. Brasseries became not only chic, spontaneous emblems of Paris' urban gaiety, but the first modern restaurants, all speed and sociability.

The roaring 20s confirmed the trend with glam Art Deco interiors, as the artistic avant-garde flocked to La Coupole, Montparnasse. Since then, cafés all over town may call themselves *café brasserie*, but few have attempted to change the genre. Fashionable **La Gare**, however, a cleverly converted railway station in the 16th, could be seen as a present-day re-interpretation, with its rôtisseried meats, late service and buzzy crowd.

If brasseries have never really gone out of style, their popularity has ebbed and flowed. Many of the young who took to the streets in 1968, the year restaurateur Jean-Paul Bucher bought Brasserie Flo, the first address in his empire, saw brasseries as dark, old-fashioned places. Bucher painstakingly restored the dark wood-panelling at Flo, and soon *le tout Paris* was heading for this seedy alleyway in the 10th *arrondissement*. Bucher continues to thrive, transforming Art Nouveau *bouillon* **Julien** and stockbrokers' Art Deco café **Vaudeville** into successful brasseries, buying up **Terminus Nord** at Gare du Nord, and **Bofinger**. Even the legendary La Coupole in Montparnasse, despite a heavy-handed restoration, remains just the place for a late-night meal of oysters and a steak.

Meanwhile, just as Parisians were starting to grumble about standardised menus and slipping quality, two shrewd Englishman recognised that the brasserie, in essence, remained quintessentially modern: Keith McNally opened L'Odéon in New York and Sir Terence Conran

launched Bibendum in London. What the English recognised was the eternal appeal of late dining in glamorous, open settings. Conran is now trying his luck with the stylish **Alcazar** brasserie, which opened in a former cabaret in St-Germain-des-Prés in November 1998. But even here the menu remains surprisingly classic – except, of course, for the fish and chips at the bar.

Le Vaudeville
29 rue Vivienne, 2nd (01.40.20.04.62). M° Bourse. **Open** noon-3.30pm, 7pm-2am daily. **Average** 250F. **Prix fixe** 132F (from 10pm), 179F. **Lunch menu** 132F. **Credit** AmEx, DC, MC, V. **Map H4**

Chez Jenny
39 bd du Temple, 3rd (01.42.74.75.75). M° République. **Open** 11.30am-1am daily. Closed mid July-mid Aug. **Average** 175F. **Prix fixe** 149F, 179F. **Lunch menu** 65F Mon-Fri. **Credit** AmEx, DC, MC, V. **Map L5**

Bofinger
5-7 rue de la Bastille, 4th (01.42.72.87.82). M° Bastille. **Open** noon-3pm, 6.30pm-1am Mon-Fri; noon-1am Sat, Sun. **Average** 230F. **Prix fixe** 179F. **Lunch menu** (Mon-Fri) 119F. **Credit** AmEx, DC, MC, V. **Map M7**

Brasserie de l'Isle St-Louis
55 quai de Bourbon, 4th (01.43.54.02.59). M° Pont-Marie. **Open** 11.30am-1am Mon, Tue, Fri-Sun; 6pm-1am Thur (all day Thur in summer). Closed Aug. **Average** 150F. **Credit** MC, V. **Map K7**

Le Balzar
49 rue des Ecoles, 5th (01.43.54.13.67). M° Cluny-La Sorbonne. **Open** noon-12.15am daily. **Average** 250F. **Credit** AmEx, MC, V. **Map J7**

Alcazar
62 rue Mazarine, 6th (01.53.10.19.99). M° Odéon. **Open** noon-3.30pm, 7pm-1am daily. **Average** 250F.

Prix fixe 100F (bar), 140F, 180F. **Credit** AmEx, DC, MC, V. **Map H7**

Brasserie Lipp
151 bd St-Germain, 6th (01.45.48.53.91). M° St-Germain-des-Prés. **Open** 8am-2am daily. **Average** 250F. **Credit** AmEx, DC, MC, V. **Map H7**

Brasserie Flo
7 cour des Petites-Ecuries, 10th (01.47.70.13.59). M° Château d'Eau. **Open** noon-3pm, 7pm-1.30am daily. **Average** 185F. **Prix fixe** 132F (after 10pm), 179F. **Lunch menu** 132F. **Credit** AmEx, DC, MC, V. **Map K3**

Julien
16 rue du Fbg-St-Denis, 10th (01.47.70.12.06). M° Strasbourg-St-Denis. **Open** noon-3pm, 7pm-1.30am daily. **Average** 200F. **Prix fixe** 132F (10pm-1.30am), 189F (dinner). **Lunch menu** 132F, 179F. **Credit** AmEx, DC, MC, V. **Map K4**

Terminus Nord
23 rue de Dunkerque, 10th (01.42.85.05.15). M° Gare du Nord. **Open** 7am-1am daily (meals served 11am-1am). **Average** 185F. **Prix fixe** 132F (after 10.30pm), 179F. **Lunch menu** 132F. **Child's menu** 60F. **Credit** AmEx, DC, MC, V. **Map K2**

Le Train Bleu
Gare de Lyon, pl Louis-Armand, 12th (01.43.43.09.06). M° Gare de Lyon. **Open** 11.30am-3pm, 7-11pm daily. **Average** 250F. **Prix fixe** 250F. **Credit** AmEx, DC, MC, V. **Map M8.** *Wheelchair access.*

La Coupole
102 bd du Montparnasse, 14th (01.43.20.14.20). M° Vavin. **Open** 11.30am-2am daily. **Average** 200F. **Prix fixe** 169F. **Credit** AmEx, DC, MC, V. **Map G9**

La Gare
19 chaussée de la Muette, 16th (01.42.15.15.31). M° La Muette. **Open** noon-3pm, 7pm-midnight daily. **Average** 150F. **Credit** AmEx, DC, MC, V. **Map A6**

The Australian Experience

Café Oz

184 RUE ST. JACQUES, 5TH. M° LUXEMBOURG. TEL: 01.43.54.30.48

18 RUE ST. DENIS, 1ST. M° CHATELET. TEL: 01.40.39.00.18

33 PL LOUISE DE BETTIGNIES. 59000 LILLE. TEL: 03.20.55.15.15

AUSTRALIAN RESTAURANT & WINE BAR

WoolLooMooLoo

36 bd Henri IV, 4th. M° Bastille. Tel: 01.42.72.32.11

A La Biche au Bois

45 av Ledru-Rollin, 12th (01.43.43.34.38). M° Gare de Lyon. **Open** noon-2pm, 7-10.30pm Mon-Fri. Closed mid July-mid Aug, 24 Dec-3 Jan. **Average** 160F. **Prix fixe** 108F, 122F. **Credit** AmEx, DC, MC, V. **Map M8**
This rustic-cum-kitsch den offers mood, food and prices to make you forget 1990s Paris. Game is a speciality and the generous 122F *menu* kicks off with homemade terrines and follows with a huge wild boar *estouffade* or wild duck with a berry sauce. Excellent cheeses and wine. Book. *Wheelchair access.*

Le Square Trousseau

1 rue Antoine-Vollon, 12th (01.43.43.06.00). M° Ledru-Rollin. **Open** noon-2.30pm, 8-11.30pm daily. **Average** 180F. **Lunch menu** 100F, 135F (Mon-Sat). **Credit** AmEx, MC, V. **Map M7**
A popular fashion-world hangout, this picture-perfect *belle époque* bistro has evolved into a gently fashionable, truly relaxed place. The food has also improved, with earthy dishes like *gigot de sept heures* and roast guinea fowl. The proprietor proudly serves wines from his friends' vineyards. Book.

Le Viaduc Café

43 av Dausmesnil, 12th (01.44.74.70.70). M° Gare de Lyon. **Open** noon-2.30pm, 7pm-3am daily. **Average** 140F. **Credit** MC, V. **Map N8**
Located in a converted railway viaduct, this address with its dramatic, high stone vault and glazed façade draws designers and suits for lunch. Typical of the modern bistro cooking are starters of a curried chicken salad, and main courses of steak with oyster mushrooms or *saumon en papillote*. Tables (and traffic) outside in summer.

La Girondine

48 bd Arago, 13th (01.43.31.64.17). M° Glacière. **Open** noon-2.30pm Mon-Fri, 7-10.30pm; 7-10.30pm Sat. **Average** 130F. **Credit** AmEx, DC, MC, V. **Map J10**
Valérie and Alain Sainsard have made a real effort here with new décor and reasonably priced food: *cuisine de terroir* with some bordelais touches. This is seen in dishes like *steak bordelais, confit de canard* and *cassoulet*. Fish is always on the blackboard, desserts are inventive and the wine list is short but well-chosen. Pleasant pavement terrace.

Le Terroir

11 bd Arago, 13th (01.47.07.36.99). M° Gobelins. **Open** noon-2pm, 7.45-10.15pm Mon-Fri; 7.45-10.15pm Sat. Closed three weeks in Aug, 23 Dec-5 Jan, Easter. **Average** 220F. **Lunch menu** 128F. **Credit** MC, V. **Map J10**
Typical of the new-style bistros that make a virtue of fine, old-fashioned food, Le Terroir draws an appreciative local audience for hearty terrines and rich, wholesome main courses, such as veal kidneys with mustard. The generous puds are old favourites: dark chocolate mousse and plum tart.

Natacha

17bis rue Campagne-Première, 14th (01.43.20.79.27). M° Raspail. **Open** 8.30pm-1am Mon-Sat. Closed three weeks in Aug. **Average** 200F. **Credit** AmEx, MC, V. **Map H9**
People (Mick Jagger, Mickey Rourke) come here late for the buzz of going where others go and for the flattering attentions of dynamic hostess Natacha. Cooking is more than decent, including *chèvre*-filled ravioli and sautéed rabbit.

Les Petites Sorcières

12 rue Liancourt, 14th (01.43.21.95.68). M° Denfert-Rochereau. **Open** noon-2pm, 8-10.30pm Mon-Fri; 8-10.30pm Sat. **Prix fixe** 170F. **Lunch menu** 120F. **Credit** MC, V. **Map F10**
This corner eatery offers bistro classics with a nod to current food fashions. Christian Teule knows what he's doing – uncomplicated pairings, direct flavours; it's simple saucery. The vibrant orange *soupe de poisson et d'étrilles au safran*

is fishy, salty and delicious, and the main of roast rabbit with snow peas, carrots and mustard another winner.

La Régalade

49 av Jean-Moulin, 14th (01.45.45.68.58). M° Alésia. **Open** noon-2pm, 7pm-midnight Tue-Fri. Closed Aug. **Prix fixe** 175F. **Credit** MC, V.
Yves Camdeborde is about the only chef in town who can pull in a crowd for dishes like duck hearts with oyster mushrooms or *hachis parmentier* done with rabbit, kidneys or even testicles. With two sittings each evening the service can be breathless, so come for the second if you don't want to be rushed – and book several days ahead.

Bistrot d'Hubert

41 bd Pasteur, 15th (01.47.34.15.50). M° Pasteur. **Open** noon-2.30pm, 7.30-11pm daily. **Prix fixe** 145F, 195F. **Credit** AmEx, MC, V. **Map E8**
Never mind the studied décor and 'innovation' vs 'tradition' *menus*. This is a place for friendly and competent service – and really good food. Tuna steak cooked in a 'caramel' of balsamic vinegar and cod with North African seasonings are both adventurous and delicious; we love the tiramisu with chicory ice cream and kumquats. The wine list is short but well-chosen.

L'Os à Moëlle

3 rue Vasco-de-Gama, 15th (01.45.57.27.27). M° Lourmel. **Open** noon-2pm, 7-11.30pm Tue-Sat. Closed Aug. **Prix fixe (dinner)** 190F. **Lunch menu** 155F. **Credit** MC, V. **Map B9**
A lace-curtained haven for young professionals unwinding after a long Métro ride home. The daily-changing dinner *menu* offers no choice (except desserts), but the risk is worth it for Thierry Faucher's six-course unveiling of such dishes as coddled eggs with asparagus and red mullet with beetroot chips.

Le Petit Plat

49 av Emile-Zola, 15th (01.45.78.24.20). M° Charles-Michel. **Open** noon-2pm, 8-10.45pm Tue-Sat. Closed two weeks in Aug. **Average** 200F. **Prix fixe** 135F. **Credit** MC, V. **Map C8**
Superb modern bistro cooking, an easygoing atmosphere and attractive, minimalist Art Deco-style décor repay a trip to a rather inconvenient part of Paris, even if the service is rather precious. The emphasis is on quality ingredients simply prepared, such as tuna steak with *tomates confites*. Gourmet Henri Gault helps select the wine list.

Le Petit Rétro

5 rue Mesnil, 16th (01.44.05.06.05). M° Victor-Hugo. **Open** noon-2.30pm, 7.45-10.30pm Mon-Fri; 7.45-10.30pm Sat. Closed two weeks in Aug. **Average** 175F. **Lunch menu** 98F. **Credit** MC, V. **Map B4**
The beautiful Art Nouveau tiles, warm, yellow-washed walls and snug dark wood tables are an ideal setting for the homely classics served here. A blackboard offers daily specials, while the menu parades a list of favourites, beautifully prepared with a few modern twists, like textbook-perfect rump steak on a disc of crispy, paper-thin slices of potato.

Bistrot de l'Etoile

13 rue Troyon, 17th (01.42.67.25.95). M° Charles de Gaulle-Etoile. **Open** noon-2pm, 7-11.30pm Mon-Fri; 7-11.30pm Sat, Sun. Closed three weeks Aug. **Average** 170F. **Prix fixe** 165F. **Credit** AmEx, DC, MC, V. **Map C3**
Chef Guy Savoy's well-priced menu at the tiny bistro-annexe of his nearby grand restaurant (*see below*, **Haute Cuisine**), offers quality and originality. A perfect example is a soup of puréed white beans blended with cream and chicken stock, served with a red wine reduction. Even humble apple crumble is distinguished.

Le Moulin à Vins

6 rue Burq, 18th (01.42.52.81.27). M° Abbesses. **Open**

6pm-2am Tue, Fri, Sat; 11am-3pm, 6pm-2am Wed, Thur.
Closed Aug. **Average** 150F. **Credit** MC, V. **Map H1**
Hidden away from the hurly-burly of Montmartre, this intimate little *bistro à vins* draws a fascinating cross-section of Parisians, from Hermès scarves to motorcycle jackets, for a seriously good, but relaxed, feed. The rabbit in mustard sauce with tagliatelle is typically generous, rustic and very good. Côtes du Rhône star on the first-rate wine list.

Au Boeuf Couronné

188 av Jean-Jaurès, 19th (01.42.39.54.54). M° Porte de Pantin. **Open** noon-3pm, 7.30pm-midnight Mon-Sat; noon-3pm Sun. **Average** 160F. **Prix fixe** 160F, 200F. **Credit** AmEx, DC, MC, V. **Map M2**
This enormous 1930s bistro offers a taste of La Villette in its meat market days. The beef now comes from top Parisian butchers, and the *pommes soufflées* are as good as ever. The skirt steak with shallots is tender and the *steak tartare* could easily satiate two – but if meat is not your thing, there is also a seafood menu during months with an 'r' in them.

Le Zéphyr

1 rue du Jourdain, 20th (01.46.36.65.81). M° Jourdain. **Open** noon-2.30pm, 8-11pm Mon-Fri; 8-11pm Sat. Closed ten days in Aug, 23 Dec-2 Jan. **Average** 170F. **Prix fixe** 150F. **Lunch menu** 69F. **Credit** MC, V. **Map P3**
The Zéphyr is worth the trip for the great food, atmosphere and classy 1930s interior complete with a grand piano that is sometimes put into use. Try interesting starters like the langoustine soup with lentils followed by *confit de canard* or veal in wine sauce. Delicious desserts are a must.

Haute Cuisine

Le Grand Véfour

17 rue de Beaujolais, 1st (01.42.96.56.27). M° Palais-Royal. **Open** 12.30-2.15pm, 7.30-10.15pm Mon-Fri. Closed Aug. **Prix fixe** 780F. **Lunch menu** 345F. **Credit** AmEx, DC, MC, V. **Map H5**
Once the scene of Revolutionary fervour, this sumptuous Palais-Royal monument (now in the hands of the Taittinger Group) strives for elegant, special-occasion cooking, as in fabulous Marennes oysters lightly poached in a beetroot sauce, and lamb *noisettes* in an intriguing fennel sauce. The cheese tray is sublime, featuring several tommes from chef Guy Martin's native Savoie. Piquant desserts include unusual combinations like spinach and cumin pie. Expensive wine list.

L'Ambroisie

9 pl des Vosges, 4th (01.42.78.51.45). M° Bastille or St-Paul. **Open** noon-1.30pm, 8-9.30pm Tue-Sat. Closed two weeks in Feb, three weeks Aug. **Average** 1000-1200F. **Credit** AmEx, MC, V. **Map M6**
Occupying a romantic townhouse on the seventeenth-century place des Vosges, L'Ambroisie's recently renovated interior drips true chic, with a high-ceilinged main room lined with gorgeous tapestries, stone floor and mini-spotlights. For a chef with a reputation as an intellectual, Bernard Pacaud's menu perhaps relies more on ingredients than real ideas. The 410F exquisitely presented *marjolaine* of truffles, *foie gras* and celeriac is delicious, but main courses can be uneven and service surprisingly erratic. It's hard to spend under 400F on wine. *Wheelchair access.*

L'Arpège

84 rue de Varenne, 7th (01.45.51.47.33). M° Varenne. **Open** noon-2pm, 7.30-10pm Mon-Fri. **Average** 700F. **Prix fixe** 690F. **Lunch menu** 390F. **Credit** AmEx, DC, MC, V. **Map F6**
The contemporary curved wall of pale wood, neo-Art Deco details and rippled glass windows are a perfect backdrop for chef Alain Passard's innovative, intellectual cuisine, which draws a sort of hushed awe as diners try to discern every

Lucas Carton: *heavy on wallet* and *waistline.*

element. Yet moments of unforgettable delight – the fabulous, pan-fried duck main course, a Passard 'invention' – may sit alongside others – an unexceptional starter of four langoustines fried in butter and finely sliced carrots with tarragon at an exceptional 220F, or the celebrated dessert of a tomato stuffed *aux douze saveurs* – that seem over-refined and exaggerated.

Le Jules Verne

Tour Eiffel, Champ de Mars, 7th (01.45.55.61.44). M° Bir-Hakeim/RER Champ de Mars. **Open** 12.15-2pm, 7.30-9.30pm daily. **Average** 775F. **Prix fixe** 680F. **Lunch menu** 290F (Mon-Fri; not holidays). **Credit** AmEx, DC, MC, V. **Map C6**
Despite the mind-blowing views from halfway up the Eiffel Tower, the black walls, halogen lamps and extravagant flower arrangements hint strongly of 1970s disco. The food succeeds in pleasing its international clientele with coquettish doses of luxuries like caviar and truffles. A starter of scallops and langoustines with potato salad is pleasant, as are main courses like swordfish with potato purée and caviar.

Les Ambassadeurs

Hôtel Crillon, 10 pl de la Concorde, 8th (01.44.71.16.16). M° Concorde. **Open** noon-2.30pm, 7-10.30pm daily. **Average** 700F. **Prix fixe** 650F. **Lunch menu** 360F (Mon-Fri). **Credit** AmEx, DC, MC, V. **Map F5**
There's almost no other dining room in Paris that has the elegance and history of Les Ambassadeurs, with its crystal chandeliers and neo-Baroque frescoes. Chef Dominique Bouchet, who took over the kitchen from Christian Constant at the start of 1997, works on a doctrine of purity, built on a base of impeccable, classical, grand French cooking that now accords well with modern tastes. Dishes like a crispy potato pancake topped with smoked salmon and a dollop of whipped cream and caviar or scallops wrapped in bacon with tomato and basil are exquisite luxury food. With its wine list

and service, this remains the best hotel restaurant in Paris. *Wheelchair access.*

Le Bristol

Hôtel Bristol, 112 rue du Fbg-St-Honoré, 8th (01.53.43.43.00). M° Miromesnil. **Open** noon-2pm, 7-10.30pm daily. **Average** 700F. **Prix fixe** 360F, 680F. **Credit** AmEx, DC, MC, V. **Map E3**
The Bristol is back in the top rank of serious gastronomic addresses. Trained by Michel Guérard and Alain Ducasse, chef Del Burgo has a respectful, but playful, approach to the luxury foods that typify grand-hotel dining. His elegant asparagus in truffle juice starter is showered with parmesan and topped by a poached egg, and the turbot with chestnuts and puréed butternut squash is doused in a delicious butter, meat juice and truffle sauce. Desserts like chocolate fritters with creamed pears and the hot chocolate soufflé are spectacular. Even the less dear bottles on the wine list are excellent, as is the service. *Wheelchair access.*

Pierre Gagnaire

6 rue Balzac, 8th (01.44.35.18.25). M° George V. **Open** noon-2pm, 8-10pm Mon-Fri; 8-10pm Sun. Closed 15 July-15 Aug. **Average** 700F. **Prix fixe** 480F, 780F, 900F. **Lunch menu** 500F. **Credit** AmEx, DC, MC, V. **Map D3**
The arrival of legendary chef Pierre Gagnaire was a great event in Parisian gastronomy. His cooking is authentically artistic and demandingly intellectual; eating one of his dishes is a mix of unexpected tastes and textures that engages every sense. The *Grand Dessert*, a five-course dessert extravaganza, is not to be missed, but the wine list is puzzlingly brief. If you are a truly serious eater with a deep curiosity about the frontiers of taste, you'll find this experience fascinating.

Laurent

41 av Gabriel, 8th (01.42.25.00.39). M° Champs-Elysées-Clemenceau. **Open** 12.30-2pm, 7.30-10pm Mon-Fri; 7.30-10pm Sat. **Average** 700F. **Lunch menu** 390F. **Credit** AmEx, DC, MC, V. **Map E4**
In its resplendent Napoléon III pavilion with cut-velvet wallpaper, brocade banquettes, *pompier* paintings and lavish flowers, Laurent looks just as an haute cuisine restaurant should. The food is generally good and politely provocative. The 390F menu is excellent value and, for once, features many dishes also listed *à la carte*, such as an explosively refreshing *fondant de légumes* (gazpacho aspic topped by avocado mousse), tuna garnished with olives, capers and peppers, and spit-roast rabbit with broad beans and artichokes. *Pièce de résistance* is the magnificent lemon macaroon and wild strawberry concoction. *Wheelchair access.*

Ledoyen

1 av Dutuit, 8th (01.47.42.35.98). M° Champs-Elysées-Clemenceau. **Open** noon-2pm, 7.30-10.15pm Mon-Fri. Closed Aug. **Average** 800F. **Prix fixe** 530F, 620F (dinner). **Lunch menu** 320F. **Credit** AmEx, DC, MC, V. **Map F5**
Young chef Christian Le Squer serves an elegant and beautifully executed menu in this Napoleon III dining room. A starter called *les coquillages* is a superb presentation of bright green herb risotto, topped with lobster, langoustine, scallop and thin slices of Jabugo ham. Two fish dishes define the classic and inventive poles of the menu – perfect line-caught turbot topped with finely chopped truffles on a bed of mashed potatoes, and sole sautéed in sage butter, filled with a refreshing, original *rémoulade* of ribbons of cucumber and fresh ginger.

Lucas Carton

9 pl de la Madeleine, 8th (01.42.65.22.90). M° Madeleine. **Open** noon-2.30pm, 8-10.30pm Tue-Fri; 8-10.30pm Mon, Sat. Closed first three weeks in Aug. **Average** 1000F. **Lunch menu** 395F. **Credit** AmEx, DC, MC, V. **Map F4**
Chef Alain Senderens, who presides over this gorgeous Art-Nouveau temple, made his name with audacious, often sweet-savoury, combos and his cooking is uncluttered, yet richly detailed. The 395F lunch *menu* excludes his famous honey-roasted duck *à l'Apicius* and vanilla-scented lobster, but includes other delights. The *millefeuille* of fresh duck *foie gras*, celeriac and apple is exquisite, the *pastilla* of cumin- and cinnamon-scented rabbit with *foie gras* amazes by its subtlety amid such strong flavours. The wine bill could easily outstrip the *menu*, but there's a lunchtime choice of affordable bottles.

Alain Ducasse

59 av Raymond-Poincaré, 16th (01.47.27.12.27). M° Victor-Hugo. **Open** noon-2pm, 7.45-10pm Mon-Fri. Closed mid July-mid Aug; 23 Dec-5 Jan. **Average** 1100F. **Prix fixe** 920F, 1490F. **Lunch menu** 480F. **Credit** AmEx, DC, MC, V. **Wheelchair access. Map B4**
Already established as a highly talented chef and maestro of Mediterranean cooking in Monte Carlo, in 1996 Ducasse audaciously, and with great fanfare, assumed the reins at retired superchef Joël Robuchon's rather gloomy *belle époque* mansion restaurant. Yet intriguing *amuse-gueules* apart, Ducasse has converted to a Bocuse-style classicism as old-fashioned and well behaved as a frogs' legs, scallops and crayfish vol-au-vent. Creamed cauliflower with caviar, retained as a tribute to the master, is a better indication of what true haute cuisine should be, while duckling subtly flavoured by cooking in fig leaves offers a teasing idea of how interesting Ducasse can be.

Le Pré Catelan

route de Suresnes, Bois de Boulogne, 16th (01.44.14.41.14). M° Porte-Maillot, then taxi. **Open** noon-2.30pm, 8-10.30pm Tue-Sat; noon-2pm Sun. Closed two weeks in Feb. **Average** 550F. **Prix fixe** 550F, 750F. **Lunch menu** 295F. **Credit** AmEx, DC, MC, V.
Enthusiastic young chef Frédéric Anton has enlivened the kitchen at this wonderfully romantic hideaway in the Bois de Boulogne. Even when the weather doesn't permit the ultimate luxury of dining on the flower-bower of a terrace, the Second Empire dining rooms are a perfect *de luxe* French setting. Anton's excellent-value 295F lunch *menu* offers rather small portions, but starters such as a spring soup of baby onions and peas and main courses of chicken breast in a mushroom *nage* or sautéed baby squid served with sweet peppers and pasta are excellent. The cheese course is superb, and desserts like cherry *clafoutis* with yoghurt ice cream are delicious. Only the rather sloppy service are a let-down.

Vivarois

192 av Victor-Hugo, 16th (01.45.04.04.31). **Open** noon-2pm, 8-10pm Mon-Fri. Closed Aug. **Average** 650F. **Lunch menu** 355F. **Credit** AmEx, DC, MC, V. **Map B4**
Though it's unfashionable to say so, we actually quite like the vintage 60s tulip chairs, warmed up in the 80s with cherrywood panelling and geometric tapestries that fit the theme. This place seems better suited to business than romance, but the food and discreet service are wholly admirable. The lunch menu features dishes from the *carte* and daily specials; roasted red pepper *bavarois* has a dreamy texture and crisp-skinned red mullet fillets come on a bed of fat lentils in a tart lemon cream sauce. Finish with homely chocolate praline cake and apple *feuilleté*.

Guy Savoy

18 rue Troyon, 17th (01.43.80.40.61). M° Charles de Gaulle-Etoile. **Open** noon-2pm, 7.30-10.30pm Mon-Fri; 7.30-10.30pm Sat. **Average** 950F. **Prix fixe** **Credit** AmEx, MC, V. **Map C3**
Although the 80s-style handkerchief halogen lamps and contemporary art look a bit tired nowadays, this is still one of Paris' top restaurants. Savoy seems clear-eyed about where haute cuisine is heading, and offers uniquely ethereal meals. A simple winter salad of razor-thin slices of black truffle and dried beetroot on lamb's lettuce and a remarkable artichoke and truffle soup are sublime. The *côte de veau* with truffled

*With its sophisticated Provençal cuisine, **Les Elysées** is a great place for a special treat.*

potato purée is heavenly, and a dessert of a 'rose' of vanilla custard with petals of dried granny smith apple in a fresh apple-juice sauce delicious. The wine list is rather grandiose – the choice of bottles at 300F-400F should be expanded. *Wheelchair access.*

Contemporary

Café Marly
93 rue de Rivoli, Cour Napoléon du Louvre, 1st (01.49.26.06.60). M° Palais-Royal. **Open** 8am-2am daily. **Credit** AmEx, DC, MC, V. **Map H5**
This corner of the Louvre is now one of Paris' choicest rendezvous. Deep red walls and a witty chandelier cleverly combine historic and contemporary. The food is pricey and notoriously uneven, but décor, crowd and view are wonderful.

Restaurant du Palais-Royal
110 Galerie Valois, 1st (01.40.20.00.27). M° Palais-Royal. **Open** 12.30-2.30pm, 7.30-10.30pm Mon-Fri; 7.30-10.30pm Sat. Closed 19 Dec-2 Jan. **Average** 250F. **Credit** AmEx, DC, MC, V. **Map H5**
The now-tranquil Palais-Royal gardens make this restaurant lovely for sitting out in summer, and a civilised refuge in winter. Bruno Hees' cooking is best described as contemporary *terroir;* a typical dish is *carré d'agneau* with an unusual ricotta and fennel lasagne. Superb ice creams and sorbets too.

Le Buddha Bar
8 rue Boissy d'Anglas, 8th (01.53.05.90.00). M° Concorde. **Open** noon-3pm Mon-Fri; 6pm-2am daily. **Average** 275F. **Lunch menu** 190F. **Credit** AmEx, DC, MC, V. **Map F4**
The cavernous, subterranean rendezvous for *le tout Paris.* A giant Buddha dominates the interior and the clientele of actors, models, designers and wannabes. Cooking spans the Pacific Rim from sashimi, tempura and Chinese chicken salad to a spicy beef fillet, but it's being seen that counts. Reserve.

Les Elysées
Hôtel Vernet, 25 rue Vernet, 8th (01.44.31.98.98). M° George V. **Open** noon-2.30pm, 7.30-10pm Mon-Fri.

Closed 25 July-25 Aug. **Average** 550F. **Prix fixe** 430F, 580F, 790F. **Lunch menu** 380F. **Credit** AmEx, DC, MC, V. **Map D4**
For a one-off splurge, try talented chef Alain Solivères' take on southern French cuisine. The 390F *menu plaisir* is truly pleasurable, with Basque-style *amuse-bouches*, sublime starters like *épeautre* (Provençal wheat grains) with baby squid and main courses of precisely cooked duck *foie gras* with rocket salad and artichokes. Great cheeses. *Wheelchair access.*

Stella Maris
4 rue Arsène-Houssaye, 8th (01.42.89.16.22). M° Charles de Gaulle-Etoile. **Open** noon-2.30pm, 7.45-10.30pm Mon-Fri; 7.45-10.30pm Sat. Closed one week in Aug. **Prix fixe** 175F, 460F. **Lunch menu** 250F, 175F. **Credit** AmEx, DC, MC, V. **Map D3**
An expense-account crowd mixes with serious French gourmets in this small vanilla-lacquered restaurant for the very subtle cuisine of Japanese chef Taderu Yoshino. Dishes such as scallops with caramel sauce and sea bass in an olive oil emulsion are delicious and delicate, if restrained.

Chez Michel
10 rue Belzunce, 10th (01.44.53.06.20). M° Gare du Nord. **Open** noon-2pm, 7-midnight Tue-Sat. Closed Aug, one week Dec/Jan. **Prix fixe** 180F. **Credit** MC, V. **Map K2**
In this very popular new-wave bistro near the Gare du Nord, chef Thierry Breton continues to offer excellent value for money, lifting bistro classics into the realm of the contemporary, as in the superb 'lasagne' of pasta atop a layered terrine of *chèvre* and artichoke hearts, main courses like monkfish with tomatoes and baby onions or seasonal game, and lovely chocolate *quenelles* for desert. He has now opened a cheaper bistro Chez Casimir almost next door; some of the same dishes, especially desserts, are served in both. *Wheelchair access.*

Les Amognes
243 rue du Fbg-St-Antoine, 11th (01.43.72.73.05). M° Faidherbe-Chaligny. **Open** 7.30-10.30pm Mon; noon-2pm, 7.30-10.30pm Tue-Fri; noon-2pm, 7.30-11pm Sat.

Closed three weeks in Aug, two weeks Dec-Jan. **Prix fixe** 200F. **Credit** MC, V. **Map N7**

Chef Thierry Coué's inventive cuisine is well thought-out and his unusual adaptations of grand classics, such as sautéed veal sweetbreads on cucumber cooked with lemon and ginger, elegantly executed. His desserts, brilliantly balancing sweetness and acidity, are equally adventurous.

Philippe Detourbe

8 rue Nicolas-Charlet, 15th (01.42.19.08.59). M° Pasteur. **Open** noon-2pm, 8-10pm Mon-Fri; 8-10pm Sat. Closed Aug, 21-28 Dec. **Dinner menu** 220F. **Lunch menu** 180F. **Credit** AmEx, MC, V. **Map E9**

Self-taught chef Detourbe delights in creating imaginative but well-reasoned dishes. His menu changes with every meal, but might be typified by a splendid cod steak with white beans on a bed of caramelised chicory. Leave room for his superb desserts. Well-chosen wine list. Book.

Branches: Detourbe-Duret, 23 rue Duret, 16th (01.45.00.10.26); Pavillon Detourbe, 6 rue Pierre Demours, 17th (01.45.72.25.25).

Le Relais du Parc

Hôtel Parc Victor Hugo, 55-57 av Raymond Poincaré, 16th (01.44.05.66.10). M° Victor Hugo. **Open** noon-2.30pm, 7.30-10.30pm daily. **Average** 275F. Credit AmEx, DC, MC, V. **Map B5**

Alain Ducasse's menu at this stylish spot is divided between traditional French and foreign-influenced; both options are equally inspired. The menu changes with the seasons, but dishes like tiny macaroni with country ham and truffles, John Dory *brochette* with Chinese noodles are characteristic of the sophisticated trip this place offers. Summer may be the best time to eat here, since the interior garden is green and quiet.

Le Restaurant d'Eric Frechon

10 rue du Général-Brunet, 19th (01.40.40.03.30). M° Danube or Botzaris. **Open** noon-2.30pm, 7pm-midnight Tue-Sat. Closed Aug, 1-5 Jan. **Prix fixe** 200F. **Credit** MC, V. **Map P2**

Young chef Eric Frechon, despite a dreary décor, packs in two sittings a night for his keenly priced, four-course *menu*. Although Scottish salmon in jelly and roast turkey don't sound cutting-edge, here they excite the tastebuds and leave you wanting more. Cheeses are perfect and desserts sumptuous. *Wheelchair access.*

Classic

Chez Pauline

5 rue Villedo, 1st (01.42.96.20.70). M° Pyramides. **Open** 12.15-2.30pm, 7.30-10.30pm Mon-Fri; 7.30-10.30pm Sat (Sept-mid-Apr only). **Average** 300F. **Prix fixe** 220F. **Credit** AmEx, DC, MC, V. **Map H5**

Gleamingly pristine décor and serious atmosphere live up to Chez Pauline's self-proclamation as a '*bistro de luxe*'. The *prix fixe* is good value, including dishes like a *feuilleté* with snails and oyster mushrooms in garlic butter and *daurade* with *citrons confits* and *beurre blanc*. First-class puddings.

Le Poquelin

17 rue Molière, 1st (01.42.96.22.19). M° Palais-Royal. **Open** noon-2pm, 7.15-10.30pm Mon-Fri. Closed three weeks in Aug. **Average** 300F. **Prix fixe** 189F. **Lunch menu** 140F. **Credit** AmEx, DC, MC, V. **Map H5**

The kitchen at this jewel-box restaurant offers classic cooking with inventive touches. Many of the best dishes are available *à la carte*, such as chicken with preserved lemon, perfectly cooked lamb chops with a Provençal garnish and ethereal *oeufs à la neige*. Wines are well-selected and fairly priced.

Pierre à la Fontaine Gaillon

pl Gaillon, 2nd (01.47.42.63.22). M° Opéra. **Open** noon-3pm, 7pm-midnight Mon-Fri; 7pm-midnight Sat. Closed

Aug. **Average** 250F. **Prix fixe** 175F. **Credit** AmEx, DC, MC, V. **Map H4**

Housed in a *hôtel particulier*, this restaurant is popular with elegantly dressed locals and tourists. The *menu* is fairly fish-heavy and main courses include the excellent *marmite bretonne en montgolifière*, a seafood stew. In summer, you can eat outside next to the eighteenth-century fountain.

Benoît

20 rue St-Martin, 4th (01.42.72.25.76). M° Hôtel-de-Ville. **Open** noon-2pm, 8-10pm daily. Closed Aug, one week in winter. **Average** 500F. **Lunch menu** 200F. **Credit** AmEx. **Map J6**

This venerable bistro remains overpriced, but it can send out some of the best classic food in Paris. Main courses are simple, seasonal and very satisfying: try the chicken cooked in a salt crust garnished with asparagus and *beurre blanc* and follow with a lavish homemade dessert. Expensive wine list.

Le Coupe-Chou

11 rue Lanneau, 5th (01.46.33.68.69). M° Maubert-Mutualité. **Open** noon-2.30pm, 7pm-1am Mon-Sat; 7pm-1am Sun. **Average** 200F. **Prix fixe** 150F, 200F. **Credit** AmEx, MC, V. **Map J7**

Located on one of the oldest streets in Paris, the fourteenth-century stone walls provide a perfect setting for this elegant restaurant. Follow a *salade Coupe-Chou* with an excellent *magret de canard aux pêches* or monkfish steak, and opt for coffee on one of the overstuffed sofas in the salon.

La Tour d'Argent

15-17 quai de la Tournelle, 5th (01.43.54.23.31). M° Maubert-Mutualité. **Open** noon-2pm, 7.30-10pm Tue-Sun. **Average** 900F. **Lunch menu** 350F. **Credit** AmEx, DC, MC, V. **Map K7**

This world-famous restaurant is worth a visit for its stunning views of Paris and the famous numbered duckling. Bernard Guillhaudin, chef since 1996, has gently re-animated this temple of gastronomy with delicate starters and grand classic main courses. Desserts are over-sugared, but the 350F lunch *menu* is a worthwhile splurge. *Wheelchair access.*

Le Violon d'Ingres

135 rue St-Dominique, 7th (01.45.55.15.05). M° Ecole-Militaire. **Open** noon-2pm, 7.15-10pm Tue-Sat. Closed three weeks in Aug; 20-28 Dec. **Average** 500F. **Dinner menu** 400F. **Lunch menu** 240F. **Credit** AmEx, DC, MC, V. **Map D6**

Christian Constant has given up the grand Hôtel Crillon for his own luxurious bistro. A well-dressed crowd tucks into very good, classic cuisine that weighs in on the top end of the bistro scale in terms of price, style and service, typified by elegant main courses, like a delicious risotto with boned chicken wings or the guinea fowl with turnip *choucroute*.

La Fermette Marbeuf 1900

5 rue Marbeuf, 8th (01.53.23.08.00). M° Alma-Marceau. **Open** noon-3pm, 7-11.30pm Sun-Wed; 7-12.30pm Thur-Sat. **Average** 280F. **Prix fixe** 178F. **Credit** AmEx, DC, MC, V. **Map D4**

This popular Frères Blanc restaurant draws a wealthy, cosmopolitan clientele to its *belle époque* dining room. Chef Gilbert Isaac plays it straight, producing light zesty starters, like the thick tomato fondant studded with artichokes, and delicious main courses including saddle of lamb with Choron sauce. Finish off with the Grand Marnier soufflé. Book.

Maxim's

3 rue Royale, 8th (01.42.65.27.94). M° Concorde. **Open** 12.30-2.15pm, 7.30-10.15pm Mon-Sat. Closed Mon in July and Aug. **Average** 600F (lunch), 1000F (dinner). **Credit** AmEx, DC, MC, V. **Map F4**

This legendary Art Nouveau sanctuary still delivers on an

CAFÉ MADELEINE

OPEN DAILY FROM 8AM TO 9PM

1 RUE TRONCHET - 35 PLACE DE LA MADELEINE, 8TH.
M° MADELEINE   TEL: 01.42.65.21.91

SOUTH-WESTERN SPECIALITIES
SPECIAL CROQUE MONSIEUR
REGIONAL WINES
VARIED CREPES

MENUS FROM 80F
COFFEES 11F, BEERS 22F
ART DECO, AQUARIUM

23 AVENUE DE LA BOURDONNAIS, 7TH.
TEL: 01.47.05.04.54
M° ECOLE MILITAIRE

CREDIT: AMEX, MC . ENGLISH SPOKEN.

old-fashioned promise of *soigné* Parisian glamour. The food remains very pricey for such uninspired main courses as turbot with deep-fried onions and a skinny and underseasoned veal chop, but still it's a real taste of *la vie en rose*. *Wheelchair access.*

Au Petit Marguery
9 bd du Port-Royal, 13th (01.43.31.58.59). Mº Gobelins. **Open** noon-2.15pm, 7.30-10.15pm Tue-Sat. Closed Aug; 24 Dec-2 Jan. **Prix fixe** 215F, 450F (game season). **Lunch menu** 165F. **Credit** AmEx, DC, MC, V. **Map J9**
You can eat guinea fowl and steaks here all year round, but in autumn the Cousin brothers' sparkling old bistro comes into its own. Try gamey terrines, tender venison in a wine sauce with raisins and pine kernels, or the house speciality, *lièvre à la royale*. Desserts go from the mildly to the wildly alcoholic. Booking advised.

Regional

Alsace: La Chope d'Alsace
4 carrefour de l'Odéon, 6th (01.43.26.67.76) Mº Odéon. **Open** noon-2am daily. **Average** 160F. **Prix fixe** 78F, 119F, 169F. **Credit** AmEx, MC, V. **Map H7**
An eclectic mix of cinema-goers, students, business travellers and locals comes to unwind here over huge mounds of excellent *choucroute garnie* and other freshly prepared Alsatian specialities. Great for a spur-of-the-moment meal.

Auvergne: La Maison du Cantal
1 pl Falguière, 15th (01.47.34.12.24). Mº Volontaires or Plaisance. **Open** noon-2pm, Mon; noon-2pm, 7-10.30pm, Tue-Sat. **Average** 200F. **Prix fixe** 149F, 159F, 189F. **Credit** AmEx, V. **Map E10**
Rather off the beaten track, this rambling, rustic restaurant offers excellent value set *menus* to a local crowd. Start with regional hams and salamis, then move on to a hearty main course such as *potée de St-Flour* (braised cabbage and *charcuterie*) or *aligot* with sausage. A chunk of cantal completes this convincing regional trip.

Basque Country: Au Bascou
38 rue Réaumur, 3rd (01.42.72.69.25). Mº Arts et Métiers. **Open** noon-2pm, 8-10.30pm Mon-Fri; 8-10.30pm Sat. Closed Aug, 24 Dec-2 Jan. **Average** 180F. **Credit** AmEx, MC, V. **Map K5**
The best Basque food in town is at this buzzy little place – innovative chef Jean-Guy Loustau's great love of his home cuisine shows in stuffed peppers and *jambon de Bayonne*, squid cooked in its own ink and roast lamb from the Pyrenees.

Brittany: Ty Breiz
52 bd de Vaugirard, 15th (01.43.20.83.72). Mº Montparnasse-Bienvenüe or Pasteur. **Open** noon-2.45pm, 7-11pm Mon-Sat. Closed first three weeks in Aug. **Average** 90F. **Lunch menu** 63F. **Credit** MC, V. **Map F9**
Ty Breiz (Breton for Brittany) offers a taste of the region's staples: *galettes* with a huge array of fillings (ham, egg, potatoes, gruyère, salmon, mushrooms) and delicious dessert *crêpes*. The relaxed atmosphere, low prices and swift service all add to its popularity. A good place to come with kids.

Burgundy: Chez Tante Louise
41 rue Boissy d'Anglas, 8th (01.42.65.06.85). Mº Madeleine or Concorde. **Open** noon-2pm, 7.30-10.pm Mon-Fri. Closed Aug. **Average** 250F. **Prix fixe** 190F. **Credit** AmEx, MC, V. **Map F4**
Famed Burgundian chef Bernard Loiseau has breathed new life into this endearing 30s-era bistro, although the cooking can be inconsistent. His menu features high-brow comfort food like poached eggs in red wine sauce, a mushroom and snail sauté, and rich Tante Louise sole fillets. There's a nice selection of Burgundies and prompt, professional service.

Catalan: Le Pavillon Puebla
corner of av Simon-Bolivar and rue Botzaris, Parc des Buttes-Chaumont (01.42.08.92.62). Mº Pyrénées or Buttes-Chaumont. **Open** noon-2.30pm, 7.30-10.30pm Tue-Sat. Closed two weeks in Aug. **Average** 350F. **Prix fixe** 180F, 250F. **Credit** AmEx, MC, V. **Map N3**
Nestling in the Parc des Buttes-Chaumont, the Pavillon Puebla is an attractive folly with a grand restaurant atmosphere and

From one fin de siècle *to another:* **La Fermette Marbeuf 1900.**

haute cuisine-style cooking. Of the two *menus*, the 180F *menu catalan* is the most interesting, featuring a meaty but delicate *boudin*, *escalivida* (a cousin of *salade niçoise*) and *piñata* (assorted Mediterranean grilled fish and shellfish). The terrace is perfect for *al fresco* dining in summer.

Corsica: Paris Main d'Or
133 rue du Fbg-St-Antoine, 11th (01.44.68.04.68).
M° Ledru-Rollin. **Open** noon-3pm, 8-11pm Mon-Sat.
Closed Aug; 24 Dec-2 Jan. **Average** 160F. **Lunch menu**
65F. **Credit** MC, V. **Map M7**
The café up front has been spiffed up, but the unique buzz remains. The herby, filling food features brocciù cheese, Corsican charcuterie, plump sardines and tender roasted *cabri* (kid goat). Island wines and even more mysterious eaux-de-vie merit investigation. Book at weekends.

Franche-Comté: Chez Maître Paul
12 rue Monsieur-le-Prince, 6th (01.43.54.74.59). M°
Odéon. **Open** 12.15-2.30pm, 7.15-10.30pm daily. Closed
Sun and Mon lunch in July and Aug. **Average** 220F. **Prix**
fixe 165F, 195F. **Credit** AmEx, DC, MC, V. **Map H7**
This pleasant, slightly dressy bistro is the best place to try the comforting, stick-to-your-ribs cooking of the Jura region, often laden with morels, cheese or *vin jaune*. Try the delicious Montbéliard sausage to start, then the free-range chicken. Finish up with the walnut meringue cake and splurge on one of the older bottles of Arbois wine.

Lyon: Le Monttessuy
4 rue de Monttessuy, 7th (01.45.55.01.90). M° Alma
Marceau or RER Pont de l'Alma. **Open** noon-2pm, 7-
10.30pm Mon-Fri; 7-10.30pm Sat. **Prix fixe** 150F. **Lunch**
menu 77F, 95F. **Credit** MC, V. **Map D6**
Red and white checked tablecloths and a mini puppet theatre give this congenial neighbourhood restaurant a cheerful, slightly haphazard air. Delicious starters include small raviolis in a basil sauce, and clams with thyme. To follow, the large slices of pink Lyonnais sausage on a heap of stodgy sautéed potatoes taste much better than they look.

Normandy: Les Fernandises
19 rue de la Fontaine-au-Roi, 11th (01.48.06.16.96).
M° République. **Open** noon-2.30pm, 7.30-10.30pm Tue-Sat.
Closed Aug, one week in May. **Average** 190F. **Prix fixe**
130F. **Lunch menu** 100F. **Credit** MC, V. **Map M4**
Boisterous locals come here for honest, homemade Normandy cuisine. The great-value *menu* lets you start with chicken liver terrine or a large crunchy salad, before main dishes like pork ribs with garlic cream sauce and grilled salmon with mashed pumpkin and celeriac. There's a fine selection of calvados.

Provence: Les Olivades
41 av de Ségur, 7th (01.47.83.70.09). M° Ecole-Militaire.
Open 7.30-11pm Mon, Sat; noon-2.30pm, 7.30-11pm
Tues-Fri. **Average** 240F. **Prix fixe** 179F. **Lunch menu**
130F. **Credit** AmEx, MC, V. **Map E7**
Refined regional cookery from chef Flora Mekula, who came here from Avignon via sophisticated Arpège. Most successful are starters such as baby mackerel on pastry with anchovy cream and knockout desserts: thyme-and-rosemary scented *crème brûlée* and *moëlleux au chocolat* with lavender ice cream.

Southwest: Sud-Ouest & Compagnie
39 bd du Montparnasse, 6th (01.42.84.35.35).
M° Montparnasse-Bienvenüe. **Open** noon-2.30pm, 7-
10pm daily. **Prix fixe** 180F. **Credit** MC, V. **Map F8**
This busy place does a good value *prix-fixe* featuring duck in various guises and other Gascon dishes. Duck breast comes in a variety of sauces, including *bordelaise* (red wine and shallots) and *quercycoise* (with its gizzards). Come dessert, skip the often dried-out rocamadour cheese in favour of a prune and armagnac parfait or apple tart.
Branch: 94 bd Malesherbes, 17th (01.42.27.61.22).

Fish & Seafood

Le Bar au Sel
49 quai d'Orsay, 7th (01.45 51 58 58). M° Invalides. **Open**
noon-2.30pm, 7-10.30pm daily. **Average** 250F. **Prix fixe**
190F. **Credit** AmEx, DC, MC, V. **Map D5**
This stylish kitchen likes to keep it simple. The house speciality, sea bass cooked in a salt crust, sees a waiter deftly removing crust and skin to present a steaming whiter-than-white fish. A trio of sorbets makes a light, pleasing dessert. When it gets busy, waiters can be hard to pin down.

Paul Minchelli
54 bd La Tour Maubourg, 7th (01.47.05.89.86).
M° La Tour Maubourg. **Open** noon-2.30pm, 8-10.30pm
Tue-Sat. Closed Aug, 25 Dec-2 Jan. **Average** 600F.
Credit MC, V. **Map E6**
A drop-dead chic crowd fills this sophisticated restaurant designed by Slavik, who has invested it with the self-assured clubbiness of the chef's former kitchen, the exorbitant Le Duc. Minchelli's fashionable minimalism is based on crucial timing – gambas with ground mixed peppers, cod steamed over seaweed, brightened with sea salt – with little other adornment.

Marines
70-72 rue du Fbg-Poissonnière, 10th (01.42.46.22.29).
M° Poissonnière. **Open** noon-2pm, 7.30-10.30pm Mon-
Fri; 7.30-10.30pm Sat. **Average** 160F. **Prix fixe** 135F.
Credit AmEx DC MC, V. **Map J4**
Given the prevailing prices of fish in Paris, the 135F three-course *menu* at this snug, bottle-blue dining room is a cracking bargain. Good bets are rich fish soup, salmon with a sweet-and-sour tomato relish or the catch of the day, maybe sea bass or cod. It's worth paying a supplement for the coffee soufflé and *crêpes suzette*, prepared tableside.

Keryado
32, rue Regnault, 13th (01.45.83.87.58). M° Porte d'Ivry
or RER Bd Massena. **Open** noon-2.30pm Mon; noon-
2.30pm, 7.30-10.30pm Tue-Sat. Closed last two weeks of
Aug. **Prix fixe** 110F, 150F **Lunch menu** 59F (Mon-Fri)
Credit MC, V.
This place's success is based on excellent value for money. At 140F, the *bouillabaisse* is a bargain, served as a tureen of tawny brown fish soup, croutons with garlicky *rouille* and a platter of squeaky fresh fish, includng half a baby lobster. Willing but unhurried service and reasonably priced wine.

La Cagouille
10 pl Constantin-Brancusi, 14th (01.43.22.09.01)
M° Gaîté. **Open** noon-2.30pm, 7.30-10.30pm daily.
Average 200F. **Prix fixe** 150F, 250F. **Credit** AmEx,
MC, V. **Map F10**
If you fancy an al fresco seafood feast, the terrace of this excellent fish house is a first-rate option. A pioneer of minimalist fish cookery in Paris, Gérard Allemandou does dishes like baby mussels cooked on a hot griddle, tuna steak wrapped in bacon and John Dory with a perfect *beurre blanc*. Consider a cognac from one of the best collections in Paris.

Le Dôme
108 bd du Montparnasse, 14th (01.43.35.25.81).
M° Vavin. **Open** noon-3pm, 70pm-12.30am daily.
Average 400F. **Credit** AmEx, DC, MC, V. **Map G9**
This legendary fish house, with slick chrome and wood décor by Slavik, silly lights and tobacco-coloured walls, is justly reputed for its shellfish and *sole meunière*. The less-formal Bistrot du Dôme (1 rue Delambre/01.43.35.32.00) offers the same quality, but with simpler preparations at lower prices.

Vin & Marée
108 av du Maine, 14th (01.43.20.29.50). M° Montparnasse-
Bienvenüe or Gaîté. **Open** noon-2pm, 7.30-11.30pm Mon,

Tue, Sun; noon-2pm, 7.30-midnight Wed-Sat. **Average** 180F. **Credit** AmEx, MC, V. **Map F9**
Even if this bistro annexe of La Luna feels suspiciously like a chain, it attracts plenty of stylish customers with its winning catch-of-the-day formula. Straightforward main courses such as whole sea bass in *beurre blanc* and skate *sauce gribiche* are served with a signature potato-and-olive-oil purée. Save room for crème caramel or a seductive fig gratin. **Branches**: 276 bd Voltaire, 11th (01.43.72.31.23); 183 bd Murat, 16th (01.46.47.91.39).
Wheelchair access.

Maison Prunier

16 av Victor-Hugo, 16th (01.44.17.35.85). M° Charles de Gaulle-Etoile. **Open** noon-3pm Tue-Sat; 7.30-11pm Mon. Closed mid-July to mid-Aug. **Average** 500F. **Credit** AmEx, DC, MC, V. **Map C3**
This 1920s offshoot of Goumard Prunier offers superb seafood and a glam night out. The recently restored, listed Art Deco mosaics are magnificent, and menu and wine list have been brilliantly revised. The seafood remains classic and fresh, like the *assiette saintongeaise* (raw oysters with grilled chipolatas) and sea bass grilled with fennel and flambéed in Ricard.
Wheelchair access.

Budget

Chez Max

47 rue St-Honoré, 1st (01.40.13.06.82). M° Châtelet-Les Halles. **Open** noon-3pm, 7pm-midnight Mon-Fri; 7pm-midnight Sat. Closed Aug. **Average** 140F. **Prix fixe** 85F, 135F. **Lunch menu** 65F, 120F. **Credit** AmEx, MC, V. **Map J5**
Charming host Max Reytet likes to mother his diners and ensure every home-cooked morsel is eaten. There's a decent choice of adventurous dishes such as prawns in pastis with rice; traditional hearty *andouillette*; roast free-range chicken in tarragon sauce; *magret de canard* with honey and lime.

Gros Minet

1 rue des Prouvaires, 1st (01.42.33.02.62). M° Châtelet-Les Halles. **Open** 7pm-midnight Mon, Sat; 11am-2pm, 7pm-midnight Tue-Fri. **Average** 150F. **Prix fixe** 95F. **Lunch menu** 78F. **Credit** AmEx, DC, MC, V. **Map J5**
This small restaurant has plenty of cranky charm: an old zinc bar, tarnished mirrors and walls adorned with rugby pennants and cartoons of politicians. Starter salads are fresh and generous, while duck features heavily in the main courses.
Wheelchair access.

Bistrot Beaubourg

25 rue Quincampoix, 4th (01.42.77.48.02). M° Châtelet-Les Halles. **Open** noon-2am daily. **Average** 80F. **Credit** MC, V. **Map J6**
Head here for hearty, unpretentious, generous food. There are plenty of potential miracles on the menu – like *cassolette d'escargots* – but go for the *plats du jour*, which offer baked, stewed or curried meats, with rice, potatoes or *frites*.

Café de la Poste

13 rue Castex, 4th (01.42.72.95.35). M° Bastille. **Open** noon-3pm, 7-11pm Mon-Fri. **Average** 110F. **Credit** MC, V. **Map L7**
This handkerchief-sized bistro in a sleepy Marais street scores high on artistic presentation. Salads are colourful and fresh, the quality of the steaks is high, and *plats du jour* are honest versions of *coq au vin*, *lapin à la moutarde* and other standards. Regulars arrive late, so book.

Les Philosophes

28 rue Vieille-du-Temple, 4th (01.48.87.49.64). M°Hôtel-de-Ville. **Open** 9am-2am daily. **Average** 150F. **Prix fixe** 85F, 104F, 136F. **Credit** MC, V. **Map K6**

Dining for la petite monnaie *at* **Gros Minet**.

It's easy to be philosophical about small flaws in the food, given the thoughtful and inventive touches that make this place stand out among budget bistros. A spicy *assiette de boudin antillais* comes with cinnamon rice, and tuna is rubbed with subtle tandoori spices. Inexpensive wines come by the glass; or choose from a good beer selection.

Chez Pento

9 rue Cujas, 5th (01.43.26.81.54). M° Cluny-La Sorbonne/ RER Luxembourg. **Open** noon-2.30pm, 7-11pm Mon-Fri; 7-11pm Sat. **Prix fixe** 112F, 149F. **Lunch menu** 87F. **Credit** AmEx, MC, V. **Map J6**
Here budget meets quality. Pento has an excellent *carte*, a delightfully old-fashioned atmosphere and mainly French clientele. The *cassolette d'escargots aux cèpes* is a perfect buttery marriage of textures and tastes, and the *rognon de veau* comes in a deliciously pungent *sauce aigre normande*.

L'Ecurie

2 rue Laplace, 5th (01.46.33.68.49). M° Maubert-Mutualité. **Open** noon-3pm, 7pm-midnight Mon, Wed-Sat; 7pm-midnight Tue, Sun. **Average** 120F. **Prix fixe** 98F. **Lunch menu** 75F. **No credit cards. Map J8**
A medieval labyrinth of dark vaults and low archways descending several levels below ground, L'Ecurie combines historic atmosphere and food for hungry carnivores, with abundant steaks, *entrecôtes*, *andouillette* and roast lamb. The wine list is hardly exhaustive, but then neither are the prices.

Bistrot Mazarin

42 rue Mazarine, 6th (01.43.29.99.03). M° Mabillon. **Open** noon-3pm, 7.15-midnight daily. **Average** 130F. **Credit** AmEx, MC, V. **Map H7**
Come here for a satisfying feed, drinkable wines, and a buzzy terrace full of students and creative types. Salads, *charcuterie*, veal chop with lemon and *boeuf bourguignon* are all fine.

Polidor

41 rue Monsieur-Le-Prince, 6th (01.43.26.95.34).
M° Odéon. **Open** noon-2.30pm, 7pm-12.30am Mon-Sat;
noon-2.30pm, 7-11pm Sun. **Average** 90F. **Prix fixe**
100F. **Lunch menu** 55F. **No credit cards. Map H7**
This picturesque budget classic has been cramming in noisy
tables of students and tourists for generations. Dishes like
guinea fowl with cabbage and bacon or *calamars à l'améri-
caine* are generously served and generally competent.

Chez Germaine

30 rue Pierre-Leroux, 7th (01.42.73.28.34). M° Duroc.
Open noon-2.30pm, 7-9.30pm Mon-Fri; noon-2.30pm Sat.
Closed Aug; 24 Dec-5 Jan. **Average** 85F. **Prix fixe** 65F
(Mon-Fri). **No credit cards. Map F7**
Chez Germaine offers an appetising taste of rural France
with sunny yellow walls, plastic tablecloths, and *maman* in
the dining room. *Papa* dishes up reliable home cooking, with
oeuf mayonnaise and lamb kebabs on the *menu*, and more
inventive dishes *à la carte*, like smoked *échine de porc.*

Au Pied de Fouet

45 rue de Babylone, 7th (01.47.05.12.27). M° Vaneau.
Open noon-2.30pm, 7-9.30pm Mon-Fri; noon-2.30pm Sat.
Closed Aug, 24 Dec-5 Jan. **Average** 75F. **No credit
cards. Map F7**
Fouet's is warm and lively, and the food reliably satisfying. The
clientele, which once included Jean Cocteau, is all cashmere –
yuppies mixed with aristos. Expect classics like herrings with
potato salad, *faux-filet* and well-prepared *confit de canard.*

Chartier

*7 rue du Fbg-Montmartre, 9th (01.47.70.86.29). M° Grands
Boulevards.* **Open** 11.30am-3pm, 7-10pm daily. **Average**
80F. **Prix fixe** 74F, 110F, 190F. **Credit MC, V. Map J4**
Once flagship of a chain of working-class *bouillons* (a form of
turn-of-the-century soup kitchen), Chartier relies more on its
period setting, reputation and bustling atmosphere than its
cuisine, but is always packed. Today the food can be rather
lacklustre, so it's best to stick to the *plats du jour.*

Chez Papa – Espace Sud-Ouest

206 rue Lafayette, 10th (01.42.09.53.87). M° Louis-Blanc.
Open 11.30am-1am daily. **Average** 70F. **Prix fixe** 50F
(Mon-Fri until 10pm). **Credit** AmEx, MC, V. **Map L2**
A young, vociferous crowd from the neighbourhood gathers
here to feast on rich, high-cholesterol Southwestern cuisine,
like traditional *cassoulet, confit de canard* and filling *salades
géantes.* Snails are a speciality and are served in three ways.
Branches: 6 rue Gassendi, 14th (01.43.22.41.19); 101 rue
de la Croix Nivert, 15th (01.48.28.31.88).

Le Petit Keller

13bis rue Keller, 11th (01.47.00.12.97). M° Ledru-Rollin.
Open noon-2pm, 7.30-midnight Mon-Sat. **Prix fixe** 70F.
Lunch menu 50F. **Credit** MC, V. **Map M6**
This friendly Bastille joint wears its vintage 1950s décor
with tongue-in-cheek cheer. The affordable, home-cooked
food includes vegetable soup, terrines and tasty main courses like *daube de boeuf à la provençale* and roast guinea fowl.

L'Ebauchoir

45 rue de Cîteaux, 12th (01.43.42.49.31).
M° Faidherbe-Chaligny. **Open** 9am-10.30pm Mon-Thur;
9am-11pm Fri, Sat. **Average** 130F. **Lunch menu** 68F,
85F. **Credit** MC, V. **Map N8**
A local crowd packs out this spacious dining hall, enjoying
its unpretentious amiability and incredibly good value. The
lunch *menu* changes daily, but might run to herrings with
potato salad, sautéed lamb and a never-fail chocolate mousse.

L'Encrier

*55 rue Traversière, 12th (01.44.68.08.16). M° Ledru-
Rollin.* **Open** noon-2.30pm; 7-11pm Mon-Fri; 7-11pm Sat.

Closed 24 Dec-2 Jan. **Average** 100F. **Prix fixe** 62F. **No
credit cards. Map M7**
A popular lunch spot with a smart crowd of filmmakers and
design bods. Exposed stone walls, beams, sleek lights and open
kitchen show how much care the owners take, as does the
remarkably priced food. Expect *plats du jour* like *daurade* with
courgettes or, *à la carte*, *noisettes* of lamb with goat's cheese.

Chez Gladines

30 rue des Cinq Diamants, 13th (01.45.80.70.10).
M° Corvisart. **Open** noon-3pm, 7pm-midnight daily. Closed
Aug. **Average** 100F. **Lunch menu** 60F. **No credit cards.**
This hectic bistro in the villagey Butte aux Cailles neigh-
bourhood is a noisy corner of the Pays Basque in Paris. Giant
salads served in earthenware bowls are popular, along with
Southwestern duck dishes and a daily 60F lunch *menu.* Or
go regional with a competent *pipérade* with *jambon de
Bayonne* and small but appealing helping of fiery red pimen-
tos stuffed with *brandade de morue* in a spicy tomato sauce.

Le Café du Commerce

*51 rue du Commerce, 15th (01.45.75.03.27). M° Emile-
Zola.* **Open** noon-midnight daily. **Average** 115F. **Prix
fixe** 82F, 117F. **Credit** AmEx, DC, MC, V. **Map C8**
This airy, three-tiered dining hall was once a cheap workers'
canteen. Now more upmarket, its prices are still reasonable
and the bustle remains as staff manipulate giant trays laden
with plates. The menu is varied if not stunning: excellent
rillettes aux deux saumons, passable *confit de canard* or
honeyed pork ribs. A good place to come in a group.

L'Etoile Verte

*13 rue Brey, 17th (01.43.80.69.34). M° Charles de Gaulle-
Etoile.* **Open** noon-3pm, 6.30-11pm Mon-Fri; 6.30pm-11pm
Sat, Sun. **Average** 130F. **Prix fixe** 74F (Mon-Fri until
9pm), 110F, 155F. **Credit** AmEx, DC, MC, V. **Map C3**
L'Etoile Verte is a useful standby for office workers and
tourists from the Arc de Triomphe, and makes more of an
effort with presentation and choice than many budget joints,
with starters, such as duck salad in raspberry vinaigrette,
preceding rather standard main courses like roast chicken.

Rendez-vous des Chauffeurs

11 rue des Portes-Blanches, 18th (01.42.64.04.17).
M° Marcadet-Poissoniers. **Open** noon-2.30pm, 7.30-11pm
Mon, Tue, Thur-Sun. Closed first two weeks in Aug.
Average 100F. **Prix fixe** 65F (until 8.30pm, Mon, Tue,
Thur-Sat). **Credit** MC, V.
Around since 1906, this simple restaurant caters mainly to
locals. The *prix fixe*, offering only four main courses (steak
tartare, kidneys, *andouillette* and *steak garni*) but with a
pichet of wine thrown in, may be the best 65F feed in Paris.

Au Virage Lepic

61 rue Lepic, 18th (01.42.52.46.79). M° Blanche.
Open noon-3pm, 6pm-2am daily. **Average** 100F.
Prix fixe 98F. **No credit cards. Map H1**
This small, shabby Montmartre bistro, all wobbly banquettes
and fading posters, seems to have been serving local students
and *baba cools* for ever. The food is closer to good café nosh
than sophistication, with simple dishes like *boudin normand*
with sautéed apple and a surprisingly good *tarte Tatin.*

Vegetarian

La Victoire Suprême du Coeur

41 rue des Bourdonnais, 1st (01.40.41.93.95).
M° Châtelet. **Open** noon-2.30pm, 6.30-10pm Mon-Thur;
noon-2.30pm, 6.30-10.30pm Fri, Sat. Closed one week in
April, two weeks in Aug. **Dinner menu** 89F. **Lunch
menu** 49F (Mon-Fri), 59F. **Credit** MC, V. **Map J6**
Run by followers of Indian guru Sri Chinmoy, the white-walled
'Heart's Supreme Victory' offers inner peace and world dishes

Saddle up your ponies for an underground feast at **L'Ecurie.** *See page 179.*

like *biryani* and *chili sin carne.* The *assiettes gourmandes* include regulars like *tapenade,* goat's cheese, salad and nuts. *Wheelchair access.*

Galerie 88
88 quai de l'Hôtel de Ville, 4th (01.42.72.17.58). *Mº Hôtel-de-Ville.* **Open** noon-2am daily. **Average** 90F. **No credit cards. Map K6**
This sly little café hides on the Right Bank waterfront, providing an offbeat breed of cosiness with its funky young clientele, ochre walls, dim lighting and jazz. The food is Mediterranean with the meat taken out – salads, *tapas,* tagliatelle and soups. Great for mint tea and a chat. *Wheelchair access.*

Les Quatre et Une Saveurs
72 rue du Cardinal-Lemoine, 5th (01.43.26.88.80). *Mº Cardinal-Lemoine.* **Open** noon-2.30pm, 7-10.30pm Tue-Sun. **Average** 100F. **Prix fixe** 130F. **Credit** MC, V. **Map K8**
An airy setting for fresh, macrobiotic, Japanese-style dishes – no dairy, no eggs, no sugar, 100 per cent organic. Miso and vegetable soups figure among the starters, while *assiettes complètes* often include pasta instead of conventional cereals.

Guen Mai
2bis rue de l'Abbaye, 6th (01.43.26.03.24). *Mº St-Germain-des-Prés.* **Open** 11.45am-3.30pm Mon-Sat. Closed Aug. **Average** 95F. **Credit** MC, V. **Map H7**
This invaluable vegetarian address pulls a trendy crowd and ladies who lunch. While prices reflect the chic St-Germain location, the salads, quiches and tofu dishes can be uneven.

La Ville de Jagannath
101 rue St-Maur, 11th (01.43.55.80.81). *Mº St-Maur.* **Open** 7.30-11.30pm Mon-Thur, Sun; 7.30pm-12.30am Fri, Sat. Closed one week in Aug. **Prix fixe** 90F, 130F, 160F. **Credit** AmEx, DC, MC, V. **Map N5**
This temple to Indian vegetarian cuisine aims to be as authentic as possible. The daily changing *menus* are based on refined *thali*-style dining, and it's the contrast between flavours, textures and colours which makes eating here so interesting. Bring your own bottle of wine (no surcharge).

Aquarius
40 rue de Gergovie, 14th (01.45.41.36.88). *Mº Pernéty.* **Open** noon-2.15pm, 7-10.30pm Mon-Sat. **Average** 85F. **Lunch menu** 65F. **Credit** MC, V. **Map F10**
This busy Paris institution has the most eclectic vegetarian menu in town. Veggie lasagne, omelettes, ravioli and *tourtes* are on the *carte,* while daily specials may run to polenta with green pepper sauce and ratatouille. Excellent desserts.

Au Grain de Folie
24 rue de Lavieuville, 18th (01.42.58.15.57). *Mº Abbesses.* **Open** 12.30-2.30pm, 7.30-10.30pm Mon-Fri; noon-2.30pm, 7-11.15pm Sat; noon-11.15pm Sun. **Average** 100F. **Prix fixe** 50F. **No credit cards. Map H1**
A slice of bohemia in touristy Montmartre, and popular with students and arty locals. Marie-Cécile's copious, homemade food includes huge main courses, like the *curieuse,* with cooked veg and a *gratin* or a *tourte.* Passable crumbles.

International
The Americas

Joe Allen
30 rue Pierre-Lescot, 1st (01.42.36.70.13). *Mº Etienne-Marcel.* **Open** noon-1am daily. **Average** 150F. **Prix fixe** 125F, 162F. **Credit** AmEx, MC, V. **Map J5**
The discreet Paris outpost of the New York theatre haunt offers a great range of neo-US dishes. Prices are a little steep; portions generous. Particular good is the skirt steak with cilantro pesto. Desserts include a rich banana *crème caramel* and fruit crumbles. Good choice of Californian wines. *Wheelchair access.*

Anahi
49 rue Volta, 3rd (01.48.87.88.24). *Mº Arts et Métiers.* **Open** 8pm-12.30am daily. **Average** 210F. **Credit** MC, V. **Map K4**
Up in the shabbiest corner of the Marais, black-clad trendsters and models pile into this South American bistro, run by fiercely elegant Spanish *patronne* Carmen and her sister Pilar. Even if dishes, like nicely spiced guacamole and high

quality Argentine *churrasco* steak are a little expensive, it's worth it for the adrenaline buzz and the glitterati.

Le Studio
41 rue du Temple, 4th (01.42.74.10.38). M° Hôtel-de-Ville. **Open** 7.30pm-midnight Mon-Fri 12.30-3pm, 7.30pm-12.30am Fri-Sun. **Average** 120F. **Credit** AmEx, MC, V. **Map K6**
The historic courtyard of the ancient Aigle d'Or inn, which Le Studio shares with dance studios and the Café de la Gare café-théâtre, is great for summer. The Tex-Mex fare is predictable and fairly average, but the atmosphere always electric – probably something to do with the Margaritas. Try the nachos and the lightly spiced beef *burritos* or chicken *tacos*.

Thanksgiving
20 rue St-Paul, 4th (01.42.77.68.28). M° St-Paul. **Open** noon-2.30pm, 7.30-10.30pm Tue-Fri; noon-4pm (brunch), 7.30-11pm Sat; 11am-4pm Sun. Closed three weeks in Aug, one week in Jan. **Average** 140F. **Dinner menu** 148F-200F. **Credit** MC, V. **Map L7**
In a far cry from the American chain experience, Judith and Frédéric Bluysen highlight authentic and inventive American fare, with an emphasis on Cajun and Louisiana dishes, among them lightly fried Maryland crabcakes, Creole *jambalaya* and New Mexican Navajo *posole* (tender pork with *jalapeños*, hominy and cilantro). The wine list is American.

Anahuacalli
30 rue des Bernardins, 5th (01.43.26.10.20). M° Maubert-Mutualité. **Open** 7.30-11pm Tue, Sat; noon-2pm, 7.30-11pm Wed-Fri, Sun. **Average** 150F. **Lunch menu** 75F. **Credit** MC, V. **Map K7**
Pale yellow walls and varnished beams make an attractive backdrop at this authentic, good-value Mexican. Try the fresh-made corn chips with green tomato sauce and excellent guacamole. Main courses are fab too: the deep-fried wheat *tortilla*, stuffed with chicken in red sauce, is fresh and appetising.

Haynes Restaurant
3 rue Clauzel, 9th (01.48.78.40.63). M° St-Georges. **Open** 7pm-12.30am Tue-Sat. Closed Aug. **Average** 150F. **Credit** AmEx, DC, MC, V. **Map H2**
This unpretentious African-American soul kitchen opened in 1949, and little has changed. Jazz legends adorn the walls, and the menu features classics like 'Ma Sutton's fried chicken', cornbread with spicy dip and gumbo, an impressive mix of gambas, chicken, okra and rice. Live jazz from 9pm (Fri, Sat). *Wheelchair access.*

The Far East

Han Lim
6 rue Blainville, 5th (01.43.54.62.74). M° Place Monge. **Open** noon-2.30pm, 7-10.30pm Tue-Sun. Closed Aug. **Average** 120F. **Lunch** 73F. **Credit** MC, V. **Map L6**
This small, family-run place is one of Paris's best Korean restaurants. Look out for the spicy sesame seed and whelk salad, buckwheat noodles in black bean sauce, deep-fried ravioli, and addictive garlic chicken wings. Book.

Dong Huong
14 rue Louis-Bonnet, 11th (01.43.57.18.88). M° Belleville. **Open** noon-11pm Mon, Wed-Sun. Closed two weeks in Aug. **Average** 80F. **Credit** MC, V. **Map M4**
The happy sound of slurping is proof enough that, at less than 40F, the big bowls of *phô* are a soul-warming steal. Try the *tonkinoise*, long white rice noodles and free-range chicken in a lemongrass-scented broth, and the *saté*, a deliciously spicy concoction of chilli pepper, peanut and beef.

New Nioullaville
32 rue de l'Orillon, 11th (01.40.21.96.18). M° Belleville. **Open** noon-3pm, 7pm-1am daily. **Average** 160F. **Lunch menu** 38F-78F (Mon-Fri). **Credit** AmEx, MC, V. **Map N4**

The kitchen at this 100-table restaurant whips up Chinese, Thai, Cambodian and Vietnamese wonders. The 18-page menu offers a rainbow of prices, while the push carts of *dim sum*, deep-fries and laquered duck are tempting. Reserve.

La Chine Masséna
Centre Commercial Masséna, 13 pl de Vénétie, 13th (01.45.83.98.88). M° Porte de Choisy. **Open** 9.30am-11.30pm Mon-Thur; 9.30am-1am Fri-Sun. **Average** 90F. **Lunch menu** 52F, 78F, 88F. **Credit** MC, V.
This over-the-top 500-seat restaurant amid the towers of Chinatown offers tasty, well-priced entertainment. The epic 280-dish menu includes Thai, Cantonese, Sichuan, Hunan, Peking and Vietnamese specialities. Great on weekend evenings, when there's dancing and a pan-Asian variety show. *Wheelchair access.*

New Hoa Khoan
15 av de Choisy, 13th (01.45.85.81.31). M° Porte de Choisy. **Open** 9am-11pm daily. **Average** 100F. **Credit** V.
The Hong Kong-style cuisine and long opening hours at this busy canteen on the ground floor of a Chinatown high-rise draw multi-generational Asian parties and astute Parisians. Try the soups, noodles, stir-fries and delicious *dim sum*.

Korean Barbecue
22 rue Delambre, 14th (01.43.35.44.32). M° Vavin. **Open** 11am-2pm, 7-11pm daily. **Average** 160F. **Prix fixe** 118F-165F (dinner). **Lunch menu** 57F-118F. **Credit** AmEx, MC, V. **Map G9**
The idea behind this place is to cook your own thin strips of beef on the burner sunk in each table. The marinated meat is wonderfully tender, and comes with a bowl of *bibambap* (rice, egg and vegetables) or ravioli, *sashimi* or crunchy prawn salad, and a lacquered bowl of peppery broth. **Branches:** 1 rue du Dragon, 6th (01.42.22.26.63); 39 rue du Montparnasse, 14th (01.43.27.69.53).

Lao Siam
49 rue de Belleville, 19th (01.40.40.09.68). M° Belleville. **Open** noon-3pm, 6pm-11.30pm Mon-Fri; noon-11.30pm Sat, Sun. **Average** 120F. **Credit** MC, V. **Map N3**
Serving a pleasant hybrid of Chinese, Laotian and Thai cooking, this is one of Belleville's most reliable and fairly priced restaurants. There's lots here for garlic and spice lovers – garlicky pork ribs and authentically seasoned Thai dishes.

Italian

L'Osteria
10 rue de Sévigné, 4th (01.42.71.37.08). M° St-Paul. **Open** noon-3pm, 8-10.30pm Mon-Fri. Closed Aug, 24 Dec-5 Jan. **Average** 200F. **Credit** MC, V. **Map L6**
A tiny, unlabelled room shrouded by a dusty lace curtain gives no hint from the street that this is an extremely successful restaurant. Osteria's renown is down to the simplicity and fine ingredients that typify good Italian cooking. The menu is based around salad starters (classic tomato and mozzarella or rocket with parmesan), a changing array of pasta and *gnocchi* dishes and a couple of meat and fish choices.

Swann et Vincent
7 rue St-Nicolas, 12th (01.43.43.49.40). M° Ledru-Rollin. **Open** noon-3pm, 7.30pm-midnight daily. **Average** 160F. **Lunch menu** 78F. **No credit cards. Map M7**
This French interpretation of Italian cuisine is not entirely convincing – *gnoccheti* with pesto is slightly sticky, although spaghetti with clams, squid and mussels make up for it. But oh, how we love the homemade herbes-de-Provence *focaccia*, brought warm to the table and the basket refilled as needed. The hubbub of animated conversations from packed tables demonstrates the popularity of this friendly, reasonably priced spot.

Japanese

Higuma

32bis rue Ste-Anne, 1st (01.47.03.38.59). M° Pyramides.
Open 11.30am-10pm daily. **Average** 70F. **Prix fixe**
63F, 65F, 70F. **Credit MC,** V. **Map H4**
Fast service, flexible hours and huge servings at excellent
prices make this the most popular noodle bar in town, among
French and Asians alike. Speciality is *ramen* noodle soups.

Orient Extrême

*4 rue Bernard-Palissy, 6th (01.45.48.92.27). M° St-Germain-
des-Prés.* **Open** noon-2.30pm, 7.30-11pm Mon-Sat. Closed
two weeks in Aug. **Average** 240F. **Prix fixe** 160F-210F.
Lunch menu 92F. **Credit** AmEx, DC, MC, V. **Map G7**
The smart ground floor is the lunch-time haunt of local publishing moguls and fashion-victim shoppers; less flash, the
cellar smoking area is nicely intimate. *Tempura* and *yakitori*
are on offer, but raw fish is the real draw. The 395F *tairyo
boune* for two comes with thrillingly fresh sushi: *tekka maki,*
fine salmon roe and chunks of raw salmon and tuna. Try the
green-tea and red-bean ice creams, rare in Paris.

Zen

18 rue du Louvre, 1st (01.42.86.95.05). M° Louvre.
Open noon-2.30pm, 7-10.30pm Tue-Sat. **Average** 250F. **Prix fixe** 180F **Lunch menu** 75F.
Credit AmEx, MC, V. **Map J5**
Ignore the anonymous facade and enter this world of zen-
like calm for some top sushi. The *prix fixe* numbers 18 big
pieces of absolutely first class fish, each seasoned with just
the right amount of wasabi. The quality of the food is upheld
in the overall attention to detail and the attentive service.

Jewish

Chez Marianne

*2 rue des Hospitalières-St-Gervais, 4th (01.42.72.18.86).
M° St-Paul.* **Open** 11am-midnight daily. **Prix fixe** 55F,
65F, 75F. **Credit MC,** V. **Map L6**

A much-loved bastion of Jewish and Eastern European cuisine, with many options for vegetarians, Marianne's deli and
adjoining dining rooms draw an international clientele. Most
people choose from a long list of tasty 'elements' or meze-like
offerings such as aubergine purée, pastrami, tzatziki, stuffed
vine leaves, *fallafel, tabouleh, kefta* and hummous. Book.

L'As du Fallafel

34 rue des Rosiers, 4th (01.48.87.63.60). M° St-Paul.
Open Sun-Thur noon-midnight, Fri noon-5pm, Sat 8pm-
midnight. **Average** 50F. **Credit** MC, V. **Map L6**
There are other things on the menu besides *fallafel* here, but
frankly we don't see the point. For a few francs more than
the extremely cheap takeaway price you can feast on *fallafel
normal,* with shredded cabbage and sesame sauce, or the
spécial with generous helpings of fried aubergine and hummous. Try the homemade lemonade.

North African

Le 404

*69 rue des Gravilliers, 3rd (01.42.74.57.81). M° Arts et
Métiers.* **Open** noon-2.30pm, 8pm-midnight Mon-Fri;
noon-4pm (brunch), 8pm-midnight Sat, Sun. Closed two
weeks in Aug. **Average** 220F. **Lunch menu** 89F;
brunch 125F. **Credit** AmEx, DC, MC, V. **Map K5**
Closed for more than a year after a fire destroyed the snug
Moorish interior, this popular showbiz haunt is back in business. The North African menu specialises in couscous and
tagines, and offers one of the best brunches in town. Book.

Chez Omar

*47 rue de Bretagne, 3rd (01.42.72.36.26). M° Arts et
Métiers.* **Open** noon-2.45pm, 7pm-midnight Mon-Sat; 7pm-
midnight Sun. **Average** 110F. **No credit cards. Map L5**
Adored by artists, gallery-folk and media types, this old
brasserie hums with a friendly buzz, carefully stoked by the
genial Omar himself. The splendid *couscous royal* entails a
buttered platter of *semoule,* unlimited broth and vegetables,
plus chicken, lamb kebab, spicy *merguez* and baked lamb.

*You can let your kids do the cooking at the **Korean Barbecue** (see also chapter **Children**).*

P'tit Cahoua

39 bd St-Marcel, 13th (01.47.07.24.42). M° St-Marcel.
Open noon-2.30pm, 7.30-11pm Mon-Fri, Sun; 7.30-11pm
Sat. Closed one week in Aug. **Average** 160F. **Prix fixe**
155F. **Lunch menu** 65F. **Credit** AmEx, MC, V. **Map L9**
With its tented ceiling, exotic bric-a-brac and burning joss
sticks, the P'tit Cahoua aims to transport you to warmer
climes. Try crisp, chicken *briouattes* and follow with a delicate *tagine* of chicken and preserved lemons or an out-of-the-
ordinary *couscous*, and sticky Moroccan pastries.
Branch: 24 rue des Taillandiers, 11th (01.47.00.20.42).

Oum el Banine

*16bis rue Dufrenoy, 16th (01.45.04.91.22). M° Rue de la
Pompe.* **Open** noon-2pm, 8-10.30pm Mon-Fri; 8-10.30pm
Sat. Closed one week in Aug. **Average** 225F. **Credit**
AmEx, MC, V. **Map A5**
Named after one of the founders of the university in Fez, this
top of the range Moroccan restaurant is fairly classical but
the quality is excellent. The pigeon *pastilla* is superb as is
the *couscous*, and the *kefta tagine* comes with spiced meat-
balls and a nearly raw egg on top.

Other

African: Chez Aïda

*48 rue Polonceau, 18th (01.42.58.26.20). M° Barbès-
Rochechouart.* **Open** noon-4pm, 7pm-midnight Mon, Tue,
Thu-Sat. **Average** 90F. **Credit** V. **Map K1**
Many small African restaurants in the Goutte d'Or guarantee a cheap and filling meal, but we particularly like this
Senegalese spot for its well-prepared food, relaxed clientele,
and genuinely warm, good-humoured waiter. Try the stuffed
crab, the chicken *yassa*, or *thiébou diene*, Senegal's robust
national dish of rice and fish with seasonal vegetables.

Belgian: Le Bouillon Racine

3 rue Racine, 6th (01.44.32.15.60). M° Cluny-La Sorbonne.
Open 11am-midnight Mon-Fri; 11am-12.30am Sat; 11am-
11pm Sun. **Average** 198F. **Prix fixe** 159F. **Lunch menu**
79F, 107F (Mon-Fri). **Credit** AmEx, MC, V. **Map J7**
Originally operated by Camille Chartier as a *bouillon*, the
lovely Art Nouveau woodwork and mirrors of Le Bouillon
Racine have now been splendidly renovated. Young chef
Olivier Simon's Belgian menu is very good and gently priced.
Start with a delicious Ardennes ham mousse, and follow with
traditional *waterzooi*, a savoury Belgian take on *poule-au-
pot*. Beer is the house quaff, of course. Book.
Wheelchair access.

British: Bertie's

*Hôtel Baltimore, 1 rue Léo-Delibes, 16th
(01.44.34.54.34).* M° Boissière. **Open** 12.30-2pm, 7.30-
10.30pm Mon-Fri. Closed three weeks in Aug. **Average**
250F. **Prix fixe** 220F. **Lunch menu** 195F. **Credit**
AmEx, DC, MC, V. **Map B4**
The menu at upmarket Bertie's is supervised by Brittany-
born Albert Roux, while Londoner Simon Gayle runs the
kitchens, using British ingredients where possible in a surprisingly successful mission to change French opinions of
Brit *bouffe*. Kentish lamb is served with mint sauce (unheard
of in France), cheese is served English style at the very end,
but the wine is reassuringly French.

Caribbean: Le Marais Cage

8 rue de Beauce, 3rd (01.48.87.31.20). M° Temple.
Open noon-2.15pm, 7-10.30pm Mon-Fri; 7-10.30pm Sat.
Closed Aug. **Average** 170F. **Prix fixe** 99F, 165F, 199F.
Lunch menu 135F. **Credit** AmEx, MC, V. **Map K5**
Hidden up one of the seedier streets of the Marais district,
this long-established restaurant serves refined food in a
wonderfully warm and welcoming setting. A mixed starter
of three typical Martinique dishes – *crabe farci*, a chunky

clove-flavoured *boudin créole*, and the avocado-and-manioc
féroce martiniquais – is a good bet, and the main-course
shark in a sweet tomato and onion sauce flavoured with bay
leaves and spicy peppers is superb.

Greek: Mavrommatis

*42 rue Daubenton, 5th (01.43.31.17.17). M° Censier-
Daubenton.* **Open** noon-2.30pm, 7-11pm Tue-Sun. Closed
Aug. **Average** 200F. **Prix fixe** 150F, 165F (for four or
more). **Lunch menu** 120F. **Credit** MC, V. **Map K9**
This is a far more sophisticated take on Greek regional cooking than up the plate-smashing, bouzouki-strumming rue
Mouffetard nearby. Dishes like quail roasted in vine leaves
and lamb-stuffed cabbage *paupiettes* are delectable, although
portions can be small. For dessert, try the sheep's yoghurt
with honey and nuts.

Indian: Pooja

*91 passage Brady, 10th (01.48.24.00.83). M° Strasbourg-
St Denis.* **Open** noon-3pm, 7-11pm Tue-Sun. **Average**
100F. **Prix fixe** 89F. **Lunch menu** 45F, 65F. **Credit**
DC, MC, V. **Map K4**
This tiny North Indian restaurant is the best of the bunch in
Passage Brady, a covered passage full of Indian shops and
gaudy restaurants. Servings are copious and good value.
The bargain lunch plate bursts with tasty chicken and veg-
etable curries, *dhal* and saffron-scented Basmati rice.

Lebanese: Fakhr el Dine

3 rue Quentin-Bouchart, 8th (01.47.23.44.42).
M° George V or Alma-Marceau. **Open** noon-3pm, 7pm-
midnight daily. **Average** 180F. **Prix fixe** 150F, 160F.
Lunch menu 95F. **Credit** AmEx, DC, MC, V. **Map D4**
This plush restaurant serves excellent Lebanese food.
Starters include *kebe* and *tabouleh*, followed by the copious
and delicious mixed grill, and lamb and marinated chicken
kebabs. End with mint tea.
Branches: 24 pl d'Italie, 13th (01.45.65.14.01); 30 rue de
Longchamp, 16th (01.47.27.90.00).

Portuguese: Chez Albert

43 rue Mazarine, 6th (01.46.33.22.57). M° Odéon. **Open**
noon-2.30pm, 7.30-11pm, Tue-Sat; 7-11pm Mon. Closed
Aug and one week at Christmas. **Average** 200F. **Prix
fixe** 135F (90F at 8pm). **Credit** MC, V. **Map G6**
Owned and run by a friendly husband-wife team, this
place has a holiday atmosphere, and dishes like rice with
shellfish may recall Iberian hols. Salt cod is served in multiple ways, and desserts are good too. A nice selection of
Portuguese wines includes a delicious if slightly pricey
white Alvarinho.

Russian: Dominique

19 rue Bréa, 6th (01.43.27.08.80). M° Vavin. **Open**
7.30pm-1am Mon-Sat (bar from noon). Closed mid July-
mid Aug. **Average** 180F. **Prix fixe** 175F. **Credit**
AmEx, DC, MC, V. **Map G8**
Blood-red walls lined with vodka bottles soon have you feeling like a cossack in this institution, around since the 1920s.
Choose from pricey Iranian caviar, *borscht*, *kebabs* and various *zakouski* (cold assortments). Mop these up with *blinis*,
washed down with one of the 60 vodkas.

Spanish: Fogon St-Julien

10 rue St-Julien-le-Pauvre, 5th (01.43.54.31.33).
M° St-Michel. **Open** Mon-Sat noon-3pm, 8pm-1am.
Average 220F. **Prix fixe** 165F. **Lunch menu** 120F.
Dinner menu 175. **Credit** MC, V **Map J7**
Here you'll find not just one authentic *paëlla* but several
different kinds, including one with seasonal vegetables
and another with squid ink, prawns and fish. Before digging in, start with a selection of fresh and very authentic
tapas (55F) or the squid cooked in its own ink. Splurge on
one of the excellent riojas.

Cafés & Bars

Paris has enough cafés and bars – and enough variety – to satisfy even the most discriminating or demanding drinker. What's yours?

What's in a name? The first place in France to have sold coffee – *qahwa* in Arabic, *kalvé* in Turkish – was probably Marseilles, in 1671. The establishment was known as a *maison de café* and, ultimately, simply *café*. The taste soon spread to Paris with the opening of le Procope in 1672 at 6 rue de l'Ancienne-Comédie. Although now mainly a restaurant, it still has a café section and (a more modern definition, this) still serves draught on tap. The pioneering cafés served exotic non-alcoholic drinks – coffee, tea, chocolate, sherbet – to an aristocratic clientele. Wine was served in *tavernes* (although theoretically one didn't drink on the premises) in *cabarets*, the forerunner of the bistro where wine was sold with a meal and in various shady operations; beer was sold by *brasseurs* but generally consumed at home. By the late eighteenth century, the distinction between these dif-

ferent venues begun to be confused and, by the early nineteenth century, a trendy new word emerged – bistro, ascribed by some to Russian Cossacks in the 1814 occupation of Paris asking for their food to be brought *bistro* (quickly). By the early nineteenth century, there were probably around 2000 cafés in Paris, including both the luxurious aristrocratic establishments – where smoking was forbidden – and humbler *tabacs* – where it was not. Smoking prevailed with the arrival of *estaminets* for the proletariat and chic *divans* for the bourgeoisie. The café craze continued, becoming places for games and popular entertainment, as well as for eating and drinking.

Cafés also played a key role in the country's political and artistic life, as the source of news for journalists, a meeting-place for the diffusion of new ideas and a place to read all sorts of papers and pamphlets. While the Procope was largely frequented by writers and actors, the Café de Foy at the Palais Royal was the seat of the *enragés* in the build-up to the 1789 French Revolution. In 1855-56 Courbet, Fantin-Latour, Manet and Degas gathered at the Café Molière after Courbet's exclusion from the Salon. In the early 1900s, Picasso and Braque frequented Les Deux Magots, before heading for Montparnasse, while during the war Café de Flore became home for Sartre and de Beauvoir. Today's cafés are expanding and adapting again, whether for the Internet, tapas, live music or comedy.

Today cafés change function over the course of a day – 'café-tabac-brasserie-bar à vins-salon de thé' – as customers whizz by for a quick coffee and croissant at the counter for breakfast, pile in at noon for a three-course lunch menu, relax over a newspaper in the mid-afternoon, or philosophise over a beer by night. Here we've chosen a selection of classic cafés, hip new bars and the best locals, but you're also sure to discover the pleasant local corner café or the tiny bar which can squeeze only a handful of people round the *zinc*. Note that prices are generally lowest standing at the bar, slightly higher seated inside and highest on the terrace outside. Prices often go up by about 2F after 10pm. Happy hours are most common in Anglo and Irish-style pubs. As well as beers, most cafés offer wines, spirits, coffee, light snacks and meals. Except in various Irish/Anglo bars, beers on tap (*pression*) are usually served as a *demi* (25cl).

Period atmos at **Café L'Epoque**.

Cafés

Bar de l'Entr'acte
47 rue Montpensier, 1st (01.42.97.57.76). M° Palais-Royal.
Open noon-midnight daily. **Credit** MC, V. **Map H5**
Hidden down a sidestreet, this café has been around for centuries under different names (notably La Pissote). Actors and spectators alike come by for a nightcap after a performance at the Comédie Française or Théâtre du Palais Royal. Food, including a daily *plat du marché*, salads and the speciality *andouillette à la moutarde*, is fresh and homemade. The cellar walls bear vintage photos – supposedly of the owner's family.

Café de l'Epoque
2 rue du Buloi, 1st (01.42.33.40.70). M° Palais-Royal.
Open Apr-Nov 7am-11pm daily; Dec-Mar 7am-9pm daily. Closed three weeks in Aug. **Credit** MC, V. **Map H5**
Opening on to the historic Galerie Véro Dodat, the Epoque's facade is an elegant series of wooden-framed arched windows and Corinthian capitals. Inside you'll find all the classic Parisian hallmarks: tall mirrors, polished brass, high ceilings, pâtisserie-display cabinets and upholstered *banquettes*. The reliable food runs to grills and salads.

Au Vide-Gousset
1 rue Vide-Gousset, 2nd (01.42.60.02.78). M° Bourse.
Open 8am-7.30pm Mon-Fri. Closed Aug. **No credit cards. Map H4**
This quaint café-*tabac*, fluttering its lacy windows on a corner of cobbled place des Petits-Pères, is a blueprint for the Parisian cliché. Inside, the mirrors and Art Nouveau lights won't disappoint, and neither will the female management and the 'closet hedonist, surface purist' company of brokers, journalists from *Le Figaro* and sky-high cheek-boned ladies.

L'Apparement Café
18 rue des Coutures-St-Gervais, 3rd (01.48.87.12.22). M° Filles de Calvaire. **Open** noon-2am Mon-Fri; 4pm-2am Sat; 12.30pm-midnight Sun. **Credit** MC, V. **Map L6**
This dimly lit retreat near the Musée Picasso aims at domestic calm; the 'salon' and 'library' are furnished with portraits, comfortable armchairs and flea-market finds. A professional but chilled crowd enhances the sense of a private club. If bored, why not whip out a board game from the 'toy cupboard', or flick through a bound copy of *Paris Match?* Fussy eaters can design their own salad for lunch by ticking them off the menu chart. There are monthly art shows here too.

Web Bar
32 rue de Picardie, 3rd (01.42.72.66.55). M° République.
Open 8.30am-2am Mon-Fri; 11am-2am Sat, Sun. **Credit** MC, V. **Map L5**
The net-plus ultra of Paris cyberspace is more than just a computer nerd's hangout. Converted out of a silversmith's atelier, the impressive space has multipersona *salles* (wickerchaired terrace, mellow-lit, airy stairwell), funky furniture and a hip clientele. It's a bit of a cultural all-rounder, with its poetry nights, concerts, dance displays and art exhibitions.

Café Beaubourg
100 rue St Martin/43 rue St-Merri, 4th (01.48.87.63.96). M° Hôtel-de-Ville/RER Châtelet-Les Halles. **Open** 8am-1am Mon-Thur, Sun; 8am-2am Fri, Sat. **Credit** AmEx, DC, MC, V. **Map K6**
Designed by architect Christian de Portzamparc, the Costes brothers' stylish, two-level reinvention of the classic café by the Centre Pompidou is a sleek, civilised postmodern affair, drawing members of the art world and other fashionable types. Fairly priced salads and excellent desserts.

La Chaise au Plafond
10 rue du Trésor, 4th (01.42.76.03.22). M° St-Paul.
Open 9am-2am daily. **Credit** MC, V. **Map K6**
This cosily trendy little haunt run by the crew from the Petit Fer à Cheval (*see below*) is a clever updating of the classic café. The ceiling is adorned with black and white Friesian cow blotches, and the wooden park-bench-style seating puts you in a relaxed, summery mood at any time of the year, even when not on the fight-for-space terrace. Check out the toilets.

Le Petit Fer à Cheval
30 rue Vieille-du-Temple, 4th (01.42.72.47.47). M° St-Paul. **Open** 9am-2am Mon-Fri; 9am-2am Sat, Sun. **MC, V. Map L6**
On one of the main thoroughfares of the Marais, this quirky vintage café is so popular that it's often impossible to squeeze inside. Almost the entire front room is taken up by a horseshoe-shaped café (hence the name), with a large mirror on either side, elaborate electric chandeliers and a vintage clocking-in machine, complete with askew clock.

L'Imprévu Café
7-9 rue Quincampoix, 4th (01.42.78.23.50). M° Hôtel-de-Ville. **Open** 11am-2am Mon-Sat; 2pm-2am Sun. **Credit** AmEx, V. **Map J6**
Students and the local arty clique have set up residence in this friendly, hip hollow which allows you to select your resting place from Aladdin's den to velvet cinema seating. The fun continues in the thirteenth-century cellar-cum-jazz venue. *Wheelchair access.*

Le Mouffetard
116 rue Mouffetard, 5th (01.43.31.42.50). M° Censier-Daubenton. **Open** 7.15am-10pm Tue-Sat; 7.15am-8pm Sun. Closed three weeks in July. **Credit** AmEx, MC, V. **Map J9**
With its open-air market, animated rue Mouffetard creates an easygoing, villagey mood around this friendly café, which featured in Kieslowski's *Trois Couleurs: Bleu.* There's a 70F *menu* which includes traditional *plats du jour*, sustenance for noisy students, bohemian locals and bemused tourists.

Le Reflet
6 rue Champollion, 5th (01.43.29.97.27). M° Cluny-La Sorbonne. **Open** 10am-2am daily. **Credit** MC, V. **Map J7**
Opposite the Reflet Médicis cinema, it's a short step from screen to caffeine in this relaxed café, full of students and film buffs, here for a chat and cheap, reliable food. The mock movie-studio lighting rig throws some light on the conversations below, with jazz playing in the background.

L'Assignat
7 rue Guénégaud, 6th (01.43.54.87.68). M° Mabillon or Pont-Neuf. **Open** Mon-Sat 9am-late. **No credit cards. Map H6**
This St-Germain local is suitably antiquated and good-value (beer 10F), with all the attributes of the classic family-run *café du quartier*: pinball, *babyfoot*, jukebox (Brel yes – Prodigy no), random barking dog, card-playing regulars. Impromptu jazz nights and cool location bring in students and literary types. Traditional menu available at lunch.

Bar du Marché
75 rue de Seine, 6th (01.43.26.55.15). M° Odéon.
Open 8am-2am daily. **Credit** MC, V. **Map H9**
The terrace attracts a trendy young crowd of students and musicians including rap star MC Solaar. There's not much scope for intellectual discussion here, with the market-stall holders along the adjoining rue de Buci yelling out the virtues of their *moules* and *haricots*, but if it's genuine atmosphere you're after, this is definitely the place to be.

Café de Flore
172 bd St-Germain, 6th (01.45.48.55.26). M° St-Germain-des-Prés. **Open** 7am-1.30am daily. **Credit** AmEx, MC, V. **Map H7**
The existentialist Mecca once frequented by Sartre and de Beauvoir is still abuzz with fervent intellectual prattle in numerous tongues. The 1930s décor hasn't changed, neither

Café Beaubourg: *arty, stylish, postmodern – and that's just the customers!*

has the waiter service, only the prices have risen (a lot). Eric Rohmer has discovered many an actress here; Karl Lagerfeld and Bernard-Henri Lévy are other famous regulars.

Café Mabillon
164 bd St-Germain, 6th (01.43.26.62.93). M° Mabillon. **Open** 7am-6am daily. **Credit** V. **Map H7**
Recently revamped, Café Mabillon is now a slick, bronzed, dimly lit exercise by Jonathan Amar, that is aiming to lure the all-night set back to the *Rive Gauche*.

Café de la Mairie
8 pl St-Sulpice, 6th (01.43.26.67.82). M° St-Sulpice. **Open** 7am-2am Mon-Sat; daily in June. **No credit cards**. **Map H7**
With the summer sun beating down on St-Sulpice church and the magnificent fountain, it is no wonder the terrace is full of students and arty intellectual types, here for the quintessential Left Bank experience.

Aux Deux Magots
6 pl St-Germain-des-Prés, 6th (01.45.48.55.25). M° St-Germain-des-Prés. **Open** 7.30am-1.30am daily. **Credit** AmEx, MC, V. **Map H7**
It's easy to sit back and be inspired by the great intellectual heritage of this famous café, which still symbolises so much of the arty myth of St-Germain, along with its neighbour Café de Flore (*see above*). Founded in 1875, the Deux Magots (named after the two wise Chinamen inside the entrance) has played host to countless writers, artists and thinkers escaping from the cold of their garrets: Picasso (who supposedly created Cubism here), Hemingway, Mallarmé, Sartre…

La Palette
43 rue de Seine, 6th (01.43.26.68.15). M° Mabillon or St Germain-des-Prés. **Open** 8am-2am Mon-Sat. Closed three weeks in Jan. **No credit cards**. **Map H7**
This classic turn-of-the-century artists' café, with faded paintings and palettes, has plenty of tables inside and out; those in the know prefer the secluded back room. The crowd is a colourful mix of local art dealers, students and glam shoppers. Some hot dishes at lunch, wines and good *tartines* all day.

Le Select
99 bd du Montparnasse, 6th (01.42.22.65.27). M° Vavin. **Open** 7am-3am Mon-Fri, Sun; 7am-4am Sat. **Credit** MC, V. **Map G9**
Opened as an 'American Bar' in the 1920s, Le Select still holds on to the image of its arty Montparnasse heyday with dignity, thanks to its décor and bohemian regulars. The pavement tables attract a more internationally cosmopolitan set. Great cocktails and a huge list of malt whiskies, as well as decent steaks, salads and snacks.

Café du Marché
38 rue Cler, 7th (01.47.05.51.27). M° Ecole-Militaire. **Open** 7am-midnight Mon-Sat; 8am-4pm Sun. **Credit** MC, V. **Map D6**
The location of this café on the bustling rue Cler, one of Paris' smartest street markets, is definitely its attraction. People clock up hours under the awnings, imbibing the hypnotic sounds and smells. Shrine status means the café is always well populated, but the prospect of lunch compiled from fresh market produce is worth braving the rush.

Le Rouquet
188 bd St-Germain, 7th (01.45.48.06.93). M° St-Germain-des-Prés. **Open** 7am-9pm Mon-Sat. **Credit** MC, V. **Map G6**
St-Germain locals prefer to patronise this café, rather than be patronised by the existential waiters of Les Deux Magots. A perfectly preserved 1950s interior, plus a terrace, make this charming café an ideal spot for idling away the afternoon.

Bar des Théâtres
6 av Montaigne, 8th (01.47.23.34.63). M° Alma-Marceau. **Open** 6am-2am daily. **Credit** AmEx, MC, V. **Map D5**
This is the unofficial Mecca for the collective radius of fashion's happy valley, RTL, France 3 and the Comédie des Champs-Elysées. Patrick and his merry band serve steak tartares to famous faces and wannabes, while a brasserie menu extends into a more formal dining area.

Café Madeleine
1 rue Tronchet, 8th (01.42.65.21.91). M° Madeleine. **Open** 8am-9pm daily. **Credit** AmEx, DC, MC, V. **Map D5**

CAFE CHARBON

'Le plus parisien des cafés parisiens'
Open 7 days a week, 9am-2am Lunch & Dinner every day
Brunch Saturday and Sunday
109 rue Oberkampf, 11th. Tel:01.43.57.55.13

The most attractive of the cafés ringing the Madeleine comes into its own when the sun hits the terrace. Stop in after visiting the square's fabled delicatessens.

Le Café Zéphyr
12 bd Montmartre, 9th (01.47.70.80.14). Mº Grands Boulevards. **Open** 8am-2am Mon-Sat; 8am-10pm Sun. **Credit** MC, V. **Map H4**
Founded in the early 1900s by Auvergnats who fell in love with Algeria, the Zéphyr preserves a bizarre combination of North African-inspired décor and dishes from the Auvergne. A pool table and terrace are good excuses to linger.

L'Armagnac
104 rue de Charonne, 11th (01.43.71.49.43). Mº Charonne. **Open** 7am-2am Mon-Fri; 10.30am-2am Sat, Sun. **Credit** V. **Map P6**
The dimly lit, deep-red interior is a perfect refuge from the hectic Bastille, attracting a trainered-up, dressed-down crowd. When the waiters actually remember they are at work and not in a night-club chill-out room, the service is friendly. The inexpensive menu offers café snacks alongside dishes such as *la Danoise*, a mixed plate of haddock, anchovies and smoked salmon. An ideal place to finish the night off.

Bar la Fontaine
1 rue de Charonne, 11th (01.56.98.03.30). Mº Bastille. **Open** 7am-2am Mon-Sat; 10am-2am Sun. **No credit cards. Map M7**
Less chic but no less crucial than other hip tips in the area, this bar attracts a casual crowd and the Radio Nova crew. The boisterous, grungy goings-on fit nicely with the décor and the salsa music keeps things swinging. The pavement terrace fills up from early morning, and there are good-value salads, *gratins* and assorted *croques* (around 35F) at lunch.

Le Bistrot du Peintre
116 av Ledru-Rollin, 11th (01.47.00.34.39). Mº Ledru-Rollin. **Open** 7am-2am Mon-Sat; 10am-8pm Sun. **Credit** AmEx, DC, MC, V. **Map N7**
Founded in 1902, this is a fine example of a sophisticated, well-restored Art Nouveau café, with a perfect corner position. The kitchen is pretty reliable with offerings that range from open sandwiches or plates of Auvergnat *charcuterie* to a full three courses. Try to squeeze in downstairs rather than the more anonymous first-floor dining room. Tables outside.

La Fabrique
53 rue du Fbg-St-Antoine, 11th (01.43.07.67.07). Mº Bastille. **Open** 10am-2am daily. **Credit** AmEx, MC, V. **Map M7**
This laidback new brasserie brews blonde and amber beers on the spot in shiny brewing tanks ranged down one side. Snack on various species of *flammeküche* on a thin crispy pastry base, rôtisseried meats and salads. Club nights. *Wheelchair access.*

Pause Café
41 rue de Charonne, 11th (01.48.06.80.33). Mº Ledru-Rollin. **Open** 7.30am-2am Mon-Sat; 7.30am-8.30pm Sun. **Credit** AmEx, MC, V. **Map M7**
A hip, light-hearted Bastille hangout *obligé* has doubled in size but is still beautified by art exhibits, cheerful 50s-style red-and-yellow formica tables and cool Parisians. The chrome terrace is well placed for people who need to see and be seen, and starred in the film, *Chacun cherche son chat*. House specialities include chilli and *tourtes*.

Café de la Place
23 rue d'Odessa, 14th (01.42.18.01.55). Mº Edgar-Quinet. **Open** 7am-2am Mon-Sat; 10.30am-9.30pm Sun. **Credit** MC, V. **Map G9**
Adorned with *pastis* jugs and old advertising plaques, this lively, revamped vintage café, with a sunny terrace, has

Au Roi du Café: *mobiles, body-piercing, neon.*

become *the* gathering place in the Montparnasse area, attracting a youthful, laidback crowd. There's an excellent choice of French regional wines and a tempting selection of Auvergnat *charcuterie*, salads and hot *plats du jour*.

Au Roi du Café
59 rue Lecourbe, 15th (01.47.34.48.50). Mº Sèvres-Lecourbe. **Open** 7.30am-2am daily. **Credit** MC, V. **Map G7**
This pretty wood-fronted corner café has just all the ingredients for a trendy spot: a kitsch pink neon sign above the bar, paintings exhibited about the café and staff into multiple body piercing. Thirsty hipsters with mobile phones pack out the pavement tables; further back an authentic bistro serves the usual *frites* to young lovers and single *demoiselles*.

L'Eté en Pente Douce
23 rue Muller, 18th (01.42.64.02.67). Mº Château-Rouge. **Open** noon-midnight daily. **Credit** MC, V. **Map J1**
Descend the eastern steps of Sacré Coeur to join the locals in this tree-shaded haven of calm and simple culinary excellence. The menu is limited – salads, *charcuterie*, smoked fish – but everything is fresh and plentiful. And there's always room for one of the legendary desserts, like *fondant au chocolat* or homemade ice cream. Friendly service.

Le Sancerre
35 rue des Abbesses, 18th (01.42.58.08.20). Mº Abbesses. **Open** 8am-2am daily. **Credit** MC, V. **Map H1**
This is the place to cool your boots after climbing up out of the wonderful Abbesses Métro station. An attractive, laidback hangout, it usually airs jazz-funk background tunes; in the evenings, it bursts at the seams with hip leather-jacketed youth, and rock takes precedence. There's a long list of wines, whiskies and beers, and good food.

Le Rendez-vous des Quais
10 quai de la Seine, 19th (01.40.37.02.81). Mº Stalingrad. **Open** *winter* 11.30am-1am daily; *summer* 10.30am-2am. **Credit** AmEx, V. **Map M1**
This modern bar-restaurant overlooking the Bassin de la Villette is part of the MK2 multiplex cinema; photos of film stars line the walls, but many of the smart thirty-somethings just come for the good food and the canal view. The149F *menu ciné* includes a cinema ticket (usable any time). *Wheelchair access.*

Le Soleil
136 bd de Ménilmontant, 20th (01.46.36.47.44). Mº Ménilmontant. **Open** 8am-2am daily. **No credit cards. Map P5**
Aptly named, as the *terrasse* catches most of the afternoon sun, this inexpensive, brightly lit café is a standby for local artists, musicians and hipsters. Totally unexceptional inside, but you want to be outside anyway. *Wheelchair access.*

Bars & Pubs

Flann O'Brien's
6 rue Bailleul, 1st (01.42.60.13.58). M° Louvre. **Open**
4pm-2am daily. **No credit cards. Map H5**
Tucked in a backstreet off rue de Rivoli, this is one of the best
Irish pubs in town. Serving arguably the creamiest pint of
Guinness in Paris as well as excellent live music most nights,
this bar buzzes constantly. With a dartboard upstairs, and
quiz night on Thursdays, there's no lack of entertainment.

Le Fumoir
6 rue de l'Amiral-de-Coligny, 1st (01.42.92.00.24).
M° Louvre. **Open** 11am-2am daily. **Credit** AmEx, MC, V.
Map H6
Brought to you by the China Club team, this is the address
of the moment. Press attachés, blazer-wearing wolves, tou-
sled, sleep-deprived young artists all stake out their turf in
the large, airy space with bare wood floors, a large brown
wood bar and a décor that seems inspired by Vienna,
Edward Hopper and Scandinavia. The food is actually pretty good. And there's a great selection of malt whiskies.
Wheelchair access.

Le Café Noir
65 rue Montmartre, 2nd (01.40.39.07.36). M° Sentier.
Open 7.30am-2am Mon-Fri; 4.30pm-2am Sat. **No credit
cards. Map J4**
Cheerful staff, whimsical sun mobiles and giant sunglasses
over the door give this unpretentious corner café an inviting
atmosphere. The young crowd is a mix of French and
Anglophones, and, with its budget prices and light meals, this
can be a good place to live it up and brush up your French.
Wheelchair access.

The Frog & Rosbif
*116 rue St-Denis, 2nd (01.42.36.34.73). M° Etienne-
Marcel.* **Open** noon-2am daily. **Credit** MC, V. **Map J5**
With all the trimmings from trad pub grub, real ale (brewed
in the basement) and the English papers to wackily named
home-brews (Inseine, Parislytic), this is the retreat of the
Englishman abroad. Live broadcasts of football and rugby.
Branch: The Frog & Princess, 9 rue Princesse, 6th
(01.40.51.77.38).

Harry's Bar
5 rue Daunou, 2nd (01.42.61.71.14). M° Opéra. **Open**
10.30am-4am Mon-Sat. **Credit** AmEx, DC, V. **Map G4**
A favourite with sozzled expats since 1911, this legendary
cocktail bar is the birthplace of the Bloody Mary, and Harry's
original remains unbeatable. Light fare is available at lunch-
time, otherwise you're down to the *chiens chauds à toute
heure*: try the bunless sushi version. Later at night the business clientele gives way to a younger international crowd.

Kitty O'Shea's
10 rue des Capucines, 2nd (01.40.15.00.30). M° Opéra.
Open noon-1.30am daily. **Credit** AmEx, MC, V. **Map G4**
The décor is imported from Ireland, as are the Guinness and
Kilkenny. Packed with bankers early on, the atmosphere
becomes more relaxed later, with a civilised mix of Irish,
English and French, except on rugby Five Nations Cup days.
A first-floor restaurant serves Irish grub.
Branch: James Joyce, 71 bd Gouvion-St-Cyr, 17th
(01.44.09.70.32).

Tigh Johnny's
55 rue Montmartre, 2nd (01.42.33.91.33). M° Sentier.
Open 4pm-1.15am daily. **No credit cards. Map J4**
The second-oldest Irish pub in Paris serves as an informal
Gaelic cultural centre. The dark saloon is decorated with photos of poets who perform in the monthly Live Poets' Society
readings (third Sun/month). Decent draught Guinness.

The Lizard Lounge
18 rue du Bourg-Tibourg, 4th (01.42.72.81.34).
M° Hôtel-de-Ville. **Open** noon-2am daily. Closed one week
in Aug. **Credit** MC, V. **Map K6**
A stylish, split level bar-restaurant designed and built by its
American owners with a heavy steel mezzanine, art on the
walls and a long flowing bar. Professionals and hip young
Anglophiles dine on deli sandwiches, *plats du jour* or Sunday
brunch. The Underground cellar bar has DJs (Thur-Sat).

Le Pick-Clops
*16 rue Vieille-du-Temple, 4th (01.40.29.02.18). M° Hôtel-
de-Ville.* **Open** 8am-2am Mon-Sat; 2pm-2am Sun. **Credit**
V. **Map K6**
Somewhat rougher and readier than its Marais neighbours,
this bar boasts outside tables perfect for people-watching.
Music policy steers towards loud, 70s rock, but has been
known to pump house and jungle over the sound of the many
languages coming from aspiring models who join the largely teenage, *parigot* rock crowd and live-in drunks.

Piment Café
15 rue de Sévigné, 4th (01.42.74.33.75). M° St-Paul.
Open 11am-2am Mon-Fri; 6pm-2am Sat, Sun. **No credit
cards Map L6**
This small café has a cast of endearing oddballs on both
sides of the *comptoir*, enjoying one of the better happy hours
in Paris. The menu, mainly French at lunch time, gets more
exotic by night, with international dishes which may coin-
cide with the exhibitions of trans-global art. The masks and
wall-hangings fit the relaxed mood, helped by the Afro-
funky music. Inexpensive and popular with local artists.

Café Oz
184 rue St-Jacques, 5th (01.43.54.30.48). RER Luxembourg.
Open 4pm-2am daily. **Credit** MC, V. **Map J8**
A healthy range of draught and bottled beers (Fosters, VA
etc), fabulous, if pricey, Australian wines, friendly, wise-
cracking staff, and an agreeably mixed French/expat crowd
make this a popular hideout. Mock aboriginal cave paintings
cover the walls and quaint Aussie mementoes fill corners.
Branch: 18 rue St-Denis, 1st (01.40.39.00.18).
Wheelchair access.

Finnegan's Wake
9 rue des Boulangers, 5th (01.46.34.23.65). M° Jussieu.
Open *term time* 11am-2am Mon-Fri; 6pm-2am Sat, Sun.
holidays 6pm-2am daily. **No credit cards. Map K8**
With black-beamed ceilings and a dresser-bar gleaming with
bottles, this spooky but friendly pub sees a cosmopolitan
staff serve Sorbonne students by day and a jolly bunch of
youths by night. With an arty exhibition space, and live Irish
music or blues most weekends, this is a ready-made local.
There's French poetry every Sunday evening, plus occasional theatre and Celtic, Gallic and Welsh language classes.

Le Piano Vache
*8 rue Laplace, 5th (01.46.33.75.03). M° Maubert-
Mutualité.* **Open** noon-2am Mon-Fri; 9pm-2am Sat, Sun.
Credit MC, V. **Map J8**
Markedly more French than its neighbours, this reliable old
student haunt, with an intimate candlelit front room, smoke-
stained walls, heavy wood beams and a large, pleasantly
seedy back bar (often closed early in the week), has a cosy
feel. Music is mainly indie rock, with a DJ on Wednesday's
Gothic night, Thursday's reggae and Friday's *rock anglais*.

Le Rallye
11 quai de la Tournelle, 5th (01.43.54.29.65). M° Jussieu.
Open 7am-2am Mon-Fri; 9.30am-2pm Sat, Sun. **No credit
cards. Map K7**
About as close as you'll come to a working-class caff in this
part of the 5th, this family-run café-tabac is a veritable shrine
to comic-book hero Tintin. Beneath giant inflatables lie 1950s

'I drink… therefore I am'

The idea of talking philosophy in a café has moved on from the days when Sartre used to hold court in the Café de Flore. The craze began in 1992 in the Café des Phares, with Sunday-morning discussions led by Marc Sautet, an ex-Trotskyist who claimed to bring philosophy back to life 'after thirty years of oblivion'. There are now around twenty *cafés philo* in Paris. About half of the *animateurs* are either teachers or ex-teachers of philosophy; the rest are amateurs, as befits the movement's principle of making philosophy accessible to all.

Despite Sautet's death last year, discussions at the Phares still attract up to 200 people. But the clinking coffee cups and the exchange of money prevent deep concentration on 'Does the ephemeral have a value?' Moderators try to probe the contributions made, struggling to get speakers to keep to the subject (which is chosen by a vote on suggestions offered by those present).

English-speakers in Paris have not been far behind. A 'philosophical dinner' on the subject of 'Emotions' led by American Gale Prawda felt like a group therapy session. Prawda also hosts a *café philo* at the Flore; if you are not too bothered about how strictly philosophical the discussion is, you may enjoy it. For a different style, try Peter Coville at trendy Café de l'Industrie. The group tends to be small, so everyone is likely to be involved in the discussion. Coville's approach is serious and unpretentious.

The philosophy spoken in the cafés of Paris today suffers from the very malaise behind the recent explosion in pop philosophy, namely that we no longer believe in guiding ideas, beyond the relativism that says that everyone has something interesting to say. However, it is worth seeing a *café philo* in action; they are not dominated by terminology-dropping students (the average age is about 40) and present an unintimidating environment in which to develop your thoughts.

Café de Flore
172 bd St-Germain, 6th (01.45.48.55.26). M° St-Germain-des-Prés. **Open** 7am-1.30am daily. **Credit** AmEx, MC, V. **Map H7**
Discussions in English, first Wed of the month at 7pm.

Café de l'Industrie
16 rue St-Sabin, 11th (01.47.00.13.53). M° Bastille. **Open** 10am-2am Sun-Fri. **Credit** DC, MC, V **Map L6**
Discussions in English on the second and fourth Sunday of the month, 11am-1pm.

Café des Phares
7 pl de la Bastille, 4th (01.42.72.04.70). M° Bastille. **Open** 7am-4am daily. **No credit cards**. **Map L7**
Discussions in French every Sunday, 11am-1pm.

L'Entrepôt
7-9 rue Francis-de-Pressensé, 14th (cinema 08.36.68.05.87; restaurant 01.45.40.60.70). M° Pernéty. **Open** 10am-midnight Mon-Thur; 11am-midnight Sun; 10am-2am Fri, Sat. **Credit** MC, V. **Map F10**
A film screening followed by a philosophical debate takes place every fortnight. In French.
Wheelchair access.

Marc Sautet, café philo *pioneer*.

mirrored walls and red vinyl banquettes and friendly, if not indulgent, staff. A steady stream of students, workers and locals from nearby houseboats jostle for space, enjoying the cheap beer and simple hot dishes, like *lapin à la moutarde*.

Chez Georges
11 rue des Cannettes, 6th (01.43.26.79.15). Mº Mabillon. **Open** noon-2am Tue-Sat. Closed Aug. **No credit cards**. **Map H7**
The street-level bar is a perfect locals' haunt – tiled floor, foam-spilling banquettes, simple food and a good selection of wines. Signed photos pay tribute to Georges' glorious past as a cabaret. The cellar, meanwhile, candlelit and low-slung, caters to a raucous beer-guzzling, Piaf-listening crowd of students, especially at weekends. (Best seats are on the raised platform that was once the cabaret stage.)

La Closerie des Lilas
171 bd du Montparnasse, 6th (01.40.51.34.50). Mº Vavin. **Open** 11.30am-1am daily. **Credit** AmEx, DC, MC, V. **Map G9**
Founded as a lilac-shaded *guinguette* dance hall in 1847, this bar has had famous clients including Man Ray, Apollinaire, Picasso and Hemingway, as little brass plaques on the tables testify. Now a classy cocktail bar, it still attracts the political world and cultural establishment, and a pianist tinkles in the background. Brasserie fare is served all day and the upmarket restaurant has been reinvigorated by a new chef.

Coolín
Marché St-Germain, 15 rue Clément, 6th (01.44.07.00.92). Mº Mabillon. **Open** 10am-2am Mon-Sat; 1pm-2am Sun. **Credit** MC, V. **Map H7**
An attractive synthesis of pub and Parisian café, with burnt-orange paintwork, blue blinds and wooden furniture, this Irish addition in the revamped St-Germain covered market has made its mark with a lively young Anglo-Irish crowd. *Wheelchair access.*

Café Thoumieux
4 rue de la Comète, 7th (01.45.51.50.40). Mº Latour-Maubourg. **Open** noon-2am Mon-Fri; 5pm-2am Sat. Closed 1-15 Aug. **Credit** AmEx, MC, V. **Map E6**
The three-year-old brother to long-established Thoumieux (*see chapter* **Restaurants**) is full of Moorish luxuriance, with a cocoon of rich yellows, reds and browns, and red velour *banquettes*. Stare at the glamorous rich kids and Eurotrash intellectuals over a glass of wine, a cocktail and excellent *tapas*. The big-screen comes into its own for sporting events.

Barfly
49-51 av George V, 8th (01.53.67.84.60). Mº George V. **Open** noon-3pm, 6.30pm-2am Mon-Fri; 6.30pm-2am Sat; noon-3pm, 7pm-2am Sun. **Credit** AmEx, MC, V. **Map D4**
This self-proclaimed fashionable bar aims at New York style, but Bukowski (from whose book the name hails) would be chuckling in his grave. Beautiful people eat internationally spun titbits (reservation only) or sushi, while older businessmen and their twenty-something women sip cocktails. *Wheelchair access*

Montecristo Café
68 av des Champs-Elysées, 8th (01.45.62.30.86). Mº Franklin D Roosevelt. **Open** 11am-6am daily. **Credit** AmEx, DC, MC, V. **Map E4**
This all-night joint has finally struck lucky with Cuba. Despite lots of tourists by day and high Champs-Elysées prices, the place now pulls in a stylish young crowd at night. The ground floor, modelled on a Havana street, is a restaurant, while they dish out *tapas* and cocktails in the basement.

Au Général Lafayette
52 rue Lafayette, 9th (01.47.70.59.08). Mº Le Peletier. **Open** 8am-4pm daily. **Credit** AmEx, MC, V. **Map H9**

A spacious bar for beer connoisseurs, with its turn-of the-century ceilings, mirrors, potted plants and mellow, jazzy atmosphere. Relaxed professionals lunch on brasserie-style dishes; come evening, drinkers snack as they work their way through some of the 130 (mostly Belgian) beers. Look out for the peach-flavoured *péché originel* (original sin) and *fruit défendu*, served in a glass depicting Adam and Eve.

Le Sainte Marthe
32 rue Ste-Marthe, 10th (01.44.84.36.96). Mº Belleville. **Open** 11am-2am Tue-Sat; noon-8pm Sun. **Credit** AmEx, MC, V. **Map M3**
Occupying the former premises of magazine *l'Affiche*, in a tree-lined square, this swish, refreshingly gimmick-free bar could represent the first step towards gentrification of this dilapidated corner of old Belleville. The lighting is great, the atmosphere chilled, and the drink cheap. The bistro also boasts a mouthwatering range of tapas at just 20F a plate, and has begun to attract aficionados of the *quartier*.

Bar des Ferailleurs
18 rue de Lappe, 11th (01.48.07.89.12). Mº Bastille. **Open** 5pm-2am Mon-Fri; 3pm-2am Sat, Sun. **Credit** MC, V. **Map M7**
This excessively hip and regularly heaving bar can do no wrong. Fashion victims squeeze on to uncomfortable high metal chairs to be amiably abused by the barmen, or gather around tables to gossip. Everything seems to be made from scrap metal: iron portholes, a scrap metal bar and metal oddities on the walls. The music tends to be acid jazz and deep house; there are photo and art expos every month too.

Boca Chica
58 rue de Charonne, 11th (01.43.57.93.13). Mº Ledru-Rollin. **Open** 11am-2am daily. **Credit** AmEx, MC, V. **Map M7**
This very successful *tapas* bar offers a sleek, burnt-colour take on Spain, with deep-red walls, round, rusty iron tables and strangely low, sub-Miró boiled-sweet seats. The menu, blaring music and impromptu dancing are more authentically Iberian. Try an assortment of *tapas* for 60F.

Café Charbon
109 rue Oberkampf, 11th (01.43.57.55.13). Mº Parmentier or Ménilmontant. **Open** 9am-2am daily. **Credit** MC, V. **Map N5**
This *fin-de-siècle* dance hall is the star of the area. Vintage booths, fab chandeliers, gas lamps and a pulley system which arranges the beer kegs add to the charm. The hip crowd is relaxed by day and lively by night, although runaway success can mean near suffocation. On Tue-Sat nights, a DJ plays a mix of funk and house. Pity about the Turkish loo.

Mecano
99 rue Oberkampf, 11th (01.40.21.35.28). Mº Parmentier. **Open** 9am-2pm Mon-Sat; 10am-2am Sun **Credit** AmEx, MC, V. **Map N5**
Check out the workshop-style interior, or fuel up with a 'Jet 27' before heading on to one of the street's other bars. Enjoy a 'sex on the beach' under a wired ceiling adorned with huge silver pipes, spanners and other mechanics' tools, as you take a seat next to a shining, full-sized car engine. Avoid when crowded.

China Club
50 rue de Charenton, 12th (01.43.43.82.02). Mº Ledru-Rollin or Bastille. **Open** 7pm-2am Mon-Thur, Sun; 7pm-3am Fri, Sat. Closed Mon, Sun July 15-Aug 15. **Credit** AmEx, V. **Map M7**
This sophisticated haven, decorated to resemble a colonial Hong Kong gentleman's club, boasts a speakeasy-style cellar bar (live jazz Fri and Sat from 11pm), a lacquered *fumoir chinois*, and a mile-long main bar with eclectic jazz standards. Great cocktails, and good, but pricey, Chinese-inspired food. *Wheelchair access.*

Le Merle Moqueur

*11 rue de la Butte-aux-Cailles, 13th (01.45.65.12.43). M°
Corvisart or Place d'Italie.* **Open** 5pm-2am daily. **Credit**
AmEx, DC, MC, V.
Following a facelift, the Merle Moqueur is trying to attract a
hipper crowd. The interior evokes a jungle vibe – leafy murals
and real bamboo adorn the walls, along with exotic plants, a
hammock and tribal paintings. Drinks remain cheap, and the
soundtrack runs from French music hall to mod alternative.
Wheelchair access.

Mustang Café

*84 bd du Montparnasse, 14th (01.43.35.36.12).
M° Montparnasse-Bienvenüe.* **Open** 11am-5am daily.
Credit MC, V. **Map G8**
A thriving Tex-Mex bar-restaurant with ranch décor, a late-
night licence and an indulgent happy hour attracts hordes
of well-behaved *lycéens* and cinema-goers. *Tacos*, burgers
and *fajitas* (49F-99F) are dished out until late and washed
down with Bud or Margaritas. Theme nights Tue and Thur.

Le Rosebud

*11bis rue Delambre, 14th (01.43.20.44.13). M° Vavin or
Edgar Quinet.* **Open** 7pm-2am daily. Closed Aug. **Credit**
MC, V. **Map G9**
This dimly lit Montparnasse cocktail haunt has become
something of a middle-aged pick-up joint, where sozzled travellers down Martinis at the bar, waiting for strangers-in-the-
night encounters. So *ringard*, it's almost chic.

L'Endroit

*67 pl du Dr-Félix-Lobligeois, 17th (01.42.29.50.00).
M° Rome.* **Open** noon-2am daily. **Credit** V. **Map F1**
L'Endroit is *the* place, at least in this area not renowned for
its bar life. Outside it has an enviable terrace; inside a cool
soundtrack and well-bred residents. Decent cocktails and salads, *magret* and sometimes even vegetarian lasagne.

Club Club

3 rue André-Antoine, 18th (01.42.54.38.38). M° Pigalle.
Open 7pm-2am Mon-Sat. **Credit** MC, V. **Map H2**
Pigalle is seeing a cultural resurgence at this former hostess
bar, helped along by Franco-American duo Nicolas and Tex.
Tuesday is Poésie 2000°, when a programme of poets is com-
plemented by spontaneous outbursts from Jo(e) public.

La Fourmi

74 rue des Martyrs, 18th (01.42.64.70.35). M° Pigalle.
Open 8.30am-2am Mon-Sat; 10am-2am Sun. **Credit** AmEx,
MC, V. **Map H2**
Industrial lighting, a long wooden bar and a Duchampian bottle rack hanging from the ceiling make this Pigalle bar more
sophisticated than its neighbours. Rich Parisian youth and
local trend-setters come from the Divan du Monde over the
road. Food includes salads, sandwiches and a *plat du jour.*

La Buvette

*4 rue des Panoyaux, 20th (01.46.36.81.79)
M° Ménilmontant.* **Open** 4.30pm-1.30am daily. **No credit
cards. Map N5**
The strong rum punch renders the barren, quirkly rear courtyard even more of an apocalyptic dreamworld than it really
is. Though loud African and Caribbean music fills the dark,
cramped interior, the bartender and gregarious, international crowd create a laidback, groovy atmosphere.

Lou Pescalou

*14 rue des Panoyaux, 20th (01.46.36.78.10).
M° Ménilmontant.* **Open** 9am-2am daily. **Credit** MC, V.
Map N5
This veteran of the Ménilmontant scene boasts friendly staff,
a nicely worn-in décor and well-sheltered terrace. The focal
point is the pool table – constantly hogged by the area's cool
crowd. Check out the chrome, spaceship-style loos.

Salons de Thé

Angelina's

226 rue de Rivoli, 1st (01.42.60.82.00). M° Tuileries.
Open 9am-7pm Mon-Fri; 9am-7.30pm Sat, Sun. Closed
Tue July 15-Aug 15. **Credit** AmEx, MC, V. **Map G5**
Near the Tuileries gardens, this is the ultimate Parisian tea
room, with rococo murals, ornate gilt plasterwork and vast
mirrors harking back to its opening in 1903. It remains the
perfect place to take your grandmother, and sit amid well-
to-do ladies and tourists. The hot chocolate is heavenly.
Branches: Galeries Lafayette (3rd floor), 40 bd
Haussmann, 9th (01.42.82.30.32); Palais de Congrès,
2 pl de la Porte-Maillot, 17th (01.40.68.22.50).

La Charlotte en l'Ile

*24 rue St-Louis-en-l'Ile, 4th (01.43.54.25.83). M° Pont-
Marie.* **Open** noon-8pm Thur-Sun. Closed July, Aug.
Credit MC, V. **Map K7**
This children's fairytale of a place has existed for 26 years
and retains all its charm. Its walls are decorated with carni-
val masks, instruments and animals; homemade chocolate
figurines adorn the entrance. The charmingly eccentric
woman who runs it serves up the 32 delicious different teas,
tarts, loose-leaf poems and recipes. They have a pianist (Fri
from 6pm) and you can reserve for puppet shows (Wed).

Les Enfants Gâtés

*43 rue des Francs-Bourgeois, 4th (01.42.77.07.63).
M° St-Paul.* **Open** noon-8pm Wed, Sun; noon-10pm Thur-
Sat. **Credit** MC, V. **Map L6**
A papier mâché chicken in a cowboy hat sits in the entrance
of this Marais outfit, the perfect place to write your Parisian
art-novel. Classical music, battered leather armchairs, low
tables, pot plants and cinema posters give a Casablanca
effect. Add to that excellent *gratins* and salads, fruit juices
and superb (pricey) pâtisseries and it's not surprising some
of the languid figures look as if they've come to stay.

La Mosquée de Paris

*39 rue Géoffroy-St-Hilaire, 5th (01.43.31.38.20).
M° Censier-Daubenton.* **Open** 9am-midnight daily.
Credit MC, V. **Map K9**
The never-ending quest for novelty has made this mosaic-
decorated tea room adjoining the mosque and *hammam* one
of the trendiest destinations in Paris. Ravers, Jussieu students
and intellectuals are among the regulars hanging out over
sweet mint tea and pastries, fig-filled or honeyed cigar *baklava.* The secluded courtyard is very popular in the summer.
Wheelchair access.

L'Heure Gourmande

22 passage Dauphine, 6th (01.46.34.00.40). M° Odéon.
Open 11.30am-7pm Tues-Sat; 1-7pm Sun. Closed two
weeks in Aug. **Credit** MC, V. **Map H6**
Tucked away in a cobbled passageway near boulevard St-
Germain, this pleasant tea room is fuller than one would
expect given its unobtrusive décor. However, its flavoursome
wares make up for this neutrality. The Betjeman and Barton
teas are organised regionally and seasonally, and the cakes
are great value: teacake, fruitcake and chocolate cake.
Wheelchair access.

Purple

*9 rue Pierre-Dupont, 10th (01.40.34.14.21). M° Château-
Landon.* **Open** 2pm-7pm Tue-Sat. **No credit cards.**
Map L2
Autumn 1998's most talked-about new arrival has bravely
set up in an inconspicuous sidestreet behind Gare de l'Est.
Elaine Fleiss of intello-trendy design consultancy and

*Check-mate all your mates
chez* **Le Soleil.**

art/fashion/fiction publishing empire *Purple Prose, Purple Fashion* and *Purple Fiction* (now published jointly as *Purple*), launched it to practise what she published. Here you can drink peculiar Flammes Glacées, Purple Milk or Fluide Floral concocted by artist Martine Aballéa, try on sculptural homespun clothes by very young designers, buy *Purple* contributors' photos, or flick through cult mags and art catalogues.

Wine bars

Juvéniles

47 rue de Richelieu, 1st (01.42.97.46.49). M° Palais-Royal. **Open** noon-11pm Mon-Sat. **Credit** MC, V. **Map H5**
British expat Tim Johnston, along with his partner Mark Williamson at Willi's Wine Bar, attract clients from all corners of the globe, to taste wines from other countries. As the bar includes a shop, this is an excellent opportunity to taste before buying. Food includes good *tapas*-style starters, standard French dishes and enlightened English pub food.

Taverne Henri IV

13 pl du Pont-Neuf, 1st (01.43.54.27.90). M° Pont-Neuf. **Open** noon-9pm Mon-Fri; noon-4pm Sat. Closed three weeks in Aug. **No credit cards.**
This bar on the tip of the Ile de la Cité and owner Robert Cointepas are as famous as each other, and after 40 years he continues to draw lawyers, judges and the odd tourist. Cointepas personally chooses his Beaujolais, Montlouis, Jurançon and Bordeaux from the vineyards and serves them in peak condition with *tartines* of *rillettes* or cheese, or a plate of snails. Beaujolais Nouveau celebrations are electric.

Le Comptoir du Relais

5 carrefour de l'Odeon, 6th (01 43 29 12 05). M° Odéon. **Open** noon-midnight Mon-Thu; noon-2am Fri, Sat; 1pm-10pm Sun. Closed first three weeks of Aug. **No credit cards. Map H7**
This is a fine refuge for cinephiles before or after a film. A broad range of modest wines includes some rarities, such as a 93 Bourgogne Irancy, a Côte Catalane from Roussillon, and a 1990 Oriu from Corsica. The menu is brief, with toasted *tartines* made of the ubiquitous *pain Poilâne* dominating, but the combination of simple savoury food and the uncorked pleasures of some good wines adequately fulfils one's needs.

Au Sauvignon

80 rue des Sts-Pères, 7th (01.45.48. 49.02). M° Sèvres-Babylone. **Open** 8am-9pm Mon-Sat. Closed Aug. **Credit** MC, V. **Map G6**
The walls are covered with pictures, photos and bawdy cartoons connected with wine. Marie-Françoise Vergne has taken over from her father Henri, but he pops in regularly. With a good range of Loire whites, this is the place to compare a glass of Muscadet, Quincy, Sancerre and Reuilly; Saturdays, it's a perfect spot to spy on the bourgeoisie at play.

Le Griffonnier

8 rue des Saussaies, 8th (01.42.65.17.17). M° Champs-Elysées-Clemenceau. **Open** 8am-9pm Mon-Wed, Fri; 8am-10.30pm Thur. **Credit** MC, V. **Map F4**
Heavily moustached Robert Savoye and his staff welcome their clientele with a smile, as French suits and pearls and the odd Canadian banker cluster in groups, or stand at the bar eating a quick lunch while reading a newspaper. The house favours Beaujolais but there are early Viognier, St-Joseph, Côtes du Roussillon and St-Estèphe for those who prefer. Food varies from sandwiches and *charcuterie* to sturdy *plats du jour.*

La Cave Drouot

8 rue Drouot, 9th (01.47.70.83.38). M° Richelieu-Drouot. **Open** 7am-9am Mon-Sat. **Credit** MC, V. **Map H4**
From 7am, the bar is surrounded by the 'red collars' from the Drouot auction house across the street popping in for a coffee or an early glass of white. Drouot specialises in wines from the Southwest, while the barrels of Beaujolais are personally chosen, then bottled and labelled in the cellar. The bar food reflects the owner's Basque roots; or you can lunch more seriously in the grape-moulded restaurant and drink *au compteur.*

Bistro Jacques Mélac

42 rue Léon-Frot, 11th (01.43.70.59.27). M° Charonne. **Open** 9am-5pm Mon; 9am-midnight Tue-Sat. Closed two weeks in Aug. **Credit** MC, V. **Map N6**
The sign, 'The water here is reserved for cooking potatoes', gives you an idea of Jacques Mélac's sense of humour and the convivial mood of this friendly wine bar. Don't be deceived by the small room: the tiny kitchen gives access to two more rooms, of which one is non-smoking.

Le Clown Bar

114 rue Amelot, 11th (01.43.55.87.35). M° Filles du Calvaire. **Open** noon-3.30pm, 7pm-1am Mon-Sat; 7pm-1am (Oct-Apr) Sun. Closed one week in Aug. **Credit** V. **Map L5**
This happy, family-run wine bar is next to the historic Cirque d'Hiver, and the listed interior runs amok with clown tiles, posters and memorabilia. Even today, famous French clowns frequent the bar during runs at the Cirque. Mr et Mme Vitte and daughter Myriam specialise in Côtes du Rhône and often have an interesting *vin du jour.* In the evening, it's advisable to book, but you can usually find room at the *zinc* if all you want is a plate of *charcuterie.* Dogs are welcome, too.

Le Baron Rouge

1 rue Théophile-Roussel, 12th (01.43.43.14.32). M° Ledru-Rollin. **Open** 10am-2pm, 5-9.30pm Tue-Thur; 10am-9.30pm Fri, Sat; 10am-3pm Sun. **Credit** MC, V. **Map M7**
With four tables at the back and a row of barrels outside, this is a true *bar à vins.* An eclectic crowd of artists, musicians, journalists and those seeking refreshment after a visit to the nearby Marché d'Aligre come for the wines and *saucisson sec, andouille, rillettes* or *chèvre.* Bernard Delis from Cap Ferrat opens his own oysters here (*Oct-Mar*, Sat, Sun). *Wheelchair access.*

Winner stays on at **Lou Pascalou** *(see p194).*

RECIPROQUE
Nicole Morel

photo: Pascal Faligot

Featured above are clothes from: CHANEL, DIOR, HERMÈS, CHRISTIAN LACROIX, HERVE LÉGER, VUITTON, GUCCI, MOSCHINO, PRADA, VERSACE, VIVIENNE WESTWOOD.

HIGH FASHION
CLOTHING
WOMEN
MEN

CONSIGNMENT SHOP
800m² Retail Space

TRINKETS-GIFTS
ACCESSORIES
JEWELLERY
FURS

The best and biggest second-hand boutique in Paris. Ladies' and men's clothing by famous fashion designers, all in perfect condition.

ALAIA - ARMANI - BOSS - CERRUTI- CHURCH'S - FAÇONNABLE - FERAUD
GALLIANO - GAULTIER - GIVENCHY - DONNA KARAN - KENZO - RALPH LAUREN
LOBB - MIYAKE - MUGLER - MONTANA - REVILLON - ROCHAS - SAINT-LAURENT
PAUL SMITH - TODD'S - WESTON - YAMAMOTO
Housewares and gifts.

88, 89, 92, 93, 95, 97, 101, 123 Rue de la Pompe, 16th. Mº Pompe.
Tel: 01.47.04.82.24 / 01.47.04.30.28 / Gift: 01.47.27.93.52

photo: Pascal Faligot

Fashion

In Paris you are where you shop, so get a grip on all the different areas and indulge your fashion tastes, from couture to street.

Shopping in Paris is an exhilarating if exhausting experience; few other cities can offer such wonderful diversity. In *couture* heartland (avenue Montaigne or rue du Faubourg St-Honoré) you'll see face-lifted 50-somethings airing their miniature terriers and credit cards while, a 20-minute cab ride away in Abbesses, the fashion landscape morphs into windows chock-a-block with street style, clubwear and bohemian chic. For an all-in-one spree, start on rue Etienne-Marcel (wall-to-wall **Comme**, Yamamoto, Joseph and **Junk**), then move on up to place des Victoires, before an afternoon's browsing in rue du Jour (**Agnès b** land). St Germain, once the haunt of chain-smoking existentialists and beret-wearing bohemians, has undergone a dramatic transformation with the arrival of the Right Bank *luxe* pack. **Vuitton**, **Dior** and **Armani** have all opened major new stores near place St-Germain-des-Prés. If affordable fashion is what you're after, however, head to rue du Four. Then nip along to rues de Grenelle, du Cherche-Midi and du Dragon for stylish shoes and bags and rue des Sts-Pères for the supermodel knicker shop Sabbia Rosa.

The Marais is shopping paradise, except on Sunday afternoon when rue des Francs-Bourgeois is invaded by hordes cashing in on the free-and-easy opening times. In rue des Rosiers, you'll find designer fashion in among kosher butchers and falafel stalls. Check out rue de Sévigné for jewellery and original gift shops, or for a break from tasteful architecture and romantic squares, head towards rue Ste-Croix de la Bretonnerie for a burst of full-on kitsch.

DETAXE (TAX REFUNDS)

Non-EU residents can claim a refund (average 13 per cent) on value-added tax if they spend over 1200F in any one shop, and if they've been in the country less than three months. At the shop ask for a *détaxe* form, and when you leave France have it stamped by customs. Then send a stamped copy back to the shop, who will refund the tax, either by bank transfer or by crediting your credit card. *Détaxe* does not cover food, drink, antiques or works of art.

Designer Names

Absinthe
74-76 rue Jean-Jacques-Rousseau, 1st (01.42.33.54.44). M° Les Halles. **Open** 11am-7.30pm Mon-Sat. Closed Aug. **Credit** DC, MC, V. **Map J5**
In a prettily designed boutique, owner Marthe Desmoulins

nurtures fresh international talent, with an emphasis on the post-grunge Belgian avant-garde. Designers include Josep Font, Julie Skarland and Christine Palmassio. Also stocked are clever bags by Jamin Puech and some shoes.

Calvin Klein
45 av Montaigne, 8th (01.47.23.62.22). M° Franklin D Roosevelt. **Open** 10am-7.30pm Mon-Sat. **Credit** AmEx, DC, MC, V. **Map E4**
No jeans or Y-fronts here, just Calvin's luxury lines to match the glam address. Behind the historic facade discover Claudio Silvestrin's temple to modern minimalism, which also showcases Klein's elegant housewear. Exorbitant prices; scary staff.

Comme des Garcons
40, 42 rue Etienne-Marcel, 2nd (women 01.42.33.05.21/ men 01.42.36.91.54). M° Etienne-Marcel. **Open** 11am-7pm Mon-Sat. **Credit** AmEx, DC, MC, V. **Map J5**
Rei Kawakubo, renowned for her severe, androgynous cuts, state-of-the-art fabrics, and post-apocalyptic vision of fashion, has started to mellow a little, even abandoning funereal black and introducing a burst of colour and print into recent collections. Her men's and women's stores, which retain their *art-brut* design, also stock Rei's protégé Junya Watanabe. (Prices start at around 7000F for men's suits, 6000F for an original woman's dress, 2000F for a line one).

Christian Dior

30 av Montaigne, 8th (01.40.73.54.44). M° Franklin D Roosevelt. **Open** 10am-7pm Mon-Sat. **Credit** AmEx, DC, MC, V. **Map E4**

After Galliano's 'pantomime' extravaganza at the Gare St Lazare in 98, critics began bitching that the Diorient Express was out of steam. But Galliano is back with a collection inspired by Russian constructivism. With army trousers, Chinese workers' caps and red armbands, John has gone for fashion for the People – if not at People's prices.

L'Eclaireur

3ter rue des Rosiers, 4th (01.48.87.10.22). M° St-Paul. **Open** 2-7pm Mon; 11am-7pm Tue-Sat. **Credit** AmEx, DC, MC, V. **Map L6**

Cutting-edge men's and women's fashions – Dries Van Noten, Ann Demeulemeester, Jil Sander, Martin Margiela, Helmut Lang and rising Dutch star Josephus Thimister – are cleverly displayed against iron girders and gleaming parquet. Miyake's famous Pleats Please collection has special prominence. Branches: 24 rue de L'Echaudé, 6th (01.44.27.08.03) (younger and trendier); 26 av des Champs-Elysées, 8th (01.45.62.12.32) (men only).

Emporio Armani

149 bd St-Germain, 6th (01.45.48.62.15). M° St-Germain-des-Prés. **Open** 10am-7.30pm Mon-Sat **Credit** AmEx, MC, V. **Map H7**

Armani sparked controversy when he sited this four-storey boutique opposite the legendary Deux Magots. Left Bank intellectuals took to the streets, claiming the Italian designer was destroying the *quartier*'s soul. But if the glamorous Ms de Beauvoir were alive she'd surely be sporting Armani shades and sipping cappuccino in the Emporio's slick new café. Branch: 25 pl Vendôme, 1st (01.42.61.02.34).

L'Epicerie

30 rue du Temple, 4th (01.42.78.12.39). M° Hôtel de Ville. **Open** 11am-9pm Tue-Sat. **No credit cards. Map K6**

Hidden in a Marais courtyard, this irreverent designer upstart combines art gallery, chill-out lounge and fashion space, with clothing exhibited on upturned packing crates. L'Epicerie stocks its own unisex basics as well as clothes by Jeremy Scott, Eric Bergère and Neil Klavers, and limited edition jewellery by Erik Halley. The owners want customers to feel they can drop by anytime they like – but be warned, opening hours may be a little erratic so as to 'disorientate the clientele'.

Franck et Fils

80 rue de Passy, 16th (01.44.14.38.00). M° Passy. **Open** 10am-7pm Mon-Sat. **Credit** AmEx, DC, MC, V. **Map B6**

Opened in 1897, Franck et Fils used to be a fusty department store for dowager duchesses and ladies who lunch. More recently it has re-invented itself, earning a reputation for its *Ab Fab* racks laden with Armani, Chanel, Givenchy, Lacroix, Ralph Lauren, Vivienne Westwood etc etc…

Galerie Gaultier

30 rue du Fbg-St-Antoine, 12th (01.44.68.84.84). M° Bastille. **Open** 11am-7.30pm Mon-Sat; 10.30am-7.30pm Tue-Fri; 11am-7.30pm Sat. Closed two weeks in Aug. **Credit** AmEx, DC, MC, V. **Map M7**

French fashion's oldest *enfant terrible* is renowned for mixing street and ethnic styles with innovative fabrics and sharp tailoring. The new couture line has been hailed a success, but you might prefer JPG, his cheaper cyber/streetwear, displayed alongside jeans, sunglasses, perfumes, watches and shoes. Branch: Boutique Jean-Paul Gaultier, 6 rue Vivienne, 2nd (01.42.86.05.05).

Givenchy

3 av George V, 8th (01.44.31.50.23). M°Alma-Marceau. **Open** 9.30am-6.30pm Mon-Fri; 10am-6.30pm Sat. **Credit** AmEx, DC, V. **Map D4**

Not long ago genteel blue-blooded designer Hubert de Givenchy was replaced by East End bad boy Alexander McQueen. Recently McQueen has softened his razor-sharp tailoring and aggressive shoulders, experimenting instead with fluid evening wear and eye-catching geometric prints.

Irié

8, 10 rue du Pré-aux-Clercs, 7th (01.42.61.18.28). M° Rue du Bac. **Open** 10.15am-7pm Mon-Sat. Closed first three weeks in Aug. **Credit** MC, V. **Map G6**

Fashion editors and chic Parisians make a bee-line for this Japanese designer's twin boutiques – possibly because, in an era when fabrics are fashion's new message, Irié boldly gambles on the newest of the new: plastic coatings, stretch wools, chenille, fake fur, sequins and hologram prints are scattered over suits, minidresses and perfectly cut jeans in stretch lycra.

Kenzo

3 pl des Victoires, 1st (01.40.39.72.03). M° Palais-Royal. **Open** 10am-7pm Mon; 10am-7pm Tue-Sat. **Credit** AmEx, DC, MC, V. **Map H5**

Kenzo has now introduced long black dresses and neutral shades to join the ebullient flower prints and bright colours. You'll also find ultra-stylish leather handbags and accessories. Branches: 16 (women/home) and 17 (men) bd Raspail, 7th (01.42.22.09.38/01.45.49.33.75); 18 av George V, 8th (01.47.23.33.49); Les 3 Quartiers, 23 bd de la Madeleine, 8th (01.42.61.04.51).

Louis Vuitton

101 av des Champs-Elysées, 8th (01.53.57.24.00). M° George V. **Open** 10am-8pm Mon-Sat. **Credit** AmEx, DC, MC, V. **Map D4**

The opening of Louis Vuitton's new flagship store (designed by American style guru Peter Marino) was celebrated by a bevy of supermodels and designers. Vuitton is now back in vogue with a vengeance, largely thanks to the chic (and ludicrously expensive) new ready-to-wear line (only at the Champs-Elysées store) designed by American Golden Boy Marc Jacobs and sold alongside the famous luggage. Branches: 6 pl St-Germain-des-Prés, 6th (01.45.49.62.32); 54 av Montaigne, 8th (01.45.62.47.00).

Maria Luisa

2 rue Cambon, 1st (01.47.03.96.15). M° Concorde. **Open** 10.30am-7pm Mon-Sat. **Credit** AmEx, DC, MC, V. **Map G5**

Venezuelan Maria Luisa Poumaillou nurtures talented young designers, and was one of Paris' original stockists for Helmut Lang, Ann Demeulemeester, John Galliano and Martine Sitbon. New labels to discover here are knits by Colette Dinnegan and suits by Eric Bergère; there are always a few finds for 1000F or less. Her new men's shop across the street at No 5 features Alexander McQueen, Lang, Demeulemeester, Vivienne Westwood and Yohji Yamamoto.

Martine Sitbon

13 rue de Grenelle, 7th (01.44.39.84.44). M° Rue du Bac or Sèvres-Babylone. **Open** 10.30am-7pm Mon-Sat. **Credit** AmEx, MC, V. **Map G7**

The coloured plexiglass entrance nods to a contemporary art influence in Sitbon's work; within, burnt-out velvet or geometrical abstract dresses bask beneath a huge skylight.

Onward

147 bd St-Germain, 6th (01.55.42.77.56). M°St-Germain-des-Prés. **Open** 10am-7pm Mon; 10am-7pm Tue-Sat. **Credit** AmEx, DC, MC, V. **Map G7**

Completely revamped, this beautiful light-filled store now boasts three levels. The ground stocks accessories and shoes (Jimmy Choo, Dolce & Gabbana, Martine Sitbon), the first showcases a mix of designers (Gaultier, Helmut Lang, Matthew Williamson, Julien McDonald…), while each season one designer gets a basement show. Groovy music, friendly staff. (Prices range from a 500F tulle top to 8000F Helmut Lang coat).

Louis Vuitton *has a new (highly expensive) ready-to-wear line to go with the fancy luggage.*

Prada

10 av Montaigne, 8th (01.53.23.99.40). M° Alma Marceau.
Open 10am-7pm Mon-Sat. **Credit** AmEx, DC, MC, V.
Map D5
In a spacious store, painted in soothing pale avocado green, you'll find menswear, womenswear, accessories, shoes and the inevitable black nylon bag. Miu Miu (10 rue du Cherche-Midi, 6th/01.45.48.63.33), Prada's second line is directional and slightly less astronomically priced.
Branch: 5 rue de Grenelle, 6th (01.45.48.53.14).

Sonia Rykiel

175 bd St-Germain, 6th (01.49.54.60.60). M° St-Germain-des-Prés. **Open** 10am-7pm Mon-Sat. **Credit** AmEx, DC, MC, V. **Map G7**
The First Lady of *Rive Gauche* fashion designs for intellectual *Parisiennes* who want to look sophisticated and relaxed all at once – hence the success of the famous velour 'lounge suit'. Clothes, accessories and cosmetics are shown off in an elegant wood-panelled boutique. And, because this is St-Germain, the windows often display Mme Rykiel's favourite reading matter alongside her designs. Menswear is at No 194.
Branch: 70 rue du Fbg-St-Honoré, 8th (01.42.65.20.81).

Ralph Kemp

18 rue Houdon, 18th (01.46.06.51.05). M° Pigalle. **Open** noon-8pm Mon-Sat **Credit** MC, V. **Map H2**
Housed in effortlessly minimalist boutiques, Parisian Kemp livens up the prescriptive tendencies of French chic with kerb-sweeping coats and radical tailoring that nod at London style. By altering a neckline or adding an unforeseen zip, his designer creations are memorable rather than ridiculous.
Branch: 13 rue du Temple, 4th (01.40.27.14.68).

Spleen

3bis rue des Rosiers, 4th (01.42.74.65.66). M° St-Paul. **Open** 3-7pm Mon; 11am-7pm Tue-Sat; 2-7pm Sun. **Credit** AmEx, DC, MC, V. **Map L6**
This trendy new Marais boutique boasts a divine wrought-iron staircase and impressive selection of designers. Cristina

Bevilacqua's aluminium cable-knits share space with Emilio Cavallini's slinky tops; John Richmond suits hang next to American sportswear by John Bartlett and leather jackets by Lawrence Steele (ex-Prada whizzkid). The space is also a gallery, selling original fashion photography (1000F-4000F).

Victoire

12 pl des Victoires, 2nd (01.42.61.09.02). M° Bourse or Palais-Royal. **Open** 10am-7pm Mon-Sat. **Credit** AmEx, DC, MC, V. **Map H5**
The well-edited mix here dependably spotlights the designer trends, including capsule collections by Donna Karan, Narcisso Rodriguez and hot Brit duo Wilson & Estella. A branch next door carries Victoire's own label at cheaper prices.
Branches: 1 rue Madame, 6th (01.45.44.28.14); 16 rue de Passy, 16th (01.42.88.20.84).

Yohji Yamamoto

3 rue de Grenelle, 6th (01.42.84.28.87). M° Sèvres-Babylone or St-Sulpice. **Open** 10.30am-7pm Mon-Sat.
Credit AmEx, DC, MC, V. **Map G7**
Yohji Yamamoto's starting point for his long asymmetric coats and trendy destructured jackets is the kimono. Y's is his simpler, less-expensive second line.
Branches: 47 rue Etienne-Marcel (mostly menswear), 1st (01.45.08.82.45). Y's: 25 rue du Louvre, 1st (01.42.21.42.93); 69 rue des Sts-Pères, 6th (01.45.48.22.56).

Affordable Chic

Abou Dhabi

10 rue des Francs-Bourgeois, 3rd (01.42.77.96.98). M°St-Paul **Open** 2-7pm Mon; 10.30am-7pm; 2-7pm Sun. **Credit** AmEx, MC, V. **Map L6**
A must for all those with mix-and-match wardrobe problems: rails of stylishly up-to-the-minute clothes (Ange, Les Petites, Tara Jarmon, Toupy, Paul et Joe, Diabless) from 290F to 890F are meticulously arranged according to fabric and colour.

Agnès b

2, 3, 6, 10, 19 rue du Jour, 1st (women 01.45.08.56.56/ men 01.42.33.04.13). Mº Châtelet-Les Halles. **Open** 10am-7pm Mon-Sat. **Credit** AmEx, MC, V. **Map J5**
Agnès b is shorthand for the French take on basic dressing and there's an Agnès b boutique for everyone on rue du Jour. The emphasis is on neutral colours, natural fabrics and durability. Staple leggings and snap-front cardigans underline the designer's real-life approach to fashion, as does the classic men's suit which kitted out the mob in *Reservoir Dogs.* Cotton shirts cost around 500F, cotton knit tops around 400F. Branches: 83 rue d'Assas (baby/child), 6th (01.43.54.69.21); 13 rue Michelet (women), 6th (01.46.33.70.20); 22 rue St-Sulpice (children), 6th (01.40.51.70.69); 6, 10, 12 rue du Vieux-Colombier (women/beauty/children/men), 6th (01.44.39.02.60); 17, 15 av Pierre 1er de Serbie (women/men), 16th (01.47.20.22.44/01.47.23.36.69).

Anne Willi

13 rue Keller, 11th, (01.48.06.74.06). Mº Bastille or Ledru-Rollin. **Open** 2-8pm Mon; 11.30am-8pm Tue-Sat. **Closed** 10-23 Aug. **Credit** MC, V **Map M6**
Designer Anne Willis' stylish boutique-atelier has already attracted a steady stream of regular clients. She makes simple, classic women's clothes in neutral colours and very small quantities. Dresses can be made to measure.

A.P.C.

3 (women) and 4 (men) rue de Fleurus, 6th (01.42.22.12.77). Mº St-Placide. **Open** 10.30am-7pm Mon-Sat. **Credit** AmEx, MC, V. **Map G8**
Atelier de Production et de Création is a fave with design students and fashion editors, with its hip leather jackets, A-line minis, drainpipe trousers and skinny-rib knits inspired by French *nouvelle vague* films, in similar versions for men and women. Colours run from black to tan. Prices are reasonable; the clothes stylish. Magasin Général APC (45 rue Madame, 6th/ 01.45.48.72.42) holds designer Jean Toitou's collection from his travels: from olive oil to New York firemen's T-shirts. Branch: 25bis rue Benjamin Franklin, 16th (01.45.53.28.28).

Diapositive

42 rue du Four, 6th (01.45.48.85.57). Mº Sèvres-Babylone. **Open** 11am-7pm Mon; 10.30am-7pm Tue-Sat. Closed two weeks in Aug. **Credit** AmEx, MC, V. **Map H7**
A well-priced collection (suits around 2500F) of own-label co-ordinated casual and career separates, both tailored and knit, that hew to a minimalist bent, with a few fun items, such as a red velvet coat. Shoes, jewellery and housewares too.

Episode

277 rue St Honoré, 8th (01.49.26.01.48). Mº Concorde. **Open** 10am-7pm Mon-Sat. **Credit** AmEx, MC, V. **Map G4**
Everything in this spacious, well-lit store is so beautifully displayed that the prices – around 1500F for a jacket – come as a surprise. The line emphasises a low-key chic, with a lot of honeyed neutrals offset by black for day, and gold for evening. The coats and jackets are the best investments here. Branch: 47 rue Bonaparte, 6th (01.43.29.13.19).

Et Vous

25 rue Royale, 8th (01.47.42.31.00). Mº Madeleine. **Open** 10.30am-7pm Mon-Sat. **Credit** AmEx, DC, MC, V. **Map F4**
Andrée Putman designed the sleek flagship of this French group, a useful source of contemporary clothes to wear to work. Fashionably cut neutral-coloured suits are set off by more flamboyant shirts, with jackets from around 1500F, dresses 1000F. Et Vous Stock at 17 rue de Turbigo, 2nd (01.40.13.04.12), sells discontinued items and collection prototypes at half price. Branches include: 6 rue des Francs-Bourgeois (women), 3rd (01.42.71.75.11); 46 rue du Four, 6th (01.45.44.70.21); 72 rue de Passy (women), 16th (01.45.20.47.15).

Heaven

83 rue des Martyrs, 18th (01.44.92.92.92) Mº Pigalle. **Open** Tue-Sat 11am-7.30pm; Mon, Sun 2pm-7pm **Credit** MC, V. Closed one-two weeks in Aug. **Map H2**
Up in offbeat Montmartre, Vivienne Westwood-style bustles, tweeds and tartans are made up at the rear of the shop. These are good value, original but not crazy clothes. Lots of aubergine and plum colours. Jewellery, too.

Antoine et Lili: *the perfect place for a designer shower curtain or Mexican good-luck charm.*

Isabel Marant

16 rue de Charonne, 11th (01.49.29.71.55).
M° Ledru-Rollin. **Open** 2-7pm Mon, 10.30am-7.30pm Tue-Sat. **Credit** AmEx, MC, V. **Map M7.**
Shooting out of nowhere, Isabel Marant offers a range characterised by long, long skirts, big knit pullovers, some ethnotrendy brocades. Marant brings in multi-cultural references to create funky, wearable clothes which are mostly long, sexy and figure-hugging, but never constricting – but what do you do with your arms in that knitted alpaca poncho dress?

Junk by Junko Shimada

54 rue Etienne-Marcel, 2nd. (01.42.36.36.97).
M° Etienne-Marcel. **Open** 10am-7pm Mon-Sat. **Credit** AmEx, MC, V. **Map J5**
Shimada's clothes have the colourful ebullience of streetwear, at street prices, and will make it through the wash. Great denim summerwear, cool T-shirts and wacky accessories for all.

Martin Grant

32 rue des Rosiers, 4th (01.42.71.39.49). M° St-Paul.
Open 1-7.30pm Tue-Sat. Closed two weeks in Aug.
Credit AmEx, MC, V. **Map L6**
The very first Australian couture outlet in Paris is on show in an old Marais hairdresser's shop. The shop's beautiful tiled floors and red velvet chairs provide the perfect setting for Grant's impeccably cut suits, exquisite evening wear and strappy summer dresses. In spite of the fact that Grant can list the likes of Claudia and Helena among his customers, prices are extremely reasonable (800F-3700F).

Mon Ami Pierlot

3 rue Montmartre, 1st (01.40.28.45.55). M° Les Halles.
Open 10.15am-7.15pm Mon-Sat. Closed three weeks in Aug. **Credit** AmEx, MC, V. **Map J5**
Claudie Pierlot's less expensive, mostly natural-fabric, basics for women, men and children. For women Claudie tends to go in for girly silhouettes – think cute little shift dresses – and retro styles – think stripey ribbed knits, seaman's sweaters and prints.

Plein Sud

21 rue des Francs-Bourgeois, 4th (01.42.72.10.60).
M° St-Paul. **Open** 11am-7pm Mon-Sat. **Credit** AmEx, MC, V. **Map L6**
Fayçal Amor appears to design with a skeletal size 8 in mind, but don't let that put you off if you're into spiky three-inch heels, extavagantly *décolleté* evening wear and skirts slit to kingdom come. Or, if you're after a more subtle effect, go for a fab full-length leather coat teamed with over-the-knee boots.
Branch: 70bis rue de Bonaparte, 6th (01.43.54.43.06).

Tara Jarmon

18 rue du Four, 6th (01.46.33.26.60). M° Mabillon. **Open** 10.30am-7.15pm Mon-Sat. **Credit** AmEx, V. **Map H7**
Modern, feminine, uncomplicated and affordable, this Canadian's designs have scored a big hit with trendy 20- and 30 somethings. Tara's sunny, two-storey boutique in the heart of St-Germain is filled with neat fitted jackets, beautifully lined skirts and fabulous winter coats.

Zadig et Voltaire

1 rue du Vieux-Colombier, 6th (01.43.29.18.29).
M° St-Sulpice. **Open** 10.30am-7.30pm Mon-Sat. **Credit** AmEx, DC, V. **Map G7**
Cool yet comfortable Yoshi Kondo, Helmut Lang Jeans, All Saints and own-label coats and casual wear (lots of navy, grey and black) are complemented by Zadig et Voltaire's fantastic handbags (from around 400F) in clever combinations of leather, suede, nylon, velvet or flannel.
Branches: 15 rue du Jour, 1st (01.42.21.88.70); 4, 12 rue Ste-Croix-de-la-Bretonnerie, 4th (01.42.72.09.55/ 01.42.72.15.20).

Club heaven chez **Kllwatch** *(see page 206).*

Highstreet, Street & Clubwear

Antoine et Lili

90 rue des Martyrs, 18th (01.42.58.10.22). M° Abbesses.
Open 11am-8pm Mon-Fri; 10.30am-8pm Sat; 2-7.30pm Sun. **Credit** AmEx, MC, V. **Map H2**
This kitsch fuschia, lime and banana-yellow store sells Antoine et Lili's popular clothes (Lurex top 249F; floor-length coat 890F), plus enticing if pricey gifts. Service with a smile.
Branches: Forum des Halles, 1st (01.42.36.89.54); 100 rue Réaumur, 2nd (01.42.36.09.81); 7 rue de l'Alboni, 16th (01.45.27.95.00)

Bonnie Cox

38 rue des Abbesses, 18th (01.42.54.95.68). M°Abbesses.
Open 11am-8pm daily. **Credit** AmEx, DC, MC, V. **Map H1**
This funky Montmartre boutique was first in Paris to stock Xúly Bet, winning a reputation as a showcase for fresh new talent. Clothes have sobered up a bit since but still run the gamut from quirky to clubby (Traoré, Sissi, Toi du Monde and Custo T-shirts), along with its own reasonably priced leather coats (2800F), denim cowboy hats (195F), and 'young designer' jewellery. A new Bonnie Cox boutique (62 galerie Vivienne, 2nd/01.42.60.05.00) stocks wacky housewares.

Le Forum des Créateurs

Forum des Halles, Porte Berger, level -1, 1st
(01.44.76.96.56). M° Châtelet-Les Halles. **Open** 11am-7.30pm Mon-Sat. **Credit** varies with shop. **Map J5**
The decline of Les Halles led to several vacant shops being let out to a group of young designers. A few like Malian father of salvage Xúly Bet were already getting known; many still await discovery. Often the boutiques are shared, with accessories as well as clothes. Look out for Pedro Williams Borquez. Emphasis is on the colourful and streetwise.

All change on the fashion front

Bernard Arnault, director of LVMH (which owns several fashion houses, along with the bubbly) started the Great Shake-Up in 1996, when he gave the top design job at Dior to Brit fashion eccentric John Galliano and installed Alexander McQueen as Galliano's successor at Givenchy. The ladies-who-lunch sat quaking at the prospect of 'bum-crack' *décolletés* and heroin chic; in fact, they ended up with a wardrobe of Masai warrior dresses and Amazonian jungle couture. A furious game of musical chairs ensued, as other top fashion houses set to revamping their image by appointing hot young designers from overseas.

The Brit invasion continued when Chloé hired Beatles offspring Stella McCartney, fresh out of St Martin's and virtually unknown, as head designer. Her highly acclaimed debut collection answered the fashion backstabbers, but critics were less gentle second time around, accusing her of sending models down the runway dressed like tacky old slappers. Was the love affair with Cool Britannia cooling?

So it proved. When Arnault decided to revamp Louis Vuitton, he passed over a new wave of British fashion eccentrics. Vuitton's much-faked monogrammed luggage was losing its cred with the international jetset and turning into an airport accessory for Japanese tourists. Noting how Italian leather-goods company Gucci had made a miraculous comeback after hiring hip young American Tom Ford, Arnault signed Marc Jacobs, the darling of New York fashion editors. Ironically, Jacobs had launched his career championing 'grunge chic', in a notorious collection of fleamarket fabrics printed to look like flannel; now he was to design cashmere sweaters and luxury silk skirts for Vuitton's very wearable (if very expensive) new *prêt-à-porter* line. But it's not all middle-aged chic: Jacobs' second show for Vuitton included wacky ponchos, funky velvet and plastic bikinis and cheeky bum-revealing shorts.

Rumours of a new era of American influence in Paris seemed confirmed when another leading French fashion house, Céline, appointed hip young New Yorker Michael Kors. Kors, who believes in 'mixing Zen-style minimalism with luxury and glamour', has completely transformed

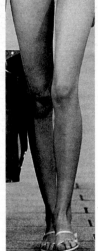

Céline's middle-aged *madame* image. His Garbo-inspired Fall/Winter 98 show was a huge hit, with models sporting huge raccoon stoles thrown over vicuna sweaters and cashmere coats. Céline's new store on avenue Montaigne reportedly did a million francs worth of sales in its first six days.

Meanwhile, Spanish leather goods company Loewe (which recently joined the LVMH stable) hired brilliant young Cuban-American designer Narciso Rodriguez to launch its ready-to-wear line. Best known for designing *that* wedding dress for Caroline Bessett-Kennedy, Rodriguez has created three collections of classic minimalist chic for Loewe, while letting the wilder streaks of his creative imagination run riot on the catwalks of Milan. Like Galliano, McQueen, Jacobs and Kors before him, his contract allows him to continue designing his own line in tandem with his house's ready-to-wear.

Guy Laroche took a different approach. Instead of appointing a star designer who would divide his time between his own line and Laroche, company president Ralph Toledano began scouting for an up-and-coming talent who would design exclusively for Guy Laroche. He came up with virtual unknown Alber Elbaz, who'd spent seven years in the US as a lowly assistant to Geoffrey Beene. Quirky 37-year-old Elbaz, born in Casablanca but raised in Tel Aviv, was soon taking international catwalks by storm with floaty, feminine, flower-stencilled dresses and sequinned tulle. 'Women can walk in my clothes and go from a cab to a party,' he says. 'They don't have to be zipped up and carried.'

Elbaz's sophisticatedly simple designs soon caught the attention of Yves Saint Laurent president Pierre Bergé; just two years on, he was hired to design the *prêt-à-porter* at YSL. (Yves, looking dreamy himself as a dream-team of models paraded his clothes at the opening ceremony of the World Cup final, will devote himself to *haute couture*). Elbaz's old job went to Ronald van der Kemp, a 33-year-old Dutch designer who'd made his name designing the women's collection for Barneys New York. Van der Kemp in turn made a major impact on the French fashion scene in March 98 with his collection of witty, well-tailored clothes.

At Balmain, natty young Singapore-born designer Andrew Gn failed to impress the buyers at his first show. He was promptly replaced by Gilles Dufour from Chanel, who promised a fashionable but wearable collection *à la française*. Other Paris fashion houses have also started looking to homegrown talent. Kenzo recently snapped up Gilles Rosier (of GR816 fame) and the young design team Mariot Chanet is now working for the famous French swimwear company Erès.

The French fashion old guard soldiers on, withstanding the onslaught from the American minimalists. Jean-Paul Gaultier, the 40-year-old *enfant terrible*, recently launched a critically acclaimed collection of *haute couture* (which has the cognoscenti whispering about Jean-Paul taking over from Yves Saint Laurent one of these days). Despite being stuck in an 80s timewarp of hourglass curves and power shoulders, Thierry Mugler also remains popular – though the one-sleeved white toga dresses at his Fall/Winter 98 show left everyone looking rather bemused.

Among France's own rising stars, 30-year-old cosmopolitan Isabel Marant (her father was French, her designer mother German and her stepmother French Caribbean) is renowned for using multi-cultural influences to create funky, wearable clothes. Young Marseillaise designer Fred Sathal is another hot talent on the indie fashion scene. One of fifteen *jeunes créateurs* invited to show at the Carrousel du Louvre in October 1998, she sent out a superbly tailored collection of wild and eccentric clothes (from asymmetric leather and suede dresses to a flamboyant beaded jacket with Elvis collar), and was listed by *Harper's Bazaar* as one of the top ten designers to watch.

Jérôme Dreyfuss, 24, is also being touted as a future great. Discovered by British style guru Isabella Blow (the woman who helped catapult Alexander McQueen to Givenchy), he made an explosive début in March 98 with a collection of raw-edged cowhide dresses. Dreyfuss displayed a penchant for stitching snake skeletons and lizard claws onto hems and seams, and says he gets 'a kick out of transforming primitive, raw materials into glamorous, structured clothes.' Other names to look for (and invest in before their prices rise) include Eric Bergère and Christian Le Dresdeno.

Finally, it remains to be seen if ultra-hyped Jeremy Scott – one American-in-Paris definitely not into clean lines and minimalist chic – will ever score a top job at a major French house. For the moment, Scott's one-legged trousers, asymmetric gold shoulders and 'nude' tutus are considered rather too outré for avenue Montaigne.

Futurware Lab

2 rue Piémontési, 18th (01.42.23.66.08). M° Abbesses.
Open 11am-8pm Mon-Sat; 2pm-8pm Sun **Credit** AmEx,
MC, V. **Map H2**

Trained in costume design, including a stint at the Comédie
Française, Tatiana Lebedev finds inspiration for her conceptual clothing in religion and folklore. The
trailing hemlines hint at Orthodox priests, the colours are
bold but earthy, while the entwining layers recall the
designer's Russian roots. Her retro-cyberesque creations
are constructed from a range of unusual (although not
uncomfortable) fabrics, including padded aluminium and
neoprene sponge. Futurware Lab takes itself a bit too seriously, but neverthless warrants recognition for its daring
convention-flouting.

Kiliwatch

*64 rue Tiquetonne, 2nd (01.42.21.17.37). M°Etienne-
Marcel.* **Open** 1-7pm Mon; 10.30am-7pm Tue-Sat. **Credit**
AmEx, MC, V. **Map J5**

The new-look Kiliwatch is a vast hangar filled with pumping techno sounds and endless clothes-rails. There is still an
extensive selection of 'quality-controlled' second-hand
clothes (leather coats 850F, jackets 350F, shirts 160F), but
also many new lines: G-star, All Saints, Futurware Lab and
its own clubby label. A kiosque is stacked with CDs, vinyl,
international magazines, flyers and Kiliwatch's club guide
Close Combat.

Kookaï

*2 rue Gustave-Courbet, 16th (01.47.55.18.00).
M° Trocadéro.* **Open** 10.30am-7.30pm Mon-Sat. Closed
two weeks in Aug. **Credit** AmEx, DC, MC, V. **Map B5**

Kookaï specialises in transferring the latest looks from catwalk
to high street – fast. Lines are often not the same as the more
upmarket exports. Stock changes frequently, ranging from
wafty floral dresses to more Goth fake fur coats. Look for coats
under 1000F; skirts, dresses and sweaters around 200F.
Branches include: pl Carrée, Forum des Halles, 1st
(01.40.26.59.11); Kookaï Stock, 82 rue Réaumur, 2nd
(01.45.08.93.69); 155 rue de Rennes, 6th (01.45.48.26.36).

Morgan

*16 rue de Turbigo,2nd (01.44.82.02.00). M° Etienne-
Marcel.* **Open** 11am-8pm Mon; 10.30am-8pm Tue-Sat
Credit AmEx, DC, MC, V. **Map J5**

Morgan used to target tacky teens (think plunging cleav-
ages and skin-tight Lycra), but in the wake of a 'sophisticated but sexy' ad campaign the Sentier label recently
underwent a major revamp to translate stylish designer
looks hot off the catwalk. Shoppers are pampered to the max
at the new flagship store, which boasts ludicrously large
changing rooms, mini-bar refreshments and a film-star red
carpet on the stairs.

Patricia Louisor

*16 rue Houdon, 18th (01.42.62.10.42). M°Abbesses or
Pigalle.* **Open** 11am-8pm daily. **Credit** MC, V. **Map H2**

This tiny Montmartre boutique soons gets you in party mood
as one of the three energetic sisters who run it is guaranteed
to be playing her favourite tapes at the till. Patricia designs
upmarket bohemian chic (wide-legged trousers, floor-length
dresses, mohair jumpers), but the boutique also stocks club-
bier pieces by young designers. See, too, Hortensia Louisor's
funky designs for babies and mothers-to-be round the corner (14 rue Clauzel, 9th/01.45.26.67.68).

Le Shop

*3 rue d'Argout, 2nd (01.40.28.95.94). M° Etienne-
Marcel.* **Open** 1-7pm Mon; 11am-7pm Tue-Sat. Closed
two weeks in Aug. **Credit** AmEx, MC, V. **Map J5**

Whether they're into riding waves, concrete or cyberspace, this
huge, market-like collection of individual outlets will keep
teenagers amused for hours. Lines include Lady Soul, Crw, and

Freaks. The café downstairs is a good place for a chill out, if
you can make yourself heard over the pounding techno music.

Terrain Vogue

13 rue Keller, 11th (01.43.14.03.23). M° Bastille. **Open**
noon-8pm Mon-Sat. Closed two weeks in Aug. **Credit**
AmEx, DC, MC, V. **Map M6**

This streetwise second-hand shop is good on 70s psychedelic
boots and skinny ribs. It has a clubwear line, plus young
designers, T-shirts from BD Curso, hologram T-shirts by
Julien Brunois, and psychedelic underwear by Eminence.

Toi du Monde

7 rue du Jour, 1st (01.40.13.09.32). M° Les Halles.
Open 1-7pm Mon; 10.30am-7pm Tue-Sat. **Credit** AmEx,
DC, MC, V. **Map J5**

Recuperated wood and suspended mini-lights set off youth-
ful female garb. Bright colours, lots of stretch.
Branches: 24 rue de Sévigné, 4th (01.42.72.24.23); 3 rue
Montfaucon, 6th (01.46.34.01.19).

Zara

2 rue Halévy, 9th (01.44.71.90.90). M° Opéra. **Open** 10am-
7.30pm Mon-Sat. **Credit** AmEx, DC, MC, V. **Map G4**

The Spanish Next has stormed Paris with affordable clothes
for women who work (dresses around 400F, jackets around
550F). The choice is wide, but fabrics can be flimsy. There's
also casualwear, menswear and trendy kids' gear.
Branches: 128 rue de Rivoli, 1st (01.44.82.64.00);
45 rue de Rennes, 6th (01.44.39.03.50); 59 rue de Sèvres,
6th (01.45.44.61.60); 44 av des Champs-Elysées, 8th
(01.45.61.52.80).

Mainly Men

See also **Agnès b**, **Sonia Rykiel**, **Et Vous** and,
below, **Jeans & Casual Wear**.

Façonnable

9 rue du Fbg-St-Honoré, 8th (01.47.42.72.60).
M° Concorde. **Open** 10am-7pm Mon-Sat.
Credit AmEx, DC, MC, V. **Map F4**

A male *BCBG* haven where new suits smell like old money.
Upstairs find executive suits (average 4500F), shoes and luggage. The ground floor stocks trad hunting jackets, jeans, an
impressive range of silk ties (450F) and Liberty-print boxers.
Branch: 174 bd St-Germain, 6th (01.40.49.02.47).

Flower

7 rue Chomel, 7th (01.42.22.11.78). M° Sèvres-Babylone.
Open noon-7pm Mon-Thur; 11am-7pm Fri, Sat. Closed
Aug. **Credit** MC, V. **Map G7**

Ousui Nakamura showcases the latest trends for men, including clothes by Alexander McQueen, Marc Le Bihan, Raf Simons
and Japan's Nepenthes, and has recently added women's
wear. Unusual accessories by Vava Dudu and Bill Amberg.

Paul Smith

22 bd Raspail, 7th (01.42.84.15.75). M° Rue du Bac.
Open 11.30am-7pm Mon; 10am-7pm Tue-Sat.
Credit AmEx, DC, MC, V. **Map G7**

Le style anglais in a wood-panelled interior. Smith's great
suits and classic shoes are on the upper floor, while women
and kids get a funkier space below.

Victoire Hommes

15 rue du Vieux-Colombier, 6th (01.45.44.28.02).
M° St-Sulpice. **Open** 10am-7pm Mon-Sat. **Credit** AmEx,
MC, V. **Map G7**

The menswear annexe of the famed Victoire women's boutiques specialises in casual sportswear, with some suits;
shoes by Sam Walker Cheaney.
Branch: 10-12 rue du Colonel-Driant, 1st (01.42.97.44.87).

Jeans & Casual Wear

Autour du Monde

*12 rue des Francs-Bourgeois, 3rd (01.42.77.16.18). M°
St-Paul.* **Open** 2-7pm Mon; 10.30am-7pm Tue-Sat; 2-7pm
Sun. **Credit** AmEx, MC, V. **Map L6**
Wholesome, casual classics for both sexes in plain colours and
natural fabrics. 8 rue des Francs-Bourgeois (01.42.77.06.08)
has younger gear and Shaker-influenced housewares.
Branch: 54 rue de Seine, 6th (01.43.54.64.47).

Blanc Bleu

14 pl des Victoires, 2nd (01.42.96.05.40). M° Bourse.
Open 11am-7pm Mon; 10am-7pm Tue-Sat. **Credit**
AmEx, DC, MC, V. **Map H5**
'Gentleman skipper' chic infuses Patrick Khayat's line of clas-
sic sportswear, including cotton tops, often in navy and white.
Branches: 18 rue Royale, 8th (01.42.96.26.10); 5 bd
Malesherbes, 8th (01.47.42.02.18).

Loft Design By

*12 rue du Fbg-St-Honoré, 8th (01.42.65.59.65).
M° Concorde or Madeleine.* **Open** 10am-7pm Mon-Sat.
Credit AmEx, DC, MC, V. **Map F4**
This is where the French came before Gap. Menswear is gen-
erally better than the women's, with lots of navy, grey and
taupe. Prices seem dear for casualwear but the cut is all French.
Branches: 12 rue de Sévigné, 4th (01.48.87.13.07); 56 rue de
Rennes, 6th (01.45.44.88.99); 22 av de la Grande Armée,
17th (01.45.72.13.53).

Lingerie & Swimwear

Capucine Puerari

*63 rue des Sts-Pères, 6th (01.42.22.14.09). M° St-
Germain-des-Prés.* **Open** 10am-7pm Mon-Sat. Closed two
weeks in Aug. **Credit** AmEx, MC, V. **Map G7**
From modern, sexy and fashionable lingerie and swimwear
to a ready-to-wear, trendy collection in the same spirit.

Erès

2 rue Tronchet, 8th (01.47.42.28.82). M°Madeleine.
Open Mon-Sat 10am-7pm Mon-Sat. **Credit** AmEx, DC,
MC, V. **Map G4**
Stylish *Parisiennes* from 18-80 will kill to own the latest Erès
swimwear. The swimsuits, cut in quality fabric, come in all
styles from demure belted one-piece to sexy Bond Girl bikini
(you can buy bikini tops and bottoms in different sizes). Erès
recently caused a major splash by hiring French design duo
Mariot Chanet to launch a range of simple yet luxury lingerie.
Branches: 4bis rue du Cherche-Midi, 6th (01.45.44.95.54); 6
rue Guichard, 16th (01.46.47.45.21).

Laurence Tavernier

*7 rue du Pré-aux-Clercs, 7th (01.49.27.03.95). M° Rue du
Bac.* **Open** 10am-7pm Mon-Sat. Closed 10-20 Aug.
Credit MC, V. **Map G6**
Some of the lingerie here looks smart enough to dine out in.
The last word in wool and cashmere bathrobes (1900F) and
slippers (900F), designed by the sister of film director Bertrand.

Sabbia Rosa

*73 rue des Sts-Pères, 6th. (01.45.48.88.37). M° St-
Germain-des-Prés.* **Open** 10am-7pm Mon-Sat. **Credit**
AmEx, MC, V. **Map G7**
Moana Moati has been steering pampered Parisian wives,
execs (50 per cent of the clientele is men) and models to the
right silk undies in varying degrees of naughtiness for the past
22 years. 800F for a string bikini; babydoll nighties for 6000F.

Designer Bargains & Vintage

Second hand can be chic if it has a designer label
attached, but don't expect it to be particularly cheap
(look for the sign *dépôt-vente*). Rue d'Alésia, in the
14th, is packed with discount factory outlets (look
for 'Stock' in the name), while trendy club outlets
like Kiliwatch and Terrain Vogue mix new and old.

Terrain Vogue: *from hologram T-shirts to psychedelic undies.*

Cécile et Jeanne *where modern art meets costume jewellery.*

Alternatives

18 rue du Roi-de-Sicile, 4th (01.42.78.31.50). M° St-Paul.
Open 11am-1pm, 2.30-7pm Tue-Sat. Closed 15 July-15
Aug. **Credit** MC, V. **Map K/L6**
Martine Bergossi accepts only the most trendy of cast-offs
in top condition, such as Jean-Paul Gaultier, Hermès, Dries
Van Noten and Comme des Garçons. Prices 400F-3000F.

La Clef des Marques

*20 pl du Marché St-Honoré, 1st (01.47.03.90.40). M°
Tuileries.* **Open** 12.30-7pm Mon; 10.30am-2.45pm, 3.30-
7pm Tue-Fri; 10.30am-7pm Sat. **Credit** MC, V. **Map G5**
In a glossy two-storey space designed by architect Ricardo
Bofill, this chain carries clothes for men, women and children,
with new merchandise arriving regularly. Clothing is a hotch
potch, often a season or more old, and can look shopworn.
Still, you might find a good pair of Ferre or Gaultier trousers
in the 300F range, ski wear or a pair of Doc Martens for 250F.
Branches: 126 bd Raspail, 6th (01.45.49.31.00); 86 rue du
Fbg-St-Antoine, 11th (01.40.01.95.15).

Didier Ludot

*20-24 galerie Montpensier, 1st (01.42.96.06.56).
M°Palais-Royal.* **Open** Mon-Sat 10.30am-7pm **Credit**
AmEx, DC, V. **Map H5**
Walk in to this wall-to-wall wardrobe of vintage couture and
try on a Jacques Fath dress, an original 50s Chanel suit, or 70s
beaded Dior. A favourite haunt of supermodels; Miuccia Prada
and Demi Moore have been known to fly in just to rifle through
the impressive collection of shoes and crocodile handbags.

L'Habilleur

*44 rue de Poitou, 3rd (01.48.87.77.12).
M° St-Sébastien-Froissart.* **Open** 11am-8pm Mon-Sat.
Credit MC, V. **Map L5**
From the smartly attired mannequins in the window, you
wouldn't guess that the clothes here are *dégriffés* – end-of-
line and off-the-catwalk clothes and accessories bought
direct from designers like Martine Sitbon, Patrick Cox, John
Richmond, Olivier Strelli and Plein Sud and sold half price.

Le Mouton à Cinq Pattes

*19 rue Grégoire de Tours, 6th (01.43.29.73.56). M°
Odéon.* **Open** 10.30am-7.30pm Mon-Fri; 10.30am-8pm
Sat. **Credit** AmEx, MC, V. **Map H7**
Shopping here can be a scrum, but many people swear by the
bargains. Many are *dégriffés* (with their label cut out), so you
need to know what you're looking for to recognise the Gaultier,
Helmut Lang, Claude Montana and Martine Sitbon pieces.
Branches: 15 rue Vieille-du-Temple, 4th (01.42.71.86.30);
138 bd St-Germain, 6th (01.43.26.49.25); 8 (women), 10
(children), 18 (women, men) and 48 (men) rue St-Placide,
6th (01.45.48.86.26).

Réciproque

*88, 89, 92, 95, 97, 101, 123 rue de la Pompe, 16th
(01.47.04.82.24/01.47.04.30.28). M° Rue de la Pompe.*
Open 11am-7.30pm Tue-Fri; 10.30am-7.30pm Sat. Closed
Aug. **Credit** AmEx, MC, V. **Map H7**
The doyenne of Paris' *dépôt-ventes*, Réciproque's side-by-side
second-hand boutiques are the answer for those with *couture*
taste and limited bank accounts. Prices are not as cheap, however, (3000F for a good-condition Dior or Chanel suit, 1300F
for a Prada dress) as you might hope. Menswear too.

Jewellery & Accessories

Cécile et Jeanne

215 rue St-Honoré, 1st (01.42.61.68.68). M° Tuileries.
Open 11am-7pm Mon-Sat. **Credit** AmEx, DC, MC, V.
Map G5
Wire-and-resin creations and modern art-inspired brooches
by two young designers in a colourful baroque setting.
Branches: Carrousel du Louvre, 1st 01.42.61.26.15); 12 rue
des Francs-Bourgeois, 3rd (01.44.61.00.99); 4 rue de Sèvres,
6th (01.42.22.82.82); 49 av Daumesnil, 12th (01.43.41.24.24).

Devana
30 rue de Sévigné, 4th (01.42.78.69.76). M°St Paul.
Open 2-7pm Mon, Sun; 11am-7pm Tue-Sat. **Credit**
AmEx, MC, V. **Map L6**
A stylish showcase for Danish designer Jacob Taga-Jorgensen,
whose jewellery ranges from chunky unisex bracelets and armbands to delicate silver chains entwined with precious stones.
Glance down as you enter and give your regards to Shamballa,
the python who lives in a glass box set into the parquet. Don't
worry: Shamballa only comes out to snack after closing time.

Hermès
24 rue du Fbg-St-Honoré, 8th (01.40.17.47.17).
M° Concorde. **Open** 10am-1pm, 2.15-6.30pm Mon;
10am-6.30pm Tue-Sat. Hours vary in July, Aug. **Credit**
AmEx, DC, MC, V. **Map F4**
The department store to end all department stores, at least
if you are seriously rich and the idea of dropping 10,000F on
a Kelly handbag doesn't faze you. Hermès sells everything
from saddles to jewellery, housewares, shoes, plus Hermès'
trademark silk scarves (about 1420F) and ready-to-wear by
invisible man Martin Margiela.

Jamin Puech
61 rue d'Hauteville, 10th (01.40.22.08.32). M° Bonne-
Nouvelle or Poissonnière. **Open** 9.30am-6.30pm Mon-Fri.
Credit MC, V. **Map K3**
Trendy handbag designers Isabelle Puech and Benoît Jamin
recently opened their first store in a former paper-goods
shop. Their unpretentious yet wildly inventive handbags
and carry-alls use a mad mix of materials from crocheted
twine to printed satin plaid canvas. Prices 90F-1800F.

Madeleine Gély
218 bd St-Germain, 7th (01.42.22.63.35). M° Rue du
Bac. **Open** 10am-7pm Tue-Sat. Closed Aug. **Credit** MC,
V. **Map G6**
This shop, spilling over with umbrellas and canes, probably
hasn't changed much since opening in 1834. Short or long,
plain or fancy, there's an umbrella or cane here for everyone.

Marie Streichenberger
23 rue du Cherche-Midi, 6th (01.45.44.93.02). M° Sèvres-
Babylone. **Open** 10am-7pm Mon-Sat. **Credit** AmEx, MC,
V. **Map G7**
Marie Streichenberger has designed for dozens of Paris fashion houses, including Dior, Kenzo and Montana, as well as
bags, belts and jewellery for Thierry Mugler and Donna
Karan. This shop showcases her own reasonably priced
lines, such as Art Deco lacework silver bracelets (440F-650F).

Les Montres
58 rue Bonaparte, 6th (01.46.34.71.38). M° Mabillon or
St-Germain-des-Prés. **Open** 10am-7pm Mon-Sat. **Credit**
AmEx, DC, MC, V. **Map H7**
Status-symbol watches for any occasion, among them Swiss
and American models for men and women. There are also
collectors' watches, such as vintage Rolexes from the 1920s.
Branch: 40 rue de Passy, 16th (01.53.92.51.61).

Naïla de Monbrison
6 rue de Bourgogne, 7th (01.47.05.11.15). M° Solférino.
Open 11.30am-1.30pm, 2.30-7pm Tue-Sat. Closed Aug.
Credit AmEx, MC, V. **Map F6**
A showcase for contemporary jewellery by world-famous
names: Juliette Polac, Dominique Biard, Marcial Berro,
Giorgio Vigna… Real works of art – at prices to match.

Pallas
21 rue St-Roch, 1st (01.42.61.13.21). M° Tuileries. **Open**
9am-7pm Mon-Fri; 2-7pm Sat. Closed first three weeks in
Aug. **Credit** AmEx, DC, MC, V. **Map G5**
Elsa Zanetti has been making handbags for the couture
houses – including Fath and Balenciaga for years. Designs

range from classic box leather shoulderbags to tassled and
embroidered evening pouches. All the handbags (400F-
3000F) are manufactured in an *atelier* in the back, and you
can order what you like in different colours.

Sac & Sac
30 rue des Abbesses, 18th (01.42.64.51.11).
M° Abbesses. **Open** 3-7.30pm Mon; 10.30am-1.30pm, 3-
7.30pm Tue-Fri; 10.30am-7.30pm Sat; 11am-2pm Sun.
Credit AmEx, DC, MC, V. **Map H2**
Sisterly duo Valérie and Gabrielle design their own line of
reasonably priced handbags and purses (100F-595F), following the fashion flow in fabric. But the
charm of this tiny Montmartre boutique lies in the glasses,
vases, jewellery and other gift ides which the sisters bring
back from trips to Spain, Vietnam and Morocco.

Sisso's
20 rue Malher, 4th (01.44.61.99.50). M°St Paul **Open**
Mon-Sat 10am-7pm. **Credit** AmEx, V. **Map L6**
One of the most talked-about addresses in town, this is a one-
stop glamour shop where you can pick up everything from
Prada and Hogan shoes to Sequoia leather clutch bags and
exquisite handmade jewellery by Kathy Korvin and the
exciting new Franco-Italian design duo Rafia & Bossa.

Ursule Beaugeste
15 rue Oberkampf, 11th (01.49.23.02.48).
M° Oberkampf. **Open** 11am-7pm Mon-Fri. **Credit** MC, V.
Map M5
Along with its trendy bars and cafés, Ménilmontant is now
moving on to the fashion map and designer Anne Grand-
Clément is one of the reasons. Elle Mcpherson and other fashion pacesetters come to this plum-coloured boutique with its
50s retro furnishings for her crocheted shopping bags and
dressy little tweed handbags.

Hats

Divine
39 rue Daguerre, 14th (01.43.22.28.10). M° Denfert-
Rochereau. **Open** 10.30am-1pm, 3-7.30pm Tue-Sat.
Closed three weeks in Aug. **Credit** DC, MC, V. **Map G10**
An unexpected treasure trove of new and vintage hats for
men and women to suit all sartorial styles, pockets and occa-
sions – including traditional straw boaters, floppy velvet, genuine Basque berets and never-worn 1920s lacy cloches.

Elvis Pompilio
62 rue des Sts-Pères, 7th (01.45 44.82.02). M° St-
Germain-des-Prés. **Open** 2-7pm Mon; 11am-7pm Tue-Sat.
Closed two weeks in Aug. **Credit** AmEx, MC, V. **Map G7**
This young Belgian hat designer is a source for creative
headgear at reasonable prices (350F-1500F). Think multi-
coloured feathers soaring from a satin stovepipe, dalmation
spots or hats stuffed with spongy yellow stars or pompoms.

Marie Mercié
23 rue St-Sulpice, 6th (01.43.26.45.83). M° Odéon. **Open**
11am-7pm Mon-Sat. **Credit** AmEx, DC, MC, V. **Map H7**
Marie Mercié is the mad hatter who put everyone in big-
crowned skypieces, revolutionising the hat industry in our
times. There are colourful felt hats in winter, straw and silks
in summer, in styles that go from classic to theatrical. One-
offs cost from 2500F, the season's lines 1000F-2500F.
Branch: 56 rue Tiquetonne, 2nd (01.40.26.60.68).

Têtes en l'Air
65 rue des Abbesses, 18th (01.46.06.71.19).
M° Abbesses. **Open** 2-7pm Mon; 10.30am-7.30pm Tue-
Sat. Closed Aug. **No credit cards. Map H1**
Attention-seeking hats, be it the lemon-yellow and lime-

green head contraption with a canary in a cage on top, or the Christmas tree. Hats can be made to measure.

Shoes

Accessoire Diffusion
6 rue du Cherche-Midi, 6th (01.45.48.36.08). M° Sèvres-Babylone or St-Sulpice **Open** 10am-7pm Mon-Sat. Closed two weeks in Aug. **Credit** AmEx, MC, V. **Map G7**
A French chain selling well-made fashionable styles at reasonable prices, including assorted sleek square-capped ankle boots. The Détente range is more casual and less expensive.
Branches: 8 rue du Jour, 1st (01.40.26.19.84); 36 rue Vieille-du-Temple 4th (01.40.29.99.49); 11 rue du Pré-aux-Clercs, 7th (01.42.84.26.85).

Christian Louboutin
19 rue Jean-Jacques-Rousseau, 1st (01.42.36.05.31). M° Palais-Royal or Louvre. **Open** 11am-7.30pm Mon-Sat. Closed Aug. Credit AmEx, MC, V.
About as close as *cordonnerie* has to a successor to Roger Vivier, his former assistant Christian Louboutin draws a gilt-edged clientele for shoes with such signature details as 18k gold-plated heels and bright red soles. Prices 1400F-3300F.
Branch: 38 rue de Grenelle, 7th (01.42.22.33.07).

Freelance
30 rue du Four, 6th (01.45.48.14.78). M° St Germain-des-Prés. **Open** 10am-7pm Mon-Sat. Credit AmEx, DC, MC, V. **Map H7**
French design duo Guy and Yvon Rautureau let their creative imagination run wild on a multi-trend collection which includes everything from funky men's shoes in rainbow colours to Gucci-style vamp stilettos for girls. Prices are not cheap, but a loud fashion statement is guaranteed.

Kabuki
25 rue Etienne-Marcel, 1st (01.42.33.55.65).
M° Etienne-Marcel **Open** 1-7.30pm Mon; 10.30am-7.30pm Tue-Sat. **Credit** AmEx, DC, MC, V. **Map J5**
Owner William Halimi has his finger firmly on the fashion pulse, changing lines every season. The ground floor showcases to-die-for Prada bags and Sergio Rossi shoes. Upstairs, drool over beautifully presented men's and women's fashion (Prada, Martine Sitbon, Barbara Bui, Helmut Lang and Costume National), and opposite there's the Kabuki Café.

Shoe Bizz
42 rue du Dragon, 6th (01.45.44.91.70). M° St-Sulpice. **Open** 2-7.30pm Mon; 10.30am-7.30pm Tue-Sat. **Credit** AmEx, MC, V. **Map G7**
Their bizz is to zero in on the most fashionable shoe shapes of the season, and recreate them at around 30 per cent cheaper than their competitors. Men's lines are slightly more sober.
Branch: 48 rue Beaubourg, 3rd (01.48.87.12.73).

Stéphane Kélian
13bis rue de Grenelle, 7th (01.42.22.93.03). M° Sèvres-Babylone. **Open** 10am-7pm Mon-Sat. **Credit** AmEx, MC, V. **Map G7**
High-fashion women's shoes from around 1000F up, as well as classic woven flats. He also designs for Martine Sitbon. Branches: 6 pl des Victoires, 2nd (01.42.61.60.74); 26 av des Champs-Elysées, 8th (01.42.56.42.26); 20 av Victor Hugo, 16th (01.45.00.44.41).

Stephen
42 rue de Grenelle, 7th (01.42.84.12.45). M° Sèvres-Babylone. **Open** 11am-2pm, 3pm-7pm Mon-Fri; 11am-12.30pm, 1-7pm Sat. Closed two weeks in Aug. **Credit** AmEx, MC, V. **Map G7**
Shoes designed by Michel Perry that cost less than his

eponymous line. Strappy high-heeled sandals and chunky-heeled slippers in patent leathers, in colours such as lime-blossom, mauve and ruby. Prices 300F-1500F.

Perfumes & Cosmetics

By Terry
21 passage Véro-Dodat, 1st (01.44.76.00.76). M° Palais-Royal. **Open** 11am-7pm Mon-Sat. **Credit** AmEx, DC, MC, V. **Map H5**
Long glass test tubes containing a rainbow of brilliantly coloured powders in the window immediately catch the eye at this sleek modern shop in an antiquated covered passage. This is the haute couture of make-up (Terry previously worked with Yves Saint Laurent); hundreds of colours can be made up specially, though there's also a ready-to-wear range. *Rouge à lèvres*, in a refillable metal container, costs 650F (refills 150F).

Guerlain
68 av des Champs-Elysées, 8th (01.45.62.52.57).
M° Franklin D Roosevelt. **Open** 9.45am-7pm Mon-Sat. **Credit** AmEx, MC, V. **Map E4**
The boutique is one of the last vestiges of the golden age of the Champs-Elysées. Many of the Guerlain fragrances were created with royal or Proustian inspirations. It's still a family concern and even today some of the scents are sold only in the Guerlain boutiques.
Branches include: 2 pl Vendôme, 1st (01.42.60.68.61); 47 rue Bonaparte, 6th (01.43.26.71.19); 29 rue de Sèvres, 6th (01.42.22.46.60); 93 rue de Passy, 16th (01.42.88.41.62).

MAC
76bis rue des Sts-Pères, 7th (01.45.48.60.24). M° Sèvres-Babylone. **Open** 10.30am-7pm Mon-Sat. **Credit** AmEx, DC, MC, V. **Map G6**
The first Paris store of the cosmetics chain owned by Estée Lauder but created by Canadian make-up artist Frank Toscan. The salespeople-cum-make-up artists will teach customers how to use the inventive products, like the mix-it-yourself lipstick. There's a stunning range of colours. Appointments can be made for a make-up lesson.

Parfums Caron
34 av Montaigne, 8th (01.47.23.40.82). M° Franklin D Roosevelt. **Open** 10am-6.30pm Mon-Sat. **Credit** AmEx, DC, MC, V. **Map E4**
In its elegant Art Deco boutique, Caron sells re-editions of its classic favourites from 1911-54, including the spicy, eastern rose scent Or et Noir.

Les Salons du Palais Royal Shiseido
142 galerie de Valois, 1st (01.49.27.09.09). M° Louvre or Palais-Royal. **Open** 9am-7pm Mon-Sat. **Credit** AmEx, DC, MC, V. **Map H5**
An Oriental treasure trove tucked under the arcades of the Palais-Royal where you can find the make-up and perfumes of the Japanese beauty line Shiseido. The interior, created by Serge Lutens, imitates a Directoire-period perfume shop.

Séphora
70 av des Champs-Elysées, 8th (01.53.93.22.50). M° Franklin D Roosevelt. **Open** 10am-midnight Mon-Sat; noon-midnight Sun. **Credit** AmEx, MC, V. **Map E4**
This cosmetic chain flagship carries 12,000 French and foreign brands of scent and slap. At the 'sampling bar' you can sniff 560 basic scents classified according to the eight basic olfactive families. At the front of the store are books on perfumes and perfume bottles; at the back are exhibitions on... perfumes.
Branches include: Forum des Halles, level -3, 1st (01.40.13.72.25); 30 av d'Italie, 13th (01.53.80.86.10).

Specialist Shops

From tasteful tradition to tasteless kitsch, Paris' eclectic emporia do their best to serve every lifestyle.

Led by the phenomenal success of **Colette**, with its brilliant global selection of the latest essentials in fashion and design, 'lifestyle stores' continue to multiply, as **Maison de Famille** and Japanese-arrival **Muji** expand from household goods to shirts, **Catherine Memmi** dictates cream, brown and black, and fashion gurus like Calvin Klein turn to housewares. Setting out not just how we should dress but what chair to sit on, towel to dry with or soap to use, the easy one-stop, no-decision limitation of choice risks becoming a tyranny if taken too seriously. In a sense it's the opposite of those small specialist stores (fantastic *papeteries*, kitchen supply shops) with which Paris abounds, or the department stores' stock-everything approach, although the latter are increasingly exchanging chaotic comprehensivity for a more sophisticated everything-that's-new. Another trend is the ever burgeoning field of kitsch – forget the discretion of the bourgeoisie in an unstoppable onslaught of day-glo orange pouffes, fake fur and lava lamps.

If you're after antiques and retro it helps to know where to go: traditional classy antiques in the Carré des Antiquaires of the 7th or Fbg-St-Honoré, Art Deco in St-Germain, 1960s plastic along rue de Charonne, antiquarian books in the covered passages, in the *bouquinistes* along the *quais* or at Parc Georges Brassens. Then, of course, there are the *Marchés aux Puces* (flea markets) at St-Ouen, Montreuil (*see chapter* **Right Bank**) and Vanves (*see chapter* **Left Bank**) and auction house Drouot (*see chapter* **Right Bank**), due soon to be challenged by the arrival of Sotheby's and Christie's. There are also frequent *brocantes* – antiques and collectors' markets, especially in summer; look for banners and notices in listings magazines.

Most shops open until at least 7pm, but some close for lunch and on Mondays, and many close for all or part of August. For information on the *détaxe* tax refund scheme, *see chapter* **Fashion**.

Bon Marché: *shooting up the stakes again.*

and car parts. It also stocks basic clothes and accessories on the ground floor, but no one really comes here for that.

Le Bon Marché

24 rue de Sèvres, 7th (01.44.39.80.00). M° Sèvres-Babylone. **Open** 9.30am-7pm Mon-Sat. **Credit** AmEx, DC, MC, V. **Map G7**
Less touristy than its Right Bank rivals, the ever-so-stylish 'good bargain' was the first department store in Paris, and Gustave Eiffel helped design its iron-framed structure. On the ground floor, Vuitton and Dior have leather goods boutiques next to the swish, wood-floored menswear department, revamped accessories and jewellery departments. The first floor is devoted to womenswear and carries avant-garde as well as classic designers, including Vanessa Bruno, John Galliano, Marc Jacobs, Paul Smith, new arrivals Dries van Noten and Isabel Marant, and a sophisticated lingerie department. The dramatically named Théâtre de la Beauté beauty spa, opened in 1998, offers aromatherapy as well as make-up sessions. The second floor houses kitchen and household items, bedlinens, curtain fabrics and furniture. The basement is divided between stationery, a large bookshop, children's toys and clothes. Shop 2 contains a food hall with one of the best selections of gourmet food in Paris (*see chapter* **Food & Drink**), bar and restaurant, and antiques arcade.

Department Stores

BHV (Bazar de l'Hôtel de Ville)

52-64 rue de Rivoli, 4th (01.42.74.90.00); tile shop 14 rue du Temple (01.42.74.92.12); DIY hire annexe 40 rue de la Verrerie (01.42.74.97.23). M° Hôtel-de-Ville. **Open** 9.30am-7pm Mon, Tue, Thur, Fri; 9.30am-10pm Wed; 9.30am-7pm Sat. **Credit** AmEx, MC, V. **Map K6**
Heaven for DIY-ers: BHV is the central Paris alternative to out-of-town warehouses, with a vast range of plumbing fittings, hardware, paints, electrical goods, furnishings, tools

Galeries Lafayette

40 bd Haussmann, 9th (01.42.82.34.56/fashion show reservations 01.42.82.30.25). Mº Chaussée d'Antin/RER Auber. **Open** 9.30am-7pm Mon-Wed, Fri, Sat; 9.30am-9pm Thur. **Credit** AmEx, DC, MC, V. **Map H3**

The Louvre of department stores carries over 75,000 brand names, and welcomes the equivalent of the entire population of Paris each month. Numerous designer concessions include Yohji Yamamoto, Claude Montana, Vivienne Westwood, Atsuro Tayama, Olivier Theysken and Clements Ribeiro. Cheaper alternatives include Agnès b, Gap and Galeries Lafayette's own women's labels Jodhpur, Avant Première and Briefing. As well as an entire floor devoted to lingerie, there's a vast perfume and cosmetics section, and enormous departments dedicated to kitchenwares, books and records, not to mention souvenirs of Paris. Lafayette Maison, a home-furnishings section, was opened on the fifth floor in 1996. There are two restaurants with panoramic views on the sixth floor, as well as a Café Sushi adjoining Lafayette Maison.
Branch: 22 rue du Départ, 14th (01.45.38.52.87).

Marks & Spencer

35 bd Haussmann, 9th (01.47.42.42.91). Mº Havre-Caumartin/RER Auber. **Open** 9am-8pm Mon-Wed, Fri-Sun; 9am-9pm Thur. **Credit** MC, V. **Map G3**

A branch of the British chain that's every bit as good for underwear and jumpers as you'd expect. The food hall is a great hit with French shoppers – cox's apples, scones and chicken *tikka masala* are best-sellers.
Branch: 88 rue de Rivoli, 4th (01.44.61.08.00).

Monoprix

Branches all over Paris. **Open** generally 9.30am-7.30pm Mon-Sat; some branches open till 10pm. **Credit** MC, V.

Sooner or later you're bound to come into a branch of dependable Monoprix, whether for food, shampoo, a notepad, a T-shirt or a pair of socks. The bigger supermarket sections have cheese, *charcuterie* and even wet fish counters, and the largest have entire fashion floors for women, men and children, plus house and kitchen accessories.

Le Printemps

64 bd Haussmann, 9th (01.42.82.50.00). Mº Havre-Caumartin/RER Auber. **Open** 9.35am-7pm Mon-Wed, Fri, Sat; 9.30am-10pm Thur. **Credit** AmEx, DC, MC, V. **Map G3**

Along with Galeries Lafayette, this is the other behemoth of Parisian department stores, with three stores devoted to the home, to menswear and to women's fashion. The women's store, renovated in 1997, now boasts the largest accessories department in Paris, including Chanel and Dior, hat creations by Marie Mercié, handbags from 31 Février and Peggy Hyunh Kinh, shoes from YSL, Patrick Cox and Marc Jacobs next to own label Editions Printemps. Espace Créateurs carries talents such as Martine Sitbon, Alexander McQueen, Hussein Chalayan, Véronique Leroy, Narcisso Rodriguez and Gaspard Yurkievich and Jeremy Scott. The third floor carries trendy looks and sportier labels, the fourth floor is more traditional. Housewares from kitchen basics to Lalique glass, Christofle cutlery and all the big Limoges porcelain houses, and stationery are also worth a look. Brummel, the rather shabby men's section, is curently undergoing an update.
Branches: 30 av d'Italie, 13th (01.40.78.17.17); 21-25 cour de Vincennes, 20th (01.43.71.12.41).

La Samaritaine

19 rue de la Monnaie, 1st (01.40.41.20.20). Mº Pont-Neuf. **Open** 9.30am-7pm Mon-Wed, Fri, Sat; 9.30am-10pm Thur. **Credit** AmEx, DC, MC, V. **Map J6**

La Samaritaine has never acquired the status of Galeries Lafayette or Printemps, but you can find just about anything in the four-store complex, from fashion and sports equipment to household goods, a large linen department and nuts 'n' bolts hardware, as well as a big toy department. Building two has a faded charm with wonderful Art Nouveau whiplash balustrades and painted peacocks around the central light well, a superb location on the Seine and one of the best views over Paris from the rooftop terrace. The view is also excellent from the fifth-floor restaurant Le Toupary.

Books

See also Fnac and Virgin Megastore in **Records, CDs, Cassettes & Hi-Fi** below.

Abbey Bookshop

29 rue de la Parcheminerie, 5th (01.46.33.16.24). Mº St-Michel. **Open** 10am-7pm Mon-Sat. **Credit** AmEx, MC, V. **Map J7**

This small Canadian-run bookshop has an extensive section of Canadian writers (including Québecois), as well as English and American titles. Regular author signings and readings.

Brentano's

37 av de l'Opéra, 2nd (01.42.61.52.50). Mº Opéra. **Open** 10am-7.30pm Mon-Sat. **Credit** AmEx, MC, V. **Map G4**

A good address for American classics, modern fiction and bestsellers, plus an excellent array of business titles. English-language books are at the front; magazines in the far corner; children's books are in the basement – storytelling, songs and crafts are on offer too (Wed afternoon and Sat morning).

La Chambre Claire

14 rue St-Sulpice, 6th (01.46.34.04.31). Mº Odéon. **Open** 10am-7pm Mon-Sat. **Credit** MC, V. **Map H7**

Specialises in photography, with plenty of titles in English and a photo gallery downstairs.

Entrée des Artistes

161 rue St-Martin, 3rd (01.48.87.78.58). Mº Rambuteau. **Open** 11am-7.30pm Mon-Sat. **Credit** MC, V. **Map K5**

This shrine to celluloid, from the most obscure movies to box-office blockbusters, is packed with film posters, photo stills and film books in French and English.

Galignani

224 rue de Rivoli, 1st (01.42.60.76.07). Mº Tuileries. **Open** 10am-7pm Mon-Sat. **Credit** MC, V. **Map G5**

Opened in 1802, Galignani was reputedly the first English-language bookshop in Europe. Today it stocks fine- and decorative arts books and literature in French and English.

Gibert Joseph

26, 30 bd St-Michel, 6th (01.44.41.88.88). Mº St-Michel. **Open** 9.30am-7.30pm Mon-Sat. **Credit** AmEx, MC, V. **Map J7**

Best known as a bookshop serving the Left Bank learning institutions, with some titles in English, as well as a place to flog text books. Also has stationery, office supplies and CDs.

La Hune

170 bd St-Germain, 6th (01.45.48.35.85). Mº St-Germain-des-Prés. **Open** 10am-11.45pm Mon-Sat. **Credit** AmEx, DC, MC, V. **Map G7**

A Left Bank institution, La Hune boasts an international selection of art and design books in the mezzanine and a superb collection of French literature and theory downstairs. Always busy until late with intellectual and arty types.

Institut Géographique National

107 rue La Boétie, 8th (01.43.98.85.00). Mº Franklin D Roosevelt. **Open** 9.30am-7pm Mon-Fri; 11am-12.30pm, 2-6.30pm Sat. Closed early Jan. **Credit** AmEx, MC, V. **Map E4**

Paris's best cartographic shop has a range of international maps, as well as detailed walking and cycling maps of France, wine maps and maps of historic Paris. It also stocks guidebooks to all regions of France, and globes.

Tati by name...

Tati, the discount department store synonymous with cheap nylon knickers, polyester trousers and dodgy household ornaments, has become as famous a Paris landmark as the Eiffel Tower. These days it's not uncommon for coachloads of tourists to join the hordes on boulevard Rochechouart, fighting to rummage through the bargain bins of tights (1F90), T-shirts (19F90) and purple Y-fronts (6F90).

The Tati concept was invented in 1948 when Jules Ouaki, a Tunisian Jewish immigrant, came up with the idea of selling clothes like vegetables on a market stall, throwing his clothes into enormous crates and introducing the notion of 'touchy-feely' shopping. Ouaki targeted Paris' immigrant community, the working-classes and the social stratum known as *les familles populaires* with a revolutionary slogan: *Les plus bas prix!* The first store was packed out within weeks, laying the foundations of an empire that now boasts an annual turnover of 1.5 billion francs.

In 1979 'Monsieur Jules' took Tati upmarket, opening a new store in the heart of the Left Bank. Bourgeois shoppers poked their disdainful noses in the air, but when Nadine de Rothschild revealed that she was a committed Tati hosiery fan, stylish Parisiennes flocked to

run their gloved fingers through the bargain bins, transferring their bargain buys to Hermès handbags as soon as they got outside (perhaps unaware that Tati's trademark pink-and-white gingham bags were inspired by that most chic French glamourpuss of all – Brigitte Bardot.)

These days, the bags have become an increasingly sought-after fashion accessory. The rise of Tati's street cred began in 91 when Jules Ouaki's son, Fabien, took over the family business. Ouaki Jr is in a radically different mould to dad. A former member of an 'underground' London rock band, now a practising Buddhist who hangs out with Richard Gere and the Dalai Lama, Fabien prides himself on an 'alternative' approach to business. Shortly after being instated as chairman, Fabien audaciously hired two young Paris designers, Claude Sabbah and Gilles Rosier, to create a line of cheap teenage clothing, 'La Rue est à Nous'. Tati's image was on the up. Later that year Azzedine Alaïa picked up on the Tati phenomenon, basing part of his spring/summer collection on the famous Vichy print. (American artist Julien Schnabel would also go on to use the Tati logo in his work).

Fabien Ouaki has since introduced Tati portable phones, disposable cameras, pick 'n' mix sweets and concert tickets for under 10F. He has opened Tati stores around the world, from Berlin and Beirut to Gdansk. But one of his most controversial moves was to open a discount jewellery store, Tati Or, on rue de la Paix – a precious stone's throw from Cartier. Fabien also celebrated Tati's 50th birthday in style, installing a Tati Bridal Store on New York's Fifth Avenue, although, according to *Women's Wear Daily*, American brides are still a little suspicious of 399F silk-and-polyester mix gowns.

Plans to extend the empire do not end there: Tati has branched out into eyewear with Tati Optic; Ouaki also intends to reopen the old Louxor cinema on boulevard Barbès as an arts centre and a Tati café chain could also be on the way. So watch out for the arrival of pink-and-white check croissants in your neighbourhood soon.

Tati

4 bd Rochechouart, 18th (01.55.29.50.00). Mᵒ Barbès-Rochechouart. **Open** 10am-7pm Mon; 9.30am-7pm Tue-Fri; 9.15am-7pm Sat. **Credit** MC, V. **Map J2 Branches:** 13 pl de la République, 3rd (01.48.87.72.81); **Tati Bonbons** 26 rue St-Denis, 1st (01.42.36.51.45); **Tati Optic** 11 rue Belhomme, 18th (01.55.79.95.00). **Tati Or** include: 19 rue de la Paix, 2nd (01.40.07.06.76); 132 bd St-Germain, 6th (01.56.24.93.15).

Librairie Gourmande

4 rue Dante, 5th (01.43.54.37.27). M° St-Michel. **Open** 10am-7pm daily. **Credit** MC, V. **Map J7**

Chefs from the world over hunt out Geneviève Baudon's bookstore dedicated to old and newly published books on cooking, gastronomy, wine and table arts. Non-French titles.

Librairie Ulysse

26 rue St-Louis-en-l'Ile, 4th (01.43.25.17.35). M° Pont-Marie. **Open** 2-8pm Tue-Sat. **No credit cards. Map K7**

Satisfy your wanderlust at this travel bookshop with new and old guidebooks, travellers' tales, back issues of *National Geographic* and maps covering the globe.

La Maison Rustique

26 rue Jacob, 6th (01.42.34.96.60). M° St-Germain-des-Prés. **Open** 10am-7pm Mon-Sat. **Credit** AmEx, DC, MC, V. **Map H6**

Paris' best selection of gardening, botanical and interior design books, with some titles in English.

Shakespeare & Co

37 rue de la Bûcherie, 5th (01.43.26.96.50). M° Maubert-Mutualité/RER St-Michel. **Open** noon-midnight daily. **No credit cards. Map J7**

A Parisian legend still packed with would-be Hemingways, even if no longer on the same site as Sylvia Beach's famous shop. New, used and antique books in English are arranged chaotically, often in heaps on the floor.

Tea & Tattered Pages

24 rue Mayet, 6th (01.40.65.94.35). M° Duroc. **Open** 11am-7pm daily; *Aug* noon-6pm Mon-Sat. **No credit cards. Map F8**

Pick up cheap secondhand paperbacks in English (most around 30F) or sell back your cast-offs and stop for tea and brownies in the American-run tea salon at the rear.

Village Voice

6 rue Princesse, 6th (01.46.33.36.47). M° Mabillon. **Open** 2-8pm Mon; 10am-8pm Tue-Sat; 2-7pm Sun. **Credit** AmEx, DC, MC, V. **Map H7**

The ever-charming Odile Hellier supports alternative literature by stocking the city's best selection of new and hard-to-get fiction and non-fiction in English, plus literary magazines. She also holds literary events and poetry readings.

WH Smith

248 rue de Rivoli, 1st (01.44.77.88.99). M° Concorde. **Open** 9.30am-7pm Mon-Sat; 1-7pm Sun. **Credit** AmEx, MC, V. **Map G5**

This long-established branch of the British chain carries over 70,000 titles, including paperback bestsellers, classics, travel guides, cookery books and videos. There are good reference and English-language teaching sections and a perpetual mob around the UK and US magazine and newspaper racks, which carry London *Time Out,* among many others.

Fabrics & Trimmings

La Droguerie

9 rue du Jour, 1st (01.45.08.93.27). M° Châtelet-Les Halles or Etienne-Marcel. **Open** 2-6.45pm Mon; 10.30am-6.45pm Tue-Sat; Aug 1-6.45pm Tue-Sat. **Credit** V. **Map J5**

Baubles, beads and buttons in all conceivable colours and shapes can be selected individually or by the scoopful. Also, ribbons, feather boas and knitting yarns galore.

Entrée des Fournisseurs

8 rue des Francs-Bourgeois, 3rd (01.48.87.58.98). M° St-Paul. **Open** 2.30-7pm Mon, Sun; 10.30am-7pm Tue-Sat. Closed two weeks in Aug. **Credit** MC, V. **Map L6**

Travaux de dame (needlecraft) heaven: from needles and yarns to tapestry canvases, mending eggs, ribbons and fancy buttons, as well as 4000 different pearls and beads. **Branch:** 9 rue Madame, 6th (01.42.84.13.97).

Maison de la Fausse Fourrure

34 bd Beaumarchais, 11th (01.43.55.24.21). M° Bastille or Chemin-Vert. **Open** 11am-7pm Mon-Sat. **Credit** AmEx, MC, V. **Map M6**

The 'House of Fake Fur' pays tribute to our furry friends, and everything here is fake and fun. There are synthetic teddy-bear coats, animal print bags and hats in your choice of chic 'leopard' or cheeky 'monkey', as well as bolts of fake fur fabric, lampshades and furniture covered with the stuff.

Marché St-Pierre

Dreyfus *2 rue Charles-Nodier, 18th (01.46.06.92.25);* **Tissus Reine** *5 pl St-Pierre, 18th (01.46.06.02.31);* **Moline** *1 pl St-Pierre, 18th (01.46.06.14.66). M° Anvers or Barbès-Rochechourt.* **Open** 1.30-6.30pm Mon; 9.30am-6.30pm Tue-Fri; 9.30am-6.45pm Sat. **Credit** V. **Map J2**

The three shops listed above have the best selections of fabrics, though you'll also find stores all around and off the place St-Pierre. Reine has selections of discounted silks and luxury fabrics. Moline specialises in upholstery fabrics. Dreyfus is a crowded, five-floor warehouse, with linens, silks, woollens, home furnishing fabrics and discounted bolts.

Florists & Garden Fittings

Christian Tortu

6 carrefour de l'Odéon, 6th (01.43.26.02.56). M° Odéon. **Open** 9am-8pm Mon-Sat; 11am-7pm Sun. Closed two weeks in Aug. **Credit** AmEx, DC, MC, V. **Map H7**

Paris' most celebrated florist is famous for combining flowers, foliage, twigs, bark and moss into still-lifes, but you can also buy his pots, minimalist zinc vases and leaf plates.

Despalles

26 rue Boissy d'Anglas, 8th (01.49.24.05 65). M° Concorde or Madeleine. **Open** 10am-7pm Mon-Sat. **Credit** AmEx, MC, V. **Map F4**

On two floors, the shop is an inviting jumble of green plants, gardening tools as well as garden and 'Anglo Indian' wooden furniture, tapestry cushions, dried flowers and sachets. **Branch:** 5 rue d'Alésia, 14th (01.45.89.05.31).

Gifts & Oddities

Deyrolle

46 rue du Bac, 7th (01.42.22.30.07). M° Rue du Bac. **Open** 10am-6.45pm Mon-Sat. **Credit** AmEx, MC, V. **Map G6**

A taxidermist's dream, this dusty shop, established 1831, overflows with stuffed animals, ranging from a polar bear to exotic birds. You can also have your own household pets lovingly stuffed here for 3800F (for a cat) upwards or hire a beast for a few days to complete your film set.

Lal Moti

30 rue de Sévigné, 4th (01.40.27.01.72). M° St-Paul. **Open** 11am-7pm Mon-Sat. **Credit** AmEx, V. **Map L6**

A small Indian boutique filled with a lovely array of handmade accessories: candleholders, wooden boxes, mirrors, traditional rugs and throws. The charming, English-speaking Indian owner will have you chatting for hours.

Nature et Découvertes

Carrousel du Louvre 99 rue de Rivoli, 1st (01.47.03.47.43). M° Palais-Royal. **Open** 10am-8pm daily. Closed Aug. **Credit** AmEx, MC, V. **Map H5**

This chain sells useful (and less so) camping and stargazing

Nature et Découvertes: *for pioneers, creatives and big kids everywhere.*

accessories, musical instruments, art supplies and nature or science games that are also beautiful objects. It has a play space where it runs kids' workshops (3.30pm Wed).
Branches include: Forum des Halles, rue Pierre Lescot, 1st (01.40.28.42.16); Trois Quartiers, 23 bd Madeleine, 8th (01.49.27.07.58).

N'O

Viaduc des Arts, 21 av Daumesnil, 12th (01.43.46.26.26). M° Gare de Lyon. **Open** noon-7pm Tue-Fri; 11am-7pm; Sun 2-7pm **Credit** AmEx, MC, V. **Map M8**
N'omades Authentic is a visual feast of what is essentially top of the range trinketry gathered by the Viladrechs on their travels around the globe. Prices are less ethnic but the selection is beautiful, from unusual bowls to pots of Polynesian lipstick. Also fabulous wrapping paper and photo albums.

Papeterie Moderne

12 rue de la Ferronerie, 1st 901.42.36.21.72). M° Châtelet. **Open** 9am-noon, 1.30-6.30pm Mon-Thur, Sat; 10.30am-noon, 1.30-6.30pm. **No credit cards. Map J5**
Not, as the name suggests, a stationer, but source of those enamel plaques that adorn Paris streets and forbidding gateways. Here you can find that Champs-Elysées sign or the guard-dog with a twist (*attention chien bizarre*) for a mere 40F.

Paris Accordéon

80 rue Daguerre, 14th (01.43.22.13.48). M° Denfert-Rochereau or Gaîté. **Open** 9am-noon, 1-7pm, Tue-Fri; 9am-6pm Sat. Closed Aug. **Credit** MC, V. **Map G10**
'Come share our passion' welcomes this yellow-painted shop, its shelves lined with the fashionable French national instrument, the accordion, from simple squeeze-box to the most beautiful tortoiseshell. Sheet music also sold here.

Paris-Musées

29bis rue des Francs-Bourgeois, 4th (01.42.74.13.02). M° Bastille. **Open** 2-7pm Mon; 11am-7pm Tue-Sun.
Credit AmEx, MC, V. **Map L6**
Run by the Ville de Paris museums, this shop has a collection of funky items, including lamps and ceramics, created

especially for them by some of Paris' top young designers, including Mathieu & Ray and Robert Le Héros, and copies of items in city museums, such as a Gallo-Roman carafe from Carnavalet or George Sand's set of glasses, carafes or flutes.
Branch: Forum des Halles, 1 rue Pierre-Lescot, 1st (01.40.26.56.65).

Des Pieds et des Mains

22 passage Molière, 3rd (01.42.77.53.50). M° Rambuteau. **Open** 2-6pm Fri, Sat. **No credit cards. Map K5**
The ultimate personal souvenir: Brigitte Massoutier will enshrine your hand (adult 1500F), foot or mouth (adult 500F) in plaster. The window is crammed with appendages of past customers from a baby of 57 minutes to a hardy 98-year-old. The process takes seconds – but allow a month for delivery.

Robin des Bois

15 rue Ferdinand-Duval, 4th (01.48.04.09.36). M° St-Paul. **Open** 10.30am-7.30pm Mon-Sat; 2-7.30pm Sun. **Credit** MC, V. **Map L6**
The Robin Hood of the environment is linked to an ecological organisation of the same name. Everything is made with recycled or ecologically sound products, including bottle-top jewellery, natural toiletries and recycled notepaper.

Why!

22 rue du Pont-Neuf, 1st (01.42.33.40.33). M° Pont-Neuf. **Open** 11am-7.30pm Mon-Sat.
Credit AmEx, DC, MC, V. **Map J6**
Alexis Lahellic lawyer-turned-jeweller has been replaced by Alexis Lahellic master of kitsch, although branches at rue Jean-Jacques-Rousseau and rue Bernard-Palissy still stock his gilt resin *bijoux*, alongside an accumulation of tack. Furry lamps and bags glow alongside shark staplers and tulips to grow in the loo. Prize for tackiness goes to the photo booth where for 20F you can be immortalised in a sunsetty postcard.
Branches: 14-16 rue Jean-Jacques-Rousseau, 1st (01.42.33.36.95); 41 rue des Francs-Bourgeois, 4th (01.44.61.72.75); 14-16 rue Bernard-Palissy, 6th (01.45.48.71.98).

E Dehillerin: *more pots and pans than you'll ever know what to do with.*

Home Accessories & Design

Avant-Scène
4 pl de l'Odéon, 6th (01.46.33.12.40). M° Odéon.
Open 10.30am-1pm, 2.30-7pm Tue-Sat. Closed 10-20
Aug. **Credit** MC, V. **Map H7**
The more baroque side of contemporary furniture and lighting is gathered by Elisabeth Delacarte, who stocks French and European designers, including Mark Brazier Jones, Franck Evennou, Hubert le Gall and Hervé Van der Straeten.

Catherine Memmi
32-34 rue St-Sulpice, 6th (01.44.07.22.28). M° Mabillon.
Open 12.30-7.30pm Mon; 10.30am-7.30pm Tue-Sat.
Credit AmEx, MC, V. **Map H7**
Impeccable and pricey good taste comes in white, cream, grey and black only. Table linens and sheets are meticulously arranged alongside shirts, dressing gowns, candles, iron lamps, fashionable knitted cushions, vases and furniture.

Cèdre Rouge
25 rue Duphot, 1st (01.42.61.81.81). M° Madeleine.
Open noon-7pm Mon; 10am-7pm Tue-Sat. **Credit**
AmEx, MC, V. **Map G4**
The garden-conservatory-interior store offers an undeniably urban interpretation of rusticity. Occasionally twee, often tasteful, china and glass, candles, planters.
Branches: 22 av Victoria, 1st (01.45.08.85.61); 116 rue du Bac, 7th (01.42.84.84.00); 1 bd Emile-Augier, 16th (01.45.24.62.62).

Chimène
25 rue de Charonne, 11th (01.43.55.55.00). M° Bastille.
Open 11am-7.30pm Tue-Sat; 3-7pm Sun. **Credit** AmEx,
MC, V. **Map M7**
Eclectic folky-ethnic outlets abound, but here the selection is impressively chosen. Tempting patchwork bedspreads and cushions, wrought-iron leafy candlesticks, neo-bamboo coffee cups and Kenyan soapstone bowls accompany bathtime goodies from Côté Bastide. Larger furniture is in the cellar.

CFOC
170 bd Haussmann, 8th (01.53.53.40.80).
M° St-Philippe-du-Roule. **Open** 10am-7.30pm Mon-Sat.
Credit AmEx, DC, MC, V. **Map E3**
La Compagnie Française de l'Orient et de la Chine is full of eastern promise from Chinese teapots and celadon bowls, lacquerware, Mongolian pottery and Iranian blown glass to slippers and silk jackets. Downstairs is a rare example of an interior by Art Deco maestro Ruhlmann.
Branches: 24 rue St-Roch, 1st (01.42.60.65.32); 163, 167 bd St-Germain, 6th (01.45.48.00.18/01.45.48.10.31); 260 bd St-Germain, 7th (01.47.05.92.82); 65 av Victor-Hugo, 16th (01.45.00.55.46); 113 av Mozart, 16th (01.42.88.36.08).

Colette
213 rue St-Honoré, 1st (01.55.35.33.90). M° Tuileries.
Open 10.30am-7.30pm Mon-Sat. **Credit** AmEx, DC, MC,
V. **Map G5**
The top story of 1997 and still a roaring success, this huge metal and white stone minimalist space showcases all that's trendy in design, art and fashion from neat glassware, Tom Dixon's modular furniture, Alexander McQueen dresses and Costume National accessories to the latest Sony radio, a high-tech scooter or perfect kids' teddy. There's a nail bar, exhibition space and a designer café in the basement specialising in mineral water.

Conran Shop
117 rue du Bac, 7th (01.42.84.10.01). M° Sèvres-Babylone. **Open** noon-7pm Mon; 10am-7pm Tue-Sat.
Credit AmEx, MC, V. **Map F7**
Fit out your flat or solve your present problems at Sir Terence Conran's elegant furniture and accessories shop, just next to Bon Marché. Sleek furniture, wonderful kitchen gadgets, handmade wrought-iron candleholders, sophisticated lighting and natural linens for the home.

Dîners en Ville
27 rue de Varenne, 7th (01.42.22.78.33). M° Rue du Bac.
Open 2-7pm Mon; 11am-7pm Tue-Sat. Closed two weeks

in Aug. **Credit** MC, V. **Map F6**
New and antique tableware gets spectacular window displays. Colourful Italian earthenware and coloured glasses are a speciality. Coordinated tablecloths and fancy cutlery.

DOM
21 rue Ste-Croix-de-la-Bretonnerie, 4th (01.42.71.08.00).
Open 11.30am-9pm Mon-Sat; 1.30-9pm Sun. **Credit** AmEx, MC, V. **Map K6**
This oh-so camp shop specialises in re-editing 70s classics at fair prices such as the 'Sacco' plastic pouffe (400F), pearl curtains (250F), fluffy lamp and many other fun items.

Edition Limitée
7 rue Bréguet, 11th (01.48.06.52.11). Mᵒ Bréguet-Sabin.
Open 10.30am-8pm Mon-Sat. Closed two weeks in Aug. **Credit** MC, V. **Map M6**
Opened in 1995 by Frédérique Caillet and Vincent Collin, this boutique combines the minimalist sculptural works of Collin with the lamps, furniture and lighting fixtures of fellow designers Olivier Gagnère (who designed the interior of Café Marly) and Memphis-originator Ettore Sottsass.

Maison de Famille
29 rue St-Sulpice, 6th (01.40.46.97.47). Mᵒ Odéon. **Open** 10.30am-7pm Mon-Sat. **Credit** AmEx, MC, V. **Map H7**
The busy three-storey boutique is filled with unusual French finds, from heavy brass garden scissors to rope-soled bedroom slippers, wicker baskets to leather luggage, home accessories, women's and men's clothing.
Branch: 10 pl de la Madeleine, 8th (01.53.45.82.00).

La Maison Ivre
38 rue Jacob, 6th (01.42.60.01.85). Mᵒ St-Germain-des-Prés. **Open** 2-7pm Mon; 10.30am-7pm Tue-Sat. **Credit** MC, V. **Map H6**
Traditional handmade pottery from all over France with a decided emphasis on yellow and green glazed Provençal styles. Also tablecloths, wicker bread dishes, hand-woven baskets, pretty eggcups and candlesticks.

Muji
27 rue St-Sulpice, 6th (01.46.34.01.10). MᵒSt-Sulpice.
Open Mon-Sat 10am-8pm Mon-Sat. **Credit** AmEx, MC, V. **Map H7**
The famous 'no brand' label has taken Paris by storm with its elegantly utilitarian stationary, plastic binders, Japanese kitchenwares, metal storage boxes, nylon shopping bags and bathroom accessories. There are also clothes, including jumpers and three-packs of vests in white, black and grey.

Muriel Grateau
130 Galerie de Valois, Jardins du Palais-Royal, 1st (01.40.20.90.30). Mᵒ Palais-Royal. **Open** 11am-7pm Mon-Sat. **Credit** AmEx, MC, V. **Map H5**
If your taste is for sobriety, then you'll love Grateau's contemporary minimalist chic. White biscuitware, deep striped tablecloths, grey porcelain and glasses, decanters and towels are elegantly displayed. Serious stuff at serious prices.
Branch: 37 rue de Beaune, 7th (01.40.20.42.82).

Rooming
Carrousel du Louvre, 99 rue de Rivoli, 1st (01.42.60.10.85). Mᵒ Palais-Royal. **Open** 11am-8pm daily. **Credit** AmEx, DC, MC, V. **Map H5**
A shop entirely dedicated to how to put stuff away: CD racks, stacking bookcases, hanging shoe pouches and tuckaway wine racks. Lots of colourful plastic – for the truly obsessive.

Sentou
26 bd Raspail, 7th (01.45.49.00.05). Mᵒ Sèvres-Babylone. **Open** 11am-2pm, 3-7pm Tue-Fri; 11am-7pm Sat. Closed mid-Aug. **Credit** DC, MC, V. **Map G7**
Sentou carries a varied selection of contemporary designs,

from minimalist Japanese wood-and-paper lamps by Osamu Noguchi and textiles by Robert Le Heros to the fun resin candlesticks and sculptural tableware by Tsé & Tsé Associés and design classics by Alvar Aalto.
Branch: 18, 24 rue du Pont-Louis-Philippe, 4th (01.42.77.44.79/01.42.71.00.01).

Kitchen & Bathroom

A Simon
36 rue Etienne-Marcel, 2nd (01.42.33.71.65).
Mᵒ Etienne-Marcel. **Open** 8.30am-6.30pm Mon-Sat. **Credit** AmEx, MC, V. **Map J5**
This professional kitchen supplier has gigantic tureens and saucepans for feeding two to 200, plus all the plates, wine *pichets*, menu holders and other trappings you could possibly want for your own bistro.

Axis
Marché St-Germain, 14 rue Lobineau, 6th (01.43.29.66.23). Mᵒ Mabillon. **Open** 10am-8pm Mon-Sat. **Credit** AmEx, MC, V. **Map H7**
Alessi kettles, Starck lemon squeezers, Pesce resin chairs, fab high-tech trolleys and lots of plastic are a mix of laughable and loveable, designer and gadget, but above all, Axis commissions series by young designers, with unusual teatrays and ceramics and curious fruit bowls.
Branch: 13 rue de Charonne, 11th (01.48.06.79.10).

Bains Plus
51 rue des Francs-Bourgeois, 4th (01.48.87.83.07).
Mᵒ Hôtel-de-Ville. **Open** 11am-7.30pm Tue-Sat; 2.30-7pm Sun. **Credit** AmEx, MC, V. **Map K6**
All your bathroom needs are served with the ultimate gentleman's shaving gear, duck-shaped loofahs, seductive dressing gowns, chrome mirrors and nicely packaged Provençal bath oils and soaps from Côté Bastide. On the pricey side.

La Chaise Longue
20 rue des Francs-Bourgeois, 3rd (01.48.04.36.37).
Mᵒ St-Paul. **Open** 11am-7pm Mon-Sat; 2-7pm Sun. **Credit** AmEx, MC, V. **Map L6**
Cheap and cheerful accessories for the kitchen and bath include colourful enamelled tole, chrome wire soap dishes and saucepan stands fashioned into horses, fish or cats, painted tumblers, kitsch chicken hot water bottles, colourful bathmats and old-fashioned electric fans and kitchen scales.
Branches: 30 rue Croix-des-Petits-Champs, 1st (01.42.96.32.14); 8 rue Princesse, 6th (01.43.29.62.39).

E Dehillerin
18 rue Coquillière, 1st (01.42.36.53.13). Mᵒ Châtelet-Les Halles. **Open** 8am-12.30pm, 2-6pm Mon; 8am-6pm Tue-Sat. **Credit** AmEx, MC, V. **Map J5**
Dehillerin has supplied many of the great European chefs since 1820, and the shop is packed with every possible cooking utensil, including huge cooking vessels.

Kitchen Bazaar
11 av du Maine, 15th (01.42.22.91.17).
Mᵒ Montparnasse-Bienvenüe. **Open** 10am-7pm Mon-Sat. **Credit** AmEx, MC, V. **Map F8**
High-design and high-tech kitchen equipment and accessories, superb chef's knives, spice racks and state-of-the-art chrome storage bins. Bath Bazaar Autrement (6 av du Maine, 15th/01.45.48.89.00), across the street, sells bathroom goodies.

Records, CDs, Cassettes & Hi-Fi

BPM
1 rue Keller, 11th (01.40.21.02.88). Mᵒ Bastille or Ledru-Rollin. **Open** noon-8pm Mon-Sat. **Credit** AmEx, MC, V.

Map N7

You can positively feel the bpm pounding out along the street at this hot vinyl outlet. There's a great selection of techno and trance and a good source of club and rave flyers.

Crocodisc

42 rue des Ecoles, 5th (01.43.54.47.95). M° Maubert-Mutualité or St-Michel. **Open** 11am-7pm Tue-Sat. Closed first two weeks of Aug. **Credit** MC, V. **Map J7**

Good value new, second-hand and offbeat records. pop, rock, funk, Oriental, African and country music and classical. Crocojazz (64 rue de la Montagne-Ste-Geneviève, 5th/ 01.46.34.78.38) specialises in jazz, blues and gospel.

Fnac

74 av des Champs-Elysées, 8th (01.53.53.64.64). M° George V. **Open** 10am-midnight Mon-Sat. **Credit** AmEx, MC, V. **Map D4**

The giant Fnac emporia are one-stop shops for books, music, electronics and computers, stereo, video and photography gear. They also develop film and sell tickets. This new flagship has late hours. Fnac Micro (71 bd St-Germain, 5th/ 01.44.41.31.50) specialises in computer gear and CD-Roms. **Branches:** Forum des Halles, 1st (01.40.41.40.00); 136 rue de Rennes, 6th (01.49.54.30.00); 24 bd des Italiens, 9th (open till midnight) (01.48.01.02.03); (music only) 4 pl de la Bastille, 11th (01.43.42.04.04); 26-30 av des Ternes, 17th (01.44.09.18.00).

Rough Trade

30 rue de Charonne, 11th (01.40.21.61.62). M° Ledru-Rollin. **Open** noon-7pm Mon-Wed; noon-8pm Thur-Sat. **Credit** MC, V. **Map N7**

This offshoot of the famed London shop stocks plenty of indie labels, with lots of noise, techno, jungle and ambient, vinyl and DCs. Good for fanzines and flyers.

Recreate the château look at **Cèdre Rouge.**

Virgin Megastore

52-60 av des Champs-Elysées, 8th (01.49.53.50.00). M° Franklin D Roosevelt. **Open** 10am-midnight Mon-Sat; noon-midnight Sun. **Credit** AmEx, DC, MC, V. **Map D4**

Virgin's huge French flagship seethes at all hours with those trying to listen to the latest CDs. The video department has some non-dubbed English films. There's a café, large bookstore and ticket desk. The Louvre branch is less hectic. **Branch:** Carrousel du Louvre, 99 rue de Rivoli, 1st (01.49.53.50.00).

Stationery & Art Supplies

Calligrane

4-6 rue du Pont-Louis-Philippe, 4th (01.48.04.31.89). M° Pont-Marie or St-Paul. **Open** 11am-7pm Tue-Sat. Closed first two weeks in Aug. **Credit** MC, V. **Map K6**

Three shops are devoted to handmade decorative paper from all over the world, including encrusted papers, designer office supplies, and writing paper, Filofaxes and notebooks.

Comptoir des Ecritures

35 rue Quincampoix, 4th (01.42.78.95.10). M° Rambuteau. **Open** 11am-7pm Tue-Sat. Closed Aug. **Credit** MC, V. **Map K5**

This shop specialises in calligraphy, with inks, pens and an incredible range of handmade papers from Asia. It also runs courses and exhibitions on the subject.

Graphigro

157 rue Lecourbe, 15th (01.42.50.45.49). M° Vaugirard. **Open** 10am-7pm Mon-Sat. Closed Mon in Aug. **Credit** MC, V. **Map D9**

The largest and cheapest chain of art and graphic supplies, covers all the essential paints and brushes. **Branches:** 133 rue de Rennes, 6th (01.42.22.51.80); 207 bd Voltaire, 11th (01.43.48.23.57); 120 rue Damrémont, 18th (01.42.58.93.40).

Marie-Papier

26 rue Vavin, 6th (01.43.26.46.44). M° Vavin or Notre-Dame des Champs. **Open** 10am-7pm Mon-Sat. **Credit** AmEx, MC, V. **Map G8**

Fine and fancy handmade stationery with an amazing range of writing and wrapping paper in every imaginable colour.

Papier +

9 rue du Pont-Louis-Philippe, 4th (01.42.77.70.49). M° St-Paul or Pont-Marie. **Open** noon-7pm Mon-Sat. **Credit** MC, V. **Map K6**

Crayons in attractive boxes, notebooks and hand-cut paper.

Sennelier

3 quai Voltaire, 7th (01.42.60.72.15). M° St-Germain-des-Prés. **Open** 2-6.30pm Mon; 9.30am-12.30pm, 2-6.30pm Tue-Fri; 9.30am-6.30pm Sat. **Credit** AmEx, DC, MC, V. **Map H6**

Old-fashioned artists' colour merchant Sennelier has been supplying artists and students since 1887. Oil paints, watercolours and pastels include rare mineral, resin and natural pigments, along with primered boards, varnishes and paper. **Branch:** 4bis rue de la Grande-Chaumière, 6th (01.46.33.72.39).

Terra Cotta – Atelier de Peinture sur Céramique

77 av Kléber, 16th (01.44.05.10.05). M° Trocadéro. **Open** 10.30am-7pm Tue, Wed, Fri, Sat; 10.30am-10pm Thur; noon-6pm Sun. **No credit cards. Map B5**

Satisfy your creative urge. Buy a terracotta soapdish, plate, piggy bank or vase (10F-120F) and then decorate it yourself (47F/hr adults; 35F/hr children) with guidance from staff. The price includes unlimited use of paints, brushes and stencils, and the firing of the pieces for you to pick up later.

Food & Drink

Tempt your tastebuds at Paris' traiteurs, fromageries, pâtisseries, boulangeries, chocolatiers *and wine shops*.

Whatever the hold of the supermarket, even Parisians with limited means will seek out the city's markets and specialist food shops, insisting on top quality. Buttery-rich *foie gras* on fig bread, fresh *chèvre* soaked in fruity Provençal olive oil, jewel-like handmade chocolates: the delights are endless. Each French region is justly proud of its specialities, and all come together here in an orgy of food decadence. Look for signs such as *fabrication maison, artisanale* or *à l'ancienne*, indicating that products are made on the premises following traditional methods.

Bakeries

A la Flûte Gana
226 rue des Pyrénées, 20th (01.43.58.42.62). M° Gambetta. **Open** 7.30am-8pm Tue-Sat. Closed Aug. **No credit cards.**
Find the trademarked *flûte* here and several other bakeries.

Gosselin
125 rue St-Honoré, 1st (01.45.08.03.59). M° Louvre-Rivoli. **Open** 7am 8pm Tue-Sun. Closed three weeks in July/Aug. Closed Aug. **No credit cards. Map H5**
The official supplier to the Elysées Palace, with a fine *rétrodor* baguette.

René-Gérard St-Ouen
111 bd Haussmann, 8th (01.42.65.06.25). (01.45.83.80.13). M° Miromesnil. **Open** 7.30am-7.30pm Mon-Sat. **No credit cards. Map F3**
For 70 kinds of bread, plus loaves in the shape of Eiffel Towers and vintage cars.

Au Levain du Marais
32 rue de Turenne, 3rd (01.42.78.07.31). M° St Paul. **Open** 7am-8pm Mon-Sat. **No credit cards. Map L6**
Organic *flûtes*, baguettes, *boules* and olive oil *fougasses*. **Branch:** 142 av Parmentier, 11th (01.43.57.36.91).

Moulin de la Vierge
166 av de Suffren, 15th (01.47.83.45.55). M° Sèvres-Lecourbe. **Open** 7am-8pm Mon-Sat. **No credit cards. Map E8**
Dense, fragrant country loaf, crisp *flûtes* and *fougasses*. **Branches:** 82, rue Daguerre, 14th (01.43.22.50.55); 105 rue Vercingétorix, 14th (01.45.43.09.84).

Au Panetier
10 pl des Petits-Pères, 2nd (01.42.60.90.23). M° Bourse. **Open** 8am-7.15pm Mon-Fri. Closed July. **No credit cards. Map H5**
Superb breads in a turn-of-the-century tiled interior.

Poilâne
8 rue du Cherche-Midi, 6th (01.45.48.42.59). M° Sèvres-Babylone or St-Sulpice. **Open** 7.15am-8.15pm Mon-Sat. **No credit cards. Map G7**
Legendary country, nut and raisin breads. **Branch:** Max Poilâne, 87 rue Brancion, 15th (01.48.28.45.90).

Jean-Luc Poujauran
20 rue Jean-Nicot, 7th (01.47.05.80.88). M° Invalides or Latour-Maubourg. **Open** 8am-8.30pm Tue-Sat. Closed Aug. **No credit cards. Map E6**
Try the *baguette biologique*, herb and apricot breads.

Pâtisseries

Couderc
6 bd Voltaire, 11th (01.47.00.58.20). M° République. **Open** 8.30am-7pm Tue-Sat; 8am-1.30pm, 3-7pm Sun. Closed mid-July to mid Aug. **Credit MC, V. Map L5**
All the cakes are beautiful here, but the speciality is chocolate – the buttery *pains au chocolat* are among the best in town, chocolate pastries are intensely flavoured and filled chocolates are made on the premises.

Dalloyau
101 rue du Fbg-St-Honoré, 8th (01.42.99.90.00). M° St. Philippe du Roule. **Open** 8.30am-9pm daily. **Credit** AmEx, DC, MC, V. **Map E4**
This temple to pastry, opened in 1802, has gone more modern, with a renovated three-level space that includes a 140-square-metre boutique, a plush tea room and a bar for quick meals.

Moulin de la Vierge: *worth a pilgrimage.*

Branches include: 25 bd des Capucines, 2nd (01.47.03.47.00); 2 pl Edmond Rostand, 6th (01.43.29.31.10); 63 rue de Grenelle, 7th (01.45.49.95.30); 69 rue de la Convention, 5th (01.45.77.84.27).

Finkelsztajn
27 rue des Rosiers, 4th (01.42.72.78.91). M° St-Paul. **Open** 10am-2pm, 3-9pm Wed-Sun **No credit cards. Map L6**
For a change from flaky *millefeuilles*, try the dense, satisfying central European pastries filled with poppy seeds, apples or cream cheese at this shop in the heart of the Jewish district.

Jean Millet
103 rue St-Dominique, 7th (01.45.51.49.80). M° Ecole-Militaire/RER Pont d'Alma. **Open** 9am-7.30pm Mon-Sat; 8am-1pm Sun. Closed two-three weeks in Aug. **Credit** MC, V. **Map D6**
Pâtissier Jean Millet displays mouth-watering chocolate-covered meringues with coffee filling, *tuile d'amande* biscuits, and apricot *bavarois* – the choice is endless.

Gérard Mulot
76 rue de Seine, 6th (01.43.26.85.77). M° Odéon. **Open** 7am-8pm Mon, Tue, Thur-Sun. Closed mid July-mid Aug. **No credit cards. Map H7**
This shop attracts local celebrities with picture-perfect cakes. Try the bitter chocolate tart, fluffy *tarte normande*, or the *mabillon*, with caramel mousse and apricot marmalade.

Pâtisserie Stohrer
51 rue Montorgueil, 2nd (01.42.33.38.20). M° Les Halles. **Open** 7.30am-8.30pm daily. Closed first two weeks in Aug. **Credit** MC, V. **Map J5**
This pâtisserie, opened in 1730 by a chef of Louis XV, is beautiful enough to stop you in your tracks. Cakes and bread are not always admirably fresh, but the romantically named *puits d'amour* (well of love) and eggy *cannelés* are good bets.

Cheese

France has a cheese for every taste, from the snowy-white, triple-cream chaource to potent wine-washed maroilles. Every *quartier* in Paris has *fromageries*, each offering a superb seasonal selection. The sign *maître fromager affineur* identifies master cheese merchants who buy young cheeses from farmers and then age them on their premises. *Fromage fermier* and *fromage au lait cru* signify farm-produced and raw (unpasteurised) milk cheeses.

Alain Dubois
80 rue de Tocqueville, 17th (01.42.27.11.38). M° Malesherbes or Villiers. **Open** 7.30am-1pm, 3.45-8pm Tue-Fri; 7.30am-8pm Sat; 8.30am-1pm Sun. **Credit** V. **Map E2**
It's difficult to choose from the bewildering display, including some 70 varieties of goats' cheese. Mr Dubois, who has built a separate cellar to age his prize St-Marcellin and St-Félicien, is the darling of the super-chefs. He also holds frequent cheese tastings, and happily ships orders.
Branch: 79 rue de Courcelles, 17th (01.43.80.36.42).

Alléosse
13 rue Poncelet, 17th (01.46.22.50.45). M° Ternes. **Open** 9am-1pm, 4-7.15pm Tue-Sat; 9am-1pm Sun. **Credit** V.
People cross town to this large shop for the range of cheeses ripened in its cellars. They include wonderful farmhouse camemberts, delicate St-Marcellins, a very good choice of *chèvres*, and rareties you've never seen before.

Androuët
6 rue Arsène-Houssaye, 8th (01.42.89.95.00). M° Charles de Gaulle Etoile. **Open** 10.30am-7.30pm Mon-Sat. Closed Aug. **Credit** AmEx, DC, MC, V. **Map D3**
This celebrated *fromagerie* claims to stock over 200 varieties, and even has an adjoining cheese restaurant. Sample pungent époisses, munsters and maroilles in the smelly corner, try camembert matured in calvados, or go for a *dégustation* of *chèvre*, rolled in pepper, mustard seeds or ash.
Branches: 19 rue Daguerre, 14th (01.43.21.19.09); 83 rue St-Dominique, 7th (01.45.50.45.75).

Barthélémy
51 rue de Grenelle, 7th (01.45.48.56.75). M° Rue du Bac. **Open** 7am-7.30pm Tue-Sat. **Credit** MC, V. **Map G7**
Roland Barthélémy has a devoted clientele in Paris and Fontainebleau, where he has a second shop. The selection is outstanding: creamy Mont d'Or from the Jura and brie de Malesherbes are particularly tempting, along with takeaway 'cheese boards', wines and cheese-related porcelain.

La Ferme St-Hubert
21 rue Vignon, 8th (01.47.42.79.20). M° Madeleine. **Open** 9am-7.30pm Mon-Sat. **Credit** AmEx, DC, MC, V. **Map G4**
Pop in here on the way home from the Fauchon and sample the delicious, well-aged cheese in this compact shop. The selection is lovingly aged in owner Henry Voy's own cellars. As well as a good choice of *chèvre*, look for the hard cow's cheeses like cantal and tomme or the house speciality 'corona' with cumin, paprika and vanilla to taste.

Jean-Claude Lillo
35 rue des Belles-Feuilles, 16th (01.47.27.69.08). M° Victor-Hugo. **Open** 8am-1pm, 4-7.30pm Tue-Sat. **Credit** MC, V.
A busy person's dream with over 200 cheeses and cooked cheese preparations like tarts, gnocchi and *croustades*, interesting pasta concoctions, apple tarts, not to mention the huge sacks of dried mushrooms lurking on the shelf overhead.

Marie-Anne Cantin
12 rue du Champs-de-Mars, 7th (01.45.50.43.94). M° Ecole-Militaire. **Open** 8.30am-7.30pm Tue-Sat; 8.30-1pm Sun. **Credit** MC, V. **Map D6**
This pristine shop sells cheeses ripened to perfection in its own cellars. Cantin, a vigourous defender of unpasteurised cheese, describes her creamy St-Marcellins, aged *chèvres* and nutty beauforts with obvious – and well-deserved – pride.

Chocolate

Cacao et Chocolat
29 rue de Buci, 6th (01.46.33.77.63). M° Mabillon. **Open** 10.30am-7.30pm Tue-Sat. **Credit** AmEx, DC, MC, V. **Map H7**
A new shop in burnt orange and ochre recalling chocolate's Aztec origins with spicy fillings (honey and chilli pepper, nutmeg, clove and citrus), chocolate masks and pyramids. Chocolates taste bold and come in lovely wooden boxes.

Christian Constant
37 rue d'Assas, 6th (01.53.63.15.15). M° St-Placide. **Open** 8am-9pm daily. **Credit** MC, V. **Map G8**
For chocolates or tea, prepared *plats* and salads, Constant is a name among *le tout Paris*. With a training in pâtisserie and chocolate, he goes as far as Asia for his ideas.

Debauve & Gallais
30 rue des Sts-Pères, 7th (01.45.48.54.67). M° St-Germain-des-Prés. **Open** 9am-7pm Mon-Sat. Closed Mon in July and Aug. **Credit** MC, V. **Map G6**
This former pharmacy, with a beautiful facade dating from

Battling for bread

Probably no image is more quintessentially French than a baguette tucked under an arm, its crunchy tip torn off to nibble on the way home. But, even if baguettes seem essential for slathering with jam at breakfast, for folding around ham and *cornichons* at lunch and for lapping up sauce at dinner, they are a relatively modern invention.

Bread has long been a beloved and essential part of the French diet – by the thirteenth century, the best bakers were experimenting with flours and shapes to produce more than 30 types of loaf. Only in the 1920s, though, did they start to mix the yeast directly with the flour to produce a fast-rising bread, initially known as *pain de fantaisie*. Gradually these long, crusty white loaves, made in cities for eating fresh from the oven, came to be known as *ficelle* ('string', for the skinny version), *bâtard* ('bastard', for the oversized version) and baguette ('stick', for the happy medium).

In the loaf-loving '30s, each French person ate an average of 450g of bread a day (equivalent to about a baguette and a half). Rationing and food shortages during World War II cut consumption by half, and the golden baguette gave way to a heavy grey bread made of whole wheat mixed with other grains. After the war, in reaction to that hated dark bread, fluffy white loaves became fashionable. Increasingly industrial bread backfired on bakers, though, when consumption gradually dropped to below the wartime ration – by the '80s the French seemed to have lost their passion for bread, eating a half-hearted 150g each a day.

Lionel **Poilâne** was one of the first bakers to get fired up – and fire up a wood-burning oven in the basement of his Left Bank bakery to produce the antithesis of the baguette, a rustic round country loaf made with stone-ground flour and the same old-fashioned rising agent bakers had abandoned for yeast when making baguettes. Dark-crusted with a springy, slightly tangy crumb, **pain Poilâne** has become so popular it's now a trademark.

Poilâne might be the best-known baker in town (and the world), but others are just as inspired craftsmen. Basile Kamir learned to bake bread after falling in love with an abandoned bakery in the 14th *arrondissement*. The **Moulin de la Vierge** bakery is now his, along with two branches, and his picture-perfect country loaf is thick-crusted, dense and fragrant. Equally devoted to country bread is Thierry Rabineau of **Au Levain du Marais**, whose open-textured baguettes and country *miches* – all produced with organic flour – attract queues that snake out the door. Another pioneer of the country-style baguette – a contradiction in terms when you consider that baguettes were originally the height of city sophistication – was the now-retired Bernard Ganachaud, whose two daughters keep up the crunchy, flour-dusted tradition at the popular **La Flûte Gana**.

Some bakers stick to a few, time-tested recipes, while others, like **Jean-Luc Poujaran**, can't resist playing with shapes and flavours. His little pink shop bursts with tempting breads studded with nuts, apricots, figs, anchovies, raisins or olives. Even his baguette recipe changes with the seasons. **René-Gérard de St-Ouen** has a different obsession: shapes. His 'bread sculptures' include horses, cats, bicycles and the Eiffel Tower.

Thanks to a new generation of bakers devoted to their art, the quality of bread in Paris has risen considerably in the past few years. As of April 1998, only bakers who mix, knead and bake their bread on the premises, and who never freeze it at any stage, can legally put up the sign 'boulangerie'. Many ordinary neighbourhood boulangeries now carry 'retro' baguettes made with high-quality flour and a starter rather than yeast, which gives the bread a more complex flavour, chewier texture and longer shelf life. Look for the sign 'rétrodor' and 'flûte Gana', or bakers who offer a 'baguette au levain'. And remember, the best bread doesn't always come from the most eye-catching bakeries.

1800, once sold chocolate for medicinal purposes. Its intense tea, honey or praline-flavoured chocolates do heal the soul. **Branches**: 33 rue Vivienne, 2nd (01.40.39.05.50); 107 rue Jouffroy d'Abbans, 17th (01.47.63.15.15).

Jadis et Gourmande

49bis av Franklin D Roosevelt, 8th (01.42.25.06.04). M° Franklin D Roosevelt or St Philippe du Roule. **Open** 1-7pm Mon; 9.30am-7pm Tue; 9.30am-7.30pm Wed-Fri; 10am-7pm Sat. **Credit** MC, V. **Map I19**
The best place for novelty chocolates. The chocolate Arcs de Triomphe, Santas and letters of the alphabet make fun presents. For inscriptions in white chocolate, order ahead. **Branches**: 39 rue des Archives, 4th (01.48.04.08.03); 88 bd du Port-Royal, 5th (01.43.26.17.75).

La Maison du Chocolat

89 av Raymond-Poincaré, 16th (01.40.67.77.83). M° Victor-Hugo. **Open** 9.30am-7pm Mon-Sat. **Credit** AmEx, MC, V. **Map B4**
This temple to the cocoa bean stocks incredibly rich truffles, wickedly bitter éclairs and chocolate tart. The music-loving owner often gives his creations suitably operatic names. **Branches include**: 19 rue de Sèvres, 6th (01.45.44.20.40); 225 rue du Fbg-St-Honoré, 8th (01.42.27.39.44); 8 bd de la Madeleine, 9th (01.47.42.86.52).

A la Petite Fabrique

12 rue St-Sabin, 11th (01.48.05.82.02). M° Bastille. **Open** 10.30am-7.30pm Tue-Sat. Closed one week in Aug. **Credit** MC, V. **Map M6**
This is truly artisanal chocolate-making – you can see the cauldron being stirred at the back. Little hazelnut or almond-studded drops are fresh and inexpensive.

Richart

258 bd St-Germain, 7th (01.45.55.66.00). M° Solférino. **Open** 10am-7pm Mon-Fri; 11am-7pm Sat. **Credit** MC, V. **Map F6**
This *chocolatier* has a sophisticated style all his own: each delicate chocolate has an intricate design, and no box is complete without a tract on how best to savour chocolate. **Branch**: 36 av de Wagram, 8th (01.45.74.94.00).

Gourmet Goodies & Traiteurs

Les Abeilles

21 rue de la Butte-aux-Cailles, 13th (01.45.81.43.48). M° Place d'Italie. **Open** 11am-7pm Tue-Sat. **Credit** MC, V.
In the villagey Butte-aux-Cailles, this shop displays 50 varieties of honey from all over France, including creamy clover, fragrant lavender, chestnut, thyme, rhododendron and holly.

Comptoir de la Gastronomie

34 rue Montmartre, 1st (01.42.33.31.32). M° Etienne-Marcel. **Open** 6am-1pm, 2.30-7pm Tue-Sat. **Credit** AmEx, MC, V. **Map J5**
An attractive, old-fashioned grocery laden with *foie gras* from Southwest France in all its forms, plus snails, caviar, *confit de canard*, hams, truffles and dried mushrooms.

La Comtesse du Barry

13 bd Haussmann, 9th (01.47.70.21.01). M° Chaussée-d'Antin. **Open** 9am-7pm Mon-Sat. **Credit** AmEx, DC, MC, V. **Map H3**
Staff will package French delicacies, like terrines, pâtés and *foie gras*, in hampers or gift wrap. The lazy can buy high-quality, ready-made stews, soups and sauces. **Branches**: 93 rue St-Antoine, 4th (01.40.29.07.14); 1 rue de Sèvres, 6th (01.45.48.32.04); 317 rue de Vaugirard, 15th (01.42.50.90.13); 88bis av Mozart, 16th (01.45.27.74.49).

Davoli – La Maison du Jambon

34 rue Cler, 7th (01.45.51.23.41). M° Ecole-Militaire. **Open** 8am-1pm, 3.30-7.30pm Tue, Thur-Sat; 8am-1pm Wed, Sun. Closed first three weeks in Aug. **Credit** MC, V. **Map D6**
French, Spanish and Italian hams hang from hooks and throng the counter, smoked salmon, blinis and *foie gras* jostle for position, while cheerful assistants slice and serve in a blur of movement. Locals crowd in for anything from a slice of *jambon du Bayonne* to ingredients for a chic dinner party.

L'Epicerie

51 rue St-Louis-en-l'Ile, 4th (01.43.25.20.14). M° Pont-Marie. **Open** 10.30am-8pm daily. **Credit** MC, V. **Map K7**
A perfect present shop crammed with pretty bottles of black-currant vinegar, five-spice mustard, orange sauce, tiny pots of jam, honey with figs and boxes of chocolate snails.

Fauchon

26, 28-30 pl de la Madeleine, 8th (01.47.42.60.11). M° Madeleine. **Open** shop 9.40am-7pm Mon-Sat; *traiteur* 9.40am-8.30pm Mon-Sat. **Credit** AmEx, DC, MC, V. **Map F4**
Paris' most famous food store is like every specialist deli rolled into one, with windows that are as much for tourists as for buyers. There is a museum-like prepared-food section, cheese, fish and exotic fruit counters, an Italian deli, wines in the *cave* and chocolates around the corner.

Flo Prestige

42 pl du Marché-St-Honoré, 1st (01.42.61.45.46). M° Pyramides. **Open** 8am-11pm daily. **Credit** AmEx, DC, MC, V. **Map G4**
A pricey but pristine *traiteur*, Flo Prestige has everything you need for a luxury picnic – salads, smoked salmon, cold meats, cheeses, cakes, desserts and hot dishes of the day. **Branches include**: 10 rue St-Antoine, 4th (01.53.01.91.91); 36 av de la Motte-Picquet, 7th (01.45.55.71.25); 211 av Daumesnil, 12th (01.43.44.86.36); 352 rue Lecourbe, 15th (01.45.54.76.94); 61 av de la Grande-Armée, 16th (01.45.00.12.10).

La Grande Epicerie de Paris

Le Bon Marché (shop 2), 38 rue de Sèvres, 7th (01.44.39.81.00). M° Sèvres-Babylone. **Open** 8.30am-9pm Mon-Sat. **Credit** MC, V. **Map G7**
A feast for the senses, this recently redesigned gourmet supermarket has beautiful cheese, Alsatian *charcuterie*, *foie gras*, fish and Italian deli counters and an excellent bakery.

Hédiard

21 pl de la Madeleine, 8th (01.43.12.88.88). M° Madeleine. **Open** shop 8am-10pm Mon-Sat; *traiteur* 8am-11pm Mon-Sat. **Credit** AmEx, DC, MC, V. **Map F4**
Paris' second most famous food store has luscious-looking fruits and veg, a huge variety of jams and beautifully packed spices and *tapenades*. Wine-wise, discreetly padlocked Petrus catches the eye, but there are affordable alternatives. **Branches**: 126 rue du Bac, 7th (01.45.44.01.98); 70 av Paul-Doumer, 16th (01.45.04.51.92); 106 bd des Courcelles, 17th (01.47.63.32.14).

Lenôtre

61 rue Lecourbe, 15th (01.42.73.20.97). M° Sèvres-Lecourbe. **Open** 8am-9pm daily. **Credit** AmEx, MC, V. **Map D8**
The Lenôtre shops are known for their prepared dishes, cakes and catering service, but don't miss their intensely flavoured chocolate truffles or Roland Durant's unusual jams. **Branches include**: 15 bd de Courcelles, 8th (01.45.63.87.63); 48 av Victor-Hugo, 16th (01.45.02.21.21); 121 av de Wagram, 17th (01.47.63.70.30).

Just what the doctor ordered at
Debavre et Gallais*.

La Maison de l'Escargot
79 rue Fondary, 15th (01.45.75.31.09). M° Emile-Zola.
Open 9am-7.30pm Tue-Sat; 9am-1pm Sun. Closed 13
July-1 Sept. Credit MC, V. Map C8
Two women sit stuffing garlic butter into the *petits gris* and
sought-after Burgundy snails. *Espace dégustation*.

La Maison de la Truffe
19 pl de la Madeleine, 8th (01.42.65.53.22).
M° Madeleine. Open 9am-8pm Mon; 9am-9pm Tue-Sat.
Credit AmEx, DC, MC, V. Map F4
Come here for fresh Périgord black truffles (9,980F/kg) – or
try the more affordable truffle oils, sauces and vinegars.

A L'Olivier
23 rue de Rivoli, 4th (01.48.04.86.59). M° St-Paul or
Hôtel-de-Ville. Open 9.30am-1pm, 2-7pm Tue-Sat.
Credit MC, V. Map K6
Attractively bottled olive oils (in various strengths) as well
as wine vinegars and its own range of olives and mustards.

Regional Specialities

L'Alpage
119 av Gambetta, 20th (01.40.31.99.13). M° Gambetta.
Open 9am-1pm, 3.45-8pm Mon-Sat. Closed mid-July to
end-Aug. Credit MC, V.
Thierry Swierz sells Savoie's delectable cheeses and wines,
plus sausages flavoured with wild mushroom or cabbage.

L'Auvergnat
60 rue Oberkampf, 11th (01.48.05.31.83). M° Parmentier.
Open 4-7.30pm Mon; 9am-1pm, 4-7.30pm Tue-Sat.
Closed two weeks in July. Credit MC, V. Map M5
Hearty specialities include beautifully displayed cheeses,
tempting homemade sausages and hare terrine with prunes.

La Campagne
111 bd de Grenelle, 15th (01.47.34.77.05). M° La Motte-
Piquet. Open 8.30am-1pm, 3.30-8pm Tue-Sat; 8.30am-
1pm Sun. Closed Aug. Credit MC, V. Map C7
Bask in all things Basque: Pyrenean sheep's cheeses,
Bayonne ham, fiery Espelette peppers and Irouléguy wines.

Charcuterie Lyonnaise
58 rue des Martyrs, 9th (01.48.78.96.45). M° Notre-
Dame de Lorette. Open 8.30am-1.30pm, 4-7.30pm Tue-
Sat; 8.30am-12.30pm Sun. Closed two weeks in Aug.
Credit MC, V. Map H2
Jean-Jacques Chrétienne prepares Lyonnais *quenelles de bro-
chet*, *jambon persillé* and *hure* (pistachio-seasoned tongue).

A la Cigogne
61 rue de l'Arcade, 8th (01.43.87.39.16). M° St Lazare.
Open 8am-7pm Mon-Fri; 10am-6pm Sat. Closed Aug. No
credit cards. Map F4
Hearty Alsatian fare here includes scrumptious tarts, strüdel
and *beravecka* fruit bread plus sausages laced with pistachios.

Le Comptoir Corrézien
8 rue des Volontaires, 15th (01.47.83.52.97).
M° Volontaires. Open 9.30am-1.30pm, 3-8pm Mon-Sat.
Closed Aug. Credit MC, V. Map E9
Le Comptoir Corrézien has fine *foie gras* joined by fresh and
dried mushrooms and a wide array of duck-based products.

Henri Ceccaldi
21 rue des Mathurins, 9th (01.47.42.66.52). M° Havre
Caumartin/RER Auber. Open 8.30am-7.30pm Mon-Fri;
2-6pm Sat (Jan, Feb, Nov, Dec only). Closed Aug. Credit
MC, V. Map G3
Ceccaldi sells freshly imported Corsican *charcuterie*, goat's
and sheep's cheese, chestnut flour, cakes and Corsican wines.

International

Donestia
20 rue de la Grange-aux-Belles, 10th (01.42.08.30.44).
M° Colonel-Fabien. Open 10am-8.30pm Tue-Sat; 10am-
1.30pm Sun. Credit AmEx, MC, V. Map M3
A small, sunny shop with specialities from the Basque country and Spain, like *paella* rice, spiced blood sausage and Rioja.

Izraël
30 rue François-Miron, 4th (01.42.72.66.23). M° Hôtel-
de-Ville. Open 9.30am-1pm, 2.30-7pm Tue-Fri; 9.30am-
7pm Sat. Closed Aug. Credit MC, V. Map K6
Exotic spices and other delights from as far afield as Mexico,
Turkey and India – juicy dates, feta cheese, *tapenades* and
a huge selection of spirits – will add a kick to your cuisine.

Kioko
46 rue des Petits-Champs, 2nd (01.42.61.33.65).
M° Pyramides. Open 10am-8pm Mon-Sat. Credit MC, V.
Map H4
Everything you need to make sushi, plus sauces, snacks,
takeaway sushi, sake, Japanese beer, tea and kitchen equipment. On Saturdays, everything's 10 per cent off.

Mexi & Co
10 rue Dante, 5th (01.46.34.14.12). M° Maubert-
Mutualité. Open 10.30am-midnight daily. No credit
cards. Map J7
Everything you need for a fiesta, including marinades for *fajitas*, dried chillis, South American beers, *cachaça* and tequilas.

Le Mille-Pâtes
5 rue des Petits-Champs, 1st (01.42.96.03.04).
M° Bourse. Open 9am-8pm Mon-Fri; 9am-7.30pm Sat.
Closed Aug. Credit AmEx, DC, MC, V. Map H4
A treasure trove of Italian delicacies with tender amaretti
biscuits, Italian *charcuterie* and takeaway hot pasta specials.

Pickwick's
8 rue Mandar, 2nd (01.40.26.06.58). M° Les Halles..
Open noon-7pm Tue-Sat. No credit cards. Map J5
This Liverpudlian grocer caters to Brits homesick for baked
beans, Ambrosia rice pudding, Hobnobs and Marmite, while
catching up on *Viz*. Also stocks English-language videos.

Sarl Velan Stores
83-87 passage Brady, 10th (01.42.46.06.06).
M° Château d'Eau. Open 9.30am-8.30pm Mon-Sat.
Credit AmEx, MC, V. Map K4
Sarl Velan, in an alley of Indian cafés and shops, stocks
spices and elusive vegetables from Kenya and India.

Saveurs d'Irlande
5 cité du Vauxhall, 10th (01.42.00.36.20). M° République
or Jacques-Bonsergent. Open 10am-7pm Tue-Sat (and
Mon from Sept-Jan). Closed Aug. Credit MC, V. Map L4
This shop is worth a detour for its real Irish soda bread,
smoked and wild salmon, beers, whiskeys and Celtic CDs.

Tang Frères
48 av d'Ivry, 13th (01.45.70.80.00). M° Porte d'Ivry.
Open 9am-7.30pm Tue-Sun. Credit MC, V.
Chinatown's biggest Asian supermarket is a great find for
flat, wind-dried duck and unidentifiable fruit and veg.

Thanksgiving
14 rue Charles V, 4th (01.42.77.68.29). M° St-Paul. Open
11am-7pm Tue-Sat; 11am-6pm Sun. Closed three weeks in
Aug. Credit MC, V. Map L7
North American delicacies such as Oreos, canned pumpkin
and Tollhouse chocolate chips, plus measuring cups and
spoons, comfort the homesick. Their eaterie (*see chapter*
Restaurants) specialises in regional dishes.

Streetwise shopping

If another day of monument- and museum-hopping seems like too much, a stroll around one of the city's food markets is a calming way to discover another side to the city. Smaller markets thrive in every *arrondissement*, often rambunctious on weekends when people toting shopping carts, prams and dogs admire the beautifully displayed food and soak up the atmosphere. Nearly every market offers a stunning array of food, but each has its own character.

Probably the most gorgeous market in Paris is along the **avenue de Saxe** (8am-1.30pm Thur, Sat) in the elegant 7th. Stand at place de Breteuil and you'll see the Eiffel Tower rising up between two tree-lined rows of stalls filled with mouthwatering goods. The **marché Président Wilson** (8am-1.30pm Wed, Sat) in the 16th has a similarly chic setting and beautiful foods to match. More laidback is the villagey but touristy **rue Mouffetard** (9am-1pm, 4-7pm Tue-Sat; 9am-1pm Sun), an ancient cobbled street. Wander up it, admiring the stalls on both

Mouthwatering goods on **avenue de Saxe.**

sides, turn right on rue Ortolan, and you'll find a more authentic neighbourhood market in the leafy **place Monge** (8am-1.30pm Wed, Fri, Sun). The famous **rue de Buci** (9am-1pm, 4-7pm Tue-Sat; 9am-1pm Sun) is dominated by supermarkets these days, but is still a good place to linger on a café terrace. Another prime people-watching market is the pedestrian **rue Montorgueil** (9am-1pm, 4-7pm Tue-Sat; 9am-1pm Sun), all that remains of the Les Halles wholesale market. Visit **place de Joinville** (8am-1.30pm Thur, Sun) for its setting next to the canal de l'Ourcq and down-to-earth crowd.

If your quest is for the best, seek out the organic markets along **boulevard Raspail** (8am-1.30pm Sun) or **boulevard des Batignolles** (8am-1.30pm Sat). Untreated fruit and veg may not have the gloss of their chemically enhanced counterparts, but their flavours are more intense. Also look for free-range chickens, farmers' goat cheeses and country-style *charcuterie*. Another market that draws the crowds is **Richard Lenoir** (8am-1.30pm Thur, Sun), near place de la Bastille. Similarly packed with gastronomic finds but more residential is the **cours de Vincennes** (8am-1.30pm Wed, Sat). More manageably sized and also a delight for the senses are the street markets at **rue Cler** and **rue Poncelet** (both 9am-1pm, 4-7pm Tue-Sat; 9am-1pm Sun), where most goods are displayed in pretty boutiques rather than stalls. In the mood for something more exotic? The boisterous North African markets at **place d'Aligre** (9am-1pm Tue-Sat; 9am-1pm Sun) or **Belleville** (8am-1.30pm Tue, Fri) often hold bargains.

Rue Daguerre (9am-1pm, 4-7pm Tue-Sat; 9am-1pm Sun), lined with beautiful shops including a branch of cheese specialist Androuet, has a festive feel. The **boulevard de Grenelle** market (8am-1.30pm Wed, Sun) livens up a residential neighbourhood, especially on Sunday when cheerful crowds cluster under the overhead Métro for Provençal oils, free-range chickens and freshly picked salads. Just as popular is **boulevard Auguste Blanqui** (8am-1.30pm Tue, Fri, Sun), a long tree-shaded market brightened with garlands of lights all year round.

When visiting markets, look for the sign 'producteur' to find merchants who are selling foods they grow or produce themselves. These are the ones to ask when you want to know more about a particular food – most are thrilled to find a willing audience.

Most *cavistes* are happy to guide their clients, so don't be afraid to ask for advice if you have a particular wine or dish in mind. To buy direct from producers, visit the Salon des Caves Particulières at Espace Champerret in March and December. The Nicolas and Le Repaire de Bacchus chains have numerous branches around town.

Les Caves Augé

116 bd Haussmann, 8th (01.45.22.16.97). M° St Augustin.
Open 1-7.30pm Mon; 9am-7.30pm Tue-Sat. Closed Mon in Aug. **Credit** AmEx, MC, V. **Map F3**
The oldest wine shop in Paris – Marcel Proust was a regular customer – is today serious and professional with *sommelier* Marc Sibard on hand to give advice.

Caves du Marais

64 rue François-Miron, 4th (01.42.78.54.64). M° St Paul.
Open 10.30am-1pm, 4-8pm Tue-Sat. Closed Aug. **Credit** MC, V. **Map K6**
Wines and cognacs from small producers are displayed like jewels in the window of this small shop. Jean-Jacques Bailly tastes everything, and offers some surprising finds.

Les Caves Taillevent

199 rue du Fbg-St-Honoré, 8th (01.45.61.14.09). M° Charles de Gaulle-Etoile or Ternes. **Open** 2-8pm Mon; 9am-8pm Tue-Fri; 9am-7.30pm Sat. Closed first two weeks in Aug.
Half a million bottles await you in the Taillevent empire. On Saturdays, head *sommelier* Michel Desroche gives tastings of wines starting at 24F a bottle. Visit the cellars for spiritual temptation by 1914 Hine cognac or 1951 chartreuse.

Le Jardin des Vignes

91 rue de Turenne, 3rd (01.42.77.05.00). M° St-Sébastien-Froissart. **Open** 2.30-7.30pm Mon-Sat.

Closed Aug. **Credit** MC, V. **Map L5**
Jean Radford has been selling wines from his seventeenth-century Marais cellar for 15 years. Most customers buy in bulk; he delivers within Paris, ships abroad and even stores wine in lockers for customers. Ask about tastings and classes.

Legrand Filles et Fils

1 rue de la Banque, 2nd (01.42.60.07.12). M° Bourse.
Open 9am-7.30pm Tue-Fri; 8.30am-1pm, 3-7pm Sat. **Credit** AmEx, MC, V. **Map H4**
This old-fashioned wine shop is a must for wine lovers, offering fine wines, brandies, tasting glasses and wine gadgets amid chocolates, teas, coffees and old-fashioned *bonbons*.

La Maison du Whisky

20 rue d'Anjou, 8th (01.42.65.03.16). M° Madeleine.
Open 9.30am-7pm Mon; 9.15am-8pm Tue-Fri; 9.30am-7.30pm Sat. **Credit** AmEx, MC, V. **Map F4**
Whisky is taken seriously and Jean-Marc Bellier is fascinating as he explains which whisky would taste good with which food or flavours such as honey and tobacco.

Le Saveur Club

125bis bd du Montparnasse, 6th (01.43.27.12.06). M° Vavin. **Open** 10am-8pm Tue-Sat; 10am-12.30pm Sun. **Credit** AmEx, DC, MC, V. **Map G9**
In this underground car park – ideal for popping cases straight into your car – you'll find a wide selection and professional staff ready to give advice. With Georges Lepré, former head *sommelier* at the Ritz, tasting the wines, quality control is very strict. They also offer courses.

Vignobles Passion

130 bd Haussmann, 8th (01.45.22.25.22). M° Miromesnil.
Open 10am-7pm Mon-Sat. **Credit** AmEx, DC, MC, V. **Map E3**
The young, enthusiastic bilingual team groups together French wine producers to sell and show their wines. Tutored tastings are given by Loick Ducrey (possible in English for groups), as well as deliveries (even to the UK) and advice on which wine to drink with which food.

Banking on wine chez **Legrand et Fils**.

Arts & Entertainment

Cabaret, Circus & Comedy

From girlie chorus lines and cross-dressers to cross-Channel stand-up and underwater circus, there's plenty of room for hilarity.

With its image of can-can girls, feathered costumes and glitzy turns, it's hard to remember that cabaret was once the universe for daring feats where snake wrestlers and an outré flash of flesh inspired awe. It's indicative of the state of the art that the Folies Bergère now serves up musicals and the **Lido's** show is largely in English. But if girlie cabarets now live on past glories for tourist audiences, something of the spirit lives on in more subversive descendants, in the thriving world of alternative circus, and in crossovers with theatre and dance.

Café-théâtre is less influential than in its post-68 heyday, but remains a spawning ground for comic talents. Musical comedy is a growing facet, at Café-Théâtres and at specialist venue **La Pepinière Opéra** or with crowd pullers like Le Quattuor, whose chamber-music spoof filled a full-scale theatre for months. English stand-up comedy has also established a niche for itself with the regular **Laughing Matters** sessions at the Hôtel du Nord.

By contrast, contemporary circus is booming. Drawing on both circus and cabaret traditions and often injecting a dose of social comment, where feats of sleight and skill often follow from a hotchpotch of intellectual subtexts, multi-cultural borrowings or political comment, these companies are far from the naff clowns of cliché; most succeed remarkably well in pleasing all age groups. Best-known of the modern circuses are Archaos, who combine circus skills, techno music, video projections and socio-political subtexts. Dazzling trapeze troupe Les Arts Sauts abet acrobatic skills with cross-cultural influences. Cirque Plume uses theatre, cabaret, music, trapezes and trampolines to make discreet social points, while Achille Tonic are closer to irreverent cabaret. Look out also for Bartabas' spectacular equestrian circus Zingaro, which performs in a wooden fort at Aubervilliers. So traditional it's modern, the gypsy circus **CirqueTzigane Romanes** has been a huge success in going back to basics. More conventional circus also abounds, especially at Christmas time when the famous French families Gruss, Bouglione and Pinder are bound to be appearing. Check the 'Enfants' section of listings publications for info.

Comedy in English

Laughing Matters
Hôtel du Nord, 102 quai de Jemmapes, 10th (01.48.06.01.20). M° République. **Shows** usually 8.30pm Mon, Tue, Sun. **Tickets** 100F; 80F students. **No credit cards. Map L4**
Up to a hundred English-speakers regularly cram into the upstairs room at the film-legend venue to catch a stream of stand-ups hot off the Eurostar, including top Brit and Irish acts from the Edinburgh Festival and a few transatlantic visitors. Eddie Izzard, Reg the Pub Landlord, Ed Byrne, Dylan Moran and Arj Barker have all performed here.

Café-Théâtre

Au Bec Fin
6 rue Thérèse, 1st (01.42.96.29.35). M° Palais-Royal or Pyramides. **Shows** usually 7pm, 8.15pm, 10pm Tue-Sat. **Restaurant** noon-2.30pm, 7.30pm-midnight Mon-Fri; 7.30pm-midnight Sat. **Tickets** 80F; 65F students (except Sat); 50F Mon auditions 9.30pm. *dinner and show* from 178F. **Credit** MC, V. **Map H5**
This 60-seat theatre and the Café de la Gare are the oldest café-théâtres in Paris. Monday-night auditions of untried acts draw a young, irreverent crowd. The quality is extremely variable. There is a ground-floor restaurant.

Café de la Gare
41 rue du Temple, 4th (01.42.78.52.51). M° Hôtel-de-Ville. **Shows** 8pm, 10pm Wed-Sat. **Tickets** 100F-120F; 50F-100F students. **Credit** MC, V. **Map K5**
30 years old, and source of inspiration for many others, the largest (seats 300) and most charming of the café-théâtres, set in a Marais courtyard, spawned such talents as Colouche and Miou-Miou. Shows range from Molière to one-man stand-up or eleven-strong team Les Voila! Turnover is high, but so are standards, as this place has a reputation to maintain.

La Pépinière Opéra
7 rue Louis-le-Grand, 2nd (01.42.61.44.16). M° Opéra. **Shows** 9pm Mon-Sat. **Tickets** 160F-200F; 70F students, under-26s (Mon-Fri). **Credit** AmEx, MC, V. **Map G4**
Music hall and musical comedy, plus some straight *chanson*, in a pretty little theatre. Acts are usually of a high standard, with newcomers sponsored by established 'godfathers'.

Mélo d'Amelie
4 rue Marie-Stuart, 2nd (01.40.26.11.11). M° Etienne Marcel. **Shows** 8pm, 9.30pm Tue-Sat. **Tickets** *one show* 100F; *two shows* 140F; students (Tue-Fri) *one show* 70F; *two shows* 120F. **No credit cards. Map J5**
Although it doesn't consider itself a café-théâtre, this cosy venue puts on a similar array of small-scale comedies.

Stand up if you think **Laughing Matters**.

Point Virgule

7 rue Ste-Croix-de-la-Bretonnerie, 4th (01.42.78.67.03).
M° Hôtel de Ville. **Shows** 8pm, 9.15pm, 10.15pm daily.
Tickets *one show* 80F; *two shows* 130F; *three shows* 150F;
65F students (Mon-Fri, Sun). **No credit cards. Map K6**
This small Marais theatre is one of the few to stay open in
summer. Its shows are almost all one- or two-person stand-
up, plus a few comic musical acts. Jean-François Derec's
send-up of man-woman relations was a notable long runner.

Théatre et Café Edgar

58 bd Edgar-Quinet, 14th (01.42.79.97.97). M° Edgar-
Quinet or Montparnasse-Bienvenüe. **Shows** usually
8.15pm, 9.30pm Mon-Sat. **Tickets** 80F-100F; 65F-70F
students, under-25s. **No credit cards. Map G9**
The tiny Théatre is easily packed; you may find yourself sitting on the stage. With the equally minuscule Café, they host
four or five productions a time, all of them one or two-man
shows designed for this degree of intimacy with the audience. *Les Babas cadres* has been a fixture since the early 80s.

Cabaret Glamour

Crazy Horse Saloon

12 av George V, 8th (01.47.23.32.32). M° Alma-Marceau
or George V. **Show** 8.30pm, 11pm Mon-Fri, Sun; 7.30pm,
9.45pm, 11.50pm Sat. **Admission** *with champagne* 290F-
660F; *with dinner* 750F-980F. **Credit** AmEx, DC, MC, V.
Map D4
The foot soldiers of fantasy at the Crazy Horse all boast uni-
formly curvaceous bodies to titillate a high-rolling clientele.
Mad names abound, as Lumina Neon, Looky Boop and Pussy
Duty-Free whet the appetite nightly. The revue *Teasing* is
subtitled 'the art of the nude', but the identikit girls are kept
at a draconian distance and weighed twice a month.

Le Lido

116bis av des Champs-Elysées, 8th (01.40.76.56.10).
M° George V. **Dinner** 8pm. **Show** 10pm, midnight.

Admission *with drink* 375F-560F; *with dinner* 795F-
995F; **Credit** AmEx, DC, MC, V. **Map D4**
Ever-popular with Japanese businessmen, the 60 Bluebell
Girls shake their endowments in a show entitled *C'est*
Magique – almost the only words in French. Special effects
include a fire-breathing dragon, an ice rink and a waterfall,
but it's most notable for the sheer number of costume
changes. The menu has been redesigned by Paul Bocuse,
without noticeable improvement.
Wheelchair access.

Moulin Rouge

82 bd de Clichy, 18th (01.53.09.82.82). M° Blanche.
Dinner 7pm, **Show** 9pm, 11pm daily. **Admission** *with*
dinner 770F-980F. **Credit** AmEx,
DC, MC, V. **Map G2**
This kitschy Pigalle venue, graced by Piaf, Montand and
Sinatra in their day, is the place to go for time-warp can-cans.
Breasts abound (with the odd pair titillatingly concealed to
maintain dramatic tension) and remain impressively pert
along with the fake lashes and toothpaste smiles throughout nearly two hours of high-kicks and nostalgic song routines. A brand new extravaganza is scheduled to replace the
current *'Formidable'* show in December 1999.

Cabaret Kinks & Turns

Les Assassins

40 rue Jacob, 6th (no telephone). M° St-Germain-des-Prés.
Open 7pm-midnight Mon-Sat. **Average** 110F.
No credit cards. Map H6
'No reservations, no cheques, no coffee, no telephone': this
bistro is a relic of a naughtier bygone age when St-Germain
was far less refined. Dine on classics like *lapin à la moutarde*,
while singer-guitarist Maurice Dulac – he and his blow-wave
equally present since the 60s – serenades with the likes of
La grosse bite de Dudul (*Little Dulac's big dick*). He's very
funny, but it takes a pretty good command of French ana-
tomical slang to keep up with the innuendos.

Caveau de la République

1 bd St-Martin, 3rd (01.42.78.44.45). M° République.
Show 9pm Tue-Sat; 3.30pm Sun. Closed July, Aug.
Admission 140F Tue-Thur; 180F Fri-Sun; 105F over-60s
(Tue-Thur); 90F students under-25s (Tue-Thur). **Credit**
MC, V. **Map L4**
A kind of cabaret that has survived the onslaught of the
twentieth century, the *chansonnier* is an ancient form of
entertainment comprising stand-up, verse-monologue and
song, much of it with a political-satirical bent. The older performers at this smart basement venue belong to that
dinosaur-genre, the 'humourist', and the middle-aged audience laps up their turns about not being able to work the
video, etc. The younger acts are exuberantly physical, both
edgier and naughtier, allowing the quintessentially Parisian-
bourgeois spectators a good belly-laugh. The Caveau's line-
up provides a slick, funny and very French three hours.

Chez Madame Arthur

*75 bis rue des Martyrs, 18th (01.42.64.48.27/
01.42.54.40.21). M° Pigalle or Abbesses.* **Dinner** 9pm.
Show 10.30pm daily. **Admission** *with one drink* 165F;
with dinner 295F-595F. **Credit** AmEx, MC, V. **Map H2**
The French equivalent of Dame Edna Everage presents a
non-stop show of drag artists and transsexuals, who mime
to female singers or camp-up historic scenes. The make-up
is as heavy as the *double entendre*. If you sit at the front, be
prepared to be teased, tantalised and kissed.

Chez Michou

80 rue des Martyrs, 18th (01.46.06.16.04). M° Pigalle.
Dinner daily 9pm. **Show** 11pm approx (ring to check).
Admission *with drink* 200F; *with dinner* 550F. **Credit**
MC, V. **Map H2**
Eccentric cabaret owner Michou has achieved the status of
a French national treasure. The routines change regularly

Suspend disbelief at **Espace Chapiteaux**.

but often feature larger-than-life incarnations of Josephine
Baker, French torch-song *chanteuse* Barbara, or Tina Turner.
Blue-clad Michou guides the proceedings from beside the
stage, launching irrepressible salvos of whoops and laugh-
ter. It's usually possible to get seats on the night if you just
want to see the show, but book ahead if you want to dine.

Au Lapin Agile

*22 rue des Saules, 18th (01.46.06.85.87). M° Lamarck-
Caulaincourt.* **Shows** 9pm Tue-Sun. **Admission**
show, one drink 130F; 90F students (Tue-Fri, Sun).
No credit cards. Map H1
This cosy parlour whisks you back to the turn of the centu-
ry, when it was a fave with Montmartre's bohemians, and
chansonnier Aristide Bruant was depicted by Toulouse-
Lautrec. It acquired its name after André Gill labelled his inn
The Rabbit (*Lapin A Gill*) in the nineteenth century. The
artists have been replaced by tourists and a team of per-
formers: accordionist Cassita, strident singer-songwriter
Arlette Denis and songster Yves Mathieu.

Contemporary Circus

Cirque d'Hiver Bouglione

*110 rue Amelot, 11th (01.47.00.12.25). M° Filles du
Calvaire.* **Box office** 9am-noonm 2-6pm Mon-Fri.
Tickets 70F-150F. **Credit** V. **Map L5**
The beautiful winter circus was built in 1852 by Hittorff,
inspired by the polychromy of Ancient Greece. Now it is used
for various visiting troupes, and possibly for the Cirque du
Demain competition; the circular pool under the ring was
recently resuscitated for former synchonised swimming
champ Muriel Hermine's aquatic extravaganza Crescend'O.

Cirque Tzigane Romanès

*passage Lathuille, 12 av de Clichy, 18th (01.43.87.16.38).
M° Place de Clichy.* **Shows** 8.30pm Tue-Fri; 3pm, 8.30pm
Sat; 3pm, 5pm, 8.30pm Sun. **Tickets** 100F; 50F under
18s, students. **No credit cards. Map G2**
Two gypsy families pitched tent five years ago on a waste-
ground. The show fuses acrobatics, comedy and sensuality
into superb physical theatre. Comprising a strongman, a
wire-walker, a contortionist, gymnasts and musicians, the
troupe are consummate showmen, beginning with small
stuff and building to a crescendo of exhilarating stunts punctuated by comic interludes. This is circus as it should be:
spectacular, gracefully executed, with a constant accompaniment of cacophonous, raggedly beautiful music. The circus tours from June to August but returns in the autumn.

Espace Chapiteaux

*Parc de la Villette, 19th (08.03.07.50.75). M° Porte de
Pantin or Porte de la Villette.* **Shows** 8.30pm Wed-Sat;
4pm Sun. **Tickets** 110F-150F; 90F-120F 16-25s; 50F-75F
4-15s; free under 4s. **Credit** MC, V. **Map inset**
Daring acrobatics meet intellectual modern circus at La
Villette's space for circus tents year-round and open-air per-
formances in summer. Recent tenants include Cirque Plume
(back Oct-Dec 1999), the Cirque du Docteur Paradi, Les Arts
Sauts, and Le Centre National des Arts du Cirque.
Wheelchair access.

Théâtre du Ranelagh

*5 rue des Vignes, 16th (01.42.88.64.44).
M° La Mouette/RER Boulainvilliers.*
Box office 11am-6pm Mon-Sat, 11am-2pm Sun.
Shows vary. **Tickets** 120F-200F; 75F-90F students,
over-60s. **Credit** AmEx, MC, V. **Map A6**
Madonna Bouglione comes from one of France's great circus
dynasties and this strange old theatre is sometimes home to
troupes of clowns and other performance artists from France
and abroad, alongside more standard theatrical fare.

Clubs

Clubbing in Paris is as much a lesson in style as in sound, but if you can master the fancy footwork the Latino nights really hot up.

There are many words for style in French, but no word for fun. Dance music is thus the finishing touch, rather than central, focus to an evening out. Chart and house music predominate; techno and trance appear in only a couple of clubs (try **Le Gibus**), perhaps because Parisian clubbers are not as into drugs as other Europeans. If you're looking for something hardcore, then seek out the 'afters' after big club nights. Most harder sounds happen outside Paris, in studenty and industrial cities, such as Nancy and Dijon, and in tolerated teknovial festivals, especially now the infamous Spiral Tribe are back. Combative French hip hop is found more in the *banlieue* (suburbs), as are semi-legal mobile phone raves (catch up with Rave Collective). Local authorities intermittently finance a 'cultural festival', a volatile platform for urban frustration. However, don't miss Mix Move's (01.42.23.00.33) scratching and mixing championships in October at Paris-Expo.

Nightclubbing in Paris has its own rules. Goonish bouncers (*physionomistes*) are, as elsewhere, a law unto themselves, and won't hesitate to turn you away in many places for *baskets* (trainers), for dirty or ripped clothes, or if you don't turn up with enough girls. Being foreign helps, but being gorgeous is the clincher, and Paris is unrivalled in the management's shameless capacity to blatantly advertise free entry to *lookées* ('in' club babes) and BPs (Beautiful People). It's de rigueur to clock up after midnight, and the really suave swan in at 3am when the suits start dropping off. Smarter clubs are often *privé* (private), and supposedly admit only members and their guests.

The choice of where to go remains fairly consistent, but when veteran promoters David and Cathy Guetta (now of **Les Bains**) or Axel (Crazy Baby!) move venue, their loyal followers go with them. Independent promoters and record labels irregularly organise one-off events, held anywhere from elegant Salles Gaveau and Wagram to barges moored on the Seine and restaurants in the Bois de Boulogne. Fashion fave Thanx God I'm a VIP (01.40.35.22.74) and ravier Magic Garden (08.36.68.68.44) are worth checking out.

Musical taste leans towards house and garage, with a sprinkling of Afro and world music, and lashings of *raï* and Latino. Jungle has a small dedicated following: don't miss the scene-makers at rue Keller's Black Label records, who run no nonsense drum 'n' bass and jungle nights at least once

The right (un)dress is club crucial.

a month on the Bateau Concorde Atlantique, regularly inviting DJs from London's Metalheadz. If trance is your cup of herbal tea look out for trance nights by Gaïa Concept (08.36.65.12.25).

Along with a constant stream of international guests, legions of French acts do exist beyond Air and Daft Punk, even if they are less well-known abroad. Techno DJs Ilana, Laurent Hô, Torgull and Manu le Malin feature large. A huge house scene includes shakers Greg Gauthier, Sven Love, Basenotic's Dimitri from Paris and DJ Deep, Erik Rug, Ivan Smagghe and Super Discounter Etienne de Crécy, Djul'z, Luck, G-Rom, Jef K, Patrick Vidal, Claude Monet, Sex Toy and Loïk. DJ Cam, Dee Nasty, Cut Killer, Chris the French Kiss and Yellow dominate hip hop/trip hop and acclaimed DJ Gilb'r, drum and bass merchant of swelling popularity is one name to watch in 1999.

KEEPING INFORMED

For on the ground info, look in *Time Out Paris* at the back of *Pariscope* or for flyers. Having a flyer helps admission chances. Check record shops (try rue Keller/rue de Charonne, 11th) and hip bars, or tune in to Radio Nova (101.5FM), daily 5-8pm, and Radio FG (98.2FM), Mon-Fri, 6.30pm and 7.30pm (infoline 08.36.78.98.20). Tekno Sphère has a pricey infoline, 08.36.68.01.09. Useful Minitel services are 3615 Party News, 3615 FG and 3615 Rave.

Note that admission prices often include one free drink (*consommation*) and that credit cards are often accepted at the bar but not on the door.

Gilded Youth

These *clubs privés* (private clubs) make up the door policy as they go along, so prices and entry depend principally on whether you look minted. Dress: Bond, black, sharp. You can't overdress.

Le Bash

67 rue Pierre-Charron, 8th (01.45.62.95.70).
Mº Franklin D Roosevelt. **Open** 11.30pm-dawn Tue-Sun.
Admission 100F with drink. **Drinks** 100F. **Credit** AmEx, V. **Map D4**
Playboy Jean-Roch's popular club-cum-money factory seems to have run out of steam. Even at 2am it looks like the last dregs of a school disco with only a handful of couples getting down to the house and hip hop. What's more the one men's and one women's loo result in leg-crossingly slow queues. The BPs have moved on to graze elsewhere.

Le Cabaret

68 rue Pierre-Charron, 8th (01.42.89.44.14).
Mº Franklin D Roosevelt. **Open** 11pm-4/5am Sat, Sun.
Admission free. **Drinks** from 70F. **Credit** AmEx, DC, MC, V. **Map D4**
Hustle your way past the hyper-picky doormen of this gilt and red velvet cabaret if you want to mix with Eurobrats and not-so-youthful monied expats. Now owned by Philippe Fatien (Queen, etc), Cabaret strives for swankiness: drinks are farcically expensive, and pouting staff reseat those who trespass on the territory of regulars. The womb-like interior is a fine setting for cabaret events (Mon-Fri), but oppressive at weekends when it heaves with self-proclaimed BPs.

Club Castel

15 rue Princesse, 6th (01.40.51.52.80). Mº Mabillon.
Open 9pm-dawn Tue-Sat. **Admission** free. Members and their guests only. **Drinks** 100F. **Credit** AmEx, DC, MC, V. **Map H7**
Classy Castel's reeks of wallet from the moment you pass the uncharacteristically relaxed door goons. So confident in their elitist door policy (to join, you must be nominated by two members), it seems if dressed like a yacht-owner you can breeze inside. Inside, the plush four-floor joint has relaxed its black tie dresscode since octogenarian Castel retired two years ago after 40 years in the saddle, though many of his flush cronies still patronise the place. The saprophytic girls are all stunning; it's only the sour-faced, *liftée* wives who look like they are not enjoying themselves.

Duplex

2bis av Foch, 16th (01.45.00.45.00). Mº Charles-de-Gaulle-Etoile. **Open** 11pm-dawn Tue-Sun. **Admission** 80F Tue, Wed, Sun; free for girls before midnight Tue-Thur, Sun; 100F Thur; 120F with drink Fri, Sat. **Drinks** 60F. **Credit** AmEx, DC, MC, V. **Map C3**

The Duplex is patronised by those who are still a little young to frequent Le Bash and Castel's: aristocratic parents have an opportunity to safely release teenage children onto the marriage market in this regimented, but chic venue, getting down to Europop anthems and charty house. At weekends the joint swells after midnight until there's a queue down the street. A pricey restaurant upstairs (from 9pm) transforms into a chillout room after diners have finished.

Cool Clubs

Pretty girls in kitteny clothes sometimes get away with free admission. Icy bouncers need convincing that you're worth admitting. Dress: Chic clubwear. Trainers are risky.

Arapaho

Centre Commercial Italie II, 30 av d'Italie, 13th (01.45.89.65.05). Mº Place d'Italie. **Open** 11pm-dawn Fri, Sat. **Admission** 40F-80F. **Drinks** 20F-50F. **Credit** V. **Map K10**
This rock venue looks like a carpark, located in the middle of Chinatown. Nevertheless, it was the first French venue to stage big beat nights, which continue intermittently. Occasional Asian pop parties, too. Women usually get in free.

Les Bains

7 rue du Bourg-l'Abbé, 3rd (01.48.87.01.80).
Mº Réaumur Sébastopol. **Open** 11.30pm-5am daily.
Restaurant 8.30pm-1am. **Admission** 100F.
Drinks 70F. **Credit** AmEx, MC, V, DC. **Map K5**
Les Bains is the benchmark by which other plush, prestigious and pretentious house clubs can be found wanting. Once past the legendary *physios* you wade through models and Cathy Guetta's *looké* 'friends' to reach the bar. The sound system is trumped only by the Rex's howitzer, and DJs spin the latest deep house and garage. Suits plague the place until 3am when those in the know swan in. Superfly's glam and funky hip hop (Wed) and housey Crazy Baby! (Fri) are regulars. To be sure of getting in, eat at the Thai restaurant beforehand, where you can starspot floating Hollywood froth.

Bus Palladium

6 rue Fontaine, 9th (01.53.21.07.33). Mº Pigalle.
Open 11pm-dawn Tue-Sat. **Admission** free girls Tue; 100F men; 100F Wed-Sat. **Drinks** 50F-80F, Tue free drinks for women. **Credit** AmEx, MC, V. **Map H2**
The sweaty Bus Palladium is aimed more at party people than music aficionados, and the tone is set by young Parisian *BCBGs* (Sloanes). On Thursday's Motown night DJs feel free to play almost anything to get the up-for-it crowd on its feet, from pop radio tracks through French accordion classics, to hot-off-the-press house. The management refuses point blank to play anything that could be called techno.

La Casbah

18-20 rue de la Forge-Royale, 11th (01.43.71.04.39).
Mº Faidherbe-Chaligny. **Open** 11.30pm-dawn Thur-Sat.
Bar/restaurant 8pm-midnight. **Admission** 100F with drink. **Drinks** 60F-80F. **No credit cards. Map N7**
This Moroccan-themed bar has lost its sheen since its trendy heyday. In maintaining a rude and elitist entrance policy, management may have shot itself in the foot, as the décor has made it a draw for office theme parties. Sheepish waiters look awkward in fezzes, while gold-ringed Arab suits sip cocktails at the bar. Look out for the glamorous belly dancer.

Le Divan du Monde

75 rue des Martyrs, 18th (01.44.92.77.66). Mº Pigalle.
Open 8.30pm/midnight-dawn daily. **Admission** free-120F. **Drinks** 25F-40F. **Credit** MC, V. **Map H2**
The Divan du Monde hosts a wacky mix of entertainment,

Jivin' jungle on board the **Bateau Concorde Atlantique.**

and appropriately eclectic mix of punters. Currently Saturday is Brazilian night, but during the week anything goes – kids' stuff, tango nights, even Creative Relaxation (with T'ai Chi), cabaret, big name indie and rock, house or hip hop nights, often with a quality line-up of local and imported DJs. It's hard to believe this place was immortalised by Toulouse-Lautrec. *See chapter* **Music: Rock, Roots & Jazz.**

Elysée Montmartre
72 bd Rochechouart, 18th (01.44.92.45.38). M° Anvers. **Open** varies. **Admission** 80F-250F. **Drinks** 25F-40F. **Credit** AmEx, DC, MC, V. **Map J2.**
The enormous sprung dancefloor makes this one of the leading concert venues in Paris, despite atrocious air conditioning. Every now and then clubbers get a look-in too, either for the gay Scream, or the new King$ night, a straight techno/house night organised by David Guetta, the Midas of the Paris club circuit. Second and fourth Saturdays each month welcomes the steadfastly popular Le Bal where an eclectic set dances and *yéyés* to a live big band, but girls should come with partners if they want to relax, as it's fiercely predatory.

L'Enfer
34 rue de Départ, 14th (01.42.79.94.94). M° Montparnasse-Bienvenüe. **Open** 11.30pm-10am Thur-Sat. **Admission** 100F. **Drinks** 50F. **Credit** V. **Map F9**
L'Enfer has earned quite a reputation for underworld misdemeanors. Closed by the police several times in the last couple of years, punters keep coming back, so obviously something is being done right. Gay and straight get down to hard and hip house and techno in the flame styled dungeon that gave the club its name. Don't mess with the bouncers who have a habit of settling business on the spot.

Folies Pigalle
11 pl Pigalle, 9th (01.48.78.35.56). M° Pigalle. **Open** midnight-dawn daily (Sat, Sun 'after' until noon). **Admission** 100F. **Drinks** 30F-50F. **Credit** V. **Map G2**
This funky ex-strip joint depends on a hardcore of dedicated regulars, resulting in a relaxed attitude to self-promotion.

Friday and Saturday sees residents spin house and techno, running into next morning's seedy Faster Pussy Cat Kill Kill. Weekdays revolve around Afro/US nights. United Colours of Gays tea dance (Sunday, 5.30-11pm) has an Oriental influence, before turning into the Sunday Groove.

Le Gibus
18 rue du Fbg-du-Temple, 11th (01.47.00.78.88). M° République. **Open** midnight-dawn Wed-Sun; occasional 'afters'. **Admission** free Wed, Thur; 100F Fri, Sat, Sun. **Drinks** 40F-50F.
The days of testosterone rock have been replaced by up-for-it gay house or full-tilt hard trance (Wed's Gaia Concept). Fridays are firin' with Chicago's Paul Johnson spinning US house and garage. Promoter Bitchy José secures some top-flight international outsiders and this year will see the return of Daft Punk, Boy George, Frankie Knuckles and more. Sunday morning sees mayhem from still-up-for-it nutters who congregate from all over Paris.

Planet Rock
The Club, 8 rue des Bernardins, 5th (01.43.36.21.66). M° Maubert Mutualité. **Open** 11.30pm-dawn Sat. **Admission** 70F; 50F with flyer. **Drinks** 20F-30F. **Credit** MC, V. **Map H2**
DJ G Grebo hosts Paris' virtually only indie night, spinning all manner of pop, alternative rock and breakbeats. The outfit has been losing out to dance culture, but it's a solid night out, and not overpriced. Be aware that Planet Rock is the night, not the club, and it has a habit of changing venue.

Le Queen
102 av des Champs-Elysées, 8th (01.53.89.08.90). M° George V. **Open** 11.30pm-dawn daily. **Admission** free Tue-Thur; 70F Mon; 100F Fri, Sat. **Drinks** from 50F. **Credit** AmEx, MC, V. **Map D4**
The worst thing that ever happened to Queen, was that it took off as *the* major Paris club. Nowadays, any night risks overcrowding, but none more so than flagship Respect (Wed) which regularly features big guns, such as Daft Punk,

Dimitri from Paris or Jef K, when wall-to-wall punters make it impossible to reach your wallet, let alone the bar. Best bets are Thursday and Saturday, both theoretically exclusively gay, when full-on erotic podium dancers and drag queens galore rule the roost. If you're superduper camp then don't miss Monday's Disco Inferno. *See chapter* **Gay & Lesbian**.

Rex Club

5 bd Poissonnière, 2nd (01.42.36.83.98). Mº Bonne-Nouvelle. **Open** 11pm-dawn Wed, Thur, Fri; 11.30pm-dawn Sat. **Admission** 60F Wed; 70F Thur-Fri; 80F Sat. *Drinks* 30F-50F. **Credit** AmEx, MC, V. **Map J4**
The Rex stands out as one of the rare clubs that refuses to kowtow to fashion, sex, sexuality or cash, but rather remains a shameless celebration of electronic music, delivered through the fat speakers of its peerless sound system. DJ Charles Schillings builds the house on Saturday night as resident, though at any time one can find a steady flow of orbiting stars from all over Europe. Wednesday and Thursday see a variety of formidable drum 'n' bass, house, and techno events, but Friday's regular hard techno night Automatik is as good a place as any to search out a BPM nosebleed.

Less trendy, and populated with a more mixed crowd, you still might not get in if you've got holes in your jeans. Dress: Casual, but clean.

La Locomotive

90 bd de Clichy, 18th (01.53.41.88.88). Mº Blanche. **Open** 11pm-dawn daily. **Admission** 55F Mon-Thur; 100F Fri-Sat. **Drinks** 40F-50F. **Credit** AmEx, MC, V. **Map G2**
La Locomotive has lost out to the techno revolution. Half-hearted attempts at techno nights have never proved popular, as the place has a chronically untrendy reputation. Still, the cavernous three-floor venue packs out with grungy teenagers, leaving any over 20s feeling old.

Le Saint

7 rue St-Séverin, 5th (01.43.25.50.04). Mº St-Michel. **Open** 11pm-dawn Tue-Sun. **Admission** 60F Thur, Sun; 80F Fri; 90F Sat. **Drinks** 30F-40F. **Credit** DC, MC, V. **Map J7**
Relaxed and unpretentious Le Saint is patronised mainly by

Reality check

Daft Punk and Air were hyped in the UK long before anyone had heard of them in France, and when an 'official Ibiza hype chart' places Stardust's 'Music Sounds Better With You' and Bob Sinclar's 'Gym Tonic' first and second, you know the Gallic influence on the dancefloor has been pervasive – right to bootlegger Spacedust's UK No 1 with 'Gym and Tonic'. So is it all hype?

Air

Hype: *Moon Safari* was described by *Muzik* magazine as 'perfect. An album that has ... surpassed just about everything else released in the Nineties'.
Reality: *Muzik* was fawning because it had gone all the way to San Francisco to do a story on the Versailles duo's first-ever live concerts. But many critics were disappointed with the album, after the promise of earlier tracks released on the Source label. Fortunately, Nicolas Godin and Jean-Benoit Dunckel had done one of the biggest media campaigns of any new act – more than 300 interviews in Europe alone – before *Moon Safari* was released.
Future? They lack the golden touch of Daft Punk, but will be around for a while.

Laurent Garnier

Hype: French dance music magazine, *Trax*, claims Laurent Garnier's live show at the Olympia in September 1998 has given him an international identity and sound.
Reality: Garnier spent the first half of 1998 retiring gradually from DJing, quitting his Rex Club residency, to concentrate on live performance. It's true that no other DJ has taken a live to this level – incorporating dancers, musicians and backdrops. The jury is still out, however, on whether it beats a ten-hour set from the techno master.
Future? Learn to love the live show, because no imminent return to the decks is expected.

Cassius & Motorbass

Hype: Industry mutterings indicate the Next Big Things are Cassius and Motorbass, playing phat, funky,

groovy, in-yer-face house.
Reality: The link between both is Philippe Zdar. As Cassius, he plays with Hubert 'Boombass' (the two previously produced MC Solaar) while as Motorbass he is teamed with Etienne de Crécy (of 'Super Discount' fame). Now that Cassius is signed to Virgin, success is assured, while everybody has their chequebooks out in the race to sign Motorbass.
Future? These guys cannot go wrong. For once the reality is truer than the hype!

Hyper hyped: so is it all hot **Air***?*

students, au pairs and backpackers. However it's cheerful and intimate, with a cute dancefloor in a cellar dating in parts to the thirteenth century, and the drinks won't break the bank. Music is a mix of French pop, disco, house and salsa.

La Scala
188bis rue de Rivoli, 1st (01.42.60.45.64). M° Palais-Royal. **Open** 10.30pm-6am daily. **Admission** free for ladies Mon-Thur, Sun; 80F Mon-Fri, Sun; 100F Sat. **Drinks** 45F-50F. **Credit** MC, V. **Map H5**
La Scala enjoyed a brief flourish in 1997, when Queen was shut by police and rumour had it that the organisers were relocating chez Scala. Despite potential as a grand venue and and an abundance of bars, the cavernous club is never filled with enough tourists to really get going. Music is charty.

Latino, Jazz & World

Latino clubs are one thing Parisians do especially well, and even if the *merengue* doesn't float your boat at home, it's worth having a look-in here. Dress: Havana cocktail umbrella.

Le Balajo
9 rue de Lappe, 11th (01.47.00.07.87). M° Bastille. **Open** 9pm-2am Wed; 10pm-2am Thur; 11.30pm-5.30am Fri, Sat; 3-7pm Sun. **Admission** 80F Wed (40F for women); 100F Thur-Sat; 50F Sun. **Drinks** 50F-60F. **Credit** AmEx, DC, MC, V. **Map M7**
The ever-so-kitsch 'bal-à-Jo' (Jo's bal) has been going for over 60 years. Wednesday's rock 'n' roll, boogie and swing session attracts some colourful customers, but it's starting to look a bit washed out. Those in the know have jumped ship long ago, leaving the dancefloor to ditzy tourists and their exploiters. Average age at the weekend tea dance is 70.

Caveau de la Huchette
5 rue de la Huchette, 5th (01.43.26.65.05). M° St-Michel. **Open** 9.30pm-2.30am Mon-Thur, Sun; 9.30pm-3.30am Fri, Sat. **Admission** 60F Mon-Thur, Sun; 70F Fri, Sat; students 55F Mon-Thur, Sun. **Drinks** from 30F. **Credit** MC, V. **Map J7**
Friendly, unpretentious, and hospitable, the Caveau has been a jazz hall since 1946 and is still high rollin'. During the week the dancefloor hosts ageing divorcées and wannabe Stones, come the weekend it packs out with a mixed age range of soulful jazz lovers enjoying a bopping rock n' roll or jazz live act. One of the only places you can catch staff dancing with the clientele. *See chapter* **Music: Rock, Roots & Jazz**.

La Chapelle des Lombards
19 rue de Lappe, 11th (01.43.57.24.24). M° Bastille. **Open** 10.30pm-dawn Thur-Sat; concert Thur 8pm (70F). **Admission** 100F Thur (women free before midnight); 120F Fri-Sat with drink. **Drinks** 35F-75F. **Credit** AmEx, MC, V. **Map M7**
A mixed crowd of tourists and Latino and African residents sweats it out in this cramped venue. DJ Natalia La Tropikal mixes salsa, merengue, zouk and tango on weekends. Live concert on Thursdays before the tango begins.

Dancing de la Coupole
102 bd du Montparnasse, 14th (01.43.20.14.20). M° Vavin. **Open** 10pm-4am Tue; 3-7pm, 9pm-4am Sat, Sun. **Admission** 40F-100F. **Drinks** 55F-70F. **Credit** AmEx, DC, MC, V. **Map G9**
The basement 'dancing' of the Art Deco brasserie was one of the first in Paris to risk the tango in the 20s. It still plays Latino tunes, but to a more touristy crowd. A place to flirt and mingle, like most salsa clubs, but it's refreshingly relaxed rather than predatory. 90-minute dance lessons before the weekend tango and retro nights are a snip at 40F.

Rex Club: *don't smile but the music's great.*

Les Etoiles
6 rue du Château d'Eau, 10th (01.47.70.60.56). M° Château d'Eau. **Open** 9pm-3.30am Thur; 9pm-4.30am Fri-Sat; 6.30pm two Sun a month. **Admission** 120F incl meal; 60F/100F without/with drink from 11pm. **Drinks** 20F-40F. **No credit cards. Map K3**
Formerly a cinema, Les Etoiles has got class. Top-notch musicians electrify a soulful crowd of Latino lovers. There's not much space, but that doesn't stop nightowl groovers giving it loads. Women are not liable to stand around for more than a couple of minutes, and veterans dish out footwork advice on-the-go as the evening unfolds.

La Java
105 rue du Fbg-du-Temple, 10th (01.42.02.20.52). M° Belleville. **Open** 11pm-6am Thur-Sat. **Admission** 60F-80F Thur; 100F Fri, Sat. **Drinks** 35F-50F. **Credit** AmEx, DC, MC, V. **Map M4**
La Java oozes style as a subterranean salsa venue with a lacquered dancefloor that hosted Piaf. Today the glamour is still brought alive by the Cuban heels of hundreds of Latino devotees. A live band is followed by DJs. The broad spectrum of talent reflects the extraordinary clientele, lending La Java an individual, as well as tropical edge. From March 1999 expect a new world music night.

Bar Clubs

Café du Trésor
5-7 rue du Trésor, 4th (01.44.78.06.60). M° Hôtel de Ville. **Open** daily 9am-2am. **Admission** free. **Drinks** 19F-40F. **Credit** MC, V.
Hip coffee hangout by day, crowded by night for quality house nights and the occasional trip hop *soirée*, this brightly coloured café is concealed down an *impasse* at the Marais

core. The in-crowd stem largely from the club/fashion world, many being pals of *patron* Rodolphe. It's popular also with young internationals, who turn up to get down to the latest house, funk and acid jazz. Look out for Tricky Situation, Patrick Vidal's funk, house and disco party on Thursday.

La Cithéa
114 rue Oberkampf, 11th (01.40.21.70.95).
M° Parmentier. **Open** 9.30pm-5am daily. **Admission** free Mon, Tue, Sun; 30F Wed, Thur; 60F Fri, Sat. **Drinks** 35F-60F. **Credit** MC, V. **Map M5**
In the heart of trendy Ménilmontant, where *branché* Parisians carve out a Saturday night, lies the hot red Cithéa, complete with glitter ball. It well suits the live (Wed-Sat) Afro-funk, earthy soul and acid jazz, and DJ mixes, that seek to recapture the fire that lit Paris in the 70s, but with a 90s slant. Packed at weekends with a sexy bohemian crowd. *See* chapter **Music: Rock, Roots & Jazz.**

La Distillerie
50 rue du Fbg-St-Antoine, 12th (01.40.01.99.00).
M°Bastille. **Open** 7pm-4am Mon-Wed; 7pm-5am Fri, Sat; 8pm-4am Sun. **Admission** free. **Drinks** 20F-50F. **Credit** MC, V. **Map M7**
It's gone 2am, when through leopardskin curtains you see a light burning in the Creole-style Distillerie. Soon the place seethes with up-for-it debris from bars all over Bastille stumbling in for another shot at the prize. With friendly service and hip tech-Latino beats, it's a soulful end to a night out.

Factory Café
20 rue du Fbg-St-Antoine, 12th (01.44.74.61.42.).
M° Bastille. **Open** 9pm-2am daily. **Admission** 40F. **Drinks** 25F-45F. **Credit** AmEx, DC, MC, V. **Map M7**
The décor bears the rhetoric of urban discomfort: exposed pipes, angry graffiti and Soviet blockhouse lettering on corrugated walls give the feeling you are stuck in an upturned submarine at the bottom of a Mad Max sea. And they are not afraid of repetitive beats, suiting the trainer-clad hip-hop followers. Fly guys, *banlieue* boys, few girls. Bring attitude.

Harlem Hotel (Café Oz)
18 rue St-Denis, 1st (01.40.39.00.18). M° Châtelet.
Open 10pm-2am Thur. **Admission** 50F. **Drinks** 22F-50F. **Credit** AmEx, MC, V. **Map J6**
On Thursday, Café Oz becomes the Harlem Hotel and a sexy, cosmopolitan crowd and music industry types soon get down to funky house and hip hop fronted by some formidable DJs. Twice a month for Sunday brunch, a string quartet vies with house DJs on an ambient trip from Radio FG and Nova. Weekend *soirées* are promised in 1999.

Sanz Sans
49 rue du Fbg-St-Antoine, 11th (01.44.75.78.78).
M° Bastille. **Open** 9am-2am daily. **Admission** free. **Drinks** 20F-40F. **Credit** AmEx, DC, MC, V. **Map M7**
Sanz Sans is as good as it gets on the Bastille strip, packed with party people getting ripped on cocktails then dancing on tables. Barstaff armed with drumsticks thrash dangling cymbals in time to the funk, Latin and hip hop hits, and a huge screen at the rear shows chilling out punters what they're missing up front. Try to hit it midweek before it gets too full.

Popin
105 rue Amelot, 11th (01.48.05.56.11). M° Filles du Calvaire. **Open** times vary. **Admission** free. **Drinks** 20F-35F. **No credit cards. Map L5**
Three small floors pack out with a relaxed overspill from nearby rue Oberkampf. Predominantly French, with more than a smattering of students, it also attracts savvy young internationals who clamour for a pint (35F for Kilkenny or Guinness, pitchers at 90F). Downstairs, the tiny dancefloor gets heaving at weekends after midnight as local DJs spin whatever they fancy, from big beat and hip hop to indie classics.

What's Up Bar
15 rue Daval, 11th (01.48.05.88.33). M° Bastille.
Open 7.30pm-6am daily. **Admission** free Mon-Thur, Sun; 50F Fri, Sat. **Drinks** 30F-50F. **Credit** AmEx, DC, MC, V. **Map M6**
Vinyl junkies and label gourmets populate this industrial-looking bunker. Regular DJ sets of hard house (Mon) and House (Fri) alternate between Cheers and Basenotique, the Paris house label which features Dimitri and DJ Deep. Look out for occasional live sets and visits from international hi-rollers, such as Ninja Tunes. It's so trendy is has its own free magazine of listings interspersed with gratuitous porn.

Guinguettes

If you want a taste of authentic dancefloor style, head to the old-fashioned *guinguette* dance halls along the Marne. Age: 7-70. Dress: floral frocks for her, *matelot* shirts for him.

Chez Gégène
162bis quai de Polangis, 94340 Joinville-le-Pont (01.48.83.29.43). RER Joinville-le-Pont. **Open** Apr-Oct 9pm-2am Fri, Sat (live band); 7pm-midnight Sun (recorded). **Admission** 90F (drink); 210F (dinner). **Credit** AmEx, MC, V.
The classic *guinguette*, unaltered for years. Elderly French dance fiends, dapper *galants*, multi-generational families and young Parisians pack the place. Eat at the front and move to the dance area later or eat around the dance floor getting up for a quick foxtrot, tango, *musette* classic or rock 'n' roll number between courses. A few disco hits are slipped in for those who don't know all the steps.

Guinguette du Martin-Pêcheur
41 quai Victor-Hugo, 94500 Champigny-sur-Marne (01.49.83.03.02). RER Champigny-sur-Marne. **Open** Mar-Nov 8pm-2am Tue-Sat; noon-8pm Sun (noon-midnight July, Aug). **Admission** 30F. **No credit cards.**
The youngest (built in the 1980s) and hippest of the dance halls are a tiny, tree-shaded island which you reach by raft. Great music, cute young trendies trying to look like Gabin and Piaf. Live band Fri, Sat, Sun in July, Aug.

Get swept off your feet at **Les Etoiles.**

Children

From John Cage at the children's theatre to the lion's cage at the zoo, Paris has something for all the ages and moods of childhood.

From *haute couture* baby clothes to *haute cuisine* sessions for kids at Cordon Bleu, young Parisians are initiated early into *l'art de vivre*. Custom-built theatres and museums have tailor-made kids' programmes, as do the major cultural Meccas such as the Louvre and the Musée d'Orsay. Young readers have their own bookshop, **Chantelivre**, and from six months on can subscribe to a vast array of graded magazines, including two daily newspapers (*Mon Quotidien* and *Les Clés de l'actualité*), and their own TV guide. They even have children's champagne – well, *pommeau* fizzy apple juice packaged like champagne – so they're not left out at family celebrations.

But even in Paris, the simple pleasures are not overlooked: there are plenty of playgrounds, pools and parks (some with avant-garde pretensions) to let off steam in. The city gets more bicycle- and rollerblade-friendly each year, so family outings on both are now feasible along the newly created bike lanes, the *promenade plantée* in eastern Paris and by the Seine and Canal St-Martin on Sundays. Another fun outing is a boat trip on the Seine. Bateaux Parisiens (01.44.11.33.52) runs trips for the 3-10s, complete with songs, games and a bit of history.

Seasonal pleasures include firework displays on summer nights and free merry-go-rounds all over the city at Christmas; Halloween has recently taken off too. Most kids' events take place on Wednesdays (when primary schools close), weekends and holidays. See the weeklies *Pariscope* or *L'Officiel des Spectacles* and the quarterly *Paris-Mômes*, a mine of eclectic suggestions (with a welcome dash of multiculturalism) that appears with the daily *Libération*. Pick up a copy at the Office de Tourisme (Champs-Elysées), Musée d'Orsay, MK2 cinemas or The Louvre's children's bookshop. For outlets in your area, call 01.49.29.01.21. The free *Guide de la Rentrée* has information about sports facilities and cultural activities for children and teenagers. (Ask for one at the local *mairie* or at the Kiosque Paris-Jeunes, 25 bd Bourdon, 4th/01.42.76.22.60. Open 10am-7pm Mon-Fri; or the CIDJ, 101 quai Branly, 15th/01.44.49.12.00. Open 9.30am-6pm Mon-Fri; 9.30am-1pm Sat). For more activities, *see chapter* **Sport & Fitness**.

Getting Around

With younger kids, it is best to use public transport between 10am and 5pm to avoid the rush. Baby backpacks and quick-folding buggies will help you negotiate turnstiles, escalators and automatic doors. Taxi drivers can refuse more than three adults, but will generally take a family of four as under-10s count as half a passenger. Add a 6F surcharge for the buggy.

The new driverless line 14 (Le Météor) is a must – aim for the front carriage with its head-on views of the tunnel so your kids can 'drive' the train themselves. Line 6 (Nation to Charles-de-Gaulle-Etoile) is mostly overground and crosses the Seine twice, once beside the Eiffel Tower. Scenic bus routes include the 24, 69 and 72, which follows the river. All three take in the Louvre and the Musée d'Orsay. The 29 and 56 have an open deck at the back. Sadly, only a few lines operate on Sundays. Both the minibus and the funicular on the Butte Montmartre are part of the public transport system, as is the Balabus (April-Sept, Sun and holidays), which takes in most of the sights. For frequent or extended visits, the Guide Paris Bus is worth investing in. The RATP's annual travel pass (the Carte 'R', price 1500 F), launched in September 1998, gives 10-26 year olds the freedom of the city — and all of Ile-de-France at weekends and on holidays.

Help & Information

The American Church (65 quai d'Orsay, 7th/ 01.40.62.05.00) noticeboard is a major source of English-speaking babysitters and au pairs.

Ababa
(01.45.49.46.46). **Open** 9am-7pm Mon-Sat.
Childminding 33F/hour plus 64F agency fee.
Ababa can provide experienced childminders or babysitters (mainly students) at the last minute.

Inter-Service Parents
(01.44.93.44.93). **Open** 9.30am-12.30pm, 1.30-5pm Mon, Tue, Fri; 9.30am-12.30pm Wed; 1.30-5pm Thur.
A free telephone service detailing babysitting agencies and kids' activities. English-speaking mums can meet at La Maison Ouverte, 5 impasse Bons-Secours, 11th (01.44.93.24.10).

Message
c/o Sallie Chaballier (01.48.04.74.61)
A helpful English-speaking support group for mothers and mothers-to-be of all nationalities living in and around Paris.

Parks & Playgrounds

Post-modern parks like Bercy, La Villette or Parc André Citroën contrast sharply with the traditional charm of the Luxembourg and Tuileries gardens where generations of kids have grown up with sand-pits, puppet shows, pony rides and boating ponds. The Bois de Vincennes and Bois de Boulogne also provide expanses of trees, picnic areas, boating lakes, cycle paths, and substantial play areas. The eighteenth-century Palais-Royal garden is home to Daniel Buren's avant-garde black-and-white striped pillars, which children can climb on or skate round. For adventures there's the artificial cave and water-

The Tuileries: *the classic childhood park.*

fall at the Parc des Buttes-Chaumont, or the suspension bridge leading to a 50-metre rock with a gazebo on top. Or try the Parc de Belleville which clings to the side of a hill with slides built into it. (Note: the grass is still out of bounds in the Luxembourg, Tuileries, Monceau and Palais-Royal parks.)

A perennial pleasure for children is the funfair. Best-known Parisian fairs include La Fête à Neu-Neu (Bois de Boulogne, autumn) and the carnivalesque Foire du Trône (late March-late May, pelouse de Reuilly, Bois de Vincennes). La Fête des Tuileries (Jardin des Tuileries, June-August) offers breathtaking views of the city from the top of the big wheel.

Jardin d'Acclimatation

Bois de Boulogne, 16th (01.40.67.90.82). M° Les Sablons, then short walk, or M° Porte Maillot and Le Petit Train (single 6F, every 15 minutes daily from behind L'Orée du Bois restaurant during holidays, and 1.30-6pm Wed, Sat, Sun). **Open** *winter* 10am-6pm daily; *summer* 10am-7pm daily. **Admission** 12F; free under-3s. The small zoo, hall of mirrors, *guignol* puppet theatre and wooden playgrounds in this classic amusement park are all free. However the caterpillar and dragon rollercoasters, the 'enchanted river', trampolines, dodgems and mini-motorbikes each cost around 10F extra. (A book of 16 tickets costs 150F.) A babysitting service is available in summer at weekends. *See also* **Musée en Herbe** *below.*

Jardin des Enfants aux Halles

105 rue Rambuteau, 1st (01.45.08.07.18). M° Châtelet-Les Halles. **Admission** 2.50F for a one-hour session. **Map J5**
This well-supervised garden with underground tunnels, rope swings, secret dens and pools of coloured ping-pong balls is great for 7-11s, and useful for parents visiting the adjoining Forum des Halles. Adults are allowed in only at 10am-2pm on Saturdays, to accompany their under-sevens.

Parc Floral de Paris

route de la Pyramide, Bois de Vincennes, 12th (01.43.43.92.95). M° Château de Vincennes, then 112 bus to Parc Floral or 15-minute walk. **Open** 9.30am-6pm or -7pm, depending on time of year **Admission** *summer* 10F; 5F 6-18s; free under-6s; *winter* 5F; 2.50F 6-18s.
A miniature train chugs around a track between the majestic conifers (6F per ride) of this highly attractive park. The huge adventure playground offers a multitude of slides, swings, climbing frames and giant spider webs. This is also the home of the Maison Paris-Nature, a nature resource cen-

tre for kids with exhibitions, books and games, and the Serre des Papillons, where children can wander among the butterflies. In summer there are free concerts and children's shows at the newly refurbished theatre (*see* Entertainment).

Promenade Plantée & Jardin de Reuilly

crossroads of av Ledru-Rollin and av Daumesnil, 12th. M° Ledru-Rollin. Jardin de Reuilly, allée Vivaldi, 12th. M° Montgallet. **Map M8**
A disused railway line has been converted into this wonderful suspended garden, running from the Bastille to the Bois de Vincennes. Biking and roller skating are possible on a parallel track between the Bois de Vincennes and the Jardin de Reuilly, itself basically an outsize lawn, great for picnics and ball games. It has the winning combination of no traffic (and no accompanying noise), a small playground, safe roller skating, and the new Piscine de Reuilly nearby.

Museums & Galleries

Some museums (Louvre, Petit Palais, Carnavalet) offer guided visits by storytellers. Others (Orsay, Monnaie, Arts et Traditions Populaires, Gustave-Moreau) provide free kids' activity sheets. Many organise Wednesday afternoon workshops (in French). The Musée du Moyen Age has both themed visits for 8-12s (children in the Middle Ages, medieval beasts, the life of a lord, etc) and ateliers for the artistically inclined on the goldsmith's craft, stained glass or medieval architecture (visits 25F, workshops 45F). However, the big museums will quickly tire younger children, so limit yourselves to a few favourites, such as the Egyptian mummies, IM Pei's pyramid and the new sculpture wing at the Louvre, or the animal statues outside the Musée d'Orsay. Better still, kids love sitting behind the giant clock in the museum café, watching the hands go round. *See chapter* **Museums**.

Espace Dalí Montmartre

11 rue Poulbot, 18th (01.42.64.40.10). M° Abbesses. **Open** 10am-6pm daily. **Admission** 35F; 25F 8-25s, students, over-60s; free under-8s. **Credit** AmEx, DC, MC, V (Shop). **Map H1**
This small Dalí museum, which has a giant thumb sculpture among its 330 exhibits, provides a ready crossover between childhood and Surrealism's prankish sense of humour.

Halle St-Pierre – Musée d'Art Naïf Max Fourny

2 rue Ronsard, 18th (01.42.58.72.89). M° Anvers. **Open** 10am-6pm daily. Closed Aug. **Admission** 40F; 30F under-26s, students, over-60s; free under-4s. **Credit** (shop) MC, V. **Map J1**
Big, inviting Halle St-Pierre specialises in popular and naïve art. The 'Outsider Art' exhibition (until 25 July 1999) is a spectacular selection from the Chicago folk art museum featuring whirligigs, totem poles and vivid scenes depicted on cardboard and corrugated iron. Check out its permanent collection too, and well-stocked, quirky bookshop. The cosy café serves light meals and is a pleasant place to pass time while the kids explore the exhibits with booklet and pencil in hand. Guided visits, workshops and puppet shows (*guignol*) are offered for children (3.30pm, 4.30pm Wed, Sat, Sun). *Wheelchair access.*

Musée de la Curiosité

11 rue St-Paul, 4th (01.42.72.13.26). M° St-Paul or Sully Morland. **Open** 2-7pm Wed, Sat, Sun plus extra days during school holidays. **Admission** 45F; 30F 3-12s; free under-3s. **Map L7**

Come here for conjuring shows, optical illusions, psychic phenomena and an exhibition of magic props including boxes for sawing ladies in two. There are English-speaking guides and children's magic courses during the holidays.

Musée en Herbe du Jardin d'Acclimatation

Jardin d'Acclimatation, Bois de Boulogne, 16th (01.40.67.97.66). M° Les Sablons, then short walk. **Open** 10am-6pm Mon-Fri, Sun; 2-6pm Sat. **Admission** 17F; 14F 4-18s, over-60s; free under-4s (12F entry to garden); two exhibitions 26F; atelier 26F; atelier and exhibition pass 36F. This museum aims to introduce kids to art history, with ateliers and well-designed, imaginative interactive exhibitions. A spacious educational centre is dedicated to European Art. *Wheelchair access.*

Musée National des Arts d'Afrique et d'Océanie

293 av Daumesnil, 12th (01.44.74.84.80). M° Porte Dorée. **Open** 10am-5.30pm Mon, Wed-Sun. **Admission** 38F (with exhibition), 30F (without exhibition); 28F 18-25s; free under-18s.

Formerly known as 'the colonial museum', there are ethnic artefacts from all over Africa and the Pacific, including some scary masks. The tropical aquarium downstairs is the real draw: a vast collection of colourful exotic fish placed at just the right height for children. Beware the crocodiles…

Palais de la Découverte

av Franklin D Roosevelt, 8th (01.40.74.80.00/ 01.40.74.81.73). M° Franklin D Roosevelt. **Open** 9.30am-6pm Tue-Sat; 10am-7pm Sun; closed some public holidays. **Admission** 27F; 17F 7-18s, students; free under-7s; for planetarium add 13F (unsuitable for under-7s). **No credit cards. Map E5.**

This elegant science museum manages to deliver the goods

A mouse for all seasons

Nowadays Disneyland gets more visitors than Notre Dame, and it's not hard to see why. Though there have been no major new attractions of late, the phenomenal scale, attention to detail and technical ingenuity of the Magic Kingdom still take the breath away. And when Mickey or Minnie wanders over to hug the kids, even cynics whip out their cameras to capture the smiles.

With young children head to Fantasyland for Peter Pan's Flight, Dumbo the Flying Elephant and Sleeping Beauty's Castle, where a terrifyingly realistic dragon is chained up in a gloomy dungeon. Two attractions with minimal queuing are the giant merry-go-round that plays Disney tunes and the kitschy Small World, also a good vantage point for parades. In Frontierland, the Pocahontas Indian village gives kids a chance to let off steam.

Parents with older children are advised to try the more popular attractions early. White-knuckle rides include Big Thunder Mountain and the Jules-Vernesque Space Mountain, where you scream around in the dark. Only children measuring over 1.4 metres can go on the really fast rides. Cinematic experiences include Star Tours, a simulated space ride, and a 15-minute, 3-D George Lucas-directed *Star Wars* clone starring Michael Jackson. The whole family will enjoy *The Pirates of the Caribbean* and the *Haunted Mansion*, with their audioanimatronic figures, sound effects and elaborate props.

Useful Information

Optimise your time and cash by combining lunch and a show. The Café Hyperion's show is usually based on the latest Disney film, while the Lucky Nugget Saloon puts on a live Western cabaret. The site is very exposed to the elements: bring botttled water, straw hats and sunblock in

summer; warm hats, gloves and scarves in winter. Wear comfortable shoes too. The park opens later in summer, but queues are longer; visiting out of season you can do much more, including return visits to favourite attractions. Five minutes from the gates, next to the RER station, the Disney Village complex appeals to teenagers and young adults with bars, restaurants, a multiplex cinema and country music. *Marne-la-Vallée (01.60.30.60.30).* **Open** *27 Mar-5 Sept 1999* 9am-8pm, *except some weekends and holidays* (9am-11pm), *and Mon-Fri 6-30 Sept* (10am-6pm). **Admission** *Day pass 220F adults; 170F children.* **Credit** AmEx, DC, MC, V. **Getting there:** *By car* (32km) A4 Metz-Nancy to exit 14; follow signs. *By train* RER A or TGV to Marne-la-Vallée/Chessy.

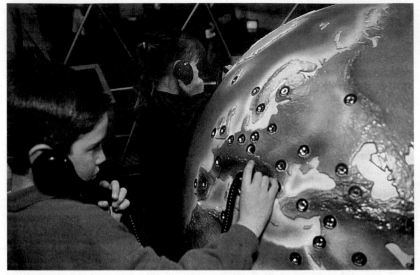

La Cité des Sciences: *the world's your oyster at Paris' sparkling futuristic science museum.*

while retaining a cosy, wood-panelled, nineteenth-century feel. Kids can see a colony of ants at work, learn about centrifugal force the hard way and play in an interactive section. The planetarium (reserve ahead) seats 200.

Cité des Sciences et de l'industrie

30 av Corentin-Cariou, 19th (01.40.05.80.00/ 01.40.05.12.12). M° Porte de la Villette. **Open** 10am-6pm Tue-Sun (visits by session, normally 3-4 daily, more frequent Wed and weekends). Closed some public holidays. **Admission** *Day pass to Cité des Sciences* 50F; 35F under-16s, students, over-60s; free under-7s. *Géode* 57F; 44F under-16s, students, over 60s. No children under 6. *Géode/Cité des Sciences combined ticket* 92F (79F outside weekends and holidays) *Cité des Enfants* 25F per session. *Techno Cité* 25F. **Credit** MC, V. **Map inset**
The Parc de la Villette is one of the largest parks in Paris, so set aside a whole day if you can. It's the setting for a futuristic science museum (*see chapter* **Museums**) with a mind-boggling choice of interactive, hands-on exhibits. A major exhibition on electricity for 5-12-year-olds (until June) shows what really goes on behind the plug, while a section on physics and the harmonics of sound features a 'sound alley' with walls that talk and whistle. A major exhibition on new technologies will offer cutting-edge software for all ages to play with. Another must is the Cité des Enfants, where three-to-five-year-olds can crawl inside a turtle's shell, grind wheat into bread, or don hard hats on a mini-construction site and transport rubber bricks with wheelbarrows and cranes. Meanwhile, six-to-12-year-olds can produce a programme in the TV studio. Sessions last 90 minutes; parents must accompany younger children. At Techno Cité, over-elevens can learn how to programme computer software into a video game. Three more hi-tech sections show them how a racing bike is made, and demonstrate the role of robotics in lifts and car washes. Particularly fun for kids are the Planetarium and the optical illusions (Jeux de Lumière). For under-fives there are workshops run by La Folie des Petits Enfants (01.40.03.75.46).

Outside, kids can clamber onto the *Argonaute*, a real sub-

marine, take in a film at the Géode (English-language headphones available) or, unless you're under six or pregnant, have a teeth-gritting experience on the Cinaxe flight simulator. The giant park has open-air sculptures, red follies (multiple-purpose pavilions) and postmodern themed gardens, from the Jardin des Voltiges obstacle course to the Jardin des Vents air mattresses. Picnics and ball games are allowed.

Zoos & Theme Parks

Château et Parc Zoölogique de Thoiry

78770 Thoiry-en-Yvelines (01.34.87.52.25). Train from Gare Montparnasse to Montfort l'Aumaury, then by taxi; phone château for taxi details and book in advance. By car A13 west, then A12, N12 and D11 (45km). **Open** *Winter* 10am-5pm daily. *Summer* 10am-6pm daily. **Admission** Park 200F; 79F 3-12s, students. *Château* 38F; 30F over-9s. **Credit** AmEx, MC, V.
Some 121 species of wild animal roam the château grounds of this safari park just 30 minutes from Paris. Less ferocious beasts can be seen from a little train that tours the gardens. There's a reptile house, tea room and pleasant picnic area.

France Miniature

25 route du Mesnil, 78990 Elancourt (01.30.62.40.79). Train from Gare Montparnasse to La Verrière, then bus 411. By car A13 direction St-Quentin-en-Yvelines/Dreux, then Elancourt Centre. **Open** *mid-Mar-mid-Nov* 10am-7pm daily (additional night openings: *May, July, Aug* 10am-midnight Sat). **Admission** 75F; 50F under-16s; free under-4s. **Credit** AmEx, MC, V.
An outdoor museum with over 200 models of monuments and sites (Tour Eiffel, Notre Dame…) reduced to one-thirtieth original size. New additions include the Stade de France. *Wheelchair access.*

Parc Astérix

60128 Plailly (recorded information 03.44.62.34.34). RER B3 Roissy-Charles de Gaulle 1, then shuttle 9.30am-

1.30pm, 4.30pm-closing time (journey plus park entry 198F/148F). By car A1 towards Lille, exit Parc Astérix. **Open** 10am-6pm daily; *July 10-Aug* 9.30am-7pm daily. Park closes various days throughout year: phone ahead. Closed mid Oct-Feb. **Admission** 170F; 120F 3-11s; 145F over-60s; free under-3s. **Credit** AmEx, MC, V.
This whimsy theme park is ideal for fans of the cartoon Gaul or students of Latin. Along with white-knuckle rides and parades, enjoy the residents of the Dolphinarium and the antics of the three musketeers and a giant baby in a self-propelled pram. Look out for artisans working in wood, stone and stained glass in a reconstructed corner of medieval Paris. A shop and restaurant are on hand too.

Zoo de Paris
53 av de St-Maurice, 12th (01.44.75.20.10/00).
M° Porte Dorée. **Open** *Apr-Sept* 9am-6pm daily; *Oct-Mar* 9am-5pm daily. **Admission** 40F; 30F 4-16s, students, over-60s; free under-4s.
A major overhaul of the signature Matterhorn-like 'mountain' means visitors can once again admire all 15 hectares of this well-loved zoo from platforms accessible by lift. Don't miss the nocturnal lemurs in their dark habitat, or the incomparable smell of hippos and rhinos in their indoor quarters. Lions, tigers and rhinos wander in relative landscaped freedom, while the monkeys leap around the trees on islands, rather than behind bars. Check at the entrance for feeding times, especially the seals. A miniature train tours the zoo and the park.

Entertainment

Three Parisian theatres are entirely devoted to young spectators; over-eights with good French may enjoy one of Ecla Company's performances of classics (01.40.27.82.05/6). A profusion of circuses, New Age or otherwise, pass through Paris, especially at Christmas (*see chapter* **Cabaret, Comedy & Circus**).

Apart from the annual must-see Hollywood/ Disney output (watch out for *Madeline*, set in Paris), the six MK2 cinemas feature children's film festivals with an international touch (Wednesdays and weekend mornings). Pick up brochures at MK2 or Fnac, (avoid the unhelpful information line). The Forum des Images runs afternoons for 5-12-year-olds on Wednesdays, Saturdays and school holidays, with a film, snack and Internet workshop (01.44.76.63.44).

ACT Theatre Company
(01.40.33.64.02). **Tickets** 50F-95F.
This English-language company performs accessible, energetic adaptations of British authors (Emily Brontë, Conan Doyle, etc) for mainly schoolgoing audiences at the Théâtre de Ménilmontant and the suburban MJC de Palaiseau.

The American Library
10 rue du Général-Camou, 7th (01.53.59.12.60).
M° Alma-Marceau or RER Pont del'Alma.
Open 10am-7pm Tue-Sat (Aug noon-6pm Tue-Fri; 10am-2pm Sat). **Map D6**
The American Library offers regular storytelling sessions for different ages: 3-5s, 2.30-3.30pm every Wed; 1-3s, 10.30-11am last Tue of month; 6-8s, 10.30-11.30am, last Sat of month. The library also lends books, magazines, cassettes, CDs and videos.

Théâtre Astral
Parc Floral de Paris, route de la Pyramide, Bois de Vincennes, 12th (01.42.41.88.33). M° Château de Vincennes. **Tickets** 28F-33F. **Park entrance** 10F

The Astral offers 3-8-year-olds epics about ogres and princesses in a bucolic setting. It's next to an adventure playground, so you may be tempted to make a day of it.

Théâtre Dunois
108 rue du Chevaleret, 13th (01.45.84.72.00).
M° Chevaleret. **Tickets** 35F-100 F. **Map M10**
Home to adventurous theatre, dance and musical creations by established children's companies such as Le Petit Théâtre. Watch out for a choreographed John Cage special in June.

Théâtre des Jeunes Spectateurs
26 pl Jean Jaurès, 93100 Montreuil (01.48.70.48.91).
M° Mairie de Montreuil. **Tickets** 40F-65 F.
Lefty Montreuil has long been into 'children's cultural rights'. Its groundbreaking kids' theatre will be in the streets, under canvas and at temporary venues after May, until its new venue is ready. In the meantime there is the annual theatre festival Enfantillages en Seine St-Denis (till end May).

Théâtre des Champs-Elysées
15 av Montaigne, 8th (01.49.52.50.50/children's programme 01.42.56.90.10). M° Alma-Marceau. **Tickets** 60F-120F (under-9s free; reservations essential). **Map D5**
Sunday mornings here involve an original package deal for music-loving families. While parents attend the 11am classical concert, the kids enjoy their own entertainments (grouped into 3-6s and 6-9s), exploring instruments or composers – thematically linked to the main concert – at their own level. Breakfast, available beforehand, costs extra.

Une Journée au Cirque
115 bd Charles de Gaulle, 92390 Villeneuve-La Garenne (01.47.99.40.40). M° Porte de Clignancourt, then 137 bus to terminus. Sessions 10am-5pm Wed, Sun, school holidays. Closed July-end Sept. **Tickets** Show 70F-155F; 45F-95F 3-11s. Day at circus and one meal 235F-295F; 195F-230F 3-11s; under-2s free. Ménagerie 10F. Reserve in advance. **Credit** MC, V.
Circus aficionado Francis Schoeller opens up his Cirque de Paris for a day-long extravaganza. Children train with circus artistes in clowning, conjuring, trapeze and tightrope skills, lunch with the performers – then watch the show. Extras include visits to the animals, the antique carousel and funfair memorabilia. Birthday parties catered for.

Puppet Theatres (*Guignol*)

Any Parisian park worth its salt has its own Théâtre de Guignol, named after its principal character, the French equivalent of Mr Punch. There is a lot of frantic audience participation, and the language can be hard to follow. With no Judy, domestic violence is absent from the plot – but the policeman always gets it. Admission to hourly shows on Wednesdays, weekends and school holidays costs around 20F. There is little to see in July and August. Here's three of many: Jardin du Luxembourg, 6th (01.43.26.46.47/ 01.43.29.50.97); Marionnettes de Montsouris, Parc Montsouris, entrance av Reille/rue Gazon, 14th (01.69.09.72.13); Marionnettes du Parc Georges Brassens, 86 rue de Brancion, 15th (01.48.42.51.80).

Meals, Snacks & Treats

Haute cuisine may be unrealistic but it doesn't have to be all burger and pizza joints: the humble streetside crêpe, with ham, egg or cheese filling, is the original fast food – and a delight for kids to watch being made. Familiarise children with standard café fare (croque-monsieur, sandwich jambon/gruyère) and how to order. The goûter, or late-afternoon snack, is a French institution consisting of sweets or viennoiseries (pain au chocolat, pain aux raisins, etc). Lemonade will never be the same after they try a diabolo menthe or diabolo grenadine – lurid green or red concoctions beloved of Parisian kids. The food court at the Carrousel du Louvre is a self-service paradise where every member of the family can eat (pizzas, burgers, kebabs, tacos, cakes, muffins, and ice cream) and still sit at the same table. Watch out for the ubiquitous Bistro Romain and Hippopotamus chains, which both have a special child's menu; the latter offers baby high-chairs and colouring books. Otherwise, go for a touch of class at Angelina's (226 rue de Rivoli, 1st/01.42.60.82.00) tea room, and sample some of their extravagant but pricey hot chocolate and pastries. Best clothes and best behaviour.

A la Mère de Famille
35 rue du Fbg-Montmartre, 9th (01.47.70.83.69). Mº Grands Boulevards. **Open** 8.30am-1.30pm, 3-7pm Tue-Sat. Closed Aug. **Credit** AmEx, V. **Map J4**
The oldest sweetshop in town offers traditional regional sweets such as Tours barley sugar, *pastilles fondantes* from Lyon, candied violet leaves from Toulouse and – the ultimate in refinement – *les bêtises de Cambrai*. Besides melt-in-the-mouth marshmallow strips, caramels and lollipops, they make their own chocolates, and do a charming line in tin boxes.

Berthillon
31 rue St-Louis-en-l'Île, 4th (01.43.54.31.61). Mº Sully-Morland. **Open** 10am-8pm Wed-Sun. Closed school holidays. **No credit cards. Map K7**
Children go dizzy trying to choose from Berthillon's home-made ice creams – *marrons glacés*, honey and nougat, etc.

Chartier
7 rue du Fbg-Montmartre, 9th (01.47.70.86.29). Mº Grands Boulevards. **Open** 11.30am-3pm, 7-10pm daily. **Average** 80F. **Credit** MC, V. **Map J4**
This noisy, crowded *belle époque* restaurant buzzes with atmosphere, and the bustling waiters are alone worth the visit. Basic French fare at unbeatable prices, but don't expect high-chairs or kids' menus. Great for children over six.

Dame Tartine
2 rue Brisemiche, 4th (01.42.77.32.22). Mº Hôtel-de-Ville. **Open** noon-11pm daily. **Average** 100F. **Credit** MC, V. **Map K6**
An ideal place for a light snack, with excellent sandwiches and a location by the zany Tinguely fountain. In fine weather, the kids can run around the whirling bowler hats and spinning snakes while the parents sip coffee outside.

Hard Rock Café
14 bd Montmartre, 9th (01.53.24.60.00). Mº Grands Boulevards. **Open** 11.30am-2am daily (boutique 10am-1am) **Credit** AmEx, DC, MC, V. **Map H4**
Choose from six 39F children's menus (with colouring books) in familiar glam décor – look out for Michael Jackson's gold lamé flares. Friendly service, great for birthdays. Book ahead.

Jadis et Gourmande
49bis av Franklin D Roosevelt, 8th, (01.42.25.06.04). Mº St-Philippe-du-Roule. **Open** 1-7pm Mon; 9.30am-7pm Tues; 9.30am-7.30pm Wed-Fri; 10-7pm Sat **Credit** MC, V. **Map E4**

This *chocolatier* makes letters like giant Scrabble tiles (6F50 each) in dark and white chocolate. You can spell your child's name or other edible message in chocolate and have the result arranged in a long, pretty box. Count 122F for 14 letters. Here you'll also find pencils, bottles, and even gift boxes made from chocolate. Try the wafer-thin frosted mints edged with dark chocolate.
Branches: 88 bd Port-Royal, 5th (01.43.26.17 75); 39 rue des Archives, 4th (01 48 04 08 03); 27 rue Boissy d'Anglas, 8th (01.42.65.23.23).

Korean Barbecue
1 rue du Dragon, 6th (01.42.22.26.63). Mº St-Germain-des-Prés. **Open** noon-2.30pm, 7pm-midnight daily. **Average** 100F. **Prix fixe** 68F. **Credit** MC, V. **Map M6**
Children who get restless at restaurants will be kept occupied here by the chance to cook their own thinly cut beef on the table grill, served with rice and a salad for 68F. Parents have a more sophisticated range of dishes to choose from.
Branches: 39 rue du Montparnasse, 14th (01.43.27.69.53); 22 rue Delambre, 14th (01.43.35.44.32).

Shopping for Children

Toys & Books

There are several branches of the supermarket La Grande Recré and branches of Toys'R'Us at La Défense and in the Forum des Halles, but small, cosy toyshops can be found in every *quartier*. The gadgets at Pier Import are a favourite with pre-teens, while shops like Nature et Découvertes (branches city-wide) blur the distinction between toys for children and desirable objects for adults.

Browsing is fun in the well-stocked children's sections of the big English-language bookshops WH Smith, Brentano's and Galignani, which also provide translations of French classics. Municipal libraries (*bibliothèques*) have comfortable children's spaces, some with a limited selection of English-language books. *Ludothèques* (toy libraries), such as the one at Espace Torcy (2 rue de Torcy, 18th, 01.40.38.67.00), allow kids to take toys (2F-10F each) home.

Au Nain Bleu
406-410 rue St-Honoré, 8th (01.42.60.39.01). Mº Concorde. **Open** 9.45am-6.30pm Mon-Sat. **Credit** AmEx, MC, V. **Map G4**
Dating from 1836 (as reportedly do some of its staff), France's most prestigious toy shop is the nearest you'll get to London's Hamley's but with a stuffier, more old-fashioned feel. There's a huge stock of toys from all around the world, from furry animals to electronic games. Note: no lifts.

La Boîte à Joujoux
41 passage Jouffroy, 9th (01.48.24.58.37). Mº Grands Boulevards. **Open** 10am-7pm Mon-Sat. **Credit** MC, V. **Map H4**
This is just the place to find miniatures and other merchandising spin-offs of cartoon characters, notably Tintin and friends. It goes in for dressing-up and disguise, and does a roaring trade at Hallowe'en. They also run La Boîte à Doudou (24-26 passage Jouffroy) which stocks anything you can think of related to comic strip characters.

Chantelivre
13 rue de Sèvres, 6th (01.45.48.87.90). Mº Sèvres-Babylone. **Open** 1-7pm Mon; 10am-7pm Tue-Sat.

Something for everyone

Botanical gardens, a small zoo, games, cafés and three excellent natural history museums — not to mention *goûter* at the nearby mosque. Dahlias the size of a six-year-old, a hill with a spiral path leading to a belvedere, a towering 250-year-old cedar of Lebanon, a roundabout featuring endangered species, a playground for under-10s, a dinosaur-skeleton climbing-frame with slides... these are just some of the attractions at the Jardin des Plantes, whose slightly severe, didactic character gives it a charm and character all of its own. The Ménagerie, one of the oldest zoos in the world, is on a perfect scale for younger kids. It's a long way from the safari park ideal of modern zoos, but still offers plenty of vultures, monkeys and big cats. The giant steamed-up greenhouses are less infant-friendly, but boast some impressive tropical plants. Cafés in the garden and zoo are pricy, so the McDonald's on the left of the entrance makes a killing, especially in picnic weather. Look out for the hollow tree near the Alpine Garden, which tiny tots love squeezing into, and the most gruesome statue in Paris, on the left before the rue Geoffroy-St-Hilaire exit.

Rather like a seventeenth-century cabinet of curiosities, the park's Paleontology museum has a renowned fossil collection. The Mineralogy museum includes some wonderful giant crystals and meteorites. Best of all is the refurbished Grande Galerie de l'Evolution, which borrows cinema techniques to recreate the atmosphere of the savannah: subtly changing light, crickets chirping, the rumble of thunder... A Noah's Ark of stuffed animals, from elephants to rats, is the centrepiece of the middle floor. Birds in flight are suspended from the upper floors, while the ground floor corresponds to the sea bed. Children love the glass lifts whizzing between the three floors, which can be seen simultaneously through cutaway vertical spaces in the gutted structure (one occupied by a suspended whale). Under-12s can play interactive games and use microscopes in the fun, if small, Espace Découverte. The shop offers do-it-yourself dinosaurs and leaf presses.

Cross rue Geoffroy-St-Hilaire behind the Grande Galerie for mint tea and almond cakes at the 1930s Moorish Mosquée de Paris. Its cool courtyard and fountain, white-walled exterior and plush, ornate interior will take you all to North Africa.

Jardin des Plantes
pl Valhubert, rue Buffon or rue Geoffroy-St-Hilaire. 5th. M° Austerlitz or Jussieu. **Map J8.** *Muséum National d'Histoire Naturelle, 57 rue Cuvier, 5th (01.40.79.30.00).* **Open** *Grande Galerie de l'Evolution* 10am-6pm Mon, Fri-Sun; 10am-10pm Thur. *Ménagerie* (01.40.79.37.04) *Apr-Sept* 10-6pm daily; *Oct-Mar* 10am-5pm daily. *Others vary.* **Admission** *Grande Galerie* 40F; 30F students, 4-16s, over-60s; free under-4s. Credit MC, V. *Ménagerie* 30F; 20F 4-16s, students, over-60s; free under-4s. **No credit cards.** *Other pavilions* each 30F; 20F 4-16s, students, over-60s. **No credit cards. Map J9.**

Chantelivre

13 rue de Sèvres, 6th (01.45.48.87.90). M° Sèvres-Babylone. **Open** 1-7pm Mon; 10am-7pm Tue-Sat.
Credit MC, V. **Map G7**
Major structural changes provided the opportunity for a total makeover of this well-loved and wide-ranging children's bookshop. Teenage reading is by the door, and successive clusters of age-related reading lead to illustrated books and the young children's section in a bright space under the sky light at the back. There are also publications on children's health and psychology for parents, together with a respectable English-language section for children, plus videos, toys, posters, stationery and party supplies.

Fnac Junior

19 rue Vavin, 6th (01.56.24.03.46). M° Vavin. **Open** 10am-7.30pm Mon-Sat. **Credit** MC, V. **Map G8**
Fnac customers have kids too and the group has adapted its specialities into books, educational toys, videos and CD-roms for the under-12s, with the chance to try them out. The shop lays on activities (mainly Wed and Sat) for two-year-olds up, from make-up, magic and mime to multimedia.
Branch: Centre Commercial Grand Ciel, 94200 Ivry-sur-Seine (01.46.58.94.86).

La Maison du Cerf-Volant

7 rue de Prague, 12th (01.44.68.00.75). M° Ledru-Rollin.
Open 10am-7pm Tue-Sat. **Credit** V. **Map M7**
You can spend between 100F and 7000F on brightly coloured kites of every kind: dragons, geometrical shapes and a nice line in miniatures. If it flies, it's here.

Pain d'Epices

29 passage Jouffroy, 9th (01.47.70.08.68). M° Grands Boulevards. **Open** 12.30-7pm Mon; 10am-7pm Tue-Sat.
Credit MC, V. **Map H4**
Along with a great selection of tiny toys and small novelties that attract parents as much as kids, this olde-worlde toyshop has everything a self-respecting doll would need in her house, including tiny cutlery and tableware.

Pylones

57 rue St-Louis-en-l'île, 4th (01.46.34,05.02). M° Pont Marie.
Open 10.30am-7.30pm daily. **Credit** AmEx, MC, V. **Map K7**
Hilarious gadgets and knick-knacks for kids and kids-at-heart. Furry pencil-cases, a stapler that looks like a biting fish, animated postcards, Wallace and Gromit toothbrushes, squeaky-toy hair-slides and keyrings and glasses with toy cars attached so you can send drinks whizzing across the table. Everything you never needed.
Branches: 54 galerie Vivienne, 2nd (01.42.61.51.60); 7 rue Tardieu, 18th (01.46.06.37.00); Galeries des Trois Quartiers, 23 bd de la Madeleine, 1st (01.42.61.08.26).

Clothes

Young trendsetters head straight for BabyGap and Gap Kids, but if you want your child to sport the classic French BCBG look, then rush to **Bonpoint**, Jacadi or Cyrillus, where you can buy smocked dresses, pleated skirts and white, round-collared blouses for girls; mini-Lacoste-style polo shirts, cardigans and Bermuda shorts for the boys. Everything in navy, bottle green or tartan, of course. Then again, you might prefer to go the cheap-and-cheerful route at **Du Pareil au Même**, **Dipaki** and Tout Compte Fait, whose solid, brightly coloured clothes are influenced by new fads and fabrics. Monoprix and Prisunic's children's sections are worth an occasional look too.

The circus *is always coming to town in Paris.*

Bonpoint

67 rue de l'Université, 7th (01.45.55.63.70).
M° Solférino. **Open** 10am-7pm Mon-Sat. Closed Mon in Aug. **Credit** AmEx, DC, MC, V. **Map E5**
For classic, conservative, BCBG clothes for children, if you like that kind of thing. Bonpoint has a shop for six-month-old babies to teenage girls and boys at 67 rue de l'Université, 7th; furniture and nursery accessories at 7 rue Solférino, 7th (01.45.51.79.22); clothes for 0-3-month-old babies at 86 rue de l'Université (01.45.51.46.28); and last season's clothing at 82 rue de Grenelle, 7th (01.45.48.05.45).
Branches include: 15 rue Royale, 8th (01.47.42.52.63); 64 av Raymond-Poincaré, 16th (01.47.27.60.81); 184 rue de Courcelles, 17th (01.47.63.87.49).

Dipaki

18 rue Vignon, 9th (01.42.66.24.74). M° Madeleine.
Open 10am-7pm Mon-Sat. **Credit** MC, V. **Map G4**
One of Paris' best shops for reasonably priced, easy-to-care-for baby and kids' clothing in bold, primary colours.
Branches: 20 rue du Pont-Neuf, 1st (01.40.26.21.00); 22 rue Cler, 7th (01.47.05.47.62); 98 rue d'Alésia, 14th (01.45.43.73.72).

Du Pareil au Même

15-17 rue des Mathurins (Maison, 23), 8th (01.42.66.93.80). M° Havre-Caumertin/RER Auber.
Open 10am-7pm Mon-Sat. **Credit** MC, V. **Map G3**
Great for cheap, colourful basics for youngsters that are also surprisingly hard-wearing. Sizing tends to be small. The 16 basic shops have been joined by new baby shops (called Du Pareil au Même Maison), which are great for gifts.
Branches include: 122 rue du Fbg-St-Antoine (Maison 120), 12th (01.43.44.67.46); 15 rue de l'Ouest, 14th (01.43.21.46.21).

Petits Petons

135 rue du Fbg-St-Antoine, 11th (01.40.19.07.19).
M° Ledru-Rollin. **Open** 10am-7pm Mon-Sat. **Credit** MC, V. **Map N7**
This simple, friendly children's shoe shop has the unusual policy of pricing by size and not by model, so that all shoes sized 25-27 cost 249F, for example. Strong, sassy shoes in bright colours include patent-leather zip ankle boots in red, yellow and black. Great styles and good value for money.
Branches: 20 rue St-Placide, 6th (01.42.84.00.05); 23 rue Tronchet, 8th (01.47.42.75.69); 115 rue d'Alésia, 14th (01.45.42.80.52).

Dance

The recent rise in 'professional' performers is not entirely welcome; the real action, meanwhile, is happening out in the suburbs.

Everything in France is linked to politics, and dance is no exception. The last few years have seen devastating changes, ever since the government instituted a mandatory state diploma training programme in ballet, contemporary and jazz open to anyone with the time and money to do it. Because the diploma pretty much guarantees a job, it has attracted countless numbers of unemployed *Bac*-less young people who see dance more as a potential nine-to-five occupation than an art. Conservatories and private schools are churning out hundreds of 'professional' performers and dance instructors each year. Technique they may have, but talent is not bought with a credit card.

In Paris alone, there are now over 300 new dance companies competing for diminishing, weary-eyed audiences and a handful of grants. Sadly, most of the creations on show in the independent theatres are disjointed movement-and-sound collages straight out of a psycho ward. As for classes, since supply exceeds demand, the more marketing-minded are succeeding by adopting names like 'Bio-danse', 'Movement & Emotion', or even 'Danse à domicile', catering to stressed-out yuppies seeking a mellow art form that heals.

The big dance factories like Studio Harmonic (5 passage des Taillandiers, 11th/01.48.07.13.39), the **Centre de Danse du Marais** and the **Centre International Danse Jazz** offer a complete menu. If you're looking for serious modern dance programmes in a more personalised setting with the pioneers that made it happen, there's Jacqueline Robinson's Atelier de la Danse, founded in 1955 in a cosy Montmartre pavilion (16 av Junot, 18th/01.46.06.44.44), and Dominique and Françoise Dupuy's historic Rencontres Internationales de Danse Contemporaine (104 bd de Clichy, 18th/01.42.64.77.71).

Meanwhile, some amazing talent has come out of the urban dance phenomenon that originated in France's suburban *cités*. Many amateur groups composed primarily of teenagers of Maghreban and African origin have benefited from government subsidies and gone professional; every major dance festival, like Paris Estivales and Paris Quartier d'Eté, invites at least one of these cheerrousing groups like Aktuel Force whose acrobatic stunts outdo anything you'd see at the circus. In fact, channelling growing gang warfare hostility into physical grassroots art forms like hip-hop continues to be a Ministry of Culture priority, as new

Getting a Handel on Auréole *at the* **Opéra**.

studios sprout up like Georges Momboye's promising Pluri-African Dance and World Culture Centre (25 rue Boyer, 20th/ 01.43.58.85.01), offering street dance, jazz and African techniques. 1998's Biennale de Lyon – one of the world's most important dance gatherings – saw a backlash, as the local extreme right majority cut funding, since the Mediterranean theme featured groups like the local hip-hop group Käfig.

On the performance front, several of Paris's independent theatres were given renewed support. To get real insight into where the dance scene is heading, though, you have to get on the RER and check out the suburban theatres. Here talented up-and-coming dancemakers – most without diplomas – are already setting the trends towards a new dance of the 21st century (*see page 247*).

Information

Centre de Ressources Musique et Danse
Cité de la Musique, 221 av Jean-Jaurès, 19th (01.44.84.45.00). M° Porte de Pantin. **Open** noon-6pm Tue-Sat; 10am-6pm Sun. **Map insert**
A great state-of-the art documentation source for both dance and music, the impressive Centre boasts over 20,000 videos, CDs, books, scores, magazines, archives and databases for consultation. You can also input and access information through their regularly updated minitel network.

Rising talent **Gigi Caciuleanu** *(see page 247).*

Centre National de la Danse
9, 15 rue Geoffroy-L'Asnier, 4th (01.42.74.44.22).
M° St-Paul. **Open** 2.30-6.30pm Mon-Fri. **Map K6**
The Centre, newly merged with the former Théâtre Contemporain de la Danse, offers documentation for dancers, rehearsal studios and a performance space hosting regular lecture-demos. Laidback studio events continue this season in the heart of the Marais, as well as various reduced-rate subscription campaigns, to make dance around town more affordable and accessible to one and all. Eventually the plan is to move to a centre in suburban Pantin.

Fédération Française de Danse
12 rue St-Germain l'Auxerrois, 1st (01.42.36.12.61). M° Châtelet-Les Halles. **Open** 9.30am-5.30pm Mon-Fri. **Map J6**
The Federation serves as a clearing house for information on the current dance scene. Call ahead for an appointment.

Major Dance Venues

Ballet de l'Opéra National de Paris
Palais Garnier *pl de l'Opéra, 9th (08.36.69.78.68). M° Opéra.* **Box office** 11am-6.30pm Mon-Sat. **Tickets** 30F-405F. **Credit** AmEx, MC, V. **Map G4**
Opéra de Paris Bastille *pl de la Bastille, 12th (08.36.69.78.68). M° Bastille.* **Box office** 11am-6.30pm Mon-Sat. **Tickets** 50F-405F. **Credit** AmEx, MC, V. **Map M7**
Since its renovation, the sumptuous Palais Garnier mainly hosts dance, keeping *balletomanes* happy with Romantic hits this season such as *Coppélia, Don Quichotte* and *La Sylphide*, alternating with more daring modern works like Pina Bausch's *Sacré du Printemps.* Dance programming at the Bastille annexe is minimal this year, as they gear more towards opera, although a scattering of shows, such as *La Bayadère,* a revival of Anglein Preljocaj's 1995 *Le Parc* and *Swan Lake* are on the bill. Among several reruns, 1999 highlights include a touring program of the Royal Danish Ballet and a creation by American iconoclast choreographer William Forsythe. *See also chapters* **Right Bank** *and* **Music: Classical & Opera.**
Wheelchair access (reserve ahead on 01.40.01.18.08).

Châtelet – Théâtre Musical de Paris
1 pl du Châtelet, 1st (01.40.28.28.40). M° Châtelet-Les Halles. **Box office** 11am-7pm daily; *telephone bookings* 10am-7pm Mon-Sat. **Tickets** 30F-345F. **Credit** AmEx, DC, MC, V. **Map J6**
The famous Châtelet theatre will be closed for renovation until October 1999, but dance will be part of its reopening season – alongside the staple opera and classical music concerts – with a new programme by Maurice Béjart's Ballet Lausanne in December. Next season it will also play host to the Ballet de l'Opéra de Lyon. *See also chapter* **Music: Classical & Opera.**
Wheelchair access.

Théâtre de la Bastille
76 rue de la Roquette, 11th (01.43.57.42.14). M° Bastille. **Box office** 10am-6pm Mon-Fri; 2-6pm Sat. Closed July, Aug. **Tickets** 120F; 80F under-26s, over-60s. **Credit** AmEx, MC, V. **Map M6**
This long-time platform for the avant-garde movement fearlessly alternates high-quality dance with theatre, and seeks out experimental choreographers, such as American-born Israeli Barak Marshall, Steve Paxton and modern buto master Carlotta Ikeda, all featured this year. *See also chapter* **Theatre.**
Wheelchair access.

Théâtre des Champs-Elysées
15 av Montaigne, 8th (01.49.52.50.50). M° Alma-Marceau. **Box office** 11am-7pm Mon-Sat; *telephone bookings* 10am-noon, 2-6pm Mon-Fri. Closed July, Aug. **Tickets** 70F-450F. **Credit** AmEx, MC, V. **Map D5**
This elegant, 1900-seat theatre was made famous before World War I by Isadora Duncan and by Nijinsky's Ballets Russes (whose stone-relief portraits adorn the facade). Mainly a classical music venue, it also holds tango and flamenco programmes. It hosts the Russian festival Les Triomphes, boasting the Bolshoi's best, and the Nouveau Festival International de Danse de Paris. This season honors Alicia Alonso and the National Ballet of Cuba after a 20-year absence. *See also chapter* **Music: Classical & Opera.**

Théâtre de la Ville
2 pl du Châtelet, 4th (01.42.74.22.77). M° Châtelet. **Box office** 11am-7pm Mon; 11am-8pm Tue-Sat; *telephone bookings* 9am-7pm Mon; 9am-8pm Tue-Sat. **Tickets** 95F-160F. **Credit** MC, V. **Map J6**
Paris' leading contemporary dance forum has doubled its dance menu since its annexe (31 rue des Abbesses, 18th) opened in 1997. The 1000-seat Châtelet auditorium has excellent sight lines, strong co-productions, a mass-pleasing attitude and popular prices. 1999 sees creations by Israel's Batheva Dance Company, Pina Bausch, Maguy Marin and DV8 Physical Theatre. *See also chapters* **Music: Classical & Opera, Music: Rock, Roots & Jazz,** *and* **Theatre.**
Wheelchair access.

Independent Dance Spaces

Centre Mandapa
6 rue Wurtz, 13th (01.45.89.01.60). M° Glacière. **Box office** 30min before performance or reserve by phone. **Tickets** 80F-100F; 60F-70F students, over-60s; free under-5s. **No credit cards. Map J1**
Dedicated to traditional Indian dance forms. Companies from Asia, the Middle East, North Africa and Eastern Europe visit regularly. It also houses a school of Indian dance. *Wheelchair access.*

Danse, Théâtre & Musique (DTM)
6 rue de la Folie-Méricourt, 11th (01.47.00.19.60). M° St-Ambroise. **Box office** 10am-7pm Mon-Sat. **Tickets** 80F; 60F students, over-60s; 40F under-12s. **No credit cards. Map M5**
A contemporary dance pioneer, the friendly 70-seat DTM offers classes plus performances by affiliated Tendanse and international companies. Tea and discussion after events.

L'Etoile du Nord
16 rue Georgette-Agutte, 18th (01.42.26.47.47). M° Guy-Môquet. **Box office** 10am-6pm Mon-Fri; *telephone bookings* 11am-7pm Mon-Fri. Closed July, Aug. **Tickets** 35F-80F. **No credit cards.**
The ex-Dix-Huit Théâtre has emerged from near extinction with the same quality of dance, alternating with theatre and kids' shows. Choreographers feature in October, January and June. *Wheelchair access.*

La Ménagerie de Verre
12-14 rue Léchevin, 11th (01.43.38.33.44). M° Parmentier.
Box office 30min before performance or reserve by phone
2-7pm Mon-Fri. **Tickets** 80F; 60F students, over-60s; free
under-6s. **No credit cards. Map M5**
A vanguard laboratory of interchange between choreographers, directors, musicians and artists since 1983, the
Ménagerie holds two annual 'Inaccoutumés' festivals of
experimental dance, attracting choreographers and performers from all over Europe and the US.
Wheelchair access.

Le Regard du Cygne
*210 rue de Belleville, 20th (Bookings answerphone
01.43.58.55.93). M° Place des Fêtes or Télégraphe.*
Tickets 70F; students, over-60s, unemployed or 30 mins
before show 50F. **No credit cards.**
Tucked off in a courtyard, this seventeenth-century stone
barn has played an important role in promoting new choreographic talent through its eclectic Worksweek festivals.
After a year-long hibernation awaiting funding, dance is in
the fore again, although alternating with theatre and music.
Also offers modern dance classes for children and adults.

Dance Classes

Académie des Arts Chorégraphiques
4bis Cité Véron, 18th (01.42.52.07.29). M° Blanche.
Open 9am-11pm daily. **Classes** average 70F; 10 classes
600F. **No credit cards. Map G2**
One of Paris' friendliest and cleanest centres, housing character dance school Tchaika, and various classical techniques.

Centre de Danse du Marais
41 rue du Temple, 4th (01.42.72.15.42). M° Hôtel-de-Ville.
Open 9am-10pm daily. Sunday workshops. **Classes**
average 85F; 12 lessons 750F. **Credit** MC, V. **Map K6**
You name the technique, this Mecca for aspiring dancers of
all ages has got it. With a dozen studios and packed classes,
this is the ultimate hypermarket for the dance consumer.

International Duncan Center/ Chorecherches
175 av Ledru-Rollin, 11th (01.43.67.31.92). M° Voltaire.
Call for information or appointment. **Regular classes**
80F; 10 classes 700 F. **No credit cards. Map N6**
This new centre promotes contemporary, modern and earlymodern dance traditions. Its La Bacchanale company performs historic modern-dance repertoires and new works.

Centre International Danse Jazz
*54a rue de Clichy, 9th (01.53.32.75.00). M° Place de
Clichy or Liège.* **Open** 9am-10pm Mon-Fri; 11am-7.30pm
Sat; 1-7pm Sun. **Classes** 78F; 10 classes 640F. **No credit
cards. Map G2**
This trendy, eight-studio dance school draws a young, highadrenalin crowd for a decade of professional and amateur
classes, with emphasis on ballet, jazz and hip-hop.

Centre Chorégraphique Blanca Li
*7 rue des Petites-Ecuries, 10th (01.53.34.04.05).
M° Château d'Eau.* **Classes** 70F; 10 classes 640F. **No
credit cards. Map K3**
Blanca Li's artsy new studios offer a mellow atmosphere
with a focus on flamenco, African dance and modern jazz.

Salle Pleyel
*252 rue du Fbg-St-Honoré, 8th (01.45.61.53.00).
M° Ternes.* **Open** 9am-7pm Mon-Fri. **Classes** ring for
details. **Map D3**
Ballet-oriented dance schools are housed in spaces straight
out of a Dégas painting, above and below the posh concert hall.

Moving out of the mainstream

Often they start out as soloists, armed with
imagination, but little formal training. One day
they take a risk, eventually finding a partner
and a small group of disciples, and start performing on the periphery of Paris in a cold,
dirty, poorly-equipped studio-theatre or prefabricated cultural centre in a satellite town in
the communist heartland. They'll probably
look back on it as their most creative period.

Such is the scenario for several ingenious
young choreographers (paradoxically foreign-born and trained), who are diligently
devoted to perfecting their craft outside the
mainstream, as opposed to building a 'career'.
One such is Spanish-born Blanca Li, who has
carved out a unique style combining flamenco,
contemporary dance, circus art and humour.
She and her company got their break at the
Centre Pompidou with a piece inspired by
Wilde's *Salomé*. Li, however, prefers to stay
independent, touring the provinces. She's
opened a new dance studio in Paris, which is
now the main source of her self-sufficiency.

Several projects provide a forum for new
performers and their works: 'Danse Dense' at
the Salle Jacques Brel in the eastern suburb of
Pantin; the Colombes MJC and Théâtre de
Suresnes (both west of La Défense), which
promote lesser-known companies year-round;
and the month-long 'Iles de Danses' autumn
fest, which programmes young troupes
throughout the Ile de France. Bucharest-born
Gigi Caciuleanu and his company have earned
acclaim thanks to this circuit, as have the
Tunisian dancer Leila Haddad, Tero Saarinen's
Toothpick Company, Mark Tompkins, and
Daniel Larrieu.

In a more classical vein, watch for choreographer Cathleen Andrews and the new ACM
Ballet Theatre, one of the rare private ballet
troupes to offer high-quality creations.

Of course, one is rarely disappointed by
new works shown in Paris by a handful of
brilliant veterans like Carolyn Carlson, Odile
Duboc, Mats Ek, buto-innovator Carlotta
Ikeda or William Forsythe. And it's well worth
thinking about making the two-hour trip to
the Lille-Roubaix area to discover the outstanding and overlooked work of Maryse
Delente and the Ballet du Nord.

Film

The French are learning to cooperate with Hollywood, but are taking steps to protect their own cinematic traditions too.

The cinecentre of Paris is shifting eastward with the arrival at the turn of the millenium, in Bercy, of the Maison du Cinema, set to become Europe's most prestigious national showcase. The deluxe former American Center will showcase Gallic cinema, grouping disparate French film institutes under one roof. The public will be welcome to consult and view the archives. In fact, the rise of cinema in Paris' traditionally deprived east end has begun already, with the opening of the city's largest multiplex, the eighteen-screen UGC Ciné Cité Bercy (2 cour St-Emilion, 12th/ 08.36.68.68.58/ M° Cour St-Emilion). Meanwhile, across the river in the 13th *arrondissement*, an arthouse MK2 multiplex opens soon, next to the new national library. The 13th already boasts the biggest screen in Paris, **Gaumont Grand Ecran** at Place d'Italie.

Elsewhere, the fourteen-screen Gaumont Aquaboulevard (4-6 rue Louis-Armond, 15th/ 01.40.30.20.10/M° Balard) has opened in the Aquaboulevard complex in the 15th *arrondissement*. Lest anyone get too carried away, however, this and the Bercy complex will be the last authorised multiplexes to open until at least 2003. After all, the authorities – pressurised by the traditional Left Bank art houses – do not want cinephile Paris to be completely overwhelmed by Hollywood product, and there is reason for concern. While 1998 saw an overall increase in bums on seats to 175 million, the audience for French fare shrank year-on-year from 51 to 44 million. As part of the plan to encourage diversity and protect French output, arthouse cinemas across the capital are benefitting from publicly-funded facelifts.

As the latest figures confirm the dominance of American film, the sacred precepts of French national cinema policy – stick to the beloved, beleaguered native language and avoid Hollywood at all costs – are gradually being eroded. With *Titanic* toppling *La Grande Vadrouille* as the biggest-ever hit at the French box office, the French film industry is learning the importance of collaboration. And so, while the infrastructure heads east, French talent is shipping out west. Hot directors Matthieu *La Haine* Kassovitz, Luc *Fifth Element* Besson and Jan *Dobermann* Kounen have set up a production company in LA. The trio's aim is to be on location to tap into the dollars that are increasingly a factor in French filmmaking. As for the stars, Gérard Depardieu has been nudged aside as Hollywood's favourite leading frog by Jean

Zonca's **La Vie Rêvée des Anges**.

Reno, while Braveheart star Sophie Marceau has announced that she is taking a Tinseltown sabbatical, as well as playing the latest Bond girl.

It's not all one-way traffic. Of late, independent American filmmakers have been looking to France for finance; recent collaborations include Lodge Kerrigan's *Claire Dolan*. Britain, too, is reaping the benefits of a more outward-looking French industry. In early 1999 Michel Blanc heads to London to direct his script, *The Wrong Blonde*, starring Daniel Auteuil and to be filmed in English.

And before anyone starts to panic about the irremediable decline of home-grown cinema, it should be remembered that 1998's two biggest sellers after *Titanic* were Veber's *Le Dîner de Cons* (soon to follow in a long tradition and get a US remake) and Pirès' (Besson-produced) *Taxi* – both through-and-through French.

Pariscope's Cinéscope section and *l'Officiel des Spectacles* list what's on; programmes change on Wednesdays. English-language films are shown at many cinemas in VO (that is, in the original language with French subtitles). VF (*version française*) means the film is dubbed in French. Allô Ciné (01.40.30.20.10), a 24-hour information line (in French), details films by category or area.

Ciné Showcases

Le Cinéma des Cinéastes
7 av de Clichy, 17th (01.53.42.40.20). M° Place Clichy.
Map G2
This three-screen showcase of world cinema (with France at the forefront) was the brainchild of Jean-Jacques *Betty Blue* Beneix and Claude Miller, president of ARP, the association of French cinema directors and producers. As well as meet-the-director sessions, the cinema has held festivals of Israeli films, gay cinema and documentaries. Short films on Fridays. *Air conditioning. Wheelchair access.*

Gaumont Grand Ecran Italie
30 pl d'Italie, 13th (08.36.68.75.13). M° Place d'Italie.
Map J10
This huge complex by Japanese architect Kenzo Tange boasts the biggest screen (24m x 10m) in the city. *Air conditioning. Wheelchair access.*

Max Linder Panorama
24 bd Poissonnière, 9th (01.48.24.88.88/ 08.36.60.00.31). M° Grands Boulevards. **Map J9**
A state-of-the-art screening facility in a house founded in 1919 by comic Max Linder. Look out for all-nighters. *Air conditioning. Wheelchair access.*

MK2 sur Seine
14 quai de la Seine, 19th (08.36.68.47.07). M° Stalingrad or Jaurès. **Map M2**
Flagship of the ever-expanding MK2 group, this stylish six-screen, canalside complex, complete with restaurant and exhibition space, offers an all-in-one night out. *Air conditioning. Café-restaurant. Wheelchair access.*

UGC Ciné Cité Les Halles
pl de la Rotonde, Nouveau Forum des Halles, 1st (08.36.68.68.58). M° Châtelet-Les Halles. **Map J5**
This ambitious 16-screen development was Paris' first multiplex and screens art movies as well as mainstream stuff. Seating in certain theatres is at a fearsome angle, adding a vertiginous *frisson* to any good film. Internet café.

The Left Bank Ciné Village

The art cinemas crowded in the 5th and 6th *arrondissements* make up a truly unique collection of screens, all within walking distance of each other. Quaint, even rundown, they offer the most diverse programming in the world.

Action
Action Christine *4 rue Christine, 6th (01.43.29.11.30). M° Odéon.* **Map H7**
Action Ecoles *23 rue des Ecoles, 5th (01.43.29.79.89). M° Maubert-Mutualité.* **Map J7**
Wheelchair access to screen 2. Air conditioning.
Grand Action *5 rue des Ecoles, 5th (01.43.29.44.40). M° Cardinal-Lemoine.* **Map K8**
Wheelchair access to salle Gine. Air conditioning. **Mac Mahon** *5 av Mac Mahon, 17th (01.43.80.24.81). M° Charles de Gaulle-Etoile.* **Map C3**
Home from home for those nostalgic for 1940s and 50s Tinseltown classics and American independents – recent series have included Cary Grant, musicals, Fritz Lang, Marx brothers and Jim Jarmusch. Showpiece is the Grand Action.

Le Champo
51 rue des Ecoles, 5th (01.43.54.51.60). M° Cluny-La Sorbonne. **Map J7**
A charming Latin Quarter veteran with a seemingly non-stop supply of Hitchcock and vintage gems, plus more recent names (Woody Allen, Jane Campion, Benigni). Neighbouring Quartier Latin (9 rue Champollion) and Reflet Médicis Logos (3 rue Champollion) are also worth checking out. *Air conditioning. Wheelchair access to salle 1.*

Diagonal Europa
13 rue Victor-Cousin, 5th (01.43.54.15.04).
M° Cluny-La Sorbonne/RER Luxembourg. **Map J7**
The former Europa Panthéon is Paris' oldest movie house, founded in 1907 in the Sorbonne gymnasium. Screenings range from Rossellini to new releases by young directors. *Air conditioning.*

Racine Odéon
6 rue de l'Ecole-de-Médecine, 6th (01.43.26.19.68).
M° Odéon or Cluny-La Sorbonne. **Map J7**
Specialises in all-night specials (two or three films, plus breakfast) from Halloween horrors to John Woo.

Ten for the century

The world's very first public film screening was held by the Lumière brothers in rue Scribe on 28 December 1895, and Paris has reigned undisputed capital of cinema ever since.

1900s *Voyage dans la lune* The man in the moon gets a poke in the eye in Méliès' dreamlike early sci-fi classic.

1910s *Les Vampires* A journalist tracks a gang of criminals, led by black-tight clad Irma Vep (actress Musidora) around Paris. Feuillade's ten-part vampire movie influenced the Surrealists. Remade in 1996 as *Irma Vep.*

1920s *Napoléon* Gance's extraordinarily lavish four-hour, triple-screen portrait is almost as megalomaniac as its subject, and was apparently an inspiration for De Gaulle.

1930s *La Bête Humaine* Renoir uses the steam trains of Zola's novel as a metaphor for destructive human passion.

1940s *Quai des Orfèvres* Clouzot's low-life detective thriller set in rundown music halls, squalid apartments and gloomy police stations.

1950s *A bout de souffle* Godard's timeless classic of waif (Seberg) meets vagabond (Belmondo), roams through Paris from the Champs to Montparnasse.

1960s *Belle de Jour* Buñuel's amoral film launched Catherine Deneuve as the bored bourgeois housewife who goes on the game.

1970s *Père Noël est une ordure* Poiré's bad-taste farce: two SOS Détresse cousellors spend Christmas coping with disasters.

1980s *Diva* Beineix's cult, ultra-stylish thriller combines great opera, fab sets and, rare for an art film, a fast-moving scenario.

1990s *La Haine* Kassovitz's scalding vision of the *banlieue*, in which three disaffected youths wrestle with frustation in a world where violence is just another fact of life.

Buñuel premiered L' Age d'Or *at* **Studio 28.**

St-André-des-Arts
30 rue St-André-des-Arts, 6th (01.43.26.48.18). 12 rue Gît-le-Coeur, 6th (01.43.26.80.25). Mº St-Michel. **Map K7**
A two-screen cinema, renowned for its quality programming – Mike Leigh, Bergman, Kieslowski, Ozu retrospectives, and a range of shorts. Occasional meet-the-director sessions.
Wheelchair access. Air conditioning.

Studio Galande
42 rue Galande, 5th (01.43.26.94.08/08.36.68.06.24). Mº St-Michel. **Map J7**
A hole-in-the-wall institution that holds high the tradition of *The Rocky Horror Picture Show,* every Friday (10.30pm) and Saturday (10.30pm, 12.30am). It also regularly shows *A Clockwork Orange,* amid a wide range of art movies.
Air conditioning.

Studio des Ursulines
10 rue des Ursulines, 5th (01.43.26.19.09/ 01.43.26.97.08). RER Luxembourg. **Map H8**
Arthouse pioneer since 1926. It went on to screen incendiary avant-garde films, but now offers a repertory programme.
Wheelchair access.

Les 3 Luxembourg
67 rue Monsieur-le-Prince, 6th (01.46.33.97.77). Mº Odéon/RER Luxembourg. **Map H7**
Not too comfortable, but source of a constant stream of international arthouse fare, plus director tributes.
Air conditioning.

Other Art Cinemas

Le Balzac
1 rue Balzac, 8th (01.45.61.10.60/08.36.68.31.23). Mº George V. **Map D4**

Built in 1935 with a mock ocean-liner foyer, Le Balzac scores highly for both design and programming.

Denfert
24 pl Denfert-Rochereau, 14th (01.43.21.41.01). Mº Denfert-Rochereau. **Map H10**
A valiant little place with an eclectic repertory selection ranging from Eisenstein to kids' films and new animation.
Air conditioning. Wheelchair access.

Elysées Lincoln
14 rue Lincoln, 8th (01.43.59.36.14/08.36.68.81.07). Mº George V or Franklin d Roosevelt. **Map D4**
Arthouse cinema showing smaller-scale and independent films. Frequent meet-the-director screenings.

L'Entrepôt
7-9 rue Francis de Pressensé, 14th (01.45.40.78.38/01.45.39.60.09/08.36.68.05.87). Mº Pernéty. **Map F10**
This converted warehouse offers three screens, a restaurant, bar and garden. New and Third World directors, shorts and gay cinema all get a look-in, including theme series that mix films with relevant food, music and exhibitions. For the fortnightly Ciné-Philo a film is followed by a philosophy debate.
Air conditioning. Bar. Wheelchair access to Salle 1.

Le Latina
20 rue du Temple, 4th (01.42.78.47.86). Mº Hôtel-de-Ville or Rambuteau. **Map K6**
Le Latina (established 1913) screens films from Italy, Spain, Portugal and Latin America. There are also Latin-themed dances, a gallery and a lively Latin American restaurant.

Studio 28
10 rue Tholozé, 18th (01.46.06.36.07). Mº Abbesses or Blanche. **Map H1**
Historic, family-run Studio 28 offers a repertory mix of classics and recent movies. Decorated with souvenirs and posters, the entrance is embedded with footprints of the great.

Cinema in the Round

Dôme IMAX
1 pl du Dôme, 92095 Paris La Défense (01.46.92.45.50/ 08.36.67.06.06). Mº La Défense. **Tickets** 57F; 44F students, over-60s. *two films* 80F; 70F Sat; free under-4s. **Map inset**
A 1114-square-metre OMNIMAX screen is the ideal locale for experiencing such startling cinema-in-the-round features as *Les Mystères de l'Egypte* and *Le Grand Frisson.*
Wheelchair access.

La Géode
26 av Corentin-Cariou, 19th (01.40.05.12.12). Mº Porte de la Villette. **Tickets** 57F; 44F, students, disabled. *two films* 60F (some nights). **Credit** MC, V. **Map inset**
An OMNIMAX cinema housed in a glorious, shiny geodesic dome at La Villette. Most films feature dizzying 3-D plunges through dramatic natural scenery. Booking is advisable.
Wheelchair access (reserve ahead).

Public Repertory Institutions

Auditorium du Louvre
entrance through Pyramid, Cour Napoléon, 1st (01.40.20.51.86). Mº Palais Royal. **Tickets** 25F; 17F under-18s; membership available. **Map H5**
Like the Louvre pyramid, this 420-seat auditorium was designed by IM Pei. Film screenings are sometimes related to the exhibitions, but can be as delightfully unintellectual as 50s 3-D sci-fi. A regular feature are silent movies with live

Short films: small is beautiful

Often neglected in Britain and the USA, short films (*courts-métrages*) have a vital, if struggling place in French cinema. 'Shorts have never made money, so it has always been difficult to finance them and creatively [the medium] is bogged down in social subjects. We want to get more films screened in the main circuits,' says Jean-Louis Gérard of quarterly short magazine *Bref*, whose very existence proves that the poor relation of full-length features is not forgotten in France. Indeed, it was the grainy handheld efforts of *nouvelle vague* giants like Godard which gave the form its enduring credibility, and recently the discipline got a high-profile boost with Erick Zonca's Oscar-nominated (admittedly feature-length) Cannes winner *La Vie Rêvée des Anges*. Zonca had struggled financing a number of short films before tackling his début feature, and still enthusiastically beats the drum for shorts.

The next generation of cinematic talent is also nurtured by various *court-métrage* competitions such as the Prix Kieslowski, which rewards winning screenwriters aged between 16 and 26 with the chance to direct their scripts, which go on to be screened in festivals. Last year's winner, a five-minute piece portraying the trials of an illegal African immigrant in an unfriendly

Social issues are the staple of shorts.

French city, was distributed and screened with Chabrol's latest flick, *Au Coeur du mensonge*.

The essential source of information for anyone trying to make a short is the Agence du Court-Métrage (74 rue Rocher, 8th/ 01.44.69.26.60). In theatre terms, arguably the most consistent supporter is the Karmitz chain **MK2**, which helps fund the Prix Kieslowski and shows shorts before every feature. Major networks Canal+, France Television and Arte provide finance and airtime. Look out also for shorts programmed at the **Cinéma des Cinéastes**, **L'Entrepôt**, **Le Denfert** and the **Forum des Images**.

Another key showcase for shorts are publicly-funded projects to heighten awareness of social issues. Three short films were commissioned for International AIDS day on December 1 1998, with directors including *Ridicule* star Charles Berling and a gala screening at the prestigious Cinéma des Cinéastes. A further high-profile series of shorts highlighted the work and continuing importance of the International Declaration of Human Rights, which celebrated its fiftieth anniversary in December 1998.

For those interested in a peep at *court-métrage* culture, the Italian restaurant-cum-cinema Rital et Courts (1-3 rue des Envierges, 20th/ restaurant 01.47.97.08.40)/films 01.47.97.08.41), serves up animation, fiction and documentary shorts after the meal; while the Web Bar (*see* chapter **Cafés & Bars**) near République shows *courts-métrages* by young filmmakers two or three times a month, usually on Friday nights. It has links with TPS, a satellite TV network run by a TF1-led consortium which devotes a programme to short films, and with makers of shorts in Quebec. Stars and directors often attend presentations here for what often effectively becomes a short film's première.

Real devotees and wannabe filmmakers can travel to the annual festival at Clermont-Ferrand in central France (04.73.91.65.73), which takes place in late January and claims to be 'the Cannes of short films'. Aside from awarding a prestigious annual prize, there is also a bustling film market attracting international product and hopefuls. Shorts are also featured at the suburban Côté Court festival (Ciné 104, 104 av Jean Lolive, 93500 Pantin/ 01.48.46.95.08) in June, featuring new and old films from 30 seconds to 30 minutes, and at the Brest festival in Brittany. There are shorts sections at other established festivals, notably Cannes.

musical accompaniment, often specially composed, which benefit from the excellent acoustics. *Wheelchair access.*

La Cinémathèque Française
Palais de Chaillot, 7av Albert de Mun, 16th (01.56.26.01.01). M° Trocadéro. **Map C5.** *Grands Boulevards, 42 bd Bonne-Nouvelle, 10th (01.56.26.01.01). M° Bonne Nouvelle.* **Admission** 29F. **Map J4**
Founded in 1936 by film fanatics Georges Franju and Henri Langlois, the Cinémathèque played a seminal role in shaping the New Wave directors at the end of the 1950s, and subsequently as meeting point for devoted cinephiles with its retrospectives (Melville, Carpenter), series (Italy, crime movies, 30s musicals), experimental films and theme nights. The Palais de Chaillot screen has reopened after the 1997 fire, but like the still-closed film museum will probably ultimately move to the new Maison du Cinéma at Bercy.

Forum des Images
2 Grand Galerie: Porte St-Eustache, Forum des Halles, 1st (01.44.76.62.00). M° Les Halles. **Open** 1-9pm Tue, Wed, Fri-Sun; 1-10pm Thur. Closed 2-17 Aug. **Admission** 30F per day; 25F under-30s, over-60s; membership available. **Map J5**
Enlarged and renamed from the Vidéothèque (presumably to take in the wider multimedia definition of images), the Forum des Images is an addictive public archive dedicated to Paris on celluloid from 1895 to the present. No matter how brief the clip – from the Eiffel Tower scene in *Superman II* to the letter of introduction scene in *Babette's Feast* – if Paris is on film, it's here, along with ads, trailers, Pathé news reels, short films, animation and documentaries. An addictive Star Trek-like consultation room has 40 video consoles with Minitel-style keyboards where you can access computerised data by theme, year or author. The auditoria show wide-ranging urban-themed series of films and videos featuring Paris and other metropolises. 1999 topics include neurosis, men and Mexico. The Forum also screens the annual Rencontres Internationales du Cinéma (*see below*) and films from the critics' selection at Cannes. *Wheelchair access.*

Festivals & Special Events

Each year there are any number of movie festivals in Paris. Listed here are some regular, easily accessible events. Also of note are the lesbian film festival (*see chapter* **Gay & Lesbian**) and Cinéma en Plein Air (*see chapter* **Paris by Season**).

Cinéma du Réel
Cinéma des Cinéastes (see above). **Dates** Mar. **Admission** 30F per film (25F film students); 60F per day; 300F per week.
Despite its billing as an 'ethnographic and sociological' festival, this international documentary survey is a compilation of impressive, fascinating or off-putting films. The featured country for 1999 is Iran.

Festival International de Films de Femmes
Maison des Arts, pl Salvador-Allende, 94000 Créteil (01.49.80.38.98). M° Créteil-Préfecture. **Dates** mid Mar. **Admission** 35F per film; 30F students, unemployed, over 60s; 250F ten films. **Credit** V.
An important women's film festival with an impressive selection of retrospectives and new international films by female directors. Held every spring in a new town just outside Paris. *Wheelchair access (reserve ahead).*

Rencontres Internationales du Cinéma
Forum des Images (see above). **Dates** end Oct-early Nov. **Admission** 30F per film; 25F students, under-30s, over-60s, unemployed.
A truly global section of new independent feature, documentary and short films in competition for a Grand Prix du Public, plus a programme of workshops.

CinéMémoire
Cinémathèque (see above) and other venues. **Dates** late Nov-Dec. **Admission** 15F-120F.
This remarkable five-week festival shows rare, restored and recently rediscovered films as they were intended, at the right speed and often with orchestral accompaniment.

MK2 sur Seine: *movies and merriment on the waterfront.*

Gay & Lesbian

Gay Paree just gets gayer: the Marais strip has become shoppers' happy valley. Even the lesbian scene shows signs of coming out.

Gay and lesbian culture continues the move mainstream in France. Hardly a week goes by without a gay or lesbian couple recounting their cosy life or troubles on TV. Increased visibility may explain the ferocity of the backlash against the PACS (Pacte Civile de Solidarité) bill. Giving legal status to unmarried couples whatever their sex, it is perceived by the Catholic right as a gay rights bill. But the legislature is moving with the times and another national politican has come out, this time in the stuffy Senate. *Oh la la.*

The rue Ste-Croix-de-la-Bretonnerie and rue du Temple in the Marais cater for all the creature comforts of modern gay life – regulation clothes shops, bars, restaurants, a piercing boutique and the first mens' beauty parlour in the French capital – and pink companies continue to put down roots and diversify all the time. The other main strip over which the rainbow flag holds sway is the bar crawl along rue des Lombards in Les Halles.

In the Gallic gay club scene, *ze* accent is on dance and fashion and the crowd trendy. Apart from the gay clubs listed, many clubs have a large gay contingent or specific gay nights. Scream at Elysée Montmartre is well worth a visit if you can stomach priapic go go dancers in the all-together. Another hit is the regular visit of London institution Queer Nation. Nuits Blanches with roving *chanteuse* at the Gibus is a monthly fixture (*see* chapter **Clubs**). Happily something of camp old yesteryear remains. Old club faithfuls Scorpion (now **Scorp**) and **L'Insolite** have had a revamp. On the Champs-Elysées, **Queen** still rules. New in town, vast no-nonsense **Le Dépôt** boasts a cavernous backroom basement.

Act Up gets it up – safely – at La Concorde.

and job hunting. The *Association des Médecins Gais* (gay doctors) mans a phone line (6-8pm Wed; 2-4pm Sat 01.48.05.81.71). The café is a pleasant place to digest the magazines and flyers on offer. Café Positif (2-7pm Sun) allows HIV+ people and their friends to socialise in a relaxed atmosphere. Also hosts Friday evening *Vendredi des Femmes*.

Act Up Paris
45 rue Sedaine, 11th (answerphone 01.48.06.13.89).
M° Bréguet-Sabin. **Map L6**
Very active branch of the worldwide anti-AIDS group, whose 'zaps' have included a flourescent pink condom over the obelisk on place de la Concorde. Weekly meeting Tuesdays at 7.30pm in amphitheatre 1 of the Ecole des Beaux-Arts, 14 rue Bonaparte, 6th. M° St-Germain-des-Prés. Publishes free monthly mag *Action*: health, news and hits.

SNEG (Syndicat National des Entreprises Gaies)
44 rue du Temple, 4th (01.44.59.81.01). M° Rambuteau.
Open 10am-6pm Mon-Fri. **Map J6**
The gay and lesbian business group unites some 950 companies across France. Organises HIV and safe-sex awareness training for staff, and hands out free condoms.

Media & Associations

Principal magazines are *Illico* (newsy), *Double Face* (lifestyle), *Têtu* (glossy), *Ex Aequo* (politics), *Idol* (young lifestyle), *Projet X* (fetish) and *Lesbia* (women). Radio FG 98.2FM is the source of house music, news, info, club notices and contacts. For information on all health services, and AIDS/HIV services *see* chapter **Directory**.

Centre Gai et Lesbien
3 rue Keller, 11th (01.43.57.21.47). M° Ledru-Rollin.
Open 2-8pm Mon-Sat; 2-7pm Sun. **Map L7**
The Lesbian and Gay Centre has become a valued community resource providing information and a meeting space, legal and other advice services, and bulletin boards for flat

Gay Bars & Cafés

Amnesia
42 rue Vieille-du-Temple, 4th (01.42.72.16.94).
Mº Hôtel-de-Ville. **Open** 10.30am-2am daily.
Credit MC, V. **Map K6**
Amnesia is now a warm meeting place with comfy sofas and easy-going clientele. Though calm in the afternoon, action hots up at night when a critical mass congregates. The popular weekend brunch (noon-4.30pm) draws a mixed crowd.

Banana Café
13 rue de la Ferronnerie, 1st (01.42.33.35.31).
Mº Châtelet-Les Halles. **Open** 4.30pm-dawn daily.
Credit AmEx, MC, V. **Map J5**
Packed and pumping nightly with hedonistic 30-somethings, gay and straight, the Banana Café's theme nights are legendary: camp, decadent and often downright silly. The terrace is great for poser-watching in summer; in the cellar bar singers diva their best through showtunes all year long.

Le Bar du Palmier
16 rue des Lombards, 4th (01.42.78.53.53).
Mº Châtelet-Les Halles. **Open** 5pm-5am daily. **Credit**
AmEx, MC, V. **Map J6**
Gets busy late, but also good during happy hour (6-8pm) when beer and copious nibbles are served. With bizarre pseudo-tropical décor and a nice terrace, this is one of the few places where women are welcome and numerous.

Le Central
33 rue Vieille-du-Temple, 4th (01.48.87.99.33).
Mº Hôtel-de-Ville. **Open** 5pm-2am Mon-Thur; 4pm-2am Fri-Sun. **Credit** MC, V. **Map K6**
Popular with tourists, one of the city's oldest gay bars (Paris's only straight gay hotel is upstairs) might seem dull compared to its sprightly neighbours, but can be a welcome respite after bar-hopping in the area. Older crowd, no attitude.

Coffee Shop
3 rue Ste-Croix-de-la-Bretonnerie, 4th (01.42.74.24.21).
Mº Hôtel-de-Ville. **Open** noon-2am daily. **No credit cards. Map K6**
The laidback Coffee Shop is a popular rendezvous and pick-up joint. MTV plays in a corner, decent bistro food is served until late, but people really come here for the gossip.

Le Cox
15 rue des Archives, 4th (01.42.72.08.00). Mº Hôtel-de-Ville. **Open** 1pm-2am daily. **No credit cards. Map K6**
Despite a name to make English-speakers cringe, this is one of the hottest and most militant Marais gay bars. Afternoons are calm, but evenings hot up with loud music, dishy barmen and a good mix of body-conscious punters.

Le Duplex
25 rue Michel-le-Comte, 3rd (01.42.72.80.86).
Mº Rambuteau. **Open** 8pm-2am daily. **Credit** AmEx, MC, V. **Map K5**
One of the oldest Marais gay bars. Monthly exhibitions and an eclectic music policy attract all sorts to this smoky bar; but don't be fooled: cruising here is down to a fine art.

Le Mercury Bar
5 rue de la Ferronnerie, 1st (01.40.41.00.10).
Mº Châtelet-Les Halles. **Open** 4pm-dawn daily.
Credit AmEx, MC, V. **Map J5**
Now renamed (from Le Bar) and under new management gaining a trendier media set. Look out for Ladies Room club events some Sundays: chill-out and house.

Mic Man
24 rue Geoffrey l'Angevin, 4th (01.42.74.39.80).
Mº Rambuteau. **Open** noon-2am Mon-Sat; 2pm-2am Sun.

Credit MC, V. **Map K6**
This bar's flowery entrance belies its true nature. Beards and moustaches abound, and the basement means business.

Mixer Bar
23 rue Ste-Croix-de-la-Bretonnerie, 4th (01.48.87.55.44).
Mº Hôtel-de-Ville. **Open** 4pm-2am daily. **Credit** MC, V. **Map K6**
In the latest attempt to make this prime spot work, the concept seems to be whooshing up juices in a shaker, hoping it will inspire the punters likewise. DJs from 5pm.

Okiwa
40 rue Vieille-du-Temple, 4th (01.48.04.30.69). Mº Hôtel-de-Ville. **Open** 11am-2am daily. **Credit** AmEx, MC, V. **Map K6**
It's amazing what some cute wooden blinds can do to the turnover in a gay bar. Opening as something like a snack bar, it has become a daytime rendezvous and bustling nighttime hangout. They even serve food at the bar. For something more formal dine in the exotically decorated basement restaurant (7.30pm-1am), so camp it's Christmas every day.

Open Bar
17 rue des Archives, 4th (01.42.72.26.18). Mº Hôtel-de-Ville. **Open** 11am-2am daily. **Credit** MC, V. **Map K6**
Thanks to the ultimate strategic location on the crossroads with Ste-Croix-de-la-Bretonnerie, the Open Bar has become a Mecca for gay boys meeting up before heading off into the night. A facelift, clearly intended to appeal to the well-heeled, has only increased its popularity, and crowds spill out onto the streets whatever the weather. Now also runs Open Bar Coffee Shop two doors down.

Quetzal
10 rue de la Verrerie, 4th (01.48.87.99.07).
Mº Hôtel-de-Ville. **Open** 5pm-5am daily. **No credit cards. Map K6**
Still the cruisiest bar in the Marais, Quetzal attracts a beefy crowd looking for a drink and company. It's at the end of the rue des Mauvais-Garçons (Bad Boy Street), so you know what to expect. There's a strategically placed terrace.

Le Tropic Café
66 rue des Lombards, 1st (01.40.13.92.62).
Mº Châtelet-Les Halles. **Open** 4.30pm-3am Mon-Thur; 4.30pm-4am Fri-Sun. **Credit** AmEx, MC, V. **Map G6**
This bright, upbeat bar is going through a renaissance with some groovy parties that draw a loyal band. Grab a table on the terrace to make the most of the people-watching.
Wheelchair access

Gay Restaurants

Au Rendezvous des Camionneurs
72 quai des Orfèvres, 1st (01.43.54.88.74).
Mº Pont-Neuf. **Open** noon-2.30pm, 7-11.30pm daily.
Average 180F. **Prix fixe** 78F, 98F (Mon-Thur).
Credit AmEx, MC, V. **Map J6**
Classic French favourites and a charming location by Pont Neuf make this restaurant a consistent gay success.

Amadeo
19 rue François-Miron, 4th (01.48.87.01.02). Mº Hôtel-de-Ville. **Open** 8-11pm Mon; noon-2pm, 8-11pm Tue-Thur; noon-2pm, 8-11.30pm Fri; 8-11.30pm Sat. Closed two weeks in Aug. **Average** 165F. **Prix fixe** 110F (Tue), 175F. **Lunch menu** 75F, 95F. **Credit** MC, V. **Map K6**
Well-informed Parisians consider this busy gay resturant a secret gem. The music is strictly Mozart and the ochre and petrol-blue colour scheme makes for typical Marais chic. Inventive *plats du jour* are typified by the *foie gras* salad,

*Good, clean fun at grande dame **Le Central**.*

goat's cheese ravioli or roast duck slivers with barley. Live opera singer first Thur of the month.

L'Amazonial
3 rue Ste-Opportune, 1st (01.42.33.53.13). M° Châtelet-Les Halles. **Open** noon-1.30am daily. **Prix fixe** 83F, 129F. **Credit** AmEx, DC, MC, V. **Map J5**
Rebuilt a couple of years ago after a fire, Paris' largest gay restaurant has now expanded its terrace even more with a lot of fake stone and tack. Decent French cuisine with a twist of the exotic and tight T-shirted waiters. Weekend brunch.

L'Eclèche et Cie
10 rue St-Merri, 4th (01.42.74.62.62). M° Hôtel-de-Ville. **Open** 8am-1am daily. **Average** 130F. **Credit** MC, V. **Map K6**
This popular gay restaurant offers breakfast (8am-noon) and traditional bistro fare like *gigot d'agneau* and *steak tartare* (noon-1am). Relaxed by day, a great hubbub prevails by mid-evening. Weather permitting, there are benches outside in a pleasant, plant-filled alley. Weekend brunch (100F).

Krokodil
20 rue de La Reynie, 4th (01.48.87.55.67). M° Châtelet-Les Halles. **Open** 7pm-2am daily (bar 5pm-2am). **Average** 160F. **Prix fixe** 130F. **Credit** AmEx, MC, V. **Map J6**
This open-plan restaurant-bar, with its ox-blood and orange interior and sheltered terrace, manages to avoid many fancy pratfalls of disco dinners. *Brochettes* are the house speciality, while for exotica, there's ostrich, but alas, no crocodile. *Wheelchair access.*

Le Rude
23 rue du Temple, 4th (01.42.74.05.15). M° Hôtel-de-Ville. **Open** noon-2am daily. **Average** 120F. **Brunch** noon-5pm Sun. **Credit** MC, V. **Map K6**

Done up in a cool minimalist style, this extremely popular restaurant feeds a mostly gay clientele, although everyone is welcome, as the party atmosphere is all-inclusive. They do good burgers and salads, as well as dishes like duck *à l'orange*. Low drink prices spur conviviality, as does chatty Jess. There's a basement bar for a quiet nightcap. *Wheelchair access.*

Gay Clubs & Discos
Check press and flyers for one-nighters and remember that not much gets going before 1am. Admission prices often include one drink.

Club 18
18 rue de Beaujolais, 1st (01.42.97.52.13). M° Palais-Royal. **Open** 11pm-dawn Thur-Sun. **Admission** free Thur, Sun; 70F Fri, Sat. **Credit** AmEx, MC, V. **Map H5**
Time travel made real: camp reigns supreme in this club. Friendly, but don't expect an adventurous music policy.

Le Dépôt
10 rue aux Ours, 3rd (01.44.54.96.96). M° Rambuteau. **Open** midnight-8am daily. **Admission** 45F Mon-Thur; 55F Fri-Sun. **Credit** DC, MC, V. **Map K5**
Since opening in October 98, this colossal disco sin-bin has been draining the hordes from the Marais bars. Rainbow flags flutter frivolously outside but inside it is hard business. Décor is blockhouse chic with jungle netting and exposed air ducts, but despite the pounding sound system and homo-erotic video walls, there's little dancing. It's clear the real action is subterranean: a labyrinth of cubicles which even Indiana Jones would find hard to navigate.

L'Insolite
33 rue des Petits-Champs, 2nd (01.40.20.98.59). M° Pyramides. **Open** 11pm-5am daily. **Admission** free Mon-Thur, Sun; 50F Fri, Sat. **No credit cards. Map H4**
Bright and brassy, this time tunnel takes you back to the 70s, save for the 90s disco glitter ball. Cosy and friendly, with a guarantee to fall into conversation (or more) with someone.

Le Queen
102 av des Champs-Elysées, 8th (01.53.89.08.90). M° George V. **Open** 11.30pm-dawn daily. **Admission** 50F Mon; free Tue-Thur, Sun; 80F Fri, Sat. **Credit** AmEx, DC, MC, V. **Map D4**
Still the pick of the crop and crammed every night. Going to Le Queen takes courage – the door staff are rude and ruthless, especially with women. Top DJs, extravagant (un)dress, drag queens and go gos galore. Generally house music and hedonism all the way or don your gaudiest shirt and flares for Monday's Disco Inferno. *See also chapter* **Clubs**.

Scorp
25 bd Poissonnière, 9th (01.40.26.28.30). M° Grands Boulevards. **Open** midnight-6.30am daily. **Admission** free Mon-Thur, Sun; 70F Fri, Sat. **Credit** AmEx, MC, V. **Map J4**
Shortened in name and sharpened in style, the former Scorpion proves that long relationships are possible in gay Paree. House and dance hits reign. Much less cool than Le Queen, but then also much less attitude.

Le Tango
13 rue au Maire, 3rd (01.42.72.17.78). M° Arts et Métiers. **Open** Thur 8pm-2am, Fri, Sat 10.30pm-5am; 6pm-2am Sun. **Admission** 60F Thur (with concert), 30F after 10.30pm; 40F Fri, Sat. **No credit cards. Map K5**
Le Tango has returned to its dancehall roots for dancing *à deux*, with a clientele that is roughly 50 per cent gay or lesbian, and their friends. Accordion concert on Thur before the *bal* takes over with *musette*, waltzes, tangos and slows.

Men-Only Clubs: The Dark Side

Banque Club
23 rue de Penthièvre, 8th (01.42.56.49.26). M° Miromesnil.
Open 4pm-2am Mon-Sat; 2pm-2am Sun. **Admission** 30F
4-6pm, 45F 6-10pm Mon-Fri, Sun; 20F Sat. **No credit
cards. Map E3**
Cruise club with three cellars, videos and private cabins.

Docks
150 rue St-Maur, 11th (01.43.57.33.82). M° Goncourt.
Open 4pm-2am daily. **Admission** 45F. **No credit cards.
Map M4**
Heavy cruise club with theme nights in meat-market labyrinth.

La Luna
28 rue Keller, 11th (01.40.21.09.91). M° Bastille.
Open 10pm-6am daily. **Admission** free. **Credit** MC, V.
Map M6
A cruise bar with a basement maze of corridors and cabins.
Busy at weekends and for Tuesday's 'Incorporo' night.

QG
*12 rue Simon-le-Franc, 4th (01.48.87.74.18).
M° Rambuteau.* **Open** 5pm-6am Mon-Thur, Sun;
5pm-8am Fri, Sat. **Credit** MC, V. **Map K6**
No entrance fee, cheap beer, late opening and a sense of
humour guarantee success for this bar. Things get tough
downstairs, and don't even ask what the bath is for.

Le Tranfert
3 rue de la Sourdière, 1st (01.42.60.48.42). M° Tuileries.
Open 11pm-dawn daily. **Credit** AmEx, MC, V. **Map G5**
Tiny, but entertaining leather/SM bar.

Le Trap
*10 rue Jacob, 6th (unlisted telephone). M° St-Germain-
des-Prés.* **Open** 11pm-4am daily. **Admission** free Mon-
Thur, Sun; 50F Fri, Sat. **No credit cards.** **Map H6**
Le Trap has been packing them in for nearly 20 years and
has become hip with the fashion crowd. Expect naked dancing ('and more!' apparently) on Mondays and Wednesdays.

Men-Only Saunas

IDM
*4 rue du Fbg-Montmartre, 9th (01.45.23.10.03).
M° Grands Boulevards.* **Open** noon-1am Mon-Thur;
noon-2am Fri-Sun. **Admission** 95F; 60F after 10pm.
No credit cards. Map J4
Paris' largest sauna has a gym, steam room and jacuzzi.

Key West
*141 rue Lafayette, 10th (01.45.26.31.74). M° Gare du
Nord.* **Open** noon-1am Mon-Thur, Sun; noon-2am Fri, Sat.
Admission 110F; 60F under-26s; 70F after 10pm. **No
credit cards. Map K2**
Europe's most beautiful sauna – as it modestly describes
itself – has a small pool, gym and large steam room. Upstairs
are cubicles with TV screens playing saucy videos.

Gay Shops

Boyz Bazzar
*5, 38 rue Ste-Croix-de-la-Bretonnerie, 4th
(01.42.71.94.00). M° Hôtel-de-Ville* **Open** noon-midnight
Mon-Sat; 2-9pm Sun. **Credit** AmEx, MC, V. **Map K6**
Now virtually a mini chain dotted along the street catering
for that boyz essential tight T-shirt or a titilating video.

Body Men Village
25 rue du Temple, 4th (01.42.72.17.16). M° Hôtel-de-

Ville. **Open** noon-10pm Mon-Fri; 10am-8pm Sat. **Credit**
AmEx, MC, V. **Map K6**
Gay boys come to buff their body shrine. Have a hand mas-
sage and facial, or go downstairs for the full (beauty) works.

Boys' Zone
*25 rue Vieille-du-Temple, 4th (01.48.87.52.54).
M° Hôtel-de-Ville.* **Open** noon-8pm Mon-Sat; 2-8pm Sun.
Credit AmEx, MC, V. **Map K6**
Garish, gay gear for those with a refined sense of over-the-
top, although you might find something more subtle.

DOM
*21 rue Ste-Croix-de-la-Bretonnerie, 4th
(01.42.71.08.00). M° Hôtel-de-Ville.* **Open** 11.30am-9pm
Mon-Thur; 11.30am-11pm Fri, Sat; 2-9pm Sun. **Credit**
AmEx, MC, V. **Map K6**
Assistants dressed in black sell essential items in screaming
colours for the home, from day-glo fish tanks to inflatable
armchairs and naughty chocs. Chic and kitsch, but not *cher.*

IEM
208 rue St-Maur, 10th (01.42.41.21.41). M° Goncourt.
Open 10am-7.30pm Mon-Sat. **Credit** AmEx, MC, V.
Map M4
This store has an enormous video section, clothes, books and
condoms. Upstairs houses all things leather and rubber.
Branches: 43 rue de l'Arbre-Sec, 1st (01.42.96.05.74);
33 rue de Liège, 9th (01.45.22.69.01).

Lionel Joubin
*10 rue des Filles-du-Calvaire, 3rd (01.42.74.37.51).
M° Filles du Calvaire.* **Open** 11am-8pm Tue-Sat.
Closed Aug. **Credit** V. **Map L5**
Famous for its extravagant window displays, florist Joubin
has decorated entire floats for the Gay Pride march.

Les Mots à la Bouche
*6 rue Ste-Croix-de-la-Bretonnerie, 4th (01.42.78.88.30).
M° Hôtel-de-Ville.* **Open** 11am-11pm Mon-Sat; 2-8pm Sun.
Credit MC, V. **Map K6**
Stocks gay-interest literature from around the world, including an English-language section, plus travel guides and magazines. Interesting community meeting board, a good
meeting place and changing art exhibitions in the basement.

Gay Services

Eurogay's
*23 rue du Bourg-Tibourg, 4th (01.48.87.37.77).
M° Hôtel-de-Ville.* **Open Oct-Mar** 10am-1.30pm, 2.30-
7pm Mon-Fri. **Apr-Sept** 10am-1.30pm, 2.30-7pm Mon-
Fri; 11am-5pm Sat. **Credit** MC, V. **Map K6**
From train tickets to world tours, this gay travel agent can
book it all, and proposes 80 gay destinations around the globe.

Hôtel Central Marais
*33 rue Vieille-du-Temple, 4th (01.48.87.56.08/fax
01.42.77.06.27). M° Hôtel-de-Ville.* **Rates** *single* 450F;
double 535F; *breakfast* 35F. **Credit** MC, V. **Map K6**
The city's only strictly gay hotel (above **Le Central**) has
seven rooms (but no private bathrooms), plus an apartment
(650F-795F). Book well in advance. English spoken.
Room services *Double glazing. Telephone.*

Hôtel Saintonge
*16 rue de Saintonge, 3rd (01.42.77.91.13/fax
01.48.87.76.41). M° Filles du Calvaire.* **Rates** *single*
410F-490F; *double* 490F-550F; *suite* 720F. **Credit** AmEx,
DC, MC, V. **Map L5**

Expect plenty of inflammatory activity at
Le Dépôt, *see p255.*

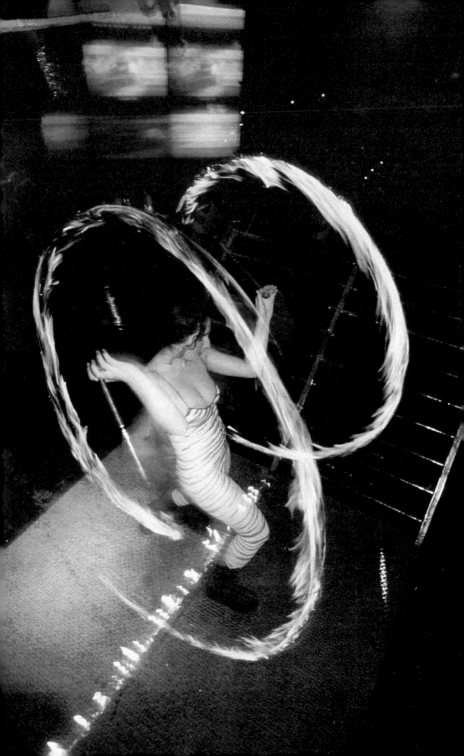

Although this hotel is open to everyone, its owners cultivate a gay clientele. All rooms have a private shower.
Room services *Hairdryer. Minibar. Safe. Telephone. TV.*

Pharmacie du Village
26 rue du Temple, 4th (01.42.72.60.71).
M° Hôtel-de-Ville. **Open** 8.30am-10pm Mon-Sat; 10am-7pm Sun. **Credit** AmEx, MC, V. **Map K6**
If the thought of having to explain intimate problems to aged men in white coats fills you with fear, this gay-staffed chemist is the answer.

Orys Image
23 bd Poissonnière, 2nd (01.42.33.05.30).
M° Grands Boulevards. **Open** 8am-7.30pm Mon-Fri; noon-7.30pm Sat. **Credit** MC, V. **Map J4**
Gay-owned photo developer, with one-hour service, total discretion and a 15 per cent reduction on film development for gay customers (upon presentation of a gay guide).

Lesbian Paris

Although discreet compared to male counterparts, lesbians in Paris have been growing more visible with a handful of trendy new bars thriving in the Marais and active campaigning for the PACS. Leading publication is long-running *Lesbia*. Lesbians share with gay men the **Centre Gai & Lesbien** (*see above*) and several militant groups are based at the Maison des Femmes (*see chapter* **Directory**). Look out also for the club nights run by **Ladies Room** at the Mercury Bar and Le Dépôt – chill out and house music.

Les Mots à la Bouche: *gay wordsmith.*

Les Archives, Recherches, Cultures Lesbiennes (ARCL)
Maison des Femmes, 163 rue de Charenton, 12th (01.43.43.41.13/01.43.43.42.13). M° Reuilly-Diderot. **Open** 7-9.30pm Tue. Closed two weeks in Aug. **Map N8**
ARCL produces audio-visual documentation, a yearbook and bulletins on lesbian and women's activities, and runs an archive of lesbian and feminist documents, essays and novels. Occasionally hosts evening parties and other events.

La Champmeslé
4 rue Chabanais, 2th (01.42.96.85.20). M° Bourse. **Open** 5pm-dawn Mon-Sat. **Credit** AmEx, MC, V. **Map H4**
With a mixed crowd in front and women-only at the back, this pillar of the lesbian bar community is busiest at weekends and on Thursday, when there's cabaret. Changing art shows and occasional fortune tellers.

Au Feu Follet
5 rue Raymond-Losserand, 14th (01.43.22.65.72). M° Gaîté. **Open** 7.30-11.30pm Mon-Thur; 7.30pm-midnight Fri, Sat. Closed Aug. **Average** 150F. **Prix fixe** 85F. **Credit** MC, V. **Map F10**
Traditional French home cooking with a Southwestern influence is served in this tiny but lively restaurant. Friendly service and a star-spangled dining room make this popular with a mixed though mainly lesbian crowd at weekends.

Pulp
25 bd Poissonnière, 2nd (01.40.26.01.93). M° Grands Boulevards. **Open** midnight-dawn Wed-Sat. **Admission** 50F Fri, Sat. **Credit** AmEx, MC, V. **Map J4**
Since it changed name (and management) from L'Entracte, Pulp has become *the* happening club – small and intimate, friendly staff. The musical mix takes in soul, funk, reggae, house, techno and Latin; regulars include DJ Sex Toy. Men admitted if accompanied. Publishes witty fanzine *Housewife*.

Quand les Lesbiennes se font du cinéma
Espace Culturel André Malraux, 2 pl Victor-Hugo, 93000 Le Kremlin-Bicêtre. M° Kremlin-Bicêtre. **Information** Cineffable 01.48.70.77.11. **Dates** late Oct-early Nov.
Women-only film festival screens mostly never-seen-before films, from documentaries and experimental videos to lesbian features, plus debates, exhibition, bar and a party.

Les Scandaleuses
8 rue des Ecouffes, 4th (01.48.87.39.26). M° Hôtel-de-Ville. **Open** 6pm-2am daily. **Credit** MC, V. **Map K6**
Les Scandaleuses has led the way among the new lesbian bars in the Marais. Chrome bar stools and high tables maximise the space, and the cellar rooms extend the mixing potential. Video monitors and changing exhibits by women artists adorn the walls. Accompanied men welcome.

Unity Bar
176-178 rue St-Martin, 3rd (01.42.72.70.59). M° Rambuteau. **Open** daily 4pm-2am. Closed one week in Dec. **No credit cards. Map K5**
A studenty clientele wears demin, plays pool and sings along to Queen and Suzanne Vega at this refreshingly visible new *bar féminin* by the Centre Pompidou. Cards and board games available at the bar. Men are welcome if accompanied.

Utopia
15 rue Michel-le-Comte, 3rd (01.42.71.63.43). M° Rambuteau. **Open** 5pm-2am Mon-Sat. **No credit cards. Map K5**
Opened by Antoinette and Anne in June 1998, the Utopia has quickly gained a reputation with house beat, billiards tournaments, pinball, music and café-théâtre showcases, and fancy dress parties. The bar is used for art shows, while the lower level resembles a subterranean garden grotto.

Music: Classical & Opera

In Paris, modernity and the Baroque are always in. There are also a couple of composer's centenaries and some divine divas to enjoy.

Paris seems set to rise to the Poulenc centenary with celebrations led by Georges Prêtre conducting a birthday concert of symphonic music at the **Palais Garnier** in April, a production of *Les Mamelles de Tiresias* at the **Opéra Comique** in May and the complete *Mélodies* at the new **Bibliothèque Nationale**. The **Cité de la Musique**, intellectual bastion of the French music establishment, is more reticent, preferring to concentrate on the Gershwin centenary. French musicologists tend to take an inflexible linear view of twentieth-century musical history: Debussy, Ravel, Messiaen, leading inexorably to Boulez. The musical movement known as 'Les Six' (Durey, Auric, Honegger, Milhaud, Taillefer and Poulenc) had Jean Cocteau as their spokesman, but he committed the cardinal sin of disregarding both German music and the sacred Debussy, suggesting that the new composers seek inspiration from such flippant sources as the music hall and the circus. This apparent lack of *sérieux* blighted Poulenc all his life. Only in France are such dramatic masterpieces as *Les Dialogues des Carmélites* or *La Voix Humaine* (based on a play by Cocteau) not fully appreciated. Composers such as Gabriel Pierné, Reynaldo Hahn or Henri Sauguet do smack more of the salon than the conservatoire, but are certainly more fun than a discussion of microtonality at the **IRCAM**.

There is another public, however, who dream of times when *The White Horse Inn* ran at **Châtelet** and who believe that popular Latin tenor Andrea Bocelli is the next Pavarotti. Someone who unites these two publics by dint of sheer joyous virtuosity is Natalie Dessay, a coloratura in the Lily Pons tradition, who has enthralled audiences around the world with her high-flying brilliance as the doll in Offenbach's *Tales of Hoffmann*, or with the death-defying arias of the Queen of the Night in Mozart's *Magic Flute*. She appears in Handel's *Alcina* in June at the Palais Garnier alongside Renée Fleming and Susan Graham. William Christie, a Baroque trendsetter if ever there was, has chosen the best Bel Canto divas in the world to float their vibrant, creamy tones over the astringent viols of the **Arts Florrisants**. Here is one ghetto door which is

opening in both directions, with talented Baroque specialist Véronique Gens now singing the classical soprano repertoire with great success. This should mean the coming together of two audiences – Opera Buff meets Early Music Fan – which can only be good news for both opera house and record companies – and, most importantly, the music itself. It remains to be seen if the contemporary music scene will manage a similar widening of its horizons. 'World' music is big at the Cité de la Musique just now, so perhaps we'll see Pierre Boulez turn his hand to a bit of Cuban jazz 'improv'...

MUSIC IN CHURCHES

The **Festival d'Art Sacré** highlights religious music in Paris in the weeks before Christmas (01.44.70.64.10). **Concertsolo** (01.44.62.70.90) offers concerts at various churches, usually St-Germain-des-Prés and Eglise St-Louis-en-l'Ile, as does **Les Grands Concerts Sacrés** (01.48.24.16.97) in Eglise St-Roch and Eglise St-Séverin, while music in Notre-Dame is taken care of by **Musique Sacrée à Notre-Dame** (01.44.41.49.99).

Generally, there is little music from late July until mid-September, except for the **Paris, Quartier d'Eté** festival. Concerts are held in gardens across the city, such as the large scale events in Parc André Citroën, or romantic candlelit concerts in the Orangerie of the Bagatelle gardens. The Carrousel du Louvre also runs high-quality chamber music concerts. *See also chapter* **Paris by Season**.

BOOKING AHEAD

For listings, see *Pariscope* and *L'Officiel des Spectacles*. The monthly *Le Monde de la Musique* and *Diapason* also list classical concerts, while *Opéra International* provides the best coverage of all things vocal. *Cadences* and *La Terrasse*, two free monthlies, are distributed outside concerts. Ticket prices and availability are largely governed by the artists performing. If Giulini is visiting the **Orchestre de Paris** then it's likely tickets will be booked up ahead and fairly pricey. Many venues offer cut-rate tickets to students (under 26) an hour before curtain. Beware of ticket touts around the Opéra and big-name concerts. For **La Fête de la**

Musique, on 21 June, events are free, as are some concerts at the **Maison de Radio France,** the **Conservatoire de Paris** and churches. If you are staying in Paris for a while, consider joining **Jeunesses Musicales de France** (01.44.61.86.86), for the equivalent of student discounts at concert halls. (For ticket agencies, *see chapter* **Directory.**)

La Flûte de Pan

49, 53, 59 rue de Rome, 8th (strings, woodwind 01.42.93.65.05/sax, brass, percussion, jazz 01.43.87.01.81/ vocal, keyboard 01.42.93.47.82). M° St-Lazare. **Open** 10am-6.30pm Mon-Sat. **Credit** MC, V. **Map E3**
This long-established music shop, among the instrument shops of Paris' *rue des luthiers*, offers the most comprehensive selection of sheet music and scores in Paris.

Orchestras & Ensembles

Les Arts Florissants

The 'Arts Flo' is France's most highly regarded Early Music group. William Christie's Handel conducting is more popular in France than it was at Glyndebourne last summer, and his purist style in Rameau and Lully has set the standard. This season orchestra and chorus will appear at the Palais Garnier in Handel's *Alcina*, by arrangement with the Opéra.

La Chapelle Royale

Philippe Herreweghe, one of the most celebrated Early Music conductors is, like Frans Brüggen, starting to conduct music of all periods with an eye for authenticity. The company's orchestral element is the Orchestre des Champs-Elysées.

Concerts Pasdeloup

This modestly accomplished orchestra (director Jean-Pierre Wallez) offers conventional fare but some interesting soloists.

Ensemble InterContemporain

Based at the Cité de la Musique, the world-famous contemporary music ensemble is led by American David Robertson, who has introduced some welcome American music, though the repertoire remains strictly avant-garde. Good news for fans of Brian Ferneyhough...

Ensemble Orchestral de Paris

Based at Salle Pleyel. John Nelson has taken over this chamber orchestra, whose repertoire ranges from Baroque to nineteenth-century operetta. Fine soloists and a visit from Fabio Biondi in April 99 should prove stimulating.

Les Talens Lyriques

Christophe Rousset's spin-off from Les Arts Florissants has established its own personality and a soaring reputation. Mostly young singers perform Baroque opera in productions as authentic as the musical presentation.

Orchestre Colonne

Based at Salle Pleyel. This orchestra often fails to live up to its past, but occasional star soloists such as glamorous diva Françoise Pollet enliven the popular 'lollipop' programming.

Orchestre Lamoureux

Based at Salle Pleyel. Director Yutaka Sado continues his fine work: not only has the orchestral playing risen, but programming is purposeful and occasionally contemporary.

Orchestre National de France

Based at the Maison de Radio France and Théâtre des Champs-Elysées. Under Canadian Charles Dutoit, an expert in the French Romantic repertoire, the orchestra can now claim to be the finest in the land. This season features visits from star maestri Riccardo Muti and Kurt Masur.

Orchestre de Paris

Based at Salle Pleyel and Châtelet, Théâtre Musical de Paris. It's finally been announced that Christophe von Dohnanyi will lead the orchestra into the next millenium with Frans Brüggen taking care of the Baroque and Early Romantic repertoire. Look out for an impressive array of guest maestri, including Sanderling, Cambreling, Prêtre and Giulini.

Orchestre Philharmonique de Radio France

Based at the Maison de Radio France and Salle Pleyel. Marek Janowski is thought one of the world's best Wagnerian conductors, as his recording of the *Ring Cycle* testifies. The orchestra continues to explore new and interesting material.

Concert Halls

The **Cité de la Musique** *auditorium can be adapted into different performance spaces.*

Théâtre des Bouffes du Nord
37bis bd de la Chapelle, 10th (01.46.07.34.50). M° La Chapelle. **Box Office** 11am-6pm Mon-Sat. **Tickets** 70F-130F. **Credit** V. **Map L2**
Peter Brook and Stéphane Lissner, keen to reinstate a musical dimension into the programming, welcome a touring double bill of Purcell's *Dido and Aeneas* and Britten's *Curlew River* in April 99, plus several tempting chamber music concerts.

Châtelet – Théâtre Musical de Paris
1 pl du Châtelet, 1st (01.40.28.28.40/recorded information 01.42.33.00.00). M° Châtelet. **Box Office** 11am-7pm daily; *telephone bookings* 10am-7pm Mon-Sat. **Tickets** phone for details. **Credit** AmEx, MC, V. **Map J6**
Converted twenty years ago, Châtelet closed in 1998 for its first major technical facelift. Its reputation is built on operatic events with top directors and conductors that have often outshone those at the Bastille. The grand reopening (October 99) promises major productions of Gluck's *Orphée et Eurydice* and *Alceste*. *Wheelchair access.*

Cité de la Musique
221 av Jean-Jaurès, 19th (01.44.84.45.45/recorded information 01.44.84.45.00/reservations 01.44.84.44.84). M° Porte de Pantin. **Box Office** noon-6pm Tue-Sun. **Tickets** 60F-160F; reduced prices under 26s, over-60s. **Credit** AmEx, DC, MC, V. **Map insert**
The complex at **La Villette** contains the new Conservatoire de Paris music school (01.40.40.45.45) and Cité de la Musique concert hall and museum designed by Christian de Portzamparc. So far the focus has been on contemporary music and Early Music; ticket holders can see rehearsals free. The museum has a smaller concert space (*see chapter* **Museums**). The Conservatoire, home to 1250 students of dance and classical, jazz and Baroque music, sees world-class performers and professors, with free concerts by the student orchestra or soloists. *Wheelchair access.*

IRCAM
1 pl Igor-Stravinsky, 4th (01.44.78.48.34). M° Hôtel de Ville. **Open** Sept-June, phone for details. **Tickets** 90F; 50F students. **Credit** AmEx, MC, V. **Map K6**

This underground musical research centre adjoining the Centre Pompidou is now largely used for musical symposiums, where modernists mull over avant-garde music. There are still some concerts here, and a general effort to reach a wider public.

Maison de Radio France
116 av du Président-Kennedy, 16th (01.42.30.22.22/ concert information 01.42.30.15.16). M° Passy/RER Kennedy Radio France. **Box Office** 11am-6pm Mon-Fri. **Tickets** free-120F. **No credit cards. Map A7**
Radio station France Musique has programmed an impressive range of classical concerts, operas and ethnic music here. Some events are free, such as Présences, the contemporary music festival (Jan-Feb). The main venue is the rather charmless Salle Olivier Messiaen, but the quality of music compensates. The Orchestre National de France and Orchestre Philarmonique de Radio France are based here. Under-26s can buy a bargain 'Passe Musique', giving four tickets for 120F. *Wheelchair access.*

Opéra Comique/Salle Favart
pl Boïeldieu, 2nd (01.42.44.45.40/reservations 01.42.44.45.46). M° Richelieu-Drouot. **Box Office** 14 rue Favart 11am-7pm Mon-Sat; *telephone bookings* 11am-6pm Mon-Sat. **Tickets** 50F-610F. **Credit** AmEx, DC, MC, V. **Map H4**
Many French operas have premiered in this charming century-old jewel box, including *Carmen,* Delibes' *Lakmé,* Massenet's *Manon* and Ravel's *L'Heure Espagnole.* Newly restored, this is a great place to hear small-scale opera, including unusual operetta in collaboration with Péniche Opéra and French Romantic rarities such as Boïeldieu's *La Dame Blanche.* This season Georges Prêtre conducts *Pelléas et Mélisande;* Puccini's *Tosca,* alternately performed in French and Italian, begins June. *Wheelchair access.*

Opéra National de Paris Bastille
pl de la Bastille, 12th (08.36.69.78.68). M° Bastille. **Box Office** 130 rue de Lyon 11am-6.30pm Mon-Sat. **Tickets** 60F-650F; *Concerts* 45F-245F. **Credit** AmEx, MC, V. **Map M7**

The Opéra Bastille has its detractors and its problems – dodgy acoustics and charmless foyers for starters – but the present team of Hugues Gall and James Conlon is making sure the house runs smoothly towards 2000. This season sees a new production of Verdi's *Macbeth* by exciting young producer Phyllida Lloyd and Wales' own Bryn Terfel as Mozart's Don Giovanni. *See chapters* **Right Bank** *and* **Dance**. *Guided visits (01.40.01.19.70); Wheelchair access (01.40.01.18.08).*

Opéra National de Paris Garnier

pl de l'Opéra, 9th (08.36.69.78.68). M° Opéra. **Box Office** 11am-6.30pm Mon-Sat. **Tickets** 60F-650F; *Concerts* 45F-245F. **Credit** AmEx, MC, V. **Map G4**
Restored to something like its glittering original, the Palais Garnier is now performing its original function as an opera house, sharing the task with the Bastille. The division of work still seems to favour the new house for suspected financial rather than artistic reasons. The perfect acoustics and undeniable glamour make an evening here a privilege, but the building's tiara shape means some seats have poor visibility. A highlight of the season is William Christie and the Arts Florissants in a stellar production of Handel's *Alcina* in June 99. *See chapters* **Right Bank**, **Museums** *and* **Dance**. *Visits 10am-4.30pm daily; guided visits (01.40.01.22.63); Wheelchair access (01.40.01.18.08).*

Péniche Opéra

facing 200 quai des Jemmapes, 10th (01.53.38.49.40/ 01.53.38.49.49). M° Jaurès. **Box Office** 10am-7pm Mon-Fri; 2-6pm Sat. **Tickets** 60F-150F. **Credit** MC, V. **Map L3**
An enterprising boat-based opera company producing a programme of chamber-scale rareties, often comic. Now occasionally coming ashore for productions at the Opéra Comique. *Wheelchair access.*

Salle Gaveau

45 rue La Boétie, 8th (01.49.53.05.07). M° Miromesnil. **Box Office** 11am-6pm Mon-Fri. **Tickets** 85F-200F. **Credit** AmEx, MC, V. **Map E3**
The charmingly antiquated Salle Gaveau has had its promised facelift reduced to the status of a *projet*. The idea is to improve the acoustics to allow larger Baroque performances. In the meantime it continues to be used for intimate recitals and chamber music; it's also the favoured venue for senior prima donnas giving that very last farewell recital.

Salle Pleyel

252 rue du Fbg-St-Honoré, 8th (01.45.61.53.00). M° Ternes. **Box Office** 11am-6pm Mon-Sat; *telephone bookings* (01.45.61.53.01) 10am-6pm Mon-Fri. **Tickets** 80F-410F. **Credit** MC, V. **Map D3**
The Salle Pleyel is vast and unatmospheric, but home to a great many orchestras and ensembles, although just for how much longer is currently the subject of much unmusical gossip. The acoustics are good for large-scale orchestral or choral concerts, but not for solo recitals, which is a pity as the hall plays host to all the great recitalists of the world, June 99 being something of a piano feast with recitals by Brendel and Perahia. Many people have subscriptions for the season, making concerts fuller than in other venues. *Wheelchair access.*

Théâtre des Champs-Elysées

15 av Montaigne, 8th (01.49.52.50.50). M° Alma-Marceau. **Box Office** 11am-7pm Mon-Sat; *telephone bookings* 10am-noon, 2-6pm Mon-Fri. **Tickets** 50F-690F. **Credit** V. **Map D5**
This beautiful theatre, designed by Auguste Perret with bas-reliefs by Bourdelle, witnessed the première of Stravinsky's *Le Sacre du Printemps* on 29 May 1913, and the riot that followed. The interior is well preserved, with the famous ceiling by Maurice Denis, the seating is old fashioned and the cheapest seats on the upper levels cramped. It's one of the

homes of the Orchestre National de France, as well as occasional visiting opera and dance companies. Invited orchestras this season include the Leipzig Gewandhaus, and in April 99 the Vienna Philharmonic conducted by Sir Roger Norrington. It remains a chic evening out for elegant Parisians.

Théâtre du Tambour-Royal

94 rue du Fbg-du-Temple, 11th (01.48.06.72.34). M° Belleville or Goncourt. **Box Office** 6.30-8pm Tue-Sat; *telephone bookings* 10am-8pm Mon-Sat. **Tickets** 80F, 100F. **No credit cards. Map M4**
A mixed programme of recitals and chamber opera has made this a popular venue for talent-spotting young French singers. Standards vary, but it's an outfit that deserves encouragement.

Théâtre de la Ville

2 pl du Châtelet, 4th (01.42.74.22.77). M° Châtelet. **Box Office** 11am-7pm Mon; 11am-8pm Tue-Sat; *telephone bookings* 9am-7pm Mon; 9am-8pm Tue-Sat. **Tickets** 95F. **Credit** MC, V. **Map J6**
The occasional concerts in this vertiginously raked concrete amphitheatre feature hip classical outfits like the avant-garde Kronos Quartet or Italian Baroque violinist Fabio Biondi. *See chapters* **Dance**, **Music: Rock, Roots & Jazz** *and* **Theatre**. *Wheelchair access.*

Music in Museums

For musical memorabilia, *see chapter* **Museums**.

Auditorium du Louvre

entrance through Pyramid, Cour Napoléon, 1st (01.40.20.51.86/reservations 01.40.20.84.00). M° Palais-Royal. **Box Office** 9am-7.30pm Mon, Wed-Fri. **Tickets** 60F-135F. **Credit** MC, V. **Map H5**
Top-quality chamber music in imaginative series, as well as music on film and silent films with live accompaniment. *Wheelchair access.*

Bibliothèque Nationale de France

quai François-Mauriac, 13th (01.53.79.40.45/reservations 01.53.79.49.49). M° Bibliothèque Nationale or Quai de la Gare. **Box Office** 10am-7pm Tue-Sat; noon-7pm Sun. **Tickets** 100F. **Credit** V. **Map M10**
The new library is building a good public for its song recitals by international artists. 1998-99 is the year of the complete songs of Poulenc and Ravel, to be followed by Fauré. *Wheelchair access.*

Musée National du Moyen Age (Cluny)

6 pl Paul-Painlevé, 5th (01.53.73.78.00). M° Cluny-La Sorbonne. **Tickets** 43F-53F (includes museum entry). **No credit cards. Map J7**
Concerts of medieval music in keeping with the collection.

Musée d'Orsay

62 rue de Lille, 7th (01.40.49.47.50). M° Solférino/RER Musée d'Orsay. **Tickets** 40F-130F, 100F students. **No credit cards. Map G6**
Attracts international artists for varied programmes focusing, like the collection, on the high nineteenth century. *Wheelchair access.*

Musée de la Vie Romantique

16 rue Chaptal, 9th (01.48.74.95.38). M° Pigalle. **Tickets** 50F. **No credit cards. Map H2**
Evocation in words and music of the life of George Sand. Chopin and Charpentier were frequent visitors here. Summer only.

Théâtre Grévin

10 bd Montmartre, 9th (01.48.24.16.97). M° Grands Boulevards. **Tickets** 90F-200F on sale 30 mins before concert. **No credit cards. Map J4**
Small-scale vocal and chamber music recitals.

Music: Rock, Roots & Jazz

Long known for jazz and world music, Paris is also a regular stop on the international circuit. And there are even signs of a home-grown revival.

France's reputation in the 'indie' rock department has always been a bit of a joke, but the scene is undergoing a massive transformation. It is now possible not only to see some of the best international acts in Paris but some excellent local bands every night of the week. There is an enormous energy surrounding independent music in Paris at the moment, with a refreshing sense of experimentation. While most musicians take their cues from anglo countries, they also mix in some of the best attributes of the *chanson* tradition. Yann Tiersen has influences in rock, folk, classical as well as *chanson*; Les Rita Mitsouko combine rock, funk and *chanson*; while Dit Terzi mixes rock and *chanson* in modes minimalist to operatic. Most bands are large, so that the sound is intense and multi-layered. Schizo rock band Jack the Ripper oscillates between impassioned darkness and lightness, with English lyrics verging on the blasphemous. Noir Désir continue to delight the masses, mixing French and English lyrics and experimenting with different techniques. Dolly and Autour de Lucie have been heavily influenced by the northern England phenomenon. World music, rap, and folk inject further variety into rock, be it percussion and violins by Orange Blossom, Louise Attaque's spirited acou-Celtic songs, or Irish and Slav elements from the Ogres de Barback.

It is an interesting experience going to a gig in Paris because, instead of the usual jostling and sardine-like crush, Parisians like to watch and absorb the music. One touring musician described the crowd as 'hard'. It can appear as if they are not engaging with the music until the end of a piece or the set, when they give such a passionate response it seems to be an entirely different audience.

Apart from nightly concerts in and around Paris, there are also many festivals including the Fête de la Musique on 21 June, Banlieues Bleues jazz festival every spring, Festival Fnac-Inrockuptibles in November and some of Africa's best musicians for Africolor at St-Denis every December (*see chapter* **Paris by Season**). In July and August don't expect any big rock names, but many of the jazz clubs, music barges and bar venues do keep going.

Jack the Ripper *tears into the indie revolution.*

FINDING OUT

Free tri-weekly booklet *Lylo* is the concert bible, with a directory for rock, *chanson*, jazz and world, plus a small techno section. It can be found at many of the venues listed below, and bars and ticket agencies. See the *Time Out Paris* pages of *Pariscope* for the hottest concerts of the week. Also handy are *Les Inrockuptibles* (indie), *Nova*, freebie *Blah, Blah*, and specialist magazine *L'Affiche* (rap, reggae).

Stadium Venues

Palais Omnisports de Paris-Bercy

8 bd de Bercy, 12th (01.44.68.44.68). M° *Bercy.* **Box office** 10am-6pm Mon-Sat. **Admission** from 150F. **Credit** MC, V. **Map N9**

With grass on the outside and 18,000 echoing seats inside,

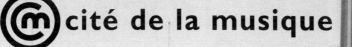

Bercy hosts sporting events and music crowdpullers from the three *raï* giants Khaled, Rachid Taha and Faudel and native rappers Stomy Bugsy to Whitney Houston. *Wheelchair access (call 01.55.93.00.56).*

Stade de France

rue Francis-de-Pressensé, St-Denis (01.44.68.44.44). M° Stade de France/RER B La Plaine Stade de France/ RER D Stade de France St Denis. **Box office** 10am-6pm daily. **Admission** from 295F. **Credit** AmEx, MC, V.
Built for the 1998 World Cup, this 100,000-seat stadium hosts such giants as the Rolling Stones and Johnny Hallyday. *Wheelchair access.*

Zénith

211 av Jean-Jaurès, 19th. M° Porte de Pantin. **No box office. Admission** from 100F. **Map inset**
A large, warehousey venue that hosts big touring bands and French groups from Eric Clapton to Fun Lovin Criminals and Marilyn Manson, Portishead or French crooner Pascal Obispo.

Rock Venues

La Bataclan

50 bd Voltaire, 11th (01.47.00.55.22). M° Oberkampf. **Box office** 11am-7pm Mon-Sat. **Concerts** 8pm most nights. **Admission** 100F-200F. **No credit cards. Map M5**
A former theatre, this ornate, medium size venue has a large dance area and a bar with good sightlines. It continuously hosts good quality bands including 16 Horsepower, Morcheeba and Placebo, plus world and *chanson* artists. *Wheelchair access.*

La Boule Noire

120 bd de Rochechouart, 18th (01.49.25.89.99). M° Pigalle. **Box office** noon-7pm Mon-Sat. **Concerts** most nights 8pm. **Admission** (1998) 80F-100F. **Credit** MC, V (box office only, not on door). **Map H2**
This small venue under La Cigale hosts up-and-coming or underground British and American rock bands. Currently being refurbished, it reopens in early 1999.

Café de la Danse

5 passage Louis-Philippe, 11th (01.47.00.57.59). M° Bastille. **Concerts** 8.30pm most nights. **Admission** 80F-120F. **No credit cards. Map M7**
This stone-walled former dance theatre is one of the best mid-size venues, although programming is totally eclectic. It has a spacious feel, with step-layered seating. Tortoise, Cornu, Cornershop and The Cramps have graced its stage recently. *Wheelchair access.*

La Cigale

120 bd Rochechouart, 18th (01.49.25.89.99). M° Pigalle. **Box office** noon-7pm Mon-Sat. **Admission** 120F-160F. **Credit** MC, V (box office only, not on door). **Map H2**
An old horseshoe-shaped vaudeville house, La Cigale holds 1900 people. It hosts many international rock bands and French groups, from The Dirty Three and Jon Spencer Blues Explosion, to Yann Tiersen and Cheb Mami, as well as the odd jazz star. The springy floor has seen the occasional stage diver land without injury. There's also a balcony.

Le Divan du Monde

75 rue des Martyrs, 18th (01.44.92.77.66). M° Pigalle. **Concerts** 7.30pm Mon-Sat; 4pm Sun. **Admission** free Mon; 60F-110F Tue-Sat. **No credit cards. Map H2**
Since it opened in 1995, this former cabaret has established itself as Paris' best medium-small venue. It hosts a diverse cast of performers from world music to rock and Brit pop in the early evening, club events later on. France Inter's long-running free Pollen sessions on Mondays showcase French bands. *See also chapter* **Clubs**.

Elysée Montmartre

72 bd Rochechouart, 18th (01.44.92.45.45). M° Anvers. **Concerts** 7.30pm most nights. Closed Aug. **Admission** 110-140F. **No credit cards. Map J2**
The veteran of musical action in Pigalle has retained its music-hall character. Latin/salsa dance nights are held here as well as vintage reggae names, international acts both established and up-and-coming (Des'Ree, Bentley Rhythm Ace, Suicidal Tendencies, Natacha Atlas, Robbie Williams), French bands like Louise Attaque and The Little Rabbits. *Wheelchair access (call ahead).*

Rock in Bars

Chesterfield Café

124 rue La Boétie, 8th (01.42.25.18.06). M° Franklin D Roosevelt. Restaurant/bar 10am-5am daily. **Concerts** 11.30pm Tue-Sat. **Admission** free. **Credit** AmEx, MC, V. **Map E4**
You'll hear narry a French voice in this cavernous bare brick Yankee bar-restaurant, but the free concerts give you a chance to catch new American rock bands before they make it to a bigger venue, as well as oldies making a comeback and some rocking curiosities (John McEnroe, David Arquette, Rolan Bolan…). Gospel at noon on Sunday.

La Flèche d'Or

102 rue de Bagnolet, 20th (01 43 72 04 23). M° Alexandre-Dumas or Gambetta. **Bar** 6pm-2am Mon, 10am-2am Tue-Sun. **Concerts** 9pm, Wed-Sat. **Admission** free-25F. **Credit** (bar only) MC, V.
This converted ex-railway station hosts everything from Celtic music festivals and industrial rock to jazz-age Japanese performers and reggae. You get the feeling that anything could happen – and probably will.

Wizards and wonders at **Elysée Montmartre.**

Le Gambetta

104 rue de Bagnolet, 20th (01 43 70 52 01). M° Alexandre-Dumas. **Bar** 9am-2am daily. **Concerts** 8pm most nights. **Admission** up to 40F. **Credit** AmEx, DC, MC, V.
This grungy Paris bar next door to La Flèche d'Or transforms itself at night to host obscure international bands like Michigan punksters The Dirtys, and their local counterparts. The emphasis is on punk, thrash, garage and some *raï*. *Wheelchair access.*

Horse's Mouth

120 rue Montmartre, 2nd (01.40.39.93.66). M° Sentier. **Bar** 10am-2am Mon-Sat. **Concerts** 9.30pm Wed-Sat. Closed Aug. **Admission** free. **Credit** MC, V. **Map J4**
Modelled on a London pub, *ze 'orzez mouz* goes for a smoky local pub feel with none of that pressure to be cool, and long happy hour (4-7pm). French rock and blues outfits dominate.

MCM Café

92 bd de Clichy, 18th (01.42.64.39.22). M° Blanche. **Bar** 9am-5am daily. **Concerts** 11pm Mon, Tue, Thur or Fri. **Admission** free. **Credit** AmEx, MC, V. **Map G2**
The former restaurant of the Moulin Rouge has had a futuristic makeover as bar, studio and concert hall by French cable music channel MCM. Established artists play on Thursday or Friday (Heather Nova, Kent, Melville), while Mondays and Tuesdays offer new acts their first live broadcast. *Wheelchair access.*

Le Réservoir

16 rue de la Forge-Royale, 11th (01.43.56.39.60). M° Faidherbe-Chaligny. **Bar** 8pm-2am daily. **Concerts** 11.30pm Tue-Sat. **Admission** free. **Credit** AmEx, MC, V. **Map N7**

This cavernous bar draws pretty young things and music industry moguls for a programme of art shows and music. Thursday sees young talents and label promos (like Jewel), Saturday tends towards groove, and Sunday is Mooviemusic, cool sounds on video. This is the sort of place where stars (Me'shell Negdellio) turn up impromptu. *Wheelchair access.*

French Chanson

Chanson has a new face. While the lyrics used to be of the upmost importance, now the music is equally important and fertile. Trickling down from the bleak realism of Bashung, punky Pigalle or whimsical Arthur H comes a new wave of musicians and bands like M, Les Ogres de Barback, Dominique A, Casse-Pipe, Les Hurleurs, or the good-time jazz-world-*chanson* line-ups Paris-Combo and the Orchestre de la Lune. One catalyst in this revival was the decision by the Ministère de la Culture that 40 per cent of music played on the radio had to be in French. Café-style venues where you can hear traditional *chanson* include Au Café Chantant (36 rue Bichat, 10th/01.42.08.83.33); La Bohème (beneath the Théâtre des Déchargeurs, 3 rue des Déchargeurs, 1st/01.42.36.10.29); Le Loup du Faubourg (21 rue de la Roquette, 11th/ 01.40.21.90.95); Paris' Aller-Retour (25 rue de Turenne, 4th/01.40.27.03.82).

Take me to the river...

As strict Parisian noise regulations make it hard to put on live music into the wee hours, a perfect solution has emerged: the *péniche*. These barges, docked on the Seine away from complaining residents, offer unpretentious fun and a spontaneous atmosphere; admission prices rarely go above 50F. The nucleus of activity is in front of the Bibliothèque Nationale in the 13th, where the existing batch are to be joined by the new Batofar in the spring; there are also boats in front of the Institut de France and opposite Notre Dame.

La Guinguette Pirate

quai François-Mauriac, 13th (01.56.29.10.20). M° Bibliothèque. **Concerts** 9pm daily. Closed Feb-Apr. **Admission** free-30F. **Credit** MC, V. **Map N10**
This wooden *péniche* junk with party lights hoisted from its masts and good-time atmosphere every night has an eclectic mix of music, performance and customers. Regulars include Paris Combo, Les Ténors de Brest, Les Alpinistes Hollandais and Les Ogres de Barback.

Péniche Makara

quai de la Gare, 13th (01.44.24.09.00). M° Quai de la Gare. **Bar** 7pm-2am Tue-Sun. **Concerts** 9pm Tue-Sun. **Admission** 30F-50F. **Credit** (bar only) MC, V. **Map M9**

Music goes from straight punk to Afro-jazz, funk and soul, often with several bands per night, as well as DJ parties and dub nights. Look out for appearances by funky Soul Finger and salsa combos Les Olives Noires and Azucar.

Péniche Blues Café

quai de la Gare, 13th (01 45 84 53 53). M° Quai de la Gare. **Concerts** 9pm/9.30pm usually daily. **Admission** 30F-60F. **No credit cards. Map M9**
This large *péniche* has recently been restored and, despite the name, hosts many musical styles, usually in theme nights that go from punk, metal, funk and hard core to zouk and reggae. Many bands from out of town play here. *Wheelchair access.*

Péniche Déclic

7 quai St-Bernard, 5th (06.12.31.02.19). M° Jussieu. **Concerts** 9pm-midnight Fri, Sat. **Admission** 40F. **No credit cards. Map L8**
This barge offers an eclectic mix of music from Franey & Zoé to percussion and didgeridoo combo Boomerang.

La Balle au Bond

(01.40.51.87.06). Oct-Mar facing 35 quai de la Tournelle, 5th. M° Maubert-Mutualité. Apr-Sept quai Malaquai, 6th. M° Pont Neuf. **Bar** 6pm-2am Mon-Sat; 6-10pm Sun. **Concerts** 10pm. **Admission** 20F-40F. **Credit** AmEx, MC, V. **Map winter K7; summer H6**
A bar and café with jazz, *chanson* and small-scale theatrical productions (8pm or 8.30pm, daily).

Soak up some home-grown French jazz talent at canal-side **L'Atmosphère**. See p268.

Cabaret Sauvage

Bord du Canal, Parc de la Villette, 19th (01.40.03.75.15)
M° Porte de la Villette. **Concerts** times vary.
Admission 50F-120F. **No credit cards. Map inset**
This round, wooden building with mirrored interior hosts a good mixture of *chanson*, rock and world music artists like Angélique Kidjo, or a festival of Algerian women singers.

Café Concert Ailleurs

13 rue Jean-Beausire, 4th (01.44.59.82.82). M° Bastille. **Bar** 6.30pm-1.30am Tue-Sun. **Concerts** 9pm Tue-Sun. Closed Aug. **Admission** up to 100F.
A small, atmospheric café where young singers and songwriters try their luck on the receptive crowd. It's a good place to catch rising talents, but some should keep their day jobs. *Wheelchair access.*

Casino de Paris

16 rue de Clichy, 9th (01.49.95.22.22/box office
01.49.95.99.99). M° Trinité. **Admission** 120F-280F. **Credit** MC, V. **Map G3**
An old-fashioned red velvet theatre welcomes the trad, easy-listening end of French *variété*.

Chez Adel

10 rue de la Grange-aux-Belles, 10th (01.42.08.24.61).
M° Gare de l'Est. **Bar** 8am-2am Mon-Fri; 5pm-2am Sat. (some Sun). **Concerts** 8pm Mon-Sat. Closed Aug. **Admission** free. **Credit** MC, V. **Map L3**
This studenty hangout in a groovy pocket of the 10th hosts a variety of musical styles, from modern and trad *chanson*, via Russian and Irish, to Afro-Cuban and rock. Reasonable drink prices. Cheap 40F *formule* and a piano bar at lunch.

La Folie en Tête

33 rue de la Butte-aux-Cailles, 13th (01.45.80.65.99). M°
Place d'Italie. **Bar** 5pm-2am Mon-Sat. **Concerts** 9pm Thur. **Admission** 40F (incl 1st drink). **Credit** AmEx, MC, V.
With over 2,572 instruments suspended in lieu of wallpaper, this is possibly the smallest feasible venue in Paris. Programming is anarchic but tends toward rock-*chanson*.

Glaz'Art

7-15 av de la Porte de la Villette, 19th (01.40.36.55.65).
M° Porte de la Villette. **Concerts** 8.30pm Thur, Fri; 10pm Sat. **Admission** 40F-80F. **Credit** AmEx, MC, V. **Map inset**
This concrete bunker provides space for many arts, including music. Expect rock and *chanson* groups with a bohemian attitude, among them Les Casse-Pipe and Ogres de Barback. *Wheelchair access.*

Au Limonaire

18 cité Bergère, 9th (01.45.23.33.33). M° Grands
Boulevards. **Bar** 6pm-2am Tue-Sun. **Concerts** 10pm Tue-Sat; 6pm Sun. **Credit** MC, V. **Map J4**
Transplanted from the 12th *arrondissement*, the Limonaire keeps the accordion-*chanson* tradition alive and well. Friendly and quintessentially French.

Olympia

28 bd des Capucines, 9th (01.55.27.10.00/telephone
bookings 01.47.42.25.49). M° Opéra. **Concerts** 8.30pm Mon-Sat; 5pm Sun. **Admission** 160F-290F. **Credit** AmEx, MC, V. **Map G4**
A spell at this listed auditorium, rebuilt a couple of doors down from the original in 1997, is still the ultimate accolade in French *variété*, a confirmation of 'living national treasure' status. Hence the long seasons here by Serge Lama and M C Solaar, plus the one-off by techno maestro Laurent Garnier. *Wheelchair access.*

Le Sentier des Halles

50 rue d'Aboukir, 2nd (01.42.36.37.27). M° Sentier.
Concerts 8pm or 10pm Mon-Sat. **Admission** 50F-120F. **No credit cards. Map J4**
Created as a café-théâtre 15 years ago by Nicole Mingasson-Londeix, this 120-seat cellar has established itself as the headquarters of everything that is most inventive and vital in French popular music. Some of the star acts who started out here – Arthur H, Mauranne – are now big enough to play the Olympia, but still come back to remind themselves what an audience looks like close up. World and tango too.

Théâtre du Tourtour

20 rue Quincampoix, 4th (01.48.87.82.48). Mº Hôtel-de-Ville. **Concerts** 10pm Tue-Sat. **Admission** 60F-100F. **No credit cards. Map J6**
A basement theatre that puts on *chanson*, world music and theatre, from new songwriters to covers of Leo Ferré.

Jazz

Paris continues to be a jazz capital, hosting a large variety of performers. Trad jazz remains concentrated in St-Germain and around Les Halles, but worthwhile venues are spread all over town from the world-famous **New Morning** to experimental **Instants-Chavirés** or streetwise **La Cithéa**. There are annual festivals at La Villette, Boulogne-Billancourt and Seine St-Denis.

All Jazz Club

7-11 rue St-Benoît, 6th (01.42.61.87.02). Mº St-Germain-des-Prés. **Concerts** 10pm-2am Fri, Sat. **Admission** 120F-160F (incl 1st drink). **Credit** AmEx, DC, MC, V. **Map H6**
The former Latitudes jazz lounge is for those who like it trad: R 'n' B, jazz, boogie-woogie and gospel from new talents and established artists, local and American, like La Velle & J Van Jones, the Tommy Flanagan Trio, or pianist Fabrice Eulry. *Wheelchair access.*

L'Atmosphère

49 rue Lucien-Sampaix, 10th (01 40 38 09 21). Mº Gare-de-l'Est. **Bar** 11am-2am Tue-Fri; 5pm-2am Sat, Sun. **Concerts** 8pm Tue-Sat; 5pm Sun. **Admission** free. **No credit cards. Map L3**
This cosy, smoky little café by the Canal St-Martin sometimes draws a queue out into the street for its adventurous programme of experimental music, especially jazz-oriented groups or jazz-folk mixes.

Le Baiser Salé

58 rue des Lombards, 1st (01 42 33 37 71). Mº Châtelet. **Concerts** 10pm Mon-Sat; 9.30pm Sun. **Admission** 60F-100F. **Credit** AmEx, MC, V. **Map J6**
This small club focuses on fusion, Latin and Afro-jazz. *Wheelchair access.*

Le Bilboquet

13 rue St-Benoît, 6th (01.45.48.81.84). Mº St-Germain-des-Prés. **Concerts** 10.30pm-2.30am daily. **Admission** 120F (incl 1st drink). **Credit** AmEx, MC, V. **Map H6**
Since Boris Vian launched it way back in 1947, this St-Germain *boîte de jazz* has received giants like Billie Holiday and Miles Davis. The club still takes care of its own, but now it's likely to be Black Jacks or Bruce Johnson redoing standards.

La Cave du Franc Pinot

1 quai Bourbon, 4th (01.46.33.60.64). Mº Pont-Marie. **Bistro/bar** 6.30pm-2am Tue-Sat. **Concerts** 10pm-2am Wed-Sat. Closed Aug. **Admission** 90F-100F (incl 1st drink). **Credit** MC, V. **Map K7**
Within the thick stone walls of a seventeenth-century listed building, the vaulted cellar is an acoustic joy where musicians perpetuate the sounds of 'good times jazz'. Bob Demeo, from New York's Blue Note, plays quality jazz that swings.

Caveau de la Huchette

5 rue de la Huchette, 5th (01.43.26.65.05). Mº St-Michel. **Open** 9.30pm-2.30am Mon-Thur, Sun; 9.30pm-3.30am Fri; 9.30-4am Sat. **Admission** 60F Mon-Thur, Sun; 55F students; 70F Fri, Sat. **Credit** V. **Map J7**
Dance to a lively mix of swing, trad, boogie and rock in a medieval cellar. Pianists like George Arvanitas and Al Copley guarantee to get you hot under the collar.

La Cithéa

112-114 rue Oberkampf, 11th (01.40.21.70.95). Mº Parmentier. **Open** 10pm-5am daily. **Concerts** 11pm Wed-Sat. **Admission** free Mon, Tue, Sun; 30F Wed, Thur; 60F Fri, Sat (with two beers). **Credit** MC, V. **Map M5**
Did the Cithéa start off rue Oberkampf cool? Possibly. At any rate its formula of concerts followed by a DJ mix is streetwise and intoxicating. By the early hours things can get very hot and steamy inside. Jazz, soul and world music predominate. Look out for Julian Lourou's Groove Gang, Ben's Berlinga and Swedish sax Sofi Hellborg. *See chapter* **Clubs**. *Wheelchair access.*

Duc des Lombards

42 rue des Lombards, 1st (01.42.33.22.88). Mº Châtelet. **Concerts** 10pm-3am daily (Fri, Sat in Aug). **Admission** 80F-100F. **Credit** MC, V. **Map J5**
Pianist Bobby Few struck gold when he introduced live jazz to the Duc (a wink to the man) in 1985. The acoustics and the stylish layout welcome visiting and local musicians like Glenn Ferris, Aldo Romano and Henri Texier or young trumpeter Eric Truffaz playing modern jazz in a great atmosphere.

Houdon Jazz Club

5 rue des Abbesses, 18th (01.46.06.35.91). Mº Abbesses. **Concerts** 10pm-2am Fri, Sat. No music in Aug. **Admission** free. **Credit** MC, V. **Map H2**
A cosmopolitan neighbourhood bistro where a conspicuously receptive audience enjoy be-bop and free jazz.

Les Instants Chavirés

7 rue Richard-Lenoir, 93100 Montreuil (01.42.87.25.91). Mº Robespierre. **Concerts** times vary Tue-Sun. Closed July, Aug. **Admission** 80F; 60F students, over-60s; free under-16s. **No credit cards.**
A bastion of improvisation and the avant-garde, this state-subsidised centre attracts contemporary jazz musicians from all over the world. There are monthly improv classes. *Wheelchair access.*

Lionel Hampton Jazz Club

Hôtel Le Méridien-Etoile, 81 bd Gouvion-St-Cyr, 17th (01.40.68.34.34). Mº Porte Maillot. **Concerts** 10.30pm-midnight, 12.30am-2am Mon-Sat. **Admission** 130F-160F (incl 1st drink). **Credit** AmEx, DC, MC, V.
A leading venue for jazz, soul, gospel and R 'n' B from mainly US musicians. The emphasis is on powerful vocalists, like big (in every sense) blues lady Marva Wright. *Wheelchair access.*

New Morning

7-9 rue des Petites-Ecuries, 10th (01.45.23.51.41). Mº Château-d'Eau. **Box Office** 4.30-7pm daily. **Concerts** 9pm daily. **Admission** 100F-150F. **Credit** V. **Map K3**
Since the New Morning (named after a Dylan song) opened in 1981, virtually all the leading exponents of jazz, blues, funk, bebop and Latin have played here, as well as renowned African musicians and ska vets. Despite an unpromising looking concrete exterior, it is a warm and user-friendly venue, where people come to listen. Chick Corea, David S Ware, John Lurie, Joshua Redman, Roy Hargrove and Elvin Jones are just a few to have played recently.

Petit Journal Montparnasse

13 rue du Commandant-Mouchotte, 14th (01.43.21.56.70). Mº Montparnasse-Bienvenüe or Gaîté. **Concert** 10pm-2am Mon-Sat. Closed three weeks in July. **Admission** 100F-120F (incl 1st drink); 280F (incl dinner, 8.30pm). **Credit** AmEx, MC, V. **Map F9**
Just look for the neon trumpeter. This is timeless French fare (the late, great Michel Petrucciani played here) as well as

Jazz luminaries from around the world flock to spend their nights at the **New Morning.**

some fave visitors like Archie Shepp and Manu Dibango when they want to play in a club setting. Classic jazz, big band and dixieland, with some Latin and R 'n' B. The more rickety Latin Quarter branch goes for New Orleans dixie. **Branch**: Petit Journal St-Michel, 71 bd St-Michel, 5th (01.43.26.28.59).

Petit Opportun
15 rue des Lavandières-Ste-Opportune, 1st (01.42.36.01.36). M° Châtelet. **Concerts** 10.30pm-3am Tue-Sat. **Admission** 50F-80F. **No credit cards. Map J6**
A little jazz cellar with a good atmosphere programming established and up-and-coming French instrumentalists playing swing, be-bop and New Orleans jazz. Look out for Eric Le Lann (trumpet) and Michel Graillier (piano) playing as a duo. Tuesday is Nuit Blanche (all-nighter), when up to twelve musicians squeeze on to the floor.

Le Slow Club
130 rue de Rivoli, 1st (01.42.33.84.30). M° Châtelet. **Concerts** 10pm-3am Tue, Thur; 10pm-4am Fri, Sat. **Admission** 60F Tue, Thur, 55F students under 25; 75F Fri, Sat. **Credit** MC, V. **Map J6**
They used to store bananas here to ripen for the market at Les Halles. This blues cellar is sister to the Caveau de la Huchette (*see above*), with a similar mix of swing, trad, boogie-woogie and rock 'n' roll.

Le Sunset
60 rue des Lombards, 1st (01.40.26.46.60). M° Châtelet-Les Halles. **Concerts** 10pm-3am Mon-Sat; 9pm-2am Sun. **Admission** 70F-100F. **Credit** MC, V. **Map K5**
Since it opened in 1980 this cosy crossover jazz cellar has been a springboard for a new generation of musicians, such as violinist Didier Lockwood. The brass-playing Belmondo brothers and drummer Aldo Romano are regulars; look out also for international visitors like Hal Singer and Dewey Redman or Americans in Paris like Steve Lacy. There are vocalists every Sunday and often salsa or Afro-Cuban on Monday.

Studio des Islettes
10 rue des Islettes, 18th (01.42.58.63.33). M° Barbès-Rochechouart. **Jam sessions** 9pm Mon-Thur. **Concerts** 9pm Fri, Sat. **Admission** 50F (incl 1st drink). **No credit cards. Map J2**
This wonderfully shabby jazz cooperative supports young players. In theory, there are formal gigs at the weekend, and jam sessions during the week, but even at concerts most the of the audience seem to end up taking their turn on a chorus.
Wheelchair access.

La Villa
29 rue Jacob, 6th (01.43.26.60.00). M° St-Germain-des-Prés. **Concerts** 10.30pm-2am Mon-Sat. Closed 25 July-30 Sept. **Admission** 120F Mon-Thur; 150F (incl 1st drink) Fri, Sat. **Credit** AmEx, DC, MC, V. **Map H6**
Sleekest of the St-Germain clubs, postmodern La Villa brings over some of the best American instrumentalists: Ravi Coltrane (sax), Billy Hart (drums) and Danilio Perez (piano).

Blues Bars

See also above **New Morning** and **Lionel Hampton Jazz Club.**

Maxwell Café
17 bd Vital-Bouhot, 92200 Neuilly-sur-Seine (01.46.24.22.00). M° Porte de Champerret, then bus 163 or 164 or M° Pont de Levallois. **Concerts** 10.30pm-1.30am Thur-Sat. Closed July, Aug. **Admission** 100F Thur Fri, Sat; 80F under-25s (Thur). **Credit** AmEx, MC, V.
This former garage now attracts African-American musicians, like Eddie King or Screamin' Jay Hawkins.

St-Louis Blues
33 rue Blomet, 15th (01.47.34.30.97). M° Volontaires. **Concerts** 9pm-2am Thur-Sat. **Admission** 60F. **No credit cards. Map D9**

Round the corner from UNESCO, this perfect den of iniquity openly contravenes all international conventions on pleasure limitation in what used to be the Bal Nègre of Montparnasse fame. Local groups often perform.

Utopia
79 rue de l'Ouest, 14th (01.43.22.79.66). M° Pernéty. **Concerts** 9.30pm, 10.30pm Mon-Sat; Sun jam session. Closed two weeks in Aug. **Admission** 50F-70F (incl 1st drink). **Credit** MC, V. **Map F10**
A live music bar with a good atmosphere which programmes blues most nights of the week.

World & Traditional Music

Traditional music from Africa, Oceania, Asia, South America and Europe all influence contemporary French music, but this continental drift also occurs in its pure traditional forms: classical Arab music at the Institut du Monde Arabe, African and Latin at the New Morning, traditional folk music at the Maison de Radio France, Latin and salsa at Les Etoiles and La Java. Paris' immigrant communities are also producing a new generation of musicians from young *raï* singer Faudel to Portuguese *fado* singer Bevinda.

Centre Mandapa
6 rue Wurtz, 13th (01.45.89.01.60). M° Glacière. **Box office** *telephone bookings 11am-7pm Mon-Sat.* **Concerts** 8.30pm. Closed Aug. **Admission** 80F; 60F students; 40F under-16s; free under-6s. **No credit cards.**
The unpretentious 100-seater hall at this Indian dance centre is Paris' oldest traditional music venue. Alongside rising stars from the subcontinent, Milena Salvini programmes fine Persian music, singers from Ireland and Bolivia, and more. Regulars include Indian sarangi star Ustad Sabri Ikram and Berber singer Houria Aïchi.

Institut du Monde Arabe
1 rue des Fossés-St-Bernard, 5th (01.40.51.38.14). M° Jussieu. **Box office** 2-5pm Tue-Sun. No concerts in Aug. **Admission** 100F; 80F students, over-60s. No under-7s. **Credit** AmEx, MC, V. **Map K7**
The basement auditorium takes airport lounge seating to new breadths and new heights, but nothing can detract from the riches of the classical Arab music on offer. They occasionally host modern Arabic music as well. *Wheelchair access.*

Maison de la Culture du Japon
101bis quai Branly 15th. (01 44 37 95 00) M° Bir-Hakeim. **Concerts** 8.30pm **Admission** 100F. Closed Aug, two weeks in Dec. **No credit cards. Map C6**
Increasingly active in bringing Japanese artists to Paris, the programme includes dance and theatre. *Wheelchair access.*

Maison des Cultures du Monde
101 bd Raspail, 6th (01.45.44.41.42). M° Notre-Dame-des-Champs. **Concerts** 8.30pm Tue-Fri; 7pm Sat; 5pm Sun. **Admission** 100F-110F; 50F under-26s. **Credit** V. **Map G8**
Music plays second fiddle to theatre most of the year, and programming is uneven, but watch out for occasional gems.

Satellit' Café
44 rue de la Folie-Méricourt, 11th (01.47.00.48.87). M° Oberkampf. **Open** 8pm-3am Tue-Thur; 8pm-6am Fri, Sat. No concerts in July, Aug. **Concerts** 9.30pm Tue-Thur. **Admission** 50F. **Credit** MC, V. **Map M5**

Friendly, adventurous bar featuring multi-ethnic acoustic concerts midweek and a mind-blowing mix of recorded sounds. An excellent place to explore Brazilian swing or Balkan folk.

Suds
55 rue de Charonne, 11th (01.43.14.06.36). M° Ledru-Rollin. **Bar** 8pm-midnight daily. **Concerts** 9.30pm Wed; Cuban bal 7.30pm Sun. **Admission** free. **Credit** MC, V. **Map M7**
A colourful restaurant dedicated to food from all points south (Mediterranean, Latin America). Concerts in the cellar bar include some fine Latin, *fado* and Afro-funk.

Théâtre de la Ville
2 pl du Châtelet, 4th (01.42.74.22.77). M° Châtelet. **Box office** (from 9am by telephone) 11am-7pm Mon; 11am-8pm Tue-Sat. **Admission** 95F. No concerts July, Aug. **Credit** MC, V. **Map J6**
Although best known for dance, the Théâtre de la Ville also puts on a magnificent programme of world music. It's strongest on traditional Indian music, but also tops in the Portuguese *fado* revival with groups like Madredeus. *Wheelchair access (call ahead).*

Celtic connection

Celtic- and folk-influenced rock bands are a prominent element in the current indie music scene. Rock and folk music have always mixed well, from Van Morrison to the Pogues, and it is the same in France, where Louise Attaque's phenomenal success has been at the crest of a movement whose roots are in Brittany, but has a more alternative feel than the traditional big names Alain Stivell or supergroup Dan Ar Braz. The strong Breton cultural identity and oral tradition are clearly attractive at this *fin de siècle*. The differences between the Irish and Breton traditions become most apparent in the dancing: that of Brittany is more earthbound – treading the earth while making circles and apparently using the body as a 'magnetic' conductor of energy (so Bretons say) – that of Ireland has more of the spirit of the air, and dancing is lighter and springier.

The traditional Celtic and folk rock music scene in Paris is relaxed and worth seeking out; much of it is centred in the Montparnasse area. As well as Louise Attaque and Miossec, look out for Tri Yann, Matmatah and Tornaod, who marry traditional Celtic sounds with rock and folk. The Mission Bretonne, 14th (01.43.21.99.86) is the local 'centre of animation', with dance lessons, cultural activities and bands playing fairly regularly. As well as various Celtic Fest Noz around town, you can see occasional bands at Ti Jos, 14th (01.43.22.57.69) and the Cadran Breton, 15th (01.45.44.03.16).

Sport & Fitness

Whether you want to tone up, tee off or trot on, or simply take time out and spectate, Paris has sporting facilities for everyone.

The best, and very often, the cheapest way to get yourself active in Paris is to make use of the plentiful sports facilities which are run by the municipal authorities. Here you'll find the standards are generally surprisingly good.

The best source of information is the comprehensive *Guide du Sport à Paris*, which is published annually by the Mairie de Paris and available from the Mairie of each *arrondissement*. The booklet covers everything from swimming pools to climbing walls or cycle routes in the Bois de Boulogne, as well as details of national and local sporting federations and top-level clubs. There's also an information line **Allô-Sports** (01.42.76.54.54; 10.30am-5pm Mon-Thur, 10.30am-4.30pm Fri) which can answer queries about sport and facilities in Paris.

To use certain sports centres, you will need a *carte* for which you must show an identity card or passport (take a photo too) and, for sports perceived as risky such as rollerblading or rock climbing, you often need proof of insurance, which you can sometimes buy in specialist shops or else may be included when you join a club.

For all kinds of sports equipment, the chains Go Sport and Decathlon have numerous branches in and around the city, and the sports sections of the department stores such as Samaritaine are also worth a look. **Au Vieux Campeur** (*see box* **Roll up, roll up**) has different shops specialising in individual pursuits: skiing, climbing, mountain walking and other outdoor sports.

Gyms & Fitness

Despite the Parisian obsession with looking good, there are actually rather fewer *clubs de forme* than you might expect. However, existing ones are well-used and usually well-equipped, with staff on hand to advise. Some clubs may pressurise you to take out a long *abonnement (subscription)* but try to negotiate, and go for a trial visit to make sure it's what you want. Also look out for promotions when membership can be half the price of official rates. For details of dance classes, *see chapter* **Dance**.

Club Quartier Latin

19 rue de Pontoise, 5th (01.55.42.77.88).
Mº Maubert-Mutualité. **Open** 9am-midnight Mon-Thur; 9am-10pm Fri; 9.30am-7pm Sat, Sun. **Membership**: Fitness section *annual* 3100F, 2200F student; *one month* 800F, student 600F; *day pass* 70F, student 60F. **Credit** AmEX, DC, MC, V.
The gym has plenty of well-maintained machines, together with a comprehensive range of stretch, cardio and other classes. There's also a squash membership (annual 2200F, 1800F students) which grants you access to the centre's

*12 July 1998… and not a dry eye in the **Stade de France** (see The Sporting Year, p273).*

four squash courts (in varying states of repair). Both memberships include access to the Piscine Pontoise (*see box* **In the swim**).

Espace Vit'Halles
48 rue Rambuteau, 3rd (01.42.77.21.71). M° Rambuteau. **Open** 8am-10pm Mon-Fri; 10am-7pm Sat; 10am-4pm Sun. **Membership** *annual* 4450F/student 3560F; *one month* 900F; *one visit* 100F **Credit** MC, V.
A friendly and professional exercise space. The gym is good if a little cluttered with machines and weights, but the instructors are knowledgeable and the crowd is non-posey. A bewildering range of fitness classes from Tai Chi to pump are run by enthusiastic and tolerant instructors. Changing rooms are surgically clean.

Gymnase Club
20 locations in and around Paris, contact 01.44.37.24.24 for full list. The most central are: **Palais Royal** *147bis rue St-Honoré, 1st (01.40.20.03.03). M° Palais-Royal.* **Champs-Elysées** *26 rue de Berri, 8th (01.43.59.04.58). M° George V.* **Grenelle** (with pool) *8 rue Frémicourt, 15th (01.45.75.34.00). M° Avenue Emile Zola.* **Membership** *annual* 4720F-5220F (reductions for some companies and organisations, and for students); *three months* 1950F; *ten visits* 1000F. **Credit** AmEx, MC, V.
The clubs are well-equipped and instruction standards are generally good, offering the usual gamut of classes plus martial arts and weight loss. There are ladies who lunch, muscle-bound men in tight shorts, and everything in between. Check if your company or organisation has an agreement with Gymnase Club – you may be able to get a hefty discount.

Gymnasium
25 locations in and around Paris. Branches include: 62 bd Sébastopol, 3rd (01.42.74.14.56). M° Etienne-

Marathon: *one way to see the sights quickly.*

Marcel; 129 bd Haussmann, 8th (01.42.89.89.14); M° Daumesnil; 226 bd Raspail, 14th (01.43.21.14.40). M° Vavin; 32 bd des Batignolles, 17th (01.42.93.77.00). M° Place de Clichy; 58 rue Ordener, 18th (01.42.51.15.15). M° Jules-Joffrin; **Membership** *approx per month* 500F.
Less-geared to bulging muscles than Gymnase Club and rather more concerned with the health aspects (weight loss as well as fitness), the Gymnasium franchise offers up-to-date rowing, cycling machines and cardio-training equipment and some branches have pools. Courses include aerobics, step, stretching and water-based workouts. L'Institut at 90 bd St-Germain, 5th, specialises in water-therapy treatments. Exact membership fees aren't revealed until you go for a look around.

Ken Club
100 av du Président-Kennedy, 16th (01.46.47.41.41). M° Passy/RER Kennedy-Radio France. **Open** 9.30am-9.30pm Mon, Wed; 7.30am-11pm Tue, Thur ; 9.30am-6pm Fri-Sun. **Membership** *annual* 7900F (+ joining fee), *three months* 3700F, *one month* 1900F, *one day* 400F.
This is a favourite hangout for media types and celebs because of its location right next door to the Maison de la Radio. Lots of Barbies. As well as the expected weights, there's a pool, jacuzzi and sauna.

Vitatop
Vitatop Plein Ciel *Hôtel Sofitel, 8 rue Louis-Armand, 15th (01.45.54.79.00); M° Balard;* **Vitatop Porte Maillot** *Hôtel Concorde Lafayette, 1 pl du Général-Koenig, 17th (01.40.68.00.21). M° Porte-Maillot.* **Membership** *one year* 7200F; *couple* 13,200F; *student* 4800F.
These posh, top-of-the line executive gyms are located in two modern, clean hotels. The Porte Maillot branch also has a swimming pool and golf-driving range.

Activities & Team Sports

All-round Sports Clubs
The Standard Athletic Club (Route Forestière du Pavé de Meudon, 92360 Meudon-la-Forêt/01.46.26.16.09) is a private, non-profit-making club aimed at Anglo-Saxons who are living in Paris. Full membership is 3800F per year plus an initial joining fee; there are also cheaper, seasonal memberships for specific sports (such as 1150F for cricket), and student rates (2600F annual). It fields a cricket side (May-Sept), men's and women's hockey, and football teams. The club is also equipped with eight tennis courts, two squash courts, a heated outdoor pool, billiards table and inexpensive bar in the clubhouse.
  Several top-level French clubs also run teams in numerous sports (athletics, basketball, football, rugby, badminton, hockey, etc), such as **Racing Club de France** (01.45.67.55.86), **Paris Université Club** (01.44.16.62.62) and **Le Stade Français** (01.40.71.33.33).

American Football
American football does happen in the Paris area, and there are six clubs to prove it. **Les Mollosses** (01.39.76.17.05; the answer machine is for a furniture business, but it's correct) has a large squad and trains at Stade Jacques Anquetil (rue Pierre Boudou, Asnières/RER Les Grésillons). You'll find plenty of hut-huts and high-fives – not to mention a top-class playing field.

Athletics & Running
If you need a track, Paris bristles with them. The municipal sites are pretty good on the whole; find your local one in the *Guide du Sport* booklet. To give an idea of the scale, Paris has eight indoor running tracks and Britain has two.

The Sporting Year

France's victory in the 1998 World Cup reawakened interest in 'le foot'. Paris' only premier division team is Paris St-Germain, based at **Parc des Princes** (24 rue du Commandant-Guilbaud, 16th/01.49.87.29.29/M° Porte d'Auteuil). Season tickets are available from the stadium (01.40.71.10.73) at 620F-6800F, or get single tickets at Fnac, Virgin or in Samaritaine's sports section (40F-600F). Internationals now take place at the **Stade de France,** (rue Francis de Pressensé, 93210 St-Denis/*switchboard* 01.55.93.00.00, *reservations* 01.44.68.44.44). Southwest France is the heart of rugby union, but Paris' Racing Club de France has been snapping up top players and can be seen at **Stade Yves du Manoir** (12 rue François Faber, 92700 Colombes/01.45.67.55.86). Tickets for the well-attended games are 60F. As well as the Five Nations Cup (spring), the Stade de France will host a Rugby World Cup quarter-final in October 1999.

For more esoteric events check out the futuristic stadium and music venue, **Palais Omnisports de Paris-Bercy** (8 bd de Bercy, 12th/*switchboard* 01.40.02.60.60; *reservations* 01.44.68.44.68), which hosts everything from figure skating to indoor mountain biking.

There are seven racecourses in the Paris area. *France Galop* publishes a full race list (01.49.10.20.30) in its Calendrier des Courses. Auteuil *Bois de Boulogne, 16th (01.40.71.47.47). M° Porte d'Auteuil.* Steeplechasing. Chantilly *41km from Paris (03.44.62.41.00). Train from Gare du Nord.* Flat racing. Enghien *18km from Paris (01.34.17.87.00). Train from Gare du Nord.* Steeplechasing and trotting. Longchamp *Bois de Boulogne, 16th (01.44.30.75.00). M° Porte d'Auteuil, then free bus.* Flat racing. Maisons-Laffitte *6 av de La Pelouse, 78600 Maisons-Laffitte. RER A Maisons-Laffitte and then bus (01.39.62.90.95).* Racing season. St Cloud *1 rue du Camp Canadien, 92210 St-Cloud. RER A Rueil-Malmaison (01.47.71.69.26).* Flat racing. Paris-Vincennes *Bois de Vincennes, 12th (01.49.77.17.17). M° Vincennes/RER Joinville le Pont.* Trotting.

January
Horse-racing: Prix d'Amérique Hippodrome de Paris-Vincennes. France's premier and glitzy trotting race.

February
Rugby: Five Nations' Cup matches are held at the Stade de France in February, March and April.
Tennis: Open Gaz de France at the Stade Pierre de Coubertin (82 av Georges-Lafont, 16th/ 01.44.31.44.31/M° Porte de St-Cloud). Big-name women players compete for fame and a lot more fortune at this WTA indoor event.

March
Cycling: The first short stage of the week-long Paris-Nice race starts outside Paris and finishes in av Foch, 16th (call Josette Leuilliot on 01.40.93.42.43 for details).
Gymnastics: Internationaux de France, at the Palais Omnisports de Paris-Bercy.
Showjumping: Jumping International de Paris, on the World Cup circuit, at Palais Omnisports de Bercy.

April
Athletics: Paris Marathon Starts 9am at av des Champs-Elysées, usually first Sun in April, with top runners finishing just after 11am at av Foch. Information or entry forms on 01.41.33.15.68. The route includes the Bois de Vincennes and Boulogne and several city sights.

Hot to trot: fast and fluid at **Vincennes.**

Horse-racing: Prix du Président de la République, a top steeplechase race, at Auteuil, third Sun of April.

May
Football: Two top matches for French football teams, the **Coupe de France** final and the **Coupe de la Ligue** final, both likely to be at the Stade de France from 1999.
Rugby: The **French Championship Final** takes place at the Stade de France.
Tennis: The **French Grand Slam** tournament at the Stade Roland-Garros (01.47.43.48.00) (*see chapter* **Paris by Season**) at the end of May/early June.

June
Horse-racing: The **Prix de Diane Hermès,** French equivalent of the Derby, is held at the pretty course of Chantilly. Watch the big hats arrive.

July
Athletics: FFA Humanité meeting Top athletes gather at the Stade de France.
Athletics: IAAF Grand Prix meeting at the Stade Charléty, bd Kellerman, 13th (01.03.80.70.00).
Cycling: The **Tour de France** arrives in Paris for a grand finale on the Champs-Elysées at the end of July or early Aug (information 01.41.33.15.00).
Golf: The **French Women's Open** at the Paris International Golf Club, 18 route du Golf, 95160 Baillet-en-France (01.34.69.90.00) in mid-July.

September
Golf: The **Lancôme Trophy,** at Golf de St-Nom-la-Brétèche, 78860 St-Nom-la-Brétèche (01.30.80.04.40).

October
Horse-racing: The **Prix de l'Arc de Triomphe** is held at Longchamp. Some of the world's best horses run.

November
Tennis: The **Paris Open,** a top-ranking international men's indoor tournament, Palais Omnisports de Paris-Bercy.
Skating: Lalique Skating Trophy at Palais Omnisports de Paris-Bercy. International ice champions and contenders skate their hearts out.

December
Showjumping: Concours hippique international at Paris-Expo, Porte de Versailles, 15th, in association with the annual Salon du Cheval, du Poney et de l'Ane.

For an open-air run the Bois de Boulogne and the Bois de Vincennes are beautiful, though some parts of the Bois de Boulogne are frequented by men cruising even in daylight hours – so take note if this does not form part of your training schedule! The Paris marathon in April and the Paris to Versailles 16km run in late September are the two main running events.

Baseball

Baseball clubs are predictably Americanised and many of the players are English-speakers. The **Patriots Baseball Club de Paris** (*recorded information 01.40.18.05.55*) has competitive and recreational sections. Annual membership will set you back 500F and kit can be borrowed for a fee for competitions). Shorter-term stays depend on the player's level. Training takes place on Saturdays (6.30-8.30pm) at Gymnase Croix Nivert (107 rue de la Croix-Nivert, 15th/Mº Commerce).

Basketball

Basketball is a hugely popular sport in Paris – and the country as a whole – and almost every municipal sports centre has at least one court and clubs that play there. For something less structured, French teenagers frequent two newish courts under the Métro tracks near the Glacière stop in the 13th *arrondissement*, at Mº Stalingrad in the 19th, and there's a hoop in the Jardins du Luxembourg in the 6th. This isn't the Bronx, but it's advisable to respect the court hierarchy nonetheless. The **Comité Parisien de Basketball** (01.53.94.27.90) can supply a list of clubs, including Racing Club de France (01.45.67.55.86) and Paris Université Club (01.44.16.62.62).

Bowling

The Paris region has more than 25 tenpin bowling centres. The two we have listed below are among the most pleasant; both rent out shoes and have restaurants, games rooms and late hours.

There are eight lanes at the very lively **Bowling-Mouffetard** (13 rue Gracieuse, 5th/01.43.31.09.35/Mº Place Monge/open 3pm-2am Mon-Fri, 10am-2am Sat, Sun). The **Bowling de Paris** (Jardin d'Acclimatation, Bois de Boulogne, 16th/ 01.53.64.93.00/ Mº Les Sablons/open 9am-2am daily) has 24 lanes plus pool, billiards and numerous video games. You have to pay 12F to get into the Jardin d'Acclimatation before you get to the centre.

Climbing

The French are big on sport climbing and on bolting climbs, so if you come from the UK tradition, there may be a culture gap to overcome. To keep those climbing muscles taut even in Paris, there are five municipal *murs d'escalade*, three outdoor and two indoor. They are often reserved for schools and climbing clubs, but facilities are also open to individuals on a one-month membership (20F, with photo, proof of insurance and passport) if you have your own gear. The wall at the **Centre Sportif Poissonnier** (2 rue Jean-Cocteau, 18th /01.42.51.24.68/Mº Porte de Clignancourt) is the largest municipal facility and has a little 'real rock' section as well as a 21m high unlit outside wall.

For more of a work-out, there is the privately-run **Mur Mur** (55 rue Cartier Bresson, 93500 Pantin/ 01.48.46.11.00/Mº Aubervilliers-Pantin Quatre Chemins), said to be the best climbing wall in Europe if not the world, with 1500 square metres of wall and 10,000 holds. It costs 33F-65F for adults, 15F-30F for under 12s per session. There's kit for hire and tuition offered. Newly added is a section of wall to practise ice-climbing (or 'dry-tooling', as they call it).

If you prefer real rock, you don't need to go far. Local climbers train on the huge, slightly surreal boulders strewn around the Forêt de Fontainebleau, 70km south of Paris. A guide to the different bouldering areas is available from climbing shops such as **Au Vieux Campeur**; there are routes around the boulders for all, from kids to lycra-clad athletes.

Cycling

Paris isn't a particularly cycle-friendly city, due to the pushy traffic, but the city's bike lanes have been ambitiously expanded, and increasing numbers of cyclists are taking to the streets. Away from the urban snarl, the Bois de Boulogne and the Bois de Vincennes offer good cycling. The quais of the Seine and the Canal St-Martin, closed to traffic most Sundays (10am-4pm), are probably the nicest stretches of all for cyclists, rollers and pedestrians. There's a law against riding on paths less than 2.5m wide (*see chapter* **Directory** for information on cycle lanes).

Paris has many cycling clubs, both in the competition-based and more leisurely categories. You can find your nearest club by phoning the **Fédération Française de Cyclotourisme** (01.44.16.88.88) or get out there and pick up a group.

Mountain biking (VTT, *vélo tout terrain* in French) is limited in Paris: Parisian MTBers head for the forests of Fontainebleau, Meudon and Montmorency. VTT Evasion guides to bike routes in various forests are produced by the Office National des Forêts and can be bought at good bookshops for 35F each. The **Stade Vélodrome Jacques-Anquetil** (Bois de Vincennes, 12th/01.43.68.01.27), is a functional racing track open to cyclists on a regular basis, if you are a licenced member of a club. For general bike needs, branches of **GoSport** should suffice. For specialist MTB, try **VTT Center** (1 pl Rungis, 13th/01.45.65.49.89), while the **Maison du Vélo** (11 rue Fénélon, 10th/ 01.42.81.24.72) sells, hires and repairs all types of bikes. There are also a number of companies offering bike tours in and around Paris (*see chapter* **Directory** for details).

Diving

If you are in Paris for some time it's worth joining a club as it works out cheaper. If time is limited, a pricier, commercial outfit will get you your certificate. For a diving shop, try **Plongespace** (80 rue Balard, 15th/01.45.57.01.01).

The **Club de Plongée du 5ème Arrondissement** (01.43.36.07.67) is a friendly club where you can train for the French licence. It organises trips to the Med and further afield and meets at the Piscine Jean-Taris (*see box* **In the swim**), although there may be a waiting list to join. There are well-qualified, experienced instructors at **Surplouf** (06.14.10.26.11/01.42.21.18.14), which offers courses in English, as well as French, aimed at a variety of underwater interests. Courses for beginners, including textbooks, insurance and scuba gear rental, cost 1680F for the French licence or 1850F for the PADI certificate.

Football

To find an amateur team to play for, call the **Ligue Ile de France de Football** (01.42.44.12.12) and ask for a contact number in your arrondissement.

Golf

Golf has become the French status-seeker's sport of choice now that tennis is more or less democratised. There are no courses in Paris, but scores in the Paris region, many of them open to non-members. Green fees are usually cheaper during the week. For a full list of courses, contact the **French Golf Federation** (68 rue Anatole France, 92309 Levallois Perret/01.41.49.77.00).

The **Golf Clément Ader** (Domaine du Château Péreire, 77220 Gretz Armainvilliers/01.64.07.80.43/SNCF Gretz Armainvilliers) is a challenging, Japanese-designed course equipped with plenty of water hazards. The **Golf Disneyland Paris Marne-la-Vallée** (77777 Marne-la-Vallée/01.60.45.68.04/RER Marne-la-Vallée/bus) has everything you'll need: 27 holes, a great clubhouse, American professionals, buggies and equipment for hire,

Splash out at the **Piscine Georges-Vallerey** *(see box* **In the Swim***).*

not to mention (Mickey) mouse-shaped bunkers. The **Golf du Réveillon** (Ferme des Hyverneaux, 77150 Lesigny/01.60.02.17.33/RER Boissy-St-Léger then taxi) is an attractive, 36-hole public course.

Closer to central Paris is the **Académie de Golf de Paris** at the Paris Country Club, Hippodrome de Saint-Cloud (1 rue du Camp Canadien, 92210 Saint-Cloud/01.47.71.39.22/SNCF Suresnes Longchamp), which has a nine-hole course within the Hippodrome horse-racing track, plus pitch and putt facilities. There are also some golf driving ranges, including the one at **Aquaboulevard** (*see box* **In the Swim**).

Horse Riding

Both the Bois de Boulogne and the Bois de Vincennes are beautiful places to ride but it must be done under the auspices of a riding club. You can join one of the following clubs: La Société d'Equitation de Paris (01.45.01.20.06), the Centre Hippique du Touring (01.45.01.20.88) or the Cercle Hippique du Bois de Vincennes (01.48.73.01.28).

Complete beginners can learn to ride in the unpretentious **Club Bayard Equitation** (Bois de Vincennes, Centre Bayard/UCPA de Vincennes, av de Polygone, 12th/01.43.65.46.87). Membership runs for three months (1233F) or you can do a five-day course in July or August (1283F).

The **Haras de Jardy** (bd de Jardy, 92430 Marnes-la-Coquette/01.47.01.35.30) is a lovely equestrian centre near Versailles, which organises accompanied group rides by the hour (119F); otherwise you can take out a three-month membership for 1586F, plus 240F insurance for a year. There are also 20 tennis courts and a nine-hole golf course at the centre.

Ice Skating

In winter (mid Dec-early Mar) the pretty **place de l'Hôtel de Ville** is transformed into an open-air ice rink. Skates

*Tennis anyone? Get lucky at the **Luxembourg**.*

can be hired (30F) and use of the rink is free. If temperatures drop extremely low and the park staff posts signs declaring the ice safe, there is skating on the Lac Supérieur in the **Bois de Boulogne**. Indoor all-year round rinks include the **Patinoire de Boulogne** (1 rue Victor Griffuelhes, Boulogne-Billancourt/01.46.94.99.74/M° Marcel Sembat) or the **Patinoire d'Asnières-sur-Seine** (bd Pierre de Coubertin, 92600 Asnières/01.47.99.96.06/M° Gabriel Péri Asnières Gennevilliers), although public opening hours are restricted due to school use.

Rowing & Watersports

In France one learns to scull before doing sweep-oar and you will be marginalised if you can't scull. Children and adults can row, canoe and kayak (Wed, Sat; equipment is provided) in the 600m x 65m basin at the **Base Nautique de la Villette** (15-17 quai de la Loire, 19th/01.42.40.29.90/M° Jaurès). La Défense-based **Société Nautique de la Basse Seine** (26 quai du President Paul Doumer, 92400 Courbevoie/ 01.43.33.03.47) has both competitive and recreational sections, good equipment and a strong history.

If you're just after some relaxing recreational rowing, you can hire boats by the hour on **Lac Daumesnil** and **Lac des Minimes** in the **Bois de Vincennes** or on **Lac Supérieur** in the **Bois de Boulogne**.

Rugby

If you want to play on a French-speaking team, call the **Comité Ile de France de Rugby** (01.43.42.51.51). Top-level rugby goes on at **Racing Club de France** (5 rue Eblé, 7th/01.45.67.55.86. Ground: Terrain Yves-du-Manoir, 12 rue François Faber, 92700 Colombes). Part of a huge multi-sport club, the top team is professional. For a good club standard try the **Athletic Club de Boulogne** (Saut du Loup, route des Tribunes, 16th/01.46.51.11.91 or 01.41.10.25.30), which fields two teams, (training 7.30pm Tue-Thur; matches on Sun). The **British Rugby Club of Paris** run by Graham Spensley (work 01.56.69.66.00/home 01.42.94.29.26) likes to describe itself as 'convivial' rather than fanatical. It runs two Saturday sides and trains on Wed at 8pm at the Standard Athletic Club (*see above*).

Snooker/Billiards

The French have their own brand of (pocketless) billiards, and many halls and bars here have only French or American pool tables. The rare snooker facilities include the **Bowling de Paris** (*see above* **Bowling**), which has one table amongst its French ones. A beer-and-Gitanes establishment, the **Académie de Billard Clichy-Montmartre** (84 rue de Clichy, 9th/01.48.78.32.85/M° Place de Clichy) has a full-size snooker table along with a room of French ones, tile floors, high ceilings and tall mirrors. There are French and American tables, a relaxing atmosphere and a bar at the **Blue-Billard** (111-113 rue St-Maur, 11th/01.43.55.87.21/M° St-Maur), and you can play for free between noon and 2pm if you have lunch. The velveteen atmosphere and the scent of cigars and cognac makes the **Hôtel Concorde St-Lazare** (108 rue St-Lazare, 8th/01.40.08.44.44/M° St-Lazare) the most elegant setting for playing French billiards. **Les Mousquetaires** (77 av du Maine, 14th/01.43.22.50.46/M° Gaîté), a popular young bar with an eleven-table pool room in the back, is a good place to shoot French or American pool.

Squash

You can play at Club Quartier Latin and the Standard Athletic Club (*see above*), or try **Squash Montmartre** (14 rue Achille-Martinet, 18th/01.42.55.38.30/M° Lamarck-Caulaincourt) which has four glazed squash courts, and offers lessons. Membership is 3400F per year or 900F for three months, plus reservation and lights each time, or you can pay each visit (80F per person per hour).

In the swim

Paris has 34 public swimming pools, patchily distributed – there are none in the 7th or 8th, for example. Municipal pools usually have restricted weekday opening hours due to school use. In term time most open early mornings (7-8am) and at lunchtimes (11.30am-1pm) on weekdays, plus Wed afternoons and all day at weekends (longer hours in the holidays). Municipal pools cost 16F (adults) and 9F (children); a ten-visit ticket costs 130F (75F children). Private pools cost more and may have longer weekday openings – phone to check.

Piscine Suzanne-Berlioux
Forum des Halles, 10 pl de la Rotonde, 1st (01.42.36.98.44). Mᵒ Les Halles. **Admission** 25F, 20F children.
This 50m private pool with tropical greenhouse in the Forum des Halles is clean and crowded. Young, hip clientele.

Piscine Saint-Merri
16 rue du Renard, 4th (01.42.72.29.45). Mᵒ Hôtel-de-Ville.
A 25m municipal pool with plants and palms.

Piscine Jean-Taris
16 rue Thouin, 5th (01.43.25.54.03). Mᵒ Cardinal Lemoine.
Look out on to the Panthéon and Lycée Henri IV gardens from this lovely if sometimes cramped 25m municipal pool.

Piscine Pontoise
19 rue de Pontoise, 5th (01.55.42.77.88). Mᵒ Maubert-Mutualité. **Admission** 25F, 19F under 16s, 22F students (+ 3F for cabin); 44F at night incl. gym access.
Vintage 33m pool has music and underwater lighting by night; classes for tots. *See above* **Club Quartier Latin.**

Piscine St-Germain
12 rue Lobineau, 6th (01.43.29.08.15). Mᵒ Mabillon.
Underground 25m municipal pool in St-Germain market.

Piscine Georges-Drigny
18 rue Bochart-de-Saron, 9th (01.45.26.86.93). Mᵒ Anvers.
A 25m x 15m municipal pool just south of Montmartre.

Piscine Château-Landon
31 rue de Château-Landon, 10th (01.46.07.34.68). Mᵒ Louis-Blanc.
Municipal facility with 25m main pool plus learners' pool.

Piscine Cour-des-Lions
11 rue Alphonse-Baudin, 11th (01.43.55.09.23). Mᵒ Richard-Lenoir.
Clean-lined 25m municipal pool not far from the Marais.

Piscine Reuilly
13 rue Hénard, 12th (01.40.02.08.08). Mᵒ Montgallet.
This bright, friendly municipal facility next to a park has the two newest pools in Paris, 25m and 15m long.

Piscine Roger-LeGall
34 bd Carnot, 12th (01.44.73.81.12). Mᵒ Porte de Vincennes. **Admission** *winter* 25F, 17.5F children, 16.5F students; *summer* 36F, 18F children, 26F students, less after 5pm.
A calm outdoor pool, covered in winter. Privately-run.

Piscine Butte-aux-Cailles
5 pl Paul-Verlaine, 13th (01.45.89.60.05). Mᵒ Place d'Italie.
Built in the 1920s with Italian tiles, the 33m main pool and two outdoor pools at this municipal centre, are fed by an artesian well.

Piscine Didot
22 av Georges-Lafenestre, 14th (01.42.76.78.14). Mᵒ Porte de Vanves.
Renovated in 1996, this 25m municipal pool welcomes diving clubs and aquagym as well as general swimmers.

Aquaboulevard
4 rue Louis-Armand, 15th (01.40.60.15.15). Mᵒ Balard. **Admission** *four hours in peak periods, or all day at other times* 77F, 3-11s 56F; *before 11am* 56F, 3-11s 50F.
An extravagant indoor-outdoor complex with tropical lagoon, wave pool and sun terrace. Great for kids. There's also a golf driving range. *See* **Club Forest Hill.**

Piscine Armand-Massard
66 bd du Montparnasse, 15th (01.45.38.65.19). Mᵒ Montparnasse-Bienvenüe.
A vast underground municipal sports centre with three pools: for beginners, swimmers (33m) and divers.

Piscine Emile-Anthoine
9 rue Jean-Rey, 15th (01.53.69.61.59). Mᵒ Bir-Hakeim.
Busy, ultra-modern 25m municipal pool with a great view of the Eiffel Tower from the deep end. Disabled access.

Piscine Henry-de-Montherlant
32 bd Lannes, 16th (01.40.72.28.30). Mᵒ Porte-Dauphine.
Popular, modern 25m municipal pool (plus beginners' pool) with chic clientele and outdoor tanning area in summer.

Piscine Bernard-Lafay
79 rue de La Jonquière, 17th (01.42.26.11.05). Mᵒ Porte de Clichy.
Another municipal centre accessible to the disabled, with a 25m main pool and smaller learners' pool.

Piscine Hébert
2 rue des Fillettes, 18th (01.46.07.60.01). Mᵒ Marx-Dormoy.
A lovely (crowded) 25m city-run pool with retractable roof.

Piscine Georges-Hermant
6, 10 rue David d'Angers, 19th (01.42.02.45.10). Mᵒ Danube. **Admission** 22F, 19F under 16s.
Privately-run, this is Paris' biggest pool (50m x 20m), complete with sliding roof for summer, plus a diving area.

Piscine Georges-Vallerey
148 av Gambetta, 20th (01.40.31.15.20). Mᵒ Porte des Lilas. **Admission** 25F, 20F children.
The original 50m pool where Johnny Weissmuller swam to 400m gold in the 1924 Olympics has now been split into two (37.5m and 12.5m long), and is still in mint condition.

Piscine en Plein Air du Parc de Sceaux
148bis av du Général de Gaulle, 92160 Antony (01.43.50.39.35). RER Croix de Berny. **Admission** 30F, less for children and students.
Three outdoor pools (with diving and kids' pools), picnic lawn and sunbathing. Open dawn to dusk, May to September.

Tennis: Public Courts

If you want to make the most of any of the some 170 city-operated courts in Paris, you can either show up and hope for the best or, if you are a resident, you can use Minitel 3615 Paris (*see chapter* **Directory**) to book a court in advance. To register, pick up an application form from one of the city's 43 tennis centres (or in the *Guide du Sport*) and post it with a copy of your identity card and two passport size photos; you'll have to wait over a month to get your Carte Paris-Tennis and a reservation number. Whether you use Minitel or just show up, the price is the same: 37F per hour, 53F per hour with lights.

The six asphalt courts in the romantic setting of the **Jardins du Luxembourg** (6th/01.43.25.79.18/M° Notre-Dame-des-Champs or RER Luxembourg) are a great place to play – and be seen playing; as a result, however, they tend to be extremely popular. Reserve via Minitel or just turn up and sign up on the booking sheet. The **Centre Sportif La Falguère** (Route de la Pyramide, Bois de Vincennes, 12th/01.43.74.40.93/M° Château de Vincennes) is a symmetrical complex, with 21 acrylic and asphalt courts in good condition. With its swimming pool and seven hard courts, the **Centre Sportif Henry-de-Montherlant** (30-32 bd Lannes, 16th/01.40.72.28.33/M° Porte-Dauphine) gets a lot of use from students and clubs – it's best to reserve via Minitel first. There's a free hitting wall for those without a partner.

You can also join a club and play on municipal courts. The cost depends on how long you're staying in Paris. Some clubs cost only 500F in membership fees, plus the 22F court rental fee. Compared to a private club, this is a bargain.

Tennis: Private Clubs

There are some lovely private clubs in and around Paris, but most are very expensive and have long waiting lists. Courts, though, are generally in superb condition and you don't have to figure out the Minitel to get a reservation.

There are some 20 red clay courts (10 indoors) at the **Stade Jean Bouin** (26 av du Général-Sarrail, 16th/01.46.51.55.40/M° Porte d'Auteuil), the site of the men's qualifying tournament for the French Open. The **Tennis de Longchamp** (19 bd Anatole-France, 92100 Boulogne/01.46.03.84.49/M° Boulogne Jean-Jaurès) has 20 well-maintained hard courts along with a new complex that includes weights and a sauna. **Club Forest Hill** (4 rue Louis-Armand, 15th/01.40.60.10.00/M° Balard or RER Boulevard Victor) has fourteen branches in the Paris region and is an affordable alternative, even if most of its locations are beyond the *Périphérique*: annual membership is around 4000F; non-members can play for 210F-255F per visit. Generally, there are indoor and outdoor courts; some are of international standard. Most sites will also have squash, gyms and fitness classes. A Forest Hill membership also gives access to **Aquaboulevard** (*see box* **In the Swim**).

Roll up, roll up

Rollerbladers are everywhere, weaving through traffic and pedestrians and taking over parks and quays at weekends. The 1998 World Cup opening ceremony even included choreographed lines of rollerbladers swaying through the streets on their way to the party in place de la Concorde.

If a fast night-time glide around Paris appeals, the free Friday Night Fever trip by **Paris Roller** leaves at 10pm each Friday from the Place d'Italie and travels up to 30km in three hours with a police escort. With up to 800 participants and a fast pace, you need to be experienced to keep up. The **Roller Squad Institut** has free beginners' trips (3pm Sat from Les Invalides), and more advanced bladers (3pm Sun, phone for more details). Wrist protection and insurance are sometimes mandatory – ask the above organisers about their annual or short-term insurance. **Roller Nomades** also do *balades*, leaving 2.15pm each Sun from their Bastille shop. To skate out on your own, try the Bois de Vincennes (12th), Promenade Plantée (12th) or the Seine quays on Sundays. For stunts, there's a ramp at the stade Suzanne-Lenglen (15th).

Rollerblading shops sell a range of kit, and will hire rollerblades and protective pads for 50F-80F a day or 60F-120F a weekend. Specialists include **Parking Bld Roller Station**, **Vertical Line** and **Bike 'n' Roller**. Most do lessons by the hour or packages of a lesson and a short tour. Generalist sports shops including **Go Sport** and **Au Vieux Campeur** also have good roller sections.

Paris Roller: *starlight express.*

Paris Roller *(01.43.36.89.81)*.
Roller Squad Institut *(01.45.88.23.75)*.
Roller Nomades, *37 bd Bourdon, 4th (01.44.54.07.44)* M° *Bastille.*
Parking Bld Roller Station, *107-109 Bld Beaumarchais, 3rd (01.42.78.33.00)*. M° *St-Sébastien Froissart.*
Vertical Line, *60bis av Raymond Poincaré, 16th (01.47.27.21.21)*. M° *Victor Hugo or Trocadero.*
Bike 'n' Roller, *6 rue St-Julien-le-Pauvre, 5th (01.44.07.35.89)*. M° *St Michel.*
Branch: *137 rue St-Dominique, 7th (01.44.18.30.39)*.
Go Sport, *Forum des Halles, 1st (01.40.26.40.52)*. M° *Les Halles.*
Au Vieux Campeur, *48 rue des Ecoles, 5th (01.53.10.48.48)*. M° *Maubert-Mutualité.*
Stade Suzanne Lenglen, *2 rue Louis-Armand, 15th (01.40.60.77.18)*. M° *Balard.* **Open** 1.30-6.30pm Tue-Sun, until 9.30pm Sat. **Admission** 45F per visit.

Theatre

French theatre offers everything from intellectual highbrow to drawing-room comedy. The key is knowing where to go for what.

Paris is home to hundreds of theatres, but with so much choice it can be difficult to know where to start. You'll soon find it's helpful and more interesting to explore theatres outside the big names which everyone recognises: there is more to Paris theatre than the original **Comédie-Française**. For professional handling of the classics it's without equal, but for a slightly more varied repertoire focusing on the contemporary, the **Studio Théâtre** (Carrousel du Louvre) and **Vieux Colombier** (both offshoots of the Comédie), as well as the **Théâtre National de la Colline**, are all reliable bets.

The French press often argue that the big public theatres should do more to please their audiences, rather than indulge their own creative whims. Luckily public theatre is much better funded in France than elsewhere, so the occasional really superb production which makes (or saves) the reputation of both theatre and director continues to be put on alongside yet more dull reinterpretations of classics or adaptations of non-theatrical texts. At least funding enables experimentation and failure – which occasionally means stunning innovation.

For a real feeling of fringe theatre, however, look to smaller venues such as the **Guichet-Montparnasse, Essaïon, Aktéon-Théâtre** or **La Main d'Or**, which produce a mixture of well-known playwrights to bring in the money, alongside new talent. Mixed-media productions can be found at the **Théâtre de la Bastille** and **Théâtre Paris-Villette**, whose programmes make a feature of the boundary-breaking, mixing theatre in with music, dance, video or special effects. Meanwhile, theatres like the **Rond-Point** balance experimental and modern (Valère Novarina, Jean Vaulthier) with classics (Claudel, Molière etc).

The big boulevard theatres rely mainly on big box office turnover to make ends meet. Theatres like the **Marigny, Rive Gauche, Montparnasse** and **Hébertot** (to name but a few) attract the crowds with a mixed diet of big-name productions, where either a star or the writer is famous – Annie Girardot, Alain Delon or Jean-Paul Belmondo are all starring in productions at the time of writing, while Eric-Emmanuel Schmitt, darling playwright of the private theatre, has three

Théatre 13's *ongoing* Saga Fin de Siècle *includes a sequel to Pinter's* The Caretaker.

Montmartre's **Les Abbesses** *was designed by Belgian architect Charles Vandenhove.*

plays on across town simultaneously. Feydeau and Labiche are as popular as ever, alongside a host of Anglophone names: Oscar Wilde, Harold Pinter, Alan Bennett, Alan Ayckbourn, Neil Simon, Ray Cooney, Tennessee Williams. All are probably better known than French counterparts, except perhaps media-friendly Schmitt and Yasmina *Art* Reza; Michel Vinaver, successfully writing since the 50s; and Bernard-Marie Koltès,who until he died in 1989 was widely seen as France's most important contemporary playwright. But still it's the classics which play best: from tiny pub theatre to the glitzy boulevards, it seems everyone is keen to profit from the public demand for reliable high culture.

Big-name directors also continue to draw in the crowds. Among the best known are Patrice Chéreau (also famous for films like *La Reine Margot*), Ariane Mnouchkine (Théâtre du Soleil, see **Cartoucherie de Vincennes**), and Peter Brook, while the younger Olivier Py and Stanislas Nordey are popular and well-respected among a more theatre-literate public.

OUT AND ABOUT

Paris' suburbs are home to a number of accessible and significant public theatres, which produce some high-profile productions, often thanks to their well-known directors. Large crowds come out from town to the Manufacture des Oeillets in Ivry-sur-Seine (01.46.71.71.10), which hosts events for the *Festival d'Automne*. Other well-known suburban theatres include: Théâtre de la Commune (2 rue Edouard Poisson, 93300 Aubervilliers/ 01.48.33.93.93; MC93 (1 bd Lénine, 93000 Bobigny/

01.41.60.72.72); Théâtre de Gennevilliers (Centre Dramatique National, 41 av des Grésillons, 92230 Gennevilliers/01.41.32.26.10); Théâtre des Amandiers (7 av Pablo Picasso, 92022 Nanterre/ 01.46.14.70.00); Théâtre des Quartiers d'Ivry-La Balance (1 rue Simon Dereure, 94200 Ivry-sur-Seine/ 01.46.72.37.43; and Théâtre Gérard Philipe (59 bd Jules Guesde, 93207 St-Denis; 01.48.13.70.00).

JOUEZ-VOUS ANGLAIS?

Interest in English language productions has now extended to the French themselves. Best example of this must be the reappearance of Yasmina Reza's *Art* on the Paris stage, not in another French run but in Christopher Hampton's English translation! Paris possesses a surprising number of resident English-language theatre companies, with Pinter and Mamet among the most performed authors. **Dear Conjunction** (bilingual company, 01.42.41.69.65) was founded in 1991 by Les Clack and Barbara Bray to perform new and established plays. Modern playwrights are also featured by **On Stage Theatre Company, Walk and Talk Productions** and Bob Meyer's **Gare St-Lazare Company**, all regulars at the Théâtre de Nesle (8 rue de Nesle, 6th/01.46.34.61.04) or at the **Petit Hébertot. ACT** (01.40.33.64.02), run by Anne and Andrew Wilson, is an educational theatre company which performs modern classics at the Théâtre de Ménilmontant (15 rue du Retrait, 20th, and other venues). The **Odéon, MC93 Bobigny** and **Bouffes du Nord** occasionally host touring English-language companies.

BOOKING TIPS

Few theatres open on Monday or Sunday evenings; many close in July and August. Matinées are usually on Sunday. Performances start between 8 and 9pm (some theatres like Théâtre National de la Colline run earlier performances once a week). For details of current programmes see *Pariscope*; the *Time Out Paris* section gives a selection in English. Tickets can be bought direct from theatres, at ticket agencies (*see chapter* **Directory**) and at the following specialist agencies: Minitel, on 3615 THEA; Agence Chèque Théâtre (33 rue Le Peletier, 9th/ 01.42.46.72.40; open 10am-6.45pm Mon-Sat) and Kiosque Théâtre (opposite 15 pl de la Madeleine, 9th, and in front of Gare Montparnasse, 15th; open noon-8pm Tue-Sun) which sells same-day tickets at half-price, plus 16F commission per seat. Many private theatres offer 50 per cent reductions on previews and students can also benefit from good same-day deals.

National Theatres

Comédie Française

Salle Richelieu *2 rue de Richelieu, 1st (01.44.58.15.15).* *M° Palais-Royal.* **Box office** 11am-6pm daily. **Tickets** 70F-190F; 65F students under 26 (1hr before play); 30F limited visibility seats. **Credit** AmEx, MC, V. **Map H5** *Guided tours. Wheelchair access (call ahead).*
Théâtre du Vieux-Colombier *21 rue du Vieux-Colombier, 6th (01.44.39.87.00). M° St-Sulpice.* **Box office** 1-6pm Mon, Sun; 11am-7pm Tue-Sat. **Tickets** 160F; 110F over-60s; 65F under-27s, students (45mins before play). **Credit** AmEx, MC, V. **Map G7** *Guided tours. Wheelchair access (call ahead).*
Studio Théâtre *pl de la Pyramide inversée, Galerie du Carrousel (entrance 99 rue de Rivoli), 1st (01.44.58.98.58).* *M° Palais-Royal.* **Box office** 5.30pm same day. **Tickets** 80F; 45F under-27s. **Credit** AmEx, MC, V. **Map H5** *Wheelchair access.*
Founded in 1680 by Louis XIV out of Molière's wandering troupe, France's oldest company moved to its building adjoining the Palais-Royal just after the French Revolution. This is the only national theatre to have its own permanent troupe, the *pensionnaires*, who perform four-plus plays a week, ranging from Molière and Racine to modern classics (Lessing, Genet, Anouilh). The company has a second theatre in the restored Théâtre du Vieux-Colombier, offering small-scale classics and contemporary works, and a studio theatre in the Carrousel complex under the Louvre, used for short classics and modern plays, salons with writers or actors (Thur evenings), plus a *théâtrothèque* showing plays on video (Sat afternoons).

Odéon, Théâtre de l'Europe

1 pl de l'Odéon, 6th (01.44.41.36.36). M° Odéon/ RER Luxembourg. **Box office** 11am-6.30pm Mon-Sat; *telephone bookings* 11am-7pm Mon-Sat (Sun when plays are on). **Tickets** 30F-170F. **Credit** MC, V. **Map H7**
Based in a beautiful Neo-Classical theatre, the Odéon, under director Georges Lavaudant, stages a contrasting mix of French and international productions, classic and contemporary. It welcomes famous visiting companies and directors. Deborah Warner has directed Ibsen here, while the repertoire features everything from Koltès readings to Racine and Ibsen. *Wheelchair access (call ahead).*

Théâtre National de Chaillot

Palais de Chaillot, 1 pl du Trocadéro, 16th (01.53.65.30.00). M° Trocadéro. **Box office** 11am-7pm

Mon-Sat; 11am-5pm Sun; *telephone bookings* 9am-7pm Mon-Sat; 11am-6pm Sun. **Tickets** 160F; 120F under-25s, over-60s. **Credit** AmEx, MC, V. **Map B5**
Flamboyant entertainment-value productions are staged here in a monumental 2800-seat, 1930s theatre. There's a helpful laptop subtitling system (various languages). *Wheelchair access (call ahead).*

Théâtre National de la Colline

15 rue Malte-Brun, 20th (01.44.62.52.52). M° Gambetta. **Box office** 11am-7pm Mon, Wed-Sat; 11am-6pm Tue; (2-5pm Sun if a play is on); *telephone bookings Mon-Sat* only. **Tickets** 160F; 130F over-60s; 110F Tue. **Credit** AmEx, MC, V. **Map Q5**
This modern theatre has a remit for twentieth-century drama, happily featuring French playwrights (Vinaver, Durringer, Milavanoff) alongside imported names. *Wheelchair access.*

Central

Théâtre de la Ville

2 pl du Châtelet, 4th (01.42.74.22.77). M° Châtelet. **Box office** 11am-7pm Mon; 11am-8pm Tue-Sat; *by telephone* 11am-7pm Mon-Sat. **Tickets** 95F-190F; half-price on day of performance under-25s, students. **Credit** MC, V. **Map J6**
Funded by the City of Paris, this major dance venue presents some plays, varying from first rate to controversial. *See also East & North). See chapters* **Dance**, **Music: Classical & Opera** *and* **Music: Rock, Roots & Jazz**.

Théâtre Essaïon de Paris

6 rue Pierre-au-Lard, 4th (01.42.78.46.42). *M° Rambuteau or Hôtel-de-Ville.* **Box office** 7-8.30pm if play on, reserve by telephone 2-10pm daily. **Tickets** 100F-150F; 60F under-25s; 80F-100F over-60s. **Credit** AmEx, MC, V. **Map K6**
Two ancient cellars converted into smallish theatre spaces play host to a proudly contemporary repertoire.

Boulevard and Champs-Elysées

Comédie des Champs-Elysées

15 av Montaigne, 8th (01.53.23.99.19). M° Alma-Marceau. **Box office** 11am-6pm Mon, Sat; 11am-7pm Tue-Fri. **Tickets** 110F-250F. **Credit** AmEx, MC, V. **Map D5**
The baby brother of the Théâtre des Champs-Elysées (*see chapter* **Music: Classical & Opera**) offers mainstream modern classics and contemporary works. *Wheelchair access (call ahead).*

Théâtre du Rond-Point

2bis av Franklin D Roosevelt, 8th (01.44.95.98.00/10). *M° Franklin D Roosevelt.* **Box office** noon-7pm Tue-Sat; noon-4pm Sun. Closed Aug. **Tickets** 180F; 120F under-26s. **Credit** V. **Map E4**
This renovated nineteenth-century skating rink features Marcel Maréchal's resident company, plus visiting productions. Maréchal's repertoire includes modern French classics (Beckett, Vauthier, Audiberti) and oodle of new work. *Wheelchair access (call ahead).*

Théâtre de l'Athénée

4 sq de l'Opéra-Louis-Jouvet, 9th (01.53.05.19.19). *M° Havre-Caumartin/RER Auber.* **Box office** 11am-7pm Mon-Fri; 1-7pm Sat. **Tickets** 40F-160F. **Credit** AmEx, DC. MC, V. **Map G4**
Beautiful old theatre hidden away in a quiet square, worth seeking out for productions of French and foreign classics. *Wheelchair access (call ahead).*

La Bruyère

5 rue la Bruyère, 9th (01.48.74.76.99). M° St-Georges.
Box office 11am-7pm Mon-Sat. **Tickets** 120F-210F;
70F under-26s (Mon-Thur); 150F over-60s (Mon-Thur).
Credit MC, V. **Map H2**
This archetypal boulevard theatre is home to countless big
box office hits from home and abroad, including Ben Elton's
Popcorn (in French) which runs until July 1999.
Wheelchair access (call ahead).

Théâtre Hébertot/Petit Hébertot

78bis bd des Batignolles, 17th (01.43.87.23.23).
M° Villiers or Rome. **Box office** 11am-5.30pm Mon;
11am-6pm Tue-Sat; 11am-2pm Sun. **Tickets** 105F-290F.
Credit MC, V. **Map F2**
This pretty, steeply raked, historic venue stages a mixed
classic international and contemporary French repertoire in
its two theatres, as well as occasional English-language productions from Paris-based companies in its studio theatre
(Petit Hébertot). The repertoire has included works by more
popular contemporary writers such as Yasmina Reza, Jean-
Marie Besset and Jean-Claude Grumberg, alongside the likes
of Pirandello and Sartre.
Wheelchair access (call ahead).

Left Bank

Théâtre de la Huchette

23 rue de la Huchette, 5th (01.43.26.38.99). M° St-Michel.
Box office 5-9pm Mon-Sat. Closed first two weeks in
Jan. **Tickets** 100F; 80F students under 25 (Mon-Fri).
No credit cards. Map J7
Home to Nicolas Bataille's original production of Ionesco's
The Bald Primadonna since 1957. Other Ionesco works (*La
Leçon*) show alongside such Fench staples as Paul Claudel.
Wheelchair access (call ahead).

Théâtre 13

24 rue Daviel, 13th (01.45.88.16.30). M° Glacière. **Box office**
reserve by telephone 2-7.30pm Mon-Fri. **Tickets** 120F; 85F
under-26s, over-60s. **No credit cards. Map J10**
'Un peu de tout' is how this municipally-funded theatre
describes its ouput. Recent years have seen Mamet, Chekhov
and Goethe, plus several contemporary French playwrights.
1999's attractions include Beaumarchais, Stendhal and Pinter.

Théâtre de la Cité Internationale

*21 bd Jourdan, 14th (01.43.13.50.50). RER Cité
Universitaire.* **Box office** 2-7pm Mon-Sat. **Tickets**
110F; 55F Mon and under-26s. **No credit cards.**
A well-equipped modern theatre offering international and
French plays, such as Hugo von Hofmannsthal and Guy Walter.
Wheelchair access (call ahead).

Guichet-Montparnasse

15 rue du Maine, 14th (01.43.27.88.61).
M° Montparnasse-Bienvenüe. **Box office** 11am-12.30pm,
2-6pm; *by telephone* 2-6pm Mon-Sat. **Tickets** 100F; 80F
students, over-60s. **No credit cards. Map F9**
Like a lively pub theatre, where the programme changes regularly and features plenty of new talent. Its tiny 50-seat auditorium stages several shortish productions each night or in rep.

Théâtre Montparnasse

31 rue de la Gaîté, 14th (01.43.22.77.74). M° Gaîté.
Box office 11am-6pm Mon; 11am-7pm Tue-Sat.
Tickets 90F-260F. **Credit** MC, V. **Map F9**
A key private theatre offering lively and accessible theatre
and musical comedy, recently hosting works by Eric-William
Gibson and Pierre Sauvil. Contact its smaller theatre, the
Petit Montparnasse, separately (01.43.22.77.30).
Wheelchair access.

East & North

Aktéon-Théâtre

11 rue du Général-Blaise, 11th (01.43.38.74.62).
M° St-Ambroise. **Box office** 1-11pm daily. **Tickets**
100F; 70F students, over 65s. **No credit cards. Map N5**
A small, lively venue with a large number of plays in rep at
any one time, from classics to unknown writers.
Wheelchair access.

Bouffes du Nord

37bis bd de la Chapelle, 10th (01.46.07.34.50).
M° La Chapelle. **Box office** 11am-6pm Mon-Sat.
Tickets 70F-130F. **Credit** V. **Map L2**
The famously shabby home of Peter Brook's experimental
theatre company; Stéphane Lissner's co-direction has added
classical and operatic programming.
Wheelchair access (call ahead).

La Ménagerie de Verre

12-14 rue Léchevin, 11th (01.43.38.33.44). M° Parmentier.
Box office 1hr before play, *reserve by telephone* 2-7pm
Mon-Fri. **Tickets** 80F; 60F under-25s, over-60s.
No credit cards. Map M5
A stylishly converted warehouse which gives small compa-
nies scope to experiment. *See also chapter* **Dance.**

Théâtre de la Bastille

*76 rue de la Roquette, 11th (01.43.57.42.14). M° Bastille
or Voltaire.* **Box office** 10am-1pm, 2-6.30pm Mon-Fri; 2-
6.30pm Sat, Sun. **Tickets** 120F; 80F under-25s, students,
over-60s. **Credit** AmEx, MC, V. **Map M6**
Hosts a mix of often experimental theatre, music and dance,
frequently worked into the same production, by playwrights
like Michel Deutsch or Valère Novarina (*see chapter* **Dance**).
Wheelchair access (salle de bas only).

Cartoucherie de Vincennes

route du Champ de Manœuvre, bois de Vincennes, 12th.
M° Château de Vincennes, then shuttle bus or bus 112.
Each theatre operates independently.
The warehouses of a former cartridge factory now house a
theatre complex that includes the famous **Théâtre du Soleil**,
opened by Ariane Mnouchkine in 1970 (01.43.74.24.08). Also:
Théâtre de l'Epée de Bois (01.48.08.39.74); **Théâtre de
la Tempête** (01.43.28.36.36); **Théâtre de l'Aquarium**
(01.43.74.99.61) **Théâtre du Chaudron** (01.43.28.97.04).

Les Abbesses

31 rue des Abbesses, 18th (01.42.74.22.77). M° Abbesses.
Box office 5-8pm Tue-Sat; *by telephone* 11am-7pm Mon-
Sat. **Tickets** 95F-190F. **Credit cards** MC, V. **Map H2**
The new Montmartre-based house of the Théâtre de la Ville
features a largely contemporary repertoire, recently includ-
ing Bernard-Marie Koltès and Véronique Olmi.

Théâtre Paris-Villette

*211 av Jean-Jaurès, 19th (01.42.02.02.68). M° Porte de
Pantin.* **Box office** from 3pm Mon-Fri; *by telephone*
10.30am-6pm Mon-Fri. **Tickets** 135F; 95F Wed nights,
over-60s; 65F under-26s. **No credit cards. Map insert.**
This stylish, popular La Villette venue hosts a varied contemporary and often multimedia programme with unknown
writers and directors in its annual *Premières Pauses* season.
Wheelchair access.

Théâtre de l'Est Parisien

*159 av Gambetta, 20th (01.43.64.80.80). M° Pelleport or
St-Fargeau.* **Box office** 10am-6pm, Mon-Fri; 10am-2pm
Sun (10am-6pm Sat, Sun if a play is on). **Tickets** 140F;
90F under-24s, over-60s. **Credit** AmEx, MC, V. **Map Q4**
A modern, vibrant venue with a popular, traditional French
repertoire (Marivaux, Crébillon fils etc).

Trips Out of Town

Trips Out of Town

Artists' hideouts, monumental follies, scenes of royal courtship, canal trips, vainglorious châteaux... they're all within easy reach.

Versailles

Until 1661 Versailles was a simple hunting lodge and boyhood refuge of Louis XIV. In a fit of envy after seeing Vaux-le-Vicomte, he decided on a building to match his ego and his dreams of absolute power over the aristocracy. Louis Le Vau and painter Charles Le Brun began transforming the château, while André Le Nôtre set about the gardens, turning marshland into terraces, pools and paths.

In 1678 Jules Hardouin-Mansart took over as principal architect and dedicated the last 30 years of his life to adding the two main wings, the **Cour des Ministres** and **Chapelle Royale**. In 1682 Louis moved in and thereafter rarely set foot in Paris. The palace could house 20,000 people, including all the courtiers and royal ministers, who were reluctantly obliged to move there. With the king holding all the strings of power, nobles had no choice but to leave their provincial châteaux or Paris mansions and pass years in service at court, at great personal expense. In the 1770s, Louis XV chose his favourite architect Jacques Ange Gabriel to add the sumptuous **Opéra Royal**, still sometimes used for concerts by the Centre de Musique Baroque (01.39.20.78.10). With the fall of the monarchy in 1792, most of the furniture was dispersed and after the 1830 Revolution only Louis-Philippe saved the château from demolition.

Voltaire described Versailles as 'a masterpiece of bad taste and magnificence', yet you can't help but be impressed at the architectural purity of the vast classical facades, before being bowled over by the 73m-long **Hall of Mirrors**, where 17 windows echo the 17 mirrors in a brilliant play of light; the **King's Bedroom**, where the King rose in the presence of the court; the **Salon de la Guerre** complete with a relief by Coysevox of Louis XIV riding to history; the **Apollo Salon**, the Sun King's appropriately named throne room; and the **Queen's bedroom**, where queens gave birth in full view of courtiers, there to confirm the sex of the child and to ensure no substitutes were slipped in.

Outside, the park stretches over 815 hectares comprising formal gardens, wooded parkland and sheep-filled pastures, dominated by the grand perspectives laid out by Le Nôtre. Statues of the seasons, elements and continents, many commissioned by Colbert in 1674, are scattered throughout the gardens, and the spectacular series of fountains is served by an ingenious hydraulic system. Near the château is Hardouin-Mansart's **Orangerie**, whose vaulted gallery could house over 2000 orange trees. The **Potager du Roi**, the King's vegetable garden, has been recently restored (01.39.24.62.62/ open Apr-Oct, Tue-Sun, tour times vary).

The main palace being a little unhomely, in 1687 Louis XIV had Hardouin-Mansart build the **Grand Trianon**, on the north of the park, a pretty, but still hardly cosy, palace of stone and pink marble, where Louis stayed with Mme de Maintenon. Napoléon also stayed there with his second empress, Marie-Louise, and had it redecorated in Empire style.

The **Petit Trianon** is a perfect example of Neo-Classicism, and was built for Louis XV's mistress Mme de Pompadour, although she died before its completion. Marie-Antoinette however, managed to take advantage of the nearby *Hameau de la Reine*, the mock farm arranged around a lake, where she could play at being a lowly milkmaid.

Each Sunday from April to October (plus Saturdays in July and August and holidays) the great fountains in the gardens are set in motion, to music, in the **Grandes Eaux Musicales**, and seven times a year the **Grandes Fêtes de Nuit** capture something of the splendeur of the celebrations of the Sun King, *see chapter* **Paris by Season**.

Further Information

(01.30.84.74.00). 20km from Paris by A13 or D10. RER C to Versailles-Rive Gauche. **Open** *Château May-Sept* 9am-6pm Tue-Sun; *Oct-Apr* 9am-5pm Tue-Sun. *Grand Trianon/Petit Trianon May-Sept* 9am-12.30pm, 2-6pm Tue-Sun; *Oct-Apr* 10am-12.30pm, 2-5.30pm Tue-Fri; 10am-5.30pm Sat-Sun. *Gardens* dawn-dusk daily except bad weather. **Admission** *Château* 45F; 35F 18-25s; free under-18s; 35F for all after 3.30pm. *Grand Trianon/Petit Trianon* 40F adults; 30F 18-25s; free under-18s. *Gardens* free (except for *Grandes Eaux, Sat 3 July-28 Aug, Sun 4 Apr-10 Oct, 8, 13 May 14 July* 11am-noon, 3.30-5.30pm 30F; free under 10s). **No credit cards.**

Chantilly

In the middle of a lake, cream-coloured Chantilly with its domes and turrets looks like the archetypal French Renaissance château. In fact, the over-the-top main wing is a largely nineteenth-century reconstruction, as much of the original was destroyed during the Revolution. Beside it the **Petit Château** – what remains of the Renaissance

*Voltaire called **Versailles** 'a masterpiece of bad taste and magnificence'.*

château built for Anne de Montmorency – seems much humbler. But Chantilly is notable for its artistic treasures – three paintings by Raphael; Filippino Lippi's *Esther and Assuarus*; a cabinet of portraits by Clouet; several mythological scenes by Poussin; and the medieval miniatures from the *Très Riches Heures du Duc de Berry* (facsimiles only are usually on show).

Today, Le Nôtre's park is rather dilapidated, but still contains an extensive canal system and an artificial 'hamlet' pre-dating that of Versailles. To one side is a nineteenth-century 'English Garden'. In summer, a ten-minute ride in a hot-air balloon gives an aerial view of château, park and forest.

Chantilly's other claim to fame is as the home of French racing: this is where the most important trainers have their stables, and the town has a major racetrack. The eighteenth-century Great Stables once housed 240 horses, 500 dogs and almost 100 palfreys and hunting birds, and today contain the 'living museum' of the horse and pony.

South of the château stetches the **Forêt de Chantilly**, which has numerous footpaths and is besieged by picnickers in summer. A pleasant walk (approx 7km) circles the four Etangs de Commelles (small lakes) and passes the 'Château de la Reine Blanche', a mill converted in the 1820s into a pseudo-medieval hunting lodge.

Senlis, 9km east of Chantilly, has been bypassed since its glory days as the royal town where Hugh Capet was elected king in 987. Its historical centre contains several old streets, some handsome mansions, a fine, predominantly Gothic cathedral, some chunks of Gallo-Roman city ramparts and the remains of a Roman amphitheatre.

Further Information

Château (Musée Condé) (03.44.62.62.62/ 03.44.62.62.60). 41km from Paris by A1, exit Chantilly, and D924, or the N16 direct. By train Gare du Nord, then 30 min walk or short taxi ride. **Open** *Mar-Oct* 10am-6pm Mon, Wed-Sun; *Nov-Feb* 10.30am-12.45pm, 2-5pm Mon, Wed-Sun. **Admission** 39F adults; 34F 12-18s; 12F 3-11s; free under 3s; *park only* 17F; 10F 3-11s. **No Credit Cards. Musée Vivant du Cheval et du Poney** *(03.44.57.13.13/ 03.44.57.40.40).* **Open** *Apr-Oct* 10.30am-6.30pm daily (closed Tue Apr, Sept and Oct; Tue morning Jul-Aug); *Nov-Mar* 2-5pm Mon, Wed-Fri; 10.30am-6.30pm Sat-Sun. **Admission** 50F; 45F students, over 60s; 35F 4-16s; free under 4s. Dressage demonstrations at 3.30pm daily; *May-June* additional shows at 11.30am and 5.15pm daily. **Montgolfière** balloon (03.44.57.29.14) *Mar-Nov* 10am-7pm daily (weather permitting).

Compiègne & Pierrefonds

North of Paris on either side of the substantial hunting forest of Compiègne stand two very different châteaux with an Imperial stamp. On the edge of the old town of Compiègne, the **Château de Compiègne** looks out over a huge park and surrounding forest, and is a monument to the French royal family's obsession with *la chasse* which brought them here each year for the hunting. Although there had been a royal residence at Compiègne since the Capetians, it was Louis XV who was responsible for the present look of the château, as in 1751 he entrusted its reconstruction to architect Jacques Ange Gabriel. In the process Gabriel created an austere, classical pleasure palace around a central *cour d'honneur*.

Although some of the decoration dates from the eighteenth century (in particular an elegant, circular bathroom), most of the interior was ruthlessly remodelled by Napoléon for his second wife Marie-Louise and is stuffed with Imperial eagles, bees, palms and busts of the great self-publicist. The Empress' state apartments include fully furnished boudoirs, the ballroom (used as a military hospital in World War I) and her bedroom with its wonderfully over-the-top gilded bed and crimson damask furnishings. The only eighteenth-century piece is a commode, which belonged to Marie-Antoinette, put there as Marie-Louise wanted a souvenir of her unfortunate aunt.

Napoléon III also left his mark at Compiègne, where he and Empress Eugénie hosted lavish house parties every autumn. His most popular legacy was the highly efficient heating system he installed which still works today and makes a visit to the château bearable even in the depths of winter.

In one wing of the château, the Musée de la Voiture is devoted to early transport. You can see Napoléon I's state coach, Napoléon III's railway car and early motorcars, including an 1899 Renault and the Jamais Contente electric car of 1899.

In a clearing in the forest 6km from Compiègne is the **Clairière de l'Armistice** (take the N31 towards Soissons, then follow signs), a memorial to the site where the Germans surrendered to Maréchal Foch, ending World War I, on 11 November, 1918 (it is also where in 1940 the French surrendered to the Germans). There's the mark where the two railway lines met, a statue of Foch, and a reconstruction of his railway-carriage office.

At the other edge of the forest, a sudden dip in the land gives a view of strange turrets. At first sight, the neo-medieval castle of **Pierrefonds** is so clearly fake it's almost grotesque. Yet it well merits a pause. Napoléon bought the ruins of a fourteenth-century castle for 2950F. In 1857, Napoléon III, staying nearby at Compiègne, asked Viollet-le-Duc to restore one of the towers as a romantic hunting lodge. But the project grew and the fervent medievalist ended up reconstructing the whole massive edifice, in part using the remaining foundations, in part borrowing elements from other castles, or simply creating medieval as he felt it should be, converting his Gothic fantasies into reality. Walk up in circles between the ramparts and fortifications, through the crenellated gateway and admire the wonderful crocodile waterspouts in the

The fingerprints of many a monarch have left their mark on **Fontainebleau.**

courtyard. The grand baronial halls harbour elaborate chimneypieces carved with beasts, dragons and figures. The magnificent Salle des Preuses was designed as a ballroom for Napoléon III, with a minstrels' gallery for the musicians; the fireplace is sculpted with figures of nine ladies (one a likeness of the Empress Eugénie). One wing has a permanent exhibition about Viollet-le-Duc. Another fantasist, Michael Jackson once expressed interest in buying the château, but it was not for sale.

Further Information

Château de Compiègne, *5 pl du Général-de-Gaulle, 60200 Compiègne (03.44.38.47.00).* 80km from Paris by A1. *By train* from Gare du Nord. **Open** *10am-5.15pm* Mon, Wed-Sun. **Admission** 35F; 23F 18-25s; free under 18s except certain holidays. **No credit cards. Clairière de l'Armistice** *route de Soissons (03.44.85.14.18).* **Open** (museum) *Apr-15 Oct* 9am-12.15pm, 2-6pm; *16 Oct-Mar* 9-11.45am, 2-5pm Mon, Wed-Sun. **Admission** 10F; 6F 7-14s; free under 7s. **No credit cards. Château de Pierrefonds** *60350 Pierrefonds (03.44.42.72.72).* 14km from Compiègne by D973. *Nov-Apr* 10am-12.30pm, 2-5pm Mon-Sat; 10am-5.30pm Sun; *May-Oct* 10am-6pm daily. **Admission** 32F; 21F students, 12-25s; free under 12s. **No credit cards.**

Fontainebleau

Fontainebleau would be just another sleepy provincial French town were it not for the sumptuous palace which dominates the town. In 1528 François 1er brought in Italian artists and craftsmen – including Rosso and Primaticcio – to help architect Gilles le Breton transform it from a neglected royal lodge into the finest Italian Mannerist palace in France. This style is noted for its grotesqueries, contorted figures and crazy fireplaces, which gave sculptors an ideal chance to show off their virtuosity, still visible in the Ballroom and Long Gallery.

Other monarchs added their own touches, so that much of the palace's charm comes from its very disunity of design. Henri IV added two courtyards and a tennis court, Louis XIII added the celebrated double-horseshoe staircase that dominates the principal 'farewell' courtyard, Louis XIV and XV added further classical trimmings, while Napoléon redecorated a suite of rooms in Empire Style.

With its ravines, rocky outcrops and mix of forest and sandy heath, the **Fontainebleau Forest**, where François 1er liked to hunt, is the wildest slice of nature near to Paris and now popular with Parisian weekenders for walking, cycling, riding and rock climbing. A free map, available from the tourist office (4 rue Royale/01.60.74.99.99), marks all the paths. Bikes can be hired from Georges Mullot at the Gare de Fontainebleau (01.64.22.36.14). A good starting-off point is off the road N7 from **Barbizon** (*see below* **Rousseau & Millet**) to the Gorges d'Apremont.

Further Information

77300 Fontainebleau (01.60.71.50.70). 60km from Paris by A6, then N7. By train Gare de Lyon to Fontainebleau-Avon (50 mins), then bus marked Château. **Open** *Nov-Apr* 9.30am-12.30pm, 2-5pm Mon, Wed-Sun; *May, June, Sept, Oct* 9.30am-5pm Mon, Wed-Sun; *July, Aug* 9.30am-6pm Mon, Wed-Sun. **Admission** 35F; 23F 18-25s, all on Sun; free under-18s. **Credit** MC, V.

Vaux-Le-Vicomte

Less well-known than Versailles or Fontainebleau, this château has a story almost as interesting as the building itself. Nicholas Fouquet (1615-1680), protégé of the ultra-powerful Cardinal Mazarin, bought the site in 1641. In 1653 he was named *Surintendant des Finances*, and set about building himself an abode to match his position. He assembled three of France's most talented men for the job: painter Charles Lebrun, architect Louis Le Vau and landscape gardener André Le Nôtre.

In 1661 Fouquet held a huge soirée to inaugurate his château and invited the King. They were entertained by jewel-encrusted elephants and spectacular imported Chinese fireworks. Lully wrote music for the occasion, and Molière a comedy. The King, who was 23 and ruling *de facto* for the first time, was outraged by the way in which Fouquet's grandeur seemed to overshadow his own. Shortly afterwards Fouquet was arrested, and his embezzlement of state funds exposed in a show trial. His personal effects were taken by the crown and the court sentenced him to exile; Louis XIV changed the sentence to solitary confinement.

As you round the moat, the square, sober frontage doesn't prepare you for the Baroque rear aspect. The most telling symbol of the fallen magnate is the unfinished, domed ceiling in the vast, elliptical Grand Salon, where Lebrun only had time to paint the cloudy sky and one solitary eagle. Fouquet's *grand projet* did live on in one way, however, as it inspired Louis XIV to build Versailles – using Fouquet's architect and workmen to do it.

Watch out for the fountains, which spout from 3pm to 6pm on the second and last Saturday of the month Apr-Oct. The biggest draw however are the candlelit evenings, which transform the château into a palatial jack-o-lantern with hundreds of flickering candles illuminating house and gardens.

Further Information

77950 Maincy (01.64.14.41.90). 60km from Paris by A6 to Fontainebleau exit; follow signs to Melun, then N36 and D215. By coach **Paris-Vision** *run half-day and day trips from Paris (see chapter* **Directory***). Open 13 Mar-11 Nov 10am-1pm, 2-6pm daily.* **Admission** *59F; 47F 6-16s, free under-6s. Candlelit visits May-Mid Oct 8pm-midnight, Thu, Sat.* **Price** *80F; 70F 6-16s.* **Credit** *MC V.*

The Châteaux of the Loire

Seat of power of the Valois kings, who preferred to rule from Amboise and Blois rather than Paris, the Loire valley became the wellspring of the French Renaissance. François 1er was the main instigator, bringing architects, artists and craftsmen from Italy to build his palaces, and musicians and poets to keep him amused. Royal courtiers followed suit with their own elaborate residences. The valley is now an easy weekend trip from Paris: we've concentrated on the area between Chambord

in the east, and Azay-le-Rideau in the west.

The enormous **Château de Chambord** (02.54.50.40.00/02.54.50.40.28) is François 1er's masterpiece, and was probably designed in part by Leonardo da Vinci. It's a magnificent, but also rather playful place, from the ingenious double staircase in the centre – it was possible to go up or down without crossing someone coming the other way – to the wealth of decoration and the 400 draughty rooms. Built in the local white stone, with decorative diamonds and other shapes applied in black slate, its extraordinary forest of turrets, domes and crazy chimneys are brilliantly seen from close up as you walk around the parapet.

In total contrast of scale is the charming **Château de Beauregard** (02.54.70.40.05) nearby at Cellettes. Its main feature is the unusual panelled portrait gallery, depicting in naive style 327 famous men and women. The precious character of the room is accentuated by its fragile, blue and white Dutch Delft tiled floor. The château also boasts the tiny panelled *Cabinet des Grelots* (bells). Outside, the park contains a modern colour-themed garden designed by Gilles Clément.

From here the road to Amboise follows an attractive stretch of the Loire valley, under the looming turrets of the **Château de Chaumont** (02.54.51.26.26) and past numerous roadside wine cellars dug into the tufa cliffs (with equally numerous opportunities to indulge). Chaumont is worth visiting for its innovative annual garden festival (mid-June-mid-Oct) when garden designers, artists and architects create special gardens on a set theme.

The lively town of Amboise, not far from Tours, grew up at a strategic crossing point on the Loire. The **Château Royal d'Amboise** (02.47.57.00.98) was built within the walls of a medieval stronghold, although today only a (still considerable) fraction of Louis XI's and Charles VIII's complex remains. The château's interiors span several styles from vaulted Gothic to Empire. Across the gardens from the main wing, the exquisite Gothic chapel has a richly carved portal, fine vaulted interior and, supposedly, the tomb of Leonardo da Vinci.

It's a short walk up the hill, past several cave dwellings, to reach the fascinating **Clos Luce** (02.47.57.62.88), the Renaissance manor house where Leonardo lived at the invitation of François 1er for the three years before his death in 1519. There's an enduring myth of a – so far undiscovered – tunnel linking the two. The museum concentrates on Leonardo as Renaissance Man: artist, engineer and inventor. It is part furnished as a period manor, part filled with models derived from Leonardo's drawings of inventions, from a helicopter to a hydraulic drilling machine. An oddity just outside town is the pagoda of **Chanteloup**, an eccentric eighteenth-century edifice built when chinoiserie was the rage, in the grounds of a now-demolished château. There's a panoramic view from the top too.

*Inside the **Cyclope** (see p292).*

South of Amboise, the **Château de Chenonceau** (02.47.23.90.07) occupies a unique site on a bridge spanning the river Cher. Henri II gave the château to his beautiful mistress Diane de Poitiers, until she was forced to give it up to a jealous Catherine de Médicis, who commissioned Philibert Delorme to add the three-storey gallery that extends across the river. Chenonceau is packed with tourists in summer, its watery views, many original ceilings and fireplaces, fine tapestries and paintings (including Diane de Poitiers by Primaticcio) are well worth seeing.

Seeming to rise directly out of the water, **Azay-le-Rideau** (02.47.45.42.04), built on an island in the river Indre west of Tours, must be everyone's idea of a fairytale castle. Built between 1518 and 1527 by Gilles Berthelot, the king's treasurer, it combines the turrets of a medieval fortress with the new style of the Italian Renaissance.

At **Villandry** (02.47.50.02.09), it's not the château but the Renaissance gardens that are of interest. One part is a typical formal garden of geometrical shapes made with neatly cut hedges and flowers; much more unusual is the *jardin potager*, where the neat patterns are done not with flowers but with artichokes, cabbages and other vegetables in what has to be the ultimate kitchen garden.

Further Information

The best way to explore the region is by car. Take the A10 to Blois (182km), or leave at Mer for Chambord. An attractive route follows the Loire from Blois to Amboise and Tours, along the D761. **Where to Stay & Eat** The small town of Amboise is a pleasant, centrally placed stopping-off point with several hotels. Within the town, try the *Lion d'Or* (17 quai Charles-Guinot/02.47.57.00.23. Double 300F-320F) which also has a restaurant. For something a little grander, try the *Château de Pray* (02.47.57.23.67) at Chargé, 3km outside the town (double 550F-720F). *L'Epicerie* (46 pl Michel-Debré /02.47.57.08.94) is a pleasant restaurant with 110F, 130F, 160F and 220F *menus*. There are more hotels and restaurants at Tours.

Artists' Haunts

Van Gogh at Auvers-sur-Oise

95430 Auvers-sur-Oise. 35km north of Paris by A15, exit 7 take N184 towards Chantilly, exit Méry-sur-Oise for Auvers. *By train* Gare du Nord or Gare St-Lazare direction Pontoise, change at Persan-Beaumont or Creil, *or* RER A Cergy-Préfecture, then bus for Butry, stopping at Auvers-sur-Oise. Paris Vision (*see chapter* **Directory**) runs coach tours from Paris. **Office de Tourisme** *Les Colombières, rue de la Sansonne* (01.30.36.10.06). **Open** 9.30am-12.30pm, 2-5pm (*Apr-Oct* until 6pm) daily. **Atelier de Daubigny** *61 rue Daubigny* (01.34.48.03.03). **Open** *Easter-1 Nov* 2-6.30pm Wed-Sun, bank holidays. **Admission** 25F; free under-12s. **Château d'Auvers** *rue de Léry* (01.34.48.48.50). **Open** *May-Oct* 10am-6.30pm Tue-Sun; *Nov-Apr* 10.30am-4pm Tue-Sun. **Admission** 55F-60F; 45-50F over-60s; 40F 6-25s; free under-6s. **Credit** AmEx, MC, V. **Musée de l'Absinthe** *44 rue Callé* (01.30.36.83.26). **Open** *June-Sept* 11am-6pm Wed-Sun; *Oct-May* 11am-6pm Sat, Sun. **Admission** 25F; 20F students, over-60s; 10F 6-15s. **Musée Daubigny** *Manoir des Colombières, rue de la Sansonne* (01.30.36.80.20). **Open** *May-Oct* 2-6pm Wed-Sun; *Nov-Apr* 2.30-6pm Wed-Sun. **Admission** 20F; free under 16s. **Maison de Van Gogh** *Auberge Ravoux, pl de la Mairie* (01.30.36.60.60). **Open** 10am-6pm Tue-Sun. **Admission** 30F; free under-18s; 60F family ticket.

Auvers-sur-Oise has become synonymous with the name of Van Gogh, who rented a room here at the **Auberge Ravoux** on 20 May 1890, to escape the noise of Paris. During his stay, he executed over 60 paintings and sketches. On 27 July, he fired a bullet into his chest, and died two days later. He is buried in the cemetery, alongside his brother, Theo. If you are not familiar with Van Gogh's works, go to the **Musée d'Orsay** first, as the visit is an evocation of the village as it was during the artist's stay, although there is also a well-prepared video. Upstairs, in perfectly preserved decrepitude, is the tiny attic room where he stayed (the cheapest at 3.50F a day) and next to it the room of a fellow artist, simply furnished as it would have been at the time: a bed, a chair and a washstand.

Equally worth visiting is the **Atelier de Daubigny**, built by the successful Barbizon school artist in 1861. The house and studio are decorated with murals painted by Daubigny, his son and daughter and his friends Corot and Daumier.

Despite being so near to Paris, Auvers retains a surprising degree of rustic charm. The cornfields, where Van Gogh executed his famous last painting *Crows*, the town hall, which he painted on Bastille day, and the medieval church, have barely changed. Cézanne also stayed here for 18 months between 1872 and 1874, not far from the house of Doctor Gachet, who was the subject of portraits by both him and Van Gogh. A system of illustrated panels around town lets you compare the paintings to their locations today.

The recently renovated seventeenth-century **Château d'Auvers** offers an audio-visual display about the Impressionists, while the **Musée de l'Absinthe** is devoted to the

Princes, paupers, *folies de grandeurs*

The Ile de France has a wealth of lesser châteaux, ranging from medieval to nineteenth-century high living. Opening times vary, so ring first. Smaller châteaux have guided tours, usually in French. No credit cards, unless otherwise stated.

East along the Marne

Château de Champs-sur-Marne
(01.60.05.24.43). 20km from Paris. **Open** *Apr-Sept* 10am-noon, 1.30pm-4.30pm Mon, Wed-Fri; 10am-noon, 1.30pm-6pm Sat-Sun; *Oct-Mar* 10am-noon, 1.30pm-4.30pm Mon, Wed-Sat; 10am-noon, 1.30pm-5pm Sun. **Admission** 32F; 21F 12-25s; free under-12s.
The richly furnished, early eighteenth-century château was built for wealthy financiers. The Salon Chinois (featured in the film *Ridicule*) is furnished with chairs covered in Beauvais tapestries illustrating the fables of La Fontaine. The oval Salon de Musique (chamber music concerts Sundays) offers a magical view over the formal gardens, a feast of perspectives and hedges.

Château de Ferrières
(01.64.66.31.25). 24km from Paris. **Guided visits** *May-Sept* 2-7pm Wed-Sun; *Oct-Apr* 2-5m Wed, Sat-Sun. **Admission** 32F; 25F over-60s, 12-16s; free under-12s. *Park only* 16F; free under-12s.
The largest 'English' country house in France, designed by Joseph Paxton of Crystal Palace fame in 1859 for banker James de Rothschild in a Victorian, Gothic revisiting of the Italian Renaissance. Guy and Marie-Hélène de Rothschild took over in 1959 and donated it to the University of Paris.

Château de Guermantes
(01.64.30.00.94). 27km from Paris. **Guided tours** *Apr-Oct* 2-6pm Sat, Sun, bank holidays. **Admission** 30F; free under-12s.
The romantic name inspired Marcel Proust, a friend of the family, to use it for one of the heroines in *A la recherche…* The early seventeenth-century château has souvenirs of the writer, as well as remarkable, unrestored Louis XIII painted rooms. The most spectacular was added a century later: a 31m-long gallery, called *La Belle inutile* because of its (highly telegenic) beauty and lack of practical purpose.

South towards Fontainebleau

Courances
(01.64.98.42.18/01.40.62.07.62). 50 km from Paris. **Open** *Apr-Oct* 2-6pm Sat, Sun, public holidays. **Admission** 40F; free under-13s; park only 20F.
Courances' famous Le Nôtre water gardens are fed by 16 different springs. The view of the sixteenth-century château, transformed under Louis XIII, mirrored in the lake and canals is exceptional. The highlight is the Galerie des Singes (monkey hall), named for the tapestries which decorate it.

Grosbois
Boissy-St-Léger (01.4510.24.24). RER A to Boissy-St-Léger then 5km by taxi. (7km from Créteil). **Guided tours** *15 Mar-15 Dec* 2-5pm Sun, bank holidays. **Admission** 25F; 20F 5-12s; free under-5s.

Maisons-Lafitte: *more than a racecourse.*

With its seventeenth-century rose-coloured brick, Grosbois is attractive from the main road. However, the interior was redesigned during the Napoleonic era for one of his stalwarts, Maréchal Berthier. Only the frescoed dining room by Abraham Bosse has retained its original Louis XIII decoration; the rest is a splendid collection of Napoleonic furniture, works by Winterhalter, Canova and Gérard, and period war memorabilia. Park closed to the public.

West along the Chevreuse

Courson
Courson-Monteloup (01.64.58.90.12). 35km from Paris. **Open** *15 Mar-15 Nov* 2-6pm Sun, public holidays. **Admission** 42F; 29F 6-14s, students, over-60s; free under-6s. Park only 22F-28F.
Courson is famous throughout Europe for its *Journées des Plantes* in May and October, with over 200 green-fingered stands. The park was redesigned *à l'anglaise* in the 1830s by Berthault, Empress Joséphine's landscape gardener, with splendid trees, rhododendrons and lilies. Château and hamlet were built in 1676 by a pupil of Le Vau, as a typically sumptuous nobleman's residence not too far from Versailles.

Le Marais
St-Chéron (01.64.58.96.01). 40km from Paris. **Open** *15 Mar-15 Nov* 2-6.30pm Sun, bank holidays. **Admission** 25F; free under-14s.
The grandiose château was designed by Barre in the 1770s in solemn Neo-Classical style. The château itself is not

open to the public, as it is still inhabited by the last of the Talleyrands, owners since 1899, but the adjacent museum is filled with family portraits and souvenirs of last century. The staff are mostly family retainers, anxious to share news of Madame in the big house; all this gives the place an unusually authentic, lived-in atmosphere. A walk round the lake in the formal grounds completes the idyll.

Breteuil

Choisiel (01.30.52.05.02/11). 35km from Paris. **Open** 2.30-5.30pm Mon-Sat; 11am-5.30pm Sun, bank holidays. **Admission** 57F; 47F 6-18s, students, over-60s; free under-6s. **Credit** MC, V.

The park's plunging view over the Chevreuse valley is worth the trip, as are its 175 acres of gardens with splendid alleys leading past a medieval dovecote to two lakes. The Louis XIII period château is fine enough, but in their zeal to bring the place to life, the family have let in a troupe of unimpressive wax figures. Prize possesion (apart from Louis XVIII's wheelchair) is the jewelled Teschen table, given to the Breteuils for mediation in the Treaty of Teschen in 1779.

Dampierre

(01.30.52.53.24). 40km from Paris. **Guided tours** *15 Apr-15 Oct* 2-6pm Mon-Sat; 11am-noon, 2-6.30pm Sun, public holidays. **Admission** 50F; 38F students, over-60s; 10F under-10s. **No credit cards.**

Dampierre nestles in a wooded dell against a lush backdrop of parkland. The château was designed 1675-83 by Jules Hardouin-Mansart. The interior boasts remarkable ornate salons, panelled dining room and royal suite, where Louis XIV, XV and XVI stayed. In the pseudo-Roman Salle de Minerve, a kitsch 3m copy of Phidias' *Minerva* is an impressive centrepiece to Ingres' vast allegorical fresco *L'Age d'Or.*

Rambouillet

(01.34.83.00.25). 50km from Paris. **Open** *château Apr-Sept* 10-11.30am, 2-5.25pm; *Oct-Mar* 10-11.30am, 2-4.20pm. **Admission** 32F; 21F 12-25s; free under-12s. **No credit cards.**

Marie Antoinette called it *'La Crapaudière'* (loosely, Toad Hall). Louis XVI, who hunted in the surrounding forest, tried to win her over with a milking parlour: the resulting Neo-Classical temple is the last word in upmarket bovine architecture. The huge park also contains the national sheep farm, set up by Louis XVI to produce fine Merino wool. The château, an ungracious mix of medieval towers and duller eighteenth-century additions, is still an official residence. From here de Gaulle ordered the final march on Paris in 1944.

North-West along the Seine

Maisons-Laffitte

(01.39.62.01.49). RER A Maisons-Laffitte. **Open** *Apr-Oct* 10am-noon, 1.30-6pm Mon, Wed-Sun. *Nov-Mar* 10am-noon; 1.20-5pm Mon, Wed-Sun. **Admission** 32F; 21F 12-25s; free under-12s.

Maisons-Laffitte is now synonymous with the nearby race-course, but the château's 1651 housewarming was attended by fourteen-year-old Louis XIV. François Mansart's design is a model of French classical architecture. If the interior appears rather austere, its proportions are magnificent and sculptures, particularly by Jacques Sarrazin, outstanding. In 1818 Laffitte, a banker, bought the château and gave it his name. Later he had to sell everything, even the park, which became a luxury housing estate.

Malmaison

av du Château, Rueil-Malmaison (01.41.29.05.55). *Mº La Défense, then bus 258.* **Open** *Apr-Sept* 10am-noon, 1.30-5pm Mon, Wed-Fri; 10am-5.30pm Sat-Sun. *Oct-Mar* 10am-5pm Sat-Sun. **Admission** 30F; 20F 18-25s; free under-18s.

Empress Joséphine bought this place in 1799 for a fortune, and spent another fortune decorating it *à la mode* and turning the entrance into a military tent to make Napoléon feel he was on a campaign. After their divorce in 1809, he left the house to Joséphine, where she lived in debt until her death in 1814. After his defeat at Waterloo Napoléon paid a wistful last visit on his way to exile.

La Roche Guyon

1 rue de l'Audience, 95780 La Roche-Guyon (01.34.79.74.42). 50km from Paris. **Guided tours** *15 Jan-15 Dec* 10am-6pm daily. **Admission** 40F; 25F 6-25s, over-60s; free under-6s. **Credit** AmEx, MC, V.

Built spectacularly into the cliffs where the Seine cuts its way through the chalk landscape, La Roche Guyon has existed since the thirteenth century. A fascinating mix of styles from medieval hilltop keep to eighteenth century salons, the château is largely empty, but the presentation is suberb and the secret troglodyte aspect delightful. During World War II, Rommel set up HQ in the tunnels, digging blockhouses which remain eerily atmospheric, as does the chapel hacked out of the side of the cliff. To get the most out of the visit you have to be good at climbing long spiral staircases.

Rambouillet, *Louis XIV's hunting ground.*

Chartres cathedral, *an inspiring sight for pilgrims ancient and modern.*

Impressionists' favourite (now banned) drink, depicted by Monet, Van Gogh and many others.

Monet at Giverny

27620 Giverny. 80km west of Paris by A13 to Bonnières and D201 to Giverny. By train from Gare St-Lazare to Vernon 45 mins; then 5km taxi or bus. **Musée Claude Monet** *(02.32.51.28.21).* **Open** *Apr-Oct* 10am-6pm Tue-Sun. Open Easter and Whit Monday. **Admission** 35F; 25F students; 20F 7-12s; free under-7s. **Credit** (gift shop only) AmEx, MC, V. **Musée Américain Giverny** *99 rue Claude Monet (02.32.51.94.65).* **Open** *Apr-Oct* 10am-6pm Tue-Sun. **Admission** 35F; 20F students, over 60s; 15F 7-12s; free under-7s. **Wheelchair access.**

In 1883, Claude Monet moved his large personal entourage (one mistress, eight children) to Giverny, a rural retreat north-west of Paris. He died in 1926, having immortalised both his flower garden and the water lilies beneath his Japanese bridge. In 1966, Michel Monet donated his father's property to the Académie des Beaux-Arts, which transformed the modest estate into the major tourist site it is today. Don't be put off by the tour buses in the car park or by the outrageously enormous gift shop – the natural charm of the pink-brick house, with its cornflower-blue and yellow kitchen, and the rare glory of the gardens survive intact. A little tunnel leads (under the road) between the flower-filled Clos Normand garden in front of the house to the Japanese water garden, with all the pools, canals, little green bridges, the punt, willows and water lilies, familiar from the paintings. Up the road, the modern **Musée Americain Giverny** is devoted to the often sugary work of American artists who came to France, inspired by the Impressionists.

Rousseau & Millet at Barbizon

77630 Barbizon. 57km from Paris by A6, then N7 and D64; 10km from Fontainebleau. **Office du Tourisme** *55 Grande rue (01.60.66.41.87).* **Open** 1-5pm Wed-Fri; 11am-12.30pm, 2-5pm Sat, Sun. **Maison et Atelier Jean-François Millet** *27 Grande rue (01.60.66.21.55).* **Open** 9.30am-12.30pm, 2-5.30pm Mon, Wed-Sun.

Admission free. **Musée de l'Auberge du Père Ganne** *92 Grande rue, (01.60.66.22.27).* **Open** *Apr-Oct* 10am-12.30pm, 2-6pm Mon, Wed-Fri; 10am-6pm Sat, Sun; *Nov-Mar* 10am-12.30pm, 2-5pm Mon, Wed-Fri; 10am-5pm Sat, Sun. **Admission** 25F, 13F 12-25s, students; free under 12s. **Credit** MC, V. **Le Cyclope** *2km outside Milly-la-Forêt.* **Open** *May-Oct* 10.15am-4.15pm Fri (must book ahead on 01.64.98.83.17)*;* 11am-5pm Sat; 11am-5.45pm Sun (*Oct* last visit Sat, Sun 4.30pm)

A rural hamlet straggling along a single country lane into the forest of **Fontainebleau**, Barbizon was an ideal sanctuary for pioneers Corot, Théodore Rousseau, Daubigny (*see above* **Auvers-sur-Oise**) and Millet. From the 1830s onwards, these artists – the Barbizon school – demonstrated a new concern in painting peasant life and landscape as they really were, and paved the way for the Impressionists. The three main sights at Barbizon are all on the Grande rue, and although it's enormously touristy, some of the atmosphere remains. Commemorative plaques point out who lived where.

Hordes of other artists soon followed them to Barbizon. Many stayed at the **Auberge du Père Ganne** inn, painting on the walls and furniture of the long-suffering (or perhaps far-sighted) Ganne, in lieu of rent. The Auberge now contains the municipal art collection as well as a near-legendary sideboard painted by some of the habitués. The **Office du Tourisme** is in the former house of Théodore Rousseau. Prints and drawings by Millet and his followers can be seen in the **Maison et atelier Jean-François Millet.** Millet moved here in 1849 to escape cholera in Paris and remained, living very simply, for the rest of his life, painting the local people and their work in the fields, to which he ascribed an almost saintly value. Millet and Rousseau are both buried in the churchyard at nearby Chailly.

Not far from Barbizon, but coming from a quite different art perspective, is an extraordinary twentieth-century monster. *The Cyclope*, a vast, shimmering, clanking confection of mirrors and iron cogs, lurks down a forest track, rumbling and spitting out balls. The creature was the life work of Swiss artist Jean Tinguely, who began it in 1969, in a rare collaboration with several fellow artists including Nikki de

Saint Phalle (with whom he also created the Stravinsky Fountain in Paris), although it was only finished after his death and opened to the public in 1994. Inside it's as if a DIY addict had gone mad, as machines carry aluminium balls up through the body before ejecting them down the tongue, and a narrow passage leads you past various art works including Spoerri's *Chambre de Bonne* and Eva Aeppli's Holocaust memorial. The exterior can be viewed from behind a fence; reserve with the Office du Tourisme to visit the interior.

Dieppe & Varengeville

Should you long for the sea, the beaches of Dieppe and the 'Alabaster Coast' of northern Normandy, an easy weekend trip, can be combined with a visit to the Norman capital of Rouen (*see below*).

An important port since the Middle Ages, **Dieppe** is also the nearest seaside town to Paris, ideal for a dip and a fish meal. The charming area around the harbour along **quai Henri IV** is lined with little fish restaurants (endless variations on mussels, skate and sole, plus cider), and prettier than ever now that ferries from Britain go to a new container port and the old railway terminal has been demolished. At one end the **Tour des Crabes** is the last remnant of fortified wall. The interesting maze of old streets between the harbour and the newer quarters fronting the promenade contains numerous sailors' houses built in brick with wrought-iron balconies, many of which are now being renovated, and the fine Gothic churches of **St-Jacques**, once a starting point for pilgrimage to Compostella (note the pilgrims' shell motifs) and **St-Rémi**. The beach is shingle except at low tide (great for swimming, less so for the feet), but the seafront offers plenty of activities for kids, with mini golf, pony rides, a children's beach and lawns filled with kite flyers. The beach is overlooked from the cliff top at one end by the gloomy **Château de Dieppe** (02.35.84.19.76), now the municipal museum, known for its collection of alabasters and paintings by Pissarro and Braque.

Leave town by the coast road for a twisting, scenic drive along the cliff. Just along the coast to the west is chic **Varengeville-sur-Mer**, celebrated for its cliff-top churchyard where Cubist painter Georges Braque (who also designed one of the stained-glass windows in the church) and composer Albert Roussel are buried, for the **Parc du Bois des Moustiers** (02.35.85.10.02), planted by Lutyens and Gertrude Jekyll, famed for its rhododendrons and views, as well as for the unusual sixteenth-century Renaissance **Manoir d'Ango** (02.35.85.14.80/open Apr-Sept, daily) which has a galleried courtyard and unusual dovecote. A steep, narrow lane leads down to a sandy cove. On the headland, the **Phare d'Ailly** lighthouse is open for visits (02.35.85.11.19).

Also just outside Dieppe (8km south) is the decorative early seventeenth-century **Château de Miromesnil** (02.35.85.02.80; open 2-6pm May-18 Oct; 20F-30F) where the writer Guy de Maupassant was born in 1850, and which has a historic kitchen garden. Nearby, dominating a little hill at **Arques la Bataille**, are the ruins of a tenth-century castle.

Further information

Getting there *By car* (170km north-west) take the A13 to Rouen and then the N27. *By train* from Gare St-Lazare (2 1/2 hours). **Office du Tourisme de Dieppe** *Pont Jehan Ango, 76204 Dieppe (02.32.14.40.60).* **Open** *Apr-Sept* 9am-noon, 2-6pm daily; *Oct-Mar* 9am-noon, 2-6pm Mon-Sat.

Cathedral Cities

Beauvais

Getting there *By car* 75km from Paris by A16 or N1. *By train* from Gare du Nord.
Office du Tourisme 1 rue Beauregard, 60000 Beauvais (03.44.15.30.30). **Open** *Apr-Oct* 10am-1pm, 2-6pm Mon, Sun; 9.30am-7pm. Tue-Sat. *Nov-Mar* 10am-1pm, 2-6pm Mon, 9.30am-6.30pm Tue-Sat; 10am-1.20pm Sun. **Where to eat** Two reliable addresses are restaurant-bar **Le Marignan** (1 rue Malherbe/ 03.44.48.15.15), and Alsatian brasserie **Taverne du Maître Kanter** (16 rue Pierre Jacoby/ 03.44.06.32.72).

Beauvais cathedral is both one of the strangest and most impressive of French cathedrals. It has the tallest Gothic vault in the world and a spectacular crown of flying buttresses. The feat entailed numerous construction problems, as first the choir had to be rebuilt – you can still see where an extra column was added between the arches – and then the spire collapsed. The nave was never built at all; the church suddenly stops in a wall at the transept, which only accentuates the impression of verticality. Left of the choir is a curious astrological clock, made in the 1860s by a local watchmaker Lucien-Auguste Vérité and a typically nineteenth-century extravagance of turned wood, gilt, dials and automata; around the corner is a clock dating from the fourteenth century. Next to the cathedral, a medieval gateway leads into the sixteenth-century bishop's palace, now the **Musée Départemental de l'Oise** (03.44.11.43.83), tracing the region's illustrious heritage in wood and stone sculptures from destroyed houses and churches, Nabis paintings and Art Nouveau furniture and the tapestries for which Beauvais was famed. The tapestry industry reached its peak in the eighteenth century and then stopped when the factory was evacuated to Aubusson in 1939, but has recently been revived at the **Manufacture Nationale de la Tapisserie** (24 rue Henri Brispot/03.44.05.14.28), where you can watch weavers making tapestries under natural light (2-4pm Tue-Thur). Most of Beauvais was flattened by bombing in World War II, but the centre was rebuilt not unpleasantly in the 50s in a series of low-rise squares and shopping streets. One other impressive medieval survivor remains, the **Eglise St-Etienne**, a mix of Romanesque and Gothic styles, elaborate gargoyles sticking out in the centre of a traffic island.

Chartres

28005 Chartres. 88km from Paris by A11 direction Le Mans, exit Chartres. *By train* from Gare Montparnasse.
Office du Tourisme *pl de la Cathédrale, (02.37.21.50.00).* **Open** *Apr-Sept* 9am-7pm Mon-Sat; 9.30am-5.30pm Sun; *Oct-Mar* 10am-6pm Mon-Sat; 10am-1pm, 2.30-4.30pm Sun. **Where to eat** *La Vieille Maison* (5 rue au Lait/ 02.37.34.10.67) is just that, but the classical cooking is excellent and desserts delicious; the 165F *menu* offers good value for cooking and service of this calibre. Simpler, but with an attractive setting facing the cathedral, the *Café Serpente* (2 Cloître Notre Dame/ 02.37.21.68.81) triples as café, tea room and restaurant.

Looming over a flat agricultural plain, **Chartres Cathedral** was described by Rodin as the 'French Acropolis'. Certainly, with its two uneven spires – the stubbier from the twelfth century, the taller one completed only in the sixteenth century – and doorways bristling with sculpture, the cathedral has an enormous amount of slightly wonky charm and is a pristine example of Early Gothic art. Chartres was a pilgrimage site long before the present cathedral was built, ever since the Sacra Camisia (said to be the Virgin Mary's lying-in garment and now displayed in the Cathedral Treasury) was donated to the city in 876 by the Carolingian King Charles I, 'the Bald'. When the church caught fire in 1194, local burghers clubbed together to reconstruct it, taking St-Denis as the model for the new west front, 'the royal portal' with its three richly sculpted doorways. On the cusp between Romanesque and Gothic, the stylised, elongated figure columns above geometric patterns still form part of the door structure. Be sure to walk all round the cathedral as there are two other interesting portals which were added slightly later: the north transept door is a curious, faintly top-heavy conconcoction of lively figures and slight columns, and there's also an unusual clock.

Inside yet another era of sculpture is represented in the lively, sixteenth-century scenes of the life of Christ that surround the choir. Note also the circular labyrinth of black and white stones in the floor; such mazes used to exist in most cathedrals but have now mostly been destroyed. Chartres is above all famed for its stained-glass windows depicting Biblical scenes, saints and medieval trades in brilliant 'Chartres blue', punctuated by rich reds. To learn all about them, take one of the erudite and entertaining tours given in English by Malcolm Miller, who specialises in deciphering the medieval picture codes. Between Easter and mid-Nov, Mr Miller's tours are at noon and 2.45pm Mon-Sat (40F adults, 20F students). At other times phone 02.37.28.15.58. The cathedral may dominate the town from a distance, but once in the town centre's narrow medieval streets, with their overhanging gables, glimpses of it are only occasional. Wander past the iron-framed market hall, down to the river Eure, crossed by a string of attractive old bridges, past the partly Romanesque **Eglise St-André** and down the rue des Tanneries that runs along the banks. There's more fine stained glass in the thirteenth-century **Eglise St-Pierre**. There's a good view from the Jardin de l'Evêché, located at the back of the cathedral and adjoining the **Musée des Beaux-Arts** (02.37.36.41.39/29 Cloître Notre-Dame). Housed in the former Bishop's palace, the collection includes fine eighteenth-century French paintings by Boucher and Watteau, and a large array of medieval sculpture.

The other main tourist attraction is very much of this century and a reminder that Chartres towers over the Beauce region, known as the 'bread basket of France' for its prairie-like expanses of wheat. The **COMPA** agricultural museum (pont de Maenvilliers/02.37.36.11.30) in a converted engine shed near the station has a small, but lively presentation of the history of agriculture and food (and consequently society) from 50,000BC to today, with the emphasis on machinery, from vintage tractors and threshing machines to old fridges. For curiosity value, you can also visit (Apr-Oct) the **Maison Picassiette** (22 rue de Repos/02.37.34.10.78) just outside the centre, a colourful naïve mosaic house constructed with broken pottery by a former civil servant.

Reims

51100 Reims. 150km by A4. *By train* from Gare de l'Est about 1/2 hour. **Office du Tourisme** *2 rue Guillaume-de-Machault, (03.26.77.45.25).* **Open** *Oct-Easter* 9am-6.30pm Mon-Sat; 9.30am-5.30pm Sun; *Easter-June, Sept* 9am-7.30pm Mon-Sat; 9.30am-6.30pm Sun; *July-Aug* 9am-8pm Mon-Sat; 9.30am-7pm Sun. **Where to eat** Haute-cuisine mecca is Gérard Boyer's *Château des Crayères* (64 bd Henri-Vanier/03.26.82.80.80) in a Second Empire château to the south-east of town. Boyer no longer owns the lively bistro *Au Petit Comptoir* (17 rue de Mars/

03.26.40.58.58), but the chef has stayed on. Within town there are numerous brasseries, restaurants and cafés around pl Drouet d'Erlon.

Begun in the thirteenth century, the **Cathédrale Notre-Dame** is of dual importance to the French, as the coronation church of most monarchs since Clovis in 496 and for the richness of its Gothic decoration. Thousands of figures on the portals and the Kings of Judea high above the rose window show how sculptural style developed over the century. Heavy shelling in World War I, together with erosion, means that many of the carvings have been replaced by copies; the originals are on show next door in the **Palais de Tau**, the Bishop's palace. It is possible that some of the masons from Chartres also worked on Reims, but the figures generally show more classical influence in their drapery and increasing expressivity. Look out in particular for the winsome 'smiling angel' sculpture and St-Joseph on the facade, while inside take a look at the capitals decorated with elaborate, naturalistic foliage with birds hiding among the leaves.

A few streets south of the cathedral, the **Musée des Beaux-Arts** (8 rue Chanzy/03.26.47.28.44) has some wonderful portraits of German princes by Cranach, 26 canvases by Corot, and the famous *Death of Marat* by Jean-Louis David. From the museum, head down rue Gambetta to the **Basilique de St-Rémi**, which honours the saint who baptised Clovis. The church, built 1007-49, is a fascinating complement to the cathedral. Subsequent alterations allow you to see how the Romanesque evolved into the Gothic. Don't miss the remarkable cycle of ten sixteenth-century tapestries depicting the life of St Rémi in the **Musée St-Rémi** (53 rue Simon/03.26.85.23.36) in the restored monastic buildings next door.

Reims is also, of course, at the heart of the Champagne region. Many of the leading producers of the famous bubbly are based in the town and offer visits of their *caves*, generally an informative insight into the laborious and skilful champagne-making process. The attractive cellars of **Champagne Pommery** (03.26.61.62.63) occupy Gallo-Roman chalk mines 30m below ground and are decorated with Art Nouveau bas-reliefs by Emile Gallé. **Champagne Taittinger** (03.26.85.45.35) doesn't look like much until you descend into the cellars: on the first level are the vaulted Gothic cellars of a former monastery; below are the strangely beautiful, Gallo-Roman chalk quarries.

Rouen

76000 Rouen. 137km west of Paris by A13. *By train* from Gare St-Lazare. **Office du Tourisme** *25 pl de la Cathédrale (02.32.08.32.40).* **Open** *May-Sept* 9am-7pm Mon-Sat; 9.30am-12.30pm, 2.30-6.30pm Sun; *Oct-Apr* 9am-6.30pm Mon-Sat; 10am-1pm Sun. **Eating** Best-known gourmet restaurant is fish specialist *Gill* (9 quai de la Bourse/02.35.71.16.14); there are several cheaper bistros, especially on pl du Vieux-Marché, or the quietly formal *L'Orangerie* (2 rue Thomas-Corneille/02.35.88.43.97).

The capital of Normandy is a cathedral town of contrasts. The centre retains lots of drunken half-timbered buildings and narrow streets, while the port areas by the Seine were almost totally destroyed by bombing during the war. Begun at the start of the thirteenth century, the **Cathédrale Notre-Dame**, depicted at all times of day by Monet, spans the Gothic periods. The north tower dates from the early period while the more Flamboyant Tour de Beurre is from the late fifteenth century. Nearby the famous Gros-Horloge gateway, with its ornamental clock over the busy medieval rue du Gros Horloge, leads to picturesque streets of half-timbered houses.

Two more Gothic churches are worth a visit, the **Eglise St-Ouen** and the **Eglise St-Maclou**, as well as an enormously fanciful Flamboyant Gothic **Palais de Justice**. The striking contemporary **Eglise Ste-Jeanne d'Arc**, adjoining a funky modern market hall on place du Vieux-Marché is a boat-shaped structure with a swooping wooden roof and stained glass windows recuperated from a bombed city church. The recently renovated **Musée des Beaux Arts**

Lille, *a provincial city with something for everyone – and it doesn't close down at 9pm.*

(26 bis rue Jean Le Canuet/02.35.71.28.40) numbers works by Gérard David, Velázquez, Perugino and Caravaggio, some wonderful oil studies by Géricault (a native of Rouen) and Impressionist paintings by Monet and Sisley.

Troyes

10014 Troyes. 150km southeast of Paris by A6 and A5. *By train* from Gare de l'Est (1 hr 15 mins). **Office du Tourisme** *16 bd Carnot, (03.25.82.62.70).* **Open** 9am-12.30pm; 2-6.30pm Mon-Sat. **Branch:** rue Mignard (03.25.82.62.70) **Open** 9am-12.30pm, 2-6.30pm Mon-Sat; 9am-12.30pm, 2-5pm Sun. **Eating** Many consider *Le Clos Juillet* (22 bd du 14-Juillet/03.25.73.31.32) to be the best table in town; its young chef specialises in modernised regional dishes.

Although better known today for its ring of clothes factory discount shops, Troyes still delights with its remarkably preserved half-timbered houses and Gothic churches. Begin your visit with a stroll along the rue Champeaux at the heart of the old city, and don't miss the ruelle des Chats, a narrow lane full of medieval atmosphere which leads to the **Eglise Ste-Madeleine**, the oldest church in the city. Entering the church, you'll be struck by the Flamboyant Gothic rood screen, but the real draw is the superb fifteenth-century stained glass.

Nearby, the **Basilique St-Urbain** was built in 1262-86 on the orders of Pope Urbain IV, a native of Troyes. This church represents an early apogee of Gothic architecture and its ambitions of replacing the heavy masonry of the Romanesque with lacy stone work and glass. Inside, the Virgin with the Grapes is a fine example of local sixteenth-century sculpture. Heading down rue Champeaux to the **Cathédrale St-Pierre St Paul**, pass through café-lined place du Maréchal-Foch, with the handsome seventeenth-century Hôtel de Ville and cross a canal into the oldest part of the city. Part of the impressive facade was done by Martin Chambiges, who also worked on the cathedrals at Sens and Beauvais. The triforium of the choir was one of the first in France to be built with windows instead of blind arcading. The stained glass is a catalogue of styles from the thirteenth to sixteenth centuries; particularly impressive are the richly coloured thirteenth-century scenes from the Virgin's life and the portraits of popes in the choir.

Next door in the former bishop's palace, the **Musée d'Art Moderne** (pl St-Pierre/03.25.76.26.80) contains numerous canvases by Derain, in both his Fauvist and late styles, in addition to works by Braque, Courbet, Degas, Seurat and Vuillard, and modern sculpture and drawings. The **Maison de l'Outil** (7 rue de la Trinité/03.25.73.28.26) has a fascinating array of craftsmen's tools. The **Musée des Beaux-Arts et d'Archéologie** in the Abbaye St-Loup (1 rue Chrétien de Troyes/03.25.76.21.68) next to the cathedral, has fine Gallo-Roman bronzes and a fantastic treasure of arms and jewellery found in a fifth-century Merovingian tomb.

Lille

Lille, one of the great wool towns of medieval Flanders, became part of France only in 1667 and its culture remains Flemish – mussels, chips, beer, gabled houses. While the region has been hit by industrial decline, Lille is a dynamic capital, a crossroads between the Netherlands, France, Belgium, Germany and Great Britain – especially with the new TGV and Channel Tunnel. It is home to futuristic **Eurolille**, the showcase business city by Dutch architect Rem Koolhaas, a lively mix of popular and high culture, from crowded karoake bars to opera, with busy restaurants, cafés and smart shops. This is one of the rare French provincial cities that does not close at 9pm; come here for **La Braderie** in September and the city doesn't close at all.

Vieux Lille is booming: many ornate red-brick and carved-stone Renaissance houses have been renovated, including the beautiful 1652-53 **Vieille Bourse** (old stock exchange), a dignified, arcaded courtyard full of ornate memorials, on the **Grand' Place** at the historic heart of the city. The

adjoining **place du Théâtre** has the nineteenth-century Nouvelle Bourse, a pretty opera house and the rang de Beauregard, a row of late seventeenth-century houses. A pedestrianised street leads from the Grand' Place to **place Rihour** with its cafés and brasseries; the tourist office is housed in the Gothic **Palais Rihour** started in 1454 by Philippe Le Bel, Duc de Bourgogne. Between here and the station is Lille's finest church, the late Gothic **Eglise St-Maurice**. Upmarket shops and antique dealers have moved into **rue de la Grande-Chaussée** and **rue des Chats-Bossus** and quirky small shops into the

Messing about in boats

An unrivalled 8500km network of waterways are a peaceful and picturesque way to discover France from Alsace to Aquitaine. You can even hire a boat in Paris from the Ile de France network from Ourcq Loisirs (bassin de la Villette, 9 quai de Loire, 19th/ 01.42.40.82.10). A more likely starting spot is Auxerre on the Yonne. The Canal du Midi in southern France (from Toulouse to the Med) and Canal du Bourgogne in Burgundy get notoriously crowded in peak summer season, with traffic jams at locks; lesser-known stretches, such as the river Doubs, are much less busy. Many locks (*écluses*) still have lock keepers – less work, but be prepared for the long lunchbreak accorded by the powerful lock keepers' union – or are mechanised, only rarely will you have to open the locks yourself. There are also such feats as Eiffel's bridge canal over the Loire at Briare and the boat-lift at Arzviller connecting the Marne to the Rhine.

Navigable waterways are run by Voies Navigables de France (VNF/03.21.63.24.24). Five companies dominate boat hire France-wide – Connoisseur Cruisers (03.84.64.95.20); Crown Blue Line (04.68.94.52.72); Locaboat Plaisance (03.86.91.72.72); Nichols (02.41.56.46.56), Rive de France (01.41.86.01.01). Boats tend to be modern and well-equipped (hot water, showers, etc) if less picturesque than British narrowboats, although life on board is pretty cramped if you fill them up to the designated capacity. Bilingual navigation manuals are supplied, and it is often possible to hire bikes for onshore exploration.

renovated **place aux Oignons**.

The **Musée de l'Hospice Comtesse** (32 rue de la Monnaie/03.20.49.50.90) in the Renaissance wards, chapel and tiled kitchen of a hospital founded in 1257 by Jeanne, Countess of Flanders, contains displays of Flemish art, local furniture and ceramics, folk art and local history.

You can visit the modest brick house where de Gaulle was born, the **Maison Natale de Charles de Gaulle** (9 rue Princesse/03.28.38.12.05). On the edge of town, across the river Deûle, the **Bois de Boulogne** hides a zoo and the imposing ramparts of the citadel built by Louis XIV's military architect Vauban and still in army use.

Sited south of the town in the boulevards of nineteenth-century Lille, the palatial **Musée des Beaux-Arts** (1 pl de la République/03.20.06.78.00) reopened after renovation with a sparkling new extension in 1997. It has one of the best fine art collections in France, including works by Rubens, Jordaens, El Greco, Goya, David, Delacroix and Courbet, and new Renaissance, medieval and sculpture galleries. East of here, the **Porte de Paris** was put up by Louis XIV after his conquest of the city, as both gateway and triumphal arch, while the **Quartier de St-Saveur**, notorious for its slums in the nineteenth century, has been rehabilitated since the 1950s, and now mixes public housing with conference and trade fair centres.

On the edge of Lille, the **Musée d'Art Moderne** (1 allée du Musée, Villeneuve-d'Ascq/03.20.19.68.68) houses the collection (Picasso, Braque, Léger, Derain, Modigliani) donated by Geneviève and Jean Masurel, along with a modern sculpture park.

La Braderie de Lille

Open First weekend in Sept, 3pm Sat-midnight Sun.
This *Grand Déballage* ('great clear out') attracts two million visitors every year. The centre is closed to vehicles and a 100km network of streets is lined with stalls of jumble and antiques (run by both amateurs and professionals), while mussel shells mount up outside cafés. The fair has existed since the Middle Ages, when townspeople were permitted to clear out their attics, and is still wonderfully anarchic – stallholders turn up a few days ahead to grab the best spot. Many stalls and bars stay open all night, with crowds getting progressively drunker. Everyone seems to lug home some treasure, from Art Deco furniture to rusty tools.

Further information

59002 Lille. 220km from Paris by A1 or 1hr by TGV from Gare du Nord. 104km from Calais or 2hr by Eurostar from London.
Office du Tourisme de Lille *Palais Rihour, pl Rihour (03.20.21.94.21).* **Open** 10am-6pm Mon-Sat; 10am-noon, 2-5pm Sun. **Hotels** *Hôtel de la Treille* (7-9 pl Louise de Bettignies/03.20.55.45.46) is a pleasant modern hotel right in the old city (double 400F), as is the simple *Hôtel de la Paix* (46bis rue de Paris/03.20.54.63.93) near eglise St-Maurice (double 390F-430F). Slightly grander is the *Carlton* (3 rue de Paris/03.20.13.33.13. Double 880F-1800F). **Eating** Vieux Lille is best: try chic if dear *L'Huîtrière* (3 rue des Chats-Bossus/03.20.55.43.41), or pretty brasserie *Alcide* (5 rue des Debris-St-Etienne/03.20.12.06.95), for mussels and other northern dishes. Numerous bistros, African and Italian eateries line the rue de Gand. Stop for tea at the pâtisserie *Méert* (27 rue Esquermoisse/03.20.57.07.44) with fab shopfront and interior.

Directory

Directory

Getting Around

Arriving in Paris

By Eurostar Train
The Eurostar train between London and Paris takes three hours. You must check in 20 minutes in advance. On arrival you are close to the centre of each city. Eurostar trains from London Waterloo (01233 617575) arrive at Gare du Nord (08.36.35.35.39, 2.23F/min; Minitel 3615 SNCF), with easy access to public transport.

Roissy-Charles-de-Gaulle Airport
Most international flights arrive at Roissy-Charles-de-Gaulle airport, 30km north-east of Paris. Its two main terminals are some way apart, so it's important to check which is the right one for your flight if you are flying out. 24-hour information service in English: 01.48.62.22.80.
The **RER B** is the quickest and most reliable way to central Paris (about 45 minutes to St-Michel; 48F single). A new station gives direct access from Terminal 2 (Air France flights); from Terminal 1 you take the free shuttle bus. RER trains run every 15 to 20 minutes, 5.24am-12.09am daily. Call the SNCF (01.53.90.20.20) for more information.
Air France buses (60F) leave every 12-20 minutes, 6am-11pm daily, from both terminals, and stop at Porte Maillot and pl Charles-de-Gaulle (35-50 min trip). Air France buses also run to Gare Montparnasse and Gare de Lyon (70F) every 30 minutes (45-60 minute trip), 7am-9.30pm daily. There is also a bus from Roissy to Orly (70F) which runs every 20-30 minutes, 5.40am-11pm daily. Call 01.41.56.89.00 for more information. The RATP's **Roissybus** (45F) runs every 15 minutes, 5.45am-11pm daily, between the airport and the corner of rue Scribe/rue Auber, near pl de l'Opéra (at least 45 minutes). Call 08.36.68.77.14 (2.23F/min) for info. Tickets are sold on the buses.
The **Airport Shuttle** is a door-to-door minibus service between the airports and your hotel, running 6am-6pm daily at 120F per person; 89F each for two or more (reserve ahead 01.45.38.55.72). **Airport Connection** (01.44.18.36.02) runs a similar service at 150F per person, 85F each for two or more.

By Eurostar Train

Taxis are the least reliable and most expensive means of transport. A **taxi** to central Paris can take 30-60 mins depending on traffic and your point of arrival. Expect to pay 170F-300F, plus 6F per piece of luggage.

Orly Airport
French domestic and several international flights use Orly airport, 18km south of the city. It also has two terminals: Orly-Sud (mainly international flights) and Orly-Ouest (mainly domestic flights). English-speaking information service on 01.49.75.15.15, 6am-11.30pm daily. **Air France buses** (01.41.56.89.00; 45F) leave both terminals every 12 minutes, 5.50am-11pm daily, and stop at Invalides and Montparnasse (30-45 minute trip). There is also a bus from Orly to Roissy-Charles-de-Gaulle (70F) which runs every 20-30 minutes, 6am-11.30pm daily.
The RATP-run **Orlybus** to Denfert-Rochereau leaves every 15 minutes, 5.35am-11pm daily (30-minute trip). Tickets (30F) are available on the bus. A **taxi** into town takes 20-40 minutes and costs 100F-170F, plus 6F per piece of luggage.
The high-speed **Orlyval shuttle train** runs every 7 minutes (6am-10.12pm Mon-Fri; 7am-11pm Sat, Sun) to RER B station Antony (Orlyval and RER together cost 57F); getting to central Paris takes about 40 minutes. Alternatively, catch the courtesy bus to RER C station Pont de Rungis, where you can get an **Orlyrail** train to central Paris (30F). Trains run every 12 minutes, 5.45am-11.10pm daily; 50-minute trip.

Beauvais Tillé Airport
Ryan Air (03.44.11.41.41) runs flights from Dublin and Glasgow to Beauvais, 70km from Paris, with a bus link (50F) to Porte Maillot in 60-90 minutes.

Pontoise-Cormeilles Airport
Debonair (01.53.77.13.39) has flights from Luton to this small airport 40km from Paris. Debonair transfers passengers to the nearest station for travelling into Paris, and hopes to organise bus transfers later in 1999.

By Coach
International coach services arrive at the Gare Routière International Paris-

Galliéni at Bagnolet, 20th (M° Galliéni). For reservations (in English) call **Eurolines** on 08.36.69.52.52 (2.23F/min), or in the UK 01582 404511.

By Car
For travelling to and from the UK with a car, travel options now include driving your car onto **Le Shuttle**, which takes about 25 mins from Folkestone to Calais (01.43.18.62.22/ 08.01.63.03.04). Ferry options include **Brittany Ferries** (08.03.828.828), **P&O Stena Line** (01.53.43.40.00) and **Sealink** (08.01.63.63.01).

Public Transport

The Paris public transport system (**RATP**) consists of **bus** routes, the **Métro** (underground) and the **RER** suburban express railway which interconnects with the Métro inside Paris. Pick up a free map at any Métro station (*see p311*, **Maps**). Paris and its suburbs are divided into five travel zones. Zones 1 and 2 cover the city centre. Information 6am-9pm daily, 08.36.68.77.14/in English 08.36.68.41.14 (2.23F/min). **SNCF**, the French national railway system, serves the French regions and international (*Grandes Lignes*) and the suburbs (*banlieue*).

Tickets & Travel Passes
RATP **tickets** and passes are valid on the Métro, bus and RER. Tickets and *carnets* can be bought at Métro stations, tourist offices and *tabacs* (tobacconists). Keep your ticket in case of spot checks and to exit from RER stations. Individual tickets cost 8F; it's more economical to buy a *carnet* of ten tickets for 52F. **Carte Orange** travel passes (passport photo needed) offer unlimited travel in the relevant zones for a week or month. A weekly *Coupon Hebdomadaire* – valid Mon-Sun inclusive, zones 1-2 – costs 80F. A *Coupon Mensuel* – valid from the first day of the month, zones 1-2 – costs 271F. The *Coupon Hebdomadaire* is better value than *Paris Visite* passes – a three-day pass for zones 1-3 is 120F; a five-day pass is 175F, with discounts on some tourist attractions. A one-day *Mobilis* pass ranges from 30F for zones 1-2 to 110F for zones 1-8 (not including airports). *Ticket Jeunes* allows

student card holders under 26 to travel in zones 1-3 for 20F (zones 1-5 40F) , but only at weekends and holidays. Children under 12 pay half. Public transport prices usually go up a little each July or August.

Métro & RER

The Paris **Métro** is at most times the quickest and cheapest means of travelling around the city. Trains run daily 5.30am-12.30am. Individual lines are numbered, with each direction named after the last stop. So Line 1 northbound is indicated Porte de Clignancourt, while southbound is designated Porte d'Orléans. Follow the orange *correspondance* signs to change lines. Some interchanges, notably Châtelet-Les Halles, Montparnasse-Bienvenüe and République involve a long walk. The exit (*sortie*) is indicated in blue. The high-speed Line 14, **Météor**, opened in the autumn of 1998, and links the new Bibliothèque Nationale to Madeleine. Beware pickpockets, especially on much-touristed Line 1. The four **RER** lines (A, B, C, D) run 5.30am-1am daily across Paris and into the Ile-de-France commuter land. Within Paris, the RER is useful for

making faster journeys – for example, Châtelet-Les Halles to Charles de Gaulle-Etoile is only two stops on the RER compared with eight on Métro Line 1. The future Line E of the RER, **EOLE**, will link the eastern and western suburbs via Gare St-Lazare and Gare du Nord-Gare de l'Est.

Buses

Buses run from 6.30am until 8.30pm, with some routes running until 12.30am, Mon-Sat, with a more limited service on selected lines on Sundays and public holidays. You can use a Métro ticket, a ticket bought from the driver (8F) or a travel pass. Tickets should be punched in the machine next to the driver; passes should be shown to the driver. When you want to get off, press the red request button, and the *arrêt demandé* (stop requested) sign above the driver will light up.

Nightbuses

After the Métro and normal bus services stop running, the only public transport – apart from taxis – are the 18 **Noctambus** lines, between pl du Châtelet and the suburbs (hourly 1.30am-5.30am Mon-Thur; half-

hourly 1am-5.30am Fri, Sat). Ranks A to H, P, T and V serve the Right Bank and northern suburbs; I to M, R and S serve the Left Bank and southern suburbs. Look out for the owl logo on bus stops. A journey costs 30F; travel passes are valid.

Useful Bus Routes

The following pass interesting places and, unless stated, run daily, some with reduced routes on Sun.
29 Gare St-Lazare, past Palais Garnier and Centre Pompidou, through the Marais, Bastille to Gare de Lyon (Mon-Sat).
38 From Gare de l'Est , past the Centre Pompidou and place du Châtelet, then via the Sainte-Chapelle one direction, Notre Dame the other, then St-Michel, the Sorbonne, Jardins du Luxembourg to the Catacombes.
42 From Gare du Nord, via Opéra, Madeleine, Concorde, Champs-Elysées, over the river, past the Eiffel Tower to Quai André Citroën (Mon-Sat).
48 Literature and art: Montparnasse, St-Germain, the Louvre, Palais-Royal to Gare du Nord (Mon-Sat).
67 From sleazy Pigalle via the Louvre, Ile St-Louis, Latin Quarter and place d'Italie to Porte de Gentilly.

Métropolitan passions

Long after London had inaugurated its Underground in 1863, Parisians were still squabbling about theirs: detractors argued it would destroy the landscape of *vieux Paris* and socialists denounced it as a capitalist plot. Work eventually began in 1898 under the supervision of civil engineer Fulgance Bienvenüe (commemorated in the station Montparnasse-Bienvenüe). The first Métro line opened on 19 July 1900 to carry passengers the 10km and 18 stations from Porte Maillot to Porte de Vincennes in 25 minutes. Despite earlier misgivings, the new transport soon became so popular that over a million people had used it by the end of the year. This line was soon followed by the first sections of lines 2 (Porte Dauphine-Etoile) and 6 (Etoile-Trocadéro). Today there are 14 lines, 370 stations and over 201km of tracks, a few above the surface, the deepest at over 50m. At peak times 570 trains circulate at once. Line 4 (Porte d'Orleans to Porte de Clignancourt) is the busiest with an estimated 127 million passengers a year. Latest arrival is the futuristic high-speed Météor (line 14), the first all-new line since 1936, which opened in autumn 1998, and with glistening new stations and driverless, computer-controlled trains, giving an added frisson to those who sit at the very front.

A few stations merit a visit in their own right:
Abbesses (Line 12) Murals run up the spiral staircase that leads up to Guimard's ornate canopied Art Nouveau Métro entrance.
Arts et Métiers (Lines 3,11) Dramatic copper-covered art. Porthole exhibits of engineering inventions from the Musée des Arts et Métiers.
Assemblée Nationale (Line 12) Giant political heads colour the stop for the parliament.
Bastille (Lines 1, 5, 8) Decorated with scenes of the storming of the Bastille; line 5 platform contains a section of the fortress foundations.
Cluny-La Sorbonne (Line 10) The vault bears mosaic signatures of an appropriately erudite selection of writers and thinkers.
Concorde (Lines 1, 8, 12) The tiles were designed by two women artists to spell out the *Déclaration des Droits de l'Homme*.
Gare de Lyon (Lines 1, 14, RER A) The spectacular new Méteor station is airy and well-lit, with a lush Amazonian hothouse of exotic plants.
Louvre (Line 1) Replicas from the Louvre include Egyptian busts and Assyrian winged beasts.
St-Germain-des-Prés (Line 4) In Paris' literary heartland, prints depict the history of printing.
Varenne (Line 13) Sculptures preview the nearby Rodin museum.

Taxi tips

Paris taxi drivers (with some agreeable exceptions) are not known for their charm, nor for infallible knowledge of the Paris street plan – if there's a route you would prefer, say so. Taxi ranks are found on numerous major roads and at stations. The white light on the roof indicates the cab is free. A glowing orange light means the cab is busy. Taxi charges are based on area and time: A (7am-7pm Mon-Sat; 3.53F/km); B (7pm-7am Mon-Sat, all day Sun; 7am-7pm Mon-Sat suburbs and airports; 5.83F/km); C (7pm-7am daily suburbs and airports; 7.16F/km). Most journeys in central Paris average 40F-80F; there's a minimum charge of 13F, plus a 6F surcharge for each piece of luggage over 5kg or bulky objects such as skis, and a 5F surcharge if picked up from certain SNCF stations. Most drivers will not take more than three people, although they should take a couple and two children. Don't feel obliged to tip, although rounding up by 2F-5F is polite. Taxis are not allowed to refuse rides because they are too short and can only refuse to take you in a particular direction during their last half-hour of service. If you want a receipt, ask for *un reçu* or *une fiche* (compulsory for journeys of 100F or more). Any complaints should be made in writing to the Bureau de la réglementation publique de Paris, 36 rue des Morillons, 75732 Paris Cedex 15.

Taxi companies

The following accept telephone bookings 24 hours daily. However, you also pay for the radioed taxi to get to where you are. If you wish to pay by credit card, mention this when you order. **Accept credit cards over 50F: Alpha** 01.45.85.85.85; **G7** 01.47.39.47.39; **accept credit cards over 100F: Artaxi** 01.42.03.50.50; **Taxis Bleus** 01.49.36.10.10.

68 From place de Clichy via Opéra, Palais-Royal, the Louvre and Musée d'Orsay, bd Raspail to Montparnasse, the Catacombes and Porte d'Orléans.
69 From Père Lachaise, via Bastille, Hôtel de Ville and Châtelet along the quais to the monuments of the 7th, the Musée d'Orsay, the Invalides and the Champ de Mars (Mon-Sat).
72 From the 16th to Hôtel de Ville, along the Seine one direction and down arcaded rue de Rivoli the other.
73 From La Défense past the Arc de Triomphe, along the Champs-Elysées to Concorde and over the river to the Musée d'Orsay (Mon-Sat).
82 From smart residential Neuilly to the Jardins du Luxembourg via the Eiffel Tower and Invalides.
84 From Parc Monceau in the 17th via the Grands Boulevards, the Madeleine, St-Germain-des-Prés and St-Sulpice to the Panthéon (Mon-Sat).
86 From Zoo de Paris via Nation, the Bastille and Institut du Monde Arabe to St-Germain-des-Prés (Mon-Sat).
87 From Gare de Lyon to the Bastille, over the Ile-St-Louis, through the Latin Quarter via the Collège de France, Odéon, St-Sulpice and on to UNESCO, ending at the

Champ de Mars (Mon-Sat).
95 One hill to another: from Montparnasse to Montmartre.
Montmartrobus Special small bus circulates around Montmartre.
PC Petite Ceinture (the 'small belt') covers the outer boulevards, just within the Périphérique.
Balabus Runs 1-8pm on Sundays Apr-Sept. It links Gare de Lyon with the Grande Arche la Défense.

Trams

Two modern tramlines operate in the suburbs, connecting at either end with the Métro or RER: T1 from St-Denis to Bobigny-Pablo Picasso, T2 from La Défense to Issy-Val de Seine. Fares are the same as for buses.

Pedestrian Tips

Exploring by foot is the very best way to discover Paris, just remember that to anything on wheels (and this includes cyclists and rollerbladers), pedestrians are the lowest form of life. Crossing Paris' multi-lane boulevards can be lethal to the uninitiated. By law drivers are only

fully obliged to stop when there is a red light. Where there is a crossing, whether or not it has a flashing amber light or a sign saying *Priorité aux Piétons*, most drivers will ignore pedestrians and keep going.

Cycle Routes

Since 1996, the Mairie de Paris has been energetically introducing cycle lanes and, in the first two years of the programme, bike traffic increased fivefold. The quais along the Seine and the Canal St-Martin are usually closed to cars on Sundays (10am-4pm), providing the nicest stretches for cyclists and rollerbladers, along with the bike path by the Canal de l'Ourcq. The Bois de Boulogne and Bois de Vincennes offer paths away from traffic although they are still criss-crossed by roads. Esplanade du Trocadéro and bd Richard-Lenoir are popular with rollerbladers.
Cycle lanes (*pistes cyclables*) run mostly N-S and E-W; you could well be fined (from 230F) if you don't use them. N-S routes include rue de Rennes, bd St-Germain, bd de Sébastopol and av Marceau, while E-W routes take in the Champs-Elysées, bd St-Germain, the rue de Rivoli, bd St-Jacques and bd Vincent-Auriol and av Daumesnil. The lanes are at the edge of the road or down *contre-allées*, but only a small percentage are actually separated from motorised traffic, so you may encounter delivery vans, scooters and pedestrians blocking your way; the 900F fine for obstructing a cycle lane is barely enforced. There were 100km of cycle lanes at the end of 1997, and the aim is 150km by 2000 (including plans for a cycle lane 'Périphérique' circling Paris). A related municipal drive to create ten or so *quartiers piétons* (pedestrianised areas) will further favour Parisian cyclists.
You can get a free map of Paris' cycle routes (*Paris à Vélo*), with advice and addresses, at any Mairie or from bike shops. For more on cycling, *see below* **Car & Bike Hire**, **Armchair & Guided Tours**, *and chapter* **Sport & Fitness**.

Car & Bike Hire

To hire a car you must normally be 25 or over and have held a licence for at least a year. Some agencies accept drivers aged 21-24, but a supplement of 50F-100F per day is usual (Valem is an exception). Take your licence and passport with you. It is easiest to pay by credit card.

Hire Companies

Ada 01.45.54.63.63/08.36.68.40.02. **Avis** 01.55.38.68.60. **Budget**

08.00.10.00.01. **Europcar** 01.30.43.82.82. **Hertz** 01.39.38.38.38. **Rent-a-Car** 01.45.22.28.28/ 08.36.69.46.95. **Valem** 01.43.14.79.79. There are often good weekend offers (Fri evening to Mon morning). Week-long deals are better at the bigger hire companies – with Avis or Budget, for example, it's around 1600F a week for a small car with insurance and 1700km included. The more expensive hire companies allow the return of a car in other French cities and abroad. Beware that supposedly bargain companies, such as Ada, may have an extremely high excess charge for dents or damage.

Chauffeur-driven Cars

Les Berlines de Paris *(01.45.33.14.14).* **Open** 8am-7pm daily. **Prices** From 800F airport transfer; 1100F for four hours. **Credit** AmEx, DC, MC, V. Chauffeur-driven car service and multi-lingual guided tours. **International Limousines** *(01.53.81.14.14).* **Open** 24 hours daily. **Prices** From 848F airport transfer; from 1100F four-hour hire. **Credit** AmEx, DC, MC, V. Limos with English-speaking drivers.

Cycles, Scooters & Motorbikes

Note that bike insurance may not cover theft: be sure to check. **Atelier de la Compagnie** *57 bd de Grenelle, 15th (01.45.79.77.24).* **Open** 10am-7pm Mon-Fri; 10am-6pm Sat. **Credit** V. Rent a scooter for 250F/day or 950F/week; motorbike from 340F/day or 1500F/week. Weekend rates (Fri-Mon) work out best. A 14,000F refundable deposit is required, plus your passport. **Bicloune** *93 bd Beaumarchais, 3rd (01.42.77.58.06).* **Mº** *St-Sébastien-Froissart.* **Open** 10am-1pm, 2-7pm Tue-Sat. **Credit** AmEx, MC, V. **Branch:** *7 rue Froment, 11th (01.48.05.47.75).* Cycle rentals from 90F/day, new and second-hand cycles for sale, repairs, accessories. **Maison du Vélo** *11 rue Fénélon, 10th (01.42.81.24.72).* **Mº** *Gare du Nord or Poissonnière.* **Open** 10am-7pm Tue-Sat. **Credit** MC, V. Bikes for hire, new and used cycles on sale, as well as repairs and accessories. **Paris-Vélo** *2 rue du Fer-à-Moulin, 5th (01.43.37.59.22).* **Mº** *Censier-Daubenton.* **Open** 10am-12.30pm, 2-6pm daily. **Credit** MC, V. Mountain bikes and 21-speed models for hire.

Driving in Paris

If you bring your car to France, you will need to bring the registration and insurance documents (an insurance green card, available from insurance companies and the AA and RAC in the UK, is not compulsory but is advisable). It's advisable to carry spare lightbulbs, a first-aid kit and a warning triangle.

As you come into Paris you will inevitably meet the *Périphérique*, the giant ring road that carries all the heavy traffic in, out and around the city. Its intersections, which lead onto other main roads, are called *portes* (gates). Driving on the *Périphérique* is not as hair-raising as you might expect, even though it's often congested, especially during rush hour and at peak holiday times. If you've come to Paris by car, it can be a good idea to park at the edge of the city and use public transport. A few hotels have parking spaces. You can get traffic information for the Ile-de-France on 01.48.99.33.33. In peak holiday periods, the organisation Bison Futé hands out brochures at the motorway *péages* (toll stations), suggesting less-crowded routes. Travelling by car is still the best way to explore France. French roads are divided into *Autoroutes* (motorways, with an 'A' in front of the number), *Routes Nationales* (national 'N' roads), *Routes Départementales* (local, 'D' roads) and tiny, rural *Routes Communales* ('C' roads). *Autoroutes* are toll roads (*péages*), although some sections, including most of the area immediately around Paris, are free. Motorways have a speed limit of 130km/h (80mph). On most *Routes Nationales* the limit is 90km/h (56mph).

Breakdown Services

The AA or RAC do not have reciprocal arrangements in France, so it is advisable to take out additional breakdown insurance cover, for example with **Europ Assistance** *(in the UK 01444 442211).* If you don't have insurance, you can use their service *(01.41.85.85.85)* but they will charge you the full cost. Other 24-hour breakdown services in Paris include **SOS Dépannage** *(01.47.07.99.99);* **Action Auto Assistance** *(01.45.58.49.58);* **Adan Dépann Auto** *(01.42.66.67.58).*

Driving Tips

• At intersections where no signposts indicate the right of way, the car coming from the right has priority. Many roundabouts now give priority to those on the roundabout. If this is not indicated (by road markings or *vous n'avez pas la priorité*), priority is for those coming from the right.
• Drivers and all passengers must wear seat belts.
• Children under ten are not allowed to travel in the front of a car, except special babyseats facing backwards.
• You should not stop on an open road; pull off to the side.

• When drivers flash their lights at you, this means that they will not slow down and are warning you to keep out of the way. Friendly drivers also flash their lights to warn you when there are gendarmes lurking on the other side of the hill.
• Carry change, as it's quicker to head for the exact-money line on *péages*; but cashiers do give change and *péages* accept credit cards.

Parking

There are still a few free on-street parking areas left in Paris, but they're usually full when you find them. If you park illegally, you risk getting your car clamped or towed away (*see below*). It is forbidden to park in zones marked for *livraisons* (deliveries) or taxis. In central zones, parking meters have been replaced by *horodateurs*, pay-and-display machines, which either take coins or cards (100F or 200F available from *tabacs*). Parking is often free at weekends and after 7pm, and in August. There are numerous underground car parks in central Paris. Most cost 12F-15F per hour; 80F-130F for 24 hours; some offer lower rates after 6pm.

Clamps & Car Pounds

If you've had the misfortune to have your car clamped, contact the local police station. There are eight car pounds (*préfourrières*) in Paris. You'll have to pay a 600F removal fee plus 30F storage charge per day; add to that a parking fine of 230F for parking in a no-parking zone. Be sure to bring your driving permit and insurance papers. If your car is confiscated at night, it goes first to *préfourrière* Bercy for southern Paris or Europe for the north; and will be sent to the car pound for the relevant *arrondissement* after 48 hours. For details call 08.36.67.22.22 (2.23F/min). **Les Halles** *1st, 2nd, 3rd, 4th (01.40.39.12.20).* **Bercy** *5th, 12th, 13th (01.53.46.69.20).* **Montparnasse** *6th, 7th, 14th (01.40.47.42.00).* **Europe** *8th, 9th (01.42.93.51.30).* **Pantin** *10th, 11th, 19th, 20th (01.44.52.52.10).* **Balard** *15th/16th (south) (01.45.58.70.30).* **Foch** *8th, 16th (north), 17th (01.53.64.11.80).* **Pouchet** *17th, 18th (01.53.06.67.68).*

Leaving Town

Travelling by Train

Several attractions in the suburbs, notably Versailles and Disneyland Paris, are served by the RER. Most locations farther from the city are served by French national railways, the SNCF; there are few long-distance bus services. The TGV (*Train à Grande Vitesse*) high-speed train has

Directory

revolutionised journey times and is gradually being extended to all the main regions. On the downside, travel by TGV requires a price supplement and reservation, and there are now fewer trains to lesser towns.

SNCF Reservations/Tickets
SNCF national reservations and information: *08.36.35.35.35* (2.23F/min). **Open** 7am-10pm daily. SNCF information (no reservations) in the Ile de France: *01.53.90.20.20*. You can buy tickets at counters and machines and at travel agents. If you reserve on Minitel 3615 SNCF or by phone, you must pick up and pay for the ticket within 48 hours. Regular trains have both full-rate White and cheaper Blue periods. You can save on TGV fares by purchasing special cards. *Carte 12/25* gives under-26s a 50 per cent reduction; without it, under-26s are entitled to 25 per cent off. Pensioners benefit from similar terms with a *Carte Vermeil*. Before you board any train, validate your ticket in the orange *composteur* machines located by the platforms, or you might have to pay a hefty fine.

Paris Mainline Stations
Gare d'Austerlitz: Central and SW France and western Spain.
Gare de l'Est: Alsace, Champagne and southern Germany.
Gare de Lyon: Burgundy, the Alps,

Provence, Italy.
Gare Montparnasse: West France, Brittany, Bordeaux, the Southwest.
Gare du Nord: Northeast France, Channel ports, Eurostar, Belgium and the Netherlands.
Gare St-Lazare: Normandy.

Major Airlines
Aer Lingus 01.47.42.12.50.
Air France 08.02.802.802.
American Airlines 01.69.32.73.07.
British Airways 08.02.802.902.
British Midland 01.48.62.55.65.
Continental 01.42.99.09.09.
KLM & **NorthWest** 01.44.56.18.25.
Tower Air 01.55.04.80.80.
USAir 01.49.10.29.00.

Travel Agencies
Cash & Go *34 av des Champs-Elysées, 8th (01.53.93.63.63). Mº Champs-Elysées-Clemenceau.* **Open** 9am-7pm Mon-Fri; 10am-6pm Sat. **Credit** AmEx, MC, V. Broker with well-priced flights around the world.
Council Travel *1 pl de l'Odéon, 6th (01.44.41.89.80). Mº Odéon.* **Open** 9.30am-6.30pm Mon-Fri; 10am-5pm Sat. **Credit** AmEx, MC, V. Specialises in student tickets.
Havas Voyages *26 av de l'Opéra, 1st (01.53.29.40.00). Mº Opéra.* **Open** 10am-7pm Mon-Sat. **Credit** AmEx, V. General travel agent with more than 15 branches in Paris.
Maison de la Grande Bretagne

19 rue des Mathurins, 9th (01.44.51.56.20). Mº Havre-Caumartin/RER Auber. **Open** 9.30am-6pm Mon-Fri; 10am-5pm Sat. **Credit** MC, V. All under one roof, the British Tourist Office and other services for travelling to or in the UK including ferry companies, Le Shuttle, British Rail (01.44.51.06.00) and a theatre ticket agency for the UK, **Global Tickets** (01.42.65.39.21). **Nouvelles Frontières** *13 av de l'Opéra, 1st. Mº Pyramides.* **Open** 9am-7pm Mon-Sat. **Credit** DC, MC, V. Large travel agent with 18 branches in Paris. Call 08.03.333.333 or 01.41.41.58.58 for reservations, information or branch addresses.
USIT *6 rue de Vaugirard, 6th (01.42.34.56.90/telephone bookings only 01.42.44.14.00). Mº Odéon.* **Open** 10am-7pm Mon-Fri; 10am-1pm, 2-6pm Sat. **Credit** MC, V. Coach, air and train tickets for under-26s and for general customers.

Hitch-hiking
Allô-Stop *8 rue Rochambeau, 9th (01.53.20.42.42).* **Open** 9am-7.30pm Mon-Fri; 9am-1pm, 2-6pm Sat. **Credit** MC, V. Call several days ahead to be put in touch with drivers. There's an initial fee (30F for under 200km; up to 70F for over 500km), plus 22 centimes/km to pay to the driver. Routes most travelled: Lyon, Toulouse, Rennes, Nantes, Cologne.

Directory A-Z

Banks & Money

Since 1 Jan 1999 there have been two currencies in France: the franc and the Euro. The French franc is usually abbreviated to F or sometimes FF after the amount. One franc is made up of 100 centimes, the smallest coin in circulation is five centimes. There are coins for five, ten, 20 and 50 centimes, one, two and five francs, and the heavier ten and 20 francs, silver-centred coins with a copper rim. There are banknotes at 20F, 50F, 100F, 200F and 500F.

The Euro
1 Jan 1999 saw the start of the transition to the Euro, when the Euro became the official currency in France (and ten other nations of the European Union) and the official exchange rate was set at 6.55957F. Shops and businesses are increasingly indicating prices in both currencies. You can open Euro accounts, and some places will accept payment in Euros by cheque or credit card, although Euro coins and notes will not be circulated until 2002. Beware high bank charges for cashing cheques for Euros from other

countries. Travellers cheques are also available in Euros (eg. from Thomas Cook).

Bureaux de Change
If you arrive in Paris early or late, you can change money at the **Travelex** Bureaux de Change at Roissy (one in each terminal; 01.48.64.37.26) and at Orly (Sud and West; 01.49.75.89.25) airports which are open 6.30am to 10.30pm or 11pm daily. **Thomas Cook** has bureaux de change at the main train stations. Hours can vary.
Gare d'Austerlitz 01.53.60.12.97. **Open** 7.15am-8.45pm Mon-Fri; 7.15am-11am, 5-8.45pm Sat, Sun.
Gare Montparnasse 01.42.79.03.88. **Open** 8am-6.55pm daily (until 8pm in summer).
Gare St-Lazare 01.43.87.72.51. **Open** 8am-7pm Mon-Sat; 9am-4.50pm Sun.
Gare du Nord 01.42.80.11.50. **Open** 6.15am-11.25pm daily.
Gare de l'Est 01.42.09.51.97. **Open** Mon-Sat 6.45am-9.50pm, 6.45am-7pm Sun.
Gare de Lyon 01.43.41.52.70. 6.30am-11pm daily.
Some banks have cash exchange

machines that accept notes of major currencies in good condition and convert them into francs. **Crédit Commercial de France (CCF)** has automatic change machines at 28 rue de Rivoli, 4th, and at 103 av des Champs-Elysées, 8th.

Banks & Banking Hours
French banks usually open 9am-5pm Mon-Fri (some close at lunch 12.30-2.30pm); some banks also open on Sat. All are closed on public holidays, and from noon on the previous day. Note that not all banks have foreign exchange counters. Commission rates vary between banks. The state Banque de France usually offers good rates. Most banks accept travellers cheques, but may be reluctant to accept personal cheques with the Eurocheque guarantee card, which is not widely used in France.

Bank Accounts
To open an account (*ouvrir un compte*), French banks require proof of identity, address and your income (if any). You'll typically need to show your passport, *Carte de Séjour*, an electricity/gas or phone bill in your name and a payslip/letter from your

employer. Students need a student card and may need a letter from their parents. Of the major banks (BNP, Crédit Lyonnais, Société Générale, Banque Populaire, Crédit Agricole), Société Générale tends to be most foreigner- and student-friendly. Most banks don't hand out a Carte Bleue/Visa until several weeks after you've opened an account. A chequebook (*chéquier*) is usually issued in about a week. The Carte Bleue is debited directly from your current account, but you can choose for purchases to be debited at the end of every month. French banks are very tough on overdrafts, so try to anticipate any cash crisis in advance and work out a deal for an authorised overdraft (*découvert autorisé*) or you risk being blacklisted as '*interdit bancaire*' – forbidden from having a current account – for up to ten years. Depositing foreign-currency cheques is slow, so use wire transfer or a bank draft in francs to receive funds from abroad.

Credit Cards & Cash Machines

Major international credit cards are widely used in France; Visa (in French *Carte Bleue*) is the most readily accepted. French-issued credit cards have a special security microchip (*puce*) in each card. The card is slotted into a card reader, and the holder keys in a PIN number to authorise the transaction. Non-French cards should be read in the conventional way. In case of credit card loss or theft, call the following 24-hour services which have English-speaking staff: **American Express** 01.47.77.72.00; **Diners Club** 01.49.06.17.17; **MasterCard** 01.45.67.84.84; **Visa** 08.36.69.08.80. Withdrawals in francs can be made from bank and post office automatic cash machines. The specific cards accepted are marked on each machine, and most give instructions in English. Credit card companies charge a fee for cash advances, but rates are often better than bank rates.

Foreign Affairs

American Express *11 rue Scribe, 9th (01.47.14.50.00). M° Opéra.* **Open** 9am-4.30pm Mon-Fri. *Bureau de change (01.47.77.79.50).* **Open** 9am-6pm Mon-Fri; 9am-5pm Sat; 10am-4pm Sun. Bureau de change, poste restante, card replacement, travellers cheque refund service, international money transfers and a cash machine for AmEx cardholders. **Barclays** *6 rond point des Champs-Elysées, 8th (01.44.95.13.80). M° Franklin D Roosevelt.* **Open** 9.15am-4.30pm Mon-Fri. As well as regular services, Barclays' international Expat Service handles direct debits, international transfer of funds, etc.

Chequepoint *150 av des Champs-Elysées, 8th (01.49.53.02.51). M° Charles de Gaulle-Etoile.* **Open** 24 hours daily. Other branches have variable hours between 8am and 11pm daily; some are closed on Sun. No commission.
Thomas Cook *52 av des Champs-Elysées, 8th (01.42.89.80.32). M° Franklin D Roosevelt.* **Open** 9am-10pm daily. Hours of other branches (over 20 in Paris) vary. They issue travellers' cheques and deal with bank drafts and bank transfers.
Western Union Money Transfer *CCF Change, 4 rue du Cloître-Notre-Dame, 4th (01.43.54.46.12). M° Cité.* **Open** 9am-6pm daily. CCF is an agent for Western Union in Paris, with several branches in the city. 48 post offices now provide Western Union services (call 01.43.35.60.60 for details). Money transfers from abroad should arrive within 10-15 minutes. Charges paid by the sender.
Citibank *125 av des Champs-Elysées, 8th (01.53.23.33.60). M° Charles de Gaulle-Etoile.* **Open** 10am-6pm Mon-Fri. Existing clients get good rates for transferring money from country to country, preferential exchange rates and no commision on on travellers cheques. European clients can make immediate on-line transfers from account to account on ATM with a Cirrus cashcard.

Beauty Spas

Women's beauty is an obsessive cult in Paris, with local cosmetic shops, beauty parlours and hairdressers around every corner, and numerous branches of affordable chains like Jean-Claude Biguine and Jean-Louis David. Look for cheap promotions on tanning or leg waxing and for cheap cuts at hairdressers if you volunteer to be a guinea pig for student stylists.
Les Bains du Marais *31-33 rue des Blancs-Manteaux, 4th (01.44.61.02.02). M° Rambuteau.* **Open** *women* 11am-8pm Mon; 11am-11pm Tue; 10am-7pm Wed; *men* 11am-11pm Thur; 10am-8pm Fri, Sat; *mixed* 7pm-midnight Wed; 11am-11pm Sun. **Credit** AmEx, MC, V. Morrocan décor provides a suitable setting for a steam bath or massage (180F).
Carita *11 rue du Fbg-St-Honoré, 8th (01.44.94.11.11). M° Concorde.* **Open** 10am-6.30pm Mon-Fri. **Credit** AmEx, DC, MC, V. A sybaritic heaven of spacious pink and black booths, reclining chairs and wafting music and scents. Treatments range from 'Prolifting' facials (700F-850F) and body 'Harmoniponcture' (690F) to a special massaging chair.
Charlie en Particulier *1 rue Goethe, 16th (01.47.20.94.01). M° Alma-Marceau.* **Open** 9.30am-6pm Mon-Fri. **Credit** AmEx, DC, MC, V.

A hair appointment with Charlie is for that special occasion when looking great is a must and money no object (cut 2000F).
Christophe Robin *7 rue du Mont-Thabor, 1st (01.42.60.99.15). M° Tuileries.* **Open** 11am-7pm Mon-Fri. **No credit cards.** The latest, very young, genius of hair colouring is responsible for Catherine Deneuve's and many lesser-known Parisians' blondeness (800F-2000F). To guard your secret, he never takes more than two clients at a time.
Guerlain Institut de Beauté *68 av des Champs-Elysées, 8th (01.45.62.11.21). M° Franklin D Roosevelt.* **Open** 9am-6.30pm Mon-Sat. **Credit** AmEx, MC, V. Art Deco touches by Cocteau and Giacometti surround the 16 cabins where miracles occur: try a facial (from 620F), a manicure (210F), a pedicure (480F) or the new 'Acti-Lift (720F).
Hammam de la Mosquée de Paris *39 rue Geoffroy-St-Hilaire, 5th (01.43.31.18.14). M° Censier-Daubenton.* **Open** *women* 10am-9pm Mon, Wed-Sat. *men* 2-9pm Tue, 10am-9pm Sun. **Admission** 85F. **Credit** MC, V. The Turkish bath at the Mosque is a perfect place to unwind and get the pollution out of your pores. Languish in steam rooms, take an invigorating massage, or lounge on mattresses. It's a favourite girls' treat; there are also men's days.
Institut Lancôme *29 rue St-Honoré, 8th (01.42.65.30.74). M° Concorde.* **Open** 10am-8pm Mon-Fri; 10am-7pm Sat. **Credit** AmEx, DC, MC, V. Art Deco elegance plus efficient and up-to-date skincare. The 90-minute 'Soin Relaxant Douceur' includes a facial, a mask and a 20-minute massage of face, shoulders, hands and feet (600F).
Institut Orlane *163 av Victor-Hugo, 16th (01.47.04.65.00). M° Victor-Hugo.* **Open** 9am-6.30pm Mon-Fri; 9am-1pm Sat. **Credit** AmEx, V. Apart from quality products and treatments, Orlane provides a small salon to repair damaged hair.
Villa Thalgo *218-220 rue du Fbg-St-Honoré, 8th (01.45.62.00.20). M° Ternes.* **Open** 8.30am-8.30pm Mon-Thur; 8.30am-7pm Fri; 9am-7pm Sat. **Credit** AmEx, DC, MC, V. Thalassotherapy without the sea. Half a day of 'anti-stress and beauty' treatment, with an Aquagym class, skin exfoliating treatment, toning seaweed wrap and facial costs 980F, including lunch served next to the swimming pool.

Bureaucracy

Anyone from abroad coming to live in Paris should be prepared for the sheer weight of bureaucracy to which

Armchair and guided tours

Boat Trips

Bateaux-Mouches
pont de l'Alma, Rive Droite, 8th (reservations 01.42.25.96.10/recorded info 01.40.76.99.99). M° *Alma-Marceau.* **Departs** *summer* every 30min 10am-11pm daily; *winter* approx every hour from 11am-9pm daily; lasts one hour. **Tickets** 40F; 20F under-15s; free under-5s. Lunch 330F; 150F; dinner (smart dress) 500F-700F **Credit** AmEx, MC, V (meal cruises only).

Bateaux Parisiens Tour Eiffel
port de la Bourdonnais, 7th (01.44.11.33.55). RER Pont de l'Alma or M° Trocadéro. **Departs** *summer & winter weekends* every 30 min 10am-10pm daily; *winter weekdays* every hour 10am-9pm daily. **Tickets** 50F; 25F under-12s. Lunch 300F, 150F under-12s; dinner 560F-750F. **Credit** AmEx, MC, V (meals only).

Bateaux Vedettes de Paris
port de Suffren, 7th (01.47.05.71.29). M° Bir-Hakeim or RER Champ de Mars. **Departs** every 30 min; *summer* 10am-11pm; *winter* 11am-6pm daily. **Tickets** 50F; 20F 5-12s; free under-4s. **Credit** AmEx, MC, V.

Les Vedettes du Pont Neuf
square du Vert-Galant, 1st (01.46.33.98.38). M° Pont-Neuf. **Departs** summer every 30min: 10am-noon, 1.30-6.30pm daily; floodlit evening trips 9-10.30pm daily; winter times depend on demand. **Tickets** 50F; 25F 4-11s; free under-4s. Lunch 290F; 200F under-10s; dinner 350F-470F. **Credit** AmEx, MC, V (meals only).

Canal Trips

Canauxrama
(01.42.39.15.00). **Departs** *Bassin de la Villette, 13 quai de la Loire, 19th. M° Jaurès.* 9.45am, 2.45pm daily. **Departs** *Port de l'Arsenal, opposite 50 bd de la Bastille, 12th. M° Bastille.* 9.45am, 2.30pm daily. Fewer trips in winter. **Tickets** 75F daily; 60F students, over-65s Mon-Fri; 45F 6-12s; free under-6s. No reductions holidays or weekend afternoons. Trips last 2-3hrs, live commentary in French; in English if enough foreigners.

Navettes de la Villette
(01.42.39.15.00). Shuttle between *Parc de la Villette (M° Porte de Pantin)* and *la Rotonde de Ledoux (5bis quai de la Loire. M° Jaurès).* **Departs** every 30 mins 11am-6pm Sat, Sun and holidays. **Tickets** 10F single; 15F return.

Paris Canal
(Reservations essential on 01.42.40.96.97). Musée d'Orsay (M° Solférino) to Parc de la Villette (M° Porte de Pantin) or reverse. **Departs** *end-Mar-mid-Nov* Musée d'Orsay 9.30am daily; Parc de la Villette 2.30pm daily. *mid-Nov-Mar* times as above but just Sun. Lasts 3 hours. **Tickets** 100F; 75F 12-25s, over-60s (except Sun pm and holidays); 60F 4-11s; free under-4s. Lively commentary in French (and English if enough demand).

Coach Tours

Cityrama
4 pl des Pyramides, 1st (01.44.55.61.00). M° Palais Royal. **Departs** *summer* hourly 9.30am-4.30pm daily; *winter* 9.30am, 10.30am, 1.30pm, 2.30pm daily. **Tickets** 150F; free under-12s. **Credit** AmEx, DC, MC, V. Two-hour tours with recorded English commentary.

Parisbus
(01.42.30.55.50). **Departs** every 30 min. *Easter-July* 10am-5pm; *Aug-mid-Oct* 9.45am-4.50pm; *mid-Oct-* *Easter* 9.55am-2.55pm daily. **Tickets** 125F; 100F students; 60F under-12s; free under-4s. **Credit** AmEx, DC. Red London doubledeckers with recorded commentary in English. You can get off and on at will at any of nine stops; tickets are valid for two days. Buses start at the Eiffel Tower, quai Branly, 7th; stops include Notre Dame, the Louvre, Opéra, Arc de Triomphe and the Grand Palais.

Paris Vision
214 rue de Rivoli, 1st (01.42.60.30.01). M° Tuileries. **Trips** hourly 9.30am-3.30pm daily (lasts 2 hours). **Tickets** first one 150F, then 100F; 75F 4-11s; free under-4s. **Credit** AmEx, DC, MC, V. Tickets from the departure point. Recorded multilingual commentaries.

Cycle Tours

Escapade Nature
3 rue Antoine Vollon, 12th (01.53.17.03.18). **Tickets** *including bike hire* 100F-250F; 80F-140F 12-25s; 50F-75F 4-12s; cheaper with own bike. Runs guided rides (1h30 min up to a full day) between Mar and Oct, in partnership with RATP's bike hire enterprise 'Roue Libre'. Tours start from place du Châtelet, the Eiffel Tower or in the Bois de Vincennes or Boulogne.

Paris à vélo, c'est sympa!
37 bd Bourdon, 4th (01.48.87.60.01). M° Bastille. **Open** 9am-6pm daily. **Tickets** *including bike hire* 150F for a half-day; 170F for a night tour; 130F, 150F under-26s; plus 20F membership. Guided tours, usually leaving at 10am, 3pm or 8.30pm. Reservations required. Also bike rental by the day or weekend.

Walking Tours
Many individual guides organise walks (in French), and details are published weekly in *Pariscope* under Promenades. The **Caisse Nationale des Monuments Historiques et des Sites** (Hôtel de Sully, 62 rue St-Antoine, 4th/ 01.44.61.20.00), does tours of monuments, museums and historic districts (in French). The tours below have English-speaking guides; their walks are usually listed in the *Time Out Paris* section in *Pariscope*, but most also organise group walks on request. Prices exclude entrance fees for sights.

Anne Hervé
(01.47.90.52.16); parisfra@altern.com. **Tours** *summer* Sat, Sun; *winter* variable. **Tickets** 50F. Claims to conduct the original Paris visits in English, since 1992.

Paris Contact
Jill Daneels (01.42.51.08.40). **Tickets** 60F; 50F students, over-60s. Guided weekly walks and customised cultural tours, including Parks and Gardens of Paris and In Jefferson's Footsteps.

Paris Walking Tours
Oriel and Peter Caine (01.48.09.21.40). **Tours** last 90 minutes, usually daily. **Tickets** 60F; 40F students; free under-10s (except sewers). Regular tours include the Louvre, the Marais, Montmartre and Latin Quarter.

Paristoric
11bis rue Scribe, 9th (01.42.66.62.06). M° Opéra. **Shows** *Apr-Oct* hourly 9am-8pm daily; *Nov-Mar* hourly 9am-6pm daily. **Admission** 50F; 40F over-60s; 30F under-18s, students. A 45-minute, audiovisual ride which flashes through 2000 years of Paris history. Headset commentary in English and other languages.

Directory

French officialdom is devoted, whether it's for acquiring a *Carte de Séjour* (resident's permit), opening a bank account, reclaiming medical expenses or getting married. Among documents regularly required are a *Fiche d'Etat Civile* (essential details translated from your passport by the embassy/consulate) and a legally approved translation of your birth certificate (embassies will provide lists of approved legal translators; for general translators, *see p320*, **Business Resources**). You need to be able to prove your identity to the police at all times, so keep your passport/*Carte de Séjour* with you.

Cartes de Séjour

Officially, all foreigners, both EU citizens and non-Europeans in France for more than three months, must apply for a *Carte de Séjour*, valid for one year. People who have had a *Carte de Séjour* for at least three years, have been paying French income tax, can show proof of income and/or are married to a French national can apply for a *Carte de Résident*, valid for ten years.
CIRA (Centre Interministeriel de Renseignements Administratifs) *(01.40.01.11.01)*. **Open** 9am-12.30pm, 2-5.30pm Mon-Fri. For enquiries concerning French administrative procedures.
Préfecture de Police de Paris *Service Étrangers, 7 bd du Palais, 1st (01.53.71.51.68)*. *M° Cité.* **Open** 8.30am-4pm Mon-Fri. Information on residency and work permits.
Cosmopolitan Services Unlimited *113 bd Pereire, 17th (01.55.65.11.65/ fax 01.55.65.11.69)*. *M° or RER Pereire.* **Office hours** 9am-6pm Mon-Thur; 9am-5pm Fri. A good but pricey relocation services. Services include getting work permits and *Cartes de Séjour* approved (*see p313*, **Removals & Relocation**).

Customs

There are no limits on the quantity of goods you can take into France from another EU country for personal use, provided tax has been paid on them in the country of origin. However, customs still has the right to question visitors. Quantities accepted as being for personal use are:
• up to 800 cigarettes, 400 small cigars, 200 cigars or 1kg of loose tobacco.
• 10 litres of spirits (over 22% alcohol), 90 litres of wine (under 22% alcohol) or 110 litres of beer.
For goods from outside the EU:
• 200 cigarettes or 100 small cigars, 50 cigars or 250g loose tobacco
• 1 litre of spirits (over 22% alcohol) and 2 litres of wine and beer (under 22% alcohol)

• 50g perfume
Visitors can carry up to 50,000F in currency. Non-EU residents can reclaim V A T (*TVA*) on some purchases on leaving France in the *Détaxe* scheme (*see chapter* **Fashion**).

Disabled Travellers

Disabled visitors to Paris are advised to buy **Access in Paris**, an excellent English-language guide by Gordon Couch and Ben Roberts, published by Quiller Press. It can be ordered from RADAR, Unit 12, City Forum, 250 City Rd, London EC1V 8AF/0171-250 3222 (£6.95, including UK postage, add £2 for Europe, £7 for rest of world). The **Office de Tourisme de Paris** produces *Tourisme pour tout le monde* (60F). A free number (08.00.03.37.48) offers advice (in French) to disabled persons living in or visiting Paris. We've put wheelchair access in the listings where applicable, but it's always wise to check beforehand. Many additional places are accessible to wheelchair users but do not have accessible or specialised toilets.
Comité national de liaison pour la réadaptation des handicapés (CNRH) *236bis rue de Tolbiac, 13th (01.53.80.66.63)*. Publishes *Paris Ile-de-France Pour Tous*, an all-purpose tourist guide for the disabled (60F in Paris; 80F if ordered from abroad), which is available in French.
Association des Paralysés de France *22 rue du Père-Guérain, 13th (01.44.16.83.83)*. *M° Place d'Italie.* **Open** 9am-12.30pm, 2-6pm Mon-Thur (until 5pm Fri). Publishes *Où ferons-nous étape?* (85F), listing French hotels and motels accessible to those with limited mobility.

Getting Around

Neither the Métro nor buses are wheelchair-accessible, except bus line 20, some No 91 buses and, from mid-1999, the PC. Forward seats on buses are intended for people with poor mobility. RER lines A and B and some SNCF trains are wheelchair-accessible in parts. All Paris taxis are obliged by law to take passengers in wheelchairs. The following offer adapted transport for the disabled. Book 48hrs in advance.
Aihrop *(01.41.29.01.29)*. **Open** 8am-noon, 1.30-6pm Mon-Fri. Transport to and from the airports.
GiHP *24 av Henri Barbusse, 93000 Bobigny (01.41.83.15.15)*. **Open** 7.30am-8pm Mon-Fri.

Electricity & Gas

Electricity in France runs on 220V. Visitors with British 240V appliances can simply change the plug or use a

converter (*adaptateur*), available at most hardware shops. For US 110V appliances, you will need to use a transformer (*transformateur*) available at the Fnac and Darty chains or in the basement of the BHV store. Gas and electricity are supplied by the state-owned EDF-GDF (Electricité de France-Gaz de France). Contact them about supply, bills, or in case of power failures or gas leaks (*see p308*, **Emergencies**).

Embassies

Before going to an embassy or consulate, phone and check opening hours. You may need to make an appointment. Otherwise, their answer-phone will usually give an emergency contact number. There's a full list of embassies and consulates in the *Pages Jaunes* under *Ambassades et Consulats*. For general enquiries or problems with passports or visas, it is usually the consulate you need.
Australian Embassy *4 rue Jean-Rey, 15th (01.40.59.33.00)*. *M° Bir-Hakeim.* **Open** 9am-6pm Mon-Fri; Visas 9.15am-12.15pm Mon-Fri.
British Embassy *35 rue du Fbg-St-Honoré, 8th (01.44.51.31.00)*. *M° Concorde.* **Open** 9.30am-1pm, 2.30-6pm Mon-Fri. Consulate *16 rue d'Anjou, 8th (01.44.51.33.01/ 01.44.51.33.03)*. *M° Concorde or Madeleine.* **Open** 2.30-5.30pm Mon-Fri.
Canadian Embassy *35 av Montaigne, 8th (01.44.43.29.00)*. *M° Franklin D Roosevelt.* **Open** 9am-noon, 2-5pm Mon-Fri. Visas *37 av Montaigne (01.44.43.29.16)*. **Open** 8.30-11am Mon-Fri.
Irish Embassy *12 av Foch, 16th.* Consulate *4 rue Rude, 16th (01.44.17.67.00)*. *M° Charles de Gaulle-Etoile.* **Open** *for visits* 9.30am-noon Mon-Fri; *by phone* 9.30am-1pm, 2.30-5.30pm Mon-Fri.
New Zealand Embassy *7ter rue Léonard de Vinci, 16th (01.45.00.24.11)*. *M° Victor-Hugo.* **Open** Visas 9am-1pm Mon-Fri.
South African Embassy *59 quai d'Orsay, 7th (01.53.59.23.23)*. *M° Invalides.* **Open** 8.30am-5.15pm Mon-Fri, by appointment. Consulate 9am-noon.
US Embassy *2 av Gabriel, 8th (01.43.12.22.22)*. *M° Concorde.* **Open** 9am-6pm Mon-Fri by appointment. Consulate/Visas *2 rue St-Florentin, 1st (01.43.12.22.22)*. *M° Concorde.* **Open** 8.45-11am Mon-Fri. Passport service 9am-3pm.

English Media

The Paris-based **International Herald Tribune** is on sale throughout the city; British dailies,

Emergencies

Most of the following services operate 24 hours daily. In a real medical emergency, call the Sapeurs-Pompiers, who are trained paramedics, rather than the SAMU.

Police	17
Fire (Sapeurs-Pompiers)	18
Ambulance (SAMU)	15

GDF (gas leaks) (01.47.54.20.20). **Open** 8am-4.30pm daily.
EDF (electricity) (01.40.42.22.22) **Open** 8am-4.30pm daily.
After-hours look in the *Pages Blanches* (heading *Urgence-Dépannage Gaz et Electricité*) for your *arrondissement*.
SOS Help (01.47.23.80.80). **Open** 3-11pm daily. An English-language crisis line with a team of trained listeners.

Sundays and **USA Today** are widely available on the day of issue at larger kiosks in the city centre. On the local front, **Time Out Paris** is a six-page supplement inside the weekly listings magazine *Pariscope*, available at all news stands, covering selected Paris events, exhibitions, films, concerts and restaurants. The quarterly **Time Out Paris Free Guide** is distributed in bars, hotels and tourist centres. **FUSAC** (France-USA Contacts) is a fortnightly small-ads free-sheet with flat rentals, job ads and appliances for sale. The monthly **Paris Free Voice** is community oriented with reasonable arts coverage. Both are available at US and English-language bookshops, bars and the American Church. You can receive the **BBC World Service** (648 KHz AM) for its English-language international news, current events, pop and drama. Also on 198KHz LW, from midnight to 5.30am daily. At other times this frequency carries **BBC Radio 4** (198 KHz LW), for British news, talk and The Archers directed at the home audience. On **RFI** (738 KHz AM), there's an English-language programme of news and music from 3-4pm daily.

Flower Delivery

Interflora *(freephone 08.00.20.32.04)*. **Open** 8am-8pm Mon-Sat. **Credit** AmEx, DC, MC, V. Prices start at 280F for a standard bouquet delivered in Paris.
Lachaume *10 rue Royale, 8th (01.42.60.57.26). M° Concorde or Madeleine.* **Open** 9am-7pm Mon-Fri; 9am-6pm Sat. **Credit** AmEx, MC, V. Paris' most regal flower shop. Call before noon for same-day delivery in the Paris area.

Health & Hospitals

All EU nationals staying in France are entitled to use of the French Social Security system, which refunds up to 70 per cent of medical expenses (but sometimes much less, eg. for dental treatment). To get a refund, British nationals should obtain form E111 before leaving the UK (or E112 for those already in treatment). Nationals of non-EU countries should take out insurance before leaving home. Consultations and prescriptions have to be paid for in full, and are reimbursed, in part, on receipt of a completed *fiche*. If you undergo treatment while in France the doctor will give you a prescription and a *feuille de soins* (statement of treatment). The medication will carry *vignettes* (little stickers) which you must stick onto your *feuille de soins*. Send this, the prescription and form E111, to the local *Caisse Primaire d'Assurance Maladie* (in the phone book under *Sécurité Sociale*). Refunds can take over a month to come through.

Doctors & Dentists

A complete list of practitioners is in the *Pages Jaunes* under *Médecins Qualifiés*. To get a Social Security refund, choose a doctor or dentist registered with the state system; look for *Médecin Conventionné* after the name. Consultations cost 115F upwards, of which a proportion can be reimbursed. To see a specialist rather than a generalist costs more.
Centre Médical Europe *44 rue d'Amsterdam, 9th (01.42.81.93.33/ dentists 01.42.81.80.00). M° St-Lazare.* **Open** 8am-7pm Mon-Fri; 8am-6pm Sat. Practitioners in all fields under one roof, charging minimal consultation fees (115F for foreigners). Appointments advisable.

Help Lines & House Calls

See also box **Emergencies.**
SOS Infirmiers (Nurses) *(01.43.57.01.26/06.08.34.08.92/ 08.36.60.50.50 beeper)*. House calls 8pm-midnight; daytime Sat-Sun; generally around 150F.
SOS Dépression *(01.45.22.44.44)*. People listen and/or give advice, and can send a counsellor or psychiatrist to your home in case of a crisis.
SOS Médecins *(01.47.07.77.77/ 01.43.37.77.77)*. Doctors make house calls. A home visit starts at 250F if you don't have French Social Security, 145F if you do, before 7pm; from 310F thereafter.
Urgences Médicales de Paris *(01.48.28.40.04)*. Doctors make house calls. Some speak English.
Urgences Dentaires de Paris *(01.47.07.44.44)*. **Open** 8am-10pm. Will offer advice by phone or refer you to nearby dentists; after 10pm all are sent to the Hôpital Salpêtrière.
SOS Dentaire *87 bd Port-Royal, 5th (01.43.37.51.00). RER Port-Royal.* **Open** 8-11.45pm. Emergency dental care.
Alcoholics Anonymous in English *(01.46.34.59.65)*. 24-hour recorded message gives details of AA meetings at the American Church or Cathedral (*see below* **Religion**) and members' phone numbers for more information.
The Counselling Center (01.47.23.61.13) based at the American Cathedral. Counselling services in English.

Hospital Specialities

For a complete list of hospitals consult the *Pages Blanches* under *Hôpital Assistance Publique*, or ring 01.40.27.30.00.
Burns: Hôpital Cochin, *27 rue du Fbg-St-Jacques, 14th (01.42.34.17.58). M° St-Jacques/RER Port-Royal.* **Open** 24 hours daily. Hôpital St-Antoine, *184 rue du Fbg-St-Antoine, 12th (01.49.28.26.09). M° Faidherbe-Chaligny or Reuilly-Diderot.*
Children: Hôpital St Vincent de Paul, *74 av Denfert Rochereau (01.40.48.81.11). M° Denfert-Rochereau.* **Open** 24 hours daily. Hôpital Necker, *149 rue de Sèvres, 15th (01.44.49.40.00). M° Duroc.*
Children's Burns: Hôpital Armand-Trousseau, *26 av du Dr-Arnold-Netter, 12th (01.44.73.74.75). M° Bel-Air.*
Dog Bites: Institut Pasteur, *209 rue de Vaugirard, 15th (01.40.61.38.48). M° Pasteur.* Service Anti-rabique **Open** 9am-noon Mon-Fri; 9-11am Sat.
Drugs: Centre Hospitalier Ste-Anne, *1 rue Cabanis, 14th (01.45.65.80.64). M° Glacière.* Hôpital Marmottan, *19 rue d'Armaillé, 17th (01.45.74.00.04). M° Argentine.*
Poisons: Hôpital Fernand Widal, *200 rue du Fbg-St-Denis, 10th*

(01.40.05.48.48). Mº Gare du Nord.
Open 24 hours.
American Hospital in Paris
*63 bd Victor-Hugo, 92202 Neuilly
(01.46.41.25.25). Mº Porte Maillot,
then bus 82 to the terminus opposite
the hospital.* **Open** 24 hours daily.
A private hospital. French Social
Security will refund only a small
percentage of treatment costs. All
staff speak English.
**Hertford British Hospital
(Hôpital Franco-Britannique)**
*3 rue Barbès, 92300 Levallois-Perret
(01.46.39.22.22). Mº Anatole-France.*
Open 24 hours daily. Most doctors
are English-speaking. Accepts BUPA.

Pharmacies

Pharmacies sport a green neon cross.
They have a monopoly on issuing
medication, and also sell sanitary
products. Most open 9am/10am-
7pm/8pm. Staff can provide basic

medical services like disinfecting and
bandaging wounds (for a small fee)
and will indicate the nearest doctor
on duty. French pharmacists are
highly trained; you can often avoid
visiting a doctor by describing your
symptoms and seeing what they
suggest. Paris has a rota system of
Pharmacies de Garde at night and on
Sunday. A closed pharmacy will
have a sign in its window indicating
the nearest open pharmacy. Ordinary
toiletries and cosmetics are often
cheaper in supermarkets

Night Chemists

Pharma Presto (01.42.42.42.50).
Open 24 hours daily. Delivery charge
150F from 8am-6pm; 250F 6pm-8am.
Delivers prescription medication
(non-prescription exceptions can be
made), in association with **Dérhy**.
Pharmacie des Halles *10 bd de
Sébastopol, 4th (01.42.72.03.23).*

Mº Châtelet. **Open** 9am-midnight
Mon-Sat; noon-midnight Sun.
Dérhy/Pharmacie des Champs
*84 av des Champs-Elysées, 8th
(01.45.62.02.41). Mº George V.*
Open 24 hours daily.
Matignon *2 rue Jean-Mermoz, 8th
(01.43.59.86.55). Mº Franklin D
Roosevelt.* **Open** 8.30am-2am daily.
Capucines *6 bd des Capucines,
9th (01.42.65.88.29). Mº Opéra.*
Open 8am-12.30am Mon-Fri; 9am-
12.30am Sat; 10am-12.30am Sun.
**Pharmacie Européenne de la
Place de Clichy** *6 pl de Clichy, 9th
(01.48.74.65.18). Mº Place de Clichy.*
Open 24 hours daily.
Lagarce *13 pl de la Nation, 11th
(01.43.73.24.03). Mº Nation.* **Open**
8am-midnight daily.
Pharmacie d'Italie *61 av d'Italie,
13th (01.44.24.19.72). Mº Tolbiac.*
Open 8am-midnight Mon-Sat; 9am-
midnight Sun.

Paris on the Web

Myriad sites cover all aspects of the city and French
culture in both English and French. Most major
magazines and newspapers have web equivalents of
their paper formats. To find out about hot new sites,
listen to RTL (104.3 FM) 8pm-midnight Mon-Fri.

News & Media

www.liberation.com *Libé*'s web site provides the
current affairs stories covered in its daily paper, plus
features on cinema, multimedia and the arts. One
section has excerpts from 250 recent books and *BD*s.
www.lemonde.com France's respected heavyweight
daily newspaper, online. Stock exchange information,
arts, cinema and literary features. In French only.
www.telerama.fr Online version of the weekly TV,
radio and cultural listings magazine, with features,
personalised programming and new film releases.

Entertainment & Culture

www.timeout.com *Time Out*'s web site contains
information about 27 cities, including Paris, with a
weekly updated list of current events and an extensive
guide to hotels, restaurants, monuments and the arts.
www.pariscope.fr The weekly online version of the
Pariscope entertainment guide. Mostly French.
www.louvre.fr Visit the building, its temporary
exhibitions and permanent collections in a
multilingual site. Lots of images.
www.musee-orsay.fr The museum and its
collections, with information on key works, but
reproductions are very small.
www.bnf.fr The real Bibliothèque National may be
beset by strikes, but the web site should be immune.
Come here for illuminated manuscripts and page-by-
page scans from first editions of literary classics.
www.chateauversailles.fr Visit the home of the
Sun King in French or English. There's a 360º view of
the Hall of Mirrors, and a wealth of eclectic
information, including the King's hot chocolate recipe.
www.tour-eiffel.fr The official Eiffel Tower site, in
English and French. Cut-away diagrams of the tower's

different levels, archive photos of its construction, tales
from its history and a nifty 360º rotating view across
Paris from the summit – not for vertigo-sufferers.
www.jazzfrance.com Jazz information site with
clubs, concerts, festivals and reviews. Bilingual.
www.johnny-hallyday.tm.fr/ The official fan site
of the legendary, leathery rocker; full discography,
excerpts from his latest album, photos, and a shot of
Johnny astride his beloved Harley.
www.pageszoom.com/ruescommercants France
Telecom's online version of the phone book and *Pages
Jaunes* has a useful search engine for Paris streets:
type in the street, and up come details of every shop,
restaurant, florist and launderette along its length,
plus photos from different angles and maps.
www.paris.org Exhaustive coverage from the state
tourist office about Paris and France. Bilingual.
www.worldmedia.fr Online magazine covers
tourism and the Paris fashion shows, live.

Officialdom

www.elysee.fr Tour the President's official
residence, keep up with his recent engagements and
speeches, or browse his family album. Multilingual
www.premier-ministre.gouv.fr After paying a
virtual visit to the Elysée, pop in to the Prime
Minister's official web site for a similar virtual tour of
the Palais Matignon, plus links to other ministries.
www.mairie-paris.fr Visit Hôtel de Ville, check out
the 2000 projects, Paris statistics and municipal info.
www.meteo.fr/temps/ The latest satellite pics and
forecasts from the French meteorological office.

Offbeat

altern.org/tidji Street art on the walls of Paris by
Mesnager, Miss-Tic, Némo, etc. Good links.
www.multimania.cim/lafouine/kata Images and
info on graffiti in the Paris catacombes by cataphiles.
www.multimania.com Read (in French) the *Journal
Intime Collectif*, a multi-author open-ended journal of
Paris *quartiers* and their inhabitants.

Opticians

Branches of **Alain Afflelou** and **Lissac** are the most abundant in Paris. They stock hundreds of styles and can have prescription glasses ready within the hour.
SOS Optique *(01.48.07.22.00)*. 24-hour repair service. Glasses repaired at your home by a certified optician.

Complementary Medicine

Most pharmacies also sell homeo-pathic medicines.
Académie d'Homéopathie et des Médecines Douces *2 rue d'Isly, 8th (01.43.87.60.33)*. *M° St-Lazare*. **Open** 10am-6pm Mon-Thur; 10am-7pm Fri. Health services include acupuncture, aromatherapy and homeopathy.
Association Française d'Acuponcture *3 rue de l'Arrivée, 15th (01.43.20.26.26)*. *M° Brochart*. **Open** 9am-12.30pm, 2-5.30pm Mon-Fri. Provides names of professional acupuncturists.
Centre d'Homéopathie de Paris *48 av Gabriel, 8th (01.45.55.12.15)*. *M° Franklin D Roosevelt*. **Open** 8am-7pm Mon-Sat.

AIDS, HIV & Sexually Transmitted Diseases

These centres carry out anonymous, free HIV (VIH) tests (*dépistages*) in addition to offering other services for AIDS (SIDA) sufferers.
AIDES *247 rue de Belleville, 19th (01.44.52.00.00)*. *M° Télégraphe*. **Open** 2-6pm Mon-Fri. Volunteers provide support for AIDS patients.
AJCS (Action jeunes conseils santé) *6 rue Dante, 5th (01.46.33.71.83/01.44.78.00.00)*. *M° Maubert-Mutualité*. **Open** Tue-Fri 10am-12.30pm, 2-6pm. Youth association offering info on AIDS, youth and health.
Centre Médico-Social *3 rue Ridder, 14th (01.45.43.83.78)*. *M° Plaisance*. **Open** 8.30am-6.30pm Mon-Fri; 9.30am-noon Sat. Free, anonymous HIV tests noon-6.30pm Mon-Fri; 9.30am-noon Sat. Other services include heart and lung diagnoses, as well as endocrinology and gynaecological exams.
Dispensaire de la Croix Rouge *43 rue de Valois, 1st (01.42.61.30.04)*. *M° Palais-Royal*. A medical centre specialising in sexually transmitted diseases. Also offers free, anonymous HIV tests (*dépistages*).
FACTS *(01.44.93.16.69)*. **Open** 6-10pm Mon, Wed, Fri. English-speaking crisis line gives information and support for those touched by HIV/AIDS and runs support groups for friends and relatives.
SIDA Info Service *(08.00.84.08.00)*. **Open** 24 hours daily. Confidential AIDS-information in French (some bilingual counsellors).

Internet Providers

After a slow start, Internet use has skyrocketed, although there are still complaints about high phone charges. It is also now possible in most of Paris to get access via cable.
America Online (freephone 08.00.903.910) or www.aol.fr.
Club-Internet (01.55.45.46.47) or www.club-internet.fr
CompuServe (08.03.00.60.00) or www.compuserve.fr.
Imaginet (01.43.38.10.24) or www.imaginet.fr.
Microsoft Network (01.69.86.47.47) or www.fr.msn.com.
Wanadoo (France Télécom) (08.01.63.34.34) or wanadoo.fr

Late Night Shops

Most areas have a local grocer that stays open until around 10pm. At other times, 24-hour garages and the shops listed provide supermarket essentials and help placate midnight munchies.

24-Hour Newsagents

include *33 av des Champs-Elysées, 8th*. *M° Franklin D Roosevelt*. and *2 bd Montmartre, 9th*. *M° Grands Boulevards*.

Shops

See also bookshops and record shops in chapter **Specialist Shops**.
L'An 2000 *82 bd des Batignolles, 17th (01.43.87.24.67)*. *M° Rome or Villiers*. **Open** 5-11 pm Mon-Fri, Sun. **Credit** MC, V. A *traiteur* where paëlla is always on the menu, as well as a *plat du jour*, cheese, *charcuterie*.
Boulangerie de l'Ancienne Comédie *10 rue de l'Ancienne-Comédie, 6th (01.43.26.89.72)*. *M° Odéon*. **Open** 24 hours daily. **Credit** AmEx, MC, V. Bread, *pâtisseries* and sandwiches, plus hot and cold snacks.
Boulangerie Pigalle *28 bd de Clichy, 18th (01.46.06.39.37)*. *M° Pigalle*. **Open** 24 hours Mon, Tue, Thur-Sun. **No credit cards**. Basic groceries and North African goods.
Elyfleur *82 av de Wagram, 17th (01.47.66.87.19)*. *M° Charles de Gaulle-Etoile*. **Open** 24 hours daily. Say it with flowers, any time.
Noura *27 av Marceau, 16th (01.47.23.02.20)*. *M° Iéna or Alma-Marceau*. **Open** 8am-midnight daily. **Credit** AmEx, DC, MC, V. Upmarket Lebanese *traiteur* stocks *meze*, bread, cheese, *charcuterie*, *baklava*, wines.
Prisunic *109 rue La Boétie, 8th (01.53.77.65.65)*. *M° Franklin D Roosevelt*. **Open** 9am-midnight Mon-Sat. **Credit** AmEx, MC, V. Full-scale supermarket for clothes, make-up, deli, grocery and liquid needs. Packed nightly with foreigners stocking up on French staples.
Select *Shell Garage, 6 bd Raspail,*

7th (01.45.48.43.12). *M° Rue du Bac*. **Open** 24 hours daily. **Credit** MC, V. Shop at the Shell Garage has a large if pricey array of supermarket standards. No alcohol sold 10pm-6am.

Tobacconists

La Brazza *86 bd du Montparnasse, 14th (01.43.35.42.65)*. *M° Montparnasse-Bienvenüe*. **Open** 6.30am-2am daily.
La Favorite *3 bd St-Michel, 5th (01.43.54.08.02)*. *M° St-Michel*. **Open** 7am-2am Mon-Fri; 8am-2am Sat, Sun.
La Havane *4 pl de Clichy, 17th (01.48.74.67.56)*. *M° Place de Clichy*. **Open** 6.30am-5am daily.

Legal Advice

Mairies also answer legal enquiries. Phone for details and times of free *consultations juridiques*.
Avocat Assistance et Recours du Consommateur *11 pl Dauphine, 1st (01.43.54.32.04)*. *M° Pont Neuf*. **Open** 2-6pm Mon-Fri. Lawyers here deal with consumer-related cases. 200F for a consultation.
Direction Départmentale de la Concurrence, de la Consommation, et de la Répression des Fraudes *8 rue Froissart, 3rd (01.40.27.16.00)*. *M° St-Sébastien-Froissart*. **Open** 9-11.30am, 2-5.30pm Mon-Fri. This subdivision of the Ministry of Finance deals with consumer complaints.
Palais de Justice *Galerie de Harlay, escalier S, 4 bd du Palais, 4th (01.44.32.48.48)*. *M° Cité*. **Open** 9.30am-noon Mon-Fri. Free legal consultation. Arrive early.
SOS Avocats *(08.03.39.63.00)*. **Open** 7-11.30pm Mon-Fri. Free legal advice by phone.
SOS Racisme *28 rue des Petites Ecuries, 10th (01.42.05.44.44)*. *M° Château d'Eau*. **Open** 9.30am-1pm, 2-6pm Mon-Fri. A non-profit association defending the rights of ethnic minorities.

Libraries

All *arrondissements* have free public libraries. For a library card, you need ID and two documents proving residency, such as a phone bill or tenancy agreement. Book and magazine loan are free; there are charges for CD and video loans. The University of Paris has library facilities for enrolled students.
American Library *10 rue du Général-Camou, 7th (01.53.59.12.60)*. *M° Alma-Marceau then cross Pont de l'Alma, or Ecole-Militaire*. **Open** 10am-7pm Tue-Sat (shorter hours in Aug). **Admission** day pass 70F; annual 570F. Claims to

be the largest English-language lending library in mainland Europe, and also organises talks and readings. Receives 350 periodicals, plus popular magazines and newspapers (mainly American).

Bibliothèque Historique de la Ville de Paris *Hôtel Lamoignon, 24 rue Pavée, 4th (01.44.59.29.40). M° St-Paul.* **Open** 9.30am-6pm Mon-Sat. Reference books and documents on Paris history in a Marais mansion.

Bibliothèque Marguerite Durand *79 rue Nationale, 13th (01.45.70.80.30). M° Tolbiac or Place d'Italie.* **Open** 2-6pm Tue-Sat. 30,000 books and 120 periodicals, some in English, on women's history and feminism, many of which were assembled by feminist pioneer Durand. The collection includes letters of Colette and Louise Michel.

Bibliothèque Nationale de France François Mitterrand *quai François-Mauriac, 13th (01.53.79.55.01). M° Bibliothèque.* **Open** 10am-7pm Tue-Sat; noon-6pm Sun. **Admission** *day pass* 20F; *annual* 200F. Books, newspapers and periodicals, plus titles in English, are on access to anyone over 18. An audio-visual room lets you browse photo, film and sound archives.

Bibliothèque Nationale de France Richelieu *58 rue de Richelieu, 2nd (01.47.03.81.26). M° Bourse.* **Open** 9am-8pm Mon-Fri (printed works), 9am-5.30pm Sat. **Admission** researchers only. The old national library now holds only stamps, photographs, medals, maps, manuscripts and music.

Bibliothèque Publique d'Information (BPI) *11 rue Brantôme (01.44.78.12.33). M° Rambuteau.* **Open** noon-10pm Mon, Wed-Fri; 10am-10pm Sat, Sun. The Centre Pompidou's vast reference library is closed until 2000, but has reopened in this temporary annexe, with selected books, reference materials and computers.

Bibliothèque Ste-Geneviève *10 pl du Panthéon, 5th (01.44.41.97.97). RER Luxembourg.* **Open** 10am-10pm Mon-Sat. This reference library, with a spectacular, iron-framed reading room, is open to students over 18. Bring ID and a photo to register (by 6pm).

BIFI (Bibliothèque du Film) *100 rue du Fbg-St-Antoine, 12th (01.53.02.22.30). M° Ledru-Rollin.* **Open** 10am-7pm Mon-Fri. Film buffs' library offers books, magazines film stills and posters, as well as films on video and CD-Rom.

BILIPO (Bibliothèque des Littératures Policières) *48-50 rue du Cardinal-Lemoine, 5th (01.42.34.93.00). M° Cardinal-Lemoine.* **Open** 2-6pm Tue-Fri; 10am-5pm Sat. Non-lending library specialised in crime, spy and detective fiction.

British Council Library *9-11 rue Constantine, 7th (01.49.55.73.00). M° Invalides.* **Open** 11am-6pm Mon-Fri (until 7pm Wed). **Admission** *day pass* 30F; *annual* 250F; 200F students. Reference and lending library. A small book selection, but it stocks British press and offers an Internet and CD-rom service.

Documentation Française *29 quai Voltaire, 7th (01.40.15.70.00). M° Rue du Bac.* **Open** 10am-6pm Mon-Wed, Fri; 10am-1pm Thur. **Admission** free. The official government archive and central reference library has information on contemporary French politics and economy since 1945.

Médiathèque de Paris *Forum des Halles, 8 porte St-Eustache, 1st (01.42.33.20.50). RER Châtelet-Les Halles.* **Open** noon-7pm Tue-Sat. **Admission** annual borrowing pass 200F. Records on vinyl, CD and cassette for loan, plus sound archives, videos and musical and choreographic literature and documents for consultation.

Maps

Free maps of the Métro, bus and RER systems are available at airports and Métro stations. Other brochures from Métro stations are *Paris Visite – Le Guide*, with details of transport tickets and a small map, and the *Grand Plan de Paris*, a fold-out map that also indicates Noctambus night bus lines (*see p301*). Métro, bus, RER and street maps are also included at the back of this Guide.

If you're staying more than a few days it's worth buying a detailed map book. The Michelin *Paris-Plan, Paris par Arrondissement* (Editions l'Indispensable), the small paperback *Plan de Paris* (Editions Leconte) and the slightly larger *Collection Plan Net* (Ponchet Plan Net) are all available from kiosks and bookshops.

Opening Times

Standard opening hours for shops are 9am/10am-7pm/8pm Mon-Sat. Some shops also close on Mon. Shops and businesses often close at lunch for an hour, sometimes more, usually 12.30-2pm. Many shops are closed for all or part of August.

Photo Labs

Photo developing is often more expensive than in the UK or USA. **Photo Station** and **Fnac Service** both have numerous branches and are reasonably priced.

Police/Lost Property

If you are robbed or attacked, you should report the incident as soon as possible. You will need to make a statement (*procès verbal*) at the *commissariat* in the *arrondissement* in which it was committed. To find the appropriate *commissariat*, phone the Préfecture Centrale (01.53.71.53.71) day or night, or look in the phone book. Stolen goods are unlikely to be recovered, but you will need the police statement for insurance purposes.

Bureau des Objets Trouvés *36 rue des Morillons, 15th (01.55.76.20.20). M° Convention.* **Open** 8.30am-7pm Mon, Wed, Fri; 8.30am-8pm Tue, Thur. Visit in person to fill in a form specifying date, time and place you lost the item.

Post

If you're simply sending a letter or postcard, it is quicker to buy stamps at a tobacconist (*tabac*) than at a post office. Post offices (*bureaux de poste*) are open 8am-7pm Mon-Fri; 9am-noon Sat. All are listed in the phone book: under *Administration des PTT* in the *Pages Jaunes*; under *Poste* in the *Pages Blanches*. Most post offices have automatic machines (in French and English) that weigh your letter, print out a stamp and give change.

Main Post Office *52 rue du Louvre, 1st (01.40.28.20.00). M° Les Halles or Louvre-Rivoli.* **Open** 24 hours daily for *Poste Restante*, telephones, telegrams, stamps and fax. This is the best place to get your mail sent if you haven't got a fixed address in Paris. Mail should be addressed to you in block capitals, followed by *Poste Restante*, then the post office's address. There is a charge of 3F for each letter received. Letters will arrive sooner if they bear the correct five-digit postcode.

Within Paris: postcodes always begin with '75'; if your address is in the 1st *arrondissement*, the postcode is 75001; in the 15th, the code is 75015. The 16th *arrondissement* is subdivided into two sectors, 75016 and 75116. Some business addresses have a more detailed postcode, followed by a Cedex number which indicates the *arrondissement*.

Press

Newspapers

The main daily papers are characterised by high prices and relatively low circulation. Only 20 per cent of the population reads a national paper; regional dailies hold the sway outside Paris.

Serious, centre-left daily **Le Monde** is essential reading for businessmen, politicians and would-be intellectuals. Despite its highbrow reputation, subject matter is surprisingly eclectic, although international coverage is selective. Co-publishes *Aden*, a weekly Paris-listings supplement with rock magazine *Les Inrockuptibles*. Founded post-68 by a group that included Sartre and de Beauvoir, trendy **Libération** is now centre-left, but still the read of the *gauche caviar*. Hit by declining circulation, but worth reading for wide-ranging news and arts coverage and guest columnists, such as Baudrillard. The conservative middle classes go for **Le Figaro**, a daily broadsheet with a devotion to politics, shopping, food and sport. Sales are boosted by a pink financial section, lots of property and job ads and the Wednesday *Figaroscope* Paris listings. Saturday's edition contains three magazines which rockets the price from 7F to 25F. Tabloid in format, the easy-read **Le Parisien-Aujourd'hui** is strong on consumer affairs, social issues, local news and events and vox pops. *Aujourd'hui* is the national edition, without the local news. Downmarket **France Soir** has recently gone tabloid to suit its spirit. **Le Croix** is a Catholic, right-wing daily. The Communist Party **L'Humanité** has kept going despite the collapse of the Party's colleagues outside France. **Le Journal du Dimanche,** a thin broadsheet, is the sole Sunday news offering. Most of France waits until Monday to read about the weekend's events. It comes with free *Femina* mag. **L'Equipe** is a big-selling sports daily, with a bias towards football while **Paris-Turf** caters just for horse-racing fans. *See also p319* **Business Resources**.

Satirical Papers

Le Canard Enchaîné is the Gallic *Private Eye*, a satirical weekly broadsheet that's full of in-jokes and breaks political and economic scandals. **Charlie Hebdo** is mainly bought for its cartoons.

News Magazines

Weekly news magazines are an important sector in France, taking the place of weighty Sunday tomes. Titles range from solidly serious **L'Express** and **Le Point** to the traditionally left-wing **Le Nouvel Observateur**, sardonic, chaotically arranged **Marianne** and recently rejuvenated **L'Evénement** (which has been redesigned and lost *du Jeudi* from its name). Similarities tend to be stronger than political differences. All summarise the main events of the week, with more limited cultural sections, but are of greatest interest

for the varied in-depth reports. **Courrier International** reprints articles from newspapers all over the world, giving fascinating perspectives from elsewhere.

Arts & Listings Magazines

Two pocket-sized publications rival for basic Wednesday to Tuesday listings information: **Pariscope** (3F), the Parisian cinema-goer's bible, which includes **Time Out Paris** in English; and the thinner **Officiel des Spectacles** (2.80F). Linked to Radio Nova, monthly **Nova** magazine is ultra-cool and it knows it: rigorously multi-ethnic information on where to drink, dance, be-seen or just hang out. Highbrow TV magazine **Télérama** has good arts and entertainment features and a Paris listings insert. *See also above* **Le Monde** *and* **Le Figaro**. There are specialist arts magazines to meet every interest (*see also* chapters **Art Galleries** and **Music: Rock, Roots & Jazz**). Film titles include intellectual **Les Cahiers du Cinéma**, glossy **Studio** and younger, celebrity-geared **Première**.

Gossip Magazines

Despite strict privacy laws, the French appear to have an almost insatiable appetite for gossip. 1998 saw two new, confusingly similar sounding (and looking) arrivals: **Oh La!** from Spain's *Hola!* (and UK's *Hello!*) group and **Allo!** from German-owned Prisma Presse, already responsible for France's juiciest scandal sheet **Voici** and glossy **Gala,** which tells the same stories without the sleaze. **Paris Match** is a national institution founded in 1948, packed with society gossip and celebrity interviews, but still regularly scoops the rest for photo shoots of international affairs. **Point de Vue** specialises in royalty and disdains showbizz fluff. Monthly **Entrevue** tends toward features on bizarre sexual practices, but still somehow clinches regular exclusives with celebs like Sharon Stone.

Women & Fashion Mags

Elle was a pioneer among liberated women's mags and has spawned editions across the globe. In France it is weekly and spot-on for interviews and fashion coverage. Publishes **Elle Décoration**. **Marie-Claire** is a monthly which takes a more feminist, campaigning line. Publishes **Marie-Claire Décoration**. **DS** aims at the intelligent reader, with lots to read and coverage of social issues. **Biba** treats fashion, sex and career topics with a younger, more urban approach. **Atmosphères** does a similar juggling act but for a slightly older readership. French **Vogue**, read both for its fashion coverage

and big-name guests, is rivalled when it comes to fashion week by **L'Officiel de la Mode** and **Dépêche Mode**. The underground go for more radical **Purple** (six-monthly tripartite art, literature and fashion tome).

A quota requiring a minimum of 40 per cent French music has led to overplay of gallic pop oldies and to the creation of dubious hybrids by local groups that mix some words in French with a refrain in English. Trash-talking phone-in shows also proliferate. Wavelengths are in MHz.
87.8 France Inter State-run, broadcasts MOR music, international news and Jean-Louis Foulquier's Pollen – concerts by rock newcomers.
90.4 Nostalgie As it sounds.
90.9 Chante France 100 per cent French *chanson*.
91.3 Cherie FM Lots of oldies.
91.7 92.1 MHz France Musique State classical music channel offers concerts, contemporary bleeps, top jazz and too much talk (*see also* Maison de la Radio *in* **Music: Classical & Opera**).
93.1 Aligre From local Paris news to highbrow literary.
93.5/93.9 France Culture Highbrow state culture station: literature, poetry, history, cinema and music.
94.8 RCJ/Radio J/Judaïque FM/ Radio Shalom Shared wavelength for Paris' Jewish stations.
96 Skyrock Pop station with loudmouth presenters. Lots of rap.
96.4 BFM Business and economics. Wall Street in English every evening.
96.9 Voltage FM Dance music.
97.4 Rire et Chansons A non-stop diet of jokes – racist, sexist or just plain lousy – and pop oldies.
97.8 Ado Local music station for ado(lescents).
98.2 Radio FG 98.2 Gay station. Techno music, rave announcements and very explicit lonely hearts.
99 Radio Latina Great Latin and salsa music, increasingly adding *raï*, Spanish and Italian pop.
101.1 Radio Classique More classical pops than France Musique, but also less pedagogical.
101.5 Radio Nova Hip hop, trip hop, world, jazz and whatever else is hopping now.
100.3 NRJ Energy: national leader with the under-30s.
101.9 Fun Radio Now embracing techno alongside Anglo pop hits.
102.3 Ouï FM Ouï rock you.
103.9 RFM Easy listening.
104.3 RTL The most popular French station nationwide mixes music and talk programmes. Grand Jury on Sunday is a debate between

journalists and a top politician.
104.7 Europe 1 News, press
reviews, sports, business, gardening,
entertainment, music. Much the best
weekday breakfast news broadcast,
with politicians interviewed live.
105.1 FIP Traffic bulletins, what's
on in Paris and a mix of jazz,
classical, world and pop, known for
the seductive-voiced *Fipettes*, its
female programme announcers.
105.5 France Info 24-hour news,
economic updates and sports
bulletins. As everything gets
repeated every 15 minutes, it's
guaranteed to drive you mad – good
though if you're learning French.
106.7 Beur FM Aimed at Paris'
North Africans.

Recycling & Rubbish

Large, green hive-shaped bottle
banks can be found on many street
corners. If your building has
recycling bins they will fall into two
categories: blue lids for newspapers
and magazines, white for glass. Your
building owner has to request bins
from the Service Technique de la
Propreté de Paris (01.40.41.87.00).
Green bins are for general household
refuse. For getting rid of furniture,
wood, and non-dangerous rubbish,
look for green skips on street corners.
Allô Propreté *(01.43.64.91.91)*.
Open 7.30am-7.30pm Mon-Fri.
Recycling information, will collect
cumbersome objects.
Mini-déchetteries Small recycling
centres which accept household
packaging, paper and disposable
batteries are at: *132 bd Vincent-
Auriol, 13th (01.45.83.06.15). M°
Nationale.* **Open** 9am-5.45pm Mon-
Fri; 9.30am-5.30pm Sat-Sun. *1 rue
Fabert, 7th (01.47.53.90.52). M°
Invalides.* **Open** 6am-1.30pm Mon;
6am-7.30pm Tue-Fri; 7am-7.30pm Sat.

Déchetteries

Poterne des Peupliers, *8 rue
Jacques Destrée (formerly rue du Val
de Marne), 13th (01.46.63.38.59).
M° Porte d'Italie.* **Open** 9.30am-7pm
daily.
*quai d'Issy-les-Moulineaux, 15th
(01.45.57.27.35). RER Issy.* **Open**
9.30am-7pm daily.
*17-25 av de la Porte de la Chapelle,
18th (01.40.35.07.90). M° Porte de
la Chapelle.* **Open** 9.30am-7pm daily.
*52 rue de Frères-Flavien, 20th
(01.43.64.91.91). M° Porte des Lilas.*
Open 8.30am-noon, 2-7.30pm Mon-
Thur; 8.30am-noon Fri, Sat.
These four recycling centres accept
all kinds of household packaging,
including cans, glass and plastic
bottles, packing boxes, aerosols,
newspapers and magazines, as well
as motor oil, fridges, car batteries, old
furniture and wood scraps.

Religion

Churches and religious centres are
listed in the phone book (*Pages
Jaunes*) under *Eglises* and *Culte*. Paris
has several English-speaking
churches and other religious
communities. The *International
Herald Tribune*'s Saturday edition
lists Sunday church services in
English.
American Cathedral *23 av George
V, 8th (01.53.23.84.00). M° George V.*
American Church in Paris
*65 quai d'Orsay, 7th
(01.40.62.05.00). M° Invalides.*
Church of Scotland *17 rue
Bayard, 8th (01.48.78.47.94). M°
Franklin D Roosevelt.*
St George's Anglican Church
*7 rue Auguste-Vacquerie, 16th
(01.47.20.22.51). M° Charles de
Gaulle-Etoile.* The YWCA-Cardew
club for under-28s meets here.
**St Joseph's Roman Catholic
Church** *50 av Hoche, 8th
(01.42.27.28.56). M° Charles de
Gaulle-Etoile.*
St Michael's Church of England
*5 rue d'Aguesseau, 8th
(01.47.42.70.88). M° Madeleine.*
Kehilat Gesher *10 rue de Pologne,
78100 St-Germain-en-Laye
(01.39.21.97.19).* The Liberal
English-speaking Jewish community
has rotating services in Paris and the
western suburbs.

Removals/Relocation

Grospiron, Arthur Pierre, Interdean,
Desbordes and Transpaq International
are the big five of removals: see
Déménagements in the *Pages Jaunes*.
Companies targeted at UK/US
removals also advertise in the free
magazine FUSAC. Relocation services
will also help with work papers, flat
hunting and opening bank accounts.
Grospiron *15 rue Danielle
Casanova, 93300 Aubervilliers
(01.48.11.71.71/fax 01.48.11.71.70).
M° Fort d'Aubervilliers.* **Open** 9am-
6pm Mon-Fri. High-class, corporate-
oriented packing, loading and
transport service moves people and
businesses all over the world.
Contact Nancy Cruse for English-
speaking service.

Packing & Shipping

Hedley's Humpers *6 bd de la
Libération, 93284 St-Denis
(01.48.13.01.02). M° Carrefour-
Pleyel.* **Open** 8am-6pm Mon-Fri. *102
rue des Rosiers, 93400 St-Ouen
(01.40.10.94.00). M° Porte de
Clignancourt.* **Open** 9am-1pm Mon;
9am-6pm Sat, Sun. English company
specialised in transporting furniture
and antiques. **In UK:** *3 Leonards Rd,
London NW10 6SX, UK (0181-965
8733).* **In USA:** *21-41 45th Road,*

*Long Island City, New York NY
11101, USA (1.718.433.4005).*
Logistic Air/Sea France
*C-O ACM BP 10232 95703 Roissy
CDG (01.48.62.13.25).* **Open** 9am-
6.30pm Mon-Fri. **Credit** MC, V.
Air shipping worldwide out of
France for roughly 12F/kg (45kg
minimum), up to 100kg. Pick-up
charge 500F. Lower rates for
shipping by boat.

Renting a Flat

The best flats often go by word of
mouth. Northern, eastern and
southeastern Paris are generally
cheaper than the western,
southwestern and central parts of the
city. Expect to pay roughly 100F per
month/m^2 (3500F/month for a 35m^2
flat, and so on). Studio and one-
bedroom flats fetch the highest prices
proportionally; lifts and central
heating will also boost the rent.

Rental laws

The legal minimum period for a
rental lease (*bail de location*) on an
unfurnished apartment is three years;
one year for a furnished flat. Both
are renewable. During this period
the landlord can only raise the rent
by the official construction inflation
index. At the end of the lease, the
rent can be adjusted, but tenants can
object before a rent board if it seems
exorbitant. Tenants can be evicted
for non-payment, or if the landlord
wishes to sell the property or use it
as his own residence. It is nearly
impossible to evict non-payers Oct-
Mar, as it's illegal to throw people
out in winter.
Before accepting you as a tenant,
agencies or landlords will probably
require you to present a *dossier* with
pay slips (*fiches de paie/bulletins de
salaire*) showing three to four times
the amount of the monthly rent, and
for foreigners, in particular, to furnish
a financial guarantee. When taking
out a lease, payments usually include
the first month's rent, a deposit (*une
caution*) equal to two month's rent,
and an agency fee, if applicable. It is
customary for an inspection of the
premises (*état des lieux*) by a bailiff
(*huissier*) at the start and end of the
rental to assess the flat's condition,
the cost of which (around 1000F) is
shared by landlord and tenant.
Landlords may try to rent their flats
non-declaré – without a written lease
and get rent in cash. This can make
it difficult for the tenant to establish
his or her rights – which, in addition
to avoiding tax, is why landlords do it.

Flat hunting

The largest lists of furnished
(*meublé*) and unfurnished (*vide*) flats
for rent are in Tuesday's *Le Figaro*.

Most ads are placed by agencies. Flats offered to foreigners are advertised in the daily *International Herald Tribune* and English-language fortnightly *FUSAC*; rents tend to be higher than in the French press. Short-term flat agencies can simplify things, but are not cheap either. Local bakeries often post notices of flats for rent direct from the owner. Non-agency listings are also available in the weekly *Particulier à Particulier*, published on Thursdays, and via Minitel 3615 PAP. There's also a commercial Minitel flat rental service on 3615 LOCAT. Landlords often list a visiting time; prepare to meet hordes of other flat-seekers on the staircase and take supporting documents and cheque book.

Bureau de l'Information Juridique des Proprietaires et des Occupants (BIPO)
6 rue Agrippa-d'Aubigné, 4th (01.42.71.31.31). M° Sully-Morland.
Open 9am-5pm Mon-Thur; 9am-4.30pm Fri. Run by the Mairie de Paris, it provides free advice (in French) about renting or buying an apartment, housing benefits, rent legislation and tenants' rights.

Centre d'Information et de Défense des Locataires
115 rue de l'Abbé-Groult, 15th (01.48.42.10.22). M° Convention.
Open 9.30am-1pm, 2.30-6pm Mon-Fri (until 8pm Thur). For problems with landlords, rent increases, etc.

Repairs & Cleaning

Most department stores provide services, such as ticket sales, watch and jewellery repairs and printing. *See chapter* **Specialist Shops**.

BHV (Bazar de l'Hôtel de Ville)
Main shop: 52-64 rue de Rivoli, 4th (01.42.74.90.00). M° Hôtel-de-Ville.
Open 9.30am-7pm Mon, Tue, Thur-Sat; 9.30am-10pm Wed. *DIY shop: 11 rue des Archives (01.42.74.94.51). DIY tool hire annexe:* 40 rue de la Verrerie, 4th (01.42.74.97.23).
Credit AmEx, MC, V. The leading department store for camera cleaning and repair, photo-developing, photocopying, shoe repair, watch repair, car parts and tool hire.

Horloger Artisan/Jean-Claude Soulage *32 rue St-Paul, 4th (01.48.87.24.75). M° St-Paul.* **Open** 9.30am-noon, 3-7pm Tue-Fri; 9.30am-noon Sat. **No credit cards**. Watch and jewellery repairs and restoration.

Nestor Pressing *10bis rue Berteaux-Dumas, Neuilly-sur-Seine (01.47.69.74.15). M° Les Sablons.* **Open** 9am-9pm Mon-Fri. **Credit** AmEx, MC, V. Full-service cleaning, clothing repair, ironing, shoe repair for most *arrondissements* and western suburbs. Home pick-up 3-10pm. 48-hour and express service.

Rainbow International
40 rue Galilée, 77380 Combs-la-Ville (01.60.60.18.16). **Open** 7am-9pm daily. **No credit cards**. Rainbow will clean carpets (around 25F/m²; 15m² minimum), sofas, leather, etc.

Emergency Repairs

Numerous 24-hour emergency repair services deal with plumbing, electricity, heating, locks, car repairs and much more. Most charge a minimum of 150F call-out and 200F per hour's labour, plus parts; more on Sunday and at night.

Allô Assistance Dépannage *(08.00.07.24.24).* No car repairs.
Numéro Un Dépannage *(01.43.31.51.51).* No car repairs.
SOS Dépannage *(01.47.07.99.99).* double the price, but claim to be twice as reliable. 320F call-out, then 320F/hour. 8am-7pm Mon-Sat; nights and Sun 400F call out, 400F/hour.

Smoking

Earnest official health campaigns have made only a slight dent in French lighting-up habits, and in most public places many people still smoke. Under a 1991 law, restaurants are obliged to provide a non-smoking area. However, if you ask to be seated in the *non-fumeurs* space you're likely to end up at the worst table in the house, tucked away next to the toilets or the stairs. Unless you're seriously allergic to tobacco you'll probably find it more pleasant to sit amid the smoke with the rest. Smoking is banned in most theatres, cinemas and on public transport.

Study & Students

The University of Paris is split into numerous units around the city and suburbs, of which the renowned Sorbonne is just one. Anyone who has passed the *baccalauréat* can apply, so over-crowded facilities and huge drop-out rates (up to 50 per cent at the end of the first year) are perennial problems. The situation is different in the prestigious, highly selective *Grandes Ecoles*, such as the Ecole National d'Administration (ENA), Ecole Normale Supérieure or Ecole Polytechnique. Students at French universities study either for a two-year *DEUG* or for a *Licence*, a three-year degree course. Many students take vocational or business-oriented courses, and many do a *stage*, a practical traineeship, after or during their degree. Other study options include private colleges, whether to learn French or make the most of Paris' cultural opportunities. Meeting other students can be difficult as most students live with

their parents and there are few organised social activities. Sport is one good way, as you can do free sports courses as part of your degree. There are cheap organised ski trips. Registration in Paris universities takes about three weeks; each course has to be signed up for separately, and involves queueing at a different office to obtain a reading list.

CROUS (Centre Régional des Oeuvres Universitaires et Scolaires) *39 av Georges-Bernanos, 5th (01.40.51.36.00/Service du Logement 01.40.51.37.17/19/21). RER Port-Royal.* **Open** 9am-5pm Mon-Fri. Manages all University of Paris student residences. Most rooms are single-occupancy (around 750F/month). Requests for rooms must be made by 1 April for the next academic year. CROUS posts ads for rooms and has a list of hostels, some of which overlap with **UCRIF**. In summer, university residences are open to under-26s (around 100F/night). CROUS also issues the ISIC card, organises excursions, sports and cultural events, provides information on jobs, and offers discount theatre, cinema and concert tickets. It is the clearing house for all *bourses* (grants) issued to foreign students. Students may qualify if they are members of the EU or if their family has lived in France for two years. Call the Service des Bourses on 01.40.51.35.50.

Exchange Schemes

Socrates-Erasmus Programme
In Britain: *UK Socrates-Erasmus Council, RND Building, The University, Canterbury, Kent CT2 7PD (0122-7762712).*
In France: *Agence Erasmus, 10 pl de la Bourse, 33081 Bordeaux Cedex (05.56.79.44.10).* The Socrates-Erasmus scheme enables EU students with a reasonable standard of written and spoken French to spend a year of their degree following appropriate courses in the French university system. The UK office publishes a brochure and helps with general enquiries, but applications must be made through the Erasmus Co-ordinator at your home university.
Students from non-EU countries should find out from their university whether it has an agreement with the Paris university system such as the US 'Junior Year Abroad' scheme via **MICEFA** (26 rue du Fbg-St-Jacques, 14th/01.40.51.76.96).

Cartes de Séjour and Housing Benefit

Centre de Réception des Etudiants Etrangers *13 rue Miollis, 15th (01.53.71.51.68). M° Cambronne.* **Open** 9am-4pm Mon-Fri. Foreign students who wish to qualify for housing benefit or to work

legally during their course in Paris must get a *Carte de Séjour*. You need to present your passport or national identity card; proof of residence; an electricity bill; student card; student social security card; visa (if applicable); a bank statement, accompanied by a parental letter (in French) proving that you receive at least 2500F per month. Add to this, three black-and-white passport photos and a 200F *timbre fiscal* (which you buy at the Centre or a *tabac*). Expect it to take around two months. Pick-up is at the Préfecture de Police at 9 bd du Palais (4th). You will then be eligible for the ALS (*Allocation Logement à Caractère Social*), which is handled by three CAFs (*Centres de gestion des allocations familiales*), depending on your *arrondissement*. They are open 8.30am-4pm/5.30pm Mon-Fri.
CAF 101 rue Nationale, 13th (01.40.77.58.00). 18 rue Viala, 15th (01.45.75.62.47); 67 av Jean-Jaurès, 19th (01.44.84.74.98). Depending on your living situation, you may receive 600F-1000F a month.

Student & Youth Discounts

Despite Paris' expensive reputation, a wide range of student discounts makes budget living possible. To claim the *tarif étudiant* (around 10F off some cinema seats, up to 50 per cent off museums and standby theatre tickets, 20 per cent in some hairdressers), you must have a French student card or an International Student Identity Card (ISIC), available from **CROUS**, student travel agents and the **Cité Universitaire**. ISIC cards are only valid in France if you are under 26. Under-26s can get up to 50 per cent off rail travel on certain trains with the *Carte 12/25*, or buy the *Carte Jeune* (120F from Fnac), which gives discounts on museums, cinema, theatre, travel, sports clubs, restaurants, insurance and some shops. Theatre, concert and opera deals usually work by buying discounted seats at the last minute. **SMEREP** *54 bd St-Michel, 6th (01.56.54.36.34).* **Open** 9am-5.30pm Mon-Fri. A 140F *Carte Jeune* offers similar reductions to the Fnac card, including the Louvre and the RATP. Look also for the magazine *JAP (Jeune à Paris)*, which has useful discount vouchers.

Student Accommodation

The simplest budget accommodation for medium-to-long stays are the Cité Universitaire and *foyers* (student hostels). An option, which is more common for women than men, is a *chambre contre travail* – free board in exchange for childcare, housework or English lessons. Look out for ads

at accommodation offices, language schools and the American Church. For cheap hotels and youth hostels, *see chapter* **Accommodation**. As students often cannot provide proof of income, a *porte-garant* (guarantor) is required, usually a parent, who must write a letter (in French) declaring that he/she guarantees payment of rent and bills. **Cité Universitaire** *19 bd Jourdan, 14th (01.42.53.51.44). RER Cité Universitaire.* **Open** administration 9am-3pm Mon-Fri. Foreign students enrolled on a university course, or current *stagiaires* who have previously done two years of career work, can apply for a place at this huge campus of halls of residence on the southern edge of Paris. Excellent facilities (lawns, tennis courts, swimming pool, gym, theatres, library, an orchestra and student restaurant) and a friendly atmosphere compensate for the rather basic rooms. Rooms must be booked for the entire academic year (Oct-June). Rents are around 1700F-2200F per month for a single room, 1200F-1625F per person for a double. Prices vary according to which *maison* you live in. UK citizens must apply to the Collège Franco-Britannique, and Americans to the Fondation des Etats-Unis. From 1 July to 30 Sept rooms are available to anybody with an ISIC card, for about 100F per night, minimum one week. **UCRIF (Union des Centres de Rencontres Internationales de France)** *27 rue de Turbigo, 2nd (01.40.26.57.64). M° Les Halles.* **Open** 9am-6pm Mon-Fri. Operates several cheap, short-stay hostels in France, including four in Paris.

Office de Tourisme de Paris

127 av des Champs-Elysées, 8th (01.36.68.31.12/recorded information in English 01.49.52.53.56). M° Charles de Gaulle-Etoile. **Open** *summer* 9am-8pm daily; *winter* 9am-8pm Mon-Sat; 11am-6pm Sun. Closed 1 May. Brochures and information on sights and events in Paris and the suburbs. It has a souvenir and bookshop, a bureau de change, hotel reservation service, and sells phonecards, museum cards, travel passes and tickets for museums, theatres, tours and other attractions. All staff are multi-lingual. Branch offices have more limited facilities. **Branches**: Eiffel Tower (01.45.51.22.15). Open May-Sept 11am-6pm daily. Gare de Lyon (01.43.43.33.24). Open 8am-8pm Mon-Sat.

Espace du Tourisme d'Ile de France

Carrousel du Louvre, 99 rue de Rivoli, 1st (08.03.03.19.98/from abroad (33)1.44.50.19.98). **Open** 10am-7pm Mon, Wed-Sun. Sleekly designed information showcase for Paris and the Ile de France, includes information on museums, châteaux, accommodation, gourmet weekends, golf and walking tours.

Resto-U

3 rue Mabillon, 6th (01.43.25.66.23). M° Mabillon. **Open** 11.30am-2pm, 6-8pm Mon-Fri. **No credit cards.** A chain of cheap university canteens run by CROUS. If you have a student card from Paris university you can buy a *carnet* of tickets at 14F per ticket (24F for ISIC cardholders).

Student Employment

Foreign students from the EU can legally work up to 39 hours per week. Non-EU members who are studying in Paris may apply for an *autorisation provisoire de travail* after one year to work a 20hr week. **CIDJ (Centre d'Information et de Documentation Jeunesse)** *101 quai Branly, 7th (01.44.49.12.00). M° Bir-Hakeim/ RER Champ de Mars.* **Open** 9.30am-6pm Mon-Fri; 9.30am-1pm Sat. The CIDJ is mainly a library giving students advice on courses and careers, but it also houses the main youth bureau of the ANPE (Agence Nationale Pour l'Emploi), the state employment service, which provides assistance with job applications. Many ANPE job offers are part-time or menial, but specialised divisions exist for professional jobs.

Language Courses

Alliance Française *101 bd Raspail, 6th (01.45.44.38.28). M° St-Placide or Notre Dame des Champs.* **Open** 9am-6pm Mon-Fri; **Fees** enrolment 250F; 1460F-3900F per month. A highly regarded, non-profit French-language school, with beginners' and specialist courses starting every month, plus a *médiathèque*, film club and lectures. **Berlitz France** *38 av de l'Opéra, 2nd (01.44.94.50.00). M° Opéra.*

Women's Paris

Paris is essentially unthreatening for women, although the usual precautions of not going out alone late at night apply as they would in any other large city. The worst problems tend to be concentrated in the suburbs, although be careful in areas like Pigalle, the rue St-Denis, the Bois de Boulogne and Bois de Vincennes. Violent crime has been on the increase, but the majority of rapes go unreported, which makes figures hard to estimate. Nonetheless counselling and support services do exist. While French men refrain from whistling and bottom-pinching, many are not shy about trying to pick women up. The best brushoff is a withering stare, well-practised among streetwise *Parisiennes*. Legislation was passed in 1992 to punish sexual harrassment in the workplace, but prosecutions are rare. Flirtatious advances are commonly accepted as consistent with male machismo or chivalry. French women got the vote only in 1948, and the pill only in 1967, but a large proportion of women in the Ile de France work, although as everywhere in Europe salaries are generally lower than male counterparts. Despite some important female ministers and judges, there are few women in top civil service or business positions. For further information on associations, try also the Annuaire au Feminin website on www.iway.fr/femmes.

Maison des Femmes

163 rue de Charenton, 12th (01.43.43.41.13/ 01.43.43.42.13). M° Reuilly-Diderot or Gare de Lyon. **Open** 4-7pm Wed, Fri, Sat; café 7-10pm Fri.
Run with heartfelt enthusiasm, the strictly women-only MdF hosts a feminist library, a café, assorted women's groups including Ruptures, a feminist theory workshop, and SOS Sexisme, an anti-sexism group, and the ARCL lesbian archives (*see chapter* **Gay & Lesbian**). Counselling about women's work rights is also offered (*Conseil Juridique Droit du Travail*). Volunteers can guide on where to look for legal or employment advice or a rape crisis centre.

Librairie des Femmes

74 rue de Seine, 6th (01.43.29.50.75). M° Mabillon. **Open** 11.30am-7pm Mon-Sat. **Credit** AmEx, MC, V.
Paris' main feminist bookshop owned by Editions des Femmes has a gallery area and leaflets on events.

Alliance des Femmes pour la Démocratie

5 rue de Lille, 7th (01.45.48.83.80). M° Rue du Bac. This groups militates against sexual discrimination, whether it be granting political asylum to feminist writers or opposing international prostitution rings.

CNIDFF

7 rue du Jura, 13th (01.42.17.12.34). M° Gobelins. **Open** 1.30-5.30pm Tue-Thur; *phone enquiries* 9am-12.30pm Tue-Thur.
The Centre National d'Information et de Documentation des Femmes et des Familles offers legal, professional and health advice for women.

Service des Droits des Femmes

31 rue Le Peletier, 9th (01.47.70.41.58). M° Le Peletier. **Open** phone calls only 9am-5pm Mon-Fri. **Library** 9am-5pm Wed, Thur (by appointment only).

Sponsored by the Ministère de l'Emploi et de la Solidarité, the service promotes women's rights and oversees the implementation of programmes aimed at achieving equal employment opportunity.

Violence conjugale: Femmes Info Service

(01.40.02.02.33). **Open** 7.30am-11.30pm Mon-Fri; 10am-8pm Sat.
Telephone hotline for battered women, directing them towards medical aid or shelters, if need be.

Viols Femmes Informations

(08.00.05.95.95). **Open** 10am-6pm Mon-Fri.
A freephone in French for dealing with rape.

WICE

20 bd du Montparnasse, 15th (01.45.66.75.50). M° Montparnasse-Bienvenüe. **Open** 9am-5pm Mon-Fri. **Membership** 350F; 500F joint; 250F students.
American expatriate cultural/educational centre runs courses ranging from art history and literature to wine tasting. Membership benefits include discounts to certain shops and leisure facilities, and a library.

Contraception

To obtain the Pill, a diaphragm or the morning-after pill, you'll need a prescription, available on appointment from the first two places below or from a *médecin généraliste* (GP) or gynaecologist. Note that the mini-pill is not reimbursed. Spermicides and condoms (*préservatifs*) are sold in pharmacies, and there are condom dispensing machines in Métros, club lavatories and on street corners. For sanitary products, supermarkets are your best bet.

Centre de Planification et d'Education Familiale *27 rue Curnonsky, 17th (01.48.88.07.28). M° Porte de Champerret.* **Open** 9am-5pm Mon-Fri.
Free consultations in French, on family planning and abortion. Abortion counselling on demand; otherwise phone for an appointment.

MFPF (Mouvement Français pour le Planning Familial) *10 rue Vivienne, 2nd (01.42.60.93.20). M° Bourse.* **Open** 9.30am-5pm Mon-Thur; 11am-4pm Fri.
Phone for an appointment for contraception advice and prescriptions. For abortion advice, just turn up at the centre. Branch at 94 bd Masséna, 13th (01.45.84.28.25), operating Fridays only.

Women's Accommodation

Union des Foyers des Jeunes Travailleurs *21 rue des Malmaisons, 13th (01.42.16.86.66). M° Maison-Blanche.* **Open** 9am-1pm, 2-5pm Mon-Fri. **Rates** per month 2500F (half-board). **No credit cards.** An organisation running around 30 *foyers* (hostels) in Paris, of which some 15 are specifically for women aged 18-25, who are either working or unemployed but looking for work.

Union Chrétienne de Jeunes Filles *22 rue de Naples, 8th (01.45.22.23.49). M° Villiers; 168 rue Blomet, 15th (01.56.56.63.00). M° Convention.* **Open** 9am-7pm daily. **Rates** *single room* per month 3150F (half-board). **No credit cards.** Individual and dormitory rooms for women aged 18-24. Breakfast and dinner are included. Shorter stays possible in summer.

Open 9.30am-6pm Mon-Fri; 9.30am-12.30pm Sat. **Fees** 7714F-29,735F. Well known and effective, individual and evening classes, but pricey; mainly used by businesses.
British Institute *9 rue Constantine, 7th (01.44.11.73.73/70). Mº Invalides*. **Open** 10am-1pm, 2-5.45pm Mon-Fri. **Fees** 1500F-6000F per term. Linked to London University, the 4000-student Institute offers both English courses for Parisians, and French courses (not beginner) in translation, commercial French, film and literature. It is possible to study at the Institute for a three-year French degree from the University of London (details from Senate House, Malet Street, London WC1/0171-636 8000).
Eurocentres *13 passage Dauphine, 6th (01.40.46.72.00). Mº Odéon*. **Open** 8.30am-6pm Mon-Fri. **Fees** four weeks 7729F. This international group offers intensive classes for a maximum of 15 students. Courses emphasise communication over grammar, and include an audiovisual *médiathèque* and lectures.
Institut Catholique de Paris *12 rue Cassette, 6th (01.44.39.52.68). Mº St-Sulpice*. **Open** 10am-2pm, 5-7pm Mon; 10am-4pm Tue; 10am-1pm Wed; 10am-4pm Thur; 10am-1pm Fri. **Fees** enrolment 500F (*dossier* test); *registration* 3750F; 15-week course (6 hrs/week) 3780F. reputable school offers traditional courses in French language and culture. The equivalent of a French *bac* is required, plus proof of residence. Students must be 18 or above, but don't have to be Catholic.
Institut Parisien *87 bd de Grenelle, 15th (01.40.56.09.53). Mº La Motte Picquet-Grenelle*. **Open** 8.30am-5pm Mon-Fri. **Fees** enrolment 250F; 990F-2900F. This dynamic private school offers courses in language (up to 25 hours per week) and French civilisation, business French and has evening courses if there's enough demand. Except for beginners, you can join a class any week.
La Sorbonne – Cours de Langue et Civilisation *47 rue des Ecoles, 5th (01.40.46.22.11 ext 2664/75). Mº Cluny-La Sorbonne/RER Luxembourg*. **Open** 10am-noon, 2-4pm Mon-Fri. **Fees** 3450F-11,550F per half-year. Classes for foreigners at the Sorbonne ride on the name of this eminent institution. Teaching is grammar-based. The main course includes lectures on politics, history and culture, as well as language-lab sessions. Courses are open to anyone over 18, and fill up very quickly.

Specialised Courses

American University of Paris *Office of Admissions, 31 av Bosquet, 7th (01.40.62.07.20). RER Pont de l'Alma*. Established in 1962, the AUP is an international college awarding four-year American liberal arts degrees (BA/BSc). It has exchange agreements with colleges in the US, Poland and Japan. A Summer Session and Division of Continuing Education (102 rue St-Dominique, 7th/01.40.62.07.20) are also offered.
Cours d'Adultes *Information: Hôtel de Ville, pl de l'Hôtel de Ville, 4th (01.44.61.16.16). Mº Hôtel-de-Ville*. **Fees** 160F-1000F. A huge range of inexpensive adult-education classes are run by the City of Paris, in town halls and colleges. To enrol, you need a *Carte de Séjour*.
CIDD Découverte du Vin *30 rue de la Sablière, 14th (01.45.45.44.20). Mº Pernéty*. **Open** 9am-8pm Mon-Fri; 11am-1pm, 2-8pm Sat. **Fees** from 420F (for 4 hrs). Wine tasting and appreciation courses (some in English) from beginner to advanced.
Cordon Bleu *8 rue Léon-Delhomme, 15th (01.53.68.22.50). Mº Vaugirard*. **Open** 8am-7pm Mon-Fri; 8.30am-4pm Sat. **Fees** 220F-4950F. Three-hour sessions on classical and regional cuisine, one-week workshops and ten-week courses aimed at those refining skills or embarking on a culinary career.
Ritz-Escoffier Ecole de Gastronomie Française *38 rue Cambon, 1st (01.43.16.31.43). Mº Madeleine*. **Fees** 275F-172,000F. From afternoon demonstrations in the Ritz kitchens to twelve-week diplomas. Classes in French with English translation.
Ecole du Louvre *Porte Jaugard, L'aile de Flore, Musée du Louvre, quai du Louvre, 1st (01.55.35.19.35)*. **Open** 9.30am-noon, 1.30-5pm Mon-Fri. **Fees** 1420F-1750F. This prestigious school runs art history and archaeology courses. Foreign students not wanting to take a full degree (*Licence*) can enrol (May-Sept) as *auditeurs* to attend lectures.
INSEAD *bd de Constance, 77305 Fontainebleau (01.60.72.40.00)*. **Open** 8.30am-5.30pm Mon-Fri. Call for information sessions 2.30pm Fri. **Fees** 155,000F. Highly regarded international business school, with 520 students from across the world, offers a ten-month MBA in English.
Parsons School of Design *14 rue Letellier, 15th (01.45.77.39.66). Mº La Motte-Picquet-Grenelle*. **Open** 9am-5pm Mon-Thur; 9am-4.30pm Fri. **Fees** 300F registration fee; 8 sessions 2000F-2500F. Subsidiary of New York art and design college offers full- and part-time courses in fine art, fashion, photography, illustration, computer, interior and communication design, in English.
Spéos – Paris Photographic Institute *7 rue Jules-Vallès, 11th (01.40.09.18.58). Mº Charonne*. **Open** 9am-6pm Mon-Fri. **Fees** 450F-35,500F. Bilingual photo school affiliated with the Rhode Island School of Design offers courses and intensive workshops in photography and photojournalism.

All French phone numbers have ten digits. Paris and Ile de France numbers begin with 01; the rest of France is divided into four zones (02-05). Portable phones start with 06. 08 indicates a special rate (see below). If you are calling France from abroad leave off the 0 at the start of the ten-digit number. To call abroad from France dial 00, then country code. Since 1998 other phone companies have been allowed to enter the market, with new prefixes (eg. Cégétel numbers starting with 7).

Special Rate Numbers

08.00 Numéro Vert Freephone.
08.01 Numéro Azur 0.74F under 3 min, then 0.28F/min.
08.02 Numéro Indigo I 0.74F under 56 secs, then 0.79F/min.
08.03 Numéro Indigo II 0.74F under 41 secs, then 1.09F/min.
08.36 numbers are charged 2.23F/min. This rate applies not just to chat lines but increasingly to cinema and transportation infolines.

Public Phones

Most public phones in Paris use phonecards (*télécartes*). Sold at post offices, tobacconists, airports and train and Métro stations, cards cost 40F for 50 units and 96F for 120 units. Cafés have coin phones, while post offices usually have card phones. In a phone box, the digital display screen should read *Décrochez*. Pick up the phone. When *Introduisez votre carte* appears, insert your card into the slot. The screen should then read *Patientez SVP*. When *Numérotez* appears, this is your signal to dial. *Crédit épuisé* means that you have no more units left. Finally, hang up (*Raccrochez*), and don't forget your card. Some public phones take credit cards. If you are using a credit card, insert the card, key in your PIN number and *Patientez SVP* should appear. Continue as above.

Phone Books

Phone books are found in all post offices and in most cafés (ask if you don't see them by the phone). The *Pages Blanches* (White Pages, two volumes) lists names of people and businesses alphabetically. The *Pages Jaunes* (Yellow Pages) lists businesses and services by category.

Telephone Charges

Local calls in Paris and Ile-de-France beginning with 01 cost 74 centimes for three minutes, standard rate, 29 centimes/minute thereafter. Calls beyond a 100km radius are charged at 74 centimes for the first 39 seconds, then 1.14F per minute. International destinations are divided into 16 zones. Reduced-rate periods for calls within France and Europe: 7pm-8am during the week; noon Sat to 8am Mon. Reduced-rate periods for the US and Canada: 7pm through to 1pm Mon-Fri; all day Sat, Sun. France Telecom's **Primaliste** offers 20 per cent off on calls to six chosen numbers.

Cheap Rate Providers

There are several companies offering low rates for overseas calls, which usually involve you dialling an access number before the number you want to reach. Some require an advance payment to establish a credit limit. Some offer itemised billing to a credit card. The following providers offer competitive rates from France: Based in France, **AXS Telecom** *(01.53.00.37.10)*; **BigBig Fone Co** *(01.46.98.20.88)*; **First Telecom** *(01.46.98.20.00)*. Good deals are offered in the UK by **AT&T Global Customer Service** and in the US by **KallMart**.

24-Hour Telephone Services

Operator assistance, French directory enquiries (*renseignements*), dial 12. To make a reverse-charge call within France, ask to make a call *en PCV*. **International directory enquiries** 00.33.12, then country code (eg. 44 for UK). **Telephone engineer** dial 13. **International news** (French recorded message, France Inter), dial 08.36.68.10.33 (2.23F/min). **Telegram** all languages, international 08.00.33.44.11; within France 36.55. **Time** dial 36.99. **Traffic news** dial 01.48.99.33.33. **Weather** dial 08.36.70.12.34 (2.23F/min) for enquiries on weather in France and abroad, in French or English; dial 08.36.68.02.75 (2.23F/min) for a recorded weather announcement for Paris and region. **Airparif** (01.44.59.47.64). Mon-Fri 9am-5.30pm. Information about pollution levels and air quality in Paris: invaluable for asthmatics.

Minitel

France Telecom's Minitel is an interactive videotext service available to any telephone subscriber, although it is gradually being superceded by the Internet. Hotels are often Minitel-equipped and most post offices offer use of the terminals for directory enquiries on 3611. Hundreds of services on the pricier 3614, 3615, 3616 and 3617

numbers give access to hotel and ticket reservations, airline and train information, weather forecasts and dozens of recreational lines that include 'dating' hook-ups. For French telephone directory information, dial 3611 on the keyboard, wait for the beep and press *Connexion*, then type in the name and city of the person or business whose number and/or address you're looking for, and press *Envoi*. Minitel directory use is free for the first free minutes, 37 centimes per minute thereafter. Minitel directory in English dial 3611, wait for the beep, press *Connexion*, type MGS, then *Envoi*. Then type *Minitel en anglais*.

Television

Everyone derides French TV, but at least cable and satellite mean an ever-growing choice of channels. **TF1** The country's biggest channel, and the first to be privatised in 1987. Game shows, dubbed soaps, celebrity gossip and audience debates are staples, although Depardieu's *Comte de Monte Cristo* showed that quality is possible. Detective series *Navarro* and *Julie Lescaut* and the political interviewees of Public draw big audiences. The 8pm news has star anchors Patrick Poivre d'Arvor ('PPDA') and Claire Chazal. **France 2** State-owned station mixes game shows, documentaries, and serious cultural chat in Bernard Pivot's literary *Bouillon de Culture*. In Michel Drucker's weekly *Studio Gabriel*, the interviewer is as famous as those he has on set. **FR3** The more heavyweight – and hence less popular – of the two state channels offers lots of local, wildlife and sports coverage, on-screen debating about social issues, and *Cinéma de Minuit*, late-night Sunday classic films in the original language. **Canal+** Subscription channel draws viewers with recent movies (sometimes in the original languague), exclusive sport and late-night porn. *Teletubbies* and amusing talk show *Nulle Part Ailleurs* with satirical puppets *Les Guignols* are available unscrambled. **Arte/La Cinquième** Franco-German hybrid Arte specialises in intelligent, often themed, evenings, for an enlightened audience. Films are often shown in their original language. Arte shares its wavelength with educational channel *La Cinquième* (5.45am-7pm). **M6** Daytime base is music videos, but M6 is winning the 20s and 30s audience, with some excellent magazine programmes, such as *Culture Pub* (about advertising), finance mag *Capital* and voyeuristic *Zone Interdite*, as well as the *X-Files*.

Cable TV & Satellite

France offers a similar range of cable and satellite channels to every European country. The basic package from Paris-Câble (01.44.25.89.99/160F per month, plus connection fee) includes **Paris Première**, excellent for fashion shows and *VO* films, TF1's continuous news programme **LC1**, documentary channel **Planète**, history channel **Histoire**, **Eurosport**, **MTV** music television, **MCM** its French imitator, woman's mag **Téva,**, **Série Club** for vintage series, and **Canal Jimmy**, which shows British and American sitcoms in the original, such as *Friends* and *Ab Fab*. You have to go to the next package (from 194F/month) for **BBC Prime**, which shows up-to-date *Eastenders* and archaic comedy repeats and CNN's 24-hours news. Other packages offer film channel and pay-as-you-view options.

Satellite potentially offers better-quality reception, lower (if any) subscription prices and a better-targeted *bouquet* of channels, but is opposed by most Paris and suburban local authorities. At present, operators include Eutelsat (capturing channels from the rest of Europe and the Middle East), Canal Satellite (linked to Canal+), Astra, TPS and AB Sat.

Ticket agencies

The following sell tickets for rock and classical concerts and theatre. *See also chapter* **Theatre**. **Fnac** *Forum des Halles, 1-5 rue Pierre-Lescot, level -3, 1st (01.40.41.40.00). M° Les Halles/RER Châtelet-Les Halles.* **Open** 10am-7.30pm Mon-Sat. **Credit** AmEx, MC, V. Bookings in person only. Branches: 136 rue de Rennes, 6th (01.49.54.30.00); 74 av des Champs-Elysées, 8th (01.53.53.64.64); 24 bd des Italiens, 9th (open till midnight) (01.48.01.02.03); 4 pl de la Bastille, 12th (01.43.42.04.04). **Ticket +** *(01.49.87.50.50)*. **Open** 9am-9pm Mon-Sat. **Credit** MC, V. Telephone bookings linked to Fnac. **Virgin Megastore** *52 av des Champs-Elysées, 8th (01.49.53.50.00). M° Franklin D Roosevelt.* **Open** 10am-midnight Mon-Sat (by telephone at the *billetterie on 01.44.68.44.08*); noon-midnight Sun. **Credit** AmEx, DC, MC, V. Branch: Carrousel du Louvre, 1st (01.49.53.50.00).

Time & the Seasons

France is one hour ahead of Greenwich Mean Time (GMT). In France time is based on the 24-hour system so that 8am is *8 heures*, noon is *12 heures (midi)*, 8pm is *20 heures* and midnight is *0 (zéro) heure (minuit)*.

Directory

Average Temperatures

January 7.5°C (5.5°F); February 7.1°C (44.8°F); March 10.2°C (50.4°F); April 15.7°C (60.3°F); May 16.6°C (61.9°F); June 23.4°C (74.1°F); July 25.1°C (77.2°F); August 25.6°C (78.1°F); September 20.9°C (69.6°F); October 16.5°C (61.7F); November 11.7°C (53.1°F); December 7.8°C (46°F).

Video Rental

Reels on Wheels *12 villa Croix-Nivert, 15th (01.45.67.64.99). M°* *Cambronne.* **Open** 11.30am-10.30pm daily. **Rates** 22F-35F for three days; membership 500F a year, 250F three months. **Credit** MC, V. Ian, a Scot, can deliver over 6000 films (most in English, subtitled if not).
Prime Time Video *24 rue Mayet, 6th (01.40.56.33.44). M° Duroc.* **Open** noon-midnight daily. **Rates** 30F for three days; free membership. **Credit** MC, V. Rents English language videos. Branch: 12 rue Leance Reynaud, 16th (01.47.20.50.01).

Visas

European Union nationals do not need a visa to enter France, nor do US, Canadian, Australian or New Zealand citizens for stays of up to three months. Nationals of other countries should enquire at the nearest French Consulate before leaving home; if they are travelling to France from one of the countries included in the Schengen agreement (most of the EU, but not Britain, Ireland, Italy or Greece), the visa from that country should be sufficient. For over three months, *see p307*, **Cartes de Séjour**.

Working in Paris

All EU nationals can work legally in France, but must apply for a French social security number and *Carte de Séjour*. Some job ads can be found at branches of the Agence National Pour l'Emploi (ANPE), the French national employment bureau. This is also the place to go to sign up as a *demandeur d'emploi*, to be placed on file as available for work and to qualify for French unemployment benefits. Britons can only claim French unemployment benefit if they were already signed on before leaving the UK. Non-EU nationals need a work permit and are not entitled to use the ANPE network without valid work papers.
CIEE *1 pl de l'Odéon, 6th (01.44.41.74.74). M° Odéon.* **Open** 9am-6pm, Mon-Fri. The Council on International Educational Exchange provides three-month work permits for US citizens and residents still at or recently graduated from university. The programme has its own job centre in Paris, mostly for sales and catering. The CIEE also provides a three-month permit to those with a pre-arranged job.
Office des Migrations Internationales (OMI) *Service de l'Expatriation-BCO, 44 rue Bargue, 75732 Paris Cedex 15 (01.53.69.53.29).* The OMI provides work permits of up to 18 months to Americans aged 18-35 and has a job placement service. *Stagiaires* should pick up permit, which takes 8-10 weeks, in their home country.

Job Ads

Help-wanted ads sometimes appear in the *International Herald Tribune*, although the 'sophisticated personal companion' make up the bulk of them. The free publication *FUSAC* carries some job ads for English-speakers, mainly English-language teaching, bar work, secretarial and child minding. Offers for English-speakers are sometimes listed on noticeboards at language schools and Anglo establishments, such as the **American Church**; most are for babysitters and language tutors. Positions as waiters and bar staff are often available at international-style watering holes. Bilingual secretarial/PA work is available for those with good written French, *see p320.* If you are looking for professional work, have your CV translated, including French equivalents for any qualifications. Most job applications require a photo and a handwritten letter; French employers are very fond of graphological analysis.

Business Resources

Information

The best first stop in Paris for anyone initiating business in France is the **Bourse du Commerce**. Most major banks can refer you to lawyers, accountants and tax consultants, and several US and British banks provide other expatriate services. For business and financial news, the French dailies *La Tribune* and *Les Echos*, and the weekly *Investir* are the tried and trusted sources. German-owned *Capital*, its sister magazine *Management* and the weightier *L'Expansion* are worthwhile monthlies. *Défis* has tips for the entrepreneur, while *Initiatives* is for the self-employed. BFM on 96.4 FM is the all-news business radio station. *Les Echos* gives stock quotes on http://www.lesechos.com and the Minitel service 3615 CD offers real-time stock quotes.
The business directories *Kompass France* and *Kompass Régional* give company details, as well as detailed French market profiles, available by Minitel on 3617 KOMPASS.
The standard English-language reference is *The French Company Handbook*, a list of all companies in the 120 Index of the Paris Bourse, published by the *International Herald Tribune* (01.41.43.93.00). It can be ordered with a cheque or credit card for £50 from Paul Baker Publishing, 37 Lambton Rd, London SW20 0LW (0181-946 0590).
Paris Anglophone Directory lists 2500 English-speaking companies, professionals and organisations. It can be ordered for 98F plus 25F postage from Paris Anglophone, 32 rue Edouard Vaillant, 93100 Montreuil (01.48.59.66.58).

Institutions

American Chamber of Commerce *21 av George V, 8th (01.40.73.89.90/ fax 01.47.20.18.62). M° George V or Alma-Marceau.* **Open** 9am-5.30pm Mon-Fri. **Library** only for members 10am-12.30pm Mon-Fri. 100F per day, 50F students. The American Chamber hosts social events for members, and has an active small-business committee. Its directory, listing Franco-American firms and organisations, is available to non-members (400F), as is its *Guide to Doing Business in France* (400F).
Bourse du Commerce *2 rue de Viarmes, 1st (01.55.65.55.65). M° Les Halles.* **Open** 9am-6pm Mon-Fri. This branch of the **CCIP** houses a wide range of services for new businesses, including L'Espace Création (01.53.40.48.50) and the Centre de Formalités des Entreprises (01.53.40.46.00).
British Embassy Commercial Library *35 rue du Fbg-St-Honoré, 8th (01.44.51.34.56/fax 01.44.51.34.01). M° Concorde.* **Open** 10am-1pm, 2.30-5pm Mon-Fri, by appointment. The library stocks trade directories, and assists British companies that wish to develop sales or set up in France.

Directory

Chambre de Commerce et d'Industrie Franco-Britannique
Promotes contacts in the Franco-British business community through talks, social events and seminars. It has three divisions:
Language Training Centre *41 rue de Turenne, 3rd (01.44.59.25.10). Mº Chemin-Vert.* Open 9am-7pm Mon-Thur; 9am-5pm Fri; 9am-1pm Sat. French and English courses in business communication.
Trade and Membership Department *31 rue Boissy d'Anglas, 8th (01.53.30.81.30). Mº Madeleine.* Open 2-5pm Mon-Fri. Annual membership 1450F. Commercial enquiries library. The annual trade directory costs 375F.
Franco-British Educational Services *1 impasse St-Claude, 3rd (01.44.59.24.11). Mº St Sébastien-Froissart.* Open 9am-1pm Mon-Thur; 2-6pm Fri; 9am-1pm, 2-5pm Sat. Administers language courses and Chamber exams.
CCIP (Chambre de Commerce et d'Industrie de Paris) *27 av de Friedland, 8th (01.42.89.70.00/fax 01.42.89.78.68). Mº George V.* Open 9am-6pm Mon-Fri. A huge organisation providing an information centre, and the best business library in the city (30F per day; 300F per year). Its publications *Business and Commerce Undertaken by Non-French Nationals* (for small businesses) and *Foreigners: Starting Up Your Company in France* (for large companies) in English, cost 48F and can be purchased at CCIP or at Presses Universitaires de France, 49 bd St-Michel, 5th (01.44.41.81.20). Trade, market and export information on Minitel 3615 CCIP and 3617 CCIPLUS.
US Embassy Commercial Section *4 av Gabriel, 8th (library 01.43.12.25.32/fax 01.43.12.21.72). Mº Concorde.* Open 9am-6pm Mon-Fri, by appointment only. Business library advises on US companies in France, as well as contacts, research and information. Minitel 3617 USATRADE will respond to enquiries within 24 hours (Mon-Fri).

Trade Fairs & Conferences

The leading centre for international trade fairs, Paris hosts over 500 exhibitions a year, from the Auto Show to the major fashion collections.
Foires et Salons de France *31 rue de Billancourt, Boulogne-Billancourt (01.48.25.66.55/ fax 01.48.25.04.55). Mº Billancourt.* Open 9am-1pm, 2-6pm Mon-Thur (5pm Fri). Distributes the calendar *Salons Nationaux et Internationaux en France* (send a 6.70F stamped envelope or pick one up in person). Consult Minitel 3616 SALONS.
CNIT *2 pl de la Défense, BP 321, 92053 Paris La Défense*

(01.46.92.28.66/ fax 01.46.92.15.78). Mº La Défense. Mainly computer fairs.
Palais des Congrès *2 pl de la Porte-Maillot, 17th (01.40.68.22.22). Mº Porte-Maillot.*
Paris-Expo *Porte de Versailles, 15th (01.43.95.37.00/fax 01.53.68.71.71). Mº Porte de Versailles.* The biggest exhibition centre from agriculture to pharmaceuticals.
Parc des Expositions de Paris-Nord Villepinte *BP 6004, Paris Nord 2, 95970 Roissy-Charles de Gaulle. (01.48.63.30.30/fax 01.48.63.33.70). RER B Parc des Expositions.*

Accountants & Lawyers

Many big UK and US accountancy and legal firms have Paris offices.
France Audit Expertise *148 bd Malesherbes, 17th (01.43.80.42.98/fax 01.47.64.03.92). Mº Wagram.* Open 9am-6pm Mon-Fri. Handles companies of all sizes.
Levine & Okoshken *51 av Montaigne, 8th (01.44.13.69.50/fax 01.45.63.24.96). Mº Franklin D Roosevelt.* Open 9am-6pm Mon-Fri. A specialist in tax and corporate law, with many US clients.
Shubert & Dusausoy *190 bd Haussmann, 8th (01.40.76.01.43/fax 01.40.76.01.44). Mº St-Philippe-du-Roule.* Open 9am-4pm Mon-Fri. Law firm helps English-speaking business people set up in France.

Translators & Interpreters

Certain documents, from birth certificates to loan applications, must be translated by certified legal translators, listed at the CCIP (*see above*) or embassies. For French-English or English/French business translations of annual reports, brochures, etc, there are dozens of reliable independents.
Association des Anciens Elèves de L'Esit
Centre Universitaire Dauphine, 16th (01.44.05.41.46). Open *phone only* 9am-6pm Mon-Fri. A translation and interpreting cooperative whose 1000 members are graduates of L'Ecole Supérieure d'Interprètes et de Traducteurs.
International Corporate Communication *3 rue des Batignolles, 17th (01.43.87.29.29/fax 01.45.22.49.13). Mº Place de Clichy.* Open 9am-1pm, 2-6pm Mon-Fri. Translators of financial and corporate documents. Also offers simultaneous translation services.

Secretarial Services

ADECCO International *4 pl de la Défense, Cedex 26, 92974 Paris La Défense (01.49.01.94.94/ fax 01.46.93.03.44). Mº Grande Arche de La Défense.* Open 8.30am-12pm, 2-

6pm Mon-Fri. This branch of the large international employment agency specialises in bilingual secretaries and office staff – permanent or temporary.
TM International *36-38 rue des Mathurins, 8th (01.47.42.71.00/fax 01.47.42.18.87). RER Auber.* Open 9am-6pm Mon-Fri. Full-time French-English bilingual secretarial staff.

Computer Equipment

Surcouf Informatique *139 av Daumesnil, 12th (01.53.33.20.00/fax 01.53.33.21.01). Mº Gare de Lyon.* Open 9.30am-7pm Tue-Sat. Credit MC, V. An impressive computer superstore, with repair service and an English-language software stall.
KA *14 rue Magellan, 8th (01.44.43.16.00/ fax 01.47.20.34.39). Mº George V.* Open *sales & rental* 9am-7pm Mon-Fri; *technical service* 9am-6pm, Mon-Fri. Credit AmEx, MC, V. Sale and rental of IBM, Apple and Compaq computers.
Prorata Services *27 rue Linné, 5th (01.45.35.94.14/ fax 01.45.35.19.13). Mº Jussieu.* Open 9am-7pm Mon-Fri; 10.30am-6pm Sat. Credit V. Use Macs and PCs on the spot (1F/min) or hire a portable. Its graphic design studio, Studio PAO is at 15 rue Jussieu.

Couriers

Chronopost *9 rue Hérold, 1st (08.03.801.801). Mº Châtelet-Les Halles or Sentier.* Open 8am-8pm Mon-Fri; 9am-3pm Sat. Credit AmEx, MC, V. This post office offshoot is the most widely used service for parcels of up to 30kg. International service.
DHL *59 av d'Iéna, 16th (08.00.20.25.25). Mº Iéna.* Open 9am-8pm Mon-Fri; 9am-5pm Sat. Credit AmEx, MC, V. One of the big names in international courier services. **Branch**: 6 rue des Colonnes, 2nd.
Flash Service *32 rue des Blancs-Manteaux, 4th (01.42.74.26.01/fax 01.42.74.11.17). Mº Rambuteau.* Open 9am-6.30pm Mon-Fri. No credit cards. A local bike messenger company.

Office Hire

CNIT *2 pl de la Défense, BP 200, 92053 Paris La Défense (01.46.92.24.24/fax 01.46.92.15.92). Mº La Défense.* Open 8.30am-7.30pm Mon-Fri. The trade centre houses 800 firms and offers a data-processing service, video-conference facilities and offices and meeting rooms.
Jones Lang Wootton *49 av Hoche, 8th (01.40.55.15.15/ fax 01.46.22.28.28). Mº Charles de Gaulle-Etoile.* Open 8am-7pm Mon-Fri. Britain's leading office-rental firm. Branch at 193-197 rue de Bercy, Tour Gamma B, 12th (01.43.43.60.61).

Essential Vocabulary

In French, as in other Latin languages, the second person singular (you) has two forms. Phrases here are given in the more polite *vous* form. The *tu* form is used with family, friends, young children and pets; you should be careful not to use it with people you do not know sufficiently well, as it is considered rude. You will also find that courtesies such as *monsieur*, *madame* and *mademoiselle* are used much more than their English equivalents. *See chapter* **Directory A-Z** for information on language courses and **Menu Lexicon** for help in deciphering menus.

General Expressions

good morning/good afternoon, hello *bonjour*
good evening *bonsoir;* **goodbye** *au revoir*
hi (familiar) *salut;* **OK** *d'accord;* **yes** *oui;* **no** *non*
How are you? *Comment allez vous?/vous allez bien?*
How's it going? *Comment ça va?/ça va?* (familiar)
Sir/Mr *monsieur (Mr);* **Madam/Mrs** *madame (Mme)*
Miss *mademoiselle (Mlle)*
please *s'il vous plaît;* **thank you** *merci;*
thank you very much *merci beaucoup*
sorry *pardon;* **excuse me** *excusez-moi*
Do you speak English? *Parlez-vous anglais?*
I don't speak French *Je ne parle pas français*
I don't understand *Je ne comprends pas*
Speak more slowly, please *Parlez plus lentement, s'il vous plaît*
Leave me alone *Laissez-moi tranquille*
how much?/how many? *combien?*
Have you got change? *Avez-vous de la monnaie?*
I would like.... *Je voudrais....*
I am going *Je vais;* **I am going to pay** *Je vais payer*
it is *c'est;* **it isn't** *ce n'est pas*
good *bon/bonne;* **bad** *mauvais/mauvaise*
small *petit/petite;* **big** *grand/grande*
beautiful *beau/belle;* **well** *bien;* **badly** *mal*
expensive *cher;* **cheap** *pas cher*
a bit *un peu;* **alot** *beaucoup;* **very** *très;* **with** *avec;*
without *sans;* **and** *et;* **or** *ou;* **because** *parce que*
who? *qui?;* **when?** *quand?;* **what?** *quoi?;* **which?** *quel?;* **where?** *où?;* **why?** *pourquoi?;* **how?** *comment?*
at what time/when? *à quelle heure?*
forbidden *interdit/défendu*
out of order *hors service (hs)/en panne*
daily *tous les jours (tlj)*

On the Phone

hello (telephone) *allô;* **Who's calling?** *C'est de la part de qui?/Qui est à l'appareil?*
Hold the line *Ne quittez pas/Patientez s'il vous plaît*

Getting Around

Where is the (nearest) Métro? *Où est le Métro (le plus proche)?;* **When is the next train for... ?** *C'est quand le prochain train pour... ?*
ticket *un billet;* **station** *la gare;* **platform** *le quai*
entrance *entrée;* **exit** *sortie*
left *gauche;* **right** *droite;* **interchange** *correspondence*
straight on *tout droit;* **far** *loin;* **near** *pas loin/près d'ici*
street *la rue;* **street map** *le plan;* **road map** *la carte*
bank *la banque;* **is there a bank near here?** *est-ce qu'il y a une banque près d'ici?*
Post Office *La Poste;* **a stamp** *un timbre*

Sightseeing

museum *un musée;* **church** *une église*
exhibition *une exposition;* **ticket** (for museum) *un billet;* (for theatre, concert) *une place*
open *ouvert;* **closed** *fermé*
free *gratuit;* **reduced price** *un tarif réduit*
except Sunday *sauf le dimanche*

Accommodation

Do you have a room (for this evening/ for two people)? *Avez-vous une chambre (pour ce soir/ pour deux personnes)?*
full *complet;* **room** *une chambre*
bed *un lit;* **double bed** *un grand lit;*
(a room with) twin beds *une chambre à deux lits*
with bath(room)/shower *avec (salle de) bain/douche*
breakfast *le petit déjeuner;* **included** *compris*
lift *un ascenseur;* **air conditioned** *climatisé*

At the Café or Restaurant

I'd like to book a table (for three/at 8pm) *Je voudrais réserver une table (pour trois personnes/à vingt heures)*
lunch *le déjeuner;* **dinner** *le dîner*
coffee (espresso) *un café;* **white coffee** *un café au lait/café crème;* **tea** *le thé;* **wine** *le vin;* **beer** *la bière*
mineral water *eau minérale;* **fizzy** *gazeuse;* **still** *plate*
tap water *eau du robinet/une carafe d'eau*
the bill, please *l'addition, s'il vous plaît*

Behind the Wheel

give way *céder le passage*
it's not your right of way *vous n'avez pas la priorité;* **no parking** *stationnement interdit/ stationnement gênant;* **deliveries** *livraisons*
toll *péage;* **speed limit 40** *rappel 40*
petrol *essence;* **unleaded** *sans plomb*
traffic jam *embouteillage/bouchon;* **speed** *vitesse*
traffic moving freely *traffic fluide*
dangerous bends *attention virages*

Numbers

0 *zéro;* 1 *un, une;* 2 *deux;* 3 *trois;* 4 *quatre;* 5 *cinq;* 6 *six;* 7 *sept;* 8 *huit;* 9 *neuf;* 10 *dix;* 11 *onze;* 12 *douze;* 13 *treize;* 14 *quatorze;* 15 *quinze;* 16 *seize;* 17 *dix-sept;* 18 *dix-huit;* 19 *dix-neuf;* 20 *vingt;* 21 *vingt-et-un;* 22 *vingt-deux;* 30 *trente;* 40 *quarante;* 50 *cinquante;* 60 *soixante;* 70 *soixante-dix;* 80 *quatre-vingts;* 90 *quatre-vingt-dix;* 100 *cent;* 1000 *mille;* 1,000,000 *un million.*

Days, Months & Seasons

Monday *lundi;* **Tuesday** *mardi;* **Wednesday** *mercredi;* **Thursday** *jeudi;* **Friday** *vendredi;* **Saturday** *samedi;* **Sunday** *dimanche.* **January** *janvier;* **February** *février;* **March** *mars;* **April** *avril;* **May** *mai;* **June** *juin;* **July** *juillet;* **August** *août;* **September** *septembre;* **October** *octobre;* **November** *novembre;* **December** *décembre.* **Spring** *printemps;* **Summer** *été;* **Autumn** *automne;* **Winter** *hiver.*

Further Reading

See also p37 War of the Words for recent books by

History, Art & Culture

Beevor, Antony, & Cooper, Artemis *Paris after the Liberation*
The city during rationing, liberation and existentialism.
Christiansen, Rupert *Tales of the New Babylon*
The Paris of Napoléon III, from sleaze, prostitution and Haussmann's bulldozer to the bloody Commune.
Cole, Robert *A Traveller's History of Paris*
A useful general introduction.
Cronin, Vincent *Napoleon*
A fine biography of the great megalomaniac.
Fitch, Noel Riley *Literary Cafés of Paris*
Who drank where and when.
Littlewood, Ian *Paris: Architecture, History, Art*
Paris' history intertwined with its treasures.
Lurie, Patty *Guide to Impressionist Paris*
Impressionist paintings matched to their exact Paris locations as they look today.
Marnham, Patrick *Crime & the Académie Française*
Quirks and scandals of Mitterrand-era Paris.
Martin, Hervé *Guide to Modern Architecture in Paris*
An accessible, bilingual illustrated guide to significant buildings in Paris since 1900, arranged by area.
Mitford, Nancy *The Sun King; Madame de Pompadour*
Mitford's biographies, although some years old, are still the best gossip accounts of the courts of the *ancien régime*.
Johnson, Douglas, & Johnson, Madeleine *Age of Illusion: Art & Politics in France 1918-1940*
Every aspect of the culture of France in an era when Paris was more than ever at the forefront of modernity.
Mann, Carol *Paris Années Folles*
A photographic view of artistic Paris in the 1930s.
Rudorff, Raymond *Belle Epoque: Paris in the Nineties*
Glamorous *fin-de-siècle* Paris.
Salvadori, Renzo *Architect's Guide to Paris*
Plans, illustrations and a guide to Paris' growth, of interest to the general reader as well as to architects.
Schama, Simon *Citizens*
Giant but wonderfully readable account of the Revolution.
Zeldin, Theodore *The French*
Idiosyncratic and entertaining survey of modern France.

French Literature

See also p37 **War of the Words** for recent books by contemporary novelists.
Abaelardus, Petrus & Heloïse *Letters*
The full details of Paris' first great drama.
Aragon, Louis *Paris Peasant*
A great Surrealist view of the city.
Balzac, Honoré de *Le Père Goriot*
All of Balzac's 'Human Comedy' deals with Paris, but the story of old Goriot is one of the most acute of his novels.
Beyala, Calixthe *Le Petit Prince de Belleville*
Entertaining chronicle of African immigrants in Paris.
Céline, Louis-Ferdinand *Mort à Crédit*
Remarkably vivid, largely autobiographical account of an impoverished Paris childhood.
Daninos, Pierre *Les Carnets de Major Thompson*
Understand why the French have such odd ideas about the English: the French as seen by a retired English major. Lots of people fell for it when published in the 1950s.
De Beauvoir, Simone *The Mandarins*

Paris intellectuals and idealists just after the Liberation.
Desforges, Régine *The Blue Bicycle*
A vivid, easy-read drama of resistance, collaboration and sex during the German occupation. First of a trilogy.
Hugo, Victor *Notre Dame de Paris*
Quasimodo and the romantic vision of medieval Paris.
Maupassant, Guy de *Bel-Ami*
Gambling and dissipation.
Modiano, Patrick *Honeymoon*
Evocative story of two lives that cross in Paris.
Perec, Georges *Life, A User's Manual*
Intellectual puzzle in a Haussmannian apartment building.
Restif de la Bretonne, Nicolas *Les Nuits de Paris*
The sexual underworld of the Paris of Louis XV, by one of France's most famous defrocked priests.
Queneau, Raymond *Zazie in the Metro*
Paris in the 1950s: bright and very *nouvelle vague*.
Sartre, Jean-Paul *Roads to Freedom*
Existential angst as the German army takes over Paris.
Simenon, Georges The Maigret series
All of Simenon's books featuring his laconic detective provide a great picture of Paris and its underworld.
Vian, Boris *Froth on the Daydream*
Wonderfully funny Surrealist satire of Paris in the goldern era of Sartre and St-Germain.
Zola, Emile *Nana, l'Assommoir, le Ventre de Paris*
These are perhaps Zola's most vivid accounts of the underside of life in the Second Empire.

The Ex-Pat Angle

Hemingway, Ernest *A Moveable Feast*
Big Ern drinks his way around 1920s writers' Paris.
Littlewood, Ian *Paris: A Literary Companion*
Great selection of pieces by all kinds of writers on Paris.
Maugham, W Somerset *The Moon & Sixpence*
Impoverished artist in Montmartre and escape to the South Seas, inspired by the life of Gauguin.
Miller, Henry *Tropic of Cancer, Tropic of Capricorn*
Low-life and lust in Montparnasse.
Nin, Anaïs *Henry & June*
Lust in Montparnasse with Henry Miller and his wife.
Orwell, George *Down & Out in Paris & London*
Exactly what the title says.
Rhys, Jean *After Mr Mackenzie*
Life as a kept woman in seedy hotels.
ed **Royle, Nicholas** *Time Out Book of Paris Short Stories*
New fiction by British, American and French writers.
Stein, Gertrude *The Autobiography of Alice B Toklas*
Ex-pat Paris, from start to finish.
Süskind, Patrick *Perfume*
Pungent murder in Paris on the eve of the Revolution.

Food & Drink

A-Z of French Food A handy pocket glossary.
Masui, Kasuko *French Cheeses*
An illustrated guide to tickle your tastebuds.
Time Out *Eating & Drinking in Paris*
Over 750 restaurants, bars, brasseries and bistros.
Toklas, Alice B *The Alice B Toklas Cookbook*
Literary and artistic life, and how to cook fish for Picasso.
Wells, Patricia *Bistro Cooking* Recipes and bistro lore.

Index

Centre Pompidou 23, 36, 60, 61, 108
Cézanne, Paul 289
Chaise Longue, La 61, 217
Chaise au Plafond, La 62, 186
chambers of commerce 319
Chambord 16
Champ de Mars 92
Champigny-sur-Marne 102
Champs-Elysées (*see* avenue des)
Chanel, Coco 138
chanson française 266
Chantilly 284
Chapelle St-Louis-de-la-Salpêtrière 99, 129
Chapelle de la Médaille Miraculeuse 91, 92
Chapelle du Martyre 73
Chapelle Expiatoire 55
Charles II, Emperor 14, 56
Charles III the Simple 14
Charles V the Wise/Dauphin 16, 33, 50, 102
Charles V, Emperor 16, 47
Charles VII 16
Charles IX 16
Charles X 20
Charles Martel 14
Chartier 27, 56, 180, 242
Chartres 31, 293
Château d'Ecouen 100
Château de Malmaison 99
Château de Monte Cristo 99-100
Château de la Reine Blanche 97
Château de Vincennes (*see* Bois de Vincennes)
Chateaubriand 120
châteaux, Ile de France 284, 287, 288, 290, 291
châteaux, Loire 288-289
Châtelet 58
Châtelet, Théâtre Musical de Paris 61, 246, 261
Châtenay-Malabry 102
Chez Gégène 101
Chez Georges (2nd) 52, 159
Chez Gladines 98
Chez Jenny 162, 163
Chez Michel 60
Chez Omar 62
Chez Paul 66, 161
children 237-244
Chinatown 98
Chirac, Jacques 30
cholera 21
Cimetière des Chiens 101
Cimetière des Innocents 58
Cimetière de Montmartre 73, 74
Cimetière de Montparnasse 94
Cimetière de Passy 70, 71
Cimetière du Père-Lachaise 15, 23, 76
cinemas 249-251
Cinémathèque Française 71, 251
Cinq Jours de l'Objet Extraordinaire 6
circus 11, 228, 230, 241
Cirque d'Hiver 33, 35, 66, 230

Cité de la Musique 36, 76, 105, 125, 245, 259, 261
Cité des Enfants, La 240
Cité des Sciences et de l'Industrie, La 76, 105, 125, 126, 240
Cité Universitaire 34, 96
Cithéa, La 78, 236, 286
Clairière de l'Armistice 286
Clovis 14, 294
clubs 231-236, 255-256
CNIT 34, 100
coaches 300, 306
Colbert, Jean-Baptiste 284
Colette 49, 78, 85
Collège de France 82
Comédie-Française 17, 52, 279, 281
comedy 23, 50, 228
Commune 1871 23, 50, 73
Compiègne 25, 286
Comptoir de la Gastronomie 58
computers 320
Conciergerie 15, 31, 45, 46
conferences 320
Conran Shop 91, 216
contraception 316
Coolín 87, 193
Cordeliers 19, 88
Coupole, La 34, 93, 158, 162, 163
Cour des Miracles 59
couriers 320
courses 315
Couvent des Cordeliers 19, 88
Couvent des Récollets 60
credit cards vi, 305
Crillon (*see* Hôtel Crillon)
Crypte Archéologique 46
customs 307
cycling 7, 274, 273, 287, 302, 303, 306, 324
Cyclope, Le 292

d

Dagobert 14
Dalí, Salvador 114
dance and dance centres 245-247
Danton, Georges-Jacques 19, 46, 55, 86
Daubigny, Charles-François 289
Dauphin, Le 16
De Beauvoir, Simone 84, 94, 185
Défense, La (*see* La Défense)
De Gaulle, Charles 26, 28
Degas, Edgar 75, 185
Delacroix, Eugène 63, 75, 78, 85, 88, 92, 110, 112, 114
Delorme, Philibert 83, 289
Denis, Maurice 109
dentists 308
department stores 27, 55, 211-212
Depression 25
Descartes, Jean-Louis 87
design galleries 136
Desmoulins, Camille 55, 88
détaxe 199

Deux Magots, Les 85, 86, 185, 187
Deyrolle 91
Diana, Princess of Wales 71, 138
Diane de Poitiers 289
Dieppe 293
Directoire 20
disabled travellers 307
Disneyland Paris 239
Divan du Monde, Le 74, 232, 265
doctors 308
Dôme, Le 93, 177
Dreyfus, Captain Alfred 24, 94, 125
Drouot 56
Duc des Lombards, Au 58, 268
Dufy, Raoul 70, 73, 109
Dumas, Alexandre, *fils* 56

e

E Dehillerin 58
Ecole Militaire 18, 92
Ecole Nationale Supérieure des Beaux-Arts (Ensb-a) 86, 87
Ecurie, L' 83
Edward III of England 15
Eglise du Dôme (*see* Invalides)
Eglise Notre-Dame-de-Lorette 75
Eglise Notre-Dame de Raincy 181
Eglise Notre-Dame-des-Victoires 52
Eglise St-Augustin 55
Eglise St-Etienne-du-Mont 14, 32, 82, 83
Eglise St-Eustache 32, 58
Eglise St-Germain l'Auxerrois 31, 48, 50
Eglise St-Germain de Charonne 78
Eglise St-Germain-des-Prés 87
Eglise St-Gervais-St-Protais 60
Eglise St-Jean de Montmartre 73
Eglise St-Julien-le-Pauvre 80, 81
Eglise St-Louis-en-l'Ile 47
Eglise St-Médard 84
Eglise St-Merri 60
Eglise St-Paul-St-Louis 32, 63
Eglise St-Pierre-de-Montmartre 73
Eglise St-Roch 20, 49, 50
Eglise St-Séverin 31, 80, 81
Eglise St-Sulpice 87, 88
Eglise St-Vincent de Paul 35, 60
Eglise de la Trinité 33, 56
Eglise du Val-de-Grâce 32, 84
Egouts de Paris 92
Egyptomania 20, 59.
Eiffel, Gustave 93
Eiffel Tower 24, 34, 92-93
Eleanor of Aquitaine 14
electricity 307, 308
Elysée Montmartre 74, 233, 265
embassies & consulates 307
emergencies 308, 314
Emperor Julian 13
Empire Style 20

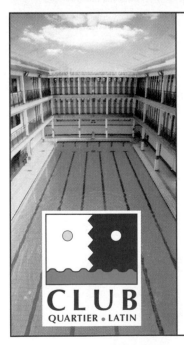

Maps

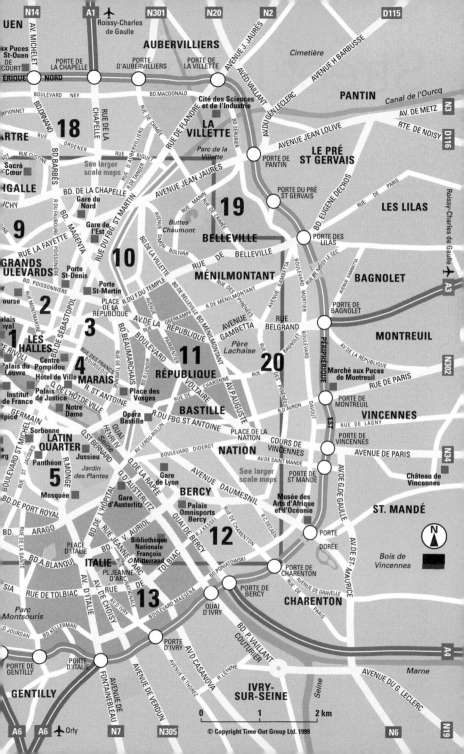

Street Index

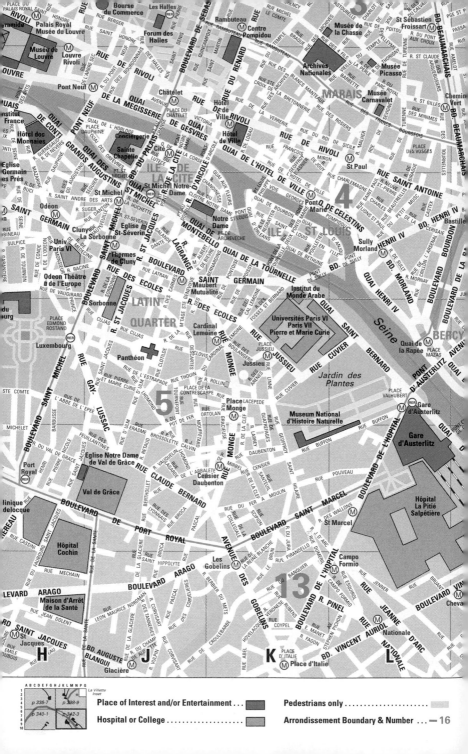

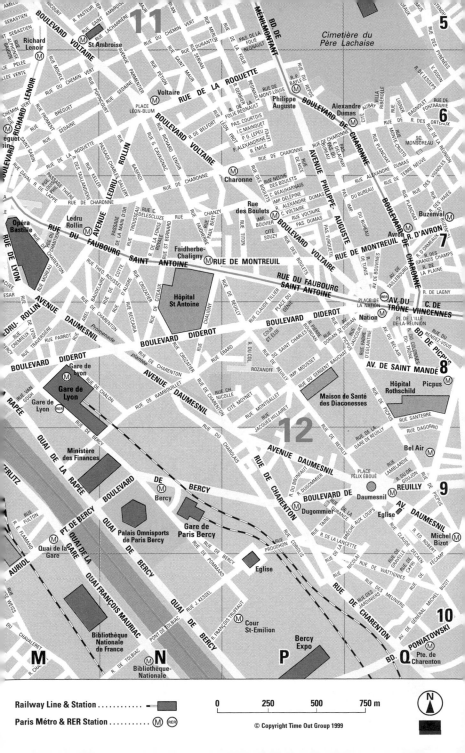

Bus

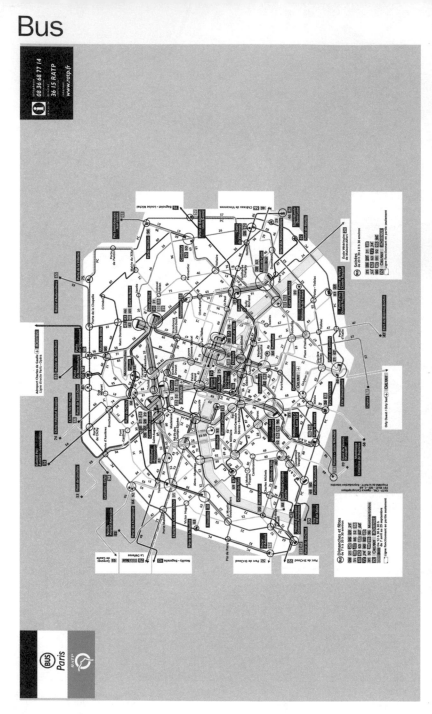

RER

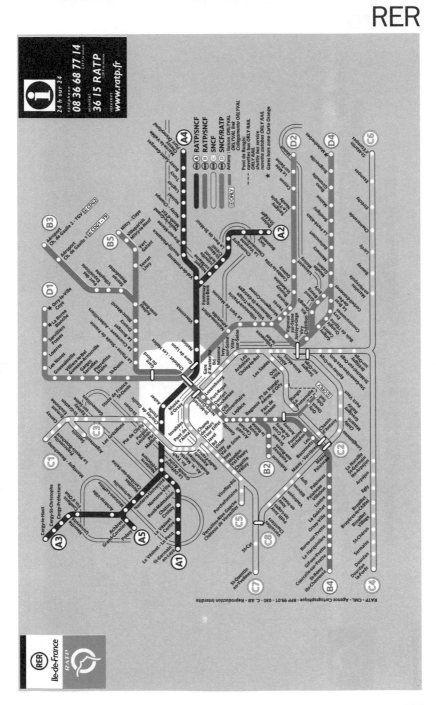

Métro

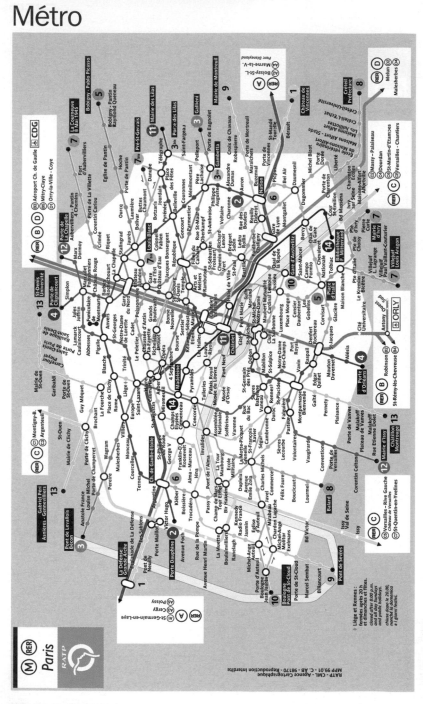

About this guide...

1. How useful did you find the following sections?

	Very	Fairly	Not very	
Paris In Context	☐	☐	☐	(5)
Sightseeing	☐	☐	☐	(6)
Accommodation	☐	☐	☐	(7)
Eating & Drinking	☐	☐	☐	(8)
Shopping	☐	☐	☐	(9)
Arts & Entertainment	☐	☐	☐	(10)
Trips	☐	☐	☐	(11)
Directory	☐	☐	☐	(12)
Maps	☐	☐	☐	(13)

2. Did you travel to Paris: (17)

Alone? ☐   With partner? ☐
As part of group? ☐   With children? ☐
On business? ☐

3. How long was your trip to Paris? (18)

Less than three days ☐
Three days to one week ☐
One to two weeks ☐
Over two weeks ☐

4. Did you visit any other destinations in France? If so, which ones?

_____
_____
_____

5. Where did you get additional travel information from? (19)

Tourist Board ☐
Internet ☐
Travel agents ☐

Another guide book (please specify)
_____

Other (20/22)
_____

6. Is there anything you'd like us to cover in greater depth?

_____
_____
_____

7. Are there any places that should/should not be included in the guide?

_____
_____
_____

8. How many other people have used this guide? (23)

none ☐   1 ☐   2 ☐   3 ☐   4 ☐   5+ ☐

About other Time Out publications...

9. Have you ever bought/used Time Out magazine? (24)

Yes ☐   No ☐

10. Have you bought any other Time Out City Guides? (25)

Yes ☐   No ☐

If yes, which ones? (26/28)
_____

11. Have you ever bought/used other Time Out publications? (29)

Yes ☐   No ☐

If yes, which ones? (30)

Film Guide ☐
Kids Out magazine ☐
London Eating & Drinking Guide ☐
London Pubs & Bars Guide ☐
London Visitors' Guide ☐
ici Londres ☐
Paris Eating & Drinking Guide ☐
Paris Free Guide ☐
London Shopping Guide ☐
Student Guide ☐
Book of Country Walks ☐
Book of London Walks ☐
Book of New York Short Stories (31)
Time Out New York magazine ☐
Time Out Roma ☐
Time Out Diary ☐
www.timeout.com ☐

About you...

12. First name:

Surname:

Address:

Postcode:

13. Year of birth (32)

14. Sex: male ☐   female ☐ (43)

15. Are you: (44)

employed full-time ☐
employed part-time ☐
self-employed ☐
unemployed ☐
student ☐
homemaker ☐

16. At the moment do you earn: (45)

under £10,000 ☐
over 10,000 and up to £14,999 ☐
over £15,000 and up to £19,999 ☐
over £20,000 and up to £24,999 ☐
over £25,000 and up to £39,999 ☐
over £40,000 and up to £49,999 ☐
over £50,000 ☐

☐ Please tick here if you don't want to receive further information on related promotions or products.

Time Out Guides

FREEPOST 20 (WC3187)
LONDON
W1E 0DQ

Time Out

City Guides are available from all good bookshops or through Penguin Direct.
Simply call 0181 899 4036 (9am-5pm) or fill out the form below, affix a stamp and return.

ISBN	title	retail price	quantity	total
0140273115	Time Out Guide to **Amsterdam**	£9.99		
0140273123	Time Out Guide to **Barcelona**	£9.99		
0140257187	Time Out Guide to **Berlin**	£9.99		
0140284052	Time Out Guide to **Boston** (published 4/99)	£9.99		
0140273166	Time Out Guide to **Brussels**	£9.99		
014026745X	Time Out Guide to **Budapest**	£9.99		
0140266879	Time Out Guide to **Dublin**	£9.99		
0140266844	Time Out Guide to **Edinburgh**	£9.99		
0140266860	Time Out Guide to **Florence & Tuscany**	£9.99		
0140270620	Time Out Guide to **Las Vegas**	£9.99		
0140273158	Time Out Guide to **Lisbon**	£9.99		
0140259767	Time Out Guide to **London**	£9.99		
0140274456	Time Out Guide to **Los Angeles**	£9.99		
014027443X	Time Out Guide to **Madrid**	£9.99		
0140266852	Time Out Guide to **Miami**	£9.99		
014027314X	Time Out Guide to **Moscow**	£9.99		
0140274480	Time Out Guide to **New Orleans**	£9.99		
0140273107	Time Out Guide to **New York**	£9.99		
0140270647	Time Out Guide to **Paris**	£9.99		
0140257160	Time Out Guide to **Prague**	£9.99		
0140266887	Time Out Guide to **Rome**	£9.99		
0140267468	Time Out Guide to **San Francisco**	£9.99		
0140259732	Time Out Guide to **Sydney**	£9.99		
0140284060	Time Out Guide to **Venice** (published 4/99)	£9.99		
		+ postage & packing		£1.50
		Total Payment		

(Please Use Block Capitals)

Cardholder's Name

Address

Town _____ Postcode

Daytime Telephone Number

Method of Payment (UK Credit cards only)

Barclaycard/Visa

Access Card/Mastercard

Signature (if paying by credit card) _____

Expiry date

Cheque
I enclose a cheque £ _____ made payable to Penguin Direct

Time Out

Penguin Direct
Penguin Books Ltd
Bath Road
Harmondsworth
West Drayton
Middlesex
UB7 0DA

AFFIX
STAMP
HERE